Cliff T. Ragsdale

Virginia Polytechnic Institute
and State University

Spreadsheet Modeling and Decision Analysis

A Practical Introduction to Management Science

Second Edition

SOUTH-WESTERN College Publishing

An International Thomson Publishing Company

Sponsoring Editor:	John R. Szilagyi
Developmental Editor:	Alice C. Denny
Production Editor:	Shelley Brewer
Cover Design:	Craig LaGesse Ramsdell
Production House:	settingPace
Marketing Manager:	Steve Scoble

Library of Congress Cataloging-in-Publication Data:
Ragsdale, Cliff T.
    Spreadsheet modeling and decision analysis: a
practical introduction to management science/Cliff T. Ragsdale—2nd ed.

        p.   cm.
    Includes index.
    ISBN 0-538-88130-5
    1. Management science—Computer simulation.   2. Operations research—Computer simulation
    3. Electronic spreadsheets   4. Decision-making—Computer simulation
I. Title
T57.62 .R34 1997
                                                                        CIP

Printed in the United States of America
4   5   6   WST   01   0   9

I ⓣ P®

International Thomson Publishing
South-Western College Publishing is an ITP Company.
The ITP trademark is used under license.

Microsoft is a registered trademark, and Excel and Windows are trademarks of Microsoft Corporation.
Screen shots are reprinted with permission from Microsoft Corporation.

Some of the product names and company names used in this book have been used for identification
purposes only and may be trademarks or registered trademarks of their respective manufacturers and sellers.

Preface

Something exciting is happening in introductory OR/MS classes. The following comments, from actual MBA and undergraduate business students, are being reported by instructors who have adopted the spreadsheet approach for teaching management science.

"This was my favorite class this semester."
"I really enjoyed this class and it will be very helpful in my job."
"This subject matter is very relevant to the business world."
"This course gave me a better understanding of how management science can be applied and used in business as opposed to just exposing me to theory."

Beyond the positive feedback from individual students, the INFORMS Business School Education Task Force recently recommended the use of spreadsheets as the "delivery vehicle" for OR/MS tools in introductory OR/MS classes (*OR/MS Today*, February 1997). Teaching OR/MS with spreadsheets is not a fad; it is our future. *Spreadsheet Modeling & Decision Analysis: A Practical Introduction to Management Science* gives you everything you need to be part of that future and successfully integrate spreadsheets into your introductory OR/MS courses.

Today, millions of business people are using spreadsheet programs to build models of the decision problems they face as a regular part of their daily work activities. Because of this, it makes sense to use spreadsheets as the vehicle for introducing undergraduate and graduate students in business and engineering to the concepts and tools covered in the introductory OR/MS course. This plan simultaneously develops students' skills with a standard tool of today's business world (spreadsheets) and opens their eyes to how a variety of OR/MS techniques can be used in this modeling environment. Spreadsheets also capture students' interest and add a new relevance to OR/MS as they see how it can be applied with popular commercial software being used in the business world.

Spreadsheet Modeling & Decision Analysis provides an introduction to the most commonly used OR/MS techniques and shows how these tools can be implemented using Microsoft Excel (versions 5.0, 7.0, or 8.0). While other spreadsheet packages can be used to accomplish the same objective, Excel currently offers the best collection of built-in analytical capabilities and, therefore, is used with this book. Prior experience with Excel is certainly helpful, but is not a requirement for using this text. In general, a student familiar with Windows and the spreadsheet concepts presented in most introductory computer courses should have no trouble using this text. Step-by-step instructions and screen shots are provided for each example, and software tips are included throughout the text as needed.

INNOVATIVE FEATURES

Aside from its strong spreadsheet orientation, *Spreadsheet Modeling & Decision Analysis* contains a number of other unique features that distinguish it from traditional OR/MS texts:

- Algebraic formulations and spreadsheets are used side-by-side to help develop conceptual thinking skills.
- Emphasis is placed on model formulation and interpretation rather than algorithms.
- Realistic examples motivate the discussion of each topic. Step-by-step instructions and numerous annotated screen shots make examples easy to follow and understand. Solutions to each example are analyzed from a managerial perspective. Spreadsheet files for all the examples are provided on a data disk bundled with the text.
- A unique and accessible chapter covering discriminant analysis is provided.
- Sections entitled "The World of Management Science" show how each topic has been applied in a real company.
- Excel add-ins and templates support decision trees and queuing.

The second edition includes a number of new materials that expand on the value of the existing features:

- In Chapter 3, new guidelines are provided for developing spreadsheets that communicate effectively.
- A new, efficient approach to modeling network flow problems is presented in Chapter 5.
- A major revision of Chapter 8 introduces several new innovative nonlinear programming applications.
- Many new examples and end-of-chapter cases are included to give students more challenging real-world problems to tackle.
- Incorporation of the latest versions of Excel and @Risk.
- New Excel add-ins for discriminant analysis and simulation.

ORGANIZATION

The table of contents for *Spreadsheet Modeling & Decision Analysis* is laid out in a fairly traditional format, but topics may be covered in a variety of ways. The text begins with an overview of OR/MS in Chapter 1. Chapters 2 through 8 cover various topics in deterministic modeling techniques: linear programming, sensitivity analysis, networks, integer programming, goal programming and multiple objective optimization, and nonlinear programming. Chapters 9 through 11 cover predictive modeling and ters, depending on whether or not their students have access to @RISK. Chapters 15 and 16 cover project management and decision theory, respectively.

The material in the text could be covered in a variety of ways. After completing Chapter 1, a quick refresher on spreadsheet fundamentals (entering and copying formulas, basic formatting and editing, etc.) is always a good idea. Suggestions for the Excel review may be found at the Decision Sciences web site, www.quant.swcollege.com. Following this, an instructor could cover the material on optimization, forecasting, or simulation depending on his or her personal preferences. The chapters on queuing and project management make general references to simulation and, therefore, should follow the discussion of that topic.

ANCILLARY MATERIALS

The new edition of *Spreadsheet Modeling & Decision Analysis: A Practical Introduction to Management Science* is accompanied by several excellent ancillaries for the instructor. Call the ITP Academic Resource Center at 1-800-423-0563 to request these items.

- An *Instructor's Manual* with *Test Bank* (ISBN: 0-538-86757-4) is available to adopters of this book. The *Instructor's Manual* contains solutions to all the text problems and cases prepared by author Cliff Ragsdale. The *Test Bank*, prepared by Lance Matheson, includes multiple choice and short answer problems for each text chapter.
- WesTest™ (ISBN: 0-538-86758-2) provides the test bank in a Windows format that allows instructors to use or modify the *Test Bank* questions as well as create original questions.
- PowerPoint slides, developed by Cliff Ragsdale, provide ready-made lectures to accompany each text chapter. These files contain over 500 screens and may be downloaded directly from the South-Western College Publishing web page for the Decision Sciences, www.quant.swcollege.com
- An upgraded version of Frontline Systems' Solver DLL offering improved optimization performance for Excel 5.0 and 7.0 users is available free of charge from the publisher (see www.quant.swcollege.com). Please note that users of Excel 8.0 (included with Office 97) do not need this upgrade.

ACKNOWLEDGMENTS

I would like to thank the following individuals who made important contributions to the development and completion of this book. The reviewers for the second edition were:

Abdelghani A. Elimam
San Francisco State University

Rahul Singh
University of Texas at Austin

Leon Lasdon
University of Texas at Austin

David W. Ashley
University of Missouri at Kansas City

Pierre Ndilikilikesha
Duke University

Cem Canel
University of North Carolina at
    Wilmington

David Ashley also provided summaries of the articles found in "The World of Management Science" feature throughout the text and created the queuing template

Leon Lasdon, University of Texas at Austin
Pierre Ndilikilikesha, Duke University
Rahul Singh, University of Texas at Austin
David W. Ashley, University of Missouri at Kansas City

David Ashley also provided summaries of the articles found in "The World of Management Science" feature throughout the text and created the queuing template used in Chapter 14. Mike Middleton, University of San Francisco, once again provided the TreePlan decision tree add-in found in Chapter 16. Jack Yurkiewicz, Pace University, contributed several of the cases found throughout the text.

I would like to extend a special word of thanks to my cyber-friend Tom Schriber at the University of Michigan who scrutinized every word in the first edition of this book and provided many valuable comments and suggestions. I also thank Alice Denny, my Developmental Editor at South-Western, without whom this project would not have been completed. I also extend my gratitude to the Palisade Corporation (**www.palisade.com**) for providing a complimentary copy of @Risk and to Dan Flystra of Frontline Systems (**www.frontsys.com**) for bringing the power of optimization to the world of spreadsheets.

Once again, I would like to thank my dear wife, Kathy, for her continued patience, support, encouragement, love, and back rubs throughout this project. You still exceed them all.

FINAL THOUGHTS

I hope you enjoy the spreadsheet approach to teaching OR/MS as much as I do and that you find this book to be very interesting and helpful. Any comments, questions, suggestions, or constructive criticism you have concerning this text are most welcome and can be sent to me using e-mail: crags@mail.vt.edu.

CLIFF T. RAGSDALE
Virginia Polytechnic Institute and State University

Contents

CHAPTER 1

Introduction to Modeling and Decision Analysis

This book is titled *Spreadsheet Modeling and Decision Analysis: A Practical Introduction to Management Science*, so let's begin by discussing exactly what this title means. By the very nature of life, all of us must continually make decisions that we hope will solve problems and lead to increased opportunities for ourselves or the organizations for which we work. But making good decisions is rarely an easy task. The problems faced by decision makers in today's competitive, fast-paced business environment are often extremely complex and can be addressed by numerous possible courses of action. Evaluating these alternatives and choosing the best course of action represents the essence of decision analysis.

During the past decade, millions of business people discovered that one of the most effective ways to analyze and evaluate decision alternatives involves using electronic spreadsheets to build computer models of the decision problems they face. A **computer model** is a set of mathematical relationships and logical assumptions implemented in a computer as a representation of some real-world decision problem or phenomenon. Today, electronic spreadsheets provide the most convenient and useful way for business people to implement and analyze computer models. Indeed, most business people would probably rate the electronic spreadsheet as their most important analytical tool apart from their brain! Using a spreadsheet model (a computer model implemented via a spreadsheet), a business person can analyze decision alternatives before choosing a specific plan for implementation.

This book introduces you to a variety of techniques from the field of management science that can be applied in spreadsheet models to assist in the decision analysis process. For our purposes, we will define **management science** as a field of study that uses computers, statistics, and mathematics to solve business problems. It involves applying the methods and tools of science to management and decision making. Management science is also sometimes referred to as operations research or decision science. Figure 1.1 summarizes how management science has been applied successfully in a number of real-world situations.

In the not too distant past, management science was a highly specialized field that could be practiced only by those who had access to mainframe computers and who

1

Figure 1.1
Examples of
successful
management
science
applications.

Home Runs in Management Science

Over the past decade, scores of operations research and management science projects saved companies millions of dollars. Each year, the Institute For Operations Research and the Management Sciences (INFORMS) sponsors the Franz Edelman Awards competition to recognize some of the most outstanding OR/MS projects during the past year. Here are some of the "home runs" from the 1995 Edelman Awards (described in *Interfaces*, Vol. 26, No. 1, January-February, 1996).

- **The Harris Corporation** is an electronics and electronics systems company based in Melbourne Florida with annual sales of approximately $3.5 billion. A computerized optimization-based production planning system called IMPReSS, developed for Harris' semiconductor manufacturing division, generates schedules for a worldwide manufacturing network and quotes product delivery dates in response to customer inquiries. **Benefits:** This system raised on-time deliveries from 75 to 95 percent without increasing inventories, enabled the division to expand its markets and market share, and helped move the division to increase profits by over $115 million annually.

- **Sadia Concordia, SA** is the largest poultry producer in Brazil, processing over 300 million chickens and 11 million turkeys a year, with annual income of more than $2.5 billion. Since 1990 the company has increasingly used mathematical models to improve decision making regarding what types of flocks to grow, when to slaughter flocks, and what products (parts) to produce at each of its processing plants. **Benefits:** The use of these models has resulted in a better conversion of feed to live bird weight, greater utilization of birds, greater flexibility and reduced lead time, and cost savings of more than $50 million over a three-year period.

- **KeyCorp**, headquartered in Cleveland, Ohio, is one of the largest bank holding companies is the United States with assets of $66.8 billion, 1,300 branch banking facilities, and earnings of $854 million in 1994. In 1991 the company began developing its Service Excellence Management System (SEMS) to measure branch activities, customer wait times, and teller productivity. This system helps managers focus reengineering efforts, schedule staff to better match customer arrivals, and enhance productivity and service. **Benefits:** Customer processing time has been reduce by 53 percent, customer wait time has been improved dramatically, and personnel expenses are expected to reduced by $98 million over five years.

- **NYNEX** provides wireline and wire-free telecommunications services, directory publishing, and information delivery services to approximately 16.5 million customers in New England, New York and selected markets around the world. Planning the expansion and augmentation of the network web to service this growing area is highly complex and results in the expenditure of millions of dollars each year. The company developed a system, called Arachne, which uses heuristic rules and optimization techniques to assist in network planning. **Benefits:** Arachne improves the quality and reliability of network plans, reduces the time required to complete the planning process, and has led to cost savings of at least $33 million to date.

possessed an advanced knowledge of mathematics and computer programming languages. However, the proliferation of powerful personal computers (PCs) and the development of easy-to-use electronic spreadsheets have made the tools of management science far more practical and available to a much larger audience. Virtually everyone who uses a spreadsheet today for model building and decision making is a practitioner of management science—whether they realize it or not. So it is only a matter of time before we begin to hear success stories about "home runs" being hit by spreadsheet-based applications using the tools of management science discussed in this book.

1.0 THE MODELING APPROACH TO DECISION MAKING

The idea of using models in problem solving and decision analysis is not new, nor is it tied to the use of computers. All of us have used a modeling approach to make a decision. For example, if you have ever moved into a dormitory, apartment, or house you faced a decision about how to arrange the furniture in your new dwelling. There were probably several arrangements to consider. One arrangement might give you the most open space but require that you build a loft. Another might give you less space but allow you to avoid the hassle and expense of building a loft. To analyze these different arrangements and make a decision, you did not build the loft. You more likely built a **mental model** of the two arrangements, picturing what each looked like in your mind's eye. Thus, a simple mental model is sometimes all that is required to analyze a problem and make a decision.

For more complex decision problems, a mental model might be impossible or insufficient and other types of models might be required. For example, a set of drawings or blueprints for a house or building provides a **visual model** of the real-world structure. These drawings help illustrate how the various parts of the structure will fit together when it is completed. A road map is another type of visual model because it assists a driver in analyzing the various routes from one location to another.

You have probably also seen car commercials on television showing automotive engineers using **physical**, or **scale**, **models** to study the aerodynamics of various car designs in order to find the shape that creates the least wind resistance and maximizes fuel economy. Similarly, aeronautical engineers use scale models of airplanes to study the flight characteristics of various fuselage and wing designs. And civil engineers might use scale models of buildings and bridges to study the strengths of different construction techniques.

Another common type of model is a **mathematical model**, which uses mathematical relationships to describe or represent an object or decision problem. Throughout this book we will study how various mathematical models can be implemented and analyzed on computers using spreadsheet software. But before we begin an in-depth discussion of spreadsheet models, let's look at some of the more general characteristics and benefits of modeling.

1.1 CHARACTERISTICS AND BENEFITS OF MODELING

Although this book focuses on mathematical models implemented in computers via spreadsheets, the examples of non-mathematical models given earlier are worth discussing a bit more because they help illustrate a number of important characteristics and benefits of modeling in general. First, the models mentioned earlier are usually simplified versions of the object or decision problem they represent. To study the aerodynamics of a car design, we do not need to build the entire car complete with engine and stereo. Such components have little or no effect on aerodynamics. So, although a model is often a simplified representation of reality, the model is useful as long as it is valid. A **valid** model is one that accurately represents the relevant characteristics of the object or decision problem being studied.

Second, it is often less expensive to analyze decision problems using a model. This is especially easy to understand with respect to scale models of big-ticket items such as cars and planes. Besides the lower financial cost of building a model, the analysis of a model can help avoid costly mistakes that might result from poor decision making. For example, it is far less costly to discover a flawed wing design using a scale model of an aircraft than after the crash of a fully loaded jet.

Frank Brock, former executive vice president of the Brock Candy Company, related the following story about blueprints his company prepared for a new production facility. After months of careful design work he proudly showed the plans to several of his production workers. When he asked for their comments, one worker responded, "It's a fine looking building Mr. Brock, but that sugar valve looks like it's about twenty feet away from the steam valve." "What's wrong with that?" asked Brock. "Well, nothing," said the worker, "except that I have to have my hands on both valves at the same time!"[1] Needless to say, it was far less expensive to discover and correct this "little" problem using a visual model before pouring the concrete and laying the pipes as originally planned.

Third, models often deliver needed information on a more timely basis. Again, it is relatively easy to see that scale models of cars or airplanes can be created and analyzed more quickly than their real-world counterparts. Timeliness is also an issue when vital data will not become available until some later point in time. In these cases, we might create a model to help predict the missing data to assist in current decision making.

Fourth, models are frequently helpful in examining things that would be impossible to do in reality. For example, human models (crash dummies) are used in crash tests to see what might happen to an actual person if a car hits a brick wall at a high speed. Likewise, models of DNA can be used to visualize how molecules fit together. Both of these are difficult, if not impossible, to do without the use of models.

Finally, and probably most importantly, models allow us to gain insight and understanding about the object or decision problem under investigation. The ultimate purpose of using models is to improve decision making. As you will see, the process of building a model can shed important light and understanding on a problem. In some cases, a decision might be made while building the model as a previously misunderstood element of the problem is discovered or eliminated. In other cases, a careful analysis of a completed model might be required to "get a handle" on a problem and gain the insights needed to make a decision. In any event, it is the insight gained from the modeling process that ultimately leads to better decision making.

1   Colson, Charles and Jack Eckerd, *Why America Doesn't Work* (Denver, Colorado: Word Publishing, 1991), 146–147.

1.2   MATHEMATICAL MODELS

As mentioned earlier, the modeling techniques in this book differ quite a bit from scale models of cars and planes or visual models of production plants. The models we will build use mathematics to describe a decision problem. We use the term "mathematics" in its broadest sense, encompassing not only the most familiar elements of math, such as algebra, but also the related topic of logic.

Now, let's consider a simple example of a mathematical model,

$$\text{PROFIT = REVENUE - EXPENSES} \qquad \qquad 1.1$$

Equation 1.1 describes a simple relationship between revenue, expenses, and profit. It is a mathematical relationship that describes the operation of determining profit—or a mathematical model of profit. Of course, not all models are this simple, but, taken piece by piece, the models we will discuss are not much more complex than this one.

Frequently, mathematical models describe functional relationships. For example, the mathematical model in equation 1.1 describes a functional relationship between revenue, expenses, and profit. Using the symbols of mathematics, this functional relationship is represented as:

$$\text{PROFIT} = f(\text{REVENUE, EXPENSES}) \qquad \qquad 1.2$$

In words, the above expression means "profit is a function of revenue and expenses." We could also say that profit *depends* (or is *dependent* on) revenue and expenses. Thus, the term PROFIT in equation 1.2 represents a **dependent variable**, whereas REVENUE and EXPENSES are **independent variables**. Frequently, compact symbols (such as A, B, and C) are used to represent variables in an equation like 1.2. For instance, if we let Y, X_1, and X_2 represent PROFIT, REVENUE, and EXPENSES, respectively, we could rewrite equation 1.2 as follows:

$$Y = f(X_1, X_2) \qquad \qquad 1.3$$

The notation $f(\cdot)$ represents the function that defines the relationship between the dependent variable Y and the independent variables X_1 and X_2. In the case of determining PROFIT from REVENUE and EXPENSES, the mathematical form of the function $f(\cdot)$ is quite simple because we know that $f(X_1, X_2) = X_1 - X_2$. However, in many other situations we will model, the form of $f(\cdot)$ will be quite complex and might involve many independent variables. But regardless of the complexity of $f(\cdot)$ or the number of independent variables involved, many of the decision problems encountered in business can be represented by models that assume the general form,

$$Y = f(X_1, X_2, \dots, X_n) \qquad \qquad 1.4$$

In equation 1.4, the dependent variable Y represents some bottom-line performance measure of the problem we are modeling. The terms $X_1, X_2, \dots, X_n$ represent the different independent variables that play some role or have some impact in determining the value of Y. Again, $f(\cdot)$ is the function (possibly quite complex) that specifies or describes the relationship between the dependent and independent variables.

The relationship expressed in equation 1.4 is very similar to what occurs in most spreadsheet models. Consider a simple spreadsheet model to calculate the monthly payment for a car loan, as shown in Figure 1.2.

The spreadsheet in Figure 1.2 contains a variety of "input" cells (for example, purchase price, down payment, trade-in, term of loan, annual interest rate) that correspond

Figure 1.2
Example of a
simple
spreadsheet
model.

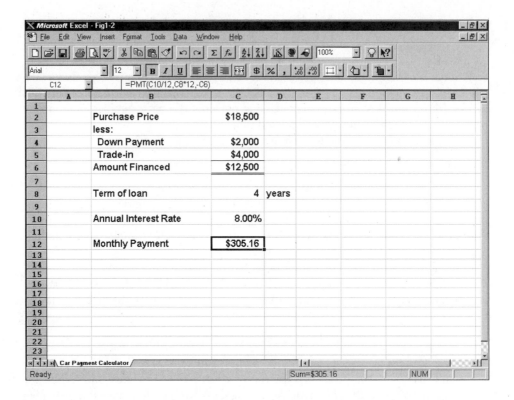

conceptually to the independent variables X_1, X_2, ... , X_n in equation 1.4. Similarly, a variety of mathematical operations are performed using these input cells in a manner analogous to the function $f(\cdot)$ in equation 1.4. The results of these mathematical operations determine the value of some output cell in the spreadsheet (for example, monthly payment) that corresponds to the dependent variable Y in equation 1.4. Thus, there is a direct correspondence between equation 1.4 and the spreadsheet in Figure 1.2. This type of correspondence exists for most of the spreadsheet models in this book.

1.3   CATEGORIES OF MATHEMATICAL MODELS

Not only does equation 1.4 describe the major elements of mathematical or spreadsheet models, it also provides a convenient means for comparing and contrasting the three categories of modeling techniques presented in this book—Prescriptive Models, Predictive Models, and Descriptive Models. Figure 1.3 summarizes the characteristics and techniques associated with each of these categories.

In some situations, a manager might face a decision problem involving a very precise, well-defined functional relationship $f(\cdot)$ between the independent variables X_1, X_2, ... , X_n and the dependent variable Y. If the values for the independent variables are under the decision maker's control, the decision problem in these types of situations boils down to determining the values of the independent variables X_1, X_2, ... , X_n that produce the best possible value for the dependent variable Y. These types of models are called **Prescriptive Models** because their solutions tell the decision maker what actions to take. For example, you might be interested in determining how

Category	Model Characteristics		
	Form of $f(\cdot)$	Values of Independent Variables	Management Science Techniques
Prescriptive Models	known, well-defined	known or under decision maker's control	Linear Programming, Networks, Integer Programming, CPM, Goal Programming, EOQ, Nonlinear Programming
Predictive Models	unknown, ill-defined	known or under decision maker's control	Regression Analysis, Time Series Analysis, Discriminant Analysis
Descriptive Models	known, well-defined	unknown or uncertain	Simulation, Queuing, PERT, Inventory Models

Figure 1.3
Categories and characteristics of management science modeling techniques.

a given sum of money should be allocated to different investments (represented by the independent variables) in order to maximize the return on a portfolio without exceeding a certain level of risk.

A second category of decision problems is one in which the objective is to predict or estimate what value the dependent variable Y will take on when the independent variables $X_1, X_2, \ldots, X_n$ take on specific values. If the function $f(\cdot)$ relating the dependent and independent variables is known, this is a very simple task—simply enter the specified values for $X_1, X_2, \ldots, X_n$ into the function $f(\cdot)$ and compute Y. In some cases however, the functional form of $f(\cdot)$ might be unknown and must be estimated in order for the decision maker to make predictions about the dependent variable Y. These types of models are called **Predictive Models**. For example, a real estate appraiser might know that the value of a commercial property (Y) is influenced by its total square footage (X_1) and age (X_2), among other things. However, the functional relationship $f(\cdot)$ that relates these variables to one another might be unknown. By analyzing the relationship between the selling price, total square footage, and age of other commercial properties, the appraiser might be able to identify a function $f(\cdot)$ that relates these variables in a reasonably accurate manner.

The third category of models you are likely to encounter in the business world are called **Descriptive Models**. In these situations, a manager might face a decision problem that has a very precise, well-defined functional relationship $f(\cdot)$ between the independent variables $X_1, X_2, \ldots, X_n$ and the dependent variable Y. However, there might be great uncertainty as to the exact values that will be assumed by one or more of the independent variables $X_1, X_2, \ldots, X_n$. In these types of problems, the objective is to describe the outcome or behavior of a given operation or system. For example, suppose a company is building a new manufacturing facility and has several choices about the type of machines to put in the new plant, as well as various options for arranging the machines. Management might be interested in studying how the various plant configurations would affect on-time shipments of orders (Y) given the uncertain number of orders that might be received (X_1), and the uncertain due dates (X_2) that might be required by these orders.

1.4　THE PROBLEM-SOLVING PROCESS

The ultimate goal in building models is to assist managers in making decisions that solve problems. The modeling techniques we will study represent a small but important part of the total problem-solving process. To become an effective modeler, it is important to understand how modeling fits into the entire problem-solving process.

Because a model can be used to represent a decision problem or phenomenon, we might be able to create a visual model of the phenomenon that occurs when people solve problems—what we call the problem-solving process. Although a variety of models could be equally valid, the one in Figure 1.4 summarizes the key elements of the problem-solving process and is sufficient for our purposes.

Figure 1.4
A visual model of the problem-solving process.

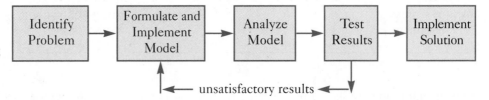

The first step of the problem-solving process, identifying the problem, is also the most important. If we do not identify the correct problem, all the work that follows will amount to nothing more than wasted effort, time, and money. Unfortunately, identifying the problem to solve is often not as easy as it seems. We know that a problem exists when there is a gap or disparity between the present situation and some desired state of affairs. However, we usually are not faced with a neat, well-defined problem. Instead, we often find ourselves facing a "mess"![2] Identifying the real problem involves gathering a lot of information and talking with many people to increase our understanding of the mess. We must then sift through all this information and try to identify the root problem or problems causing the mess. Thus, identifying the real problem (and not just the symptoms of the problem) requires insight, some imagination, time, and a good bit of detective work.

The result of the problem identification step is a well-defined statement of the problem. Simply defining a problem well will often make it much easier to solve. Having identified the problem, we turn our attention to creating or formulating a model of the problem. Depending on the nature of the problem, we might use a

2　This characterization is borrowed from Chapter 5, James R. Evans, *Creative Thinking in the Decision and Management Sciences* (Cincinnati, Ohio: South-Western Publishing, 1991), 89–115.

mental model, a visual model, a scale model, or a mathematical model. Although this book focuses on mathematical models, this does not mean that mathematical models are always applicable or best. In most situations, the *best* model is the simplest model that accurately reflects the relevant characteristic or essence of the problem being studied. We will discuss several different management science modeling techniques in this book. It is important that you not develop too strong a preference for any one technique. Some people have a tendency to want to formulate every problem they face as a model that can be solved by their favorite management science technique. This simply will not work.

As indicated in Figure 1.3, there are fundamental differences in the types of problems a manager might face. Sometimes the values of the independent variables affecting a problem are under the manager's control; sometimes they are not. Sometimes the form of the functional relationship $f(\cdot)$ relating the dependent and independent variables is well-defined, and sometimes it is not. These fundamental characteristics of the problem should guide your selection of an appropriate management science modeling technique. Your goal at the model formulation stage is to select a modeling technique that fits your problem, rather than trying to fit your problem into the required format of a preselected modeling technique.

After you select an appropriate representation or formulation of your problem, the next step is to implement this formulation as a spreadsheet model. We will not dwell on the implementation process now because that is the focus of the remainder of this book. After you verify that your spreadsheet model has been implemented accurately, the next step in the problem-solving process is to use the model to analyze the problem it represents. The main focus of this step is to generate and evaluate alternatives that might lead to a solution of the problem. This often involves playing out a number of scenarios or asking several "What if?" questions. Spreadsheets are particularly helpful in analyzing mathematical models in this manner. In a well-designed spreadsheet model, it should be fairly simple to change some of the assumptions in the model to see what might happen in different situations. As we proceed, we will highlight some techniques for designing spreadsheet models that facilitate this type of "what if" analysis. "What if" analysis is also very appropriate and useful when working with nonmathematical models.

The result of analyzing a model does not always provide a solution to the actual problem being studied. As we analyze a model by asking various "What if?" questions, it is important to test the feasibility and quality of each potential solution. The blueprints Frank Brock showed to his production employees represented the result of his analysis of the problem he faced. He wisely tested the feasibility and quality of this alternative before implementing it, and discovered an important flaw in his plans. Thus, the testing process can give important new insights into the nature of a problem. The testing process is also important because it provides the opportunity to double check the validity of the model. At times we might discover an alternative that appears to be too good to be true. This could lead us to find that some important assumption has been left out of the model. Testing the results of the model against known results (and simple common sense) helps ensure the structural integrity and validity of the model. After analyzing the model we might discover that we need to go back and modify the model.

The last step of the problem-solving process, implementation, is often the most difficult. By their very nature, solutions to problems involve people and change. For better or for worse, most people resist change. However, there are ways to minimize the seemingly inevitable resistance to change. For example, it is wise, if possible, to involve anyone who will be affected by the decision in all steps of the problem-solving process. This not only helps develop a sense of ownership and understanding of the ultimate solution, but it also can be the source of important information throughout the problem-solving process. As the Brock Candy story illustrates, even if it is impossible to include those affected by the solution in all steps, their input should be solicited and considered before a solution is accepted for implementation. Resistance to change and new systems can also be eased by creating flexible, user-friendly interfaces for the mathematical models that are often developed in the problem-solving process.

Throughout this book, we focus mostly on the model formulation, implementation, analysis, and testing steps of the problem-solving process, summarized in Figure 1.4. Again, this does not imply that these steps are more important than the others. If we do not identify the correct problem, the best we can hope for from our modeling effort is "the right answer to the wrong question," which does not solve the real problem. Similarly, even if we do identify the problem correctly and design a model that leads to a perfect solution, if we cannot implement the solution, we still have not solved the problem. Developing the interpersonal and investigative skills required to work with people in defining the problem and implementing the solution are as important as the mathematical modeling skills you will develop by working through this book.

1.5   GOOD DECISIONS VS. GOOD OUTCOMES

The goal of the modeling approach to problem solving is to help individuals make good decisions. But good decisions do not always result in good outcomes. For example, suppose the weather report on the evening news predicts a warm, dry, sunny day tomorrow. When you get up and look out the window tomorrow morning suppose there is not a cloud in sight. If you decide to leave your umbrella at home and

Figure 1.5
A good decision with a bad outcome.

> Andre-Francois Raffray thought he had a great deal in 1965 when he agreed to pay a 90-year-old woman named Jeanne Calment $500 a month until she died to acquire her grand apartment in Arles, northwest of Marseilles in the south of France—a town Vincent Van Gogh once roamed. Buying apartments "for life" is common in France. The elderly owner gets to enjoy a monthly income from the buyer who gambles on getting a real estate bargain—betting the owner doesn't live too long. Upon the owner's death, the buyer inherits the apartment, regardless of how much was paid. But in December of 1995, Raffray died at age 77, having paid more than $180,000 for an apartment he never got to live in.
>
> On the same day, Calment, then the world's oldest living person at 120, dined on foie gras, duck thighs, cheese and chocolate cake at her nursing home near the sought-after apartment. And she need not worry about losing her $500 monthly income. Although the amount Raffray already paid is twice the apartment's current market value, his widow is obligated to keep sending the monthly check to Calment. If Calment also outlives her, then the Raffray children will have to pay. "In life, one sometimes makes bad deals," said Calment of the outcome of Raffray's decision.
>
> Source: *The Savannah Morning News*, 12/29/95.

subsequently get soaked in an unexpected afternoon thundershower did you make a bad decision? Certainly not. Unforeseeable circumstances beyond your control caused you to experience a bad outcome, but it would be unfair to say that you made a bad decision. Good decisions sometimes result in bad outcomes. See Figure 1.5 for the story of another good decision having a bad outcome.

The modeling technique presented in this book can help you make good decisions, but cannot guarantee that good outcomes will always occur as a result of those decisions. Even when a good decision is made, luck often plays a role in determining whether a good or bad outcome occurs. However, using a structured, modeling approach to decision making should produce good outcomes more frequently than making decisions in a more haphazard manner.

THE WORLD OF MANAGEMENT SCIENCE
Business Analysts Trained in Management Science Can Be a Secret Weapon in a CIO's Quest for Bottom-Line Results

Efficiency nuts. Perhaps you've seen one at a cocktail party, explaining that the host could disperse that crowd around the popular shrimp dip if he would just divide the dip into three bowls and place them around the room.

As she sketches the improved traffic pattern on the back of a paper napkin, you notice that her favorite word is "optimize"—a sure-fire sign she has been trained in the field of "operations research" or "management science."

These folks are driven to solve logistics problems, a trait that may not make them sparkle on the party circuit but may be exactly what today's information systems departments need to deliver more business value. Experts say smart information systems (IS) executives will learn to exploit the talents of these mathematical wizards in their quest to boost a company's bottom line.

"If IS departments had more participation from operations research analysts, they would be building much better, richer IS solutions," declares Ron J. Ponder, chief information officer (CIO) at Sprint Corp. in Kansas City, MO, and former CIO at Federal Express Corp. Ponder and others say analysts trained in operations research or management science can turn ordinary information systems into money-saving decision-support systems and are ideally suited to be members of the business process re-engineering team.

"I've always had an operations research department reporting to me, and it's been invaluable. Now I'm building one at Sprint," Ponder says. As someone who has a Ph.D. in operations research and who built the legendary package-tracking systems at Federal Express, Ponder is a true believer in something that many IS professionals have never even heard of.

Mathematical Reasoning

So what is operations research? It's the use of advanced analytical techniques (such as mathematical models) to improve or optimize the performance of an organization. Management science is virtually the same, only academic research papers in this field have a higher ratio of text to equations. Together, they go by the acronym OR/MS.

In either case, OR/MS analysts just love to solve business problems—and the more complex the puzzle, the more they like it. A classic example is the crew scheduling problem at United Airlines. How do you plan the itineraries of 8,000 pilots and 17,000 flight attendants when there is an astronomical number of combinations of planes, crews, and cities?

The OR/MS analysts at United came up with a client/server-based scheduling system, called Paragon, that seeks to minimize the amount of paid time that crews spend waiting for flights. Their model even factors in constraints such as union rules and Federal Aviation Administration regulations. It is expected to save the airline at least $1 million a year.

Over the years, some of the best CIOs have had operations research backgrounds. For example, Joseph T. Brophy, the award-winning former CIO at The Travelers Corp., previously worked as an operations research analyst on the Polaris submarine weapons system.

Operations research got its start in World War II, when the military had to make decisions about allocating scarce resources to various military operations. Since then, the analytic sciences have spread throughout business and government, from designing efficient drive-thru window service for Burger King Corp. to ultra-sophisticated computerized stock trading.

Somewhere along the way, perhaps in the 1970s, the operations research and IS disciplines went on separate tracks. "The IS profession has had less and less contact with the operations research folks...and IS lost a powerful intellectual driver," says Peter G. W. Keen, executive director of the International Center for Information Technologies in Washington, D.C.

The split is ironic, considering that one of the first business applications for computers in the 1950s was to solve operations research problems for the petroleum industry. A technique called linear programming was used to figure out how to blend gasoline for the right flash point, the right viscosity and the right octane and in the cheapest possible way.

The 1990s may be an ideal time for the two disciplines to rebuild some bridges, Keen and other observers say. Today's OR/MS professionals are involved in a variety of IS-related fields, including inventory management, electronic data interchange, computer-integrated manufacturing, network management and practical applications of expert systems and neural networks.

Furthermore, each side needs something the other side has. OR/MS analysts need the corporate data to plug into their models, and the IS folks need to plug the OR/MS models into their strategic information systems. Meanwhile, CIOs need to build smart applications that enhance the bottom line and make them heroes with the chief executive officer.

Not People Persons

However, Keen says, there are some barriers to collaboration. Some OR/MS professionals lack communication skills and tend to focus on esoteric mathematics rather than real-world business problems. "On the other hand, they are very, very bright people. If you can get them away from what I call 'rigor without relevance' and get them onto relevant projects, their rigor is very valuable," Keen says.

Perhaps the biggest barrier is an undercurrent of rivalry between some IS and OR/MS groups as they compete for internal customers, budgets, and glory. But failure to cooperate could be suicidal for both professions, experts says. At a time when some OR/MS groups are facing budget cuts and CIOs are getting fired left and right, it would behoove the two camps to cooperate on some CEO-pleasing "home runs," says consultant Donald B. Brout, president of Quality Technology Decisions, Inc. in New York.

"Operations research and management science have a lot to offer the CIO," says Brout, who has a background in both management science and IS. "We can all be heroes."

OR/MS analysts can develop a model of the way a business process works now and simulate how it could work more efficiently in the future, he says. Therefore, it makes sense to have an OR/MS analyst on the interdisciplinary team that tackles business process re-engineering projects.

In essence, OR/MS professionals add more value to the IS infrastructure by building "tools that really help decision-makers analyze complex situations," says Andrew B. Whinston, director of the Center for Information Systems Management at the University of Texas at Austin.

Thomas M. Cook, president of American Airlines Decision Technologies, Inc. in Forth Worth, Texas, puts it in even stronger terms. IS departments typically believe their job is done if they deliver accurate and timely information. But Cook says that adding OR/MS skills to the team can produce intelligent systems that actually recommend solutions to business problems.

One of the big success stories at Cook's operations research shop is a "yield management" system, which decides how much to overbook and how to set prices for each seat so that a plane is filled up and profits are maximized. The yield management system, which deals with more than 250 decision variables, accounts for a whopping 5% of American Airlines' revenue. The airline's Sabre reservation system "got a lot of great press, but the value of things like yield management might even dwarf Sabre's benefits," Brout says.

Where To Start

So how can the CIO start down the road toward collaboration with OR/MS analysts? Brout says that if the company already has a group of OR/MS professionals, the IS department can draw on their expertise as internal consultants. Otherwise he says, the CIO can simply hire a few OR/MS wizards, throw a problem at them and see what happens. The payback may come surprisingly fast. As one former OR/MS professional put it: "If I couldn't save my employer the equivalent of my own salary in the first month of the year, then I wouldn't feel like I was doing my job."

SUMMARY

This book introduces you to a variety of techniques from the field of management science that can be applied in spreadsheet models to assist in decision analysis and problem solving. This chapter discussed how spreadsheet models of decision problems can be used to analyze the consequences of possible courses of action before a particular alternative is selected for implementation. It described how models of decision problems differ in a number of important characteristics and how you should select a modeling technique that is most appropriate for the type of problem being faced. Finally, it discussed how spreadsheet modeling and analysis fit into the problem-solving process.

QUESTIONS AND PROBLEMS

1. What is meant by the term decision analysis?

2. Define the term computer model.

3. What is the difference between a spreadsheet model and a computer model?

4. Define the term management science.

5. What is the relationship between management science and spreadsheet modeling?

6. What kinds of spreadsheet applications would not be considered management science?

7. In what ways do spreadsheet models facilitate the decision-making process?

8. What are the benefits of using a modeling approach to decision making?

9. What is a dependent variable?

10. What is an independent variable?

11. Can a model have more than one dependent variable?

12. Can a decision problem have more than one dependent variable?

13. In what ways are prescriptive models different from descriptive models?

14. In what ways are prescriptive models different from predictive models?

15. In what ways are descriptive models different from predictive models?

16. How would you define the words description, prediction, and prescription? Carefully consider what is unique about the meaning of each word.

17. Identify one or more mental models you have used. Can any of them be expressed mathematically? If so, identify the dependent and independent variables in your model.

18. Consider the spreadsheet model shown in Figure 1.2. Is this model descriptive, predictive, or prescriptive in nature, or does it not fall into any of these categories?

19. What are the steps in the problem-solving process?

20. Which step in the problem-solving process do you think is most important? Why?

21. Must a model accurately represent every detail of a decision situation to be useful? Why or why not?

22. If you were presented with several different models of a given decision problem, which would you be most inclined to use? Why?

23. Give an example where a well-known business, political, or military leader made a good decision that resulted in a bad outcome, or a bad decision that resulted in a good outcome.

REFERENCES

Forgione, G. "Corporate MS Activities: An Update." *Interfaces*, vol. 13, no. 1, 1983.
Grayson, C. "Management Science and Business Practice." *Harvard Business Review*, vol. 51, 1973.
Hall, R. "What's So Scientific about MS/OR?" *Interfaces*, vol. 15, 1985.
Wysoki, R. "OR/MS Implementation Research: A Bibliography." *Interfaces*, vol. 9, no. 2, 1979.

Introduction to Optimization and Linear Programming

O ur world is filled with limited resources. The amount of oil we can pump out of the earth is limited. The amount of land available for garbage dumps and hazardous waste is limited and, in many areas, diminishing rapidly. On a more personal level, each of us has a limited amount of time in which to accomplish or enjoy the activities we schedule each day. Most of us have a limited amount of money to spend while pursuing these activities. Businesses also have limited resources. A manufacturing organization employs a limited number of workers. A restaurant has a limited amount of space available for seating.

Deciding how best to use the limited resources available to an individual or a business is a universal problem. In today's competitive business environment, it is increasingly important to make sure that a company's limited resources are used in the most efficient manner possible. Typically, this involves determining how to allocate the resources in such a way as to maximize profits or minimize costs. **Mathematical programming** (MP) is a field of management science that finds the optimal, or most efficient, way of using limited resources to achieve the objectives of an individual or a business. For this reason, mathematical programming is often referred to as **optimization**.

2.1 APPLICATIONS OF MATHEMATICAL OPTIMIZATION

To help you understand the purpose of optimization and the types of problems in which it can be used, let's consider several examples of decision-making situations in which MP techniques have been applied.

2.1.1 Determining Product Mix

Most manufacturing companies can make a variety of products. However, each product usually requires different amounts of raw materials and labor. Similarly, the amount of profit generated by the products varies. The manager of such a company must decide how many of each product to produce in order to maximize profits or to satisfy demand at minimum cost.

2.1.2 Manufacturing

Printed circuit boards, like those used in most computers, often have hundreds or thousands of holes drilled in them to accommodate the different electrical components that must be plugged into them. To manufacture these boards, a computer-controlled drilling machine must be programmed to drill in a given location, then move the drill bit to the next location and drill again. This process is repeated hundreds or thousands of times to complete all the holes on a circuit board. Manufacturers of these boards would benefit from determining the drilling order that minimizes the total distance the drill bit must be moved.

2.1.3 Routing and Logistics

Many retail companies have warehouses around the country that are responsible for keeping stores supplied with merchandise to sell. The amount of merchandise available at the warehouses and the amount needed at each store tends to fluctuate, as does the cost of shipping or delivering merchandise from the warehouses to the retail locations. Large amounts of money can be saved by determining the least costly method of transferring merchandise from the warehouses to the stores.

2.1.4 Financial Planning

The federal government requires individuals to begin withdrawing money from individual retirement accounts (IRAs) and other tax-sheltered retirement programs no later than age 70.5. There are various rules that must be followed to avoid paying penalty taxes on these withdrawals. Most individuals want to withdraw their money in a manner that minimizes the amount of taxes they must pay while still obeying the tax laws.

2.2 CHARACTERISTICS OF OPTIMIZATION PROBLEMS

These examples represent just a few areas in which MP has been used successfully. We will consider many other examples throughout this book. However, these examples give you some idea of the issues involved in optimization. For instance, each example involves one or more *decisions* that must be made: How many of each product should be produced? Which hole should be drilled next? How much of each product should be shipped from each warehouse to the various retail locations? How much money should an individual withdraw each year from various retirement accounts?

Also in each example, restrictions, or *constraints*, are likely to be placed on the alternatives available to the decision maker. In the first example, when determining the number of products to manufacture, a production manager is probably faced with a limited amount of raw materials and a limited amount of labor. In the second example, the drill should never return to a position where a hole has already been drilled. In the third example, there is a physical limitation on the amount of merchandise a truck can carry from one warehouse to the stores on its route. In the fourth example, laws determine the minimum and maximum amounts that can be withdrawn from retirement accounts without incurring a penalty. Many other constraints also can be identified for these examples. Indeed, it is not unusual for real-world optimization problems to have hundreds or thousands of constraints.

A final common element in each of the examples is the existence of some goal or *objective* that the decision maker considers when deciding which course of action is best. In the first example, the production manager can decide to produce several different product mixes given the available resources, but the manager will probably choose the mix of products that maximizes profits. In the second example, a large number of possible drilling patterns can be used, but the ideal pattern will probably involve moving the drill bit the shortest total distance. In the third example, there are numerous ways merchandise can be shipped from the warehouses to supply the stores, but the company will probably want to identify the routing that minimizes the total transportation cost. Finally, in the fourth example, individuals can withdraw money from their retirement accounts in many ways without violating the tax laws, but they probably want to find the method that minimizes their tax liability.

2.3   EXPRESSING OPTIMIZATION PROBLEMS MATHEMATICALLY

From the preceding discussion we know that optimization problems involve three elements: decisions, constraints, and an objective. If we intend to build a mathematical model of an optimization problem, we will need mathematical terms or symbols to represent each of these three elements.

2.3.1   Decisions

The decisions in an optimization problem are often represented in a mathematical model by the symbols $X_1, X_2, \ldots, X_n$. We will refer to $X_1, X_2, \ldots, X_n$ as the **decision variables** (or simply the variables) in the model. These variables might represent the quantities of different products the production manager can choose to produce. They might represent the amount of different pieces of merchandise to ship from a warehouse to a certain store. They might represent the amount of money to be withdrawn from different retirement accounts.

The exact symbols used to represent the decision variables are not particularly important. You could use $Z_1, Z_2, \ldots, Z_n$ or symbols like Dog, Cat, and Monkey to represent the decision variables in the model. The choice of which symbols to use is largely a matter of personal preference and might vary from one problem to the next.

2.3.2   Constraints

The constraints in an optimization problem can be represented in a mathematical model in a number of ways. Three general ways of expressing the possible constraint relationships in an optimization problem are:

A less than or equal to constraint: $\quad f(X_1, X_2, \ldots, X_n) \le b$

A greater than or equal to constraint: $\quad f(X_1, X_2, \ldots, X_n) \ge b$

An equal to constraint: $\quad f(X_1, X_2, \ldots, X_n) = b$

In each case, the constraint is some function of the decision variables that must be less than or equal to, greater than or equal to, or equal to some specific value (represented above by the letter b). We will refer to $f(X_1, X_2, \ldots, X_n)$ as the left-hand side (LHS) of the constraint and to b as the right-hand side (RHS) value of the constraint.

For example, we might use a less than or equal to constraint to ensure that the total labor used in producing a given number of products does not exceed the amount of available labor. We might use a greater than or equal to constraint to ensure that the total amount of money withdrawn from a person's retirement accounts is at least the minimum amount required by the IRS. You can use any number of these constraints to represent a given optimization problem depending on the requirements of the situation.

2.3.3 Objective

The objective in an optimization problem is represented mathematically by an objective function in the general format:

$$\text{MAX (or MIN):} \qquad f(X_1, X_2, \ldots, X_n)$$

The **objective function** identifies some function of the decision variables that the decision maker wants to either MAXimize or MINimize. In our earlier examples, this function might be used to describe the total profit associated with a product mix, the total distance the drill bit must be moved, the total cost of transporting merchandise, or a retiree's total tax liability.

The mathematical formulation of an optimization problem can be described in the general format:

$$\text{MAX (or MIN):} \qquad f_0(X_1, X_2, \ldots, X_n) \qquad\qquad \textbf{2.1}$$
$$\text{Subject to:} \qquad f_1(X_1, X_2, \ldots, X_n) \leq b_1 \qquad\qquad \textbf{2.2}$$
$$\vdots$$
$$f_k(X_1, X_2, \ldots, X_n) \geq b_k \qquad\qquad \textbf{2.3}$$
$$\vdots$$
$$f_m(X_1, X_2, \ldots, X_n) = b_m \qquad\qquad \textbf{2.4}$$

This representation identifies the objective function (equation 2.1) that will be maximized (or minimized) and the constraints that must be satisfied (equations 2.2 through 2.4). Subscripts added to the f and b in each equation emphasize that the functions describing the objective and constraints can all be different. The goal in optimization is to find the values of the decision variables that maximize (or minimize) the objective function without violating any of the constraints.

2.4 MATHEMATICAL PROGRAMMING TECHNIQUES

Our general representation of an MP model is just that—general. There are many kinds of functions you can use to represent the objective function and the constraints in an MP model. Of course, you should always use functions that accurately describe the objective and constraints of the problem you are trying to solve. Sometimes the functions in a model are linear in nature (that is, form straight lines or flat surfaces); other times they are nonlinear (that is, form curved lines or curved surfaces). Sometimes the optimal values of the decision variables in a model must take on integer values (whole numbers); other times the decision variables can assume fractional values.

Given the diversity of MP problems that can be encountered, many techniques have been developed to solve different types of MP problems. In the next several chapters, we will look at these MP techniques and develop an understanding of how they differ and when each should be used. We will begin by examining a technique called **linear programming** (LP), which involves creating and solving optimization problems with linear objective functions and linear constraints. LP is a very powerful tool that can be applied in many business situations. It also forms a basis for several other techniques discussed later and is, therefore, a good starting point for our investigation into the field of optimization.

2.5 AN EXAMPLE LP PROBLEM

We will begin our study of LP by considering a simple example. You should not interpret this to mean that LP cannot solve more complex or realistic problems. LP has been used to solve extremely complicated problems, saving companies millions of dollars. However, jumping directly into one of these complicated problems would be like starting a marathon without ever having gone out for a jog—you would get winded and could be left behind very quickly. So we'll start with something simple.

Blue Ridge Hot Tubs manufactures and sells two models of hot tubs: the Aqua-Spa and the Hydro-Lux. Howie Jones, the owner and manager of the company, needs to decide how many of each type of hot tub to produce during his next production cycle. Howie buys prefabricated fiberglass hot tub shells from a local supplier and adds the pump and tubing to the shells to create his hot tubs. (This supplier has the capacity to deliver as many hot tub shells as Howie needs.) Howie installs the same type of pump into both hot tubs. He will have only 200 pumps available during his next production cycle. From a manufacturing standpoint, the main difference between the two models of hot tubs is the amount of tubing and labor required. Each Aqua-Spa requires 9 hours of labor and 12 feet of tubing. Each Hydro-Lux requires 6 hours of labor and 16 feet of tubing. Howie expects to have 1,566 production labor hours and 2,880 feet of tubing available during the next production cycle. Howie earns a profit of $350 on each Aqua-Spa he sells and $300 on each Hydro-Lux he sells. He is confident that he can sell all the hot tubs he produces. The question is, how many Aqua-Spas and Hydro-Luxes should Howie produce if he wants to maximize his profits during the next production cycle?

2.6 FORMULATING LP MODELS

The process of taking a practical problem—such as determining how many Aqua-Spas and Hydro-Luxes Howie should produce—and expressing it algebraically in the form of an LP model is known as formulating the model. Throughout the next several chapters you will see that formulating an LP model is as much an art as a science.

2.6.1 Steps in Formulating an LP Model

There are some general steps you can follow to help make sure your formulation of a particular problem is accurate. We will walk through these steps using the hot tub example.

1. **Understand the problem.** This step appears to be so obvious that it hardly seems worth mentioning. However, many people try to write the objective function and constraints before they really understand the problem. If you do not fully understand the problem you face, it is unlikely that your formulation of the problem will be correct.

    The problem in our example is fairly easy to understand: how many Aqua-Spas and Hydro-Luxes should Howie produce to maximize his profit, while using no more than 200 pumps, 1,566 labor hours, and 2,880 feet of tubing?

2. **Identify the decision variables.** After you are sure you understand the problem, you need to identify the decision variables. That is, what are the fundamental decisions that must be made in order to solve the problem? The answers to this question often will help you identify appropriate decision variables for your model. Identifying the decision variables means determining what the symbols X_1, X_2, ..., X_n represent in your model.

    In our example, the fundamental decision Howie faces is this: how many Aqua-Spas and Hydro-Luxes should be produced? In this problem we will let X_1 represent the number of Aqua-Spas to produce and X_2 represent the number of Hydro-Luxes to produce.

3. **State the objective function as a linear combination of the decision variables.** After determining the decision variables you will use, the next step is to create the objective function for the model. This function expresses the mathematical relationship between the decision variables in the model to be maximized or minimized.

    In our example, Howie earns a profit of $350 on each Aqua-Spa ($X_1$) he sells and $300 on each Hydro-Lux ($X_2$) he sells. Thus, Howie's objective of maximizing the profit he earns is stated mathematically as:

$$\text{MAX:} \qquad 350X_1 + 300X_2$$

For whatever values might be assigned to X_1 and X_2, the above function calculates the associated total profit that Howie would earn. Obviously, Howie wants to maximize this value.

4. **State the constraints as linear combinations of the decision variables.** As mentioned earlier, there are usually some limitations on the values that can be assumed by the decision variables in an LP model. These restrictions must be identified and stated in the form of constraints.

    In our example, Howie faces three major constraints. Because only 200 pumps are available and each hot tub requires one pump, Howie cannot produce more than a total of 200 hot tubs. This restriction is stated mathematically as:

$$1X_1 + 1X_2 \leq 200$$

This constraint indicates that each unit of X_1 produced (that is, each Aqua-Spa built) will use one of the 200 pumps available—as will each unit of X_2 produced (that is, each Hydro-Lux built). The total number of pumps used (represented by $1X_1 + 1X_2$) must be less than or equal to 200.

Another restriction Howie faces is that he has only 1,566 labor hours available during the next production cycle. Because each Aqua-Spa he builds (each unit of X_1) requires 9 labor hours and each Hydro-Lux (each unit of X_2) requires 6 labor hours, the constraint on the number of labor hours is stated as:

$$9X_1 + 6X_2 \leq 1,566$$

The total number of labor hours used (represented by $9X_1 + 6X_2$) must be less than or equal to the total labor hours available, which is 1,566.

The final constraint specifies that only 2,880 feet of tubing is available for the next production cycle. Each Aqua-Spa produced (each unit of X_1) requires 12 feet of tubing, and each Hydro-Lux produced (each unit of X_2) requires 16 feet of tubing. The following constraint is necessary to ensure that Howie's production plan does not use more tubing than is available:

$$12X_1 + 16X_2 \leq 2,880$$

The total number of feet of tubing used (represented by $12X_1 + 16X_2$) must be less than or equal to the total number of feet of tubing available, which is 2,880.

5. **Identify any upper or lower bounds on the decision variables.**   Often, simple upper or lower bounds apply to the decision variables. You can view upper and lower bounds as additional constraints in the problem.

In our example, there are simple lower bounds of zero on the variables X_1 and X_2 because it is impossible to produce a negative number of hot tubs. Therefore, the following two constraints also apply to this problem:

$$X_1 \geq 0$$
$$X_2 \geq 0$$

Constraints like these are often referred to as nonnegativity conditions, and are quite common in LP problems.

2.7   SUMMARY OF THE LP MODEL FOR THE EXAMPLE PROBLEM

The complete LP model for Howie's decision problem can be stated as:

MAX:	$350X_1$	$+$	$300X_2$			**2.5**
Subject to:	$1X_1$	$+$	$1X_2$	$\leq$	200	**2.6**
	$9X_1$	$+$	$6X_2$	$\leq$	1,566	**2.7**
	$12X_1$	$+$	$16X_2$	$\leq$	2,880	**2.8**
	$1X_1$			$\geq$	0	**2.9**
			$1X_2$	$\geq$	0	**2.10**

In this model, the decision variables X_1 and X_2 represent the number of Aqua-Spas and Hydro-Luxes to produce, respectively. Our goal is to determine the values for X_1 and X_2 that maximize the objective in equation 2.5 while simultaneously satisfying all the constraints in equations 2.6 through 2.10.

2.8   THE GENERAL FORM OF AN LP MODEL

The technique of linear programming is so-named because the MP problems to which it applies are linear in nature. That is, it must be possible to express all the functions in an LP model as some weighted sum (or linear combination) of the decision variables. So, an LP model takes on the general form:

MAX (or MIN): $c_1X_1 + c_2X_2 + \dots + c_nX_n$ 2.11

Subject to: $a_{11}X_1 + a_{12}X_2 + \dots + a_{1n}X_n \leq b_1$ 2.12

$$\vdots$$

$a_{k1}X_1 + a_{k2}X_2 + \dots + a_{kn}X_n \geq b_k$ 2.13

$$\vdots$$

$a_{m1}X_1 + a_{m2}X_2 + \dots + a_{mn}X_n = b_m$ 2.14

Up to this point, we have suggested that the constraints in an LP model represent some type of limited resource. Although this is frequently the case, in later chapters you will see examples of LP models in which the constraints represent things other than limited resources. The important point here is that any problem that can be formulated in the above fashion is an LP problem.

The symbols c_1, c_2, ..., c_n in equation 2.11 are called **objective function coefficients** and might represent the marginal profits (or costs) associated with the decision variables X_1, X_2, ..., X_n, respectively. The symbol a_{ij} found throughout equations 2.12 through 2.14 represents the numeric coefficient in the ith constraint for variable X_j. The objective function and constraints of an LP problem represent different weighted sums of the decision variables. The b_i symbols in the constraints, once again, represent values that the corresponding linear combination of the decision variables must be less than or equal to, greater than or equal to, or equal to.

You should now see a direct connection between the LP model we formulated for Blue Ridge Hot Tubs in equations 2.5 through 2.10 and the general definition of an LP model given in equations 2.11 through 2.14. In particular, note that the various symbols used in equations 2.11 through 2.14 to represent numeric constants (that is, the c_j, a_{ij}, and b_i) were replaced by actual numeric values in equations 2.5 through 2.10. Also, note that our formulation of the LP model for Blue Ridge Hot Tubs did not require the use of equal to constraints. Different problems require different types of constraints, and you should use whatever types of constraints are necessary for the problem at hand.

2.9   SOLVING LP PROBLEMS: AN INTUITIVE APPROACH

After an LP model has been formulated, our interest naturally turns to solving it. But before we actually solve our example problem for Blue Ridge Hot Tubs, what do you think is the optimal solution to the problem? Just by looking at the model, what values for X_1 and X_2 do you think would give Howie the largest profit?

Following one line of reasoning, it might seem that Howie should produce as many units of X_1 (Aqua-Spas) as possible because each of these generates a profit of $350, whereas each unit of X_2 (Hydro-Luxes) generates a profit of only $300. But what is the maximum number of Aqua-Spas that Howie could produce?

Howie can produce the maximum number of units of X_1 by making no units of X_2 and devoting all his resources to the production of X_1. Suppose we let $X_2 = 0$ in the model in equations 2.5 through 2.10 to indicate that no Hydro-Luxes will be produced. What then is the largest possible value of X_1? If $X_2 = 0$ then the inequality in equation 2.6 tells us:

$$X_1 \leq 200 \hspace{4cm} \textbf{2.15}$$

So we know that X_1 cannot be any greater than 200 if $X_2 = 0$. However, we also have to consider the constraints in equations 2.7 and 2.8. If $X_2 = 0$ then the inequality in equation 2.7 reduces to:

$$9X_1 \leq 1,566 \hspace{4cm} \textbf{2.16}$$

If we divide both sides of this inequality by 9, we find that the previous constraint is equivalent to:

$$X_1 \leq 174 \hspace{4cm} \textbf{2.17}$$

Now consider the constraint in equation 2.8. If $X_2 = 0$ then the inequality in equation 2.8 reduces to:

$$12X_1 \leq 2,880 \hspace{4cm} \textbf{2.18}$$

Again, if we divide both sides of this inequality by 12, we find that the previous constraint is equivalent to:

$$X_1 \leq 240 \hspace{4cm} \textbf{2.19}$$

So, if $X_2 = 0$, the three constraints in our model imposing upper limits on the value of X_1 reduce to the values shown in equations 2.15, 2.17, and 2.19. The most restrictive of these constraints is equation 2.17. Therefore, the maximum number of units of X_1 that can be produced is 174. In other words, 174 is the largest value X_1 can take on and still satisfy all the constraints in the model.

If Howie builds 174 units of X_1 (Aqua-Spas) and 0 units of X_2 (Hydro-Luxes), he will have used all of the labor that is available for production ($9X_1 = 1,566$ if $X_1 = 174$). However, he will have 26 pumps remaining ($200 - X_1 = 26$, if $X_1 = 174$) and 792 feet of tubing remaining ($2,880 - 12X_1 = 792$, if $X_1 = 174$). Also, notice that the objective function value (or total profit) associated with this solution is:

$$\$350X_1 + \$300X_2 = \$350 \times 174 + \$300 \times 0 = \$60,900$$

From this analysis, we see that the solution $X_1 = 174$, $X_2 = 0$ is a **feasible solution** to the problem because it satisfies all the constraints of the model. But is it the **optimal solution**? In other words, is there any other possible set of values for X_1 and X_2 that also satisfies all the constraints *and* results in a higher objective function value? As you will see, the intuitive approach to solving LP problems that we have taken here cannot be trusted because there actually is a better solution to Howie's problem.

2.10   SOLVING LP PROBLEMS: A GRAPHICAL APPROACH

The constraints of an LP model define the set of feasible solutions—or the **feasible region**—for the problem. The difficulty in LP is determining which point or points in the feasible region correspond to the best possible value of the objective function.

For simple problems with only two decision variables, it is fairly easy to sketch the feasible region for the LP model and locate the optimal feasible point graphically. Because the graphical approach can be used only if there are two decision variables, it has limited practical use. However, it is an extremely good way to develop a basic understanding of the issues involved in solving LP problems. Therefore, we will use the graphical approach to solve the simple problem faced by Blue Ridge Hot Tubs. Chapter 3 shows how to solve this and other LP problems using a spreadsheet.

To solve an LP problem graphically, you first must plot the constraints for the problem and identify its feasible region. This is done by plotting the *boundary lines* of the constraints and identifying the points that will satisfy all the constraints. So how do we do this for our example problem (repeated below)?

$$
\begin{array}{lllll}
\text{MAX:} & 350X_1 & + & 300X_2 & & & \textbf{2.20} \\
\text{Subject to:} & 1X_1 & + & 1X_2 & \leq & 200 & \textbf{2.21} \\
& 9X_1 & + & 6X_2 & \leq & 1{,}566 & \textbf{2.22} \\
& 12X_1 & + & 16X_2 & \leq & 2{,}880 & \textbf{2.23} \\
& 1X_1 & & & \geq & 0 & \textbf{2.24} \\
& & & 1X_2 & \geq & 0 & \textbf{2.25}
\end{array}
$$

2.10.1 Plotting the First Constraint

The boundary of the first constraint in our model, which specifies that no more than 200 pumps can be used, is represented by the straight line defined by the equation:

$$X_1 + X_2 = 200 \qquad\qquad \textbf{2.26}$$

If we can find any two points on this line, the entire line can be plotted easily by drawing a straight line through these points. If $X_2 = 0$, we can see from equation 2.26 that $X_1 = 200$. Thus, the point $(X_1, X_2) = (200, 0)$ must fall on this line. If we let $X_1 = 0$, from equation 2.26, it is easy to see that $X_2 = 200$. So the point $(X_1, X_2) = (0, 200)$ must also fall on this line. These two points are plotted on the graph in Figure 2.1 and connected to form the straight line representing equation 2.26.

Note that the graph of the line associated with equation 2.26 actually extends beyond the X_1 and X_2 axes shown in Figure 2.1. However, we can disregard the points beyond these axes because the values assumed by X_1 and X_2 cannot be negative (because we also have the constraints given by $X_1 \geq 0$ and $X_2 \geq 0$).

The line connecting the points (0, 200) and (200, 0) in Figure 2.1 identifies the points (X_1, X_2), which satisfy the equality $X_1 + X_2 = 200$. But recall that the first constraint in the LP model is the inequality $X_1 + X_2 \leq 200$. Thus, after plotting the boundary line of a constraint we must determine which area on the graph corresponds to feasible solutions for the original constraint. This can be done easily by picking an arbitrary point on either side of the boundary line and checking whether it satisfies the original constraint. For example, if we test the point $(X_1, X_2) = (0, 0)$ we see that this point satisfies the first constraint. Therefore, the area of the graph on the same side of the boundary line as the point (0, 0) corresponds to the feasible solutions of our first constraint. This area of feasible solutions is shaded in Figure 2.1.

2.10.2 Plotting the Second Constraint

Some of the feasible solutions to one constraint in an LP model usually will not satisfy one or more of the other constraints in the model. For example, the point

Figure 2.1
Graphical
representation of
the pump
constraint.

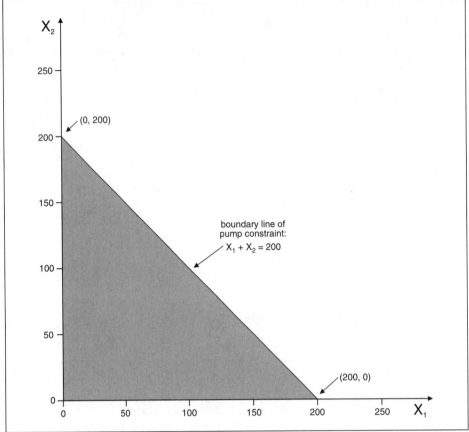

$(X_1, X_2) = (200, 0)$ satisfies the first constraint in our model, but it does not satisfy the second constraint, which requires that no more than 1,566 labor hours be used (because $9 \times 200 + 6 \times 0 = 1,800$). So, what values for X_1 and X_2 will simultaneously satisfy both of these constraints? To answer this question, we need to plot the second constraint on the graph as well. This is done in the same manner as before—by locating two points on the boundary line of the constraint and connecting these points with a straight line. The boundary line for the second constraint in our model is given by:

$$9X_1 + 6X_2 = 1,566 \qquad\qquad 2.27$$

If $X_1 = 0$ in equation 2.27, then $X_2 = 1,566/6 = 261$. So the point $(0, 261)$ must fall on the line defined by equation 2.27. Similarly, if $X_2 = 0$ in equation 2.27 then $X_1 = 1,566/9 = 174$. So the point $(174, 0)$ must also fall on this line. These two points are plotted on the graph and connected with a straight line representing equation 2.27, as shown in Figure 2.2.

The line drawn in Figure 2.2 representing equation 2.27 is the boundary line for our second constraint. To determine the area on the graph that corresponds to feasible solutions to the second constraint, we again need to test a point on either side of this line to see if it is feasible. The point $(X_1, X_2) = (0, 0)$ satisfies $9X_1 + 6X_2 \leq 1,566$. Therefore, all points on the same side of the boundary line satisfy this constraint.

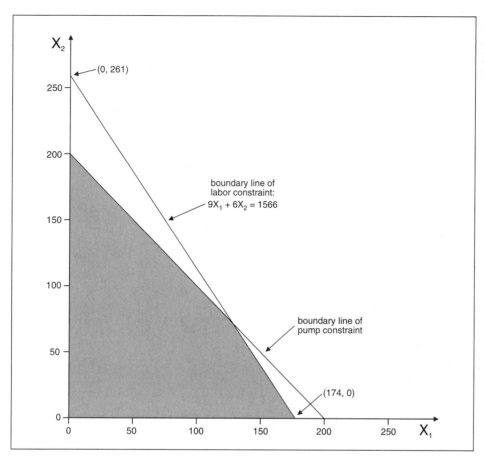

Figure 2.2
Graphical representation of the pump and labor constraints.

2.10.3   Plotting the Third Constraint

To find the set of values for X_1 and X_2 that satisfies all the constraints in the model we need to plot the third constraint. This constraint requires that no more than 2,880 feet of tubing be used in producing the hot tubs. Again, we will find two points on the graph that fall on the boundary line for this constraint and connect them with a straight line. The boundary line for the third constraint in our model is:

$$12X_1 + 16X_2 = 2,880 \qquad\qquad \textbf{2.28}$$

If $X_1 = 0$ in equation 2.28, then $X_2 = 2,880/16 = 180$. So the point $(0, 180)$ must fall on the line defined by equation 2.28. Similarly, if $X_2 = 0$ in equation 2.28, then $X_1 = 2,880/12 = 240$. So the point $(240, 0)$ must also fall on this line. These two points are plotted on the graph and connected with a straight line representing equation 2.28, as shown in Figure 2.3.

Again, the line drawn in Figure 2.3 representing equation 2.28 is the boundary line for our third constraint. To determine the area on the graph that corresponds to feasible solutions to this constraint, we need to test a point on either side of this line to see if it is feasible. The point $(X_1, X_2) = (0, 0)$ satisfies $12X_1 + 16X_2 \leq 2,880$. Therefore, all points on the same side of the boundary line satisfy this constraint.

Figure 2.3
Graphical
representation
of the feasible
region.

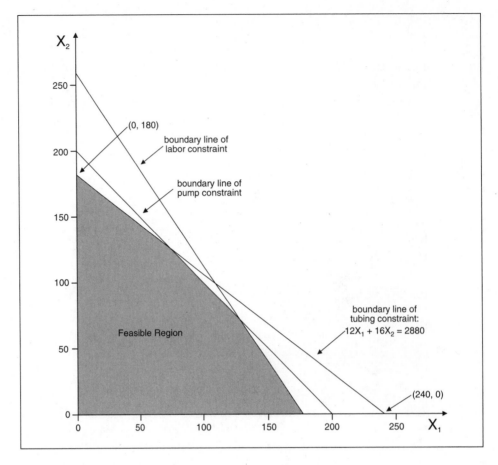

2.10.4   The Feasible Region

It is now easy to see which points satisfy all the constraints in our model. These points correspond to the shaded area in Figure 2.3, labeled "Feasible Region." The **feasible region** is the set of points or values that the decision variables can assume and simultaneously satisfy all the constraints in the problem. Take a moment now to carefully compare the graphs in Figures 2.1, 2.2, and 2.3. In particular, notice that when we added the second constraint in Figure 2.2 some of the feasible solutions associated with the first constraint were eliminated because these solutions did not satisfy the second constraint. Similarly, when we added the third constraint in Figure 2.3 another portion of the feasible solutions for the first constraint was eliminated.

2.10.5   Plotting the Objective Function

Now that we have isolated the set of feasible solutions to our LP problem, we need to determine which of these solutions is best. That is, we must determine which point in the feasible region will maximize the value of the objective function in our model. At first glance, it might seem that trying to locate this point is like searching for a needle in a haystack. After all, as shown by the shaded region in Figure 2.3, there are an *infinite* number of feasible solutions to this problem. Fortunately, we can easily eliminate most of the feasible solutions in an LP problem from consideration. It can be shown that if an LP problem has an optimal solution with a finite objective function value, this solution will always occur at a point in the feasible region where two or more of the boundary lines of the constraints intersect. These points of intersection are sometimes called **corner points** or **extreme points** of the feasible region.

To see why the finite optimal solution to an LP problem occurs at an extreme point of the feasible region, consider the relationship between the objective function and the feasible region of our example LP model. Suppose we are interested in finding the values of X_1 and X_2 associated with a given level of profit, such as $35,000. Then, mathematically, we are interested in finding the points (X_1, X_2) for which our objective function equals $35,000, or where:

$$\$350X_1 + \$300X_2 = \$35,000 \qquad \textbf{2.29}$$

This equation defines a straight line, which we can plot on our graph. Specifically, if $X_1 = 0$ then, from equation 2.29, $X_2 = 116.67$. Similarly, if $X_2 = 0$ in equation 2.29, then $X_1 = 100$. So, the points $(X_1, X_2) = (0, 116.67)$ and $(X_1, X_2) = (100, 0)$ both fall on the line defining a profit level of $35,000. (Note that all the points on this line produce a profit level of $35,000.) This line is shown in Figure 2.4.

Now suppose we are interested in finding the values of X_1 and X_2 that produce some higher level of profit, such as $52,500. Then, mathematically, we are interested in finding the points (X_1, X_2) for which our objective function equals $52,500, or where:

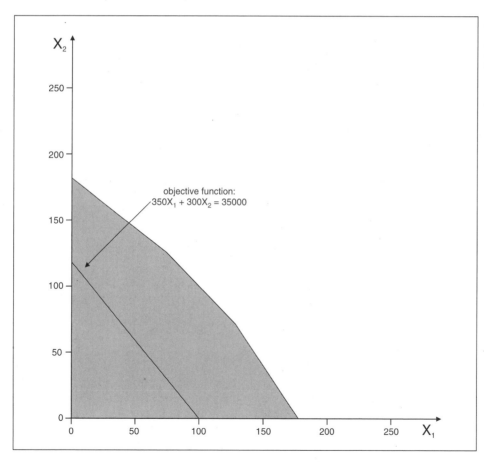

Figure 2.4
Graph showing values of X_1 and X_2 that produce an objective function value of $35,000.

objective function:
$350X_1 + 300X_2 = 35000$

$$\$350X_1 + \$300X_2 = \$52,500 \qquad\qquad \textbf{2.30}$$

This equation also defines a straight line, which we could plot on our graph. If we do this, we'll find that the points $(X_1, X_2) = (0, 175)$ and $(X_1, X_2) = (150, 0)$ both fall on this line, as shown in Figure 2.5.

2.10.6   *Finding the Optimal Solution Using Level Curves*

The lines in Figure 2.5 representing the two objective function values are sometimes referred to as **level curves** because they represent different levels or values of the objective. Note that the two level curves in Figure 2.5 are parallel to one another. If we repeat this process of drawing lines associated with larger and larger values of our objective function, we will continue to observe a series of parallel lines shifting away from the origin (that is, away from the point $(0, 0)$). The very last level curve we can draw that still intersects the feasible region will determine the maximum profit we can achieve. This point of intersection, shown in Figure 2.6, represents the optimal feasible solution to the problem.

As shown in Figure 2.6, the optimal solution to our example problem occurs at the point where the largest possible level curve intersects the feasible region at a single point. This is the feasible point that produces the largest profit for Blue Ridge Hot Tubs. But how do we figure out exactly what point this is and how much profit it provides?

Figure 2.5
Parallel level curves for two different objective function values.

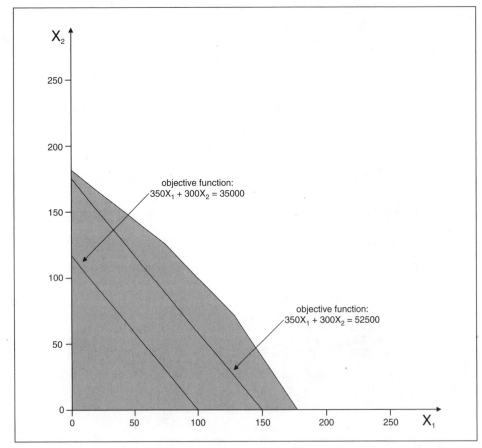

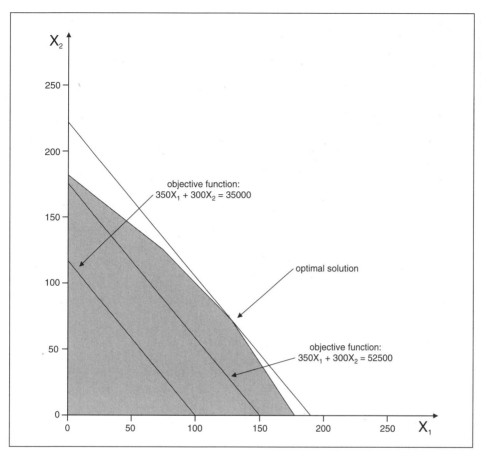

Figure 2.6
Graph showing
optimal solution
where the level
curve is tangent
to the feasible
region.

If you compare Figure 2.6 to Figure 2.3, you see that the optimal solution occurs at the point where the boundary lines of the pump and labor constraints intersect (or are equal). Thus, the optimal solution is defined by the point (X_1, X_2) that simultaneously satisfies equations 2.26 and 2.27, which are repeated below:

$$X_1 + X_2 = 200$$

$$9X_1 + 6X_2 = 1,566$$

From the first equation we easily conclude that $X_2 = 200 - X_1$. If we substitute this definition of X_2 into the second equation we obtain:

$$9X_1 + 6(200 - X_1) = 1,566$$

Using simple algebra, we can solve this equation to find that $X_1 = 122$. And because $X_2 = 200 - X_1$ we can conclude that $X_2 = 78$. Therefore, we have determined that the optimal solution to our example problem occurs at the point $(X_1, X_2) = (122, 78)$. This point satisfies all the constraints in our model and corresponds to the point in Figure 2.6 identified as the optimal solution.

The total profit associated with this solution is found by substituting the optimal values of $X_1 = 122$ and $X_2 = 78$ into the objective function. Thus, Blue Ridge Hot

Tubs can realize a profit of $66,100 if it produces 122 Aqua-Spas and 78 Hydro-Luxes ($350 × 122 + $300 × 78 = $66,100). Any other production plan would result in a lower total profit. In particular, note that the solution we found earlier using the intuitive approach (which produced a total profit of $60,900) is inferior to the optimal solution identified here.

2.10.7   Finding the Optimal Solution by Enumerating the Corner Points

Earlier we indicated that if an LP problem has a finite optimal solution, this solution will always occur at some corner point of the feasible region. So, another way of solving an LP problem is to identify all the corner points, or extreme points, of the feasible region and calculate the value of the objective function at each of these points. The corner point with the largest objective function value is the optimal solution to the problem.

This approach is illustrated in Figure 2.7, where the X_1 and X_2 coordinates for each of the extreme points are identified along with the associated objective function values. As expected, this analysis also indicates that the point $(X_1, X_2) = (122, 78)$ is optimal.

Figure 2.7
Objective function values at each extreme point of the feasible region.

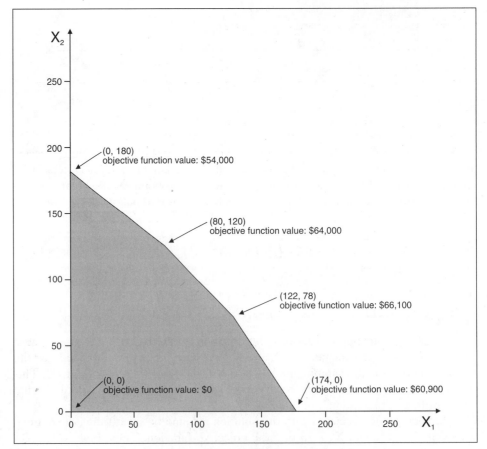

Enumerating the corner points to identify the optimal solution is often more difficult than the level curve approach because it requires that you identify the coordinates for all the extreme points of the feasible region. If there are many intersecting constraints, the number of extreme points can become rather large, making this procedure very tedious. Also, a special condition exists for which this procedure will not work. This condition, known as an unbounded solution, will be described shortly.

2.10.8   Summary of Graphical Solution to LP Problems

To summarize this section, a two-variable LP problem is solved graphically by performing these steps:

1. Plot the boundary line of each constraint in the model.
2. Identify the feasible region, that is, the set of points on the graph that simultaneously satisfy all the constraints.
3. Locate the optimal solution by one of the following methods:
   a. Plot one or more level curves for the objective function and determine the direction in which parallel shifts in this line produce improved objective function values. Shift the level curve in a parallel manner in the improving direction until it intersects the feasible region at a single point. Then find the coordinates for this point. This is the optimal solution.
   b. Identify the coordinates of all the extreme points of the feasible region and calculate the objective function values associated with each point. If the feasible region is bounded, the point with the best objective function value is the optimal solution.

2.11   SPECIAL CONDITIONS IN LP MODELS

Several special conditions can arise in LP modeling: alternate optimal solutions, redundant constraints, unbounded solutions, and infeasibility. The first two conditions do not prevent you from solving an LP model and are not really problems—they are just anomalies that sometimes occur. On the other hand, the last two conditions represent real problems that prevent us from solving an LP model.

2.11.1   Alternate Optimal Solutions

Some LP models can actually have more than one optimal solution, or alternate optimal solutions. That is, there can be more than one feasible point that maximizes (or minimizes) the value of the objective function.

For example, suppose Howie can increase the price of Aqua-Spas to the point where each unit sold generates a profit of $450 rather than $350. The revised LP model for this problem is:

$$
\begin{array}{llrclcr}
\text{MAX:} & & 450X_1 & + & 300X_2 & & \\
\text{Subject to:} & & 1X_1 & + & 1X_2 & \leq & 200 \\
& & 9X_1 & + & 6X_2 & \leq & 1,566 \\
& & 12X_1 & + & 16X_2 & \leq & 2,880 \\
& & 1X_1 & & & \geq & 0 \\
& & & & 1X_2 & \geq & 0
\end{array}
$$

Because none of the constraints changed, the feasible region for this model is the same as for the earlier example. The only difference in this model is the objective function. Therefore, the level curves for the objective function are different from what we observed earlier. Several level curves for this model are plotted with its feasible region in Figure 2.8.

Notice that the final level curve in Figure 2.8 intersects the feasible region along an edge of the feasible region rather than at a single point. All the points on the line segment joining the corner point at (122, 78) to the corner point at (174, 0) produce the same optimal objective function value of $78,300 for this problem. Thus, all these points are alternate optimal solutions to the problem. If we used a computer to solve this problem, it would identify only one of the corner points of this edge as the optimal solution.

The fact that alternate optimal solutions sometimes occur is really not a problem because this anomaly does not prevent us from finding an optimal solution to the problem. In fact, in chapter 7, Goal Programming and Multiple Objective Optimization, you will see that alternate optimal solutions are sometimes very desirable.

2.11.2 Redundant Constraints

Redundant constraints present another special condition that sometimes occurs in an LP model. A **redundant constraint** is a constraint that plays no role in determining

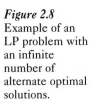
Figure 2.8
Example of an LP problem with an infinite number of alternate optimal solutions.

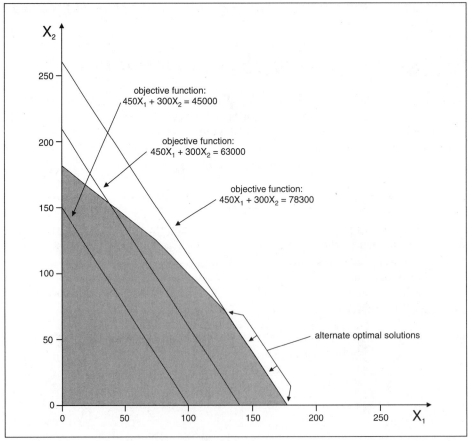

the feasible region of the problem. For example, in the hot tub example, suppose that 225 hot tub pumps are available instead of 200. The earlier LP model can be modified as follows to reflect this change:

$$
\begin{array}{llrcrcr}
\text{MAX:} & & 350X_1 & + & 300X_2 & & \\
\text{Subject to:} & & 1X_1 & + & 1X_2 & \leq & 225 \\
& & 9X_1 & + & 6X_2 & \leq & 1{,}566 \\
& & 12X_1 & + & 16X_2 & \leq & 2{,}880 \\
& & 1X_1 & & & \geq & 0 \\
& & & & 1X_2 & \geq & 0
\end{array}
$$

This model is identical to the original model we formulated for this problem except for the new upper limit on the first constraint (representing the number of pumps that can be used). The constraints and feasible region for this revised model are shown in Figure 2.9.

Notice that the pump constraint in this model no longer plays any role in defining the feasible region of the problem. That is, as long as the tubing constraint and labor constraints are satisfied (which is always the case for any feasible solution), then the pump constraint will also be satisfied. Therefore, we can remove the pump constraint from the model without changing the feasible region of the problem—the constraint is simply redundant.

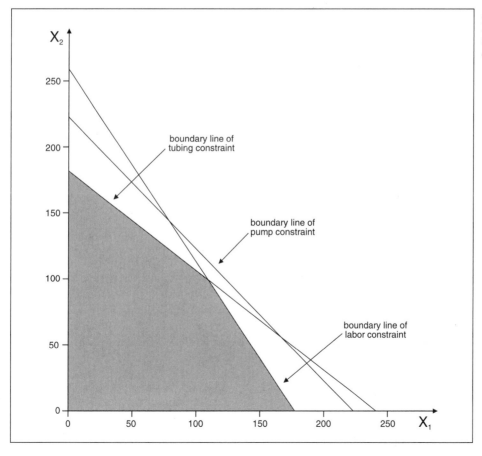

Figure 2.9
Example of a redundant constraint.

The fact that the pump constraint does not play a role in defining the feasible region in Figure 2.9 implies that there will always be an excess number of pumps available. Because none of the feasible solutions identified in Figure 2.9 fall on the boundary line of the pump constraint, this constraint will always be satisfied as a strict inequality ($1X_1 + 1X_2 < 225$) and never as a strict equality ($1X_1 + 1X_2 = 225$).

Again, redundant constraints are not really a problem. They do not prevent us (or the computer) from finding the optimal solution to an LP problem. However, they do represent "excess baggage" for the computer; so if you know that a constraint is redundant, eliminating it will save the computer this excess work. On the other hand, if the model you are working with will be modified and used repeatedly, it might be best to leave any redundant constraints in the model because they might not be redundant in the future. For example, from Figure 2.3 we know that if the availability of pumps is returned to 200, then the pump constraint again will play an important role in defining the feasible region (and optimal solution) of the problem.

2.11.3   Unbounded Solutions

When attempting to solve some LP problems, you might encounter situations in which the objective function can be made infinitely large (in the case of a maximization problem) or infinitely small (in the case of a minimization problem). As an example, consider this LP problem:

$$
\begin{array}{llrcrcr}
\text{MAX:} & & X_1 & + & X_2 & & \\
\text{Subject to:} & & X_1 & + & X_2 & \geq & 400 \\
& & -X_1 & + & 2X_2 & \leq & 400 \\
& & X_1 & & & \geq & 0 \\
& & & & X_2 & \geq & 0
\end{array}
$$

The feasible region and some level curves for this problem are shown in Figure 2.10. From this graph, you can see that as the level curves shift farther and farther away from the origin, the objective function increases. Because the feasible region is not bounded in this direction, you can continue shifting the level curve by an infinite amount and make the objective function infinitely large.

Although, it is not unusual to encounter an **unbounded solution** when solving an LP model, such a solution indicates that there is something wrong with the formulation—for example, one or more constraints were omitted from the formulation, or a less than constraint was erroneously entered as a greater than constraint.

While describing how to find the optimal solution to an LP model by enumerating corner points, we noted that this procedure will not always work if the feasible region for the problem is unbounded. Figure 2.10 provides an example of such a situation. The only extreme points for the feasible region in Figure 2.10 occur at the points (400, 0) and ($13\overline{3}3$, $266.\overline{6}$). The objective function value at both of these points (and at any point on the line segment joining them) is 400. By enumerating the extreme points for this problem we might erroneously conclude that alternate optimal solutions to this problem exist that produce an optimal objective function value of 400. This is true if the problem involved *minimizing* the objective function. However, the goal here is to *maximize* the objective function value, which, as we have seen, can be done without limit. So, when trying to solve an LP problem by enumerating the extreme points of an unbounded feasible region, you must also check whether or not the objective function is unbounded.

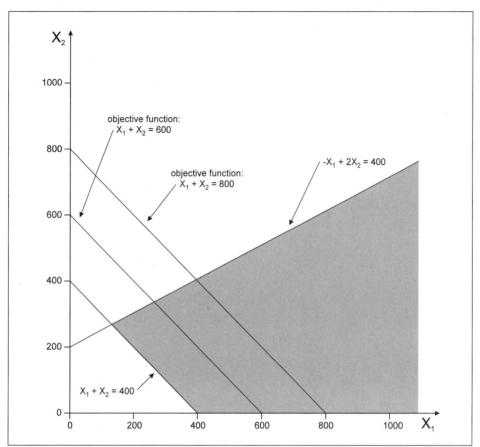

Figure 2.10
Example of an
LP problem with
an unbounded
solution.

2.11.4   Infeasibility

An LP problem is **infeasible** if there is no way to simultaneously satisfy all the constraints in the problem. As an example, consider the LP model:

$$\begin{array}{rrcll}
\text{MAX:} & X_1 & + & X_2 & \\
\text{Subject to:} & X_1 & + & X_2 & \leq \quad 150 \\
& X_1 & + & X_2 & \geq \quad 200 \\
& X_1 & & & \geq \quad 0 \\
& & & X_2 & \geq \quad 0
\end{array}$$

The feasible solutions for the first two constraints in this model are shown in Figure 2.11. Notice that the feasible solutions to the first constraint fall on the left side of its boundary line, whereas the feasible solutions to the second constraint fall on the right side of its boundary line. Therefore, no possible values for X_1 and X_2 exist that simultaneously satisfy both constraints in the model. In such a case, there are no feasible solutions to the problem.

Infeasibility can occur in LP problems, perhaps due to an error in the formulation of the model—such as unintentionally making a less than or equal to constraint a greater than or equal to constraint. Or there just might not be a way to satisfy all the

Figure 2.11
Example of an
LP problem
with no feasible
solution

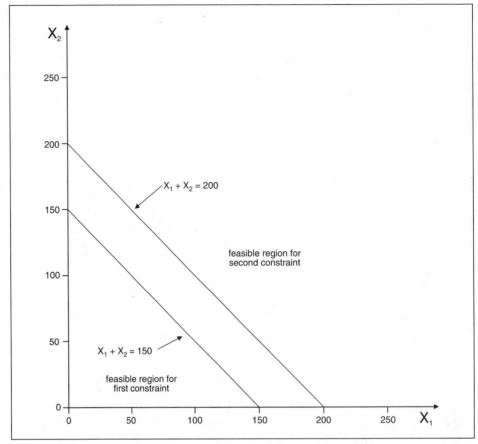

constraints in the model. In this case, constraints will have to be eliminated or loosened in order to obtain a feasible region (and feasible solution) for the problem.

Loosening constraints involves increasing the upper limits (or reducing the lower limits) to expand the range of feasible solutions. For example, if we loosen the first constraint in the previous model by changing the upper limit from 150 to 250, there is a feasible region for the problem. Of course, loosening constraints should not be done arbitrarily. In a real model, the value 150 would represent some actual characteristic of the decision problem (such as the number of pumps available to make hot tubs). We obviously cannot change this value to 250 unless it is appropriate to do so that is, unless we know another 100 pumps can be obtained.

SUMMARY

This chapter provided an introduction to an area of management science known as mathematical programming (MP), or optimization. Optimization covers a broad range of problems that share a common goal—determining the values for the decision variables in a problem that will maximize (or minimize) some objective function while satisfying various constraints. Constraints impose restrictions on the values that can be assumed by the decision variables and define the set of feasible options (or the feasible region) for the problem.

Linear programming (LP) problems represent a special category of MP problems in which the objective function and all the constraints can be expressed as linear combinations of the decision variables. Simple, two-variable LP problems can be solved graphically by identifying the feasible region and plotting level curves for the objective function. An optimal solution to an LP problem always occurs at a corner point of its feasible region (unless the objective function is unbounded).

Some anomalies can occur in optimization problems; these include alternate optimal solutions, redundant constraints, unbounded solutions, and infeasibility.

QUESTIONS AND PROBLEMS

1. An LP model can have more than one optimal solution. Is it possible for an LP model to have exactly two optimal solutions? Why or why not?

2. In the solution to the Blue Ridge Hot Tubs problem, the optimal values for X_1 and X_2 turned out to be integers (whole numbers). Is this a general property of the solutions to LP problems? In other words, will the solution to an LP problem always consist of integers? Why or why not?

3. To determine the feasible region associated with less than or equal to constraints or greater than or equal to constraints, we graphed these constraints as if they were equal to constraints. Why is this possible?

4. Are the following objective functions for an LP model equivalent? That is, if they are both used, one at a time, to solve a problem with exactly the same constraints, will the optimal values for X_1 and X_2 be the same in both cases? Why or why not?

$$\text{MAX:} \quad 2X_1 + 3X_2$$
$$\text{MIN:} \quad -2X_1 - 3X_2$$

5. Which of the following constraints are not linear or cannot be included as a constraint in a linear programming problem?

   a. $2X_1 + X_2 - 3X_3 \geq 50$

   b. $2X_1 + \sqrt{X_2} \geq 60$

   c. $4X_1 - \frac{1}{3}X_2 = 75$

   d. $\dfrac{3X_1 + 2X_2 - 3X_3}{X_1 + X_2 + X_3} \leq 0.9$

   e. $3X_1^2 + 7X_2 \leq 45$

6. Solve the following LP problem graphically by enumerating the corner points.

$$\begin{array}{llrcrcr}
\text{MAX:} & & 3X_1 & + & 4X_2 & & \\
\text{Subject to:} & X_1 & & & & \leq & 12 \\
& & & & X_2 & \leq & 10 \\
& 4X_1 & + & 6X_2 & & \leq & 72 \\
& & & X_1, X_2 & & \geq & 0
\end{array}$$

7. Solve the following LP problem graphically using level curves.

$$
\begin{array}{llrll}
\text{MIN:} & 2X_1 & + & 3X_2 & \\
\text{Subject to:} & 2X_1 & + & 1X_2 & \geq & 3 \\
& 4X_1 & + & 5X_2 & \geq & 20 \\
& 2X_1 & + & 8X_2 & \geq & 16 \\
& 5X_1 & + & 6X_2 & \leq & 60 \\
& X_1, X_2 & & & \geq & 0
\end{array}
$$

8. Solve the following LP problem graphically using level curves.

$$
\begin{array}{llrll}
\text{MAX:} & 2X_1 & + & 5X_2 & \\
\text{Subject to:} & 6X_1 & + & 5X_2 & \leq & 60 \\
& 2X_1 & + & 3X_2 & \leq & 24 \\
& 3X_1 & + & 6X_2 & \leq & 48 \\
& X_1, X_2 & & & \geq & 0
\end{array}
$$

9. Solve the following LP problem graphically by enumerating the corner points.

$$
\begin{array}{llrll}
\text{MIN:} & 5X_1 & + & 20X_2 & \\
\text{Subject to:} & X_1 & + & X_2 & \geq & 12 \\
& 2X_1 & + & 5X_2 & \geq & 40 \\
& X_1 & + & X_2 & \leq & 15 \\
& X_1, X_2 & & & \geq & 0
\end{array}
$$

10. Consider the following LP problem.

$$
\begin{array}{llrll}
\text{MAX:} & 3X_1 & + & 2X_2 & \\
\text{Subject to:} & 3X_1 & + & 3X_2 & \leq & 300 \\
& 6X_1 & + & 3X_2 & \leq & 480 \\
& 3X_1 & + & 3X_2 & \leq & 480 \\
& X_1, X_2 & & & \geq & 0
\end{array}
$$

   a. Sketch the feasible region for this model.
   b. What is the optimal solution?
   c. Identify any redundant constraints in this model.

11. Solve the following LP problem graphically by enumerating the corner points.

$$
\begin{array}{llrll}
\text{MAX:} & 10X_1 & + & 12X_2 & \\
\text{Subject to:} & 8X_1 & + & 6X_2 & \leq & 98 \\
& 6X_1 & + & 8X_2 & \leq & 98 \\
& X_1 & + & X_2 & \geq & 14 \\
& X_1, X_2 & & & \geq & 0
\end{array}
$$

12. Solve the following LP problem using level curves.

$$
\begin{aligned}
\text{MAX:} \quad & 4X_1 + 5X_2 \\
\text{Subject to:} \quad & 2X_1 + 3X_2 \leq 120 \\
& 4X_1 + 3X_2 \leq 140 \\
& X_1 + X_2 \geq 80 \\
& X_1, X_2 \geq 0
\end{aligned}
$$

13. The Electrotech Corporation manufactures two industrial-sized electrical devices: generators and alternators. Both of these products require wiring and testing during the assembly process. Each generator requires 2 hours of wiring and 1 hour of testing and can be sold for a $250 profit. Each alternator requires 3 hours of wiring and 2 hours of testing and can be sold for a $150 profit. There are 260 hours of wiring time and 140 hours of testing time available in the next production period.

   a. Formulate an LP model for this problem.
   b. Sketch the feasible region for this problem.
   c. Determine the optimal solution to this problem using level curves.

14. Refer to question 13. Suppose that Electrotech's management decides that they need to make at least 20 generators and at least 20 alternators.

   a. Reformulate your LP model to account for this change.
   b. Sketch the feasible region for this problem.
   c. Determine the optimal solution to this problem by enumerating the corner points.

15. Refer to question 14. Suppose that Electrotech can acquire additional wiring time at a very favorable cost. Should it do so? Why or why not?

16. Bill's Grill is a popular college restaurant that is famous for its hamburgers. The owner of the restaurant, Bill, mixes fresh ground beef and pork with a secret ingredient to make delicious quarter-pound hamburgers that are advertised as having no more than 25% fat. Bill can buy beef containing 80% meat and 20% fat at $0.85 per pound. He can buy pork containing 70% meat and 30% fat at $0.65 per pound. Bill wants to determine the most economical way to blend the beef and pork to make hamburgers that have no more than 25% fat.

   a. Formulate an LP model for this problem. (Hint: The decision variables for this problem represent the percentage of beef and the percentage of pork to combine.)
   b. Sketch the feasible region for this problem.
   c. Determine the optimal solution to this problem by enumerating the corner points.

17. The Springer Dog Food Company makes dry dog food from two ingredients. The two ingredients (A and B) provide different amounts of protein and vitamins. Ingredient A provides 16 units of protein and 4 units of vitamins per pound. Ingredient B provides 8 units of protein and 8 units of vitamins per pound. Ingredients A and B cost $0.50 and $0.20 per pound, respectively. The company wants its dog food to contain at least 12 units of protein and 6 units of vitamins per pound.

   a. Formulate an LP model for this problem.
   b. Sketch the feasible region for this model.
   c. Find the optimal solution to the problem by enumerating the corner points.

18. Refer to question 17. How will the optimal solution change if the company requires only 5 units of vitamins per pound rather than 6?

19. A farmer in Georgia has a 100 acre farm on which to plant watermelons and cantaloupes. Every acre planted with watermelons requires 50 gallons of water per day and must be prepared for planting with 20 pounds of fertilizer. Every acre planted with cantaloupes requires 75 gallons of water per day and must be prepared for planting with 15 pounds of fertilizer. The farmer estimates that it will take 2 hours of labor to harvest each acre planted with watermelons and 2.5 hours to harvest each acre planted with cantaloupes. He believes that watermelons will sell for about $3 each, and cantaloupes will sell for about $1 each. Every acre planted with watermelons is expected to yield 90 salable units. Every acre planted with cantaloupes is expected to yield 300 salable units. The farmer can pump about 6,000 gallons of water per day for irrigation purposes from a shallow well. He can buy as much fertilizer as he needs at a cost of $10 per 50-pound bag. Finally, the farmer can hire laborers to harvest the fields at a rate of $5 per hour. If the farmer sells all the watermelons and cantaloupes he produces, how many acres of each crop should the farmer plant in order to maximize profits?

    a. Formulate an LP model for this problem.
    b. Sketch the feasible region for this model.
    c. Find the optimal solution to the problem using level curves.

20. PC-Express is a computer retail store that sells two kinds of microcomputers: desktops and laptops. The company earns $600 on each desktop computer it sells and $900 on each laptop. The microcomputers PC-Express sells are actually manufactured by another company. This manufacturer has a special order to fill for another customer and cannot ship more than 80 desktop computers and 75 laptops to PC-Express next month. The employees at PC-Express must spend about 2 hours installing software and checking each desktop computer they sell. They spend roughly 3 hours to complete this process for laptop computers. They expect to have about 300 hours available for this purpose during the next month. The store's management is fairly certain that they can sell all the computers they order, but are unsure how many desktops and laptops they should order to maximize profits.

    a. Formulate an LP model for this problem.
    b. Sketch the feasible region for this model.
    c. Find the optimal solution to the problem by enumerating the corner points.

REFERENCES

Bazaraa, M. and J. Jarvis. *Linear Programming and Network Flows*. New York: Wiley, 1990.
Dantzig, G. *Linear Programming and Extensions*. Princeton, NJ: Princeton University Press, 1963.
Eppen, G., F. Gould and C. Schmidt. *Introduction to Management Science*. Englewood Cliffs, NJ: Prentice Hall, 1993.
Shogan, A. *Management Science*. Englewood Cliffs, NJ: Prentice Hall, 1988.
Winston, W. *Operations Research: Applications and Algorithms*. Belmont, CA: Duxbury Press, 1994.

CHAPTER 3

Modeling and Solving LP Problems in a Spreadsheet

Chapter 2 discussed how to formulate linear programming (LP) problems and how to solve simple, two-variable LP problems graphically. As you might expect, very few real-world LP problems involve only two decision variables. So the graphical solution approach is of limited value in solving LP problems. However, the discussion of two-variable problems provides a basis for understanding the issues involved in all LP problems and the general strategies for solving them.

For example, every solvable LP problem has a feasible region, and an optimal solution to the problem can be found at some extreme point of this region (assuming the problem is not unbounded). This is true of all LP problems regardless of the number of decision variables. Although it is fairly easy to graph the feasible region for a two-variable LP problem, it is difficult to visualize or graph the feasible region of an LP problem with three variables because such a graph would be three-dimensional. If there are more than three variables it is virtually impossible to visualize or graph the feasible region for an LP problem because such a graph involves more than three dimensions.

Fortunately, several mathematical techniques exist to solve LP problems involving almost any number of variables without visualizing or graphing their feasible regions. These techniques are now built into spreadsheet packages in a way that makes solving LP problems a fairly simple task. So using the appropriate computer software, you can solve almost any LP problem easily. The main challenge is ensuring that you formulate the LP problem correctly and communicate this formulation to the computer accurately. This chapter shows you how to do this using spreadsheets.

3.1 SPREADSHEET SOLVERS

The importance of LP (and optimization in general) is underscored by the fact that the latest versions of Excel, Quattro Pro, and Lotus 1-2-3 come with built-in spreadsheet optimization tools called solvers. Several spreadsheet add-in packages are also available to bring the power of optimization to older versions of these spreadsheet packages. This book uses Excel to illustrate how spreadsheet solvers can solve optimization problems. However, the same concepts and techniques presented here apply to other spreadsheet packages, although certain details of implementation may differ.

You can also solve optimization problems without using a spreadsheet by using a specialized mathematical programming package. A partial list of these packages includes: LINDO, MPSX, AMPL, CPLEX, and MathPro. Typically, these packages are used by researchers and businesses interested in solving extremely large problems that do not fit conveniently in a spreadsheet.

The Spreadsheet Solver Company

Frontline Systems Inc. created the Solvers in Microsoft Excel, Lotus 1-2-3 97, and Corel Quattro Pro. This company markets enhanced versions of these spreadsheet solvers which offer greater capacity, much faster speed, and several ease-of-use features. You can find out more about Frontline Systems and their Solver products by visiting their website at http://www.frontsys.com.

3.2   SOLVING LP PROBLEMS IN A SPREADSHEET

We will demonstrate the mechanics of using the Solver in Excel by solving the problem faced by Howie Jones, described in Chapter 2. You will recall that Howie owns and operates Blue Ridge Hot Tubs, a company that sells two models of hot tubs: the Aqua-Spa and the Hydro-Lux. Howie purchases prefabricated fiberglass hot tub shells and installs a common water pump and the appropriate amount of tubing into each hot tub. Every Aqua-Spa requires 9 hours of labor and 12 feet of tubing; every Hydro-Lux requires 6 hours of labor and 16 feet of tubing. Demand for these products is such that each Aqua-Spa produced can be sold to generate a profit of $350, and each Hydro-Lux produced can be sold to generate a profit of $300. The company expects to have 200 pumps, 1,566 hours of labor, and 2,880 feet of tubing available during the next production cycle. The problem is to determine the optimal number of Aqua-Spas and Hydro-Luxes to produce in order to maximize profits.

Chapter 2 developed the following LP formulation for the problem Howie faces. In this model, X_1 represents the number of Aqua-Spas to be produced, and X_2 represents the number of Hydro-Luxes to be produced.

$$
\begin{array}{llllllll}
\text{MAX:} & 350X_1 & + & 300X_2 & & & \} \text{ profit} \\
\text{Subject to:} & 1X_1 & + & 1X_2 & \leq & 200 & \} \text{ pump constraint} \\
& 9X_1 & + & 6X_2 & \leq & 1{,}566 & \} \text{ labor constraint} \\
& 12X_1 & + & 16X_2 & \leq & 2{,}800 & \} \text{ tubing constraint} \\
& 1X_1 & & & \geq & 0 & \} \text{ simple lower bound} \\
& & & 1X_2 & \geq & 0 & \} \text{ simple lower bound}
\end{array}
$$

So how do you solve this problem in a spreadsheet? First you must implement, or build, this model in the spreadsheet.

3.3   THE STEPS IN IMPLEMENTING AN LP MODEL IN A SPREADSHEET

The following four steps summarize what must be done to implement any LP problem in a spreadsheet.

1. **Organize the data for the model on the spreadsheet.**   The data for the model consist of the coefficients in the objective function, the various coefficients in the constraints, and the right-hand side (RHS) values for the constraints. There is usually more than one way to organize the data for a particular problem on a spreadsheet, but you should keep in mind some general guidelines. First, the goal is to organize the data so their purpose and meaning are as clear as possible. Think of your spreadsheet as a management report that needs to communicate clearly the important factors of the problem being solved. To this end, you should spend some time organizing the data for the problem by visualizing how the data can be laid out logically before you start typing values in the spreadsheet. Descriptive labels should be placed in the spreadsheet to clearly identify the various data elements. Often, row and column structures of the data in the model can be used in the spreadsheet to facilitate model implementation. (Note that some or all of the coefficients and values for an LP model might be calculated from other data, often referred to as the primary data. It is best to maintain primary data in the spreadsheet and use appropriate formulas to calculate the coefficients and values that are needed for the LP formulation. Then, if the primary data change, appropriate changes will be made automatically in the coefficients for the LP model.)

2. **Reserve separate cells in the spreadsheet to represent each decision variable in the algebraic model.**   Although you can use any empty cells in a spreadsheet to represent the decision variables, it is usually best to arrange the cells representing the decision variables in a way that parallels the structure of the data. This is often helpful in setting up formulas for the objective function and constraints. When possible, it is also a good idea to keep the cells representing decision variables in the same area of the spreadsheet. And you should use descriptive labels to clearly identify the meaning of these cells.

3. **Create a formula in a cell in the spreadsheet that corresponds to the objective function in the algebraic model.**   The spreadsheet formula corresponding to the objective function is created by referring to the data cells where the objective function coefficients have been entered (or calculated) and to the corresponding cells representing the decision variables.

4. **For each constraint, create a formula in a separate cell in the spreadsheet that corresponds to the left-hand side (LHS) of the constraint.**   The formula corresponding to the LHS of each constraint is created by referring to the data cells where the coefficients for these constraints have been entered (or calculated) and to the appropriate decision variable cells. Many of the constraint formulas have a similar structure. Thus, when possible, you should create constraint formulas that can be copied to implement other constraint formulas. This not only reduces the effort required to implement a model, but also helps avoid hard-to-detect typing errors.

While each of the above steps must be performed to implement an LP model in a spreadsheet, they do not have to be performed in the order indicated. It is usually wise to perform step 1 first, followed by step 2. But the order in which steps 3 and 4 are performed will often vary from problem to problem.

Also, it is often wise to use shading, background colors, and/or borders to identify the cells representing decision variables, constraints, and the objective function in a model. This allows the user of a spreadsheet to more readily distinguish between cells representing raw data (that can be changed) and other elements of the model. We will have more to say about how to design and implement effective spreadsheet models for LP problems. But first, let's see how the above steps can be used to implement a spreadsheet model using our example problem.

3.4   A SPREADSHEET MODEL FOR THE BLUE RIDGE HOT TUBS PROBLEM

One possible spreadsheet representation for our example problem is given in Figure 3.1 (and in the file named Fig3-1.xls on your data disk). Let's walk through the creation of this model step-by-step so you can see how it relates to the algebraic formulation of the model.

Figure 3.1
A spreadsheet model for the Blue Ridge Hot Tub production problem.

X_2

X_1

Objective Function =
B6 × B5 + C6 × C5

LHS of 1st constraint =
B9 × B5 + C9 × C5

LHS of 2nd constraint =
B10 × B5 + C10 × C5

LHS of 3rd constraint =
B11 × B5 + C11 × C5

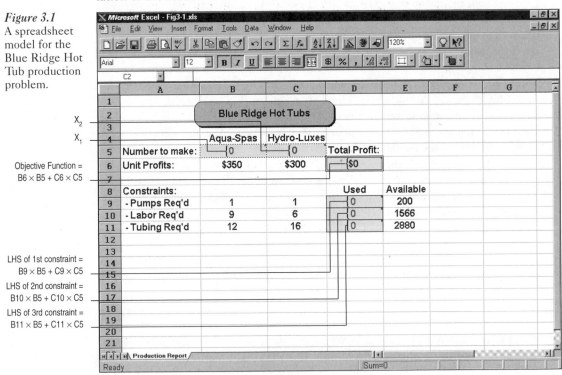

3.4.1   Organizing the Data

One of the first steps in building any spreadsheet model for an LP problem is to organize the data for the model on the spreadsheet. In Figure 3.1 we entered the data for the unit profits for Aqua-Spas and Hydro-Luxes in cells B6 and C6, respectively. Next, the number of pumps, labor hours, and feet of tubing required to produce each type of hot tub are entered in cells B9 through C11. The values in cells B9 and C9 indicate that one pump is required to produce each type of hot tub. The values in cells B10 and C10 show that each Aqua-Spa produced requires 9 hours of labor, and each Hydro-Lux requires 6 hours. Cells B11 and C11 indicate that each Aqua-Spa produced requires 12 feet of tubing, and each Hydro-Lux requires 16 feet. The available number of pumps, labor hours, and feet of tubing are entered in cells E9 through E11. Notice that appropriate labels are also entered to identify all the data elements for the problem.

3.4.2   Representing the Decision Variables

As indicated in Figure 3.1, cells B5 and C5 represent the decision variables X_1 and X_2 in our algebraic model. These cells are shaded and outlined with dashed borders to visually distinguish them from other elements of the model. Values of zero were placed in cells B5 and C5 because we do not know how many Aqua-Spas and Hydro-Luxes should be produced. Shortly, we will use Solver to determine the optimal values for these cells. Figure 3.2 summarizes the relationship between the decision variables in the algebraic model and the corresponding cells in the spreadsheet.

Decision Variables:	X_1	X_2	
	↓	↓	
Spreadsheet Cells:	B5	C5	

Figure 3.2
Summary of the relationship between the decision variables and corresponding spreadsheet cells.

3.4.3   Representing the Objective Function

The next step in implementing our LP problem is to create a formula in a cell of the spreadsheet to represent the objective function. We can accomplish this in many ways. Because the objective function is $350X_1 + 300X_2$, you might be tempted to enter the formula =350 * B5+300 * C5 in the spreadsheet. However, if you wanted to change the coefficients in the objective function, you would have to go back and edit this formula to reflect the changes. Because the objective function coefficients are entered in cells B6 and C6, a better way of implementing the objective function is to refer to the values in cells B6 and C6 rather than entering numeric constants in the formula. The formula for the objective function is entered in cell D6 as:

Formula for cell D6:   =B6*B5+C6*C5

As shown in Figure 3.1, cell D6 initially returns the value 0 because cells B5 and C5 both contain zeros. Figure 3.3 summarizes the relationship between the algebraic objective function and the formula entered in cell D6. By implementing the objective function in this manner, if the profits earned on the hot tubs ever change, the spreadsheet model can be changed easily and the problem can be re-solved to determine the impact of this change on the optimal solution. Note that D6 has been shaded and outlined with a double border to distinguish it from other elements of the model.

Algebraic Objective:	350 X_1	+	300 X_2	
	↓ ↓		↓ ↓	
Formula in cell D6:	=B6*B5	+	C6*C5	

Figure 3.3
Summary of the relationship between the decision variables and corresponding spreadsheet cells.

3.4.4 Representing the Constraints

The next step in building the spreadsheet model involves implementing the constraints of the LP model. Earlier we said that for each constraint in the algebraic model, you must create a formula in a cell of the spreadsheet that corresponds to the LHS of the constraint. The LHS of each constraint in our model is:

LHS of the pump constraint

$$\boxed{1X_1 + 1X_2} \leq 200$$

LHS of the labor constraint

$$\boxed{9X_1 + 6X_2} \leq 1{,}566$$

LHS of the tubing constraint

$$\boxed{12X_1 + 16X_2} \leq 2{,}880$$

We need to set up three cells in the spreadsheet to represent the LHS formulas of the three constraints. Again, this is done by referring to the data cells containing the coefficients for these constraints and to the cells representing the decision variables. The LHS of the first constraint is entered in cell D9 as:

Formula for cell D9:   =B9*B5+C9*C5

Similarly, the LHS of the second and third constraints are entered in cells D9 and D10 as:

Formula for cell D10:   =B10*B5+C10*C5

Formula for cell D11:   =B11*B5+C11*C5

These formulas calculate the number of pumps, hours of labor, and feet of tubing required to manufacture the number of hot tubs represented in cells B5 and C5. Note that cells D9 through D11 were shaded and outlined with solid borders to distinguish them from the other elements of the model.

Figure 3.4 summarizes the relationship between the LHS formulas of the constraints in the algebraic formulation of our model and their spreadsheet representations.

Figure 3.4
Summary of the relationship between the LHS formulas of the constraints and their spreadsheet representations.

LHS formula for the pump constraint:	$1 \; X_1 \;\; + \;\; 1 \; X_2$
	$\downarrow \; \downarrow \;\;\;\;\;\; \downarrow \; \downarrow$
Formula in cell D9:	=B9*B5 + C9*C5
LHS formula for the labor constraint:	$9 \; X_1 \;\; + \;\; 6 \; X_2$
	$\downarrow \; \downarrow \;\;\;\;\;\; \downarrow \; \downarrow$
Formula in cell D10:	=B10*B5 + C10*C5
LHS formula for the tubing constraint:	$12 \; X_1 \;\; + \;\; 16 \; X_2$
	$\downarrow \; \downarrow \;\;\;\;\;\; \downarrow \; \downarrow$
Formula in cell D11:	=B11*B5 + C11*C5

We know that Blue Ridge Hot Tubs has 200 pumps, 1,566 labor hours, and 2,880 feet of tubing available during its next production cycle. In our algebraic formulation of the LP model, these values represent the RHS values for the three constraints. Therefore, we entered the available number of pumps, hours of labor, and feet of tubing in cells E9, E10, and E11, respectively. These terms indicate the upper limits on the values cells D9, D10, and D11 can assume.

3.4.5 Representing the Bounds on the Decision Variables

Now what about the simple lower bounds on our decision variables represented by $X_1 \geq 0$ and $X_2 \geq 0$? These conditions are quite common in LP problems and are referred to as **nonnegativity conditions** because they indicate that the decision variables can assume only nonnegative values. These conditions might seem like constraints and can, in fact, be implemented like the other constraints. However, Solver allows you to specify simple upper and lower bounds for the decision variables by referring directly to the cells representing the decision variables. Thus, at this point, we have taken no specific action to implement these bounds in our spreadsheet.

3.5 HOW SOLVER VIEWS THE MODEL

After implementing our model in the spreadsheet, we can use Solver to find the optimal solution to the problem. But first, we need to define the following three components of our spreadsheet model for Solver:

1. **Target cell**—the cell in the spreadsheet that represents the *objective function* in the model (and whether its value should be maximized or minimized)
2. **Changing cells**—the cells in the spreadsheet that represent the *decision variables* in the model
3. **Constraint cells**—the cells in the spreadsheet that represent the *LHS formulas* of the constraints in the model (and any upper and lower bounds that apply to these formulas)

These components correspond directly to the cells in the spreadsheet we established when implementing the LP model. For example, in the spreadsheet for our example problem, the target cell is represented by cell D6, the changing cells are represented by cells B5 and C5, and the constraint cells are represented by cells D9, D10, and D11. Figure 3.5 shows these relationships. Figure 3.5 also shows a cell note documenting the purpose of cell D6. Cell notes can be a very effective way of describing details about the purpose or meaning of various cells in a model.

By comparing Figure 3.1 with Figure 3.5, you can see the direct connection between the way we formulate LP models algebraically and how Solver views the spreadsheet implementation of the model. The decision variables in the algebraic model correspond to the changing cells for Solver. The LHS formulas for the different constraints in the algebraic model correspond to the constraint cells for Solver. Finally, the objective function in the algebraic model corresponds to the target cell for Solver. So although the terminology Solver uses to describe spreadsheet LP models is different from the terminology we use to describe LP models algebraically, the concepts are the same. Figure 3.6 summarizes these differences in terminology.

Figure 3.5
Summary of
Solver's view of
the model.

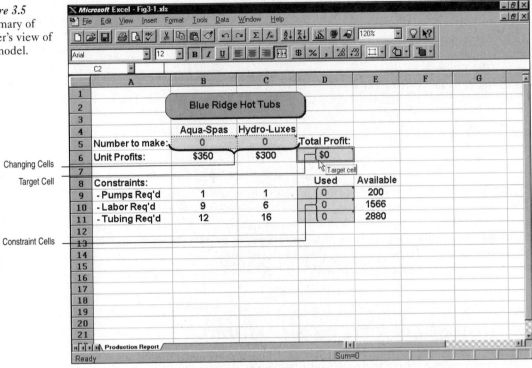

A Note About Creating Cell Notes...

It is easy to create cell notes (or comments in Excel 8.0) like the one shown for cell D6 in Figure 3.5. To create a note for a cell:

1. Click the cell to select it.
2. Choose the Note (or Comment) command on the Insert menu (or press Shift and F2 simultaneously).
3. Type the note for the cell.

The display of cells notes can be turned on or off as follows:

1. Choose the Options command on the Tools menu.
2. Select or deselect the Note (or Comment) Indicator option on the View card.
3. Click the OK button.

To copy a cell note from one cell to a series of other cells:

1. Click the cell containing the note you wish to copy.
2. Choose the Copy command on the Edit menu (or press the Ctrl and C keys simultaneously).
3. Select the cells you want to copy the note to.
4. Select the Paste Special command on the Edit menu (or click the right mouse button and select Paste Special).
5. Select the Notes (or Comments) option button.
6. Click the OK button.

Terms used to describe LP models algebraically	Corresponding terms used by Solver to describe spreadsheet LP models
objective function	target cell
decision variables	changing cells
LHS formulas of constraints	constraint cells

Figure 3.6
Summary of Solver terminology.

3.6 USING SOLVER

After implementing an LP model in a spreadsheet, we still need to solve the model. To do this we must first indicate to Solver which cells in the spreadsheet represent the objective function (or target cell), the decision variables (or changing cells), and the constraints (or constraint cells). To invoke Solver in Excel, choose the Solver command from the Tools menu, as shown in Figure 3.7. This displays the Solver Parameters dialog box shown in Figure 3.8. Then complete the options in the Solver Parameters dialog box.

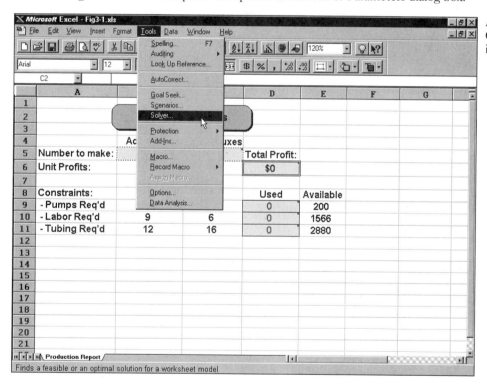

Figure 3.7
Command for invoking Solver.

Important Software Note

If you are using Excel 8.0 (in Office 97) the Solver Parameters dialog box will look slightly different than the one shown in Figure 3.8, but it works in essentially the same way as described here.

Figure 3.8
The Solver
Parameters
dialog box.

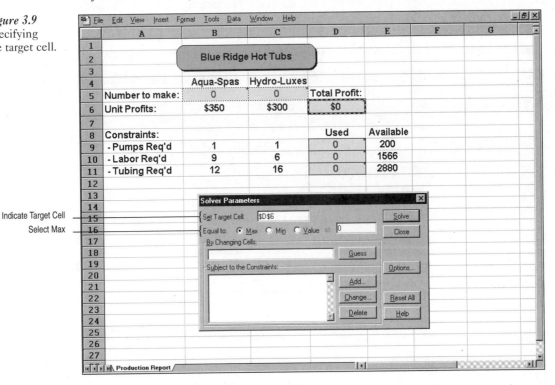

3.6.1 Defining the Target Cell

In the Solver Parameters dialog box, specify the location of the cell that represents the objective function by entering it in the Set Target Cell box, as shown in Figure 3.9.

Figure 3.9
Specifying
the target cell.

Notice that cell D6 is the target cell and that we instructed Solver to set the target cell value equal to the maximum possible value, as specified by the Max button. Select the Min button when you want Solver to find a solution that minimizes the value of the target cell. The Value button finds a solution where the objective function has a specific value.

3.6.2 Defining the Changing Cells

To solve our LP problem, we also need to indicate which cells represent the decision variables in the model. Again, Solver refers to these cells as changing cells. The changing cells for our example problem are specified as shown in Figure 3.10.

Guess What?

The Guess button in the Solver Parameters dialog box (or the Variables button if you are using Excel 8.0) instructs Solver to make a educated guess regarding which cells in the spreadsheet represent decision variables. If you press this button, Solver will display all the cells upon which the value of the target cell depends. In some cases this will only be the changing cells. In other cases this will be the changing cells plus some additional cells that you will have to edit out of the changing cells box before continuing. In general, it is probably a good idea for you to enter the changing cells manually by clicking on the appropriate cells in your spreadsheet. But if you use the Guess button, remember that you will usually need to remove some of the cells it identifies as changing cells.

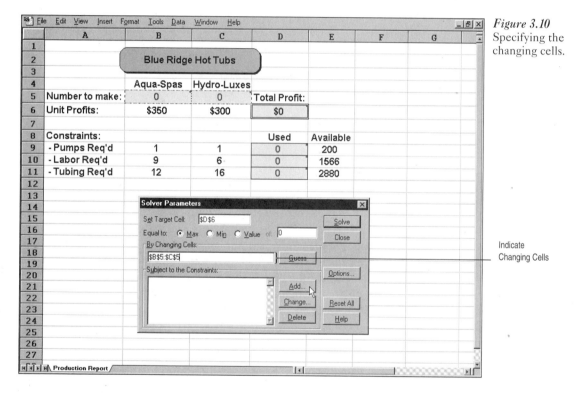

Figure 3.10
Specifying the changing cells.

Indicate Changing Cells

Cells B5 and C5 represent the decision variables (or changing cells) for the model. Solver will determine the optimal values for these cells. If the decision variables were not in a contiguous range, we would have to list the individual decision variable cells separated by commas in the By Changing Cells box. Whenever possible, it is best to use contiguous cells to represent the decision variables.

3.6.3 Defining the Constraint Cells

Next we must define the constraint cells in the spreadsheet and the restrictions that apply to these cells. As mentioned earlier, the constraint cells are the cells in which we implemented the LHS formulas for each constraint in our model. To define the constraint cells, click the Add button shown in Figure 3.10, then complete the Add Constraint dialog box shown in Figure 3.11. In the Add Constraint dialog box, click the Add button again to define additional constraints. Click the OK button when you have finished defining constraints.

Figure 3.11
Specifying the constraint cells.

Indicate LHS Formula Cells

Indicate RHS Formula Cells

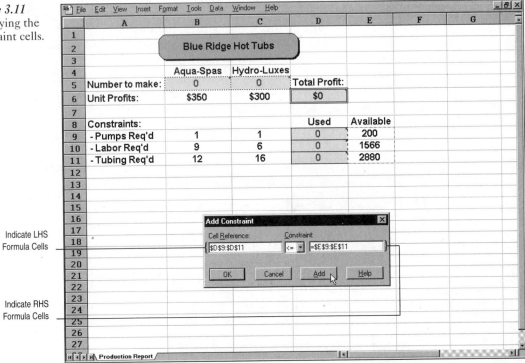

Cells D9 through D11 represent constraint cells whose values must be less than or equal to the values in cells E9 through E11, respectively. If the constraint cells were not in contiguous cells in the spreadsheet, we would have to define the constraint cells repeatedly. As with the changing cells, it is usually best to choose contiguous cells in your spreadsheet to implement the LHS formulas of the constraints in a model.

If you want to define more than one constraint at the same time, as in Figure 3.11, all the constraint cells you select must be the same type (that is, they must all be ≤, ≥, or =). Therefore, it is a good idea to keep constraints of a given type grouped in contiguous cells so you can select them at the same time. However, this consideration should not take precedence over setting up the spreadsheet in the way that communicates its purpose most clearly.

3.6.4   Defining the Nonnegativity Conditions

One final specification we need to make for our model is that the decision variables must be greater than or equal to zero. As mentioned earlier, we can impose these conditions as constraints by placing appropriate restrictions on the values that can be assigned to the cells representing the decision variables (in this case, cells B5 and C5). To do this, we simply add another set of constraints to the model, as shown in Figure 3.12.

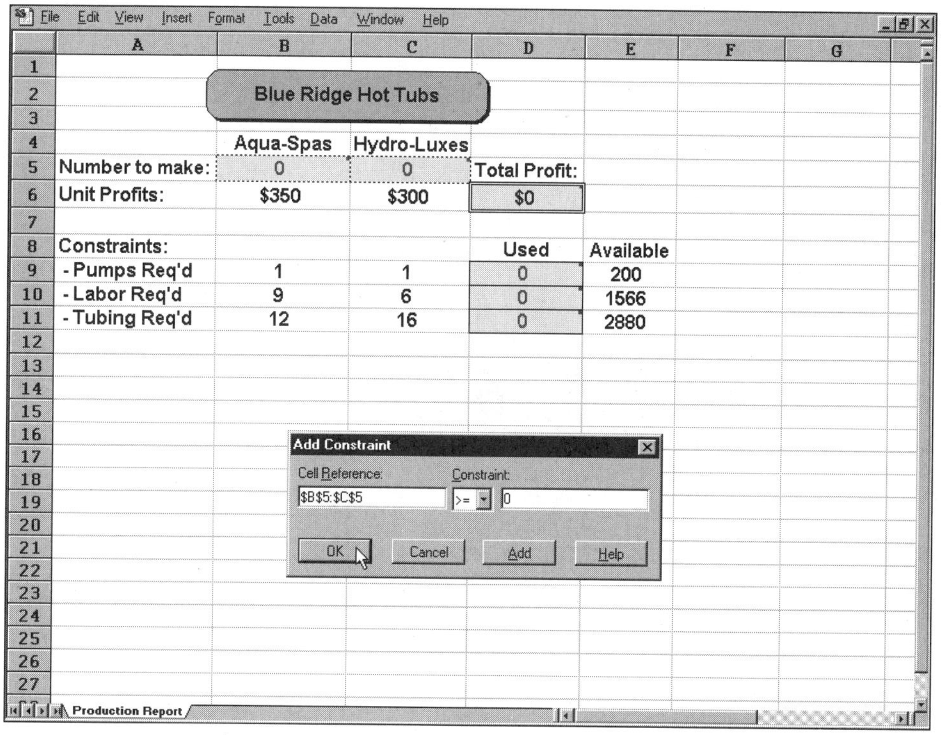

Figure 3.12
Adding the
nonnegativity
conditions for
the problem.

Figure 3.12 indicates that cells B5 and C5, which represent the decision variables in our model, must be greater than or equal to zero. Notice that the RHS value of this constraint is a numeric constant that is entered manually. The same type of constraints can also be used if we placed some strictly positive lower bounds on these variables (for example, if we wanted to produce at least 10 Aqua-Spas and at least 10 Hydro-Luxes). However, in that case it probably would be best to place the minimum required production amounts on the spreadsheet so that these restrictions are clearly displayed. We can then refer to those cells in the spreadsheet when specifying the RHS values for these constraints.

Important Software Note

If you are using Excel 8.0, there is another way to impose nonnegativity conditions simply by checking the Assume Non-Negative check box in the Solver Options dialog box. Checking this box tells Solver to assume that all the variables (or changing cells) in your model that have not been assigned explicit lower bounds should have lower bounds of zero.

3.6.5 Reviewing the Model

After specifying all the constraints for our model, the final Solver Parameters dialog box appears, as shown in Figure 3.13. This dialog box provides a summary of how Solver views our model. It is a good idea to review this information before solving the model to make sure you entered all the parameters accurately and to correct any errors before proceeding.

Figure 3.13
Summary of how
Solver views the
model.

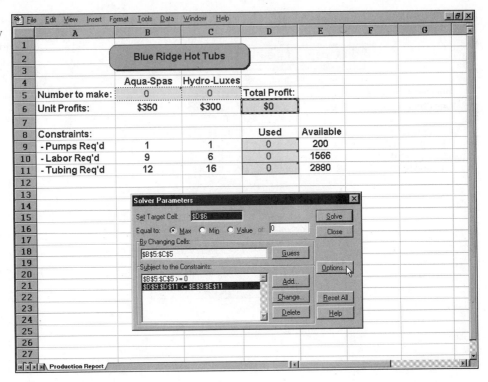

3.6.6   Options

Solver provides a number of options that affect how it solves a problem. These options are available in the Solver Options dialog box, which you display by clicking the Options button in the Solver Parameters dialog box. Figure 3.14 shows the Solver Options dialog box.

Notice the option named Assume Linear Model. If the problem you are trying to solve is an LP problem (that is, an optimization problem with a linear objective function and linear constraints), Solver can use a special algorithm known as the **simplex method** to solve the problem. The simplex method provides an efficient way of solving LP problems and, therefore, requires less solution time. Furthermore, using the simplex method allows for expanded sensitivity information about the solution obtained. (Chapter 4 discusses this in detail.) In any event, when using Solver to solve an LP problem, it is a good idea to select the Assume Linear Model option as indicated in Figure 3.14.

The Max Time and Iterations options determine how much time and effort Solver is allowed in attempting to solve the problem. The default settings for these options work well and should be changed only if Solver runs out of time while trying to solve a particular problem.

The Precision option specifies how much rounding error is allowed in the solutions Solver obtains. Whenever you use a computer to solve a difficult math problem, slight rounding or precision errors can enter the solution. For example, Solver might obtain an optimal solution that requires the use of 200.00000906 pumps, which *technically* violates the upper bound of 200 specified for the number of pumps available. However, because there is no *practical* difference between the value 200 and 200.00000906, you might consider this solution to be close enough or within an acceptable tolerance of

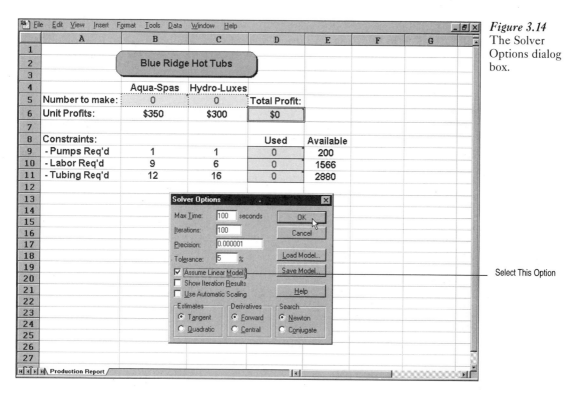

Figure 3.14
The Solver Options dialog box.

satisfying the constraints. This type of precision problem is common and seldom poses a practical problem. If you need a more precise solution to a problem, you can use the Precision option to control the level of precision Solver uses in checking the feasibility of its solutions.

The Tolerance option relates to solving integer programming problems, and is discussed in detail in Chapter 6. The Estimates, Derivatives, and Search options are discussed in Chapter 8.

Important Software Note

If you are using Excel 8.0 the Solver Options dialog box looks slightly different than the one shown in Figure 3.14. In addition to the options described here, there is a check box labeled Assume Non-Negative that you may use to tell Solver to assume that all the variables (or changing cells) in your model that have not been assigned explicit lower bounds should have lower bounds of zero. There is also a Convergence setting that will be discussed in Chapter 8.

3.6.7 Solving the Model

After entering all the appropriate parameters and choosing any necessary options for our model, the next step is to solve the problem. Click the Solve button in the Solver Parameters dialog box to solve the problem. When Solver finds the optimal solution, it displays the Solver Results dialog box shown in Figure 3.15. If the values on your screen do not match those in Figure 3.15, click the Restore Original Values option button, click OK, then re-enter the parameters and options.

This dialog box provides options for keeping the solution found by Solver or restoring the spreadsheet to its original condition. Most often you'll want to keep Solver's solution unless there is an obvious problem with it. Notice that the Solver Results dialog box also provides options for generating Answer, Sensitivity, and Limits reports. Chapter 4 discusses these options.

Figure 3.15
Optimal solution for the Blue Ridge Hot Tubs problem.

Optimal Objective Function Value

Optimal Values of Decimal Variables

Amount of Resources Used in the Optimal Solution

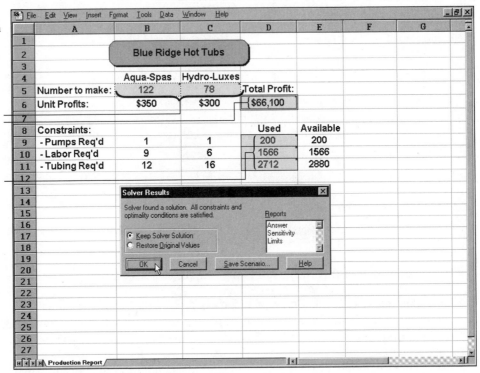

As shown in Figure 3.15, Solver determined that the optimal value for cell B5 is 122 and the optimal value for cell C5 is 78. These values correspond to the optimal values for X_1 and X_2 that we determined graphically in chapter 2. The value of the target cell (D6) now indicates that if Blue Ridge Hot Tubs produces and sells 122 Aqua-Spas and 78 Hydro-Luxes, the company will earn a profit of $66,100. Cells D9, D10, and D11 indicate that this solution uses all the 200 available pumps, all the 1,566 available labor hours, and 2,712 of the 2,880 feet of available tubing.

3.7   GOALS AND GUIDELINES FOR SPREADSHEET DESIGN

Now that you have a basic idea of how Solver works and how to set up an LP model in a spreadsheet, we'll walk through several more examples of formulating LP models and solving them with Solver. These problems highlight the wide variety of business problems in which LP can be applied and will also show you some helpful "tricks of the trade" that should help you solve the problems at the end of this chapter. When you work through the end of the chapter problems, you will better appreciate how much thought is required to find a good way to implement a given model.

As we proceed, keep in mind that you can set up these problems more than one way. Creating spreadsheet models that effectively communicate their purpose is very much an art—or at least an acquired skill. Spreadsheets are inherently free-form and impose no particular structure on the way we model problems. As a result, there is no one "right" way to model a problem in a spreadsheet; but some ways are certainly better (or more logical) than others. To achieve the end result of a logical spreadsheet design, your modeling efforts should be directed toward the following goals:

- **Communication**—A spreadsheet's primary business purpose is that of communicating information to managers. As such, the primary design objective in most spreadsheet modeling tasks is to communicate the relevant aspects of the problem at hand in as clear and intuitively appealing a manner as possible.
- **Reliability**—The output a spreadsheet generates should be correct and consistent. This has an obvious impact on the degree of confidence a manager places in the results of the modeling effort.
- **Auditability**—A manager should be able to retrace the steps followed to generate the different outputs from the model in order to understand the model and verify results. Models that are setup in an intuitively appealing, logical layout tend to be the most auditable.
- **Modifiability**—The data and assumptions upon which we build spreadsheet models can change frequently. A well-designed spreadsheet should be easy to change or enhance in order to meet dynamic user requirements.

In most cases, the spreadsheet design which communicates its purpose most clearly will also be the most reliable, auditable, and modifiable design. As you consider different ways of implementing a spreadsheet model for a particular problem, consider how well the modeling alternatives compare in terms of these goals. Some practical suggestions and guidelines for creating effective spreadsheet models are given in Figure 3.16.

3.8   MAKE VS. BUY DECISIONS

As mentioned at the beginning of Chapter 2, LP is particularly well suited to problems where scarce or limited resources must be allocated or used in an optimal manner. Numerous examples of these types of problems occur in manufacturing organizations. For example, LP might be used to determine how the various components of a job should be assigned to multi-purpose machines in order to minimize the time it takes to complete the job. As another example, a company might receive an order for several items that it cannot fill entirely with its own production capacity. In such a case, the company must determine which items to produce and which items to subcontract (or buy) from an outside supplier. The following is an example of this type of make vs. buy decision.

The Electro-Poly Corporation is the world's leading manufacturer of slip rings. A slip ring is an electrical coupling device that allows current to pass through a spinning or rotating connection—such as a gun turret on a ship, aircraft, or tank. The company recently received a $750,000 order for various quantities of three types of slip rings. Each slip ring requires a certain amount of time to wire and harness. The following table summarizes the requirements for the three models of slip rings.

Figure 3.16
Guidelines for
effective
spreadsheet
design.

Spreadsheet Design Guidelines

- **Organize the data, then build the model around the data.** Once the data is arranged in a visually appealing manner, logical locations for decision variables, constraints and objective function tend to naturally suggest themselves. This also tends to enhance the reliability, auditability and maintainability of the model.

- **Do not embed numeric constants in formulas.** Numeric constants should be placed in individual cells and labeled appropriately. This enhances the reliability and modifiability of the model.

- **Things which are logically related (e.g., left-hand sides and right-hand sides of constraints) should be arranged in close physical proximity to one another and in the same columnar or row orientation.** This enhances reliability and auditability of the model.

- **A design that results in formulas that can be copied is probably better than one that does not.** A model with formulas that can copied to complete a series of calculations in a range is less prone to error (more reliable) and tends to be more understandable (auditable). Once a user understands the first formula in a range, he/she understands all the formulas in a range.

- **Column or row totals should be in close proximity to the columns or rows being totaled.** Spreadsheet users often expect numbers at the end of a column or row to represent a total or some other summary measure involving the data in the column or row. Numbers at the ends of columns or rows that do not represent totals can easily be misinterpreted (reducing auditability).

- **The English-reading human eye scans left to right, top to bottom.** This fact should be considered and reflected in the spreadsheet design to enhance the auditability of the model.

- **Use color, shading, borders and protection to distinguish changeable parameters from other elements of the model.** This enhances the reliability and modifiability of the model.

- **Use text boxes and cell notes to document various elements of the model.** These devises can be used to provide greater detail about a model or particular cells in a model than labels on a spreadsheet may allow.

	Model 1	*Model 2*	*Model 3*
Number ordered	3,000	2,000	900
Hours of wiring required per unit	2	1.5	3
Hours of harnessing required per unit	1	2	1

Unfortunately, Electro-Poly does not have enough wiring and harnessing capacity to fill the order by its due date. The company has only 10,000 hours of wiring capacity and 5,000 hours of harnessing capacity available to devote to this order. However, the company can subcontract any portion of this order to one of its competitors. The unit costs of producing each model in-house and buying the finished products from a competitor are summarized on the next page.

	Model 1	Model 2	Model 3
Cost to Make	$50	$83	$130
Cost to Buy	$61	$97	$145

Electro-Poly wants to determine the number of slip rings to make and the number to buy in order to fill the customer order at the least possible cost.

3.8.1 Defining the Decision Variables

To solve the Electro-Poly problem, we need six decision variables to represent the alternatives under consideration. The six variables are:

M_1 = number of model 1 slip rings to make in-house

M_2 = number of model 2 slip rings to make in-house

M_3 = number of model 3 slip rings to make in-house

B_1 = number of model 1 slip rings to buy from competitor

B_2 = number of model 2 slip rings to buy from competitor

B_3 = number of model 3 slip rings to buy from competitor

As mentioned in Chapter 2, we do not have to use the symbols X_1, X_2, ..., X_n for the decision variables. If other symbols better clarify the model, you are certainly free to use them. In this case, the symbols M_i and B_i help distinguish the **M**ake in-house variables from the **B**uy from competitor variables.

3.8.2 Defining the Objective Function

The objective in this problem is to minimize the total cost of filling the order. Recall that each model 1 slip ring made in-house (each unit of M_1) costs $50; each model 2 slip ring made in-house (each unit of M_2) costs $83; and each model 3 slip ring (each unit of M_3) costs $130. Each model 1 slip ring bought from the competitor (each unit of B_1) costs $61; each model 2 slip ring bought from the competitor (each unit of B_2) costs $97; and each model 3 slip ring bought from the competitor (each unit of B_3) costs $145. Thus, the objective is stated mathematically as:

$$\text{MIN:} \quad 50M_1 + 83M_2 + 130M_3 + 61B_1 + 97B_2 + 145B_3$$

3.8.3 Defining the Constraints

Several constraints affect this problem. Two constraints are needed to ensure that the number of slip rings made in-house does not exceed the available capacity for wiring and harnessing. These constraints are stated as:

$$2M_1 + 1.5M_2 + 3M_3 \leq 10{,}000 \quad \} \text{ wiring constraint}$$
$$1M_1 + 2M_2 + 1M_3 \leq 5{,}000 \quad \} \text{ harnessing constraint}$$

Three additional constraints ensure that 3,000 model 1 slip rings, 2,000 model 2 slip rings, and 900 model 3 slip rings are available to fill the order. These constraints are stated as:

$$M_1 \; + \; B_1 \; = \; 3{,}000 \quad \} \text{ demand for model 1}$$
$$M_2 \; + \; B_2 \; = \; 2{,}000 \quad \} \text{ demand for model 2}$$
$$M_3 \; + \; B_3 \; = \; 900 \quad \} \text{ demand for model 3}$$

Finally, because none of the variables in the model can assume a value of less than zero, we also need the following nonnegativity condition:

$$M_1, M_2, M_3, B_1, B_2, B_3 \geq 0$$

3.8.4   Implementing the Model

The LP model for Electro-Poly's make vs. buy problem is summarized as:

MIN: $50M_1 + 83M_2 + 130M_2 + 61B_1 + 97B_2 + 145B_3$ } total cost

Subject to:

$$
\begin{array}{ccccccccl}
M_1 & + & B_1 & & & = & 3{,}000 & \} \text{ demand for model 1} \\
M_2 & + & B_2 & & & = & 2{,}000 & \} \text{ demand for model 2} \\
M_3 & + & B_3 & & & = & 900 & \} \text{ demand for model 3} \\
2M_1 & + & 1.5M_2 & + & 3M_3 & \leq & 10{,}000 & \} \text{ wiring constraint} \\
1M_1 & + & 2M_2 & + & 1M_3 & \leq & 5{,}000 & \} \text{ harnessing constraint} \\
\multicolumn{5}{c}{M_1, M_2, M_3, B_1, B_2, B_3} & \geq & 0 & \} \text{ nonnegativity condition}
\end{array}
$$

The data for this model are implemented in the spreadsheet shown in Figure 3.17 (and in the file Fig3-17.xls on your data disk). The coefficients that appear in the objective function are entered in the range B10 through D11. The coefficients for the LHS formulas for the wiring and harnessing constraints are entered in cells B17 through D18, and the corresponding RHS values are entered in cells F17 and F18. Because the LHS formulas for the demand constraints involve simply summing the decision variables, we do not need to list the coefficients for these constraints in the spreadsheet. The RHS values for the demand constraints are entered in cells B14 through D14.

Cells B6 through D7 are reserved to represent the six variables in our algebraic model. So the objective function could be entered in cell E11 as:

Formula for cell E11:   =B10*B6+C10*C6+D10*D6+B11*B7+C11*C7+D11*D7

In this formula, the values in the range B6 through D7 are multiplied by the corresponding values in the range B10 through D11; these individual products are then added together. Therefore, the formula is simply the sum of a collection of products— or a *sum of products*. It turns out that this formula can be implemented in an equivalent (and easier) way as:

Equivalent formula for cell E11:   =SUMPRODUCT(B10:D11,B6:D7)

The preceding formula takes the values in the range B10 through D11, multiplies them by the corresponding values in the range B6 through D7, and adds (or sums) these products. The SUMPRODUCT( ) function greatly simplifies the implementation of many formulas required in optimization problems and will be used extensively throughout this book.

Because the LHS of the demand constraint for model 1 slip rings involves adding variables M_1 and B_1, this constraint is implemented in cell B13 by adding the two cells in the spreadsheet that correspond to these variables—cells B6 and B7:

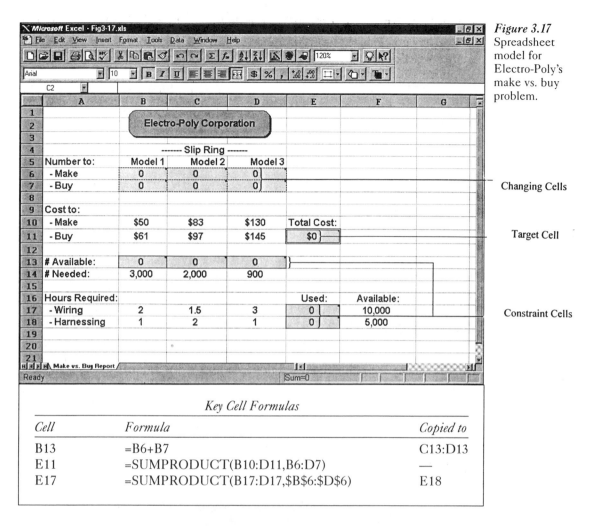

Figure 3.17
Spreadsheet model for Electro-Poly's make vs. buy problem.

Key Cell Formulas

Cell	Formula	Copied to
B13	=B6+B7	C13:D13
E11	=SUMPRODUCT(B10:D11,B6:D7)	—
E17	=SUMPRODUCT(B17:D17,$B$6:$D$6)	E18

Formula for cell B13:   =B6+B7
(copy to C13 through D13)

The formula in cell B13 is then copied to cells C13 and D13 to implement the LHS formulas for the constraints for model 2 and model 3 slip rings.

The coefficients for the wiring and harnessing constraints are entered in cells B17 through D17. The LHS formula for the wiring constraint is implemented in cell E17 as:

Formula for cell E17:   =SUMPRODUCT(B17:D17,$B$6:$D$6)
(copy to cell E18)

This formula is then copied to cell E18 to implement the LHS formula for the harnessing constraint. (In the preceding formula, the dollar signs denote absolute cell references. An **absolute cell reference** will not change if the formula containing the reference is copied to another location.)

3.8.5   Solving the Model

To solve this model we need to specify the target cell, changing cells, and constraint cells identified in Figure 3.17, just as we did earlier in the Blue Ridge Hot Tubs example.

Figure 3.18 shows the Solver parameters and options required to solve Electro-Poly's make vs. buy problem.

After we click the Solve button in the Solver Parameters dialog box, Solver finds the optimal solution shown in Figure 3.19.

3.8.6   Analyzing the Solution

The optimal solution shown in Figure 3.19 indicates that Electro-Poly should make (in-house) 3,000 model 1 slip rings, 550 model 2 slip rings, and 900 model 3 slip rings (that is, $M_1 = 3,000$, $M_2 = 550$, $M_3 = 900$). Additionally, it should buy 1,450 model 2 slip rings from its competitor (that is, $B_1 = 0$, $B_2 = 1,450$, $B_3 = 0$). This solution allows Electro-Poly to fill the customer order at a minimum cost of $453,300. This solution uses 9,525 of the 10,000 hours of available wiring capacity and all 5,000 hours of the harnessing capacity.

At first glance, this solution might seem a bit surprising. Electro-Poly has to pay $97 for each model 2 slip ring it purchases from its competitor. This represents a $14 premium over its in-house cost of $83. On the other hand, Electro-Poly has to pay a premium of $11 over its in-house cost to purchase model 1 slip rings from its competitor. It seems as if the optimal solution would be to purchase model 1 slip rings from its competitor rather than model 2 slip rings because the additional cost premium for model 1 slip rings is smaller. However, this argument fails to consider the fact that each model 2 slip ring produced in-house uses twice as much of the company's harnessing capacity as does each model 1 slip ring. Making more model 2 slip rings in-house would deplete the company's harnessing capacity more quickly, and would require buying an excessive number of model 1 slip rings from the competitor. Fortunately, the LP technique automatically considers such trade-offs in determining the optimal solution to the problem.

Figure 3.18
Solver parameters and options for the make vs. buy problem.

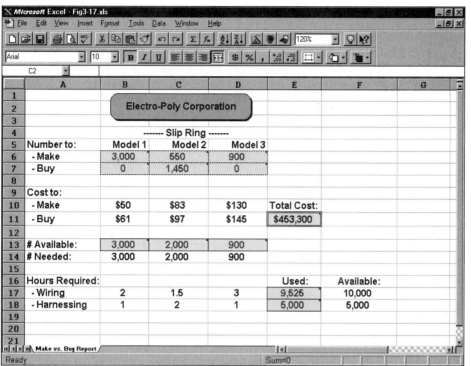

Figure 3.19
Optimal solution to Electro-Poly's make vs. buy problem.

3.9 AN INVESTMENT PROBLEM

There are numerous problems in the area of finance where various optimization techniques can be applied. These problems often involve attempting to maximize the return on an investment while meeting certain cashflow requirements and risk constraints. Alternatively, we may wish to minimize the risk on an investment while maintaining a certain level of return. We'll consider one such problem here and discuss several other financial engineering problems throughout this text.

Brian Givens is a Chartered Financial Planner (CFP) for Retirement Planning Services, Inc. who specializes in designing retirement income portfolios for retirees using corporate bonds. He has just completed a consultation with a client who expects to have $750,000 in liquid assets to invest when she retires next month. Brian and his client agreed to consider upcoming bond issues from the following six companies:

Company	Return	Years to Maturity	Rating
Acme Chemical	8.65%	11	1-Excellent
DynaStar	9.50%	10	3-Good
Eagle Vision	10.00%	6	4-Fair
MicroModeling	8.75%	10	1-Excellent
OptiPro	9.25%	7	3-Good
Sabre Systems	9.00%	13	2-Very Good

The column labeled "Return" in this table represents the expected annual yield on each bond, the column labeled "Years to Maturity" indicates the length of time over which the bonds will be payable, and the column labeled "Rating" indicates an independent underwriter's assessment of the quality or risk associated with each issue.

Brian believes that all of the companies are relatively safe investments. However, to protect his client's income, Brain and his client agreed that no more than 25% of her money should be invested in any one investment and at least half of her money should be invested in long-term bonds which mature in ten or more years. Also, even though DynaStar, Eagle Vision, and OptiPro offer the highest returns it was agreed that no more than 35% of the money should be invested in these bonds since they also represent the highest risks (i.e., they were rated lower than "very good"). Brian needs to determine how to allocate his client's investments to maximize her income while meeting their agreed upon investment restrictions.

3.9.1 Defining the Decision Variables

In this problem, Brian must decide how much money to invest in each type of bond. Because there are six different investments alternatives, we need the following six decision variables:

$$X_1 = \text{amount of money to invest in Acme Chemical}$$
$$X_2 = \text{amount of money to invest in DynaStar}$$
$$X_3 = \text{amount of money to invest in Eagle Vision}$$
$$X_4 = \text{amount of money to invest in MicroModeling}$$
$$X_5 = \text{amount of money to invest in OptiPro}$$
$$X_6 = \text{amount of money to invest in Sabre Systems}$$

3.9.2 Defining the Objective Function

The objective in this problem is to maximize the investment income for Brian's client. Because each dollar invested in Acme Chemical (X_1) earns 8.65% annually, each dollar invested in DynaStar (X_2) earns 9.50%, and so on, the objective function for the problem is expressed as:

MAX: $.0865X_1 + .095X_2 + .10X_3 + .0875X_4 + .0925X_5 + .09X_6$ } total annual investment return

3.9.3 Defining the Constraints

Again, there are several constraints that apply to this problem. First, we must ensure that exactly $750,000 is invested. This is accomplished by the following constraint:

$$X_1 + X_2 + X_3 + X_4 + X_5 + X_6 = 750,000$$

Next, we must ensure that no more than 25% of the total be invested in any one investment. Twenty-five percent of $750,000 is $187,500. Therefore, Brian can put no more than $187,500 in any one investment. The following constraints enforce this restriction:

$$X_1 \leq 187{,}500$$
$$X_2 \leq 187{,}500$$
$$X_3 \leq 187{,}500$$
$$X_4 \leq 187{,}500$$
$$X_5 \leq 187{,}500$$
$$X_6 \leq 187{,}500$$

Because the bonds for Eagle Vision (X_3) and OptiPro (X_5) are the only ones that mature in fewer than 10 years, the following constraint will ensure that at least half the money ($375,000) is placed in investments maturing in ten or more years:

$$X_1 + X_2 + X_4 + X_6 \geq 375{,}000$$

Similarly, the following constraint will ensure that no more than 35% of the money ($262,500) is placed the bonds for DynaStar (X_2), Eagle Vision (X_3), and OptiPro (X_5):

$$X_2 + X_3 + X_5 \leq 262{,}500$$

Finally, because none of the variables in the model can assume a value of less than zero, we also need the following nonnegativity condition:

$$X_1, X_2, X_3, X_4, X_5, X_6 \geq 0$$

3.9.4   Implementing the Model

The LP model for the Retirement Planning Services, Inc. investment problem is summarized as:

MAX: $.0865X_1 + .095X_2 + .10X_3 + .0875X_4 + .0925X_5 + .09X_6$ } total annual investment return

Subject to:
$X_1 \leq 187{,}500$ } 25% restriction per investment
$X_2 \leq 187{,}500$ } 25% restriction per investment
$X_3 \leq 187{,}500$ } 25% restriction per investment
$X_4 \leq 187{,}500$ } 25% restriction per investment
$X_5 \leq 187{,}500$ } 25% restriction per investment
$X_6 \leq 187{,}500$ } 25% restriction per investment
$X_1 + X_2 + X_3 + X_4 + X_5 + X_6 = 750{,}000$ } total amount invested
$X_1 + X_2 + X_4 + X_6 \geq 375{,}000$ } long-term investment
$X_2 + X_3 + X_5 \leq 262{,}500$ } higher-risk investment
$X_1, X_2, X_3, X_4, X_5, X_6 \geq 0$ } non-negativity conditions

A convenient way of implementing this model is shown in Figure 3.20 (file Fig3-20.xls on your data disk). Each row in this spreadsheet corresponds to one of the investment alternatives. Cells C6 through C11 correspond to the decision variables for the problem ($X_1, ..., X_6$). The maximum value that each of these cells can take on is listed in cells D6 through D11. These values correspond to the RHS values for the first six constraints. The sum of cells C6 through C11 is computed in cell C12 as follows and will be restricted to equal the value shown in cell C13:

Formula for cell C12: =SUM(C6:C11)

Figure 3.20
Spreadsheet model for Retirement Planning Services, Inc. bond selection problem.

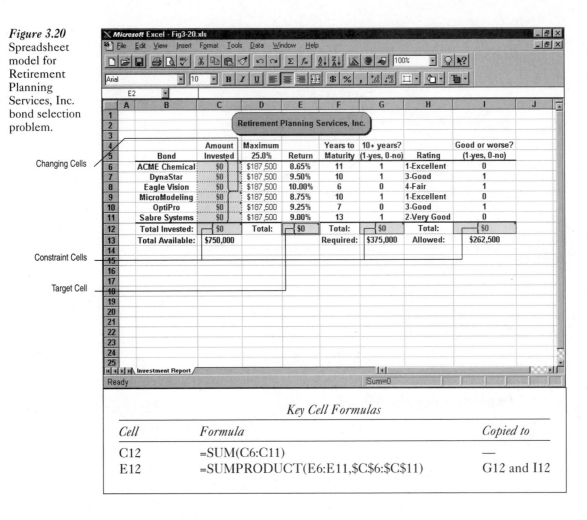

Cell	Formula	Copied to
C12	=SUM(C6:C11)	—
E12	=SUMPRODUCT(E6:E11,$C$6:$C$11)	G12 and I12

Key Cell Formulas

The annual returns for each investment are listed in cells E6 through E11. The objective function is then implemented conveniently in cell E12 as follows:

Formula for cell E12: =SUMPRODUCT(E6:E11,$C$6:$C$11)

The values in cells G6 through G11 indicate which of these rows correspond to "long-term" investments. Note that the use of ones and zeros in this column makes it convenient to compute the sum of the cells C6, C7, C9, and C11 (X_1, X_2, X_4, and X_6) representing the LHS of the "long-term" investment constraint. This is done in cell G12 as follows:

Formula for cell G12: =SUMPRODUCT(G6:G11,$C$6:$C$11)

Similarly, the zeros and ones in cells I6 through I11 indicate the higher-risk investments and allow us to implement the LHS of the "higher-risk investment" constraint as follows:

Formula for cell I12: =SUMPRODUCT(I6:I11,$C$6:$C$11)

Note that the use of zeros and ones in columns G and I to compute the sums of selected decision variables is a very useful modeling technique that makes it easy for the user to change the variables being included in the sums. Also note that the formula for the objective in cell E12 could be copied to cells G12 and I12 to implement LHS formulas for these constraint cells.

3.9.5 Solving the Model

To solve this model we need to specify the target cell, changing cells, and constraint cells identified in Figure 3.20. Figure 3.21 shows the Solver parameters and options required to solve this problem. After we click the Solve button in the Solver Parameters dialog box, Solver finds the optimal solution shown in Figure 3.22.

3.9.6 Analyzing the Solution

The solution shown in Figure 3.22 indicates the optimal investment plan places \$112,500 in Acme Chemical (X_1), \$75,000 in DynaStar (X_2), \$187,500 in Eagle Vision (X_3), \$187,500 in MicroModeling (X_4), \$0 in OptiPro (X_5), and \$187,500 in Sabre Systems (X_6). It is interesting to note that more money is being invested in Acme Chemical than DynaStar and OptiPro even though the return on Acme Chemical is lower than on the returns for DynaStar and OptiPro. This is due to the fact that DynaStar and OptiPro are both "higher-risk" investments and the 35% limit on "higher-risk" investments is a binding constraint (or is met as a strict equality in the optimal solution). Thus, the optimal solution could be improved if we could put more than 35% of the money into the higher-risk investments.

3.10 AN EMPLOYEE SCHEDULING PROBLEM

Anyone responsible for creating work schedules for a number of employees can appreciate the difficulties in this task. It can be very difficult to develop a feasible schedule,

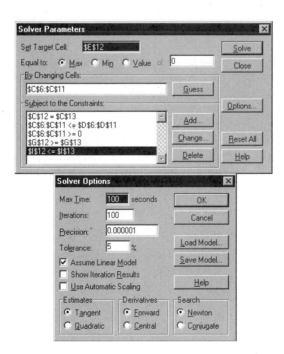

Figure 3.21
Solver parameters and options for the bond selection problem.

Figure 3.22
Optimal solution
to the bond
selection
problem.

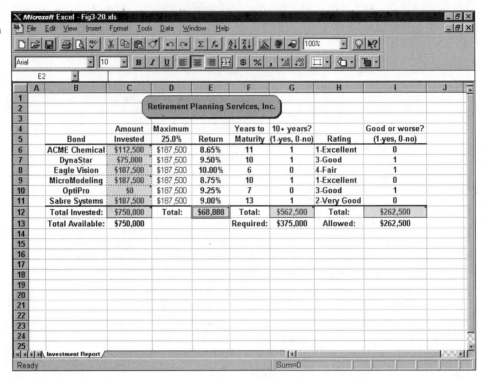

much less an optimal schedule. Trying to ensure that a sufficient number of workers is available when needed is a complicated task when you must consider multiple shifts, rest breaks, and lunch or dinner breaks. However, some sophisticated LP models have been devised to solve these problems. Although a discussion of these models is beyond the scope of this text, we will consider a simple example of an employee scheduling problem to give you an idea of how LP models are applied in this area.

Air-Express is an express shipping service that guarantees overnight delivery of packages anywhere in the continental United States. The company has various operations centers, called hubs, at airports in major cities across the country. Packages are received at hubs from other locations and then shipped to intermediate hubs or to their final destinations.

The manager of the Air-Express hub in Baltimore, Maryland, is concerned about labor costs at the hub and is interested in determining the most effective way to schedule workers. The hub operates seven days a week, and the number of packages it handles each day varies. Using historical data on the average number of packages received each day, the manager estimates the number of workers needed to handle the packages as:

Day of Week	Workers Required
Sunday	18
Monday	27
Tuesday	22
Wednesday	26
Thursday	25
Friday	21
Saturday	19

The package handlers working for Air-Express are unionized and are guaranteed a five-day work week with two consecutive days off. The base wage for the handlers is $655 per week. Because most workers prefer to have Saturday or Sunday off, the union has negotiated bonuses of $25 per day for its members who work on these days. The possible shifts and salaries for package handlers are:

Shift	Days Off	Wage
1	Sunday and Monday	$680
2	Monday and Tuesday	$705
3	Tuesday and Wednesday	$705
4	Wednesday and Thursday	$705
5	Thursday and Friday	$705
6	Friday and Saturday	$680
7	Saturday and Sunday	$655

The manager wants to keep the total wage expense for the hub as low as possible. With this in mind, how many package handlers should be assigned to each shift if the manager wants to have a sufficient number of workers available each day?

3.10.1 Defining the Decision Variables

In this problem, the manager must decide how many workers to assign to each shift. Because there are seven possible shifts, we need the following seven decision variables:

X_1 = the number of workers assigned to shift 1
X_2 = the number of workers assigned to shift 2
X_3 = the number of workers assigned to shift 3
X_4 = the number of workers assigned to shift 4
X_5 = the number of workers assigned to shift 5
X_6 = the number of workers assigned to shift 6
X_7 = the number of workers assigned to shift 7

Another way to represent this is:

X_i = the number of workers assigned to shift i, for i = 1, 2, ..., 7

3.10.2 Defining the Objective Function

The objective in this problem is to minimize the total wages paid. Each worker on shift 1 and 6 is paid $680 per week, and each worker on shift 7 is paid $655. All other workers are paid $705 per week. Thus, the objective of minimizing the total wage expense is expressed as:

MIN: $680X_1 + 705X_2 + 705X_3 + 705X_4 + 705X_5 + 680X_6 + 655X_7$ } total wage expense

3.10.3 Defining the Constraints

The constraints for this problem must ensure that at least 18 workers are scheduled for Sunday, at least 27 are scheduled for Monday, and so on. We need one constraint for each day of the week.

To make sure that at least 18 workers are available on Sunday, we must determine which decision variables represent shifts that are scheduled to work on Sunday. Because shifts 1 and 7 are the only shifts that have Sunday scheduled as a day off, the remaining shifts, 2 through 6, all are scheduled to work on Sunday. The following constraint ensures that at least 18 workers are available on Sunday:

$$0X_1 + 1X_2 + 1X_3 + 1X_4 + 1X_5 + 1X_6 + 0X_7 \geq 18 \quad \} \text{ workers required on Sunday}$$

Because workers on shifts 1 and 2 have Monday off, the constraint for Monday should ensure that the sum of the variables representing the number of workers on the remaining shifts, 3 through 7, is at least 27. This constraint is expressed as:

$$0X_1 + 0X_2 + 1X_3 + 1X_4 + 1X_5 + 1X_6 + 1X_7 \geq 27 \quad \} \text{ workers required on Monday}$$

Constraints for the remaining days of the week are generated easily by applying the same logic used in generating the previous two constraints. The resulting constraints are stated as:

$$1X_1 + 0X_2 + 0X_3 + 1X_4 + 1X_5 + 1X_6 + 1X_7 \geq 22 \quad \} \text{ workers required on Tuesday}$$
$$1X_1 + 1X_2 + 0X_3 + 0X_4 + 1X_5 + 1X_6 + 1X_7 \geq 26 \quad \} \text{ workers required on Wednesday}$$
$$1X_1 + 1X_2 + 1X_3 + 0X_4 + 0X_5 + 1X_6 + 1X_7 \geq 25 \quad \} \text{ workers required on Thursday}$$
$$1X_1 + 1X_2 + 1X_3 + 1X_4 + 0X_5 + 0X_6 + 1X_7 \geq 21 \quad \} \text{ workers required on Friday}$$
$$1X_1 + 1X_2 + 1X_3 + 1X_4 + 1X_5 + 0X_6 + 0X_7 \geq 19 \quad \} \text{ workers required on Saturday}$$

All our decision variables must assume nonnegative values. This nonnegativity condition is stated as:

$$X_1, X_2, X_3, X_4, X_5, X_6, X_7 \geq 0$$

3.10.4   A Note About the Constraints

At this point you might wonder why the constraints for each day are greater than or equal to rather than equal to constraints. For example, if Air-Express needs only 19 people on Saturday, why do we have a constraint that allows *more* than 19 people to be scheduled? The answer to this question relates to feasibility. Suppose we restate the problem so that all the constraints are equal to constraints. There are two possible outcomes for this problem: (1) it might have a feasible optimal solution, or (2) it might not have a feasible solution.

In the first case, if the formulation using equal to constraints has a feasible optimal solution, this same solution also must be a feasible solution to our formulation using greater than or equal to constraints. Because both formulations have the same objective function, the solution to our original formulation could not be worse (in terms of the optimal objective function value) than a formulation using equal to constraints.

In the second case, if the formulation using equal to constraints has no feasible solution, there is no schedule where the *exact* number of employees required can be scheduled each day. To find a feasible solution in this case, we would need to make the constraints less restrictive by allowing for more than the required number of employees to be scheduled (that is, using greater than or equal to constraints).

Therefore, using greater than or equal to constraints does not preclude a solution where the exact number of workers needed is scheduled for each shift, if such a schedule is feasible and optimal. If such a schedule is not feasible or not optimal, the formulation using greater than or equal to constraints also guarantees that a feasible optimal solution to the problem will be obtained.

3.10.5 Implementing the Model

The LP model for the Air-Express scheduling problem is summarized as:

MIN: $680X_1 + 705X_2 + 705X_3 + 705X_4 + 705X_5 + 680X_6 + 655X_7$ } total wage expense
Subject to:

$0X_1 + 1X_2 + 1X_3 + 1X_4 + 1X_5 + 1X_6 + 0X_7 \geq 18$ } workers required on Sunday
$0X_1 + 0X_2 + 1X_3 + 1X_4 + 1X_5 + 1X_6 + 1X_7 \geq 27$ } workers required on Monday
$1X_1 + 0X_2 + 0X_3 + 1X_4 + 1X_5 + 1X_6 + 1X_7 \geq 22$ } workers required on Tuesday
$1X_1 + 1X_2 + 0X_3 + 0X_4 + 1X_5 + 1X_6 + 1X_7 \geq 26$ } workers required on Wednesday
$1X_1 + 1X_2 + 1X_3 + 0X_4 + 0X_5 + 1X_6 + 1X_7 \geq 25$ } workers required on Thursday
$1X_1 + 1X_2 + 1X_3 + 1X_4 + 0X_5 + 0X_6 + 1X_7 \geq 21$ } workers required on Friday
$1X_1 + 1X_2 + 1X_3 + 1X_4 + 1X_5 + 0X_6 + 0X_7 \geq 19$ } workers required on Saturday
$X_1, X_2, X_3, X_4, X_5, X_6, X_7 \geq 0$ } nonnegativity conditions

A convenient way of implementing this model is shown in Figure 3.23 (and in the file Fig3-23.xls on your data disk). Each row in the table shown in this spreadsheet

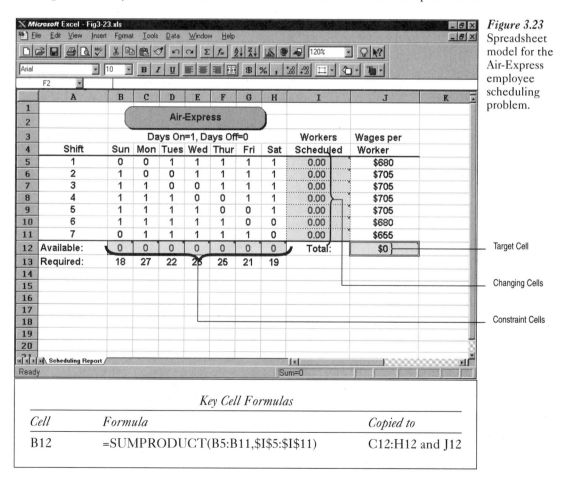

Figure 3.23
Spreadsheet model for the Air-Express employee scheduling problem.

Cell	Formula	Copied to
B12	=SUMPRODUCT(B5:B11,$I$5:$I$11)	C12:H12 and J12

Key Cell Formulas

corresponds to one of the seven shifts in the problem. For each day of the week, entries have been made to indicate which shifts are scheduled to be on or off. For example, shift 1 is scheduled off Sunday and Monday, and on the remaining days of the week. Notice that the values for each day of the week in Figure 3.23 correspond directly to the coefficients in the constraint in our LP model for the same day of the week. The required number of workers for each day is listed in cells B13 through H13 and corresponds to the RHS values of each constraint. The wages to be paid to each worker on the various shifts are listed in cells J5 through J11 and correspond to the objective function coefficients in our model.

Cells I5 through I11 indicate the number of workers assigned to each shift, and correspond to the decision variables X_1 through X_7 in our algebraic formulation of the LP model. The LHS formula for each constraint is implemented easily using the SUMPRODUCT( ) function. For example, the formula in cell B12 implements the LHS of the constraint for the number of workers needed on Sunday as:

Formula for cell B12:   =SUMPRODUCT(B5:B11,$I$5:$I$11)
(copy to C12 through H12 and J12)

This formula is then copied to cells C12 through H12 to implement the LHS formulas of the remaining constraints. With the coefficients for the objective function entered in cells J5 through J11, the previous formula is also copied to cell J12 to implement the objective function for this model.

3.10.6   Solving the Model

Figure 3.24 shows the Solver parameters and options required to solve this problem. The optimal solution is shown in Figure 3.25.

Figure 3.24
Solver parameters and options for the Air-Express scheduling problem.

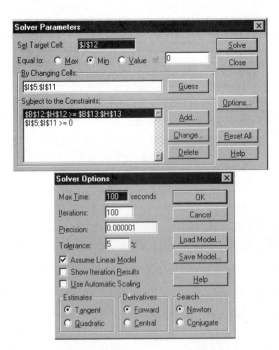

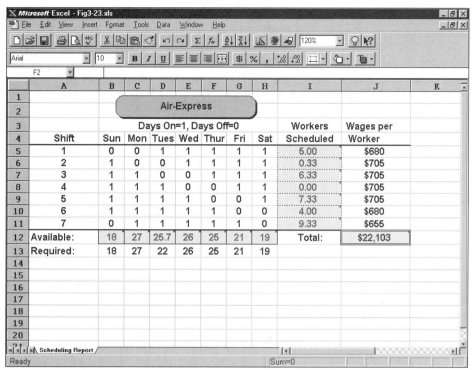

Figure 3.25
Optimal solution to the Air-Express employee scheduling problem.

3.10.7 *Analyzing the Solution*

As shown in Figure 3.25, the optimal solution to this problem ensures that the available number of employees is at least as great as the required number of employees for each day, and that the minimum total wage expense associated with this solution is $22,103. Notice that this solution calls for 5 workers to be assigned to shift 1 ($X_1 = 5.00$), 0.33 workers to be assigned to shift 2 ($X_2 = 0.33$), 6.33 workers to be assigned to shift 3 ($X_3 = 6.33$), and so on. So, although workers generally come in whole units, the solution we obtained suggests that fractional workers be assigned to various shifts. Thus, it would be helpful if we could determine the best possible solution where all the decision variables assume integer values.

Many optimization problems exist in which we might want to restrict the decision variables to assume only integer values. Such problems are known as **integer programming** problems, and they can be quite difficult to solve. We devote an entire chapter to this topic later. However, to appreciate the difficulty in integer programming problems, let's consider how we might obtain an integer solution for our current problem.

One way to get an integer solution to the Air-Express problem is to manually round all the fractional solution values to the next largest integer value. Because we are increasing the number of workers by this process, this should still give us a feasible solution. If all the fractional values in column I in Figure 3.25 are manually rounded to the next largest integer, we obtain the spreadsheet shown in Figure 3.26.

The solution shown in Figure 3.26 is feasible because the available number of workers in each time period is at least as great as the required number of workers. However, the total wage expense associated with this solution increased from $22,103 to $23,950. Although rounding up the fractional values gives us a feasible integer solution, we cannot be certain that this is the best possible integer solution to the problem.

Figure 3.26
An integer
solution to the
Air-Express
problem
obtained by
rounding up.

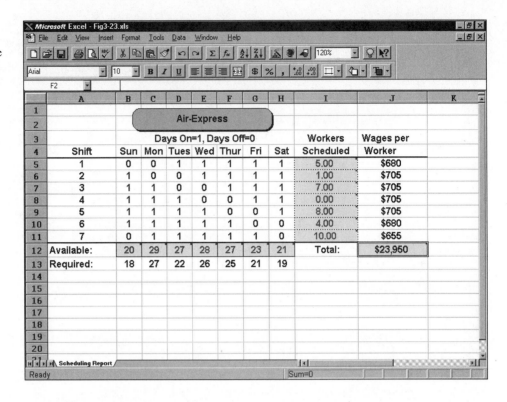

From the solution in Figure 3.25, we know that there is no feasible integer solution with an objective function value better than $22,103. If there were, the solution to the original LP problem would have favored this solution over the one it found with an objective function of $22,103. So, although we might not know the optimal integer solution to the problem, we know with certainty that its objective function value is no less than $22,103. In other words, $22,103 is a lower bound on the objective function value for the optimal integer solution to the problem. If the best possible integer solution has an objective function value of no less than $22,103 and we know an integer feasible solution to the problem that has an objective function value of $23,950, the maximum percentage difference between our known integer solution and the optimal integer solution is:

$$\frac{23,950 - 22,103}{22,103} = 8.3\%$$

Thus, even though we do not know if our rounded integer solution is the optimal integer solution, we are certain that it is within 8.3% of the optimal integer solution.

As it turns out, the integer solution we generated by rounding is *not* the optimal integer solution to this problem. A better integer solution, in fact, the optimal integer solution, is shown in Figure 3.27. The optimal integer solution to this problem is $X_1 = 6$, $X_2 = 0$, $X_3 = 6$, $X_4 = 0$, $X_5 = 7$, $X_6 = 5$, $X_7 = 9$ with a total wage expense of $22,540. The technique used to obtain this solution is described in Chapter 6, which discusses integer programming.

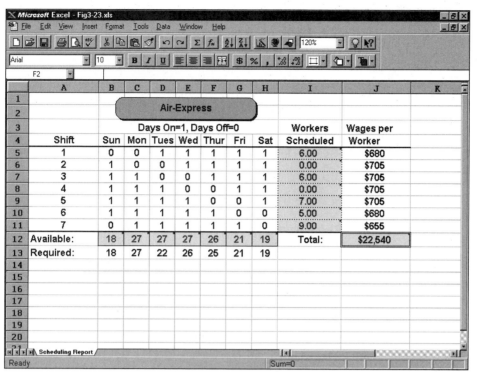

Figure 3.27
Optimal integer
solution to the
Air-Express
scheduling
problem.

3.11 A TRANSPORTATION PROBLEM

Many transportation and logistics problems faced by businesses fall into a category of problems known as network flow problems. We will consider one such example here and study this area in more detail in Chapter 5.

Tropicsun is a leading grower and distributor of fresh citrus products with three large citrus groves scattered around central Florida in the cities of Mt. Dora, Eustis, and Clermont. Tropicsun currently has 275,000 bushels of citrus at the grove in Mt. Dora, 400,000 bushels at the grove in Eustis, and 300,000 at the grove in Clermont. Tropicsun has citrus processing plants in Ocala, Orlando, and Leesburg with processing capacities to handle 200,000, 600,000, and 225,000 bushels, respectively. Tropicsun contracts with a local trucking company to transport its fruit from the groves to the processing plants. The trucking company charges a flat rate for every mile that each bushel of fruit must be transported. Each mile a bushel of fruit travels is known as a bushel-mile. The following table summarizes the distances (in miles) between the groves and processing plants:

Distances (in miles) Between
Groves and Plants

Grove	Ocala	Orlando	Leesburg
Mt. Dora	21	50	40
Eustis	35	30	22
Clermont	55	20	25

Tropicsun wants to determine how many bushels to ship from each grove to each processing plant in order to minimize the total number of bushel-miles the fruit must be shipped.

3.11.1   Defining the Decision Variables

In this situation, the problem is to determine how many bushels of fruit should be shipped from each grove to each processing plant. The problem is summarized graphically in Figure 3.28.

The circles (or nodes) in Figure 3.28 correspond to the different groves and processing plants in the problem. Note that a number has been assigned to each node. The arrows (or arcs) connecting the various groves and processing plants represent different shipping routes. The decision problem faced by Tropicsun is to determine how many bushels of fruit to ship on each of these routes. Thus, one decision variable is associated with each of the arcs in Figure 3.28. We can define these variables in general as:

$$X_{ij} = \text{number of bushels to ship from node } i \text{ to node } j$$

Specifically, the nine decision variables are:

X_{14} = number of bushels to ship from Mt. Dora (node 1) to Ocala (node 4)

X_{15} = number of bushels to ship from Mt. Dora (node 1) to Orlando (node 5)

X_{16} = number of bushels to ship from Mt. Dora (node 1) to Leesburg (node 6)

X_{24} = number of bushels to ship from Eustis (node 2) to Ocala (node 4)

Figure 3.28
Diagram for the Tropicsun transportation problem.

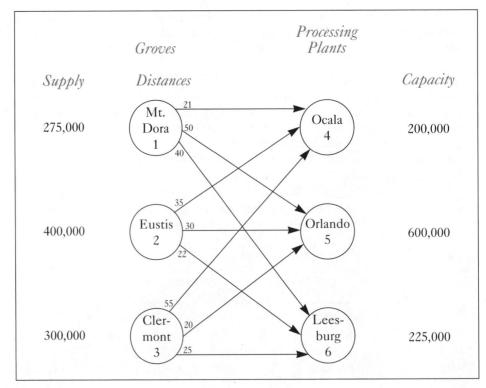

X_{25} = number of bushels to ship from Eustis (node 2) to Orlando (node 5)

X_{26} = number of bushels to ship from Eustis (node 2) to Leesburg (node 6)

X_{34} = number of bushels to ship from Clermont (node 3) to Ocala (node 4)

X_{35} = number of bushels to ship from Clermont (node 3) to Orlando (node 5)

X_{36} = number of bushels to ship from Clermont (node 3) to Leesburg (node 6)

3.11.2   Defining the Objective Function

The goal in this problem is to determine how many bushels to ship from each grove to each processing plant while minimizing the total distance (or total number of bushel-miles) the fruit must travel. The objective function for this problem is represented by:

$$\text{MIN:} \quad 21X_{14} + 50X_{15} + 40X_{16} + 35X_{24} + 30X_{25} + 22X_{26} + 55X_{34} + 20X_{35} + 25X_{36}$$

The term $21X_{14}$ in this function reflects the fact that each bushel shipped from Mt. Dora (node 1) to Ocala (node 4) must travel 21 miles. The remaining terms in the function express similar relationships for the other shipping routes.

3.11.3   Defining the Constraints

Two types of physical constraints apply to this problem. First, there is a limit on the amount of fruit that can be shipped to each processing plant. Tropicsun can ship no more than 200,000, 600,000, and 225,000 bushels to Ocala, Orlando, and Leesburg, respectively. These restrictions are reflected by the following constraints:

$$X_{14} + X_{24} + X_{34} \leq 200{,}000 \quad \} \text{ capacity restriction for Ocala}$$
$$X_{15} + X_{25} + X_{35} \leq 600{,}000 \quad \} \text{ capacity restriction for Orlando}$$
$$X_{16} + X_{26} + X_{36} \leq 225{,}000 \quad \} \text{ capacity restriction for Leesburg}$$

The first constraint indicates that the total bushels shipped to Ocala (node 4) from Mt. Dora (node 1), Eustis (node 2), and Clermont (node 3) must be less than or equal to Ocala's capacity of 200,000 bushels. The other two constraints have similar interpretations for Orlando and Leesburg. Notice that the total processing capacity at the plants (1,025,000 bushels) exceeds the total supply of fruit at the groves (975,000 bushels). Therefore, these constraints are less than or equal to constraints because not all the available capacity will be used.

The second set of constraints ensures that the supply of fruit at each grove is shipped to a processing plant. That is, all of the 275,000, 400,000, and 300,000 bushels at Mt. Dora, Eustis, and Clermont, respectively, must be processed somewhere. This is accomplished by the following constraints:

$$X_{14} + X_{15} + X_{16} = 275{,}000 \quad \} \text{ supply available at Mt. Dora}$$
$$X_{24} + X_{25} + X_{26} = 400{,}000 \quad \} \text{ supply available at Eustis}$$
$$X_{34} + X_{35} + X_{36} = 300{,}000 \quad \} \text{ supply available at Clermont}$$

The first constraint indicates that the total amount shipped from Mt. Dora (node 1) to the plants in Ocala (node 4), Orlando (node 5), and Leesburg (node 6) must equal the total amount available at Mt. Dora. This constraint indicates that all the fruit available at Mt. Dora must be shipped somewhere. The other two constraints play similar roles for Eustis and Clermont.

3.11.4   Implementing the Model

The LP model for Tropicsun's fruit transportation problem is summarized as:

$$\text{MIN:} \qquad \left. \begin{array}{l} 21X_{14} + 50X_{15} + 40X_{16} \\ + 35X_{24} + 30X_{25} + 22X_{26} + \\ 55X_{34} + 20X_{35} + 25X_{36} \end{array} \right\} \begin{array}{l} \text{total distance fruit is shipped} \\ \text{(in bushel-miles)} \end{array}$$

$$\begin{array}{lll} \text{Subject to:} & X_{14} + X_{24} + X_{34} \le 200{,}000 & \} \text{ capacity restriction for Ocala} \\ & X_{15} + X_{25} + X_{35} \le 600{,}000 & \} \text{ capacity restriction for Orlando} \\ & X_{16} + X_{26} + X_{36} \le 225{,}000 & \} \text{ capacity restriction for Leesburg} \\ & X_{14} + X_{15} + X_{16} = 275{,}000 & \} \text{ supply available at Mt. Dora} \\ & X_{24} + X_{25} + X_{26} = 400{,}000 & \} \text{ supply available at Eustis} \\ & X_{34} + X_{35} + X_{36} = 300{,}000 & \} \text{ supply available at Clermont} \\ & X_{ij} \ge 0, \text{ for all } i \text{ and } j & \} \text{ nonnegativity conditions} \end{array}$$

The last constraint, as in previous models, indicates that all the decision variables must be nonnegative.

A convenient way to implement this model is shown in Figure 3.29 (and in the file Fig3-29.xls on your data disk). In this spreadsheet, the distances between each grove and plant is summarized in a tabular format in cells C7 through E9. Cells C14 through E16 are reserved for representing the number of bushels of fruit to ship from each grove to each processing plant. Notice that these nine cells correspond directly to the nine decision variables in the algebraic formulation of the model.

The LHS formulas for the three capacity constraints in the model are implemented in cells C17, D17, and E17 in the spreadsheet. To do this, the following formula is entered in cell C17 and copied to cells D17 and E17:

> Formula for cell C17:   =SUM(C14:C16)
> (copy to D17 and E17)

These cells represent the total bushels of fruit being shipped to the plants in Ocala, Orlando, and Leesburg, respectively. Cells C18 through E18 contain the RHS values for these constraint cells.

The LHS formulas for the three supply constraints in the model are implemented in cells F14, F15, and F16 as:

> Formula for cell F14:   =SUM(C14:E14)
> (copy to F15 and F16)

These cells represent the total bushels of fruit being shipped from the groves at Mt. Dora, Eustis, and Clermont, respectively. Cells G14 through G16 contain the RHS values for these constraint cells.

Finally, the objective function for this model is entered in cell E20 as:

> Formula for cell E20:   =SUMPRODUCT(C7:E9,C14:E16)

The SUMPRODUCT() function multiplies each element in the range C7 through E9 by the corresponding element in the range C14 through E16 and then sums the individual products.

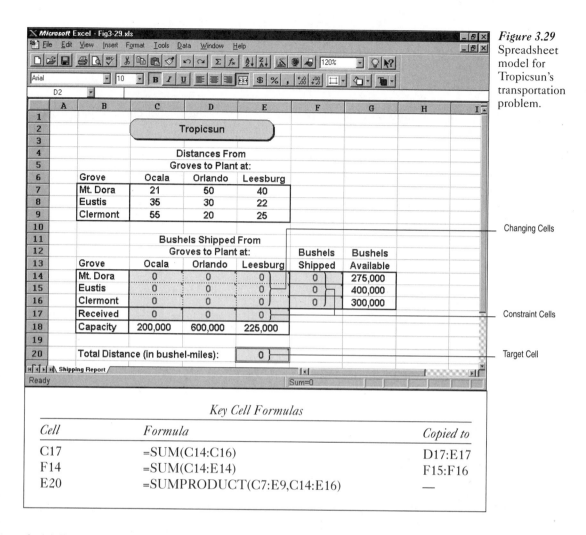

Figure 3.29
Spreadsheet
model for
Tropicsun's
transportation
problem.

Key Cell Formulas

Cell	Formula	Copied to
C17	=SUM(C14:C16)	D17:E17
F14	=SUM(C14:E14)	F15:F16
E20	=SUMPRODUCT(C7:E9,C14:E16)	—

3.11.5   Heuristic Solution for the Model

To appreciate what Solver is accomplishing, let's consider how we might try to solve this problem manually using a heuristic. A **heuristic** is a rule-of-thumb for making decisions that might work well in some instances, but is not guaranteed to produce optimal solutions or decisions. One heuristic we can apply to solve Tropicsun's problem is to always ship as much as possible along the next available path with the shortest distance (or least cost). Using this heuristic, we solve the problem as follows:

1. Because the shortest available path between any grove and processing plant is between Clermont and Orlando (20 miles), we first ship as much as possible through this route. The maximum we can ship through this route is the smaller of the supply at Clermont (300,000 bushels) or the capacity at Orlando (600,000 bushels). So we would ship 300,000 bushels from Clermont to Orlando. This depletes the supply at Clermont.

2. The next shortest available route occurs between Mt. Dora and Ocala (21 miles). The maximum we can ship through this route is the smaller of the supply at Mt. Dora (275,000 bushels) or the capacity at Ocala (200,000 bushels). So we would ship 200,000 bushels from Mt. Dora to Ocala. This depletes the capacity at Ocala.

3. The next shortest available route occurs between Eustis and Leesburg (22 miles). The maximum we can ship through this route is the smaller of the supply at Eustis (400,000 bushels) or the capacity at Leesburg (225,000 bushels). So we would ship 225,000 bushels from Eustis to Leesburg. This depletes the capacity at Leesburg.

4. The next shortest available route occurs between Eustis and Orlando (30 miles). The maximum we can ship through this route is the smaller of the remaining supply at Eustis (175,000 bushels) or the remaining capacity at Orlando (300,000 bushels). So we would ship 175,000 bushels from Eustis to Orlando. This depletes the supply at Eustis.

5. The only remaining route occurs between Mt. Dora and Orlando (because the processing capacities at Ocala and Leesburg have both been depleted). This distance is 50 miles. The maximum we can ship through this route is the smaller of the remaining supply at Mt. Dora (75,000 bushels) and the remaining capacity at Orlando (125,000 bushels). So we would ship the final 75,000 bushels at Mt. Dora to Orlando. This depletes the supply at Mt. Dora.

As shown in Figure 3.30, the solution identified with this heuristic involves shipping the fruit a total of 24,150,000 bushel-miles. All the bushels available at each grove have been shipped to the processing plants and none of the capacities at the processing plants have been exceeded. Therefore, this is a *feasible* solution to the problem. And the logic used to find this solution might lead us to believe it is a reasonably good solution—but is it the *optimal* solution? Is there no other feasible solution to this problem that can make the total distance the fruit has to travel less than 24,150,000 bushel-miles?

Figure 3.30
A heuristic solution to the transportation problem.

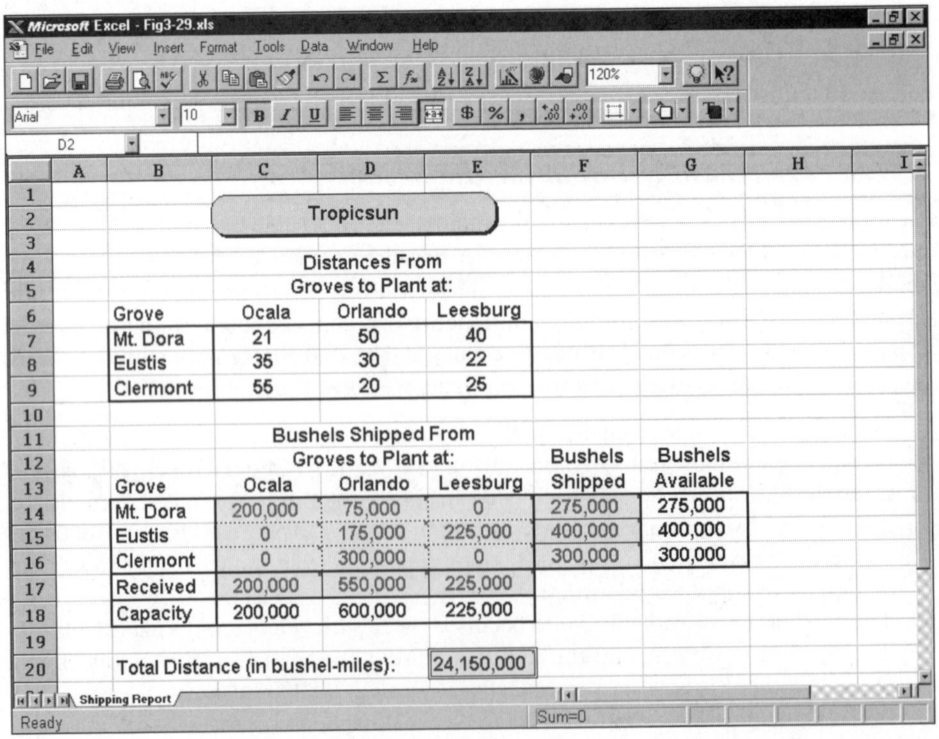

3.11.6 Solving the Model

To find the optimal solution to this model we must indicate to Solver the target cell, changing cells, and constraint cells identified in Figure 3.29. Figure 3.31 shows the Solver parameters and options required to solve this problem. The optimal solution is shown in Figure 3.32.

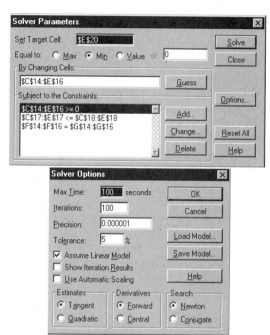

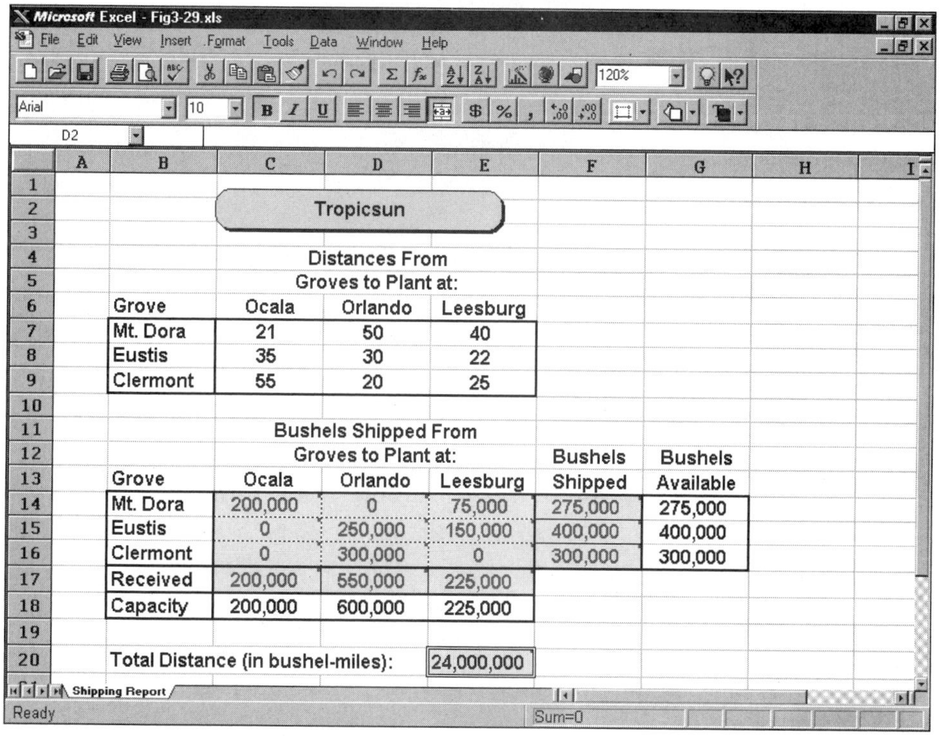

Figure 3.31 Solver parameters and options for the transportation problem.

	Grove	Ocala	Orlando	Leesburg		
		Distances From Groves to Plant at:				
	Mt. Dora	21	50	40		
	Eustis	35	30	22		
	Clermont	55	20	25		
		Bushels Shipped From Groves to Plant at:			Bushels Shipped	Bushels Available
	Grove	Ocala	Orlando	Leesburg		
	Mt. Dora	200,000	0	75,000	275,000	275,000
	Eustis	0	250,000	150,000	400,000	400,000
	Clermont	0	300,000	0	300,000	300,000
	Received	200,000	550,000	225,000		
	Capacity	200,000	600,000	225,000		
	Total Distance (in bushel-miles):			24,000,000		

Figure 3.32 Optimal solution to Tropicsun's transportation problem.

3.11.7   Analyzing the Solution

The optimal solution in Figure 3.32 indicates that 200,000 bushels should be shipped from Mt. Dora to Ocala ($X_{14} = 200,000$) and 75,000 bushels should be shipped from Mt. Dora to Leesburg ($X_{16} = 75,000$). Of the 400,000 bushels available at the grove in Eustis, 250,000 bushels should be shipped to Orlando for processing ($X_{25} = 250,000$) and 150,000 bushels should be shipped to Leesburg ($X_{26} = 150,000$). Finally, all 300,000 bushels available in Clermont should be shipped to Orlando ($X_{35} = 300,000$). None of the other possible shipping routes will be used.

The solution shown in Figure 3.32 satisfies all the constraints in the model and results in a minimum shipping distance of 24,000,000 bushel-miles, which is better than the heuristic solution identified earlier. Therefore, simple heuristics can sometimes solve LP problems, but as this example illustrates, there is no guarantee that a heuristic solution is the best possible solution.

3.12   A BLENDING PROBLEM

Many business problems involve determining an optimal mix of ingredients. For example, major oil companies must determine the least costly mix of different crude oils and other chemicals to blend together to produce a certain grade of gasoline. Lawn care companies must determine the least costly mix of chemicals and other products to blend together to produce different types of fertilizer. The following is another example of this kind of blending problem.

Agri-Pro is a company that sells agricultural products to farmers in a number of states. One service it provides to customers is custom feed mixing, whereby a farmer can order a specific amount of livestock feed and specify the amount of corn, grain, and minerals the feed should contain. This is an important service because the proper feed for various farm animals changes regularly depending on the weather, pasture conditions, and so on.

Agri-Pro stocks bulk amounts of four types of feeds that it can mix to meet a given customer's specifications. The following table summarizes the four feeds; their composition of corn, grain, and minerals; and the cost per pound for each type.

| | Percent of Nutrient in | | | |
Nutrient	Feed 1	Feed 2	Feed 3	Feed 4
Corn	30%	5%	20%	10%
Grain	10%	30%	15%	10%
Minerals	20%	20%	20%	30%
Cost per pound	$0.25	$0.30	$0.32	$0.15

Agri-Pro has just received an order from a local chicken farmer for 8,000 pounds of feed. The farmer wants this feed to contain at least 20% corn, 15% grain, and 15% minerals. What should Agri-Pro do to fill this order at minimum cost?

3.12.1   Defining the Decision Variables

In this problem, Agri-Pro must determine how much of the various feeds to blend together in order to meet the customer's requirements at minimum cost. An algebraic formulation of this problem might use the following four decision variables:

$$X_1 = \text{pounds of feed 1 to use in the mix}$$
$$X_2 = \text{pounds of feed 2 to use in the mix}$$
$$X_3 = \text{pounds of feed 3 to use in the mix}$$
$$X_4 = \text{pounds of feed 4 to use in the mix}$$

3.12.2 Defining the Objective Function

The objective in this problem is to fill the customer's order at the lowest possible cost. Because each pound of feed 1, 2, 3, and 4 costs $0.25, $0.30, $0.32, and $0.15, respectively, the objective function is represented by:

$$\text{MIN:} \quad .25X_1 + .30X_2 + .32X_3 + .15X_4$$

3.12.3 Defining the Constraints

Four constraints must be met to fulfill the customer's requirements. First, the customer wants a total of 8,000 pounds of feed. This is expressed by the constraint:

$$X_1 + X_2 + X_3 + X_4 = 8,000$$

The customer also wants the order to consist of at least 20% corn. Because each pound of feed 1, 2, 3, and 4 consists of 30%, 5%, 20%, and 10% corn, respectively, the total amount of corn in the mix is represented by:

$$.30X_1 + .05X_2 + .20X_3 + .10X_4$$

To ensure that *corn* constitutes at least 20% of the 8,000 pounds of feed, we set up the following constraint:

$$\frac{.30X_1 + .05X_2 + .20X_3 + .10X_4}{8,000} \geq .20$$

Similarly, to ensure that *grain* constitutes at least 15% of the 8,000 pounds of feed, we use the constraint:

$$\frac{.10X_1 + .30X_2 + .15X_3 + .10X_4}{8,000} \geq .15$$

Finally, to ensure that *minerals* constitute at least 15% of the 8,000 pounds of feed, we use the constraint:

$$\frac{.20X_1 + .20X_2 + .20X_3 + .30X_4}{8,000} \geq .15$$

3.12.4 Some Observations About Constraints, Reporting, and Scaling

We need to make some important observations about the constraints for this model. First, these constraints look somewhat different from the usual linear sum of products. However, these constraints are equivalent to a sum of products. For example, the constraint for the required percentage of corn can be expressed as:

$$\frac{.30X_1 + .05X_2 + .20X_3 + .10X_4}{8{,}000} \geq .20$$

or as:

$$\frac{.30X_1}{8{,}000} + \frac{.05X_2}{8{,}000} + \frac{.20X_3}{8{,}000} + \frac{.10X_4}{8{,}000} \geq .20$$

or, if you multiply both sides of the inequality by 8,000, as:

$$.30X_1 + .05X_2 + .20X_3 + .10X_4 \geq 1{,}600$$

All these constraints define exactly the same set of feasible values for X_1, ..., X_4. Theoretically, we should be able to implement and use any of these constraints to solve the problem. However, we need to consider a number of practical issues in determining which form of the constraint to implement.

Notice that the LHS formulas for the first and second versions of the constraint represent the *proportion* of corn in the 8,000 pound order, whereas the LHS in the third version of the constraint represents the *total pounds* of corn in the 8,000 pound order. Because we must implement the LHS formula of one of these constraints in the spreadsheet, we need to decide which number to display in the spreadsheet—the *proportion* (or percentage) of corn in the order, or the total pounds of corn in the order. If we know one of these values, we can easily set up a formula to calculate the other value. But, when more than one way to implement a constraint exists (as is usually the case), we need to consider what the value of the LHS portion of the constraint means to the user of the spreadsheet so that the results of the model can be reported as clearly as possible.

Another issue to consider involves scaling the model so that it can be solved accurately. For example, suppose we decide to implement the LHS formula for the first or second version of the corn constraint given earlier so that the proportion of corn in the 8,000 pound feed order appears in the spreadsheet. The coefficients for the variables in these constraints are very small values. In either case, the coefficient for X_2 is 0.05/8,000 or 0.000006250.

As Solver tries to solve an LP problem, it must perform intermediate calculations that make the various coefficients in the model larger or smaller. As numbers become extremely large or small, computers often run into storage or representation problems that force them to use approximations of the actual numbers. This opens the door for problems to occur in the accuracy of the results and, in some cases, can prevent the computer from solving the problem at all. So if some coefficients in the initial model are extremely large or extremely small, it is a good idea to re-scale the problem so that all the coefficients are of similar magnitudes.

3.12.5　Re-scaling the Model

To illustrate how a problem is re-scaled, consider the following equivalent formulation of the Agri-Pro problem:

X_1 = amount of feed 1 *in thousands of pounds* to use in the mix

X_2 = amount of feed 2 *in thousands of pounds* to use in the mix

X_3 = amount of feed 3 *in thousands of pounds* to use in the mix

X_4 = amount of feed 4 *in thousands of pounds* to use in the mix

The objective function and constraints are represented by:

MIN: $250X_1 + 300X_2 + 320X_3 + 150X_4$ } total cost

Subject to: $X_1 + X_2 + X_3 + X_4 = 8$ } pounds of feed required

$$\frac{.30X_1 + .05X_2 + .20X_3 + .10X_4}{8} \geq .20 \quad \} \text{ min \% of corn required}$$

$$\frac{.10X_1 + .30X_2 + .15X_3 + .10X_4}{8} \geq .15 \quad \} \text{ min \% of grain required}$$

$$\frac{.20X_1 + .20X_2 + .20X_3 + .30X_4}{8} \geq .15 \quad \} \text{ min \% of minerals required}$$

$X_1, X_2, X_3, X_4 \geq 0$ } nonnegativity conditions

Each unit of X_1, X_2, X_3, and X_4 now represents 1,000 pounds of feed 1, 2, 3, and 4, respectively. So the objective now reflects the fact that each unit (or each 1,000 pounds) of X_1, X_2, X_3, and X_4 costs $250, $300, $320, and $150, respectively. The constraints have also been adjusted to reflect the fact that the variables now represent thousands of pounds of the different feeds. Notice that the smallest coefficient in the constraints is now 0.05/8 = 0.00625 and the largest coefficient is 8 (that is, the RHS value for the first constraint). In our original formulation, the smallest coefficient was 0.00000625 and the largest coefficient was 8,000. By re-scaling the problem, we dramatically reduced the range between the smallest and largest coefficients in the model.

Automatic Scaling

In solving some earlier problems in this chapter, you might have noticed that the Solver Parameters dialog box provides an option called Use Automatic Scaling. If you select this option, Solver attempts to rescale the data automatically before solving the problem. Although this option is effective, you should not rely solely on it to solve all scaling problems that occur in your models.

The Assume Linear Model Option

When the Assume Linear Model option is selected, Solver conducts a number of internal tests to verify that the model is truly linear in the objective and constraints. If this option is selected and Solver's tests indicate that the model is not linear, a dialog box appears indicating that the conditions for linearity are not satisfied. The internal tests Solver applies are not always 100% accurate and sometimes indicate that the model is not linear when, in fact, it is. This often occurs when a model is poorly scaled. If you encounter this message and you are certain that your model is linear, re-solving the model might result in Solver identifying the optimal solution. If this doesn't work, try reformulating your model so that it is more evenly scaled.

3.12.6   Implementing the Model

One way to implement this model in a spreadsheet is shown in Figure 3.33 (and in the file Fig3-33.xls on your data disk). In this spreadsheet, cells B5 through E5 contain the costs of the different types of feeds. The percentage of the different nutrients found in each type of feed is listed in cells B10 through E12.

Cell G6 contains the total amount of feed (in 1,000s of pounds) required for the order and the minimum percentage of the three types of nutrients required by the customer order are entered in cells G10 through G12. Notice that the values in column G correspond to the RHS values for the various constraints in the model.

In this spreadsheet, cells B6, C6, D6, and E6 are reserved to represent the decision variables X_1, X_2, X_3, and X_4. These cells will ultimately indicate how much of each type of feed should be mixed together to fill the order. The objective function for the problem is implemented in cell F5 using the formula:

Formula for cell F5:   =SUMPRODUCT(B5:E5,B6:E6)

Figure 3.33
Spreadsheet model for Agri-Pro's blending problem.

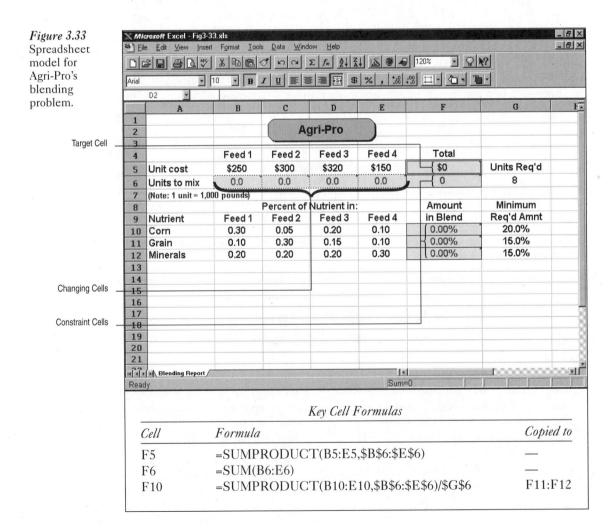

Key Cell Formulas		
Cell	*Formula*	*Copied to*
F5	=SUMPRODUCT(B5:E5,$B$6:$E$6)	—
F6	=SUM(B6:E6)	—
F10	=SUMPRODUCT(B10:E10,$B$6:$E$6)/$G$6	F11:F12

The LHS formula for the first constraint involves calculating the sum of the decision variables. This relationship is implemented in cell F6 as:

Formula for cell F6:   =SUM(B6:E6)

The RHS for this constraint is in cell G6. The LHS formulas for the other three constraints are implemented in cells F10, F11, and F12. Specifically, the LHS formula for the second constraint (representing the proportion of corn in the mix) is implemented in cell F10 as:

Formula for cell F10:   =SUMPRODUCT(B10:E10,$B$6:$E$6)/$G$6
(copy to F11 through F12)

This formula is then copied to cells F11 and F12 to implement the LHS formulas for the remaining two constraints. Again, cells G10 through G12 contain the RHS values for these constraints.

Notice that this model is implemented in a user-friendly way. Each constraint cell has a logical interpretation that communicates important information. For any given values for the changing cells (B6 through E6) totaling 8,000, the constraint cells (F10 through F12) indicate the *actual* percentage of corn, grain, and minerals in the mix.

3.12.7 Solving the Model

Figure 3.34 shows the Solver parameters and options required to solve this problem. The optimal solution is shown in Figure 3.35.

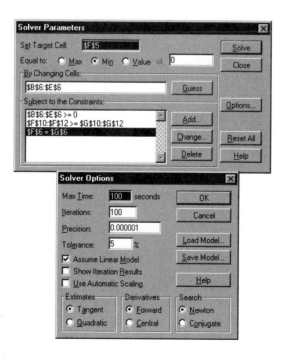

Figure 3.34
Solver parameters and options for the blending problem.

Figure 3.35
Optimal solution
to Agri-Pro's
blending
problem.

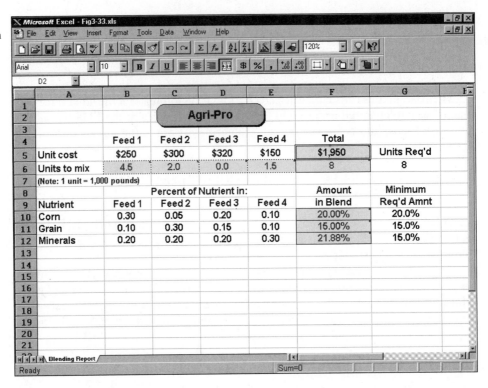

3.12.8   Analyzing the Solution

The optimal solution shown in Figure 3.35 indicates that the 8,000 pound feed order is produced at the lowest possible cost by mixing 4,500 pounds of feed 1 ($X_1 = 4.5$) with 2,000 pounds of feed 2 ($X_2 = 2$) and 1,500 pounds of feed 4 ($X_4 = 1.5$). Cell F6 indicates this produces exactly 8,000 pounds of feed. Furthermore, cells F10 through F12 indicate this mix contains 20% corn, 15% grain, and 21.88% minerals. The total cost of producing this mix is $1,950, as indicated by cell F5.

3.13 A PRODUCTION AND INVENTORY PLANNING PROBLEM

A fundamental problem facing manufacturing companies is that of planning their production and inventory levels. This process considers demand forecasts and resource constraints for the next several time periods and determines production and inventory levels for each of these time periods in order to meet the anticipated demand in the most economical way. As the following example illustrates, the multi-period nature of these problems can be handled very conveniently in a spreadsheet to greatly simplify the production planning process.

The Upton Corporation manufactures heavy-duty air compressors for the home and light industrial markets. Upton is presently trying to plan its production and inventory levels for the next six months. Because of seasonal fluctuations in utility and raw material costs, the per unit cost of producing air compressors varies from month to month—as does the demand for air compressors. Production capacity also varies from month to month due to differences in the number of working days, vacations, and scheduled maintenance and training. The following table summarizes the monthly production costs, demand, and production capacity Upton's management expects to face over the next six months.

	Month					
	1	2	3	4	5	6
Unit Production Cost	$240	$250	$265	$285	$280	$260
Units Demanded	1,000	4,500	6,000	5,500	3,500	4,000
Maximum Production	4,000	3,500	4,000	4,500	4,000	3,500

Given the size of Upton's warehouse, a maximum of 6,000 units can be held in inventory at the end of any month. The owner of the company likes to keep at least 1,500 units in inventory as safety stock to meet unexpected demand contingencies. To maintain a stable workforce, the company wants to produce at no less than one half of its maximum production capacity each month. Upton's controller estimates that the cost of carrying a unit in any given month is approximately equal to 1.5% of the unit production cost in the same month. Upton estimates the number of units carried in inventory each month by averaging the beginning and ending inventory for each month.

There are 2,750 units currently in inventory. Upton would like to identify the production and inventory plan for the next six months that will meet the expected demand each month while minimizing production and inventory costs.

3.13.1 Defining the Decision Variables

The basic decision Upton's management team faces is how many units to manufacture in each of the next six months. We will represent these decision variables as follows,

P_1 = number of units to produce in month 1

P_2 = number of units to produce in month 2

P_3 = number of units to produce in month 3

P_4 = number of units to produce in month 4

P_5 = number of units to produce in month 5

P_6 = number of units to produce in month 6

3.13.2   Defining the Objective Function

The objective in this problem is to minimize the total production and inventory costs. The total production cost is computed easily as:

$$\text{Production Cost} = 240P_1 + 250P_2 + 265P_3 + 285P_4 + 280P_5 + 260P_6$$

The inventory cost is a bit more tricky to compute. The cost of holding a unit in inventory each month is 1.5% of the production cost in the same month. So the unit inventory cost is \$3.60 in month 1 (i.e., 1.5% × \$240 = \$3.60), \$3.75 in month 2 (i.e., 1.5% × \$250 = \$3.75), and so on. The number of units held each month is to be computed as the average of the beginning and ending inventory for the month. Of course, the beginning inventory in any given month is equal to the ending inventory from the previous month. So if we let B_i represent the beginning inventory for month i, the total inventory cost is given by,

$$\text{Inventory Cost} = 3.6(B_1+B_2)/2 + 3.75(B_2+B_3)/2 + 3.98(B_3+B_4)/2 +$$
$$4.28(B_4+B_5)/2 + 4.20(B_5+B_6)/2 + 3.9(B_6+B_7)/2$$

Note that the first term in the above formula computes the inventory cost for month 1 using B_1 as the beginning inventory for month 1 and B_2 as the ending inventory for month 1. Thus, the objective function for this problem is given as,

MIN: $240P_1 + 250P_2 + 265P_3 + 285P_4 + 280P_5 + 260P_6 + 3.6(B_1+B_2)/2 +$
$3.75(B_2+B_3)/2 + 3.98(B_3+B_4)/2 + 4.28(B_4+B_5)/2 + 4.20(B_5+B_6)/2 +$ } total cost
$3.9(B_6+B_7)/2$

3.13.3   Defining the Constraints

There are two sets of constraints that apply to this problem. First, the number of units produced each month cannot exceed the maximum production levels stated in the problem. However, we must also make sure that the number of units produced each month is no less than one half of the maximum production capacity for the month. These conditions can be expressed concisely as follows,

$2{,}000 \le P_1 \le 4{,}000$ } production level for month 1

$1{,}750 \le P_2 \le 3{,}500$ } production level for month 2

$2{,}000 \le P_3 \le 4{,}000$ } production level for month 3

$2{,}250 \le P_4 \le 4{,}500$ } production level for month 4

$2{,}000 \le P_5 \le 4{,}000$ } production level for month 5

$1{,}750 \le P_6 \le 3{,}500$ } production level for month 6

The above restrictions simply place the appropriate lower and upper limit on the values each of the decision variables may assume. Similarly, we must ensure that the ending inventory each month falls between the minimum and maximum allowable inventory levels of 1,500 and 6,000, respectively. In general, the ending inventory for any month is computed as,

$$\text{Ending Inventory} = \text{Beginning Inventory} + \text{Units Produced} - \text{Units Sold}$$

Thus, the following restrictions indicate that the ending inventory in each of the next six months (after meeting the demand for the month) must fall between 1,500 and 6,000.

$$1,500 \le B_1 + P_1 - 1,000 \le 6,000 \quad \} \text{ ending inventory for month 1}$$
$$1,500 \le B_2 + P_2 - 4,500 \le 6,000 \quad \} \text{ ending inventory for month 2}$$
$$1,500 \le B_3 + P_3 - 6,000 \le 6,000 \quad \} \text{ ending inventory for month 3}$$
$$1,500 \le B_4 + P_4 - 5,500 \le 6,000 \quad \} \text{ ending inventory for month 4}$$
$$1,500 \le B_5 + P_5 - 3,500 \le 6,000 \quad \} \text{ ending inventory for month 5}$$
$$1,500 \le B_6 + P_6 - 4,000 \le 6,000 \quad \} \text{ ending inventory for month 6}$$

Finally, to ensure that the beginning balance in one month equals the ending balance from the previous month we have the following additional restrictions,

$$B_2 = B_1 + P_1 - 1,000$$
$$B_3 = B_2 + P_2 - 4,500$$
$$B_4 = B_3 + P_3 - 6,000$$
$$B_5 = B_4 + P_4 - 5,500$$
$$B_6 = B_5 + P_5 - 3,500$$
$$B_7 = B_6 + P_6 - 4,000$$

3.13.4 Implementing the Model

The LP problem for Upton's production and inventory planning problem may be summarized as:

MIN: $240P_1 + 250P_2 + 265P_3 + 285P_4 + 280P_5 + 260P_6 + 3.6(B_1 + B_2)/2 +$
$3.75(B_2 + B_3)/2 + 3.98(B_3 + B_4)/2 + 4.28(B_4 + B_5)/2 + 4.20(B_5 + B_6)/2 +$ $\Big\}$ total cost
$3.9(B_6 + B_7)/2$

Subject to:
$2,000 \le P_1 \le 4,000$ } production level for month 1
$1,750 \le P_2 \le 3,500$ } production level for month 2
$2,000 \le P_3 \le 4,000$ } production level for month 3
$2,250 \le P_4 \le 4,500$ } production level for month 4
$2,000 \le P_5 \le 4,000$ } production level for month 5
$1,750 \le P_6 \le 3,500$ } production level for month 6
$1,500 \le B_1 + P_1 - 1,000 \le 6,000$ } ending inventory for month 1
$1,500 \le B_2 + P_2 - 4,500 \le 6,000$ } ending inventory for month 2
$1,500 \le B_3 + P_3 - 6,000 \le 6,000$ } ending inventory for month 3
$1,500 \le B_4 + P_4 - 5,500 \le 6,000$ } ending inventory for month 4

$$1{,}500 \leq B_5 + P_5 - 3{,}500 \leq 6{,}000 \quad \} \text{ ending inventory for month 5}$$
$$1{,}500 \leq B_6 + P_6 - 4{,}000 \leq 6{,}000 \quad \} \text{ ending inventory for month 6}$$

where:

$$B_2 = B_1 + P_1 - 1{,}000$$
$$B_3 = B_2 + P_2 - 4{,}500$$
$$B_4 = B_3 + P_3 - 6{,}000$$
$$B_5 = B_4 + P_4 - 5{,}500$$
$$B_6 = B_5 + P_5 - 3{,}500$$
$$B_7 = B_6 + P_6 - 4{,}000$$

A convenient way of implementing this model is shown in Figure 3.36 (and file Fig3-36.xls on your data disk). Cells C7 through H7 in this spreadsheet represent the number of air compressors to produce in each month and therefore correspond to the decision variables (P_1 through P_6) in our model. We will place appropriate upper and

Figure 3.36
Spreadsheet
model for
Upton's
production
problem.

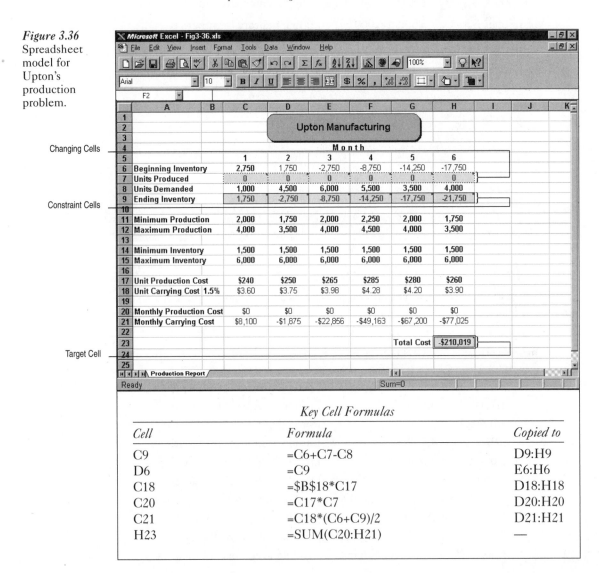

Key Cell Formulas		
Cell	Formula	Copied to
C9	=C6+C7-C8	D9:H9
D6	=C9	E6:H6
C18	=$B$18*C17	D18:H18
C20	=C17*C7	D20:H20
C21	=C18*(C6+C9)/2	D21:H21
H23	=SUM(C20:H21)	—

lower bounds on these cells to enforce the restrictions represented by the first six constraints in our model. The estimated demands for each time period are listed just below the decision variables in cells C8 through H8.

With the beginning inventory level of 2,750 entered in cell C6, the ending inventory for month 1 is computed in cell C9 as follows:

Formula for cell C9:   =C6+C7-C8
(copy to cells D9 through H9)

This formula can be copied to cells D9 through H9 to compute the ending inventory levels for each of the remaining months. We will place appropriate lower and upper limits on these cells to enforce the restrictions indicated by the second set of six constraints in our model.

To ensure that the beginning inventory in month 2 equals the ending inventory from month 1, we place the following formula in cell D6,

Formula for cell D6:   =C9
(copy to cells E6 through H6)

This formula can be copied to cells E6 through H6 to ensure that the beginning inventory levels in each month equal the ending inventory levels from the previous month. It is important to note that because the beginning inventory levels can be calculated directly from the ending inventory levels there is no need to specify these cells as constraint cells to Solver.

With the monthly unit production costs entered in cell C17 through H17, the monthly unit carrying costs are computed in cells C18 through H18 as follows,

Formula for cell C18:   =$B$18*C17
(copy to cells D18 through H18)

The total monthly production and inventory costs are then computed in rows 20 and 21 as follows,

Formula for cell C20:   =C17*C7
(copy to cells D20 through H20)

Formula for cell C21:   =C18*(C6+C9)/2
(copy to cells D21 through H21)

Finally, the objective function representing the total production and inventory costs for the problem is implemented in cell H23 as follows:

Formula for cell H23:   =SUM(C20:H21)

3.13.5 Solving the Model

Figure 3.37 shows the Solver parameters and options required to solve this problem. The optimal solution is shown in Figure 3.38.

3.13.6 Analyzing the Solution

The optimal solution shown in Figure 3.38 indicates Upton should produce 4,000 units in period 1, 3,500 units in period 2, 4,000 units in period 3, 4,250 units in period 4, 4,000 units in period 5, and 3,500 units in period 6. Although the demand for air compressors in month 1 can be met by the beginning inventory, production in month 1 is required to build inventory for future months in which demand exceeds the available production

Figure 3.37
Solver
parameters and
options for the
production
problem.

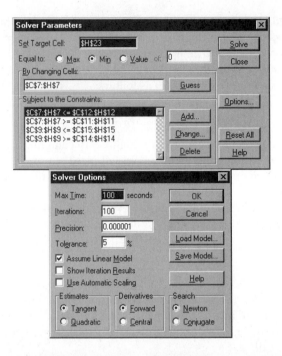

Figure 3.38
Optimal solution
to Upton's
production
problem.

A	B	C	D	E	F	G	H	I	J	K
1										
2			Upton Manufacturing							
3										
4			Month							
5		1	2	3	4	5	6			
6 Beginning Inventory		2,750	5,750	4,750	2,750	1,500	2,000			
7 Units Produced		4,000	3,500	4,000	4,250	4,000	3,500			
8 Units Demanded		1,000	4,500	6,000	5,500	3,500	4,000			
9 Ending Inventory		5,750	4,750	2,750	1,500	2,000	1,500			
10										
11 Minimum Production		2,000	1,750	2,000	2,250	2,000	1,750			
12 Maximum Production		4,000	3,500	4,000	4,500	4,000	3,500			
13										
14 Minimum Inventory		1,500	1,500	1,500	1,500	1,500	1,500			
15 Maximum Inventory		6,000	6,000	6,000	6,000	6,000	6,000			
16										
17 Unit Production Cost		$240	$250	$265	$285	$280	$260			
18 Unit Carrying Cost 1.5%		$3.60	$3.75	$3.98	$4.28	$4.20	$3.90			
19										
20 Monthly Production Cost		$960,000	$875,000	$1,060,000	$1,211,250	$1,120,000	$910,000			
21 Monthly Carrying Cost		$15,300	$19,688	$14,906	$9,084	$7,350	$6,825			
22										
23							Total Cost	$6,209,403			
24										
25										

capacity. Notice that this production schedule calls for the company to operate at full production capacity in all months except month 4. Month 4 is expected to have the highest per unit production cost. Therefore it is more economical to produce extra units in prior months and hold them in inventory for sale in month 4.

It is important to note that although the solution to this problem provides a production plan for the next six months it does not bind Upton's management team to implement this particular solution throughout the next six months. At an operational level, the management team is most concerned with the decision that must be made now–namely the number of units to schedule for production in month 1. At the end of month 1, Upton's management should update the inventory, demand, and cost estimates and re-solve the model to identify the production plan for the next six months (months 2 through 7). At the end of month 2 this process should be repeated again. Thus, multi-period planning models such as this should be used repeatedly on a periodic basis as part of a rolling planning process.

3.14   A MULTI-PERIOD CASH FLOW PROBLEM

Numerous business problems involve decisions that have a ripple effect on future decisions. In the previous example we saw how the manufacturing plans for one time period can impact the amount of resources available and the inventory carried in subsequent time periods. Similarly, many financial decisions involve multiple time periods because the amount of money invested or spent at one point in time directly affects the amount of money available in subsequent time periods. In these types of multi-period problems it can be difficult to account for the consequences of a current decision on future time periods without an LP model. The formulation of such a model is illustrated below in an example from the world of finance.

Taco-Viva is a small but growing restaurant chain specializing in Mexican fast food. The management of the company has decided to build a new location in Wilmington, North Carolina, and wants to establish a construction fund (or sinking fund) to pay for the new facility. Construction of the restaurant is expected to take six months and cost $800,000. Taco-Viva's contract with the construction company requires it to make payments of $250,000 at the end of the second and fourth months, and a final payment of $300,000 at the end of the sixth month when the restaurant is completed. The company can use four investment opportunities to establish the construction fund; these investments are summarized in the following table:

Investment	Available in Month	Months to Maturity	Yield at Maturity
A	1, 2, 3, 4, 5, 6	1	1.8%
B	1, 3, 5	2	3.5%
C	1, 4	3	5.8%
D	1	6	11.0%

The table indicates that investment A will be available at the beginning of each of the next six months, and funds invested in this manner mature in one month with a yield of 1.8%. Funds can be placed in investment C only at the beginning of months 1 and/or 4, and mature at the end of three months with a yield of 5.8%.

The management of Taco-Viva needs to determine the investment plan that allows them to meet the required schedule of payments while placing the least amount of money in the construction fund.

This is a multi-period problem because a six-month planning horizon must be considered. That is, Taco-Viva must plan which investment alternatives to use at various times during the next six months.

3.14.1   Defining the Decision Variables

The basic decision faced by the management of Taco-Viva is how much money to invest in each investment vehicle during each time period when the investment opportunities are available. To model this problem, we need different variables to represent each investment/time period combination. This can be done as:

$A_1, A_2, A_3, A_4, A_5, A_6$ = the amount of money (in $1,000s) placed in investment A at the beginning of months 1, 2, 3, 4, 5 and 6, respectively

B_1, B_3, B_5 = the amount of money (in $1,000s) placed in investment B at the beginning of months 1, 3, and 5, respectively

C_1, C_4 = the amount of money (in $1,000s) placed in investment C at the beginning of months 1 and 4, respectively

D_1 = the amount of money (in $1,000s) placed in investment D at the beginning of month 1

Notice that all variables are expressed in units of thousands of dollars to maintain a reasonable scale for this problem. So, keep in mind that when referring to the amount of money represented by our variables, we mean the amount in thousands of dollars.

3.14.2   Defining the Objective Function

Taco-Viva's management wants to minimize the amount of money it must initially place in the construction fund in order to cover the payments that will be due under the contract. At the beginning of month 1 the company wants to invest some amount of money that, along with its investment earnings, will cover the required payments without an additional infusion of cash from the company. Because A_1, B_1, C_1, and D_1 represent the initial amounts invested by the company in month 1, the objective function for the problem is:

MIN: $A_1 + B_1 + C_1 + D_1$ } total cash invested at the beginning of month 1

3.14.3   Defining the Constraints

To formulate the cash flow constraints for this problem it is important to clearly identify: (1) when the different investments can be made, (2) when the different investments will mature, and (3) how much money will be available when each investment matures. Figure 3.39 summarizes this information.

The negative values, represented by –1 in Figure 3.39, indicate when dollars can flow *into* each investment. The positive values indicate how much these same dollars will be worth when the investment matures, or when dollars flow *out* of each investment. The symbols indicate time periods in which funds remain in a particular investment. For example, the third row of the table in Figure 3.39 indicates that every dollar placed in investment C during month 1 will be worth $1.058 when this investment matures three

	Cash Inflow/Outflow at the Beginning of Month							*Figure 3.39*
Investment	1	2	3	4	5	6	7	Cash flow summary table for Taco-Viva's investment opportunities.
A_1	−1	1.018						
B_1	−1	⟷	1.035					
C_1	−1	⟷	⟷	1.058				
D_1	−1	⟷	⟷	⟷	⟷	⟷	1.11	
A_2		−1	1.018					
A_3			−1	1.018				
B_3			−1	⟷	1.035			
A_4				−1	1.018			
C_4				−1	⟷	⟷	1.058	
A_5					−1	1.018		
B_5					−1	⟷	1.035	
A_6						−1	1.018	
Req'd Payments (in $1,000s)	$0	$0	$250	$0	$250	$0	$300	

months later—at the *beginning* of month 4. (Note that the beginning of month 4 occurs at virtually the same instant as the *end* of month 3. Thus, there is no practical difference between the beginning of one time period and the end of the previous time period.)

Assuming that the company invests the amounts represented by A_1, B_1, C_1, and D_1 at the beginning of month 1, how much money will be available to reinvest or make the required payments at the beginning of months 2, 3, 4, 5, 6, and 7? The answer to this question allows us to generate the set of cash flow constraints needed for this problem.

As indicated by the second column of Figure 3.39, the only funds maturing at the beginning of month 2 are those placed in investment A at the beginning of month 1 (A_1). The value of the funds maturing at the beginning of month 2 is $1.018A_1$. Because no payments are required at the beginning of month 2, all the maturing funds must be reinvested. But the only new investment opportunity available at the beginning of month 2 is investment A (A_2). Thus, the amount of money placed in investment A at the beginning of month 2 must be $1.018A_1$. This is expressed by the constraint:

$$1.018A_1 = A_2 + 0 \quad \} \text{ cash flow for month 2}$$

This constraint indicates that the total amount of money maturing at the beginning of month 2 ($1.018A_1$) must equal the amount of money reinvested at the beginning of month 2 (A_2) plus any payment due in month 2 (0).

Now let's consider the cash flows that will occur during month 3. At the beginning of month 3, any funds that were placed in investment B at the beginning of month 1 (B_1) will mature and be worth a total of $1.035B_1$. Similarly, any funds placed in investment A at the beginning of month 2 (A_2) will mature and be worth a total of $1.018A_2$. Because a payment of $250,000 is due at the beginning of month 3, we must ensure that the funds maturing at the beginning of month 3 are sufficient to cover this payment, and that any remaining funds are placed in the investment opportunities available at the beginning of month 3 (A_3 and B_3). This requirement can be stated algebraically as:

$$1.035B_1 + 1.018A_2 = A_3 + B_3 + 250 \quad \} \text{ cash flow for month 3}$$

This constraint indicates that the total amount of money maturing at the beginning of month 3 ($1.018A_2 + 1.035B_1$) must equal the amount of money reinvested at the beginning of month 3 ($A_3 + B_3$) plus the payment due at the beginning of month 3 ($250,000).

The same logic we applied to generate the cash flow constraints for months 2 and 3 can also be used to generate cash flow constraints for the remaining months. Doing so produces a cash flow constraint for each month that takes on the general form:

$$\begin{pmatrix} \text{Total \$ amount} \\ \text{maturing at the} \\ \text{beginning} \\ \text{of the month} \end{pmatrix} = \begin{pmatrix} \text{Total \$ amount} \\ \text{reinvested at the} \\ \text{beginning} \\ \text{of the month} \end{pmatrix} + \begin{pmatrix} \text{Payment} \\ \text{due at the} \\ \text{beginning} \\ \text{of the month} \end{pmatrix}$$

Using this general definition of the cash flow relationships, the constraints for the remaining months are represented by:

$$1.058C_1 + 1.018A_3 = A_4 + C_4 \qquad\qquad \} \text{ cash flow for month 4}$$
$$1.035B_3 + 1.018A_4 = A_5 + B_5 + 250 \qquad \} \text{ cash flow for month 5}$$
$$1.018A_5 = A_6 \qquad\qquad\qquad\qquad\quad \} \text{ cash flow for month 6}$$
$$1.11D_1 + 1.058C_4 + 1.035B_5 + 1.018A_6 = 300 \quad \} \text{ cash flow for month 7}$$

To implement these constraints in the spreadsheet, we must express them in a slightly different (but algebraically equivalent) manner. Specifically, to conform to our general definition of an equality constraint ($f(X_1, X_2, \ldots, X_n) = b$) we need to rewrite the cash flow constraints so that all the *variables* in each constraint appear on the LHS of the equal sign, and a numeric constant appears on the RHS of the equal sign. This can be done as:

$$1.018A_1 - 1A_2 = 0 \qquad\qquad\qquad\qquad\qquad\quad \} \text{ cash flow for month 2}$$
$$1.035B_1 + 1.018A_2 - 1A_3 - 1B_3 = 250 \qquad\quad \} \text{ cash flow for month 3}$$
$$1.058C_1 + 1.018A_3 - 1A_4 - 1C_4 = 0 \qquad\quad \} \text{ cash flow for month 4}$$
$$1.035B_3 + 1.018A_4 - 1A_5 - 1B_5 = 250 \qquad\quad \} \text{ cash flow for month 5}$$
$$1.018A_5 - 1A_6 = 0 \qquad\qquad\qquad\qquad\qquad\quad \} \text{ cash flow for month 6}$$
$$1.11D_1 + 1.058C_4 + 1.035B_5 + 1.018A_6 = 300 \quad \} \text{ cash flow for month 7}$$

There are two important points to note about this alternate expression of the constraints. First, each constraint takes on the following general form, which is algebraically equivalent to our previous general definition for the cash flow constraints:

$$\begin{pmatrix} \text{Total \$ amount} \\ \text{maturing at the} \\ \text{beginning} \\ \text{of the month} \end{pmatrix} - \begin{pmatrix} \text{Total \$ amount} \\ \text{reinvested at the} \\ \text{beginning} \\ \text{of the month} \end{pmatrix} = \begin{pmatrix} \text{Payment} \\ \text{due at the} \\ \text{beginning} \\ \text{of the month} \end{pmatrix}$$

Although the constraints look slightly different in this form, they enforce the same relationships among the variables as expressed by the earlier constraints.

Second, the LHS coefficients in the alternate expression of the constraints correspond directly to the values listed in the cash flow summary table in Figure 3.39. That is, the coefficients in the constraint for month 2 correspond to the values in the column for month 2 in Figure 3.39; the coefficients for month 3 correspond to the values in the column for month 3, and so on. This relationship is true for all the constraints and will be very helpful in implementing this model in the spreadsheet.

3.14.4 Implementing the Model

The LP model for Taco-Viva's construction fund problem is summarized as:

$$\text{MIN: } A_1 + B_1 + C_1 + D_1 \qquad \} \text{ cash invested at beginning of month 1}$$

Subject to:

$$
\begin{aligned}
1.018A_1 - 1A_2 &= 0 &&\} \text{ cash flow for month 2}\\
1.035B_1 + 1.018A_2 - 1A_3 - 1B_3 &= 250 &&\} \text{ cash flow for month 3}\\
1.058C_1 + 1.018A_3 - 1A_4 - 1C_4 &= 0 &&\} \text{ cash flow for month 4}\\
1.035B_3 + 1.018A_4 - 1A_5 - 1B_5 &= 250 &&\} \text{ cash flow for month 5}\\
1.018A_5 - 1A_6 &= 0 &&\} \text{ cash flow for month 6}\\
1.11D_1 + 1.058C_4 + 1.035B_5 + 1.018A_6 &= 300 &&\} \text{ cash flow for month 7}\\
A_i, B_i, C_i, D_i &\geq 0, \text{ for all } i &&\} \text{ nonnegativity conditions}
\end{aligned}
$$

One approach to implementing this model is shown in Figure 3.40 (and file Fig3-40.xls on your data disk). The first three columns of this spreadsheet summarize the different investment options that are available and the months in which money may flow in to and out of these investments. Cells D6 through D17 represents the decision variables in our model and indicate the amount of money (in $1,000s) to be placed in each of the possible investments.

The objective function for this problem requires that we compute the total amount of money being invested in month 1. This was done in cell D18 as follows:

Formula for cell D18: =SUMIF(B6:B17,1,D6:D17)

This SUMIF function compares the values in cells B6 through B17 to the value 1 (its second argument). If any of the values in B6 through B17 equal 1, it sums the corresponding values in cells D6 through D17. In this case, the values in cells B6 through B9 all equal 1, therefore the function returns the sum of the values in cells D6 through D9. Note that while we could have implemented the objective using the formula SUM(D6:D9), the above SUMIF formula makes for a more modifiable and reliable model. If any of the values in column B are changed to or from 1, the SUMIF function continues to represent the appropriate objective function whereas the SUM function would not.

Our next job is to implement the cash inflow/outflow table described earlier in Figure 3.39. Recall that each row in Figure 3.39 corresponds to the cash flows associated with a particular investment alternative. This table can be implemented in our spreadsheet using the following formula,

Formula for cell F6: =IF($B6=F$5,-1,IF($C6=F$5,1+$E6,IF(AND($B6<F$5,$C6>F$5),"<---->","")))
(copy to cells F6 through L17)

This formula first checks to see if the "month of cash inflow" value in column B matches the month indicator value in row 5. If so, the formula returns the value -1. Otherwise, it goes on to check to see if the "month of cash outflow" value in column

Figure 3.40
Spreadsheet
model for
Taco-Viva's
construction
fund problem.

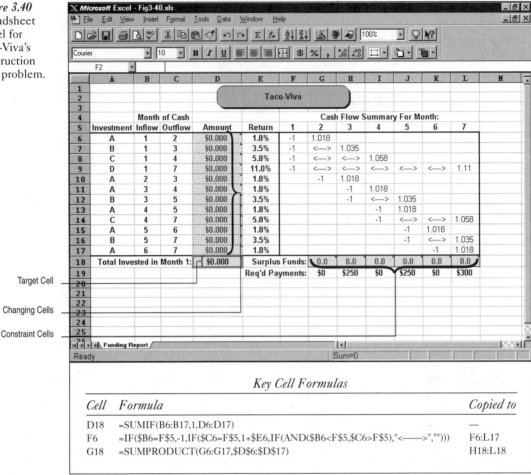

Key Cell Formulas

Cell	Formula	Copied to
D18	=SUMIF(B6:B17,1,D6:D17)	—
F6	=IF($B6=F$5,-1,IF($C6=F$5,1+$E6,IF(AND($B6<F$5,$C6>F$5),"<——>","")))	F6:L17
G18	=SUMPRODUCT(G6:G17,$D$6:$D$17)	H18:L18

C matches the month indicator value in row 5. If so, the formula returns a value equal to 1 plus the return for the investment (from column E). If neither of the first two condition are met, the formula next checks whether the current month indicator in row 5 is larger than the "month of cash inflow" value (column B) and smaller than the "month of cash outflow" value (column C). If so, the formula returns the characters "<----->" to indicate periods in which funds neither flow into or out of a particular investment. Finally, if none of the previous three condition are met, the formula simply returns an empty (or null) string "". While this formula looks a bit intimidating, it is simply a set of three nested IF functions. More importantly, it automatically updates the cash flow summary if any of the values in columns B, C, or E are changed, increasing the reliability and modifiability of the model.

Earlier we noted that the values listed in columns 2 through 7 of the cash inflow/outflow table correspond directly to the coefficients appearing in the various cash flow constraints. This property allows us to implement the cash flow constraints in the spreadsheet conveniently. For example, the LHS formula for the cash flow constraint for month 2 is implemented in cell G18 through the formula:

Formula in cell G18:   =SUMPRODUCT(G6:G17,$D$6:$D$17)
(copy to H18 through L18)

This formula multiplies each entry in the range G6 through G17 by the corresponding entry in the range D6 through D17 and then sums these individual products. This formula is copied to cells H18 through L18. (Notice that the SUMPRODUCT() formula treats cells containing labels and null strings as if they contained the value zero.) Take a moment now to verify that the formulas in cells G18 through L18 correspond to the LHS formulas of the cash flow constraints in our model. Cells G19 through L19 list the RHS values for the cash flow constraints.

3.14.5 Solving the Model

To find the optimal solution to this model, we must indicate to Solver the target cell, changing cells, and constraint cells identified in Figures 3.40. Figure 3.41 shows the Solver parameters and options required to solve this model. The optimal solution is shown in Figure 3.42.

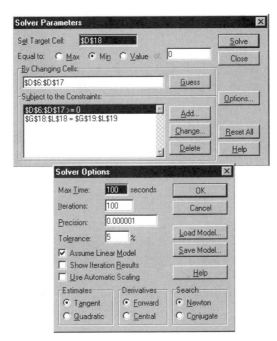

Figure 3.41
Solver parameters and options for the construction fund problem.

3.14.6 Analyzing the Solution

The value of the target cell (D18) in Figure 3.42 indicates that a total of $741,363 must be invested to meet the payments on Taco-Viva's construction project. Cells D6 and D8 indicate that approximately $241,237 should be placed in investment A at the beginning of month 1 ($A_1 = 241.237$) and approximately $500,126 should be placed in investment C ($C_1 = 500.126$).

At the beginning of month 2, the funds placed in investment A at the beginning of month 1 will mature and be worth $245,580 ($241,237 \times 1.018 = 245,580$). The value in cell D10 indicates these funds should be placed back into investment A at the beginning of month 2 ($A_2 = 245.580$).

At the beginning of month 3, the first $250,000 payment is due. At that time, the funds placed in investment A at the beginning of month 2 will mature and be worth $250,000 ($1.018 \times 245,580 = 250,000$) – allowing us to makes this payment.

Figure 3.42
Optimal solution
to Taco-Viva's
construction
fund problem.

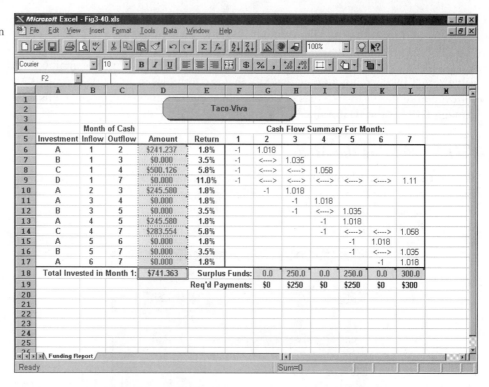

At the beginning of month 4, the funds placed in investment C at the beginning of month 1 will mature and be worth $529,134. Our solution indicates that $245,580 of this amount should be placed in investment A (A_4 = 245.580) and the rest should be re-invested in investment C (C_4 = 283.554).

If you trace through the cash flows for the remaining months, you will discover that our model is doing exactly what it was designed to do. The amount of money scheduled to mature at the beginning of each month is exactly equal to the amount of money scheduled to be reinvested after required payments are made. Thus, out of an infinite number of possible investment schedules, our LP model found the one schedule that requires the least amount of money up front.

3.14.7   Modifying The Taco-Viva Problem to Account for Risk (Optional)

In investment problems like this, it is not uncommon for decision makers to place limits on the amount of risk they are willing to assume. For instance, suppose the chief financial officer (CFO) for Taco-Viva assigned the following risk ratings to each of the possible investments on a scale from 1 to 10 (where 1 represents the least risk and 10 the greatest risk). We will also assume that the CFO wants to determine an investment plan where the weighted average risk level does not exceed 5.

Investment	Risk Rating
A	1
B	3
C	8
D	6

We will need to formulate an additional constraint for each time period to ensure the weighted average risk level never exceeds 5. To see how this can be done, let's start with month 1.

In month 1, funds can be invested in A_1, B_1, C_1, and/or D_1, and each investment is associated with a different degree of risk. To calculate the weighted average risk during month 1, we must multiply the risk factors for each investment by the proportion of money in that investment. This is represented by:

$$\text{Weighted average risk in month 1} = \frac{1A_1 + 3B_1 + 8C_1 + 6D_1}{A_1 + B_1 + C_1 + D_1}$$

We can ensure that the weighted average risk in month 1 does not exceed the value 5 by including the following constraint in our LP model:

$$\frac{1A_1 + 3B_1 + 8C_1 + 6D_1}{A_1 + B_1 + C_1 + D_1} \leq 5 \quad \} \text{ risk constraint for month 1}$$

Now let's consider month 2. According to the column for month 2 in our cash inflow/outflow table, the company can have funds invested in B_1, C_1, D_1, and/or A_2 during this month. Thus, the weighted average risk that occurs in month 2 is defined by:

$$\text{Weighted average risk in month 2} = \frac{3B_1 + 8C_1 + 6D_1 + 1A_2}{B_1 + C_1 + D_1 + A_2}$$

Again, the following constraint ensures that this quantity never exceeds 5:

$$\frac{3B_1 + 8C_1 + 6D_1 + 1A_2}{B_1 + C_1 + D_1 + A_2} \leq 5 \quad \} \text{ risk constraint for month 2}$$

The risk constraints for months 3 through 6 are generated in a similar manner, and appear as:

$$\frac{8C_1 + 6D_1 + 1A_3 + 3B_3}{C_1 + D_1 + A_3 + B_3} \leq 5 \quad \} \text{ risk constraint for month 3}$$

$$\frac{6D_1 + 3B_3 + 1A_4 + 8C_4}{D_1 + B_3 + A_4 + C_4} \leq 5 \quad \} \text{ risk constraint for month 4}$$

$$\frac{6D_1 + 8C_4 + 1A_5 + 3B_5}{D_1 + C_4 + A_5 + B_5} \leq 5 \quad \} \text{ risk constraint for month 5}$$

$$\frac{6D_1 + 8C_4 + 3B_5 + 1A_6}{D_1 + C_4 + B_5 + A_6} \leq 5 \quad \} \text{ risk constraint for month 6}$$

Although the risk constraints listed above have a very clear meaning, it is easier to implement these constraints in the spreadsheet if we state them in a different (but algebraically equivalent) manner. In particular, it is helpful to eliminate the fractions on the LHS of the inequalities by multiplying each constraint through by its denominator and re-collecting the variables on the LHS of the inequality. The following steps show how to rewrite the risk constraint for month 1:

1. Multiply both sides of the inequality by the denominator:

$$(A_1 + B_1 + C_1 + D_1) \frac{1A_1 + 3B_1 + 8C_1 + 6D_1}{A_1 + B_1 + C_1 + D_1} \leq (A_1 + B_1 + C_1 + D_1)5$$

to obtain:

$$1A_1 + 3B_1 + 8C_1 + 6D_1 \leq 5A_1 + 5B_1 + 5C_1 + 5D_1$$

2. Re-collect the variables on the LHS of the inequality sign:

$$(1 - 5)A_1 + (3 - 5)B_1 + (8 - 5)C_1 + (6 - 5)D_1 \leq 0$$

to obtain:

$$-4A_1 - 2B_1 + 3C_1 + 1D_1 \leq 0$$

Thus, the following two constraints are algebraically equivalent:

$$\frac{1A_1 + 3B_1 + 8C_1 + 6D_1}{A_1 + B_1 + C_1 + D_1} \leq 5 \quad \} \text{ risk constraint for month 1}$$

$$-4A_1 - 2B_1 + 3C_1 + 1D_1 \leq 0 \quad \} \text{ risk constraint for month 1}$$

The set of values for A_1, B_1, C_1, and D_1 that satisfies the first of these constraints also satisfies the second constraint (that is, these constraints have exactly the same set of feasible values). So, it does not matter which of these constraints we use to find the optimal solution to the problem.

The remaining risk constraints are simplified in the same way, producing the following constraints:

$$-2B_1 + 3C_1 + 1D_1 - 4A_2 \leq 0 \quad \} \text{ risk constraint for month 2}$$
$$3C_1 + 1D_1 - 4A_3 - 2B_3 \leq 0 \quad \} \text{ risk constraint for month 3}$$
$$1D_1 - 2B_3 - 4A_4 + 3C_4 \leq 0 \quad \} \text{ risk constraint for month 4}$$
$$1D_1 + 3C_4 - 4A_5 - 2B_5 \leq 0 \quad \} \text{ risk constraint for month 5}$$
$$1D_1 + 3C_4 - 2B_5 - 4A_6 \leq 0 \quad \} \text{ risk constraint for month 6}$$

Notice that the coefficient for each variable in these constraints is simply the risk factor for the particular investment minus the maximum allowable weighted average risk value of 5. That is, all A_j variables have coefficients of $1 - 5 = -4$; all B_j variables have coefficients of $3 - 5 = -2$; all C_j variables have coefficients of $8 - 5 = 3$; and all D_j variables have coefficients of $6 - 5 = 1$. This observation will help us implement these constraints efficiently.

3.14.8   Implementing the Risk Constraints

Figure 3.43 (and file Fig3-43.xls on your data disk) shows a split screen that illustrates an easy way to implement the risk constraints for this model. Earlier we noted that the coefficient for each variable in each risk constraint is simply the risk factor for the particular investment minus the maximum allowable weighted average risk value. Thus, the strategy in Figure 3.43 is to generate these values in the appropriate columns and rows of the spreadsheet so that the SUMPRODUCT() function can implement the LHS formulas for the risk constraints.

Recall that the risk constraint for each month involves only the variables representing investments that actually held funds during that month. For any given month, the investments that actually held funds during that month have the value –1 or contain a text entry starting with the "<" symbol (the first character of the "<---->" entries) in the corresponding column of the cash inflow/outflow summary table. For example, during month 2, funds can be invested in B_1, C_1, D_1, and/or A_2. The corresponding cells for month 2 in Figure 3.43 (cells G7, G8, G9, and G10, respectively) each contain either the value -1 or a text entry starting with the "<" symbol. Therefore, to generate

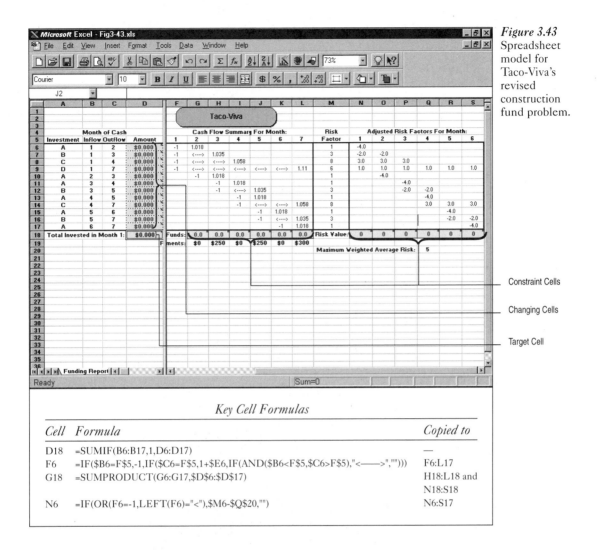

Figure 3.43
Spreadsheet model for Taco-Viva's revised construction fund problem.

Constraint Cells

Changing Cells

Target Cell

Key Cell Formulas

Cell	Formula	Copied to
D18	=SUMIF(B6:B17,1,D6:D17)	—
F6	=IF($B6=F$5,-1,IF($C6=F$5,1+$E6,IF(AND($B6<F$5,$C6>F$5),"<——>","")))	F6:L17
G18	=SUMPRODUCT(G6:G17,$D$6:$D$17)	H18:L18 and N18:S18
N6	=IF(OR(F6=-1,LEFT(F6)="<"),$M6-$Q$20,"")	N6:S17

the appropriate coefficients for the risk constraints, we can instruct the spreadsheet to scan the cash inflow/outflow summary for cells containing the value –1 or text entries starting with the "<" symbol, and return the correct risk constraint coefficients in the appropriate cells. To do this we enter the following formula in cell N6:

Formula in cell N6:   =IF(OR(F6=-1,LEFT(F6)="<"),$M6-$Q$20,"")
(copy to N6 through S17)

To generate the appropriate value in cell N6, the above formula checks if cell F6 is equal to –1 or contains a text entry that starts with the "<" symbol. If either of these conditions is true, the function takes the risk factor for the investment from cell M6 and subtracts the maximum allowable risk factor found in cell Q20; otherwise, the function returns a null string (with a value of zero). This formula is copied to the remaining cells in the range N6 through S17 as shown in Figure 3.43.

The values in cells N6 through S17 in Figure 3.43 correspond to the coefficients in the LHS formulas for each of the risk constraints formulated earlier. Thus, the LHS formula for the risk constraint for month 1 is implemented in cell N18 as:

Formula in cell N18:   =SUMPRODUCT(N6:N17,$D$6:$D$17)
(copy to O18 through S18)

The LHS formulas for the remaining risk constraints are implemented by copying this formula to cells O18 through S18. We will tell Solver that these constraint cells must be less than or equal to zero.

3.14.9   Solving the Model

To find the optimal solution to this model, we must communicate the appropriate information about the new risk constraints to Solver. Figure 3.44 shows the Solver parameters and options required to solve this model. The optimal solution is shown in Figure 3.45.

3.14.10   Analyzing the Solution

The optimal solution to the revised Taco-Viva problem with risk constraints is quite different than the solution obtained earlier. In particular, the new solutions requires that funds be placed in investment A in every time period. This is not too surprising given that investment A has the lowest risk rating. What may be somewhat surprising is that investments B and D are never used. Although these investments have lower risk ratings than investment C, the combination of funds placed in investment A and C allows for the least amount of money to be invested in month 1 while meeting the scheduled payments and keeping the weighted average risk at or below the specified level.

Figure 3.44
Solver
parameters and
options for the
revised
construction
fund problem.

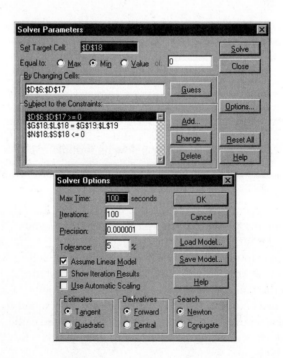

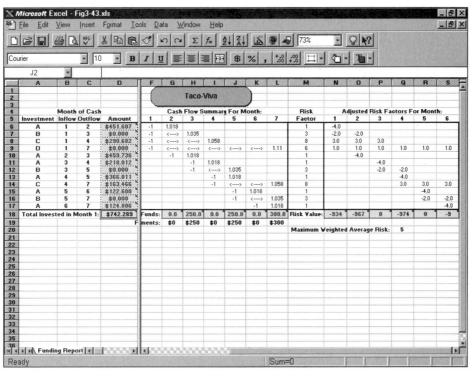

Figure 3.45
Optimal solution to Taco-Viva's revised construction fund problem.

Excel's Solver provides one of the most effective ways to handle LP models in a spreadsheet, but it was not the first. Spreadsheet solvers such as What's Best! and LP88 were being used increasingly at the time that the most popular spreadsheet programs began to bundle a solver with their new releases. LP88 can be used as a standalone program or with a spreadsheet. What's Best! was designed initially as an add-in to Lotus 1-2-3, but current releases also work with Microsoft Excel and Quattro Pro.

The Wall Street Journal reported that the availability of solvers for personal computers allow many businesses to transfer LP models from mainframe computers. Newfoundland Energy Ltd., for example, evaluated its mix of crude oils to purchase with LP on a mainframe for 25 years. Since it began using a personal computer for this application, the company has saved thousands of dollars per year in mainframe access time charges.

The expansion of access to LP also spawned new applications. Therese Fitzpatrick, a nursing administrator at Grant Hospital in Chicago, used What's Best! to create a staff scheduling model that was projected to save the hospital $80,000 per month in overtime and temporary hiring costs. The task of scheduling 300 nurses so that those with appropriate skills were in the right place at the right time had required 20 hours per month. The LP model enabled Therese to do the job in four hours, even with such complicating factors as leaves, vacations, and variations in staffing requirements at different times and days of the week.

Hawley Fuel Corp., a New York wholesaler of coal, found that it could minimize its cost of purchases while still meeting customers' requirements for sulfur and ash content by optimizing a spreadsheet LP model. Charles Howard of Victoria, British Columbia, developed an LP model to increase electricity generation from a dam just by opening and closing the outlet valves at the right time.

Source: Bulkely, William M., "The Right Mix: New Software Makes the Choice Much Easier," *The Wall Street Journal*, March 27, 1987, p. 17.

SUMMARY

This chapter described how to formulate an LP problem algebraically, implement it in a spreadsheet, and solve it using Solver. The decision variables in the algebraic formulation of a model correspond to the changing cells in the spreadsheet. The LHS formulas for each constraint in an LP model must be implemented in different cells in the spreadsheet. Also, a cell in the spreadsheet must represent the objective function in the LP model. Thus, there is a direct relationship between the various components of an algebraic formulation of an LP problem and its implementation in a spreadsheet.

There are many ways a given LP problem can be implemented in a spreadsheet. The process of building spreadsheet models is more an art than a science. A good spreadsheet model represents the problem in a way that clearly communicates its purpose while being reliable, auditable, and modifiable.

QUESTIONS AND PROBLEMS

1. In creating the spreadsheet models for the problems in this chapter, cells in the spreadsheets had to be reserved to represent each of the decision variables in the algebraic models. We reserved these cells in the spreadsheets by entering values of zero in them. Why didn't we place some other value or formula in these cells? Would doing so have made any difference?

2. Four goals should be considered when trying to design an effective spreadsheet model: communication, reliability, auditability, and maintainability. We also noted that a spreadsheet design that results in formulas that can be copied is usually more effective than other designs. Briefly describe how using formulas that can be copied supports the four spreadsheet modeling goals.

3. Refer to question 13 at the end of Chapter 2. Implement a spreadsheet model for this problem and solve it using Solver.

4. Refer to question 16 at the end of Chapter 2. Implement a spreadsheet model for this problem and solve it using Solver.

5. Refer to question 17 at the end of Chapter 2. Implement a spreadsheet model for this problem and solve it using Solver.

6. Refer to question 19 at the end of Chapter 2. Implement a spreadsheet model for this problem and solve it using Solver.

7. Refer to question 20 at the end of Chapter 2. Implement a spreadsheet model for this problem and solve it using Solver.

8. Valu-Com Electronics manufactures five different models of telecommunications interface cards for personal and laptop computers. As summarized in the following table, each of these devices requires differing amounts of printed circuit (PC) board, resistors, memory chips, and assembly.

	Per Unit Requirements				
	HyperLink	FastLink	SpeedLink	MicroLink	EtherLink
PC Board (square inches)	20	15	10	8	5
Resistors	28	24	18	12	16
Memory Chips	8	8	4	4	6
Assembly Labor (in hours)	0.75	0.6	0.5	0.65	1

The unit wholesale price and manufacturing cost for each model are as follows.

	Per Unit Revenues and Costs				
	HyperLink	FastLink	SpeedLink	MicroLink	EtherLink
Wholesale Price	$189	$149	$129	$169	$139
Manufacturing Cost	$136	$101	$96	$137	$101

In their next production period, Valu-Com has 80,000 square inches of PC board, 100,000 resistors, 30,000 memory chips, and 5,000 hours of assembly time available. They can sell all the product they can manufacture but the marketing department wants to be sure they produce at least 500 units of each product and at least twice as many FastLink cards as HyperLink cards.

a. Formulate an LP model for this problem.
b. Create a spreadsheet model for this problem and solve it using Solver.
c. What is the optimal solution?
d. Could Vaul-Com make more money if they schedule their assembly workers to work overtime?

9. A trust officer at the Blacksburg National Bank needs to determine how to invest $100,000 in the following collection of bonds.

Bond	Annual Return	Maturity	Risk	Tax-Free
A	9.5%	Long	High	Yes
B	8.0%	Short	Low	Yes
C	9.0%	Long	Low	No
D	9.0%	Long	High	Yes
E	9.0%	Short	High	No

The officer wants to invest at least 50% of the money in short-term issues and no more than 50% in high-risk issues. At least 30% of the funds should go in tax-free investments and at least 40% of the total annual return should be tax-free.

    a.   Formulate an LP model for this problem.

    b.   Create a spreadsheet model for this problem and solve it using Solver.

    c.   What is the optimal solution?

10. The Weedwacker Company manufactures two types of lawn trimmers: an electric model and a gas model. The company has contracted to supply a national discount retail chain with a total of 30,000 electric trimmers and 15,000 gas trimmers. However, Weedwacker's production capability is limited in three departments: production, assembly, and packaging. The following table summarizes the hours of processing time available and the processing time required by each department, for both types of trimmers:

	Hours Required per Trimmer		
	Electric	Gas	Hours Available
Production	0.20	0.40	10,000
Assembly	0.30	0.50	15,000
Packaging	0.10	0.10	5,000

The company makes its electric trimmer in-house for $55 and its gas trimmer for $85. Alternatively, it can buy electric and gas trimmers from another source for $67 and $95, respectively. How many gas and electric trimmers should Weedwacker make and how many should it buy from its competitor in order to fulfill its contract in the least costly manner?

    a.   Formulate an LP model for this problem.

    b.   Create a spreadsheet model for this problem and solve it using Solver.

    c.   What is the optimal solution?

11. A manufacturer of prefabricated homes has decided to subcontract four components of the homes. Several companies are interested in receiving this business, but none can handle more than one subcontract. The bids made by the companies for the various subcontracts are summarized in the following table.

Bids by Companies (in $1,000s) for Various Subcontracts

	Company			
Component	A	B	C	D
1	185	225	193	207
2	200	190	175	225
3	330	320	315	300
4	375	389	425	445

Assuming all the companies can perform each subcontract equally well, to which company should each subcontract be assigned if the home manufacturer wants to minimize payments to the subcontractors?

    a.   Formulate an LP model for this problem.

    b.   Create a spreadsheet model for this problem and solve it using Solver.

    c.   What is the optimal solution?

12. Tarmac Chemical Corporation produces a special chemical compound—called CHEMIX—that is used extensively in high school chemistry classes. This compound must contain at least 20% sulfur, at least 30% iron oxide, and at least 30% but no more than 45% potassium. Tarmac's marketing department has estimated that it will need at least 600 pounds of this compound to meet the expected demand during the coming school session. Tarmac can buy three compounds to mix together to produce CHEMIX. The makeup of these compounds is given below.

Compound	Sulfur	Iron Oxide	Potassium
1	20%	60%	20%
2	40%	30%	30%
3	10%	40%	50%

Compounds 1, 2, and 3 cost $5.00, $5.25, and $5.50 per pound, respectively. Tarmac wants to use an LP model to determine the least costly way of producing enough CHEMIX to meet the demand expected for the coming year.

a. Formulate an LP model for this problem.
b. Create a spreadsheet model for this problem and solve it using Solver.
c. What is the optimal solution?

13. Riverside Oil Company in eastern Kentucky produces regular and supreme gasoline. Each barrel of regular sells for $21 and must have an octane rating of at least 90. Each barrel of supreme sells for $25 and must have an octane rating of at least 97. Each of these types of gasoline are manufactured by mixing different quantities of the following three inputs:

Input	Cost per barrel	Octane rating	Barrels available (in 1000s)
1	$17.25	100	150
2	$15.75	87	350
3	$17.75	110	300

Riverside has orders for 300,000 barrels of regular and 450,000 barrels of supreme. How should the company allocate the available inputs to the production of regular and supreme gasoline if they want to maximize profits?

a. Formulate an LP model for this problem.
b. Create a spreadsheet model for this problem and solve it using Solver.
c. What is the optimal solution?

14. Maintenance at a major theme park in central Florida is an on-going process that occurs 24 hours a day. Because it is a long drive from most residential areas to the park, employees do not like to work shifts of fewer than eight hours. These 8-hour shifts start every four hours throughout the day. The number of maintenance workers needed at different times throughout the day varies. The following table summarizes the minimum number of employees needed in each 4-hour time period.

Time Period	Minimum Employees Needed
12 a.m. to 4 a.m.	90
4 a.m. to 8 a.m.	215
8 a.m. to 12 p.m.	250
12 p.m. to 4 p.m.	165
4 p.m. to 8 p.m.	300
8 p.m. to 12 a.m.	125

The maintenance supervisor wants to determine the minimum number of employees to schedule that meets the minimum staffing requirements.

   a. Formulate an LP model for this problem.
   b. Create a spreadsheet model for this problem and solve it using Solver.
   c. What is the optimal solution?

15. Radmore Memorial Hospital has a problem in its fluids analysis lab. The lab has available three machines that analyze various fluid samples. Recently, the demand for analyzing blood samples has increased so much that the lab director is having difficulty getting all the samples analyzed quickly enough and still completing the other fluid work that comes into the lab. The lab works with five types of blood specimens. Any machine can be used to process any of the specimens. However, the amount of time required by each machines varies depending on the type of specimen being analyzed. These times are summarized in the following table.

Required Specimen Processing Time in Minutes

	Specimen Type				
Machine	1	2	3	4	5
A	3	4	4	5	3
B	5	3	5	4	5
C	2	5	3	3	4

Each machine can be used a total of 8 hours a day. Blood samples collected on given day arrive at the lab and are stored over night and processed the next day. So at the beginning of each day the lab director must determine how to allocate the various samples to the machines for analysis. This morning the lab has 80 type 1 specimens, 75 type 2 specimens, 80 type 3 specimens, 120 type 4 specimens, and 60 type 5 specimens awaiting processing. The lab director wants to know how many of each type of specimen should be analyzed on each machine in order to minimize the total time the machines are devoted to analyzing blood samples.

   a. Formulate an LP model for this problem.
   b. Create a spreadsheet model for this problem and solve it using Solver.
   c. What is the optimal solution?
   d. How much processing time will be available on each machine if this solution is implemented?
   e. How would the model and solution change if the lab director wanted to balance the use of each machine so that each machine were used approximately the same amount of time?

16. Virginia Tech operates its own power generating plant. The electricity generated by this plant supplies power to the university and to local businesses and residences in the Blacksburg area. The plant burns three types of coal which produce steam that drives the turbines that generate the electricity. The Environmental Protection Agency (EPA) requires that for each ton of coal burned, the emissions from the coal furnace smoke stacks contain no more than 2,500 parts per million (ppm) of sulfur and no more than 2.8 kilograms (kg) of coal dust. The following table summarizes the amounts of sulfur, coal dust, and steam that result from burning a ton of each type of coal.

Coal	Sulfur (in ppm)	Coal Dust (in kg)	Pounds of Steam Produced
1	1,100	1.7	24,000
2	3,500	3.2	36,000
3	2,700	2.4	28,000

The three types of coal can be mixed and burned in any combination. The resulting emission of sulfur or coal dust and the pounds of steam produced by any mixture are given as the weighted average of the values shown in the table for each type of coal. For example, if the coals are mixed to produce a blend that consisted of 35% of coal 1, 40% of coal 2, and 25% of coal 3, the sulfur emission (in ppm) resulting from burning one ton of this blend is:

$$0.35 \times 1,100 + 0.40 \times 3,500 + 0.25 \times 2,700 = 2,460$$

The manager of this facility wants to determine the blend of coal that will produce the maximum pounds of steam per ton without violating the EPA requirements.

a. Formulate an LP model for this problem.
b. Create a spreadsheet model for this problem and solve it using Solver.
c. What is the optimal solution?
d. If the furnace can burn up to 30 tons of coal per hour, what is the maximum amount of steam that can be produced per hour?

17. A real estate developer is planning to build an apartment building specifically for graduate students on a parcel of land adjacent to a major university. Three types of apartments can be included in the building: efficiencies, and one-, two-, or three-bedroom units. Each efficiency requires 500 square feet; each one-bedroom apartment requires 700 square feet; each two-bedroom apartment requires 800 square feet; and each three-bedroom unit requires 1,000 square feet.

The developer believes that the building should include no more than 15 one-bedroom units, 22 two-bedroom units, and 10 three-bedroom units. Local zoning ordinances do not allow the developer to build more than 40 units in this particular building location, and restrict the building to a maximum of 40,000 square feet. The developer has already agreed to lease 5 one-bedroom units and 8 two-bedroom units to a local rental agency that is a "silent partner" in this endeavor. Market studies indicate that efficiencies can be rented for $350 per month, one-bedrooms for $450 per month, two-bedrooms for $550 per month, and three-bedrooms for $750 per month. How many rental units of each type should the developer include in the building plans in order to maximize the potential rental income from the building?

    a. Formulate an LP model for this problem.

    b. Create a spreadsheet model for this problem and solve it using Solver.

    c. What is the optimal solution?

    d. Which constraint in this model limits the builder's potential rental income from increasing any further?

18. Kentwood Electronics manufactures three components for stereo systems: CD players, tape decks, and stereo tuners. The wholesale price and manufacturing cost of each item are given below.

Component	Wholesale Price	Manufacturing Cost
CD Player	$150	$75
Tape Deck	$85	$35
Stereo Tuner	$70	$30

Each CD player produced requires 3 hours of assembly; each tape deck requires 2 hours of assembly; and each tuner requires 1 hour of assembly. The marketing department has indicated that it can sell no more than 150,000 CD players, 100,000 tape decks, and 90,000 stereo tuners. However, the demand is expected to be at least 50,000 units of each item, and Kentwood wants to meet this demand. If Kentwood has 400,000 hours of assembly time available, how many CD players, tape decks, and stereo tuners should it produce in order to maximize profits while meeting the minimum demand figures?

    a. Formulate an LP model for this problem.

    b. Create a spreadsheet model for this problem and solve it using Solver.

    c. What is the optimal solution?

19. The Rent-A-Dent car rental company allows its customers to pick up a rental car at one location and return it to any of its locations. Currently, two locations (1 and 2) have 16 and 18 surplus cars, respectively, and four locations (3, 4, 5, and 6) each need 10 cars. The costs of getting the surplus cars from locations 1 and 2 to the other locations are summarized below.

Costs of Transporting Cars Between Locations				
	Location 3	Location 4	Location 5	Location 6
Location 1	$54	$17	$23	$30
Location 2	$24	$18	$19	$31

Because 34 surplus cars are available at locations 1 and 2, and 40 cars are needed at locations 3, 4, 5, and 6, some locations will not receive as many cars as they need. However, management wants to make sure that all the surplus cars are sent where they are needed, and that each location needing cars receives at least five.

    a. Formulate an LP model for this problem.

    b. Create a spreadsheet model for this problem and solve it using Solver.

    c. What is the optimal solution?

20. The Sentry Lock Corporation manufactures a popular commercial security lock at plants in Macon, Louisville, Detroit and Phoenix. The per unit cost of production at each plant is $35.50, $37.50, $39.00 and $36.25, respectively, while the annual production capacity at each plant is 18,000, 15,000, 25,000 and 20,000, respectively.

Sentry's locks are sold to retailers through wholesale distributors in seven cities across the United States. The unit cost of shipping from each plant to each distributor is summarized in the following table along with the forecasted demand from each distributor for the coming year.

Plants	Tacoma	San Diego	Dallas	Denver	St. Louis	Tampa	Baltimore
	Unit Shipping Cost to Distributor in						
Macon	$2.50	$2.75	$1.75	$2.00	$2.10	$1.80	$1.65
Louisville	$1.85	$1.90	$1.50	$1.60	$1.00	$1.90	$1.85
Detroit	$2.30	$2.25	$1.85	$1.25	$1.50	$2.25	$2.00
Phoenix	$1.90	$0.90	$1.60	$1.75	$2.00	$2.50	$2.65
Demand	8,500	14,500	13,500	12,600	18,000	15,000	9,000

Sentry would like to determine the least expensive way of shipping locks from their manufacturing plants to their distributors. Because the total demand from distributors exceeds the total production capacity for all the plants, Acme realizes they will not be able to satisfy all the demand for their product; but would like to make sure each distributor will have the opportunity to fill at least 80% of the orders they receive.

a. Create a spreadsheet model for this problem and solve it.
b. What is the optimal solution?

21. A paper recycling company converts newspaper, mixed paper, white office paper, and cardboard into pulp for newsprint, packaging paper, and print stock quality paper. The following table summarizes the yield for each kind of pulp recovered from each ton of recycled material.

	Newsprint	Packaging	Print Stock
	Recycling Yield		
Newspaper	85%	80%	—
Mixed Paper	90%	80%	70%
White Office Paper	90%	85%	80%
Cardboard	80%	70%	—

For instance, a ton of newspaper can be recycled using a technique that yields 0.85 tons of newsprint pulp. Alternatively, a ton of newspaper can be recycled using a technique that yields 0.80 tons of packaging paper. Similarly, a ton of cardboard can be recycled to yield 0.80 tons of newsprint or 0.70 tons of packaging paper pulp. Note that newspaper and cardboard cannot be converted to print stock pulp using the techniques available to the recycler.

The cost of processing each ton of raw material into the various types of pulp is summarized below along with the amount of each of the four raw materials that can be purchased and their costs.

	Processing Costs per Ton			Purchase Cost Per Ton	Tons Available
	Newsprint	Packaging	Print Stock		
Newspaper	$6.50	$11.00	—	$15	600
Mixed Paper	$9.75	$12.25	$9.50	$16	500
White Office Paper	$4.75	$7.75	$8.50	$19	300
Cardboard	$7.50	$8.50	—	$17	400

The recycler would like to determine the least costly way of producing 500 tons of newsprint pulp, 600 tons of packaging paper pulp, and 300 tons of print stock quality pulp.

a. Create a spreadsheet model for this problem and solve it.
b. What is the optimal solution?

22. A winery has the following capacity to produce an exclusive dinner wine at either of its two vineyards at the indicated costs:

Vineyard	Capacity	Cost per Bottle
1	3,500 bottles	$23
2	3,100 bottles	$25

Four Italian restaurants around the country are interested in purchasing this wine. Because the wine is exclusive, they all want to buy as much as they need but will take whatever they can get. The maximum amounts required by the restaurants and the prices they are willing to pay are summarized below.

Restaurant	Maximum Demand	Price
1	1,800 bottles	$69
2	2,300 bottles	$67
3	1,250 bottles	$70
4	1,750 bottles	$66

The costs of shipping a bottle from the vineyards to the restaurants are summarized below.

	Restaurant			
Vineyard	1	2	3	4
1	$7	$8	$13	$9
2	$12	$6	$8	$7

The winery needs to determine the production and shipping plan that allows it to maximize its profits on this wine.

a. Formulate an LP model for this problem.
b. Create a spreadsheet model for this problem and solve it using Solver.
c. What is the optimal solution?

23. Bellows Lumber Yard, Inc. stocks standard length 25-foot boards, which it cuts to custom lengths to fill individual customer orders. An order has just come in for

5,000 7-foot boards, 1,200 9-foot boards, and 300 11-foot boards. The lumber yard manager has identified six ways to cut the 25-foot boards to fill this order. The six cutting patterns are summarized below:

Cutting Pattern	Number of Boards Produced		
	7 ft	9 ft	11 ft
1	3	0	0
2	2	1	0
3	2	0	1
4	1	2	0
5	0	1	1
6	0	0	2

One possibility (cutting pattern 1) is to cut a 25-foot board into three 7-foot boards, and not to cut any 9- or 11-foot boards. Note that cutting pattern 1 uses a total of 21 feet of board and leaves a 4-foot piece of scrap. Another possibility (cutting pattern 4) is to cut a 25-foot board into one 7-foot board and two 9-foot boards (using all 25 feet of the board). The remaining cutting patterns have similar interpretations. The lumber yard manager wants to fill this order using the fewest number of 25-foot boards as possible. To do this, the manager needs to determine how many 25-foot boards to run through each cutting pattern.

a. Formulate an LP model for this problem.
b. Create a spreadsheet model for this problem and solve it using Solver.
c. What is the optimal solution?

24. Howie's Carpet World has just received an order for carpets for a new office building. The order is for 4,000 yards of carpet 4-feet wide, 20,000 yards of carpet 9-feet wide, and 9,000 yards of carpet 12-feet wide. Howie can order two kinds of carpet rolls, which he will then have to cut to fill this order. One type of roll is 14-feet wide, 100-yards long, and costs $1,000 per roll; the other is 18-feet wide, 100-yards long, and costs $1,400 per roll. Howie needs to determine how many of the two types of carpet rolls to order and how they should be cut. He wants to do this in the least costly way possible.

a. Formulate an LP model for this problem.
b. Create a spreadsheet model for this problem and solve it using Solver.
c. What is the optimal solution?

25. The Pitts Barbecue Company makes three kinds of barbecue sauce: Extra Hot, Hot, and Mild. Pitts's vice president of marketing estimates that the company can sell 8,000 cases of its Extra Hot sauce plus 10 extra cases for every dollar it spends promoting this sauce; 10,000 cases of Hot sauce plus 8 extra cases for every dollar spent promoting this sauce; and 12,000 cases of its Mild sauce plus 5 extra cases for every dollar spent promoting this sauce. Although each barbecue sauce sells for $10 per case, the cost of producing the different types of sauce varies. It costs the company $6 to produce a case of Extra Hot sauce, $5.50 to produce a case of Hot sauce, and $5.25 to produce a case of Mild sauce. The president of the company wants to make sure the company manufactures at least the minimum amounts of each sauce that the marketing vice president thinks the company can

sell. A budget of $25,000 total has been approved for promoting these items of which at least $5,000 must be spent advertising each item. How many cases of each type of sauce should be made and how do you suggest that the company allocate the promotional budget if it wants to maximize profits?

a. Formulate an LP model for this problem.
b. Create a spreadsheet model for this problem and solve it using Solver.
c. What is the optimal solution?

26. Acme Manufacturing makes a variety of household appliances at a single manufacturing facility. The expected demand for one of these appliances during the next four months is shown in the following table along with the expected production costs and the expected capacity for producing these items.

		Month		
	1	2	3	4
Demand	420	580	310	540
Production Cost	$49.00	$45.00	$46.00	$47.00
Production Capacity	500	520	450	550

Acme estimates it costs $1.50 per month for each unit of this appliance carried in inventory (estimated by averaging the beginning and ending inventory levels each month). Currently, Acme has 120 units in inventory on hand for this product. To maintain a level workforce, the company wants to produce at least 400 units per month. They also want to maintain a safety stock of at least 50 units per month. Acme wants to determine how many of each appliance to manufacture during each of the next four months to meet the expected demand at the lowest possible total cost.

a. Formulate an LP model for this problem.
b. Create a spreadsheet model for this problem and solve it using Solver.
c. What is the optimal solution?
d. How much money could Acme save if they were willing to drop the restriction about producing at least 400 units per month?

27. A furniture manufacturer produces two types of tables (country and contemporary) using three types of machines. The time required to produce the tables on each machine is given in the following table.

Machine	Country	Contemporary	Total Machine Time Available per Week
Router	1.5	2.0	1,000
Sander	3.0	4.5	2,000
Polisher	2.5	1.5	1,500

Country tables sell for $350 and contemporary tables sell for $450. Management has determined that at least 20% of the tables made should be country and at least 30% should be contemporary. How many of each type of table should the company produce if it wants to maximize its revenue?

a. Formulate an LP model for this problem.
b. Create a spreadsheet model for this problem and solve it using Solver.

   c. What is the optimal solution?

   d. How will your spreadsheet model differ if there are 25 types of tables and 15 machine processes involved in manufacturing them?

28. Carter Enterprises is involved in the soybean business in South Carolina, Alabama, and Georgia. The president of the company, Earl Carter, goes to a commodity sale once a month where he buys and sells soybeans in bulk. Carter uses a local warehouse for storing his soybean inventory. This warehouse charges $10 per average ton of soybeans stored per month (based on the average of the beginning and ending inventory each month). The warehouse guarantees Carter the capacity to store up to 400 tons of soybeans at the end of each month. Carter has estimated what he believes the price per ton of soybeans will be during each of the next six months. These prices are summarized in the table below.

Month	Price per Ton
1	$135
2	$110
3	$150
4	$175
5	$130
6	$145

Assume Carter currently has 70 tons of soybeans stored in the warehouse. How many tons of soybeans should Carter buy and sell during each of the next six months to maximize his profit trading soybeans?

   a. Formulate an LP model for this problem.

   b. Create a spreadsheet model for this problem and solve it using Solver.

   c. What is the optimal solution?

29. Jack Potts recently won $1,000,000 in Las Vegas and is trying to determine how to invest his winnings. He has narrowed his decision down to five investments, which are summarized in the following table.

	Summary of Cash Inflows and Outflows (at beginning of years)			
	1998	1999	2000	2001
A	−1	0.50	0.80	
B		−1	⟷	1.25
C	−1	⟷	⟷	1.35
D			−1	1.13
E	−1	⟷	1.27	

If Jack invests $1 in investment A at the beginning of 1998, he will receive $0.50 at the beginning of 1999 and another $0.80 at the beginning of 2000. Alternatively, he can invest $1 in investment B at the beginning of 1999 and receive $1.25 at the beginning of 2001. Entries of "⟷" in the table indicate times when no cash inflows or outflows can occur. At the beginning of any year, Jack can place money in a money market account that is expected to yield 8% per year. He would like to keep at least $50,000 in the money market account at all times and doesn't want to place any more than $500,000 in any single investment. How would you advise Jack invest his winnings if he wants to maximize the amount of money he'll have at the beginning of 2001?

a. Formulate an LP model for this problem.
b. Create a spreadsheet model for this problem and solve it using Solver.
c. What is the optimal solution?

30. Fred and Sally Merrit recently inherited a substantial amount of money from a deceased relative. They would like to use part of this money to establish an account to pay for their daughter's college education. Their daughter, Lisa, will be starting college in 6 years. The Merrits estimate that her first year college expenses will amount to $12,000 and increase $2,000 per year during each of the remaining three years of her education. The following investments are available to the Merrits:

Investment	Available	Matures	Return at Maturity
A	Every year	1 year	6%
B	1, 3, 5, 7	2 years	14%
C	1, 4	3 years	18%
D	1	7 years	65%

The Merrits would like to determine an investment plan will provide the necessary funds to cover Lisa's anticipated college expenses with the smallest initial investment.

a. Formulate an LP model for this problem.
b. Create a spreadsheet model for this problem and solve it using Solver.
c. What is the optimal solution?

31. Refer to the previous question. Suppose the investments available to the Merrits have the following levels of risk associated with them.

Investment	Risk Factor
A	1
B	3
C	6
D	8

If the Merrits want the weighted average risk level of their investments to not exceed 4, how much money will they need to set aside for Lisa's education and how should they invest it?

a. Formulate an LP model for this problem.
b. Create a spreadsheet model for this problem and solve it using Solver.
c. What is the optimal solution?

CASE 3.1   THE WOLVERINE RETIREMENT FUND

Kelly Jones is a financial analyst for Wolverine Manufacturing, a company that produces engine bearings for the automotive industry. Wolverine is in the process of ham-
mering out a new labor agreement with its unionized workforce. One of the major
concerns of the labor union is the funding of Wolverine's retirement plan for their
hourly employees. The union believes the company has not been contributing
enough money to this fund to cover the benefits it will need to pay to retiring employees. Because of this, the union wants the company to contribute approximately $1.5
million dollars in additional money to this fund over the next 20 years. These extra
contributions would begin with an extra payment of $20,000 at the end of one year
with annual payments increasing by 12.35% per year for the next 19 years.

   The union has asked the company to set up a sinking fund to cover the extra
annual payments to the retirement fund. The Wolverines' Chief Financial Officer and
the union's chief negotiator have agreed that AAA rated bonds recently issued by
three different companies may be used to establish this fund. The following table
summarizes the provisions of these bonds.

Company	Maturity	Coupon Payment	Price	Par Value
AC&C	15 years	$80	$847.88	$1,000
IBN	10 years	$90	$938.55	$1,000
MicroHard	20 years	$85	$872.30	$1,000

   According to this table, Wolverine may buy bonds issued by AC&C for $847.88
per bond. Each AC&C bond will pay the bondholder $80 per year for the next 15
years, plus an extra payment of $1,000 (the par value) in the fifteenth year. Similar
interpretations apply to the information for the IBN and MicroHard bonds. A money
market fund yielding 5% may be used to hold any coupon payments that are not
needed to meet the company's required retirement fund payment in any given year.

   Wolverine's CFO has asked Kelly to determine how much money the company
would have to invest and which bonds the company should buy in order to meet the
labor union's demands.

1. If you were Kelly, what would you tell the CFO?
2. Suppose the union insists on including one of the following stipulations in the
   agreement:
   a. No more than half of the total number of bonds purchased may be purchased
      from a single company.
   b. At least 10% of the total number of bonds must be purchased from each of the
      companies.

Which stipulation should Wolverine agree to?

CASE 3.2   SAVING THE MANATEES

"So how am I going to spend this money," thought Tom Wieboldt as he sat staring at
the pictures and posters of manatees around his office. An avid environmentalist, Tom
is the president of "Friends of the Manatees," a non-profit organization trying to help
pass legislation to protect manatees.

Manatees are large, gray-brown aquatic mammals with bodies that taper to a flat, paddle-shaped tail. These gentle and slow-moving creatures grow to an average adult length of 10 feet and weigh an average of 1,000 pounds. Manatees are found in shallow, slow-moving rivers, estuaries, saltwater bays, canals, and coastal areas. In the United States, manatees are concentrated in Florida in the winter, but can be found in summer months as far west as Alabama and as far north as Virginia and the Carolinas. They have no natural enemies, but loss of habitat is the most serious threat facing manatees today. Most human-related manatee deaths occur from collisions with motor boats.

Tom's organization has been supporting a bill before the Florida legislature to restrict the use of motor boats in areas known to be inhabited by manatees. This bill is scheduled to come up for a vote in the legislature. Tom recently received a phone call from a national environmental protection organization indicating that they are going to donate $300,000 to Friends of the Manatees to help increase public awareness about the plight of the manatees and to encourage voters to urge their representatives in the state legislature to vote for this bill. Tom intends to use this money to purchase various types of advertising media to "get the message out" during the four weeks immediately preceding the vote.

Tom is considering several different advertising alternatives: newspapers, TV, radio, billboards, and magazines. A marketing consultant provided Tom with the following data on the costs and effectiveness of the various types of media being considered.

Advertising Medium	Unit Cost	Unit Impact Rating
Half-page, Daily paper	$800	55
Full-page, Daily paper	$1,400	75
Half-page, Sunday paper	$1,200	65
Full-page, Sunday paper	$1,800	80
Daytime TV spot	$2,500	85
Evening TV spot	$3,500	100
Highway Billboards	$750	35
15-second Radio spot	$150	45
30-second Radio spot	$300	55
Half-page, magazine	$500	50
Full-page, magazine	$900	60

According to the marketing consultant, the most effective type of advertising for this type of problem would be short TV ads during the evening prime-time hours. Thus, this type of advertising was given a "unit impact rating" of 100. The other types of advertising were then given assigned unit impact ratings that reflect their expected effectiveness relative to an evening TV ad. For instance, a half-page magazine ad is expected to be have half the effectiveness of an evening TV ad and is therefore given an impact rating of 50.

Tom would like to allocate the $300,000 to these different advertising alternatives in a way that will maximize the impact achieved. However, he realizes it is important to spread his message via several different advertising channels as not everyone listens to the radio and not everyone watches TV in the evenings.

The two most widely read newspapers in the state of Florida are the *Orlando Sentinel* and the *Miami Herald*. During the four weeks prior to the vote, Tom would like to have half-page ads in the daily (Monday–Saturday) versions of each of these papers at least three times per week. He also wants to have one full-page ad in the daily version of each paper the week before the vote and he is willing to run more full-page ads if this would be helpful. He also wants to run full-page ads in the Sunday editions of each paper the Sunday before the vote. Tom never wants to run a full-page and half-page ad in a paper on the same day. So the maximum number of full and half-page ads that can be run in the daily papers should be 48 (i.e., 4 weeks x 6 days per week x 2 papers = 48). Similarly, the maximum number of full and half-page ads that can be run in the Sunday papers is 8.

Tom would like to have at least one and no more than three daytime TV ads every day during the four week period. He also wants to have at least one ad on TV every night but no more than two per night.

There are ten billboards locations throughout the state that are available for use during the four week before the vote. Tom definitely wants to have at least one billboard in each of the cities of Orlando, Tampa, and Miami.

Tom believes that the ability to show pictures of the cute, pudgy, lovable manatees in the print media offers a distinct advantage over radio ads. However, the radio ads are relatively inexpensive and may reach some people that the other ads will not reach. Thus, Tom would like to have at least two 15-second and at least two 30-second ads on radio each day. However, he would like to limit the number of radio ads to five 15-second ads and five 30-second ads per day.

There are three different weekly magazines in which Tom can run ads. Tom wants to run full-page ads in each of the magazines at some point during the four week period. However, he never wants to run full and half-page ads in the same magazine in a given week. Thus, the total number of full and half-page magazine ads selected should not exceed 12 (i.e., 4 weeks × 3 magazines × 1 ad per magazine per week = 12 ads).

While Tom has some ideas about the minimum and maximum number of ads to run in the various types of media, he's not sure how much money this will take. And if he can afford to meet all the minimums, he's really confused about the best way to spend the remaining funds. So again Tom asks himself, "How am I going to spend this money?"

1. Create a spreadsheet model for this problem and solve it. What is the optimal solution?

2. Of the constraints Tom placed on this problem, which are "binding" or preventing the objective function from being improved further?

3. Suppose Tom was willing to increase the allowable number of evening TV ads. How much would this improve the solution?

4. Suppose Tom was willing to double the allowable number of radio ads aired each day. How much would this improve the solution?

CASE 3.3   REMOVING SNOW IN MONTREAL

Snow removal and disposal are important and expensive activities in Montreal and many northern cities. While snow can be cleared from streets and sidewalks by plowing and shoveling, in prolonged sub-freezing temperatures the resulting banks of accumulated snow can impede pedestrian and vehicular traffic and must be removed.

To allow timely removal and disposal of snow, the city is divided up into several sectors and snow removal operations are carried out concurrently in each sector. In Montreal, accumulated snow is loaded into trucks and hauled away to disposal sites (e.g., rivers, quarries, sewer chutes, surface holding areas). The different types of disposal sites can accommodate different amounts of snow due to either the physical size of the disposal facility or environmental restrictions on the amount of snow (often contaminated by salt and de-icing chemicals) that can be dumped into rivers. The annual capacities for five different snow disposal sites are given below (in 1,000s of cubic meters).

	Disposal Site				
	1	2	3	4	5
Capacity	350	250	500	400	200

The cost of removing and disposing of snow depends mainly on the distance it must be trucked. For planning purposes, the City of Montreal uses the straight-line distance between the center of each sector to each of the various disposal sites as an approximation of the cost involved in transporting snow between these locations. The following table summarizes these distances (in kilometers) for ten sectors in the city.

	Disposal Site				
Sector	1	2	3	4	5
1	3.4	1.4	4.9	7.4	9.3
2	2.4	2.1	8.3	9.1	8.8
3	1.4	2.9	3.7	9.4	8.6
4	2.6	3.6	4.5	8.2	8.9
5	1.5	3.1	2.1	7.9	8.8
6	4.2	4.9	6.5	7.7	6.1
7	4.8	6.2	9.9	6.2	5.7
8	5.4	6	5.2	7.6	4.9
9	3.1	4.1	6.6	7.5	7.2
10	3.2	6.5	7.1	6	8.3

Using historical snow fall data, the city is able to estimate the annual volume of snow requiring removal in each sector as four times the length of streets in the sectors in meters (i.e., it is assumed each linear meter of street generates four cubic meters of snow to remove over an entire year). The following table estimates the snow removal requirements (in 1000s of cubic meters) for each sector in the coming year.

Estimated Annual Snow Removal Requirements									
1	2	3	4	5	6	7	8	9	10
153	152	154	138	127	129	111	110	130	135

1.   Implement your model in a spreadsheet and solve it. What is the optimal solution?

Based on: James Campbell and Andre Langevin, "The Snow Disposal Assignment Problem," *Journal of the Operational Research Society*, 1995, pp. 919–929.

REFERENCES

Hilal, S., and W. Erickson. "Matching Supplies to Save Lives: Linear Programming the Production of Heart Valves." *Interfaces*, vol. 11, no. 6, 1981.

Lanzenauer, C., et al. "RRSP Flood: LP to the Rescue." *Interfaces*, vol. 17, no. 4, 1987.

McKay, A. "Linear Programming Applications on Microcomputers." *Journal of the Operational Research Society*, vol. 36, July 1985.

Roush, W., et al. "Using Chance-Constrained Programming for Animal Feed Formulation at Agway." *Interfaces*, vol. 24, no. 2, 1994.

Shogan, A. *Management Science*. Englewood Cliffs, NJ: Prentice Hall, 1988.

Williams, H. *Model Building in Mathematical Programming*. New York: Wiley, 1985.

CHAPTER 4

Sensitivity Analysis and the Simplex Method

In chapters 2 and 3 we studied how to formulate and solve LP models for a variety of decision problems. However, formulating and solving an LP model does not necessarily mean that the original decision problem has been solved. After solving a model, a number of questions often arise about the optimal solution to the LP model. In particular, we might be interested in how sensitive the optimal solution is to changes in various coefficients of the LP model.

Businesses rarely know with certainty what costs will be incurred or the exact amount of resources that will be consumed or available in a given situation or time period. Thus, optimal solutions obtained using models that assume all relevant factors are known with certainty might be viewed with skepticism by management. Sensitivity analysis can help overcome this skepticism and provide a better picture of how the solution to a problem will change if different factors in the model change. Sensitivity analysis also can help answer a number of practical managerial questions that might arise about the solution to an LP problem.

4.1 THE PURPOSE OF SENSITIVITY ANALYSIS

As noted in chapter 2, any problem that can be stated in the following form is an LP problem:

$$\text{MAX (or MIN):} \quad c_1X_1 + c_2X_2 + \ldots + c_nX_n$$

$$\text{Subject to:} \quad a_{11}X_1 + a_{12}X_2 + \ldots + a_{1n}X_n \leq b_1$$

$$\vdots$$

$$a_{k1}X_1 + a_{k2}X_2 + \ldots + a_{kn}X_n \geq b_k$$

$$\vdots$$

$$a_{m1}X_1 + a_{m2}X_2 + \ldots + a_{mn}X_n = b_m$$

All the coefficients in this model (the c_j, a_{ij}, and b_i) represent numeric constants. So, when we formulate and solve an LP problem, we implicitly assume that we can

128

specify the exact values for these coefficients. However, in the real world these coefficients might change from day to day or minute to minute. For example, the price a company charges for its products can change on a daily, weekly, or monthly basis. Similarly, if a skilled machinist calls in sick, a manufacturer might have less capacity to produce items on a given machine than was originally planned.

Realizing that such uncertainties exist, a manager should consider how sensitive an LP model's solution is to changes or estimation errors that might occur in: (1) the objective function coefficients (the c_j), (2) the constraint coefficients (the a_{ij}), and (3) the RHS values for the constraints (the b_i). A manager also might ask a number of "What if?" questions about these values. For example, What if the cost of a product increases by 7%? What if a reduction in setup time allows for additional capacity on a given machine? What if a worker's suggestion results in a product requiring only two hours of labor rather than three? Sensitivity analysis addresses these issues by assessing the sensitivity of the solution to uncertainty or errors in the model coefficients, as well as the solution's sensitivity to changes in model coefficients that might occur because of human intervention.

4.2 APPROACHES TO SENSITIVITY ANALYSIS

You can perform sensitivity analysis on an LP model in a number of ways. If you want to determine the effect of some change in the model, the most direct approach is to simply change the model and re-solve it. This approach is suitable if the model does not take an excessive amount of time to change or solve. And if you are interested in studying the consequences of *simultaneously* changing several coefficients in the model, this might be the only practical approach to sensitivity analysis.

Solver also provides some sensitivity information after solving an LP problem. As mentioned in chapter 3, one of the benefits of using the simplex method to solve LP problems is its speed—it is considerably faster than the other optimization techniques offered by Solver. However, another advantage of using the simplex method is that it provides more sensitivity analysis information than the other techniques. In particular, the simplex method provides us with information about:

- the range of values the objective function coefficients can assume without changing the optimal solution
- the impact on the optimal objective function value of increases or decreases in the availability of various constrained resources
- the impact on the optimal objective function value of forcing changes in the values of certain decision variables away from their optimal values
- the impact that changes in constraint coefficients will have on the optimal solution to the problem

4.3 AN EXAMPLE PROBLEM

We will again use the Blue Ridge Hot Tubs problem to illustrate the types of sensitivity analysis information available using Solver. The LP formulation of the problem is repeated below, where X_1 represents the number of Aqua-Spas and X_2 represents the number of Hydro-Luxes to be produced:

$$\text{MAX:} \qquad 350X_1 + 300X_2 \qquad \} \text{ profit}$$
$$\text{Subject to:} \quad 1X_1 + 1X_2 \le 200 \qquad \} \text{ pump constraint}$$
$$9X_1 + 6X_2 \le 1{,}566 \qquad \} \text{ labor constraint}$$
$$12X_1 + 16X_2 \le 2{,}880 \qquad \} \text{ tubing constraint}$$
$$X_1, X_2 \ge 0 \qquad \qquad \} \text{ nonnegativity conditions}$$

This model is implemented in the spreadsheet shown in Figure 4.1 (and in the file Fig 4-1.xls on your data disk). (See chapter 3 for details on the procedure used to create and solve this spreadsheet model.)

Figure 4.1
Spreadsheet model for the Blue Ridge Hot Tubs product mix problem.

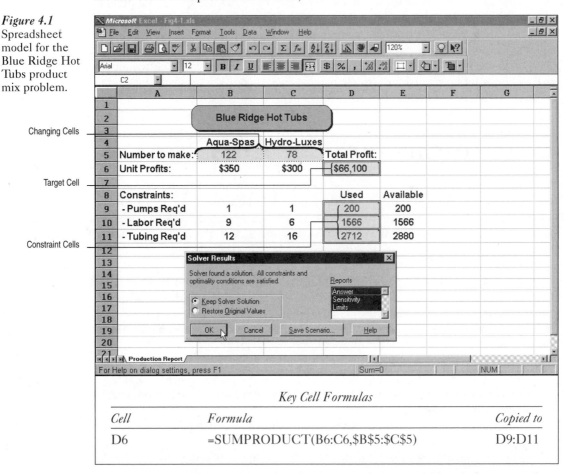

Key Cell Formulas		
Cell	*Formula*	*Copied to*
D6	=SUMPRODUCT(B6:C6,$B$5:$C$5)	D9:D11

After solving the LP model, Solver displays the Solver Results dialog box, shown in Figure 4.1. This dialog box provides three report options: Answer, Sensitivity, and Limits. You can select any of these reports after a model has been solved. To select all three reports, highlight the reports, then click OK. To access each report, click the appropriate tab at the bottom of the screen.

4.4   THE ANSWER REPORT

Figure 4.2 shows the Answer Report for the Blue Ridge Hot Tubs problem. This report summarizes the solution to the problem and is fairly self-explanatory. The first

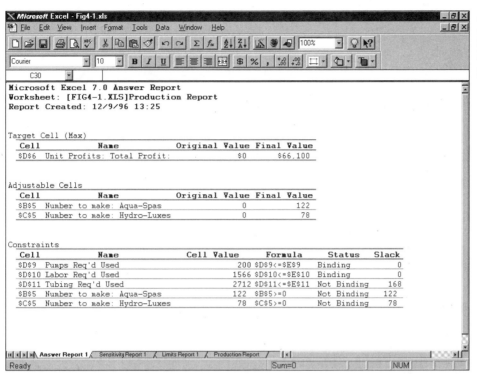

Figure 4.2
Answer Report
for the Blue
Ridge Hot Tubs
problem.

section of the report summarizes the original and final (optimal) value of the target cell. The next section summarizes the original and final (optimal) values of the adjustable (or changing) cells representing the decision variables.

The final section of this report provides information about the constraints. In particular, the Cell Value column shows the final (optimal) value assumed by each constraint cell. Note that these values correspond to the final value assumed by the LHS formula of each constraint. The Formula column indicates the upper or lower bounds that apply to each constraint cell. The Status column indicates which constraints are binding and which are nonbinding. A constraint is **binding** if it is satisfied as a strict equality in the optimal solution; otherwise, it is **nonbinding.** Notice that the constraints for the number of pumps and amount of labor used are both binding, meaning that *all* the available pumps and labor hours will be used if this solution is implemented. Therefore, these constraints are preventing Blue Ridge Hot Tubs from achieving a higher level of profit.

Finally, the values in the Slack column indicate the difference between the LHS and RHS of each constraint. By definition, binding constraints have zero slack and nonbinding constraints have some positive level of slack. The values in the Slack column indicate that if this solution is implemented, all the available pumps and labor hours will be used, but 168 feet of tubing will be left over. The slack values for the nonnegativity conditions indicate the amounts by which the decision variables exceed their respective lower bounds of zero.

The Answer Report does not provide any information that could not be derived from the solution shown in the spreadsheet model. However, the format of this report gives a convenient summary of the solution that can be incorporated easily into a word processing document as part of a written report to management.

Report Headings

When creating the reports described in this chapter, Solver will try to use various text entries from the original spreadsheet to generate meaningful headings and labels in the reports. Given the various ways in which a model can be implemented, Solver might not always produce meaningful headings. However, you can change any text entry to make the report more meaningful or descriptive.

4.5   THE SENSITIVITY REPORT

Figure 4.3 shows the Sensitivity Report for the Blue Ridge Hot Tubs problem. This report summarizes information about the changing cells and constraints for our model. This information is useful in evaluating how sensitive the optimal solution is to changes in various coefficients in the model.

Figure 4.3
Sensitivity Report for the Blue Ridge Hot Tubs problem.

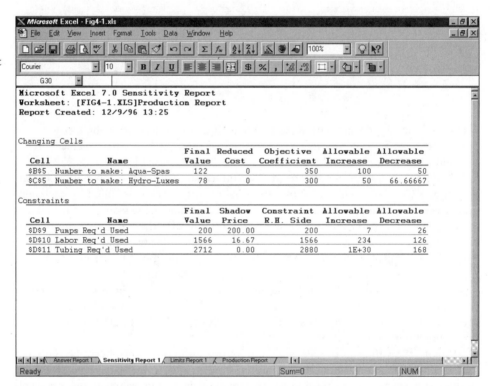

Microsoft Excel 7.0 Sensitivity Report
Worksheet: [FIG4-1.XLS]Production Report
Report Created: 12/9/96 13:25

Changing Cells

Cell	Name	Final Value	Reduced Cost	Objective Coefficient	Allowable Increase	Allowable Decrease
$B$5	Number to make: Aqua-Spas	122	0	350	100	50
$C$5	Number to make: Hydro-Luxes	78	0	300	50	66.66667

Constraints

Cell	Name	Final Value	Shadow Price	Constraint R.H. Side	Allowable Increase	Allowable Decrease
$D$9	Pumps Req'd Used	200	200.00	200	7	26
$D$10	Labor Req'd Used	1566	16.67	1566	234	126
$D$11	Tubing Req'd Used	2712	0.00	2880	1E+30	168

4.5.1   Changes in the Objective Function Coefficients

Chapter 2 introduced the level curve approach to solving a graphical LP problem and showed how to use this approach to solve the Blue Ridge Hot Tubs problem. This graphical solution is repeated in Figure 4.4.

The slope of the original level curve in Figure 4.4 is determined by the coefficients in the objective function of the model (the values 350 and 300). In Figure 4.4, we can see that if the slope of the level curve were different, the corner point

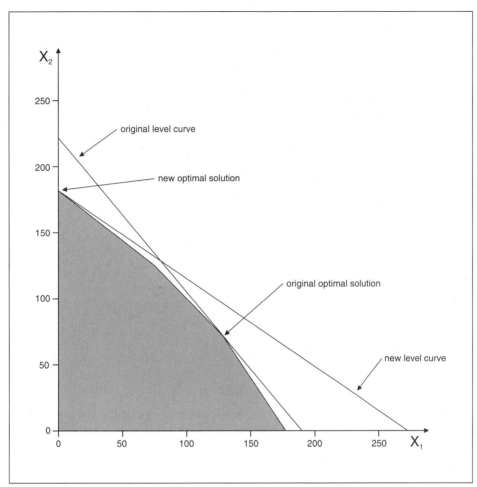

represented by $X_1 = 0$, $X_2 = 180$ would be the optimal solution. Of course, the only way to change the level curve for the objective function is to change the coefficients in the objective function. So if the objective function coefficients are at all uncertain, we might be interested in determining how much these values could change before the optimal solution would change.

For example, if the owner of Blue Ridge Hot Tubs does not have complete control over the costs of producing hot tubs (which is likely because he purchases the fiberglass hot tub shells from another company), the profit figures in the objective function of our LP model might not be the exact profits earned on hot tubs produced in the future. So before the manager decides to produce 122 Aqua-Spas and 78 Hydro-Luxes, he might want to determine how sensitive this solution is to the profit figures in the objective. That is, the manager might want to determine how much the profit figures could change before the optimal solution of $X_1 = 122$, $X_2 = 78$ would change. This information is provided in the Sensitivity Report shown in Figure 4.3.

The original objective function coefficients associated with the changing cells are listed in the Objective Coefficient column in Figure 4.3. The next two columns show the allowable increases and decreases in these values. For example, the objective function value associated with Aqua-Spas (or variable X_1) can increase by as much as $100 or decrease by as much as $50 without changing the optimal solution, assuming all other coefficients remain constant. (You can verify this by changing the profit coefficient for Aqua-Spas to any value in the range from $300 to $450 and re-solving the model.) Similarly, the objective function value associated with Hydro-Luxes (or variable X_2) can increase by $50 or decrease by approximately $66.67 without changing the optimal values of the decision variables, assuming all other coefficients remain constant. (Again, you can verify this by re-solving the model with different profit values for Hydro-Luxes.)

4.5.2   A Note About Constancy

The phrase "assuming all other coefficients remain constant" in the previous paragraph underscores the fact that the allowable increases and decreases shown in the Sensitivity Report apply only if *all* the other coefficients in the LP model do not change. The objective coefficient for Aqua-Spas can assume any value from $300 to $450 without changing the optimal solution—*but this is guaranteed to be true only if all the other coefficients in the model remain constant (including the objective function coefficient for X_2).* Similarly, the objective function coefficient for X_2 can assume any value between $233.33 and $350 without changing the optimal solution—*but this is guaranteed to be true only if all the other coefficients in the model remain constant (including the objective function coefficient for X_1).* Later in this chapter, you will see how to determine whether the current solution remains optimal if changes are made in two or more objective coefficients at the same time.

4.5.3   Alternate Optimal Solutions

Sometimes the allowable increase or allowable decrease for the objective function coefficient for one or more variables will equal zero. In the absence of degeneracy (to be described later), this indicates that alternate optimal solutions exist. You can usually get Solver to produce an alternate optimal solution (when they exist) by: (1) adding a constraint to your model that holds the objective function at the current optimal value, and then (2) attempting to maximize or minimize the value of one of the decision variables that had an objective function coefficient with an allowable increase or decrease of zero. This approach sometimes involves some "trial and error" in step 2, but should cause Solver to produce an alternate optimal solution to your problem.

4.5.4   Changes in the RHS Values

As noted earlier, constraints that have zero slack in the optimal solution to an LP problem are called **binding constraints.** Binding constraints prevent us from further improving (that is, maximizing or minimizing) the objective function. For example, the Answer Report in Figure 4.2 indicates that the constraints for the number of pumps and hours of labor available are binding, whereas the constraint on the amount of tubing available is nonbinding. This is also evident in Figure 4.3 by comparing the Final Value column with the Constraint R.H. Side column. The values in the Final Value column represent the LHS values of each constraint at the optimal solution. A constraint is binding if its Final Value is equal to its Constraint R.H. Side value.

After solving an LP problem, you might want to determine how much better or worse the solution would be if we had more or less of a given resource. For example, Howie Jones might wonder how much more profit could be earned if additional pumps or labor hours were available. The Shadow Price column in Figure 4.3 provides the answers to such questions.

The **shadow price** for a constraint indicates the amount by which the objective function value changes given a unit *increase* in the RHS value of the constraint, assuming all other coefficients remain constant. If a shadow price is positive, a unit increase in the RHS value of the associated constraint results in an increase in the optimal objective function value. If a shadow price is negative, a unit increase in the RHS of the associated constraint results in a decrease in the optimal objective function value. To analyze the effects of decreases in the RHS values, you reverse the sign on the shadow price. That is, the negated shadow price for a constraint indicates the amount by which the optimal objective function value changes given a unit **decrease** in the RHS value of the constraint, assuming all other coefficients remain constant. The shadow price values apply provided that the increase or decrease in the RHS value falls within the allowable increase or allowable decrease limits in the Sensitivity Report for each constraint.

For example, Figure 4.3 indicates that the shadow price for the labor constraint is 16.67. Therefore, if the number of available labor hours increased by any amount in the range from 0 to 234 hours, the optimal objective function value changes (increases) by $16.67 for each additional labor hour. If the number of available labor hours decreased by any amount in the range from 0 to 126 hours, the optimal objective function value changes (decreases) by –$16.67 for each lost labor hour. A similar interpretation holds for the shadow price for the constraint on the number of pumps. (It is coincidental that the shadow price for the pump constraint [200] is the same as that constraint's RHS and Final Values.)

4.5.5 Shadow Prices for Nonbinding Constraints

Now let's consider the shadow price for the nonbinding tubing constraint. The tubing constraint has a shadow price of zero with an allowable increase of infinity and an allowable decrease of 168. Therefore, if the RHS value for the tubing constraint increases by *any* amount, the objective function value does not change (or changes by zero). This result is not surprising. Because the optimal solution to this problem leaves 168 feet of tubing unused, *additional* tubing will not produce a better solution. Furthermore, because the optimal solution includes 168 feet of unused tubing, we can reduce the RHS value of this constraint by 168 without affecting the optimal solution.

As this example illustrates, the shadow price of a nonbinding constraint is always zero. There is always some amount by which the RHS value of a nonbinding constraint can be changed without affecting the optimal solution.

4.5.6 A Note About Shadow Prices and Their Ranges

One important point needs to be made concerning shadow prices. To illustrate this point, let's suppose that the RHS of the labor constraint for our example problem increases by 162 hours (from 1,566 to 1,728) due to the addition of new workers. Because this increase is within the allowable increase listed for the shadow price for the labor constraint, you might expect that the optimal objective function value would increase by $16.67 × 162 = $2,700. That is, the new optimal objective function value would be approximately $68,800 ($66,100 + $16.67 × 162 = $68,800). Figure 4.5 shows the re-solved model after increasing the RHS value for the labor constraint by 162 labor hours to 1,728.

Figure 4.5
Solution to the
revised Blue
Ridge Hot Tubs
problem with
162 additional
labor hours.

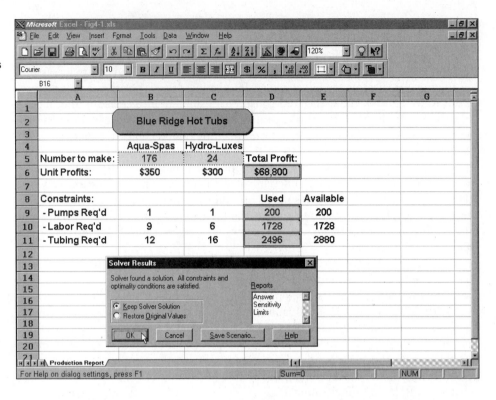

In Figure 4.5, the new optimal objective function value is $68,800, as expected. But this solution involves producing 176 Aqua-Spas and 24 Hydro-Luxes. That is, the optimal solution to the revised problem is *different* from the solution to the original problem shown in Figure 4.1. This is not surprising because changing the RHS of a constraint also changes the feasible region for the problem. The effect of increasing the RHS of the labor constraint is summarized graphically in Figure 4.6.

So, although shadow prices indicate how the objective function value changes if a given RHS value changes, they *do not* tell you which values the decision variables need to assume in order to achieve this new objective function value. Determining the new optimal values for the decision variables requires that you make the appropriate changes in the RHS value and re-solve the model.

4.5.7   Shadow Prices and the Value of Additional Resources

In the previous example, an additional 162 hours of labor allowed us to increase profits by $2,700. A question might then arise as to how much we should be willing to pay to acquire these additional 162 hours of labor. The answer to this question is, "It depends. . . ."

If labor is a *variable* cost that was subtracted (along with other variable costs) from the selling price of the hot tubs to determine the marginal profits associated with each type of tub, we should be willing to pay up to $2,700 *beyond* what we would ordinarily pay to acquire 162 hours of labor. In this case, notice that both the original and revised profit figures of $66,100 and $68,800, respectively, represent the profit earned *after* the normal labor charge has been paid. Therefore, we could pay a premium of up to $2,700 to acquire the additional 162 hours of labor (or an extra $16.67 per additional

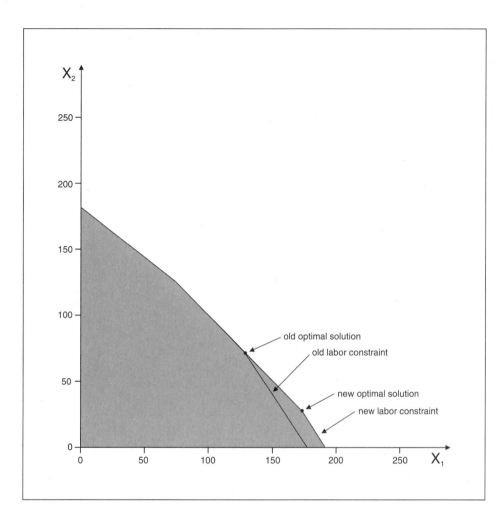

Figure 4.6
Illustration of how changes in the RHS values of a constraint can change the feasible region and optimal solution to a problem.

Another Interpretation of Shadow Prices

Unfortunately, there is no one universally accepted way of reporting shadow prices for constraints. In some software packages, the signs of the shadow prices do not conform to the convention used by Solver. Regardless of which software package you use, there is another way to look at shadow prices that should always lead to a proper interpretation. The absolute value of the shadow price always indicates the amount by which the objective function will be *improved* if the corresponding constraint is *loosened*. A less than or equal to constraint is loosened by *increasing* its RHS value, whereas a greater than or equal to constraint is loosened by *decreasing* its RHS value. (The absolute value of the shadow price can also be interpreted as the amount by which the objective will be made *worse* if the corresponding constraint is *tightened*.)

labor hour) and still earn at least as much profit as we would have without the additional 162 hours of labor. Thus, if the normal labor rate is $12 per hour, we could pay up to $28.67 per hour to acquire each of the additional 162 hours of labor.

On the other hand, if labor is a *sunk* cost, which must be paid regardless of how many hot tubs are produced, it would not (or should not) have been subtracted from the selling price of the hot tubs in determining the marginal profit coefficients for each tub produced. In this case, we should be willing to pay a maximum of $16.67 per hour to acquire each of the additional 162 hours of labor.

4.5.8   Other Uses of Shadow Prices

Because shadow prices represent the marginal values of the resources in an LP problem, they can help us answer a number of other managerial questions that might arise. For example, suppose Blue Ridge Hot Tubs is considering introducing a new model of hot tub called the Typhoon-Lagoon. Suppose that each unit of this new model requires 1 pump, 8 hours of labor, and 13 feet of tubing, and can be sold to generate a marginal profit of $320. Would production of this new model be profitable?

Because Blue Ridge Hot Tubs has limited resources, the production of any Typhoon-Lagoons would consume some of the resources currently devoted to the production of Aqua-Spas and Hydro-Luxes. So, producing Typhoon-Lagoons will reduce the number of pumps, labor hours, and tubing available for producing the other types of hot tubs. The shadow prices in Figure 4.3 indicate that each pump taken away from production of the current products will reduce profits by $200. Similarly, each labor hour taken away from the production of the current products will reduce profits by $16.67. The shadow price for the tubing constraint indicates that the supply of tubing can be reduced without adversely affecting profits.

Because each Typhoon-Lagoon requires 1 pump, 8 hours of labor, and 13 feet of tubing, the diversion of resources required to produce one unit of this new model would cause a reduction in profit of $200 \times 1 + $16.67 \times 8 + $0 \times 13 \approx 333.33. This reduction would be partially offset by the $320 increase in profit generated by each Typhoon-Lagoon. The net effect of producing each Typhoon-Lagoon would be a $13.33 reduction in profit ($320 – $333.33 = –$13.33). Therefore, the production of Typhoon-Lagoons would not be profitable (although the company might choose to produce a small number of Typhoon-Lagoons to enhance its product line for marketing purposes).

Another way to determine whether or not Typhoon-Lagoons should be produced is to add this alternative to our model and solve the resulting LP problem. The LP model for this revised problem is represented as follows, where X_1, X_2, and X_3 represent the number of Aqua-Spas, Hydro-Luxes, and Typhoon-Lagoons to be produced, respectively:

MAX: $350X_1 + 300X_2 + 320X_3$ } profit
Subject to: $1X_1 + 1X_2 + 1X_3 \leq 200$ } pump constraint
        $9X_1 + 6X_2 + 8X_3 \leq 1,566$ } labor constraint
        $12X_1 + 16X_2 + 13X_3 \leq 2,800$ } tubing constraint
        $X_1, X_2, X_3 \geq 0$ } nonnegativity conditions

This model is implemented and solved in the spreadsheet, as shown in Figure 4.7 (and in the file Fig 4-7.xls on your data disk). Notice that the optimal solution to this problem involves producing 122 Aqua-Spas ($X_1 = 122$), 78 Hydro-Luxes ($X_2 = 78$), and no Typhoon-Lagoons ($X_3 = 0$). So, as expected, the optimal solution does not involve producing Typhoon-Lagoons. Figure 4.8 shows the Sensitivity Report for our revised model.

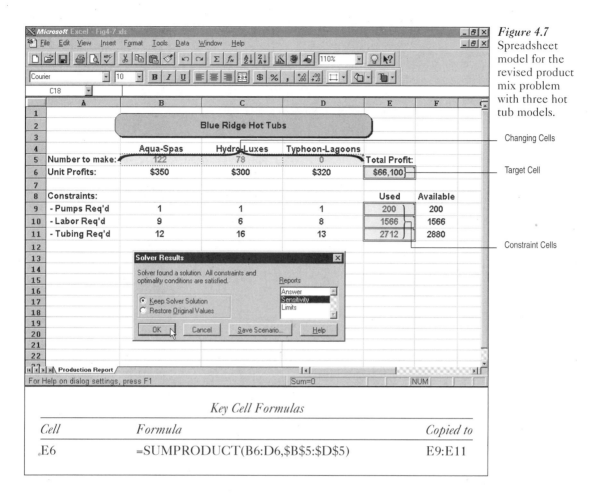

Figure 4.7
Spreadsheet model for the revised product mix problem with three hot tub models.

Key Cell Formulas

Cell	Formula	Copied to
E6	=SUMPRODUCT(B6:D6,$B$5:$D$5)	E9:E11

4.5.9 The Meaning of the Reduced Costs

The Sensitivity Report in Figure 4.8 for our revised model is identical to the Sensitivity Report for our original model *except* that it includes an additional row in the Changing Cells section. This row reports sensitivity information on the number of Typhoon-Lagoons to produce. Notice that the Reduced Cost column indicates that the reduced cost value for Typhoon-Lagoons is –13.33. This is the same number that we calculated in the previous section when determining whether or not it would be profitable to produce Typhoon-Lagoons.

The reduced cost for each variable is equal to the per-unit amount the product contributes to profits minus the per-unit value of the resources it consumes (where the consumed resources are priced at their shadow prices). For example, the reduced cost of each variable in this problem is calculated as:

Reduced cost of Aqua-Spas $\qquad = 350 - 200 \times 1 - 16.67 \times 9 - 0 \times 12 = 0$

Reduced cost of Hydro-Luxes $\qquad = 300 - 200 \times 1 - 16.67 \times 6 - 0 \times 16 = 0$

Reduced cost of Typhoon-Lagoons $\qquad = 320 - 200 \times 1 - 16.67 \times 8 - 0 \times 13 = -13.33$

The allowable increase in the objective function coefficient for Typhoon-Lagoons equals 13.33. This means that the current solution will remain optimal provided that the marginal profit on Typhoon-Lagoons is less than or equal to $320 + $13.33 \approx$ $333.33

Figure 4.8
Sensitivity
Report for the
revised product
mix problem
with three hot
tub models.

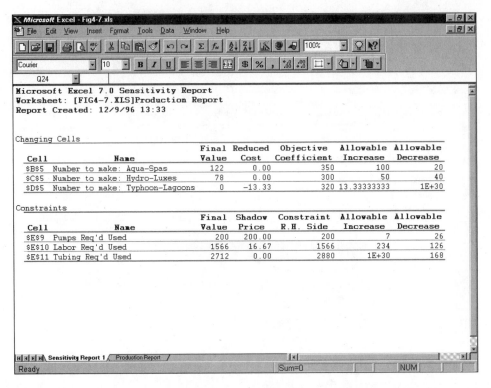

(because this would keep its reduced cost less than or equal to zero). However, if the marginal profit for Typhoon-Lagoons is more than $333.33, producing this product would be profitable and the optimal solution to the problem would change.

It is interesting to note that the shadow prices (marginal values) of the resources equate exactly with the marginal profits of the products that, at optimality, assume values between their simple lower and upper bounds. This will always be the case. In the optimal solution to an LP problem, the variables that assume values between their simple lower and upper bounds always have reduced cost values of zero. (In our example problem, all the variables have implicit simple upper bounds of positive infinity.) The variables with optimal values equal to their simple lower bounds have reduced cost values that are less than or equal to zero for maximization problems, or greater than or equal to zero for minimization problems. Variables with optimal values equal to their simple upper bounds have reduced cost values that are greater than or equal to zero for maximization problems, or less than or equal to zero for minimization problems. Figure 4.9 summarizes these relationships.

Figure 4.9
Summary of
optimal reduced
cost values.

Type of Problem	Optimal Value of Decision Variable	Optimal Value of Reduced Cost
Maximization	at simple lower bound	≤ 0
	between lower and upper bounds	$= 0$
	at simple upper bound	≥ 0
Minimization	at simple lower bound	≥ 0
	between lower and upper bounds	$= 0$
	at simple upper bound	≤ 0

Generally, at optimality, a variable assumes its largest possible value (or is set equal to its simple upper bound) if this variable helps improve the objective function value. In a maximization problem, the variable's reduced cost must be nonnegative to indicate that if the variable's value increased, the objective value would increase (improve). In a minimization problem, the variable's reduced cost must be nonpositive to indicate that if the variable's value increased, the objective value would decrease (improve).

Similar arguments can be made for the optimal reduced costs of variables at their lower bounds. At optimality, a variable assumes its smallest (lower bound) value if it cannot be used to improve the objective value. In a maximization problem, the variable's reduced cost must be nonpositive to indicate that if the variable's value increased, the objective value would decrease (worsen). In a minimization problem, the variable's reduced cost must be nonnegative to indicate that if the variable's value increased, the objective value would increase (worsen).

Key Points

Our discussion of Solver's sensitivity report highlights some key points concerning shadow prices and their relationship to reduced costs. These key points are summarized as:

- The shadow prices of resources equate the marginal value of the resources consumed with the marginal benefit of the goods being produced.
- Resources in excess supply have a shadow price (or marginal value) of zero.
- The reduced cost of a product is the difference between its marginal profit and the marginal value of the resources it consumes.
- Products whose marginal profits are less than the marginal value of the goods required for their production will not be produced in an optimal solution.

4.5.10 Analyzing Changes in Constraint Coefficients

Given what we know about reduced costs and shadow prices, we can now analyze how changes in some constraint coefficients affect the optimal solution to an LP problem. For example, it is unprofitable for Blue Ridge Hot Tubs to manufacture Typhoon-Lagoons assuming that each unit requires eight hours of labor. However, what would happen if the product could be produced in only seven hours? The reduced cost value for Typhoon-Lagoons is calculated as:

$$320 - 200 \times 1 - 16.67 \times 7 - 0 \times 13 = 3.31$$

Because this new reduced cost value is positive, producing Typhoon-Lagoons would be profitable in this scenario and the solution shown in Figure 4.7 would no longer be optimal. We could also reach this conclusion by changing the labor requirement for Typhoon-Lagoons in our spreadsheet model and re-solving the problem. In fact, we have to do this to determine the new optimal solution if each Typhoon-Lagoon requires only seven hours of labor.

As another example, suppose that we wanted to know the maximum amount of labor that is required to assemble a Typhoon-Lagoon while keeping its production economically justifiable. The production of Typhoon-Lagoons would be profitable provided that the reduced cost for the product is greater than or equal to zero. If L_3 represents the amount of labor required to produce a Typhoon-Lagoon, we want to find the maximum value of L_3 that keeps the reduced cost for Typhoon-Lagoons greater than or equal to zero. That is, we want to find the maximum value of L_3 that satisfies the inequality:

$$320 - 200 \times 1 - 16.67 \times L_3 - 0 \times 13 \geq 0$$

If we solve this inequality for L_3, we obtain:

$$L_3 \leq \frac{120}{16.67} = 7.20$$

Thus, the production of Typhoon-Lagoons would be economically justified provided that the labor required to produce them does not exceed 7.20 hours per unit. Similar types of questions can be answered using knowledge of the basic relationships between reduced costs, shadow prices, and optimality conditions.

4.5.11   Simultaneous Changes in Objective Function Coefficients

Earlier, we noted that the values in the Allowable Increase and Allowable Decrease columns in the Sensitivity Report for the objective function coefficients indicate the maximum amounts by which each objective coefficient can change without altering the optimal solution—*assuming all other coefficients in the model remain constant*. A technique known as **The 100% Rule** determines whether the current solution remains optimal when more than one objective function coefficient changes. The following two situations could arise when applying this rule:

Case 1. All variables whose objective function coefficients change have nonzero reduced costs.
Case 2. At least one variable whose objective function coefficient changes has a reduced cost of zero.

In case 1, the current solution remains optimal provided that the objective function coefficient of each changed variable remains within the limits indicated in the Allowable Increase and Allowable Decrease columns of the Sensitivity Report.
Case 2 is a bit more tricky. In case 2 we must perform the following analysis where:

c_j = the original objective function coefficient for variable X_j
Δc_j = the planned change in c_j
I_j = the allowable increase in c_j given in the Sensitivity Report
D_j = the allowable decrease in c_j given in the Sensitivity Report

$$r_j = \begin{cases} \dfrac{\Delta c_j}{I_j}, & \text{if } \Delta c_j \geq 0 \\[2ex] \dfrac{-\Delta c_j}{D_j}, & \text{if } \Delta c_j < 0 \end{cases}$$

Notice that r_j measures the ratio of the planned change in c_j to the maximum allowable change for which the current solution remains optimal. If only one objective function coefficient changed, the current solution remains optimal provided that

$r_j \leq 1$ (or, if r_j is expressed as a percentage, it must be less than or equal to 100%). Similarly, if more than one objective function coefficient changes, the current solution will remain optimal provided that $\Sigma r_j \leq 1$. (Note that if $\Sigma r_j > 1$, the current solution, might remain optimal, but this is not guaranteed.)

4.5.12 A Warning About Degeneracy

The solution to an LP problem sometimes exhibits a mathematical anomaly known as **degeneracy**. The solution to an LP problem is degenerate if the shadow prices of any of the constraints have an allowable increase or allowable decrease of zero. The presence of degeneracy impacts our interpretation of the values on the Sensitivity Report in a number of important ways:

1. When the solution is degenerate, the methods mentioned earlier for detecting alternate optimal solutions cannot be relied upon.
2. When a solution is degenerate, the reduced costs for the changing cells may not be unique. Additionally, in this case, the objective function coefficients for changing cells must change by at least as much as (and possibly more than) their respective reduced costs before the optimal solution would change.
3. When the solution is degenerate, the allowable increases and decreases for the objective function coefficients still hold and, in fact, the coefficients may have to be changed substantially beyond the allowable increase and decrease limits before the optimal solution changes.
4. When the solution is degenerate, the given shadow prices and their ranges may still be interpreted in the usual way but they may not be unique. That is, a different set of shadow prices and ranges may also apply to the problem (even if the optimal solution is unique).

So before interpreting the results on a Sensitivity Report, you should always first check to see if the solution is degenerate because this has important ramifications on how the numbers on the report should be interpreted. A complete description of the degeneracy anomaly goes beyond the intended scope of this book. However, degeneracy is sometimes caused by having redundant constraints in an LP model. *Extreme caution* (and perhaps consultation with an expert in mathematical programming) is in order if important business decisions are being made based on the Sensitivity Report for a degenerate LP problem.

4.6   THE LIMITS REPORT

The Limits Report for the original Blue Ridge Hot Tubs problem is shown in Figure 4.10. This report lists the optimal value of the target cell. It then summarizes the optimal values for each changing cell and indicates what values the target cell assumes if each changing cell is set to its upper or lower limits. The values in the Lower Limit column indicate the smallest value each changing cell can assume while the values of all other changing cells remain constant and all the constraints are satisfied. The values in the Upper Limit column indicate the largest value each changing cell can assume while the values of all other changing cells remain constant and all the constraints are satisfied.

Figure 4.10
Limits Report
for the original
Blue Ridge Hot
Tubs problem.

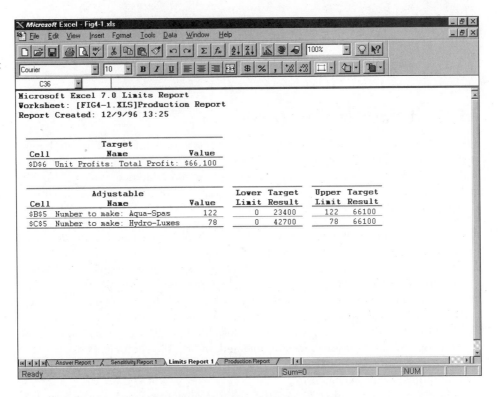

4.7   THE SIMPLEX METHOD (optional)

We have repeatedly mentioned that the simplex method is the preferred method for
solving LP problems. This section provides an overview of the simplex method and
shows how it relates to some of the items that appear on the Answer Report and the
Sensitivity Report.

4.7.1   Creating Equality Constraints Using Slack Variables

Because our original formulation of the LP model for the Blue Ridge Hot Tubs problem has only two decision variables (X_1 and X_2), you might be surprised to learn that
Solver actually used *five* variables to solve this problem. As you saw in chapter 2 when
we plotted the boundary lines for the constraints in an LP problem, it is easier to work
with equal to conditions rather than less than or equal to, or greater than or equal to
conditions. Similarly, the simplex method requires that *all* constraints in an LP model
be expressed as equalities.

To solve an LP problem using the simplex method, Solver temporarily turns all
inequality constraints into equality constraints by adding one new variable to each less
than or equal to constraint and subtracting one new variable from each greater than or
equal to constraint. The new variables used to create equality constraints are called
slack variables.

For example, consider the less than or equal to constraint:

$$a_{k1}X_1 + a_{k2}X_2 + \ldots + a_{kn}X_n \leq b_k$$

Solver can turn this constraint into an equal to constraint by adding the nonnegative slack variable S_k to the LHS of the constraint:

$$a_{k1}X_1 + a_{k2}X_2 + \ldots + a_{kn}X_n + S_k = b_k$$

The variable S_k represents the amount by which $a_{k1}X_1 + a_{k2}X_2 + \ldots + a_{kn}X_n$ is less than b_k. Now consider the greater than or equal to constraint:

$$a_{k1}X_6 + a_{k2}X_2 + \ldots + a_{kn}X_n \geq b_k$$

Solver can turn this constraint into an equal to constraint by subtracting the nonnegative slack variable S_k from the LHS of the constraint:

$$a_{k1}X_1 + a_{k2}X_2 + \ldots + a_{kn}X_n - S_k = b_k$$

In this case, the variable S_k represents the amount by which $a_{k1}X_1 + a_{k2}X_2 + \ldots + a_{kn}X_n$ exceeds b_k.

To solve the original Blue Ridge Hot Tubs problem using the simplex method, Solver actually solved the following modified problem involving *five* variables:

MAX: $350X_1 + 300X_2$ } profit
Subject to: $1X_1 + 1X_2 + S_1 = 200$ } pump constraint
          $9X_1 + 6X_2 + S_2 = 1{,}566$ } labor constraint
          $12X_1 + 16X_2 + S_3 = 2{,}880$ } tubing constraint
          $X_1, X_2, S_1, S_2, S_3 \geq 0$ } nonnegativity conditions

We will refer to X_1 and X_2 as the **structural variables** in the model to distinguish them from the slack variables.

Recall that we did not set up slack variables in the spreadsheet or include them in the formulas in the constraint cells. Solver automatically sets up the slack variables it needs to solve a particular problem. The only time Solver even mentions these variables is when it creates an Answer Report like the one shown in Figure 4.2. The values in the Slack column in the Answer Report correspond to the optimal values of the slack variables.

4.7.2   Basic Feasible Solutions

After all the inequality constraints in an LP problem have been converted into equalities (by adding or subtracting appropriate slack variables), the constraints in the LP model represent a system (or collection) of linear equations. If there are a total of n variables in a system of m equations, one strategy for finding a solution to the system of equations is to select any m variables and try to find values for them that solve the system, assuming all other variables are set equal to their lower bounds (which are usually zero). This strategy requires more variables than constraints in the system of equations—or that $n \geq m$.

The m variables selected to solve the system of equations in an LP model are sometimes called **basic variables,** while the remaining variables are called **nonbasic variables.** If a solution to the system of equations can be obtained using a given set of basic variables (while the nonbasic variables are all set equal to zero), that solution is called a **basic feasible solution.** Every basic feasible solution corresponds to one of the extreme points of the feasible region for the LP problem, and we know that the optimal solution to the LP problem also occurs at an extreme point. So the challenge in LP is to find the set of basic variables (and their optimal values) that produce the basic feasible solution corresponding to the optimal extreme point of the feasible region.

Because our modified problem involves three constraints and five variables, we could select three basic variables in ten different ways to form possible basic feasible solutions for the problem. Figure 4.11 summarizes the results for these ten options.

Figure 4.11
Possible basic feasible solutions for the original Blue Ridge Hot Tubs problem.

	Basic Variables	Nonbasic Variables	Solution	Objective Value
1	S_1, S_2, S_3	X_1, X_2	$X_1=0, X_2=0,$ $S_1=200, S_2=1566, S_3=2880$	0
2	X_1, S_1, S_3	X_2, S_2	$X_1=174, X_2=0,$ $S_1=26, S_2=0, S_3=792$	60,900
3	X_1, X_2, S_3	S_1, S_2	$X_1=122, X_2=78,$ $S_1=0, S_2=0, S_3=168$	66,100
4	X_1, X_2, S_2	S_1, S_3	$X_1=80, X_2=120,$ $S_1=0, S_2=126, S_3=0$	64,000
5	X_2, S_1, S_2	X_1, S_3	$X_1=0, X_2=180,$ $S_1=20, S_2=486, S_3=0$	54,000
6*	X_1, X_2, S_1	S_2, S_3	$X_1=108, X_2=99,$ $S_1=-7, S_2=0, S_3=0$	67,500
7*	X_1, S_1, S_2	X_2, S_3	$X_1=240, X_2=0,$ $S_1=-40, S_2=-594, S_3=0$	84,000
8*	X_1, S_2, S_3	X_2, S_1	$X_1=200, X_2=0,$ $S_1=0, S_2=-234, S_3=480$	70,000
9*	X_2, S_2, S_3	X_1, S_1	$X_1=0, X_2=200,$ $S_1=0, S_2=366, S_3=-320$	60,000
10*	X_2, S_1, S_3	X_1, S_2	$X_1=0, X_2=261,$ $S_1=-61, S_2=0, S_3=-1296$	78,300

Note: * denotes infeasible solutions

The first five solutions in Figure 4.11 are feasible and, therefore, represent basic feasible solutions to this problem. The remaining solutions are infeasible because they violate the nonnegativity conditions. The best feasible alternative shown in Figure 4.11 corresponds to the optimal solution to the problem. In particular, if X_1, X_2, and S_3 are selected as basic variables and S_1 and S_2 are nonbasic and assigned their lower bound values (zero), we try to find values for X_1, X_2, and S_3 that satisfy the following constraints:

$$1X_1 + 1X_2 = 200 \qquad \text{} \text{pump constraint}$$
$$9X_1 + 6X_2 = 1,566 \qquad \text{} \text{labor constraint}$$
$$12X_1 + 16X_2 + S_3 = 2,880 \qquad \text{} \text{tubing constraint}$$

Notice that S_1 and S_2 in the modified equal to constraints are not included in the above constraint equations because we are assuming that the values of these nonbasic variables are equal to zero (their lower bounds). Using linear algebra, the simplex method determines that the values $X_1 = 122$, $X_2 = 78$, and $S_3 = 168$ satisfy the equations given above. So, a basic feasible solution to this problem is $X_1 = 122$, $X_2 = 78$, $S_1 = 0$, $S_2 = 0$, $S_3 = 168$. As indicated in Figure 4.11, this solution produces an objective function value of \$66,100. (Notice that the optimal values for the slack variables S_1, S_2, and S_3 also correspond to the values shown in the answer report in Figure 4.2 in the slack column for constraint cells D9, D10, and D11.) Figure 4.12 shows the relationships between the basic feasible solutions listed in Figure 4.11 and the extreme points of the feasible region for this problem.

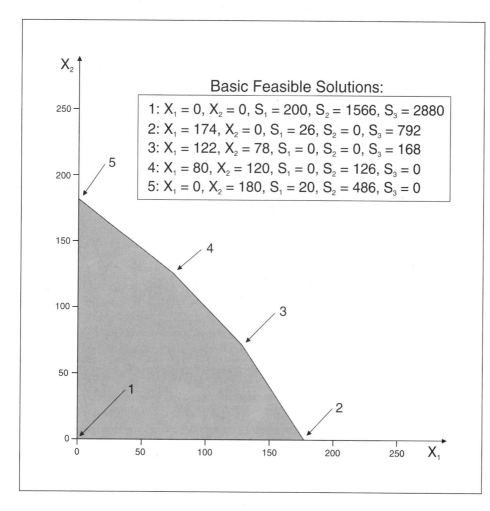

Figure 4.12
Illustration of the relation between basic feasible solutions and extreme points.

4.7.3   Finding the Best Solution

The simplex method operates by first identifying any basic feasible solution (or extreme point) for an LP problem, then moving to an adjacent extreme point, if such a move improves the value of the objective function. When no adjacent extreme point has a better objective function value, the current extreme point is optimal and the simplex method terminates.

The process of moving from one extreme point to an adjacent one is accomplished by switching one of the basic variables with one of the nonbasic variables to create a new basic feasible solution that corresponds to the adjacent extreme point. For example, in Figure 4.12, moving from the first basic feasible solution (point 1) to the second basic feasible solution (point 2) involves making X_1 a basic variable and S_2 a nonbasic variable. Similarly, we can move from point 2 to point 3 by switching basic variables with nonbasic variables. So starting at point 1 in Figure 4.12, the simplex method could move to point 2, then to the optimal solution at point 3. Alternatively, the simplex method could move from point 1 through points 5 and 4 to reach the optimal solution at point 3. Thus, although there is no guarantee that the simplex method will take the shortest route to the optimal solution of an LP problem, it will find the optimal solution eventually.

To determine whether or not switching a basic and nonbasic variable will result in a better solution, the simplex method calculates the reduced cost for each nonbasic variable to determine if the objective function could be improved if any of these variables are substituted for one of the basic variables. (Note that unbounded solutions are detected easily in the simplex method by the existence of a nonbasic variable that could improve the objective value by an infinite amount if it were made basic.) This process continues until no further improvement in the objective function value is possible.

THE WORLD OF MANAGEMENT SCIENCE
Fuel Management and Allocation Model Helps National Airlines Adapt to Cost and Supply Changes

Fuel is a major component in the cost structure of an airline. Price and availability of fuel can vary from one air terminal to the next, and it is sometimes advantageous for an aircraft to carry more than the necessary minimum for the next leg of its route. Fuel loaded for the purpose of taking advantage of price or availability at a specific location is said to be tankered. A disadvantage of tankering is that fuel consumption increases when an aircraft is carrying more weight.

The use of LP to determine when and where to fuel aircraft saved National Airlines several million dollars during the first two years of implementation. In particular, National Airlines saw its average fuel costs drop 11.75% during a period when the average fuel cost for all domestic trunk airlines increased by 2.87%.

The objective function in the Fuel Management and Allocation Model consists of fuel costs and increases in operating costs from tankering. The constraints in the model address availability, minimum reserves, and aircraft capacities.

A particularly useful feature of the Fuel Management and Allocation Model is a series of reports that assist management in modifying the fuel-loading plan when sudden changes occur in availability or price. Shadow prices, along with the associated range of applicability, provide information about supply changes. Information about changes in price per gallon comes from the allowable increase and decrease for objective function coefficients.

For example, the availability report might indicate that the optimal quantity to purchase at Los Angeles from Shell West is 2,718,013 gallons; but if its supply decreases and fuel must be purchased from the next most attractive vendor, total cost would increase at the rate of $0.0478 per gallon (the shadow price). This fuel would be replaced by a prior purchase of up to 159,293 gallons from Shell East at New Orleans, tankered to Los Angeles.

The price report shows, for example, that vendor substitutions should be made if the current price of Shell West at Los Angeles, $0.3074, increases to $0.32583 or decreases to $0.27036. The report also indicates what that substitution should be.

Source: Darnell, D. Wayne and Carolyn Loflin, "National Airlines Fuel Management and Allocation Model," *Interfaces*, vol. 7, no. 2, February 1977, pages 1–16.

SUMMARY

This chapter described the methods for assessing how sensitive an LP model is to various changes that might occur in the model or its optimal solution. The impact of changes in an LP model can be analyzed easily by re-solving the model. Solver also provides a significant amount of sensitivity information automatically. For LP problems, the maximum amount of sensitivity information is obtained by solving the problem using the simplex method. Before using the information on the Sensitivity Report, you should always first check for the presence of degeneracy because this can have a significant impact on how one should interpret the numbers on this report.

The simplex method considers only the extreme points of the feasible region and is an efficient way of solving LP problems. In this method, slack variables are first introduced to convert all constraints to equal to constraints. The simplex method systematically moves to better and better corner point solutions until no adjacent extreme point provides an improved objective function value.

QUESTIONS AND PROBLEMS

1. Howie Jones used the following information to calculate the profit coefficients for Aqua-Spas and Hydro-Luxes: pumps cost $225 each, labor costs $12 per hour, tubing costs $2 per foot. In addition to pumps, labor, and tubing, the production of Aqua-Spas and Hydro-Luxes consumes, respectively, $243 and $246 per unit in other resources that are not in short supply. Using this information, Howie calculated the marginal profits on Aqua-Spas and Hydro-Luxes as:

	Aqua-Spas	Hydro-Luxes
Selling Price	$950	$875
Pump Cost	–$225	–$225
Labor Cost	–$108	–$72
Tubing Cost	–$24	–$32
Other Variable Costs	–$243	–$246
Marginal Profit	$350	$300

Howie's accountant reviewed these calculations and thinks Howie made a mistake. For accounting purposes, factory overhead is assigned to products at a rate of $16 per labor hour. Howie's accountant argues that because Aqua-Spas require nine labor hours, the profit margin on this product should be $144 less. Similarly, because Hydro-Luxes require six labor hours, the profit margin on this product should be $96 less. Who is right and why?

2. A variable that assumes an optimal value between its lower and upper bounds has a reduced cost value of zero. Why must this be true? (Hint: What if such a variable's reduced cost value is not zero? What does this imply about the value of the objective function?)

3. Implement the following LP problem in a spreadsheet. Use Solver to solve the problem and create a Sensitivity Report. Use this information to answer the following questions:

$$\text{MAX:} \qquad 4X_1 + 2X_2$$
$$\text{Subject to:} \quad 2X_1 + 4X_2 \le 20$$
$$3X_1 + 5X_2 \le 15$$
$$X_1, X_2 \ge 0$$

   a. What range of values can the objective function coefficient for variable X_1 assume without changing the optimal solution?
   b. Is the optimal solution to this problem unique, or are there alternate optimal solutions?
   c. How much does the objective function coefficient for variable X_2 have to increase before it enters the optimal solution at a strictly positive level?
   d. What is the optimal objective function value if X_2 equals 1?
   e. What is the optimal objective function value if the RHS value for the second constraint changes from 15 to 25?
   f. Is the current solution still optimal if the coefficient for X_2 in the second constraint changes from 5 to 1? Explain.

4. Implement the following LP model in a spreadsheet. Use Solver to solve the problem and create a Sensitivity Report. Use this information to answer the following questions:

$$\text{MAX:} \qquad 2X_1 + 4X_2$$
$$\text{Subject to:} \quad -X_1 + 2X_2 \le 8$$
$$X_1 + 2X_2 \le 12$$
$$X_1 + X_2 \ge 2$$
$$X_1, X_2 \ge 0$$

   a. Which of the constraints are binding at the optimal solution?
   b. Is the optimal solution to this problem unique, or is there an alternate optimal solution?
   c. What is the optimal solution to this problem if the value of the objective function coefficient for variable X_1 is zero?
   d. How much can the objective function coefficient for variable X_2 decrease before changing the optimal solution?
   e. Given the objective in this problem, if management could increase the RHS value for any of the constraints for identical costs, which would you choose to increase and why?

5. Implement the following LP model in a spreadsheet. Use Solver to solve the problem and create a Sensitivity Report. Use this information to answer the following questions:

$$\text{MIN:} \qquad 5X_1 + 3X_2 + 4X_3$$

$$\text{Subject to:} \quad X_1 + X_2 + 2X_3 \geq 2$$
$$5X_1 + 3X_2 + 2X_3 \geq 1$$
$$X_1, X_2, X_3 \geq 0$$

a. What is the smallest value the objective function coefficient for X_3 can assume without changing the optimal solution?

b. What is the optimal objective function value if the objective function coefficient for X_3 changes to -1? (Hint: The answer to this question is not given in the Sensitivity Report. Consider what the new objective function is relative to the constraints.)

c. What is the optimal objective function value if the RHS value of the first constraint increases to 7?

d. What is the optimal objective function value if the RHS value of the first constraint decreases by 1?

e. Will the current solution remain optimal if the objective function coefficients for X_1 and X_3 both decrease by 1?

6. The CitruSun Corporation ships frozen orange juice concentrate from processing plants in Eustis and Clermont to distributors in Miami, Orlando, and Tallahassee. Each plant can produce 20 tons of concentrate each week. The company has just received orders of 10 tons from Miami for the coming week, 15 tons for Orlando, and 10 tons for Tallahassee. The cost per ton for supplying each of the distributors from each of the processing plants is given below.

	Miami	Orlando	Tallahassee
Eustis	$260	$220	$290
Clermont	$230	$240	$310

The company would like to determine the least costly plan for filling their orders for the coming week.

a. Formulate an LP model for this problem.
b. Implement the model in a spreadsheet and solve it.
c. What is the optimal solution?
d. Is the optimal solution degenerate?
e. Is the optimal solution unique? If not, identify an alternate optimal solution for the problem.
f. How would the solution change if the plant in Clermont is forced to shut for one day resulting in a loss of four tons of production capacity?
g. What would the optimal objective function value be if the processing capacity in Eustis was reduced by five tons?
h. Interpret the reduced cost for shipping from Eustis to Miami.

7. Use Solver to create Answer and Sensitivity Reports for question 13 at the end of chapter 2 and answer the following questions:

a. How much excess wiring and testing capacity exists in the optimal solution?
b. What is the company's total profit if it has 10 additional hours of wiring capacity?
c. By how much does the profit on alternators need to increase before their production is justified?

d. Does the optimal solution change if the marginal profit on generators decreases by $50 and the marginal profit on alternators increases by $75?

e. Suppose the marginal profit on generators decreases by $25. What is the maximum profit that can be earned on alternators without changing the optimal solution?

f. Suppose the amount of wiring required on alternators is reduced to 1.5 hours. Does this change the optimal solution? Why or why not?

8. Use Solver to create Answer and Sensitivity reports for question 19 at the end of chapter 2, and answer the following questions.

a. How much can the price of watermelons drop before it is no longer optimal to plant any watermelons?

b. How much does the price of cantaloupes have to increase before it is optimal to only grow cantaloupes?

c. Suppose the price of watermelons drops by $60 per acre and the price of cantaloupes increases by $50 per acre. Is the current solution still optimal?

d. Suppose the farmer can lease up to 20 acres of land from a neighboring farm to plant additional crops. How many acres should the farmer lease and what is the maximum amount he should pay to lease each acre?

9. Use Solver to create a Sensitivity Report for question 8 at the end of chapter 3 and answer the following questions:

a. Which of the constraints in the problem are binding?

b. If the company was going to eliminate one of its products, which should it be?

c. If the company could buy 1,000 additional memory chips at the usual cost, should they do it? If so, how much would profits increase?

d. Suppose the manufacturing costs used in this analysis were estimated hastily and are known to be somewhat imprecise. Which products would you be most concerned about having more precise cost estimates for before implementing this solution?

10. Use Solver to create a Sensitivity Report for question 10 at the end of chapter 3 and answer the following questions:

a. How much would electric trimmers have to cost in order for the company to consider purchasing these items rather than making them?

b. If the cost to make gas trimmers increased to $90 per unit, how would the optimal solution change?

c. How much should the company be willing to pay to acquire additional capacity in the assembly area? Explain.

d. How much should the company be willing to pay to acquire additional capacity in the production area? Explain.

11. Use Solver to create a Sensitivity Report for question 12 at the end of chapter 3 and answer the following questions.

a. Suppose the cost of the first two compounds increases by $1.00 per pound and the cost of the third compound increases by $0.50 per pound. Does the optimal solution change?

b. How does the solution change if the maximum amount of potassium allowed decreases from 45% to 40%?

c. How much does the cost of the mix increase if the specifications for CHEMIX change to require at least 31% sulfur? (Hint: Remember that the shadow price indicates the impact on the objective function if the RHS value of the associated constraint increases by 1.)

12. Use Solver to create a Sensitivity Report for question 13 at the end of chapter 3 and answer the following questions:

    a. Are there alternate optimal solutions to this problem? Explain.
    b. What is the highest possible octane rating for regular gasoline, assuming the company wishes to maximize its profits? What is the octane rating for supreme gasoline at this solution?
    c. What is the highest possible octane rating for supreme gasoline, assuming the company wishes to maximize its profits? What is the octane rating for regular gasoline at this solution?
    d. Which of the two profit maximizing solutions identified in parts b and c would you recommend the company implement? Why?
    e. If the company could buy another 150 barrels of input 2 at a cost of $17 per barrel, should they do it? Why?

13. Use Solver to create a Sensitivity Report for question 17 at the end of chapter 3 and answer the following questions:

    a. How many more three-bedroom units can be built in the development if the zoning board does not restrict the developer to 40 units?
    b. By how much does the developer's monthly rental income increase if the zoning board allows the developer to build five more units in the complex?
    c. If the developer built one efficiency unit, what effect does this have on the total rental income?

14. Use Solver to create a Sensitivity Report for question 18 at the end of chapter 3 and answer the following questions:

    a. What total profit level is realized if 100 extra hours of labor are available?
    b. Assume a marginal labor cost of $11 per hour in determining the unit profits of each of the three products. How much should management pay to acquire 100 additional labor hours?
    c. Interpret the reduced cost value for tuners. Why are more tuners not being produced?

15. Use Solver to create a Sensitivity Report for question 19 at the end of chapter 3 and answer the following questions:

    a. Is the optimal solution unique? How can you tell?
    b. Which location is receiving the fewest cars?
    c. Suppose a particular car at location 1 must be sent to location 3 in order to meet a customer's request. How much does this increase costs for the company?
    d. Suppose location 6 must have at least eight cars shipped to it. What impact does this have on the optimal objective function value?

16. Refer to the previous question. Suppose location 1 has 15 cars available rather than 16. Create a Sensitivity Report for this problem and answer the following questions:

    a. Is the optimal solution unique? How can you tell?
    b. According to the Sensitivity Report, by how much should the total cost increase if we force a car to be shipped from location 1 to location 3?

    c. Add a constraint to the model to force one car to be shipped from location 1 to location 3. By how much did the total cost increase?

17. Use Solver to create a Sensitivity Report for question 20 at the end of chapter 3 and answer the following questions:

    a. Is the solution unique?

    b. If Sentry wants to increase their production capacity in order to meet more of the demand for their product, which plant should they use? Explain.

    c. If the cost of shipping from Phoenix to Tacoma increased to \$1.98 per unit, would the solution change? Explain.

    d. Could the company make more money if they relaxed the restriction that each distributor must receive at least 80% of the predicted demand? Explain.

    e. How much extra should the company charge the distributor in Tacoma if this distributor insisted on receiving 8,500 units?

18. Use Solver to create a Sensitivity Report for question 21 at the end of chapter 3 and answer the following questions:

    a. Is the solution degenerate?

    b. Is the solution unique?

    c. How much should the recycler be willing to pay to acquire more cardboard?

    d. If the recycler could buy 50 more tons of newspaper at a cost of \$18 per ton, should they do it? Why or why not?

    e. What is the recycler's marginal cost of producing each of the three different types of pulp?

    f. By how much would the cost of converting white office paper into newsprint have to drop before it would become economical to use white office paper for this purpose?

    g. By how much would the yield of newsprint pulp per ton of cardboard have to increase before it would become economical to use cardboard for this purpose?

19. Consider the following LP problem:

$$\begin{aligned} \text{MAX:} \quad & 4X_1 + 2X_2 \\ \text{Subject to:} \quad & 2X_1 + 4X_2 \le 20 \\ & 3X_1 + 5X_2 \le 15 \\ & X_1, X_2 \ge 0 \end{aligned}$$

    a. Use slack variables to rewrite this problem so that all its constraints are equal to constraints.

    b. Identify the different sets of basic variables that might be used to obtain a solution to the problem.

    c. Of the possible sets of basic variables, which lead to feasible solutions and what are the values for all the variables at each of these solutions?

    d. Graph the feasible region for this problem and indicate which basic feasible solution corresponds to each of the extreme points of the feasible region.

    e. What is the value of the objective function at each of the basic feasible solutions?

    f. What is the optimal solution to the problem?

    g. Which constraints are binding at the optimal solution?

20. Consider the following LP problem:

$$\text{MAX:} \quad 2X_1 + 4X_2$$
$$\text{Subject to:} \quad -X_1 + 2X_2 \leq 8$$
$$X_1 + 2X_2 \leq 12$$
$$X_1 + X_2 \geq 2$$
$$X_1, X_2 \geq 0$$

a. Use slack variables to rewrite this problem so that all its constraints are equal to constraints.
b. Identify the different sets of basic variables that might be used to obtain a solution to the problem.
c. Of the possible sets of basic variables, which lead to feasible solutions and what are the values for all the variables at each of these solutions?
d. Graph the feasible region for this problem and indicate which basic feasible solution corresponds to each of the extreme points of the feasible region.
e. What is the value of the objective function at each of the basic feasible solutions?
f. What is the optimal solution to the problem?
g. Which constraints are binding at the optimal solution?

21. Consider the following LP problem:

$$\text{MIN:} \quad 5X_1 + 3X_2 + 4X_3$$
$$\text{Subject to:} \quad X_1 + X_2 + 2X_3 \geq 2$$
$$5X_1 + 3X_2 + 2X_3 \geq 1$$
$$X_1, X_2, X_3 \geq 0$$

a. Use slack variables to rewrite this problem so that all its constraints are equal to constraints.
b. Identify the different sets of basic variables that might be used to obtain a solution to the problem.
c. Of the possible sets of basic variables, which lead to feasible solutions and what are the values for all the variables at each of these solutions?
d. What is the value of the objective function at each of the basic feasible solutions?
e. What is the optimal solution to the problem?
f. Which constraints are binding at the optimal solution?

22. Consider the following constraint, where S is a slack variable:

$$2X_1 + 4X_2 + S = 16$$

a. What was the original constraint before the slack variable was included?
b. What value of S is associated with each of the following points?

   i) $X_1 = 2, X_2 = 2$
   ii) $X_1 = 8, X_2 = 0$
   iii) $X_1 = 1, X_2 = 3$
   iv) $X_1 = 4, X_2 = 1$

23. Consider the following constraint, where S is a slack variable:

$$3X_1 + 4X_2 - S = 12$$

a.   What was the original constraint before the slack variable was included?
b.   What value of S is associated with each of the following points:

i) $X_1 = 5, X_2 = 0$

ii) $X_1 = 2, X_2 = 2$

iii) $X_1 = 7, X_2 = 1$

iv) $X_1 = 4, X_2 = 0$

CASE 4.1   PARKET SISTERS

Contributed by Jack Yurkiewicz, Lubin School of Business, Pace University, New York

Computers and word processors notwithstanding, the art of writing by hand recently entered a boom era. People are buying fountain pens again, and mechanical pencils are becoming more popular than ever. Joe Script, the president and CEO of Parket Sisters, a small but growing pen and pencil manufacturer, wants to establish a better foothold in the market. The writing market is divided into two main sectors. One, dominated by Mont Blanc, Cross, Parker Brothers, Waterman, Schaffer, and a few others, caters to people who want writing instruments. The product lines from these companies consist of pens and pencils of elaborate design, lifetime warranty, and high price. At the other end of the market are manufacturers like BIC, Pentel, and many companies from the Far East, offering good quality items, low price, few trims, and limited diversity. These pens and pencils are meant to be used for a limited time and disposed of when the ink in a ballpoint pen runs out, or when the lead in a mechanical pencil won't retract or extend. In short, these items are not meant for repair.

Joe thinks that there must be a middle ground, and that is where he wants to position his company. Parket Sisters makes high-quality items, with limited trim and diversity, but also offers lifetime warranties. Furthermore, its pens and pencils are ergonomically efficient. Joe knows that some people want the status of the Mont Blanc Meisterstuck pen, for example, but he has never met a person who said that writing with such a pen is enjoyable. The pen is too large and clumsy for smooth writing. Parket Sisters' products, on the other hand, have a reputation for working well, are easy to hold and use, and cause limited "writer's fatigue."

Parket Sisters makes only three items—a ballpoint pen, a mechanical pencil, and a fountain pen. All are available in just one color, black, and are sold mostly in specialty stores and from better catalog companies. The per-unit profit of the items is $3.00 for the ballpoint pen, $3.00 for the mechanical pencil, and $5.00 for the fountain pen. These values take into account labor, the cost of materials, packing, quality control, and so on.

The company is trying to plan its production mix for each week. Joe believes that the company can sell any number of pens and pencils it produces, but production is currently limited by the available resources. Because of a recent strike and certain cash-flow problems, the suppliers of these resources are selling them to Parket Sisters in limited amounts. In particular, Joe can count on getting at most 1,000 ounces of plastic, 1,200 ounces of chrome, and 2,000 ounces of stainless steel each week from his suppliers, and these figures are not likely to change in the near future. Because of Joe's excellent reputation, the suppliers will sell Joe any amount (up to his limit) of the resources he needs when he requires them. That is, the suppliers do not require Joe to buy some fixed quantities of resources in advance of his production of pens and pencils; therefore, these resources can be considered variable costs rather than fixed costs for the pens and pencils.

Each ballpoint pen requires 1.2 ounces of plastic, 0.8 ounces of chrome, and 2 ounces of stainless steel. Each mechanical pencil requires 1.7 ounces of plastic, no chrome, and 3 ounces of stainless steel. Each fountain pen requires 1.2 ounces of plastic, 2.3 ounces of chrome, and 4.5 ounces of stainless steel. Joe believes LP could help him decide what his weekly product mix should consist of.

Getting his notes and notebooks, Joe grapples with the LP formulation. In addition to the constraints of the available resources, he recognizes that the model should include many other constraints (such as labor time availability and materials for packing). However, Joe wants to keep his model simple. He knows that eventually he'll have to take other constraints into account, but as a first-pass model, he'll restrict the constraints to just the three resources: plastic, chrome, and stainless steel.

With only these three constraints, Joe can formulate the problem easily as:

$$\text{Max} \quad 3.0X_1 + 3.0X_2 + 5.0X_3$$
$$\text{Subject to:} \quad 1.2X_1 + 1.7X_2 + 1.2X_3 \le 1,000$$
$$0.8X_1 + 0X_2 + 2.3X_3 \le 1,200$$
$$2.0X_1 + 3.0X_2 + 4.5X_3 \le 2,000$$
$$X_1, X_2, X_3 \ge 0$$

where:

X_1 = the number of ballpoint pens

X_2 = the number of mechanical pencils

X_3 = the number of fountain pens

Joe's knowledge of Excel and the Solver feature is limited, so he asks you to enter and solve the problem for him, then answer the following questions. (Assume each question is independent unless otherwise stated.)

1. What should the weekly product mix consist of, and what is the weekly net profit?

2. Is the optimal solution to question 1 degenerate? Explain your response.

3. Is the optimal solution from question 1 unique, or are there alternate answers to this question? Explain your response.

4. What is the marginal value of one more unit of chrome? Of plastic?

5. A local distributor has offered to sell Parket Sisters an additional 500 ounces of stainless steel for $0.60 per ounce more than it ordinarily pays. Should the company buy the steel at this price? Explain your response.

6. If Parket Sisters buys the additional 500 ounces of stainless steel noted in question 5, what is the new optimal product mix and what is the new optimal profit? Explain your response.

7. Suppose that the distributor offers to sell Parket Sisters some additional plastic at a price of only $1.00 over its usual cost of $5.00 per ounce. However, the distributor will sell the plastic only in lot sizes of 500 ounces. Should Parket Sisters buy one such lot? Explain your response.

8. The distributor is willing to sell the plastic in lots of just 100 ounces instead of the usual 500-ounce lots, still at $1.00 over Parket Sisters' cost of $5.00 per ounce.

How many lots (if any) should Parket Sisters buy? What is the optimal product mix if the company buys these lots, and what is the optimal profit?

9. Parket Sisters has an opportunity to sell some of its plastic for $6.50 per ounce to another company. The other company (which does not produce pens and pencils and, therefore, is not a competitor) wants to buy 300 ounces of plastic from Parket Sisters. Should Parket Sisters sell the plastic to the other company? What happens to Parket Sisters' product mix and overall profit if it does sell the plastic? Be as specific as possible.

10. The chrome supplier might have to fill an emergency order and would be able to send only 1,000 ounces of chrome this week instead of the usual 1,200 ounces. If Parket Sisters receives only 1,000 ounces of chrome, what is the optimal product mix and optimal profit? Be as specific as possible.

11. The R&D department at Parket Sisters has been redesigning the mechanical pencil to make it more profitable. The new design requires 1.1 ounces of plastic, 2.0 ounces of chrome, and 2.0 ounces of stainless steel. If the company can sell one of these pencils at a net profit of $3.00, should it approve the new design? Explain your response.

12. If the per-unit profit on ballpoint pens decreases to $2.50, what is the optimal product mix and what is the company's total profit?

13. The Marketing department suggested introducing a new felt-tip pen that requires 1.8 ounces of plastic, 0.5 ounces of chrome, and 1.3 ounces of stainless steel. What profit must this product generate in order to make it worthwhile to produce?

14. What must the minimum per-unit profit of mechanical pencils be in order to make them worthwhile to produce?

15. Management believes that the company should produce at least 20 mechanical pencils per week to round out its product line. What effect would this have on overall profit? Give a numerical answer.

16. If the profit on a fountain pen is $6.75 instead of $5.00, what is the optimal product mix and optimal profit?

REFERENCES

Bazaraa, M. and J. Jarvis. *Linear Programming and Network Flows*. New York: Wiley, 1990.

Eppen, G., F. Gould and C. Schmidt. *Introductory Management Science*. 4th edition. Englewood Cliffs, NJ: Prentice-Hall, 1993.

Shogan, A. *Management Science*. Englewood Cliffs, NJ: Prentice Hall, 1988.

Wagner, H. and D. Rubin. "Shadow Prices: Tips and Traps for Managers and Instructors." *Interfaces*, vol. 20, no. 4, 1990.

Winston, W. *Operations Research: Applications and Algorithms*. Belmont, CA: Duxbury Press, 1994.

CHAPTER 5

Network Modeling

Anumber of practical decision problems in business fall into a category known as **network flow problems**. These problems share a common characteristic—they can be described or displayed in a graphical form known as a network. This chapter focuses on several types of network flow problems: transshipment problems, shortest path problems, maximal flow problems, transportation/assignment problems, and generalized network flow problems. Although specialized solution procedures exist for solving network flow problems, we will consider how to formulate and solve these problems as LP problems. We will also consider a different type of network problem known as the **minimum spanning tree problem.**

5.1 THE TRANSSHIPMENT PROBLEM

Let's begin our study of network flow problems by considering the transshipment problem. As you will see, most of the other types of network flow problems can be viewed as simple variations of the transshipment problem. So, once you understand how to formulate and solve transshipment problems, the other types of problems will be easy to solve. The following example illustrates the transshipment problem.

The Bavarian Motor Company (BMC) manufactures expensive luxury cars in Hamburg, Germany, and exports cars to sell in the United States. The exported cars are shipped from Hamburg to ports in Newark, New Jersey, and Jacksonville, Florida. From these ports, the cars are transported by rail or truck to distributors located in Boston, Massachusetts; Columbus, Ohio; Atlanta, Georgia; Richmond, Virginia; and Mobile, Alabama. Figure 5.1 shows the possible shipping routes available to the company, along with the transportation cost for shipping each car along the indicated path.

Currently, 200 cars are available at the port in Newark and 300 are available in Jacksonville. The numbers of cars needed by the distributors in Boston,

Figure 5.1
Network
representation of
the BMC
transshipment
problem.

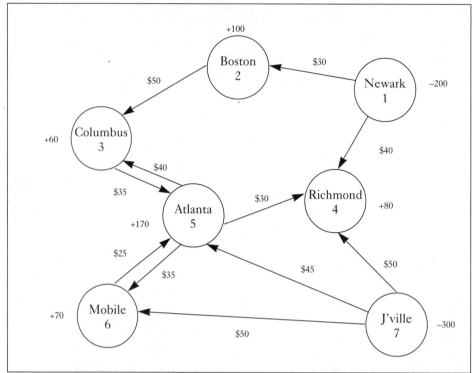

Columbus, Atlanta, Richmond, and Mobile are 100, 60, 170, 80, and 70, respectively. BMC would like to determine the least costly way of transporting cars from the ports in Newark and Jacksonville to the cities where they are needed.

5.1.1   Characteristics of Network Flow Problems

Figure 5.1 illustrates a number of characteristics common to all network flow problems. All network flow problems can be represented as a collection of nodes connected by arcs. The larger circles in Figure 5.1 are called nodes in the terminology of network flow problems, and the lines connecting the nodes are called **arcs.** The arcs in a network indicate the valid paths, routes, or connections between the nodes in a network flow problem. When the lines connecting the nodes in a network are arrows that indicate a direction, the arcs in the network are called **directed arcs.** This chapter discusses directed arcs primarily but, for convenience, refers to them as arcs.

The notion of **supply nodes** (or sending nodes) and **demand nodes** (or receiving nodes) is another common element of network flow problems illustrated in Figure 5.1. The nodes representing the port cities of Newark and Jacksonville are both supply nodes because each has a supply of cars to send to other nodes in the network. Richmond represents a demand node because it demands to receive cars from the other nodes. All the other nodes in this network are transshipment nodes. **Transshipment nodes** can both send to and receive from other nodes in the network. For example, the node representing Atlanta in Figure 5.1 is a transshipment node because it can receive cars from Jacksonville, Mobile, and Columbus, and it can also send cars to Columbus, Mobile, and Richmond.

The net supply or demand for each node in the network is indicated by a positive or negative number next to each node. **Positive numbers** represent the *demand* at a given node, and **negative numbers** represent the *supply* available at a node. For example, the value +80 next to the node for Richmond indicates that the number of cars needs to increase by 80—or that Richmond has a *demand* for 80 cars. The value −200 next to the node for Newark indicates that the number of cars can be reduced by 200—or that Newark has a *supply* of 200 cars. A transshipment node can have either a net supply or demand, but not both. In this particular problem, all the transshipment nodes have demands. For example, the node representing Mobile in Figure 5.1 has a demand for 70 cars.

5.1.2   The Decision Variables for Network Flow Problems

The goal in a network flow model is to determine how many items should be moved (or flow) across each of the arcs. In our example, BMC needs to determine the least costly method of transporting cars along the various arcs shown in Figure 5.1 to distribute cars where they are needed. Thus, each of the arcs in a network flow model represents a decision variable. Determining the optimal flow for each arc is the equivalent of determining the optimal value for the corresponding decision variable.

It is customary to use numbers to identify each node in a network flow problem. In Figure 5.1 the number 1 identifies the node for Newark, 2 identifies the node for Boston, and so on. You can assign numbers to the nodes in any manner, but it is best to use a series of consecutive integers. The node numbers provide a convenient way to identify the decision variables needed to formulate the LP model for the problem. For each arc in a network flow model, you need to define one decision variable as:

X_{ij} = the number of items shipped (or flowing) *from* node *i to* node *j*

The network in Figure 5.1 for our example problem contains 11 arcs. Therefore, the LP formulation of this model requires the following 11 decision variables:

X_{12} = the number of cars shipped *from* node 1 (Newark) *to* node 2 (Boston)

X_{14} = the number of cars shipped *from* node 1 (Newark) *to* node 4 (Richmond)

X_{23} = the number of cars shipped *from* node 2 (Boston) *to* node 3 (Columbus)

X_{35} = the number of cars shipped *from* node 3 (Columbus) *to* node 5 (Atlanta)

X_{53} = the number of cars shipped *from* node 5 (Atlanta) *to* node 3 (Columbus)

X_{54} = the number of cars shipped *from* node 5 (Atlanta) *to* node 4 (Richmond)

X_{56} = the number of cars shipped *from* node 5 (Atlanta) *to* node 6 (Mobile)

X_{65} = the number of cars shipped *from* node 6 (Mobile) *to* node 5 (Atlanta)

X_{74} = the number of cars shipped *from* node 7 (Jacksonville) *to* node 4 (Richmond)

X_{75} = the number of cars shipped *from* node 7 (Jacksonville) *to* node 5 (Atlanta)

X_{76} = the number of cars shipped *from* node 7 (Jacksonville) *to* node 6 (Mobile)

5.1.3   The Objective Function for Network Flow Problems

Each unit that flows from node *i* to node *j* in a network flow problem usually incurs some cost, c_{ij}. This cost might represent a monetary payment, a distance, or some other type of penalty. The objective in most network flow problems is to minimize the total cost, distance, or penalty that must be incurred to solve the problem. Such problems are known as **minimum cost network flow problems.**

In our example problem, different monetary costs must be paid for each car shipped across a given arc. For example, it costs \$30 to ship each car from node 1 (Newark) to node 2 (Boston). Because X_{12} represents the number of cars shipped from Newark to Boston, the total cost incurred by cars shipped along this path is determined by $\$30X_{12}$. Similar calculations can be done for the other arcs in the network. Because BMC is interested in minimizing the total shipping costs, the objective function for this problem is expressed as:

$$\text{MIN: } 30X_{12} + 40X_{14} + 50X_{23} + 35X_{35} + 40X_{53} + 30X_{54} + 35X_{56} + 25X_{65} + 50X_{74} + 45X_{75} + 50X_{76}$$

5.1.4   The Constraints for Network Flow Problems

Just as the number of arcs in the network determines the number of variables in the LP formulation of a network flow problem, the number of nodes determines the number of constraints. In particular, there must be one constraint for each node. A simple set of rules, known as the **Balance-of-Flow Rules,** applies to constructing the constraints for minimum cost network flow problems. These rules are summarized as follows:

For Minimum Cost Network Flow Problems Where:	*Apply This Balance-of-Flow Rule at Each Node:*
Total Supply > Total Demand	Inflow – Outflow ≥ Supply or Demand
Total Supply < Total Demand	Inflow – Outflow ≤ Supply or Demand
Total Supply = Total Demand	Inflow – Outflow = Supply or Demand

It should be noted that if the total supply in a network flow problem is less than the total demand, then it will be impossible to satisfy all of the demand. The balance-of-flow rule listed above for this case assumes that you would want to determine the least costly way to distribute the available supply—knowing that it is impossible to satisfy all of the demand.

So, to apply the correct balance-of-flow rule, we must first compare the total supply in the network to the total demand. In our example problem, there is a total supply of 500 cars and a total demand for 480 cars. Because the total supply exceeds the total demand, we will use the first balance-of-flow rule to formulate our example problem. That is, at each node we will create a constraint of the form:

Inflow – Outflow ≥ Supply or Demand

For example, consider node 1 (Newark) in Figure 5.1. No arcs flow into this node but two arcs (represented by X_{12} and X_{14}) flow out of the node. According to the balance-of-flow rule, the constraint for this node is:

Constraint for node 1: $-X_{12} - X_{14} \geq -200$

Notice that the supply at this node is represented by -200 following the convention we established earlier. If we multiply both sides of this equation by -1, we see that it is equivalent to $+X_{12} + X_{14} \leq +200$. (Note that multiplying an inequality by -1 reverses the sign of the inequality.) Both of these constraints indicate that the total number of cars flowing out of Newark must not exceed 200. So if we include either of these constraints in the model, we can ensure that no more than 200 cars will be shipped from Newark.

Now consider the constraint for node 2 (Boston) in Figure 5.1. Because Boston has a demand for 100 cars, the balance-of-flow rule requires that the total number of cars coming into Boston from Newark (via X_{12}) minus the total number of cars being shipped out of Boston to Columbus (via X_{23}) must leave at least 100 cars in Boston. This condition is imposed by the constraint:

$$\text{Constraint for node 2: } +X_{12} - X_{23} \geq +100$$

Note that this constraint makes it possible to leave more than the required number of cars in Boston (e.g., 200 cars could be shipped into Boston and only 50 shipped out, leaving 150 cars in Boston). However, because our objective is to minimize costs, we can be sure that an excess number of cars will never be shipped to any city, because that would result in unnecessary costs being incurred.

Using the balance-of-flow rule, the constraints for each of the remaining nodes in our example problem are represented as:

$$\text{Constraint for node 3: } +X_{23} + X_{53} - X_{35} \geq +60$$
$$\text{Constraint for node 4: } +X_{14} + X_{54} + X_{74} \geq +80$$
$$\text{Constraint for node 5: } +X_{35} + X_{65} + X_{75} - X_{53} - X_{54} - X_{56} \geq +170$$
$$\text{Constraint for node 6: } +X_{56} + X_{76} - X_{65} \geq +70$$
$$\text{Constraint for node 7: } -X_{74} - X_{75} - X_{76} \geq -300$$

Again, each constraint indicates that the flow into a given node minus the flow out of that same node must be greater than or equal to the supply or demand at the node. So, if you draw a graph of a network flow problem like the one in Figure 5.1, it is easy to write out the constraints for the problem by following the balance-of-flow rule. Of course, we also need to specify the following nonnegativity condition for all the decision variables because negative flows should not occur on arcs:

$$X_{ij} \geq 0 \text{ for all } ij$$

5.1.5   Implementing the Model in a Spreadsheet

The formulation for the BMC transshipment problem is summarized as:

MIN: $30X_{12} + 40X_{14} + 50X_{23} + 35X_{35} + 40X_{53} +$
       $30X_{54} + 35X_{56} + 25X_{65} + 50X_{74} + 45X_{75} +$
       $50X_{76}$ } total shipping cost

Subject to:

$$-X_{12} - X_{14} \geq -200 \qquad \text{\} flow constraint for node 1}$$
$$+X_{12} - X_{23} \geq +100 \qquad \text{\} flow constraint for node 2}$$
$$+X_{23} + X_{53} - X_{35} \geq +60 \qquad \text{\} flow constraint for node 3}$$
$$+X_{14} + X_{54} + X_{74} \geq +80 \qquad \text{\} flow constraint for node 4}$$
$$+X_{35} + X_{65} + X_{75} - X_{53} - X_{54} - X_{56} \geq +170 \qquad \text{\} flow constraint for node 5}$$
$$+X_{56} + X_{76} - X_{65} \geq +70 \qquad \text{\} flow constraint for node 6}$$
$$-X_{74} - X_{75} - X_{76} \geq -300 \qquad \text{\} flow constraint for node 7}$$
$$X_{ij} \geq 0 \text{ for all } ij \qquad \text{\} nonnegativity conditions}$$

A convenient way of implementing this type of problem is shown in Figure 5.2 (and in the file FIG5-2.xls on your data disk). In this spreadsheet, cells B6 through B16 are used to represent the decision variables for our model (or the number of cars that should flow between each of the cities listed). The unit cost of transporting cars between each city is listed in column G. The objective function for the model is then implemented in cell G18 as follows:

Formula for cell G18: =SUMPRODUCT(B6:B16,G6:G16)

To implement the LHS formulas for the constraints in this model, we need to compute the total inflow minus the total outflow for each node. This is done in cells K6 through K12 as follows:

Formula for cell K6:   =SUMIF($E$6:$E$16,I6,$B$6:$B$16)-
(Copy to cells K7 through K12.)   SUMIF($C$6:$C$16,I6,$B$6:$B$16)

The first SUMIF function in this formula compares the values in the range E6 through E16 to the value in I6 and, if a match occurs, sums the corresponding value

Figure 5.2
Spreadsheet implementation of the BMC transshipment problem.

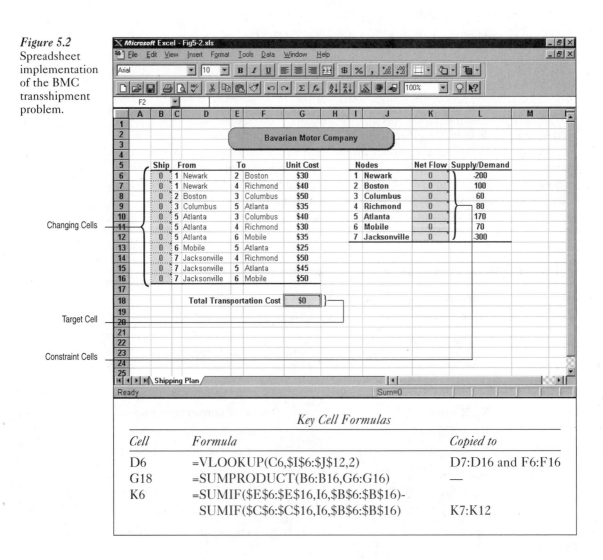

Key Cell Formulas		
Cell	*Formula*	*Copied to*
D6	=VLOOKUP(C6,$I$6:$J$12,2)	D7:D16 and F6:F16
G18	=SUMPRODUCT(B6:B16,G6:G16)	—
K6	=SUMIF($E$6:$E$16,I6,$B$6:$B$16)- SUMIF($C$6:$C$16,I6,$B$6:$B$16)	K7:K12

in the range B6 through B16. Of course, this gives us the total number of cars flowing *into* Newark (which in this case will always be zero since none of the values in E6 through E16 match the value in I6). The next SUMIF function compares the values in the range C6 through C16 to the value in I6 and, if a match occurs, sums the corresponding values in the range B6 through B16. This gives us the total number of cars flowing *out of* Newark (which in this case will always equal the values in cells B6 and B7 since these are the only arcs flowing out of Newark). Copying this formula to cells K7 though K12 allows us to easily calculate the total inflow minus the total outflow for each of the nodes in our problem. The RHS values for these constraint cells are shown in cells L6 though L12.

Figure 5.3 shows the Solver parameters and options required to solve this model. The optimal solution to the problem is shown in Figure 5.4.

5.1.6 Analyzing the Solution

Figure 5.4 shows the optimal solution for BMC's transshipment problem. The solution indicates that 120 cars should be shipped from Newark to Boston ($X_{12} = 120$), 80 cars from Newark to Richmond ($X_{14} = 80$), 20 cars from Boston to Columbus ($X_{23} = 20$), 40 cars from Atlanta to Columbus ($X_{53} = 40$), 210 cars from Jacksonville to Atlanta ($X_{75} = 210$), and 70 cars from Jacksonville to Mobile ($X_{76} = 70$). Cell G18 indicates that the total cost associated with this shipping plan is $22,350. The values of the constraint cells in K6 and K12 indicate, respectively, that all 200 cars available at Newark are being shipped and only 280 of the 300 cars available at Jacksonville are being shipped. A comparison of the remaining constraint cells in K7 through K11 with their RHS values in L7 through L11 reveals that the demand at each of these cities is being met by the net flow of cars through each city.

This solution is summarized graphically, as shown in Figure 5.5. The values in the boxes next to each arc indicate the optimal flows for the arcs. The optimal flow for all

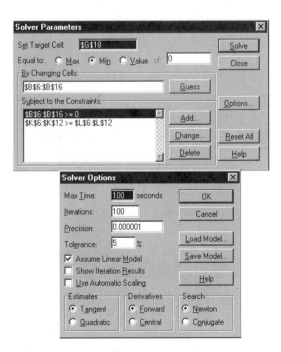

Figure 5.3
Solver parameters and options for the BMC transshipment problem.

Figure 5.4
Optimal solution to the BMC transshipment problem.

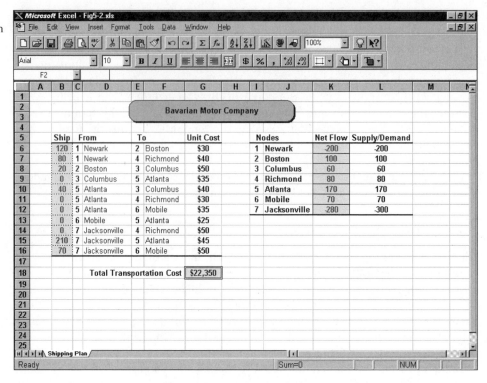

Figure 5.5
Network representation of the optimal solution for the BMC transshipment problem.

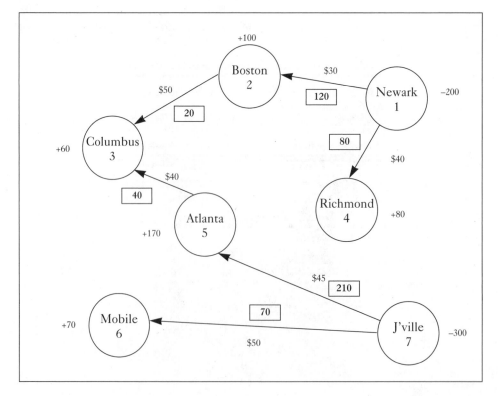

the other arcs in the problem, which are not shown in Figure 5.5, is 0. For example, 210 cars are being shipped from Jacksonville to Atlanta. Atlanta will keep 170 of the cars (to satisfy the demand at this node) and send the extra 40 to Columbus.

5.2   THE SHORTEST PATH PROBLEM

In many decision problems, we need to determine the shortest (or least costly) route or path through a network from a starting node to an ending node. For example, many cities are developing computerized models of their highways and streets to help emergency vehicles identify the quickest route to a given location. Each street intersection represents a potential node in a network, and the streets connecting the intersections represent arcs. Depending on the day of the week and the time of day, the time required to travel various streets can increase or decrease due to changes in traffic patterns. Road construction and maintenance also affect traffic flow patterns. So the quickest route (or shortest path) for getting from one point in the city to another can change frequently. In emergency situations, lives or property can be lost or saved depending on how quickly emergency vehicles arrive where they are needed. The ability to quickly determine the shortest path to the location of an emergency situation is extremely useful in these situations. The following example illustrates another application of the shortest path problem.

> The American Car Association (ACA) provides a variety of travel-related services to its members, including information on vacation destinations, discount hotel reservations, emergency road assistance, and travel route planning. This last service, travel route planning, is one of its most popular services. When members of the ACA are planning to take a driving trip, they call the organization's toll-free 800 number and indicate what cities they will be traveling from and to. The ACA then determines an optimal route for traveling between these cities. The ACA's computer databases of major highways and interstates are kept up to date with information on construction delays and detours and estimated travel times along various segments of roadways.
>
> Members of the ACA often have different objectives in planning driving trips. Some are interested in identifying routes that minimize travel times. Others, with more leisure time on their hands, wish to identify the most scenic route to their desired destination. The ACA would like to develop an automated system for identifying an optimal travel plan for its members.

To see how the ACA could benefit by solving shortest path problems, consider the simplified network shown in Figure 5.6 for an ACA member who wants to drive from Birmingham, AL to Virginia Beach, VA. The nodes in this graph represent different cities and the arcs indicate the possible travel routes between the cities. For each arc, Figure 5.6 lists both the estimated driving time to travel the road represented by each arc and the number of points that route has received on the ACA's system for rating the scenic quality of the various routes.

Solving this problem as a network flow model requires the various nodes to have some supply or demand. In Figure 5.6, node 1 (Birmingham) has a supply of 1, node 11 (Virginia Beach) has a demand of 1, and all other nodes have a demand (or supply) of 0. If we view this model as a transshipment problem, we want to find either the quickest way or the most scenic way of shipping one unit of flow from node 1 to node 11.

Figure 5.6
Network of
possible routes
for the ACA's
shortest path
problem.

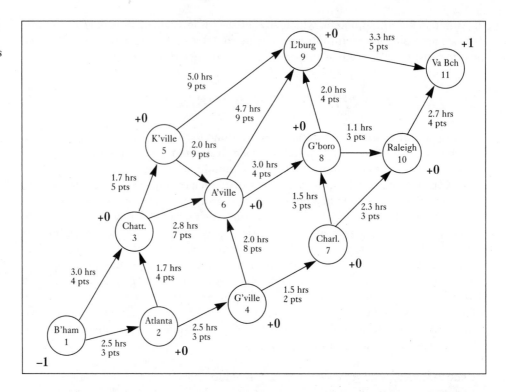

The route this unit of supply takes corresponds to either the shortest path or the most scenic path through the network, depending on which objective is being pursued.

5.2.1 An LP Model for the Example Problem

Using the balance-of-flow rule, the LP model to minimize the driving time in this problem is represented as:

MIN: $2.5X_{12} + 3X_{13} + 1.7X_{23} + 2.5X_{24} + 1.7X_{35} + 2.8X_{36} + 2X_{46} + 1.5X_{47} + 2X_{56}$
$+ 5X_{59} + 3X_{68} + 4.7X_{69} + 1.5X_{78} + 2.3X_{7,10} + 2X_{89} + 1.1X_{8,10} + 3.3X_{9,11} + 2.7X_{10,11}$

Subject to:

$$-X_{12} - X_{13} \qquad\qquad\qquad = -1 \quad \} \text{ flow constraint for node 1}$$
$$+X_{12} - X_{23} - X_{24} \qquad\qquad = 0 \quad \} \text{ flow constraint for node 2}$$
$$+X_{13} + X_{23} - X_{35} - X_{36} \qquad = 0 \quad \} \text{ flow constraint for node 3}$$
$$+X_{24} - X_{46} - X_{47} \qquad\qquad = 0 \quad \} \text{ flow constraint for node 4}$$
$$+X_{35} - X_{56} - X_{59} \qquad\qquad = 0 \quad \} \text{ flow constraint for node 5}$$
$$+X_{36} + X_{46} + X_{56} - X_{68} - X_{69} = 0 \quad \} \text{ flow constraint for node 6}$$
$$+X_{47} - X_{78} - X_{7,10} \qquad\qquad = 0 \quad \} \text{ flow constraint for node 7}$$
$$+X_{68} + X_{78} - X_{89} - X_{8,10} \qquad = 0 \quad \} \text{ flow constraint for node 8}$$
$$+X_{59} + X_{69} + X_{89} - X_{9,11} \qquad = 0 \quad \} \text{ flow constraint for node 9}$$
$$+X_{7,10} + X_{8,10} - X_{10,11} \qquad = 0 \quad \} \text{ flow constraint for node 10}$$
$$+X_{9,11} + X_{10,11} \qquad\qquad\qquad = +1 \quad \} \text{ flow constraint for node 11}$$
$$X_{ij} \geq 0 \text{ for all } i \text{ and } j \qquad\qquad \} \text{ nonnegativity conditions}$$

Because the total supply equals the total demand in this problem, each constraint is stated as an equality. The first constraint in this model ensures that the one unit of supply available at node 1 is shipped to node 2 or node 3. The next nine constraints indicate that anything flowing to nodes 2 though node 10 must also flow out of these nodes because each has a demand of 0. For example, if the unit of supply leaves node 1 for node 2 (via X_{12}), the second constraint ensures that it will leave node 2 for node 3 or node 4 (via X_{23} or X_{24}). The last constraint indicates that the unit must ultimately flow to node 11. Thus, the solution to this problem indicates the quickest route for getting from node 1 (Birmingham) to node 11 (Virginia Beach).

5.2.2 The Spreadsheet Model and Solution

The optimal solution to this problem shown in Figure 5.7 (and in the file FIG5-7.xls on your data disk) was obtained using the Solver parameters and options shown in Figure 5.8. Notice that this model includes calculations of both the total expected driving time (cell G26) and total scenic rating points (cell H26) associated with any

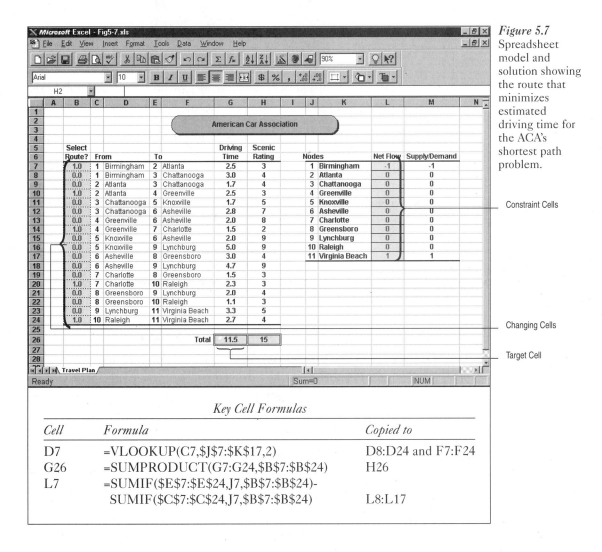

Figure 5.7 Spreadsheet model and solution showing the route that minimizes estimated driving time for the ACA's shortest path problem.

Key Cell Formulas

Cell	Formula	Copied to
D7	=VLOOKUP(C7,$J$7:$K$17,2)	D8:D24 and F7:F24
G26	=SUMPRODUCT(G7:G24,$B$7:$B$24)	H26
L7	=SUMIF($E$7:$E$24,J7,$B$7:$B$24)-SUMIF($C$7:$C$24,J7,$B$7:$B$24)	L8:L17

Figure 5.8
Solver
parameters and
options for the
ACA's shortest
path problem.

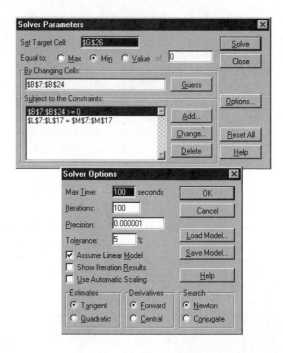

solution. Either of these cells can be chosen as the objective function according to the client's desires. However, the solution shown in Figure 5.7 minimizes the expected driving time.

The optimal solution shown in Figure 5.7 indicates that the quickest travel plan involves driving from node 1 (Birmingham) to node 2 (Atlanta), then to node 4 (Greenville), then to node 7 (Charlotte), then to node 10 (Raleigh), and finally to node 11 (Virginia Beach). The total expected driving time along this route is 11.5 hours. Also note that this route receives a rating of 15 points on the ACA's scenic rating scale.

Using this spreadsheet, we can also determine the route that would be most scenic by instructing Solver to maximize the value in cell H26. Figure 5.9 shows the optimal solution obtained in this case. This travel plan involves driving from Birmingham to Atlanta, to Chattanooga, to Knoxville, to Asheville, to Lynchburg, and finally, to Virginia Beach. This itinerary receives a rating of 35 points on the ACA's scenic rating scale but takes almost 16 hours of driving time.

5.2.3   Network Flow Models and Integer Solutions

Up to this point, each of the network flow models we have solved generated integer solutions. If you use the simplex method to solve any minimum cost network flow model having integer constraint RHS values, then the optimal solution automatically assumes integer values. This property is helpful because the items flowing through most network flow models represent discrete units (such as cars or people).

Sometimes it is tempting to place additional constraints (or side-constraints) on a network model. For example, in the ACA problem, suppose that the customer wants to get to Virginia Beach in the most scenic way possible within 14 hours of driving time. We can easily add a constraint to the model to keep the total driving time G26 less than or equal to 14 hours. If we then re-solve the model to maximize the scenic rating in cell H26, we obtain the solution shown in Figure 5.10.

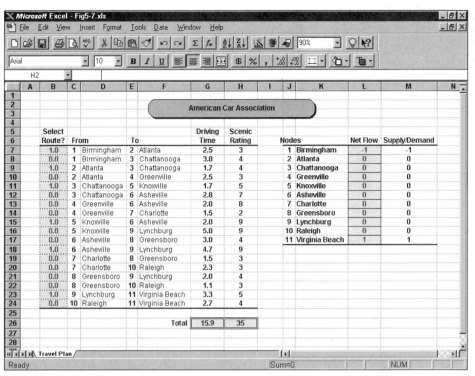

Figure 5.9
Solution showing the most scenic route.

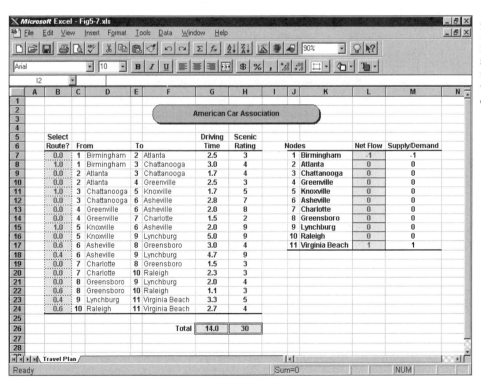

Figure 5.10
Example of a noninteger solution to a network problem with side-constraints.

Unfortunately, this solution is useless because it produces fractional results. Thus, if we add *side-constraints* to network flow problems that do not obey the balance-of-flow rule, we can no longer ensure that the solution to the LP formulation of the problems will be integral. If integer solutions are needed for such problems, the integer programming techniques discussed in Chapter 6 must be applied.

5.3   THE EQUIPMENT REPLACEMENT PROBLEM

The equipment replacement problem is a common type of business problem that can be modeled as a shortest path problem. This type of problem involves determining the least costly schedule for replacing equipment over a specified length of time. Consider the following example:

Jose Maderos is the owner of Compu-Train, a small company that provides hands-on software education and training for businesses in and around Boulder, Colorado. Jose leases the computer equipment used in his business and he likes to keep the equipment up to date so that it will run the latest state-of-the-art software in an efficient manner. Because of this, Jose wants to replace his equipment at least every two years.

Jose is currently trying to decide between two different lease contracts his equipment supplier has proposed. Under both contracts Jose would be required to pay $62,000 initially to obtain the equipment he needs. However, the two contracts differ in terms of the amount Jose would have to pay in subsequent years to replace his equipment. Under the first contract, the price to acquire new equipment would increase by 6% per year, but he would be given a trade-in credit of 60% for any equipment that is one year old and 15% for any equipment that is two years old. Under the second contract, the price to acquire new equipment would increase by just 2% per year, but he would be given a trade-in credit of only 30% for any equipment that is one year old and 10% for any equipment that is two years old.

Jose realizes that no matter what he does, he will have to pay $62,000 to obtain the equipment initially. However, he wants to determine which contract would allow him to minimize the remaining leasing costs over the next five years and when he should replace his equipment under the selected contract.

Each of the two contracts Jose is considering can be modeled as a shortest path problem. Figure 5.11 shows how this would be accomplished for the first contract under consideration. Each node corresponds to a point in time during the next five years when Jose can replace his equipment. Each arc in this network represents a choice available to Jose. For example, the arc from node 1 to node 2 indicates that Jose can keep the equipment he initially acquires for one year and then replace it (at the beginning of year 2) for a net cost of $28,520 ($62,000 × 1.06 − 0.6 × $62,000 = $28,520). Alternatively, the arc from node 1 to node 3 indicates that Jose can keep his initial equipment for two years and replace it at the beginning of year 3 for a net cost of $60,363 ($62,000 × 1.06^2 − 0.15 × $62,000 = $60,363).

The arc from node 2 to node 3 indicates that if Jose replaces his initial equipment at the beginning of year 2, he can keep the new equipment for one year and replace it at the beginning of year 3 at a net cost of $30,231 ($62,000 × 1.06^2 − 0.60 × ($62,000 × 1.06) = $30,231). The remaining arcs and costs in the network can be interpreted in the same

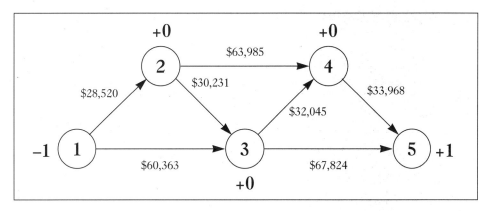

Figure 5.11
Network representation of Compu-Train's first contract alternative for its equipment replacement problem.

way. Jose's decision problem is to determine the least costly (or shortest) way of getting from node 1 to node 5 in this network.

5.3.1 The Spreadsheet Model and Solution

The LP formulation of Jose's decision problem can be generated from the graph in Figure 5.11 using the balance-of-flow rule in the same manner as the previous network flow problems. The spreadsheet model for this problem was implemented as shown in Figure 5.12 (and in the file FIG5-12.xls on your data disk) and solved using the setting shown in Figure 5.13. To assist Jose in comparing the two alternatives he faces, notice that an area of the spreadsheet in Figure 5.12 has been reserved to represent assumptions about the annual increase in leasing costs (cell G5), and the trade-in values for one- and two-year-old equipment (cells G6 and G7). The rest of the spreadsheet model uses these assumed values to compute the various costs. This enables us to change any of the assumptions and re-solve the model very easily.

The optimal solution to this problem shows that under the provisions of the first contract, Jose should replace his equipment at the beginning of each year at a total cost of $124,764. This amount is in addition to the $62,000 he has to pay up front at the beginning of year 1.

To determine the optimal replacement strategy and costs associated with the second contract, Jose could simply change the assumptions at the top of the spreadsheet and re-solve the model. The results of this are shown in Figure 5.14.

Summary of Shortest Path Problems

You can model any shortest path problem as a transshipment problem by assigning a supply of 1 to the starting node, a demand of 1 to the ending node, and a demand of 0 to all other nodes in the network. Because the examples presented here involved only a small number of paths through each of the networks, it might have been easier to solve these problems simply by enumerating the paths and calculating the total distance of each one. However, in a problem with many nodes and arcs, an automated LP model is preferable to a manual solution approach.

Figure 5.12
Spreadsheet
model and
solution for
Compu-Train's
first lease
contract
alternative.

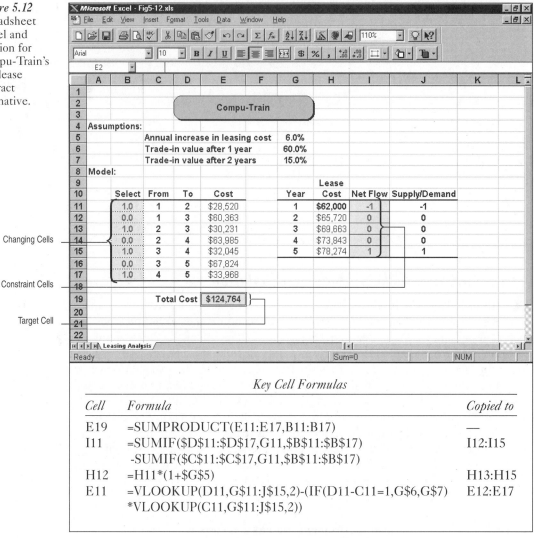

Key Cell Formulas

Cell	Formula	Copied to
E19	=SUMPRODUCT(E11:E17,B11:B17)	—
I11	=SUMIF($D$11:$D$17,G11,$B$11:$B$17)	I12:I15
	-SUMIF($C$11:$C$17,G11,$B$11:$B$17)	
H12	=H11*(1+$G$5)	H13:H15
E11	=VLOOKUP(D11,G$11:J$15,2)-(IF(D11-C11=1,G$6,G$7)	E12:E17
	*VLOOKUP(C11,G$11:J$15,2))	

Figure 5.13
Solver
parameters and
options for
Compu-Train's
equipment
replacement
problem.

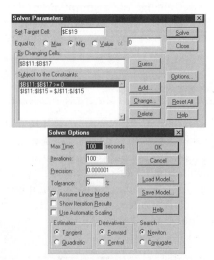

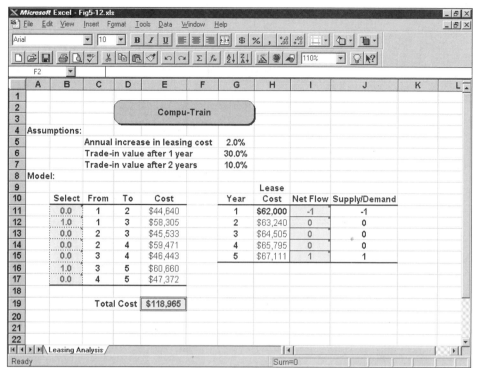

Figure 5.14
Solution for
Compu-Train's
second lease
contract
alternative.

The optimal solution to this problem shows that under the provisions of the second contract, Jose should replace his equipment at the beginning of each of years 3 and 5 at a total cost of $118,965. Again, this amount is in addition to the $62,000 he has to pay up front at the beginning of year 1. While the total costs under the second contract are lower than under the first, under the second contract Jose would be working with older equipment during years 2 and 4. Thus, while the solution to these two models makes the financial consequences of the two different alternatives clear, Jose still must decide for himself whether the benefits of the financial cost savings under the second contract outweigh the nonfinancial costs associated with using slightly out-of-date equipment during years 2 and 4. Of course, regardless of which contract Jose decides to go with, at the beginning of each of the next four years he will get to reconsider whether or not to upgrade his equipment.

5.4 TRANSPORTATION/ASSIGNMENT PROBLEMS

Chapter 3 presented an example of another type of network flow problem known as the transportation/assignment problem. The example involved the Tropicsun Company—a grower and distributor of fresh citrus products. The company wanted to determine the least expensive way of transporting freshly picked fruit from three citrus groves to three processing plants. The network representation of the problem is repeated in Figure 5.15.

The network shown in Figure 5.15 differs from the earlier network flow problems in this chapter because it contains no transshipment nodes. Each node in Figure 5.15 is either a sending node or a receiving node. The lack of transshipment nodes is the key

Figure 5.15
Network
representation of
Tropicsun's
transportation/
assignment
problem

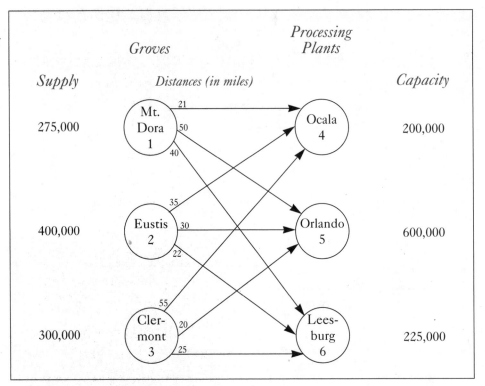

feature that distinguishes transportation/assignment problems from other types of network flow problems. As you saw in Chapter 3, this property allows you to set up and solve transportation/assignment problems conveniently in a matrix format in the spreadsheet. Although it is possible to solve transportation/assignment problems in the same way in which we solved general network flow problems, it is much easier to implement and solve these problems using the matrix approach described in Chapter 3.

Sometimes transportation/assignment problems are **sparse** or not fully interconnected (meaning that not all the supply nodes have arcs connecting them to all the demand nodes). These "missing" arcs can be handled conveniently in the matrix approach to implementation by assigning arbitrarily large costs to the changing cells representing these arcs so that flow on these arcs becomes prohibitively expensive. However, as the number of missing arcs increases, the matrix approach to implementation becomes less and less computationally efficient compared to the procedure described in this chapter.

5.5   GENERALIZED NETWORK FLOW PROBLEMS

In all of the network problems we have considered so far, the amount of flow that exited an arc was always the same as the amount that entered the arc. For example, if we put 40 cars on a train in Jacksonville and sent them to Atlanta, the same 40 cars came off the train in Atlanta. However, there are numerous examples of network flow problems in which a gain or loss occurs on flows across arcs. For instance, if oil or gas is shipped through a leaky pipeline, the amount of oil or gas arriving at the intended destination will be less than the amount originally placed in the pipeline. Similar loss-of-flow examples occur as a result of evaporation of liquids, spoilage of foods and other perishable items, or imperfections in raw materials entering production processes that result in a certain amount of scrap. Many financial cash flow problems can be modeled as network flow problems in which flow gains occur in the form of interest or dividends as money flows through various investment. The following example illustrates the modeling changes required to accommodate these types of problems.

Nancy Grant is the owner of Coal Bank Hollow Recycling, a company that specializes in collecting and recycling paper products. Nancy's company uses two different recycling processes to convert newspaper, mixed paper, white office paper, and cardboard into paper pulp. The amount of paper pulp extracted from the recyclable materials and the cost of extracting the pulp differs depending on which recycling process is used. The following table summarizes the recycling processes:

Material	Recycling Process 1		Recycling Process 2	
	Cost per ton	Yield	Cost per ton	Yield
Newspaper	$13	90%	$12	85%
Mixed Paper	$11	80%	$13	85%
White Office Paper	$9	95%	$10	90%
Cardboard	$13	75%	$14	85%

For instance, every ton of newspaper subjected to recycling process 1 costs $13 and yields 0.9 tons of paper pulp. The paper pulp produced by the two different recycling processes goes through other operations to be transformed into pulp for newsprint, packaging paper, or print stock quality paper. The yields associated with transforming the recycled pulp into pulp for the final products is summarized below:

Pulp Source	Newsprint Pulp		Packaging Paper Pulp		Print Stock Pulp	
	Cost per ton	Yield	Cost per ton	Yield	Cost per ton	Yield
Recycling Process 1	$5	95%	$6	90%	$8	90%
Recycling Process 2	$6	90%	$8	95%	$7	95%

For instance, a ton of pulp exiting recycling process 2 can be transformed into 0.95 tons of packaging paper pulp at a cost of $8.

Nancy currently has 70 tons of newspaper, 50 tons of mixed paper, 30 tons of white office paper, and 40 tons of cardboard. She would like to determine the most efficient way of converting these materials into 60 tons of newsprint pulp, 40 tons of packaging paper pulp, and 50 tons of print stock pulp.

Figure 5.16 shows how Nancy's recycling problem can be viewed as a generalized network flow problem. The arcs in this graph indicate the possible flow of recycling material through the production process. On each arc we have listed both the cost of flow along the arc and the reduction factor that applies to flow along the arc. For instance, the arc from node 1 to node 5 indicates that each ton of newspaper going to recycling process 1 costs $13 and yields 0.90 tons of paper pulp.

Figure 5.16
Graphical
representation
of Coal Bank
Hollow
Recycling's
generalized
network flow
problem.

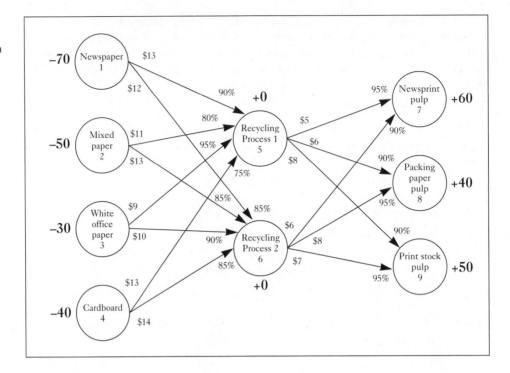

5.5.1   Formulating an LP Model for the Recycling Problem

To formulate the LP model for this problem algebraically, we defined the decision variable X_{ij} to represent the tons of product flowing from node i to node j. The objective is then stated in the usual ways as follows:

MIN: $13X_{15} + 12X_{16} + 11X_{25} + 13X_{26} + 9X_{35} + 10X_{36} + 13X_{45} + 14X_{46} + 5X_{57}$
         $+ 6X_{58} + 8X_{59} + 6X_{67} + 8X_{68} + 7X_{69}$

The constraints for this problem may be generated using the balance-of-flow rule for each node. The constraints for the first four nodes (representing the supply of newspaper, mixed paper, white office paper, and cardboard, respectively) we obtain are:

$$-X_{15} - X_{16} \geq -70 \ \} \text{ flow constraint for node 1}$$
$$-X_{25} - X_{26} \geq -50 \ \} \text{ flow constraint for node 2}$$
$$-X_{35} - X_{36} \geq -30 \ \} \text{ flow constraint for node 3}$$
$$-X_{45} - X_{46} \geq -40 \ \} \text{ flow constraint for node 4}$$

These constraints simply indicate that amount of product flowing out of each of these nodes may not exceed the supply available at each node. (Recall that the constraint given above for node 1 is equivalent to $+X_{15} + X_{16} \leq +70$.)

Applying the balance-of-flow rule at nodes 5 and 6 (representing the two recycling processes), we obtain,

$$+0.9X_{15} + 0.8X_{25} + 0.95X_{35} + 0.75X_{45} - X_{57} - X_{58} - X_{59} \geq 0 \ \} \text{ flow constraint for node 5}$$
$$+0.85X_{16} + 0.85X_{26} + 0.9X_{36} + 0.85X_{46} - X_{67} - X_{68} - X_{69} \geq 0\} \text{ flow constraint for node 6}$$

To better understand the logic of these constraints, we will rewrite them in the following algebraically equivalent manner:

$+0.9X_{15} + 0.8X_{25} + 0.95X_{35} + 0.75X_{45} \geq +X_{57} + X_{58} + X_{59}$ } equivalent flow constraint for node 5

$+0.85X_{16} + 0.85X_{26} + 0.9X_{36} + 0.85X_{46} \geq +X_{67} + X_{68} + X_{69}$ } equivalent flow constraint for node 6

Notice that the constraint for node 5 requires that the amount being shipped from node 5 (given by $+ X_{57} + X_{58} + X_{59}$) cannot exceed the net amount that would be available at node 5 (given by $+0.9X_{15} + 0.8X_{25} + 0.95X_{35} + 0.75X_{45}$). Thus, here the yield factors come into play in determining the amount of product that would be available from the recycling processes. A similar interpretation applies to the constraint for node 6.

Finally, applying the balance-of-flow rule to nodes 7, 8, and 9, we obtain the constraints:

$+0.95X_{57} + 0.90X_{67} \geq +60$ } flow constraint for node 7

$+0.9X_{58} + 0.95X_{68} \geq +40$ } flow constraint for node 8

$+0.9X_{59} + 0.95X_{69} \geq +50$ } flow constraint for node 9

The constraint for node 7 ensures that final amount of product flowing to node 7 ($+0.95X_{57} + 0.90X_{67}$) is sufficient to meet the demand for pulp at this nodes. Again, similar interpretations apply to the constraints for nodes 8 and 9.

5.5.2 Implementing the Model

The model for Coal Bank Hollow Recycling's generalized network flow problem is summarized as:

MIN: $13X_{15} + 12X_{16} + 11X_{25} + 13X_{26} + 9X_{35} + 10X_{36} + 13X_{45} + 14X_{46} + 5X_{57}$
      $+ 6X_{58} + 8X_{59} + 6X_{67} + 8X_{68} + 7X_{69}$

Subject to:

$-X_{15} - X_{16} \geq -70$ } flow constraint for node 1

$-X_{25} - X_{26} \geq -50$ } flow constraint for node 2

$-X_{35} - X_{36} \geq -30$ } flow constraint for node 3

$-X_{45} - X_{46} \geq -40$ } flow constraint for node 4

$+0.9X_{15} + 0.8X_{25} + 0.95X_{35} + 0.75X_{45} - X_{57} - X_{58} - X_{59} \geq 0$ } flow constraint for node 5

$+0.85X_{16} + 0.85X_{26} + 0.9X_{36} + 0.85X_{46} - X_{67} - X_{68} - X_{69} \geq 0$ } flow constraint for node 6

$+0.95X_{57} + 0.90X_{67} \geq 60$ } flow constraint for node 7

$+0.9X_{58} + 0.95X_{68} \geq 40$ } flow constraint for node 8

$+0.9X_{59} + 0.95X_{69} \geq 50$ } flow constraint for node 9

$X_{ij} \geq 0$ for all i and j

In all the other network flow models we have seen up to this point, all the coefficients in all the constraints were implicitly always +1 or -1. This is not true in the above model. Thus, we must give special attention to the coefficients in the constraints as we implement this model in the spreadsheet. One approach to implementing this problem is shown in Figure 5.17 (and the file FIG5-17.xls on your data disk).

The spreadsheet in Figure 5.17 is very similar those of the other network flow problems we have solved. Cells A6 through A19 represent the decision variables (arcs) for our model, and the corresponding unit cost associated with each variable is listed

Figure 5.17
Spreadsheet
model for Coal
Bank Hollow
Recycling's
generalized
network flow
problem.

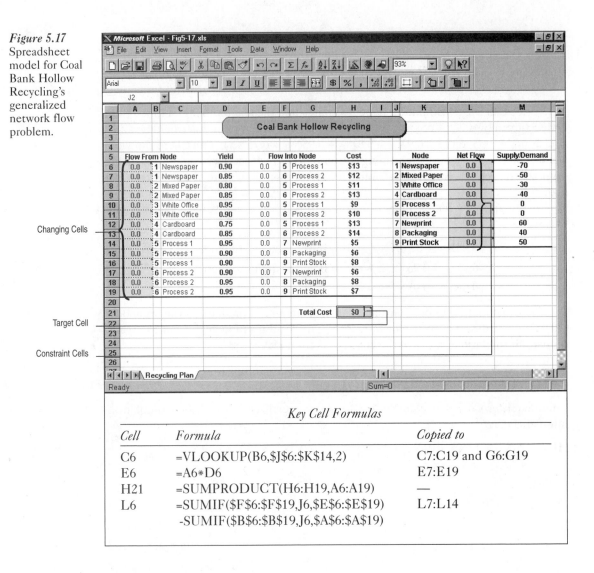

Key Cell Formulas

Cell	Formula	Copied to
C6	=VLOOKUP(B6,$J$6:$K$14,2)	C7:C19 and G6:G19
E6	=A6*D6	E7:E19
H21	=SUMPRODUCT(H6:H19,A6:A19)	—
L6	=SUMIF($F$6:$F$19,J6,$E$6:$E$19)	L7:L14
	-SUMIF($B$6:$B$19,J6,$A$6:$A$19)	

in the range from H6 through H19. The objective function is implemented in cell H21 as:

Formula for cell H21:   =SUMPRODUCT(H6:H19,A6:A19)

To implement the LHS formulas for our constraints we can no longer simply sum the variables flowing into each node and subtract the variables flowing out of the nodes. Instead, we need to first multiply the variables flowing into a node by the appropriate yield factor. With the yield factors entered in column D, the yield-adjusted flow for each arc is computed in column E as follows:

Formula for cell E6:   =A6*D6
(Copy to cells E7 through E19.)

Now to implement the LHS formulas for each node in cells L6 through L14, we will sum the yield-adjusted flows into each node and subtract the raw flow out of each node. This may be done as follows:

Formula for cell L6:	=SUMIF($F$6:$F$19,J6,$E$6:$E$19)-
(Copy to cells L7 through L14.)	SUMIF($B$6:$B$19,J6,$A$6:$A$19)

Notice that the first SUMIF function in this formula sums the appropriate yield-adjusted flows in column E while the second SUMIF sums the appropriate raw flow values from column A. Thus, while this formula is very similar to the ones used in earlier models, there is a critical difference here that must be carefully noted and understood. The RHS values for these constraint cells are listed in cells M6 through M14.

5.5.3 Analyzing the Solution

The Solver options and parameters used to solve this problem are shown in Figure 5.18 and the optimal solution is shown in Figure 5.19.

In this solution, 43.4 tons of newspaper, 50 tons of mixed paper, and 30 tons of white office paper are assigned to recycling process 1 (i.e., $X_{15} = 43.4$, $X_{25} = 50$, $X_{35} = 30$). This recycling process then yields a total of 107.6 tons of pulp (i.e., $0.9*43.3 + 0.8*50 + 0.95*30 = 107.6$) of which 63.2 tons are allocated to the production of newsprint pulp ($X_{57} = 63.2$) and 44.4 tons are allocated to the production of pulp for packaging paper ($X_{58} = 44.4$). This allows us to meet the demand for 60 tons of newsprint pulp ($0.95*63.2 = 60$) and 40 tons of packaging paper ($0.90*44.4 = 40$).

The remaining 26.6 tons of newspaper are combined with 35.4 tons of cardboard in recycling process 2 (i.e., $X_{16} = 26.6$, $X_{46} = 35.4$). This results in a yield of 52.6 tons of pulp (i.e., $0.85*26.6 + 0.85*35.4 = 52.6$) which is all devoted to the production of 50 tons of print stock quality pulp ($0.95*52.6 = 50$).

It is important for Nancy to note that this production plan calls for the use of all her supply of newspaper, mixed paper, and white office paper, but leaves about 4.6 tons of cardboard left over. Thus, she should be able to lower her total costs further

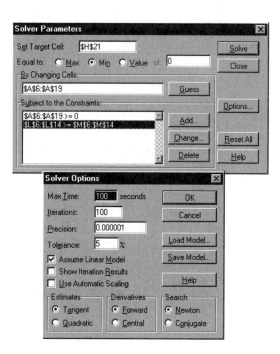

Figure 5.18
Solver parameters and options for the recycling problem.

Figure 5.19
Optimal solution
to Coal Bank
Hollow
Recycling's
generalized
network flow
problem.

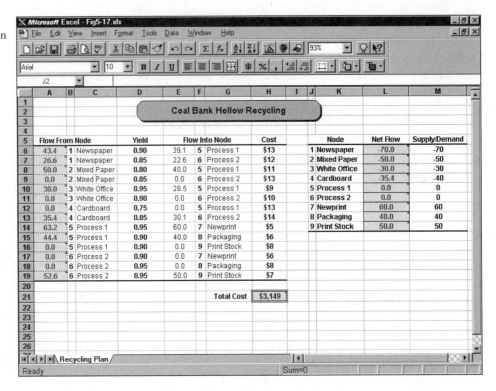

by acquiring more newspaper, mixed paper, or white office paper. It would be wise for her to see if she could trade her surplus cardboard to another recycler for the material she is running short on.

5.6   MAXIMAL FLOW PROBLEMS

The **maximal flow problem** (or max flow problem) is another type of network flow problem where the goal is to determine the maximum amount of flow that can occur in the network. In a maximal flow problem, the amount of flow that can occur over each arc is limited by some capacity restriction. This type of network might be used to model the flow of oil in a pipeline (where the amount of oil that can flow through a pipe in a unit of time is limited by the diameter of the pipe). Traffic engineers also use this type of network to determine the maximum number of cars that can travel through a collection of streets with different capacities imposed by the number of lanes in the streets and speed limits. The following example illustrates a max flow problem.

5.6.1   An Example of a Maximal Flow Problem

The Northwest Petroleum Company operates an oil field and refinery in Alaska. The crude obtained from the oil field is pumped through the network of pumping substations shown in Figure 5.20 to the company's refinery located 500 miles from the oil field. The amount of oil that can flow through each of the pipelines, represented by the arcs in the network, varies due to differing pipe diameters. The numbers next to the arcs in the network indicate the maximum amount of oil that can flow through the various pipelines (measured in thousands of barrels per hour). The company wants to determine the maximum number of barrels per hour that can flow from the oil field to the refinery.

The max flow problem appears to be very different from the network flow models described earlier because it does not include specific supplies or demands for the nodes. However, you can solve the max flow problem in the same way as a transshipment problem if you add a return arc from the ending node to the starting node, assign a demand of 0 to all the nodes in the network, and attempt to maximize the flow over the return arc. Figure 5.21 shows these modifications to the problem.

To understand the network in Figure 5.21, suppose that k units are shipped from node 6 to node 1 (where k represents some integer). Because node 6 has a supply of 0, it can send k units to node 1 only if these units can be returned through the network to node 6 (to balance the flow at node 6). The capacities on the arcs limit how many units can be returned to node 6. Therefore, the maximum flow through the network corresponds to the largest number of units that can be shipped from node 6 to node 1 and then returned through the network to node 6 (to balance the flow at this node). We can solve an LP model to determine the maximal flow by maximizing the flow from node 6 to node 1, given appropriate upper bounds on each arc and the usual balance-of-flow constraints. This model is represented as:

MAX: X_{61}

Subject to: $+X_{61} - X_{12} - X_{13} = 0$ } flow constraint for node 1

$+X_{12} - X_{24} - X_{25} = 0$ } flow constraint for node 2

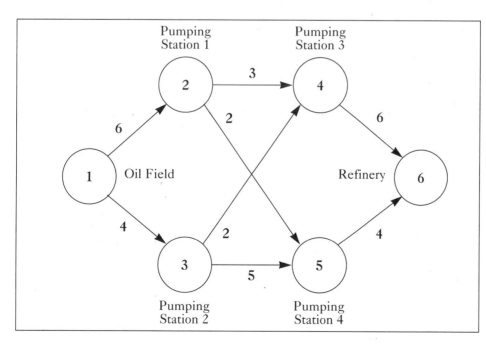

Figure 5.20
Network representation of Northwest Petroleum's oil refinery operation.

Figure 5.21
Network
structure of
Northwest
Petroleum's max
flow problem.

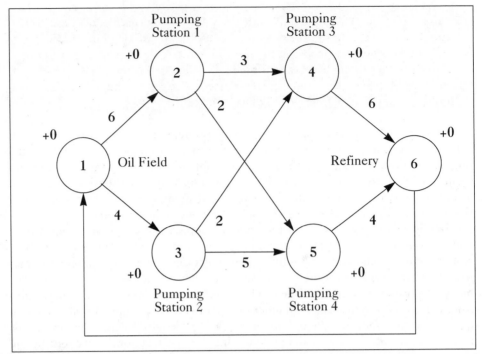

$$+X_{13} - X_{34} - X_{35} = 0 \quad \} \text{ flow constraint for node 3}$$
$$+X_{24} + X_{34} - X_{46} = 0 \quad \} \text{ flow constraint for node 4}$$
$$+X_{25} + X_{35} - X_{56} = 0 \quad \} \text{ flow constraint for node 5}$$
$$+X_{46} + X_{56} - X_{61} = 0 \quad \} \text{ flow constraint for node 6}$$

with the following bounds on the decision variables:

$$0 \leq X_{12} \leq 6 \quad 0 \leq X_{25} \leq 2 \quad 0 \leq X_{46} \leq 6$$
$$0 \leq X_{13} \leq 4 \quad 0 \leq X_{34} \leq 2 \quad 0 \leq X_{56} \leq 4$$
$$0 \leq X_{24} \leq 3 \quad 0 \leq X_{35} \leq 5 \quad 0 \leq X_{61} \leq \infty$$

5.6.2   The Spreadsheet Model and Solution

This model is implemented in the spreadsheet shown in Figure 5.22 (and in the file FIG5-22.xls on your data disk). This spreadsheet model differs from the earlier network models in a few minor, but important, ways. First, column G in Figure 5.22 represents the upper bounds for each arc. Second, the objective function (or target cell) is represented by cell B16, which contains the formula:

Formula in cell B16:   =B14

Cell B14 represents the flow from node 6 to node 1 (or X_{61}). This cell corresponds to the variable we want to maximize in the objective function of the LP model. The Solver parameters and options shown in Figure 5.23 are used to obtain the optimal solution shown in Figure 5.22.

Because the arcs leading to node 6 (X_{46} and X_{56}) have a total capacity for ten units of flow, it might be surprising to learn that only nine units can flow through the

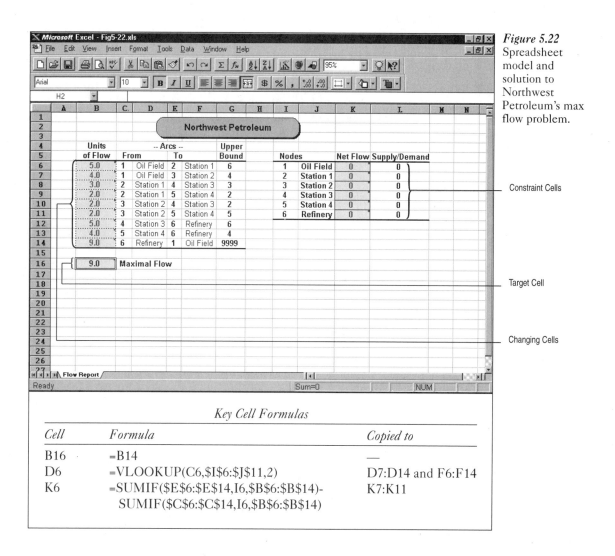

Figure 5.22
Spreadsheet model and solution to Northwest Petroleum's max flow problem.

Constraint Cells

Target Cell

Changing Cells

Key Cell Formulas

Cell	Formula	Copied to
B16	=B14	—
D6	=VLOOKUP(C6,$I$6:$J$11,2)	D7:D14 and F6:F14
K6	=SUMIF($E$6:$E$14,I6,$B$6:$B$14)-SUMIF($C$6:$C$14,I6,$B$6:$B$14)	K7:K11

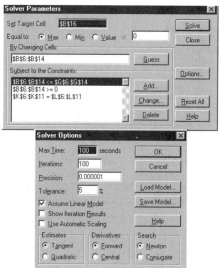

Figure 5.23
Solver parameters and options for Northwest Petroleum's max flow problem.

network. However, the optimal solution shown in Figure 5.22 indicates that the max-imal flow through the network is just nine units.

The optimal flows identified in Figure 5.22 for each arc are shown in the boxes next to the capacities for each arc in Figure 5.24. In Figure 5.24, the arc from node 5 to node 6 is at its full capacity of four units, whereas the arc from node 4 to node 6 is one unit below its full capacity of six units. Although the arc from node 4 to node 6 can carry one additional unit of flow, it is prevented from doing so because all the arcs flowing to node 4 (X_{24} and X_{34}) are at full capacity.

A graph like Figure 5.24, which summarizes the optimal flows in a max flow prob-lem, is helpful in identifying where increases in flow capacity would be most effec-tive. For example, from this graph we can see that even though X_{24} and X_{34} are both at full capacity, increasing their capacity will not necessarily increase the flow through the network. Increasing the capacity of X_{24} would allow for an increased flow through the network because an additional unit could then flow from node 1 to node 2 to node 4 to node 6. However, increasing the capacity of X_{34} would not allow for an increase in the total flow because the arc from node 1 to node 3 is already at full capacity.

5.7   MINIMAL SPANNING TREE PROBLEMS

Another type of network problem is known as the **minimal spanning tree problem.** This type of problem cannot be solved as an LP problem, but is solved easily using a simple manual algorithm.

For a network with *n* nodes, a **spanning tree** is a set of *n* – 1 arcs that connects all the nodes and contains no loops. A minimal spanning tree problem involves deter-mining the set of arcs that connects all the nodes in a network while minimizing the total length (or cost) of the selected arcs. Consider the example on the next page:

Figure 5.24
Network representation of the solution to Northwest Petroleum's max flow problem.

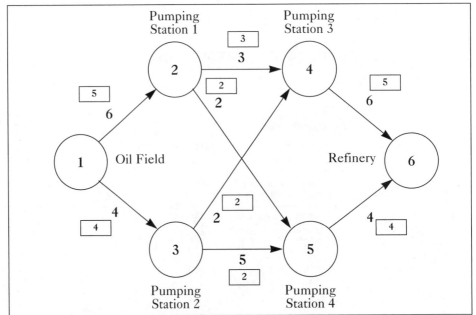

Jon Fleming is responsible for setting up a local area network (LAN) in the design engineering department of Windstar Aerospace Company. A LAN consists of a number of individual computers connected to a centralized computer or file server. Each computer in the LAN can access information from the file server and communicate with the other computers in the LAN.

Installing a LAN involves connecting all the computers together with coaxial cables. Individual computers do not have to be connected directly to the file server, but there must be some link between each computer in the network. Figure 5.25 summarizes all the possible connections that Jon can make. Each node in this figure represents one of the computers to be included in the LAN. Each line connecting the nodes represents a possible connection between pairs of computers. The dollar amount on each line represents the cost of making the connection.

The arcs in Figure 5.25 have no specific directional orientation, indicating that information can move in either direction across the arcs. Also note that the communication links represented by the arcs do not exist yet. Jon's challenge is to determine which links to establish. Because the network involves $n = 6$ nodes, a spanning tree for this problem consists of $n - 1 = 5$ arcs that results in a path existing between any pair of nodes. The objective is to find the minimal (least costly) spanning tree for this problem.

5.7.1 An Algorithm for the Minimal Spanning Tree Problem

You can apply a simple algorithm to solve minimal spanning tree problems. The steps to this algorithm are shown on the next page.

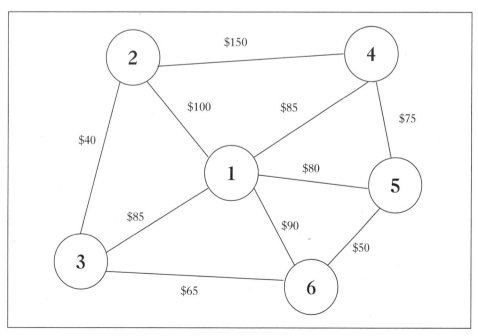

Figure 5.25
Network representation of Windstar Aerospace's minimal spanning tree problem.

1. Select any node. Call this the current subnetwork.
2. Add to the current subnetwork the cheapest arc that connects any node within the current subnetwork to any node not in the current subnetwork. (Ties for the cheapest arc can be broken arbitrarily.) Call this the current subnetwork.
3. If all the nodes are in the subnetwork, stop; this is the optimal solution. Otherwise, return to step 2.

5.7.2   Solving the Example Problem

You can program this algorithm easily or, for simple problems, execute it manually. The following steps illustrate how to execute the algorithm manually for the example problem shown in Figure 5.25.

Step 1.   If we select node 1 in Figure 5.25, then node 1 is the current subnetwork.

Step 2.   The cheapest arc connecting the current subnetwork to a node not in the current subnetwork is the $80 arc connecting nodes 1 and 5. This arc and node 5 are added to the current subnetwork.

Step 3.   Four nodes (nodes 2, 3, 4, and 6) remain unconnected—therefore, return to step 2.

Step 2.   The cheapest arc connecting the current subnetwork to a node not in the current subnetwork is the $50 arc connecting nodes 5 and 6. This arc and node 6 are added to the current subnetwork.

Step 3.   Three nodes (nodes 2, 3, and 4) remain unconnected—therefore, return to step 2.

Step 2.   The cheapest arc connecting the current subnetwork to a node not in the current subnetwork is the $65 arc connecting nodes 6 and 3. This arc and node 3 are added to the current subnetwork.

Step 3.   Two nodes (nodes 2 and 4) remain unconnected—therefore, return to step 2.

Step 2.   The cheapest arc connecting the current subnetwork to a node not in the current subnetwork is the $40 arc connecting nodes 3 and 2. This arc and node 2 are added to the current subnetwork.

Step 3.   One node (node 4) remains unconnected—therefore, return to step 2.

Step 2.   The cheapest arc connecting the current subnetwork to a node not in the current subnetwork is the $75 arc connecting nodes 5 and 4. This arc and node 4 are added to the current subnetwork.

Step 3.   All the nodes are now connected. Stop; the current subnetwork is optimal.

Figure 5.26 shows the optimal (minimal) spanning tree generated by this algorithm. The algorithm described here produces the optimal (minimal) spanning tree regardless of which node is selected initially in step 1. You can verify this by solving the example problem again starting with a different node in step 1.

SUMMARY

This chapter presented several business problems modeled as network flow problems, including transshipment problems, shortest path problems, maximal flow problems, transportation/assignment problems, and generalized network flow models. It also introduced the minimal spanning tree problem and presented a simple algorithm for solving this type of problem manually.

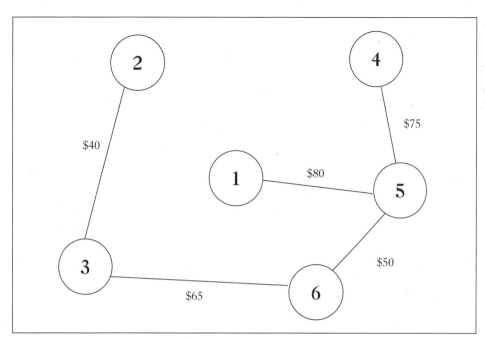

Figure 5.26
Optimal solution to Windstar Aerospace's minimal spanning tree problem.

Although special algorithms exist for solving network flow problems, you can also formulate and solve them as LP problems. The constraints in an LP formulation of a network flow problem have a special structure that enables you to implement and solve these models easily in a spreadsheet. Although there might be more efficient ways of solving network flow problems, the methods discussed in this chapter are often the most practical. For extremely complex network flow problems, you might need to use a specialized algorithm. Unfortunately, you are unlikely to find this type of software at your local software store. However, various network optimization packages can be found in the technical/scientific directories on the Internet.

THE WORLD OF MANAGEMENT SCIENCE
Yellow Freight System Boosts Profits and Quality with Network Optimization

One of the largest motor carriers in the United States, Yellow Freight System, Inc. of Overland Park, Kansas, uses network modeling and optimization to assist management in load planning, routing empty trucks, routing trailers, dropping or adding direct service routes, and strategic planning of terminal size and location. The system, called SYSNET, operates on a network of Sun workstations optimizing over a million network flow variables. The company also uses a tactical planning room equipped with graphical display tools that allow planning meetings to be conducted interactively with the system.

The company competes in the less-than-truckload (LTL) segment of the trucking market. That is, they contract for shipments of any size, regardless of whether the shipment fills the trailer. To operate efficiently, Yellow Freight must consolidate and transfer shipments at 23 break-bulk terminals located throughout the United States. At these terminals, shipments might be reloaded into different trailers depending on the final destination. Each break-bulk terminal serves several end-of-line terminals, in a hub-and-spoke network. Normally, shipments are sent by truck to the break-bulk dedicated to the origination point. Local managers occasionally try to save costs by loading direct, which means bypassing a break-bulk and sending a truckload of consolidated shipments directly to the final destination. Before SYSNET, these decisions were made in the field without accurate information on how they would affect costs and reliability in the entire system.

Since its implementation in 1989, SYSNET has scored high with upper management. Often, the first response to a new proposal is, "Has it been run through SYSNET?" The benefits attributed to the new system include:

- an increase of 11.6% in freight loaded directly, saving $4.7 million annually
- better routing of trailers, saving $1 million annually
- savings of $1.42 million annually by increasing the average number of pounds loaded per trailer
- reduction in claims for damaged merchandise
- a 27% reduction in the number of late deliveries
- tactical planning projects with SYSNET in 1990 that identified $10 million in annual savings

Equally important has been the effect on the management philosophy and culture at Yellow Freight. Management now has greater control over network operations; tradition, intuition, and "gut feel" have been replaced with formal analytical tools; and Yellow Freight is better able to act as a partner with customers in total quality management and just-in-time inventory systems.

Source: Braklow, John W., William W. Graham, Stephen M. Hassler, Ken E. Peck and Warren B. Powell, "Interactive Optimization Improves Service and Performance for Yellow Freight System," *Interfaces*, 22:1, January–February 1992, pages 147–172.

QUESTIONS AND PROBLEMS

1. This chapter followed the convention of using negative numbers to represent the supply at a node and positive numbers to represent the demand at a node. Another convention is just the opposite—using positive numbers to represent supply and negative numbers to represent demand. How would the balance-of-flow rules presented in this chapter need to be changed to accommodate this alternate convention?

√ 2. To use the balance-of-flow rules presented in this chapter, constraints for supply nodes must have negative RHS values. Some LP software packages cannot solve problems in which the constraints have negative RHS values. How should the balance-of-flow rules be modified to produce LP models that can be solved with such software packages?

3. Consider the generalized transportation problem shown in Figure 5.27. How can this problem be transformed into an equivalent transportation problem? Draw the network for the equivalent problem.

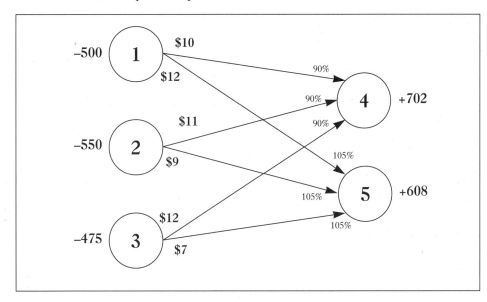

Figure 5.27
Graph of a generalized network flow problem.

4. Draw the network representation of the following network flow problem.

MIN: $+7X_{12} + 6X_{14} + 3X_{23} + 4X_{24} + 5X_{32} + 9X_{43} + 8X_{52} + 5X_{54}$

Subject to:

$$-X_{12} - X_{14} = -5$$
$$+X_{12} + X_{52} + X_{32} - X_{23} - X_{24} = +4$$
$$-X_{32} + X_{23} + X_{43} = +8$$
$$+X_{14} + X_{24} + X_{54} - X_{43} = +0$$
$$-X_{52} - X_{54} = -7$$

$X_{ij} \geq 0$ for all i and j

5. Draw the network representation of the following network flow problem. What kind of network flow problem is this?

MIN: $+2X_{13} + 6X_{14} + 5X_{15} + 4X_{23} + 3X_{24} + 7X_{25}$

Subject to:

$$-X_{13} - X_{14} - X_{15} = -8$$
$$-X_{23} - X_{24} - X_{25} = -7$$
$$+X_{13} + X_{23} = +5$$
$$+X_{14} + X_{24} = +5$$
$$+X_{15} + X_{25} = +5$$

$X_{ij} \geq 0$ for all i and j

6. Refer to the equipment replacement problem discussed in this chapter. In addition to the lease costs described for the problem, suppose that it costs Compu-Train $2,000 extra in labor costs whenever they replace their existing computers with new ones. What effect does this have on the formulation and solution of the problem? Which of the two leasing contracts is optimal in this case?

7. Acme Manufacturing makes a variety of household appliances at a single manufacturing facility. The expected demand for one of these appliances during the
next four months is shown in the following table along with the expected production costs and the expected capacity for producing these items.

	Month			
	1	2	3	4
Demand	420	580	310	540
Production Cost	$49.00	$45.00	$46.00	$47.00
Production Capacity	500	520	450	550

Acme estimates it costs $1.50 per month for each unit of this appliance carried in
inventory at the end of each month. Currently, Acme has 120 units in inventory
on hand for this product. To maintain a level workforce, the company wants to
produce at least 400 units per month. They also want to maintain a safety stock of
at least 50 units per month. Acme wants to determine how many of each appliance
to manufacture during each of the next four months to meet the expected demand
at the lowest possible total cost.

a. Draw a network flow model for this problem.
b. Create a spreadsheet model for this problem and solve it using Solver.
c. What is the optimal solution?
d. How much money could Acme save if they were willing to drop the restriction
   about producing at least 400 units per month?

8. A construction company wants to determine the optimal replacement policy for
the earth mover it owns. The company has a policy of not keeping an earth mover
for more than five years and has estimated the annual operating costs and trade-
in values for earth movers during each of the five years they might be kept as:

	Age in Years				
	0–1	1–2	2–3	3–4	4–5
Operating Cost	$8,000	$9,100	$10,700	$9,200	$11,000
Trade-in Value	$14,000	$9,000	$6,000	$3,500	$2,000

Assume that new earth movers currently cost $25,000 and are increasing in cost by
4.5% per year. The company wants to determine when it should plan on replacing its current, two-year-old earth mover. Use a five-year planning horizon.

a. Draw the network representation of this problem.
b. Solve the problem using Solver. Interpret your solution.
c. What other economic factors should the company consider including in this
   model?

9. The Ortega Food Company needs to ship 100 cases of hot tamales from its warehouse in San Diego to a distributor in New York City at minimum cost. The costs
associated with shipping between various cities are:

| | To | | | | | |
From	*Los Angeles*	*Denver*	*St. Louis*	*Memphis*	*Chicago*	*New York*
San Diego	5	13	—	45	—	105
Los Angeles	—	27	19	50	—	95
Denver	—	—	14	30	32	—
St. Louis	—	14	—	35	24	—
Memphis	—	—	35	—	18	25
Chicago	—	—	24	18	—	17

    a.   Draw the network representation of this problem.

    b.   Write out the LP formulation of this problem.

    c.   Solve the problem using Solver. Interpret your solution.

10. A furniture manufacturer has warehouses in cities represented by nodes 1, 2, and 3 in Figure 5.28. The values on the arcs indicate the per-unit shipping costs required to transport living room suites between the various cities. The supply of living room suites at each warehouse is indicated by the negative number next to nodes 1, 2, and 3. The demand for living room suites is indicated by the positive number next to the remaining nodes.

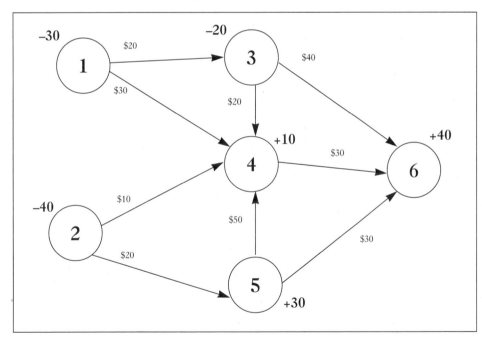

Figure 5.28
Network flow model for the furniture manufacturing problem.

    a.   Identify the supply, demand, and transshipment nodes in this problem.

    b.   Use Solver to determine the least costly shipping plan for this problem.

11. The graph in Figure 5.29 represents various flows that can occur through a sewage treatment plant, with the numbers on the arcs representing the maximum flow (in tons of sewage per hour) that can be accommodated. Formulate an LP model to determine the maximum tons of sewage per hour that can be processed by this plant.

Figure 5.29
Network flow
model for the
sewage
treatment plant.

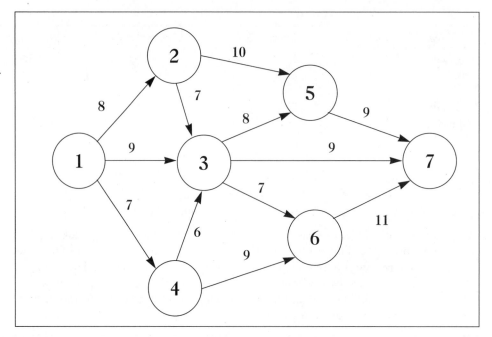

12. A company has three warehouses that supply four stores with a given product. Each warehouse has 30 units of the product. Stores 1, 2, 3, and 4 require 20, 25, 30, and 35 units of the product, respectively. The per-unit shipping costs from each warehouse to each store are:

	Store			
Warehouse	*1*	*2*	*3*	*4*
1	5	4	6	5
2	3	6	4	4
3	4	3	3	2

   a. Draw the network representation of this problem. What kind of problem is this?
   b. Formulate an LP model to determine the least expensive shipping plan to fill the demands at the stores.
   c. Solve the problem using Solver.
   d. Suppose that shipments are not allowed between warehouse 1 and store 2 or between warehouse 2 and store 3. What is the easiest way to modify the spreadsheet so that you can solve this modified problem? What is the optimal solution to the modified problem?

13. A used-car broker needs to transport his inventory of cars from locations 1 and 2 in Figure 5.30 to used-car auctions being held at locations 4 and 5. The costs of transporting cars along each of the routes are indicated on the arcs. The trucks used to carry the cars can hold a maximum of 10 cars. Therefore, the maximum number of cars that can flow over any arc is 10.

   a. Formulate an LP model to determine the least costly method of distributing the cars from locations 1 and 2 so that 20 cars will be available for sale at location 4, and 10 cars will be available for sale at location 5.
   b. Use Solver to find the optimal solution to this problem.

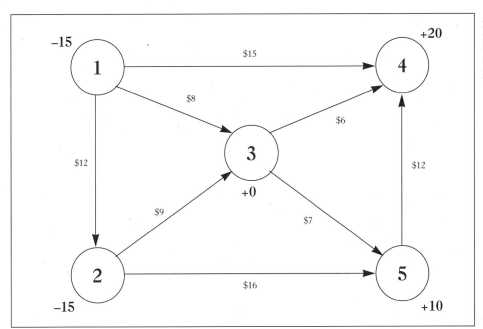

Figure 5.30
Network flow
model for the
used car
problem.

14. A information systems consultant who lives in Dallas must spend the majority of the month of March on site with a client in San Diego. Her travel schedule for the month is as follows:

Leave Dallas	Leave San Diego
Monday, March 2	Friday, March 6
Monday, March 9	Thursday, March 12
Tuesday, March 17	Friday, March 20
Monday, March 23	Wednesday, March 25

The usual round-trip ticket price between Dallas and San Diego is $750. However, the airline offers a 25% discount if the dates on a round-trip ticket cover less than seven nights and include a weekend. A 35% discount is offered for round-trip tickets covering ten or more nights, and a 45% discount is available for round-trip tickets covering 20 or more nights. The consultant can purchase four round-trip tickets in any manner that allows her to leave Dallas and San Diego on the days indicated above.

a. Draw a network flow model for this problem.
b. Implement the problem in a spreadsheet and solve it.
c. What is the optimal solution? How much does this save for four full-cost round-trip tickets?

15. Omega Airlines has several nonstop flights between Atlanta and Los Angeles every day. The schedules of these flights are given on the next page. Omega would like to determine the optimal way of assigning flight crews to these different flights. The company wants to ensure that the crews always return to the city from which they left each day. FAA regulations require at least one hour of rest for flight crews between flights. However, flight crews become irritated if they are

Flight	Departs Atlanta	Arrives in L.A.		Flight	Departs L.A.	Arrives in Atlanta
1	6 am	8 am		1	5 am	9 am
2	8 am	10 am		2	6 am	10 am
3	10 am	Noon		3	9 am	1 pm
4	Noon	2 pm		4	Noon	4 pm
5	4 pm	6 pm		5	2 pm	6 pm
6	6 pm	8 pm		6	5 pm	9 pm
7	7 pm	9 pm		7	7 pm	11 pm

forced to wait for extremely long periods of time between flights, so Omega would like to find an assignment of flight schedules that minimizes these wait periods.

a. Draw a network flow model for this problem.
b. Implement the problem in a spreadsheet and solve it.
c. What is the optimal solution? What is the longest period of time a flight crew has to wait between flights according to your solution?
d. Is there another solution to this problem where the longest layover time is less than seven hours?

16. Joe Jones would like to establish a construction fund (or sinking fund) to pay for a new bowling alley he is having built. Construction of the bowling alley is expected to take six months and cost $300,000. Joe's contract with the construction company requires him to make payments of $50,000 at the end of the second and fourth months, and a final payment of $200,000 at the end of the sixth month when the restaurant is completed. Joe has identified four investments he can use to establish the construction fund; these investments are summarized in the following table:

Investment	Available in Month	Months to Maturity	Yield at Maturity
A	1, 2, 3, 4, 5, 6	1	1.2%
B	1, 3, 5	2	3.5%
C	1, 4	3	5.8%
D	1	6	11.0%

The table indicates that investment A will be available at the beginning of each of the next six months, and funds invested in this manner mature in one month with a yield of 1.2%. Similarly, funds can be placed in investment C only at the beginning of months 1 and/or 4, and mature at the end of three months with a yield of 5.8%. Joe would like to minimize the amount of money he must invest in month 1 to meet the required payments for this project.

a. Draw a network flow model for this problem.
b. Create a spreadsheet model for this problem and solve it.
c. What is the optimal solution?

17. Telephone calls for the YakLine, a discount long-distance carrier, are routed through a variety of switching devices that interconnect various network hubs in different cities. The maximum number of calls that can be handled by each segment of its network is shown on the next page.

Network Segments	Calls (in 1,000s)
Washington, D.C. to Chicago	800
Washington, D.C. to Kansas City	650
Washington, D.C. to Dallas	700
Chicago to Dallas	725
Chicago to Denver	700
Kansas City to Denver	750
Kansas City to Dallas	625
Denver to San Francisco	900
Dallas to San Francisco	725

YakLine wishes to determine the maximum number of calls its network can handle.

a. Draw a network flow model for this problem.
b. Create a spreadsheet model for this problem and solve it.
c. What is the optimal solution?

18. Union Express has 60 tons of cargo that need to be shipped from Boston to Dallas. The shipping capacity on each of the routes Union Express planes fly each night is shown in the following table:

Nightly Flight Segments	Capacity (in tons)
Boston to Baltimore	30
Boston to Pittsburgh	25
Boston to Cincinnati	35
Baltimore to Atlanta	10
Baltimore to Cincinnati	5
Pittsburgh to Atlanta	15
Pittsburgh to Chicago	20
Cincinnati to Chicago	15
Cincinnati to Memphis	5
Atlanta to Memphis	25
Atlanta to Dallas	10
Chicago to Memphis	20
Chicago to Dallas	15
Memphis to Dallas	30
Memphis to Chicago	15

Will Union Express be able to move all 60 tons from Boston to Dallas in one night?

a. Draw a network flow model for this problem.
b. Create a spreadsheet model for the problem and solve it.
c. What is the maximum flow for this network?

19. A new airport being built will have three terminals and two baggage pickup areas. An automated baggage delivery system has been designed to transport the baggage from each terminal to the two baggage pickup areas. This system is depicted graphically in Figure 5.31, where nodes 1, 2, and 3 represent the terminals, and nodes 7 and 8 represent the baggage pickup areas. The maximum number of bags per minute that can be handled by each part of the system is indicated by the value on each arc in the network.

Figure 5.31
Network flow
model for the
airport terminal
problem.

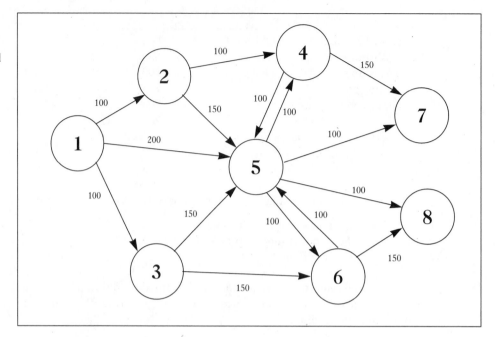

a. Formulate an LP model to determine the maximum number of bags per minute that can be delivered by this system.
b. Use Solver to find the optimal solution to this problem.

20. Bull Dog Express runs a small airline that offers commuter flights between several cities in Georgia. The airline flies into and out of small airports only. These airports have limits on the number of flights Bull Dog Express can make each day. The airline can make five round-trip flights daily between Savannah and Macon, four round-trip flights daily between Macon and Albany, two round-trip flights daily between Macon and Atlanta, two round-trip flights daily between Macon and Athens, two round-trip flights daily between Athens and Atlanta, and two round-trip flights daily from Albany to Atlanta. The airline wants to determine the maximum number of times connecting flights from Savannah to Atlanta can be offered in a single day.

a. Draw the network representation of this problem.
b. Formulate an LP model for this problem. What kind of problem is this?
c. Use Solver to determine the optimal solution to this problem.

21. The U.S. Department of Transportation (DOT) is planning to build a new interstate to run from Detroit, Michigan, to Charleston, South Carolina. A number of different routes have been proposed and are summarized in Figure 5.32, where node 1 represents Detroit and node 12 represents Charleston. The numbers on the arcs indicate the estimated construction costs of the various links (in millions of dollars). It is estimated that all of the routes will require approximately the same total driving time to make the trip from Detroit to Charleston. Thus, the DOT is interested in identifying the least costly alternative.

a. Formulate an LP model to determine the least costly construction plan.
b. Use Solver to determine the optimal solution to this problem.

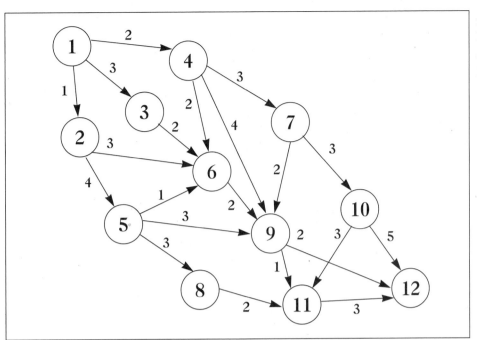

Figure 5.32
Possible routes
for the interstate
construction
problem.

✓ 22. A building contractor is designing the ductwork for the heating and air condition-
ing system in a new, single-story medical building. Figure 5.33 summarizes the
possible connections between the primary air handling unit (node 1) and the various air outlets to be placed in the building (nodes 2 through 9). The arcs in the
network represent possible ductwork connections, and the values on the arcs represent the feet of ductwork required.

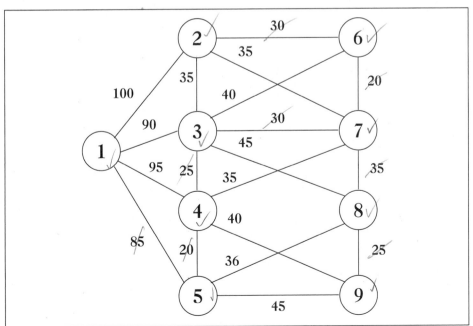

Figure 5.33
Network
representation of
the ductwork
problem.

Starting at node 1, use the minimal spanning tree algorithm to determine how much ductwork should be installed to provide air access to each vent while requiring the least amount of ductwork.

23. As rush coordinator for the Alpha Beta Chi (ABC) sorority, Kim Grant asked each pledge to identify five existing members of ABC whom she would most like to have as a big sister. Kim then asks the pledges to rank these potential big sisters from 5 down to 1, where 5 represents the person they most want as a big sister, 4 represents their next choice, and so on. These rankings are summarized in the following table:

	Big Sisters														
Pledges	1	2	3	4	5	6	7	8	9	10	11	12	13	14	15
1			5		3			1			2	·			4
2		5		2		1		4		3					
3	2		3			4		5				1			
4		5	4				1		2						3
5		3			5				2				4	1	

After much consideration, Kim decides that this problem is similar to some of the problems she encountered in a management science class she took during her sophomore year. She knows that every pledge must be assigned a big sister, and each potential big sister can be assigned no more than one pledge. Ideally, Kim wants to assign each pledge to the big sister to whom she gave a ranking of 5. The sum of the rankings for such an assignment is 25 because each of the five pledges would be assigned to the big sister they ranked as number 5. But in the above table, that would involve assigning pledges 2 and 4 to the same big sister, which is not allowable. Kim figures that the next best strategy is to determine the assignment that maximizes the sum of the rankings.

a. Create a spreadsheet model for Kim's problem and solve it.
b. Which pledges should be assigned to which big sisters?
c. Can you think of another objective that Kim might use to solve her problem?

24. The manager of catering services for the Roanoker Hotel has a problem. The banquet hall at the hotel is booked each evening during the coming week for groups who have reserved the following numbers of tables:

Day	Monday	Tuesday	Wednesday	Thursday	Friday
Tables Reserved	400	300	250	400	350

The hotel has 500 tablecloths that can be used for these banquets. However, the tablecloths used at each banquet will have to be cleaned before they can be used again. A local cleaning service will pick up the soiled tablecloths each evening after the banquet and offers overnight cleaning for $2 per tablecloth, or two-day service for $1 per tablecloth (i.e., a cloth picked up Monday night can be ready Tuesday for $2 or ready for use Wednesday for $1). Due to the cleaner's capacity restrictions, the overnight service can be performed on only up to 250 tablecloths, and overnight service is not available on tablecloths picked up Friday night. The hotel would like to determine the least costly plan for having its tablecloths cleaned.

a. Draw a network flow model for this problem. (Hint: Express the supplies and demands as minimum required and maximum allowable flows over selected arcs.)

b. Create a spreadsheet model for this problem and solve it. What is the optimal solution?

CASE 5.1 THE MAJOR ELECTRIC CORPORATION

Henry Lee is the Vice President of Purchasing for the consumer electronics division of the Major Electric Corporation (MEC). The company recently introduced a new type of video camcorder that has taken the market by storm. While Henry is pleased with the strong demand for this product in the marketplace, it has been a challenge to keep up with MEC's distributors' orders of this camcorder. His current challenge is how to meet requests from MEC's major distributors in Pittsburgh, Denver, Baltimore, and Houston who have placed orders of 10,000, 20,000, 30,000, and 25,000 units, respectively, for delivery in two months. (There is a one-month manufacturing and a one-month shipping lead time for this product.)

MEC has contracts with companies in Hong Kong, Korea, and Singapore who manufacture camcorders for the company under the MEC label. These contracts require MEC to order a specified minimum number of units each month at guaranteed per unit cost. The contracts also specify the maximum number of units that may be ordered at this price. The following table summarizes these contracts:

Monthly Purchasing Contract Provisions

Supplier	Unit Cost	Minimum Required	Maximum Allowed
Hong Kong	$375	20,000	30,000
Korea	$390	25,000	40,000
Singapore	$365	15,000	30,000

MEC also has a standing contract with a shipping company to transport product from each of these suppliers to ports in San Francisco and San Diego. The cost of shipping from each supplier to each port is given in the following table along with the minimum required and maximum allowable number of shipping cartons each month:

Monthly Shipping Contract Provisions

	San Francisco Requirements			San Diego Shipping Requirements		
Supplier	Cost per Container	Minimum Containers	Maximum Containers	Cost per Container	Minimum Containers	Maximum Containers
Hong Kong	$2,000	5	20	$2,300	5	20
Korea	$1,800	10	30	$2,100	10	30
Singapore	$2,400	5	25	$2,200	5	15

Under the terms of this contract, MEC guarantees it will send at least 20 but no more than 65 shipping containers to San Francisco each month, and at least 30 but no more than 70 shipping containers to San Diego each month.

Each shipping container can hold 1,000 video cameras and will ultimately be trucked from the seaports to the distributors. Again, MEC has a standing contract with a trucking company to provide trucking services each month. The cost of trucking a shipping container from each port to each distributor is summarized below.

Unit Shipping Cost per Container

	Pittsburgh	Denver	Baltimore	Houston
San Francisco	$1,100	$850	$1,200	$1,000
San Diego	$1,200	$1,000	$1,100	$900

As with the other contracts, to obtain the prices given above, MEC is required to use a certain minimum amount of trucking capacity on each route each month and may not exceed certain maximum shipping amounts without incurring cost penalties. These minimum and maximum shipping restrictions are summarized below:

Minimum Required and Maximum Allowable Number of Shipping Containers per Month

	Pittsburgh		Denver		Baltimore		Houston	
	Min	Max	Min	Max	Min	Max	Min	Max
San Francisco	3	7	6	12	10	18	5	15
San Diego	4	6	5	14	5	20	10	20

So Henry is left with the task of sorting through all this information to determine the least costly purchasing and distribution plan to fill the distributors' requests. But because he and his wife have tickets to the symphony for this evening, he has asked you to take a look at this problem and give him your recommendations at 9:00 tomorrow morning.

1. Create a network flow model for this problem. (Hint: Consider inserting intermediate nodes in your network to assist in meeting the minimum monthly purchase restrictions for each supplier and the minimum monthly shipping requirements for each port.)

2. Implement a spreadsheet model for this problem and solve it.

3. What is the optimal solution?

CASE 5.2   TURNER AIRLINES

Fred Turner is a successful entrepreneur in Atlanta, Georgia, who has just hit upon his next-money making idea. Recently, Fred was planning to fly to Washington, D.C., early one morning for a business meeting. Fred's own personal Leer jet happened to have a mechanical problem that morning, which forced Fred to try to book a flight on a commercial carrier. Much to his dismay, Fred learned that all the flights to D.C. were overbooked, but he was told he might be able to get a seat if he waited at the gate as a standby passenger. When Fred arrived at the gate, he was surprised to find several people waiting, hoping to get on a flight as standby passengers.

When Fred saw this situation, he immediately saw a business opportunity. He knew that the route from Atlanta to Washington, D.C., was a popular one because these airports are two of the busiest in the world. And the frustration he saw on the faces of those waiting in line with him convinced him that there was money to be made here. Fred knew that it would be difficult to compete head to head against the established, full-service, international airlines. But he figured he could begin a flight service to fill the niche to business travelers wanting to travel between Atlanta and D.C.

Fred called some of his business associates and put some people to work on this idea. A month later, their marketing research revealed that there were several times during every business day when travelers would like to hop a plane going between Atlanta and D.C. They also discovered that many business travelers would prefer to fly to Dulles Airport in Washington while most airlines fly to Washington's National Airport. The following table summarizes the flight schedules where there is considerable unmet demand and the estimated revenues and variable costs that would be incurred in operating these flights.

Depart	Time	Arrive	Time	Est. Revenue	Variable Cost
Atlanta	8 am	Dulles	10 am	$1,600	$850
Atlanta	10 am	Dulles	12 noon	$1,400	$900
Atlanta	1 pm	Dulles	3 pm	$1,450	$920
Atlanta	4 pm	Dulles	6 pm	$1,900	$950
Dulles	9 am	Atlanta	11 am	$1,400	$850
Dulles	11 am	Atlanta	1 pm	$1,650	$1,080
Dulles	1 pm	Atlanta	3 pm	$1,700	$900
Dulles	5 pm	Atlanta	7 pm	$1,900	$1,025

In addition to the costs given above, the airport in Atlanta charges a $600 servicing charge for planes left there overnight, while this charge at Dulles is $700. Of course, there are also the costs of buying or leasing aircraft, hiring pilots, etc. Before pursuing this any further, Fred would like to know if the proposed flight schedule is profitable and how many planes it would take to implement it. And he has turned to you for help.

1. Draw the graph of the network flow problem Fred should solve to determine the minimum number of planes required to implement the proposed flight schedule in the most efficient manner.

2. Implement a model for this network in a spreadsheet and solve it.

3. Describe the optimal solution to the problem.

4. Suppose there was adequate demand to run two flights from Atlanta to Washington leaving Atlanta at 4 p.m. and arriving at Dulles at 6 p.m. Would this be more profitable than the current schedule? Should Fred be willing to sacrifice any of the current flights to add this second flight out of Atlanta at 4 p.m.?

CASE 5.3   MANEUVERS IN THE SENATE

Contributed by Jack Yurkiewicz, Lubin School of Business, Pace University

Sherill Wiley, the only reporter from Channel Four covering United States congressional proceedings, knows that the public's perception of partisan politics in the Senate is not entirely correct. Although Republicans and Democrats are often at loggerheads over many national issues—such as the crime bill and healthcare reform—members of the two parties frequently vote together on bills that are considered beneficial to both. Sherill was surprised at the level of cooperation between the parties when passing legislation that benefits a particular region. For example, if a Democratic senator from the West is sponsoring a bill that would provide funding to divert water from a river so that part of his sun-drenched state would eventually receive it, quite a few Republican senators would vote for such a bill. The Republican senators know that when they need votes for a project that would be advantageous for their states, the Democratic senators would return the favor and vote for that bill.

Richard Kennely, the leading Republican in the Senate and a strong conservative from a midwest state, has little if any direct interaction with Robin Doll. Doll, a senator from a New England state, is the Senate's most liberal Democrat. The two senators have never served on a committee together or participated in a joint task force. Yet the two often rely on each other and their respective parties when voting on many fiscal issues.

Senator Doll recently added an amendment to a finance bill that would provide funding for research on the effects of using a mouse when working on a computer. Several universities from Doll's state submitted grant proposals to do this research, citing the widespread use of the mouse and the growing number of people who complain of wrist and arm fatigue as a result. If the bill and the attached amendment pass, the universities in Doll's state would be the main beneficiaries of the funding. Sherill knows that Senator Kennely, who was recently on national television railing against what he referred to as "excessive spending for trivial research," would be the main opponent to the bill. Senator Doll cannot directly influence Senator Kennely's position or vote. But she can contact other senators with whom she has influence, pleading her case and hoping that they, in turn, will influence others who might eventually influence Senator Kennely to vote in favor of the bill.

After many years as a reporter in Washington, Sherill has developed a sense of the amount of influence one senator has on another, based on party affiliation, school ties, past favors, mutual interests, and so on. She even developed a numerical system, on a scale from 0 to 10 that quantifies the amount of influence one senator has on another. A 10 means that a particular senator is almost guaranteed to secure the vote of another senator, and a 0 means that there is no interaction at all between two senators. Sherill created a table that shows the senators' names and the amount of influence each has on the other.

Sherill saw Senators Abbott, Bartle, Crumb, Dodge, and Fernandez leave Senator Doll's office one morning last week. Looking at her influence table, she notes that Doll's influence on Abbott rates a 7, on Bartle a 6, a 9 for Crumb, only a 3 for Dodge, and a 4 for Fernandez. Later that week, Senator Abbott called in Senators Bartle and Dodge for a strategy meeting. Abbott's influence on Bartle is a 7 and on Dodge a 5.

Bartle next met with Senators Dodge, Evans, and Fernandez. Bartle's influence rating on these senators is a 4 on Dodge and on Evans, and a 5 on Fernandez. The senators continued to hold meetings with each other and with Senators Gene and

Harris. Sherill summarized the influence rating of all the senators in the following table:

From–To	Abbott	Bartle	Crumb	Dodge	Evans	Fernandez	Gene	Harris	Kennely
Doll	7	6	9	3	4				
Abbott		7		5					
Bartle				4	4	5			
Crumb		5			3				
Dodge					6		5		6
Evans				6		8			7
Fernandez					8			2	5
Gene									8
Harris									2

Sherill believes that if all the senators (other than Doll) bear at least 20 total units of influence on Senator Kennely, he would not be able to resist and he would have to vote for Senator Doll's bill. With Kennely's support, the bill would definitely pass because the rest of the Republicans and Democrats will follow their leaders.

Considering the amount of networking that takes place between the senators, Sherill thinks she can build and solve a network model to predict if the bill will pass or not.

Formulate a network model for Sherill and solve it. Will the bill pass? (Hint: Make a node for each senator.)

REFERENCES

Glassey, R. and V. Gupta. "A Linear Programming Analysis of Paper Recycling." *Studies in Mathematical Programming*. New York: North-Holland, 1978.

Glover, F. and D. Klingman. "Network Applications in Industry and Government." *AIIE Transactions*, vol. 9, no. 4, 1977.

Glover, F., D. Klingman, and N. Phillips. *Network Models and Their Applications in Practice*. New York: Wiley, 1992.

Hansen, P. and R. Wendell. "A Note on Airline Commuting." *Interfaces*, vol 11, no. 12, 1982.

Phillips, D. and A. Diaz. *Fundamentals of Network Analysis*. Englewood Cliffs, NJ: Prentice Hall, 1981.

Vemuganti, R., et al. "Network Models for Fleet Management." *Decision Sciences*, vol. 20, Winter 1989.

CHAPTER 6

Integer Linear Programming

When some or all of the decision variables in an LP problem are restricted to assuming only integer values, the resulting problem is referred to as an **integer linear programming (ILP) problem.** Many practical business problems need integer solutions. For example, Chapter 3 presented an employee scheduling problem for the Air-Express Company in which we determined the optimal number of employees to assign to each shift. When we formulated this problem as an LP problem, its optimal solution involved allocating fractional numbers of workers (for example, 7.33 workers) to different shifts; this is not an integer feasible solution. Similarly, if an airline is trying to decide how many 757s, 747s, and 737s to purchase, it must obtain an integer solution because the airline cannot buy fractions of planes.

This chapter discusses how to solve optimization problems in which some decision variables must assume only integer values. This chapter also shows how the use of integer variables allows us to build more accurate models for a number of business problems.

6.1 INTEGRALITY CONDITIONS

To illustrate some of the issues involved in an ILP problem, let's consider again the decision problem faced by Howie Jones, the owner of Blue Ridge Hot Tubs, described in Chapters 2, 3, and 4. This company sells two models of hot tubs, the Aqua-Spa and the Hydro-Lux, which it produces by purchasing prefabricated fiberglass hot tub shells and installing a common water pump and an appropriate amount of tubing. Each Aqua-Spa produced requires 1 pump, 9 hours of labor, and 12 feet of tubing, and contributes $350 to profits. Each Hydro-Lux produced requires 1 pump, 6 hours of labor, and 16 feet of tubing, and contributes $300 to profits. Assuming the company has 200 pumps, 1,566 labor hours, and 2,880 feet of tubing available, we created the following LP formulation for this problem where X_1 and X_2 represent the number of Aqua-Spas and Hydro-Luxes to produce:

$$
\begin{aligned}
\text{MAX:} \quad & 350X_1 + 300X_2 && \text{\} profit} \\
\text{Subject to:} \quad & 1X_1 + 1X_2 \leq 200 && \text{\} pump constraint} \\
& 9X_1 + 6X_2 \leq 1,566 && \text{\} labor constraint} \\
& 12X_1 + 16X_2 \leq 2,880 && \text{\} tubing constraint} \\
& X_1, X_2 \geq 0 && \text{\} nonnegativity conditions}
\end{aligned}
$$

Blue Ridge Hot Tubs is undoubtedly interested in obtaining the best possible *integer solution* to this problem because hot tubs can be sold only as discrete units. Thus, we can be sure the company wants to find the *optimal integer solution* to this problem. So, in addition to the constraints stated above, we add the following integrality condition to the formulation of the problem:

$$X_1 \text{ and } X_2 \text{ must be integers}$$

An **integrality condition** indicates that some (or all) of the variables in the formulation must assume only **integer values.** We refer to such variables as the integer variables in a problem. In contrast, variables that are not required to assume strictly integer values are referred to as **continuous variables.** Although it is easy to state integrality conditions for a problem, such conditions often make a problem more difficult (and sometimes impossible) to solve.

6.2   RELAXATION

One approach to finding the optimal integer solution to a problem is to relax, or ignore, the integrality conditions and solve the problem as if it were a standard LP problem where all the variables are assumed to be continuous. This model is sometimes referred to as the **LP relaxation** of the original ILP problem. Consider the following ILP problem:

$$
\begin{aligned}
\text{MAX:} \quad & 2X_1 + 3X_2 \\
\text{Subject to:} \quad & X_1 + 3X_2 \leq 8.25 \\
& 2.5X_1 + X_2 \leq 8.75 \\
& X_1, X_2 \geq 0 \\
& X_1, X_2 \text{ must be integers}
\end{aligned}
$$

The LP relaxation for this problem is represented by:

$$
\begin{aligned}
\text{MAX:} \quad & 2X_1 + 3X_2 \\
\text{Subject to:} \quad & X_1 + 3X_2 \leq 8.25 \\
& 2.5X_1 + X_2 \leq 8.75 \\
& X_1, X_2 \geq 0
\end{aligned}
$$

The only difference between the ILP and its LP relaxation is that all integrality conditions imposed by the ILP are dropped in the relaxation. However, as illustrated in Figure 6.1, this change has a significant impact on the feasible regions for the two problems.

As shown in Figure 6.1, the feasible region for the ILP consists of only 11 discrete points. On the other hand, the feasible region for its LP relaxation consists of an infinite number of points represented by the shaded area. This figure illustrates an

Figure 6.1
Integer feasible
region vs. LP
feasible region.

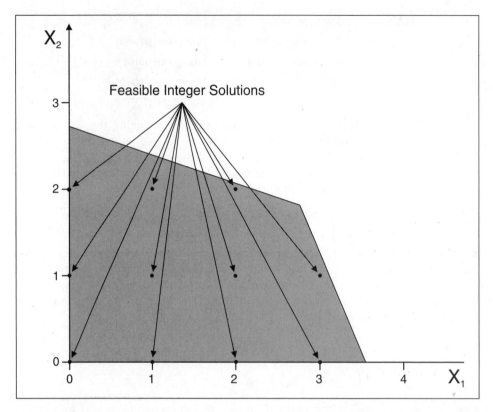

important point about the relationship between the feasible region of an ILP and its LP relaxation. The feasible region of the LP relaxation of an ILP problem *always* encompasses *all* the feasible integer solutions to the original ILP problem. Although the relaxed feasible region might include additional noninteger solutions, it will not include any integer solutions that are not feasible solutions to the original ILP.

6.3   SOLVING THE RELAXED PROBLEM

The LP relaxation of an ILP problem is often easy to solve using the simplex method. As explained in Chapter 2, an optimal solution to an LP problem occurs at one of the corner points of its feasible region (assuming that the problem has a bounded optimal solution). Thus, if we are extremely lucky, the optimal solution to the LP relaxation of an ILP problem might occur at an integer corner point of the relaxed feasible region. In this case, we find the optimal integer solution to the ILP problem simply by solving its LP relaxation. This is exactly what happened in earlier chapters when we originally solved the relaxed LP model for the hot tub problem. Figure 6.2 (and the file FIG6-2.xls on your data disk) shows the solution to this problem.

The optimal solution to the relaxed LP formulation of the hot tub problem assigns integer values to the decision variables ($X_1 = 122$ and $X_2 = 78$). So in this case, the relaxed LP problem happens to have an integer-valued optimal solution. However, as you might expect, this will not always be the case.

Suppose, for example, that Blue Ridge Hot Tubs has only 1,520 hours of labor and 2,650 feet of tubing available during their next production cycle. The company might be interested in solving the following ILP problem:

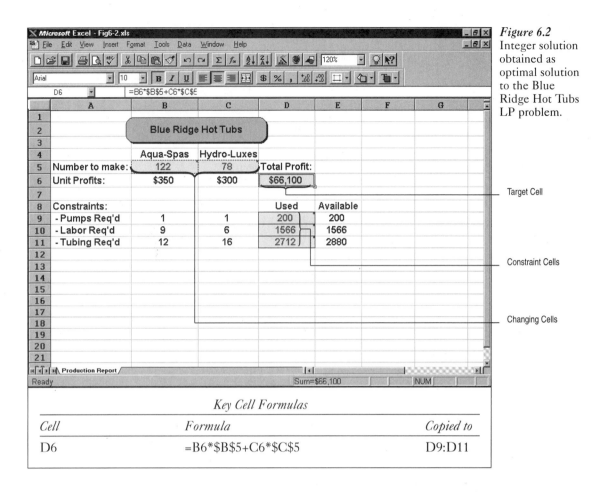

Figure 6.2
Integer solution obtained as optimal solution to the Blue Ridge Hot Tubs LP problem.

	Key Cell Formulas	
Cell	*Formula*	*Copied to*
D6	=B6*$B$5+C6*$C$5	D9:D11

MAX: $350X_1 + 300X_2$ } profit
Subject to: $1X_1 + 1X_2 \leq 200$ } pump constraint
             $9X_1 + 6X_2 \leq 1,520$ } labor constraint
             $12X_1 + 16X_2 \leq 2,650$ } tubing constraint
             $X_1, X_2 \geq 0$ } nonnegativity conditions
             X_1, X_2 must be integers   } integrality conditions

If we relax the integrality conditions and solve the resulting LP problem, we obtain the solution shown in Figure 6.3. This solution indicates that producing 116.9444 Aqua-Spas and 77.9167 Hydro-Luxes will generate a maximum profit of $64,306. But this solution violates the integrality conditions stated in the original problem. As a general rule, the optimal solution to the LP relaxation of an ILP problem is not guaranteed to produce an integer solution. In such cases, other techniques must be applied to find the optimal integer solution for the problem being solved. (There are some exceptions to this rule. In particular, the network flow problems discussed in Chapter 5 often can be viewed as ILP problems. For reasons that go beyond the scope of this text, the LP relaxation of these network problems will always have integer solutions if the supplies and/or demands at each node are integers and the problem is solved using the simplex method.)

Figure 6.3
Noninteger
solution
obtained as
optimal solution
to the revised
Blue Ridge Hot
Tubs LP
problem.

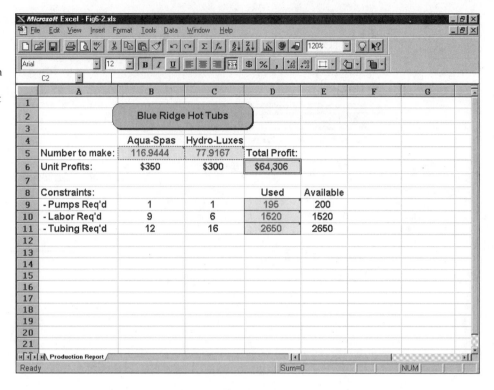

6.4 BOUNDS

Before discussing how to solve ILP problems, an important point must be made about the relationship between the optimal solution to an ILP problem and the optimal solution to its LP relaxation: *The objective function value for the optimal solution to the ILP problem can never be better than the objective function value for the optimal solution to its LP relaxation.*

For example, the solution shown in Figure 6.3 indicates that if the company could produce (and sell) fractional numbers of hot tubs, it could make a maximum profit of $64,306 by producing 116.9444 Aqua-Spas and 77.9167 Hydro-Luxes. No other feasible solution (integer or otherwise) could result in a better value of the objective function. If a better feasible solution existed, the optimization procedure would have identified this better solution as optimal because our aim was to maximize the value of the objective function.

Although solving the LP relaxation of the revised hot tub problem might not provide the optimal integer solution to our original ILP problem, it does indicate that the

---

Key Concept

For *maximization* problems, the objective function value at the optimal solution to the LP relaxation represents an *upper bound* on the optimal objective function value of the original ILP problem. For *minimization* problems, the objective function value at the optimal solution to the LP relaxation represents a *lower bound* on the optimal objective function value of the original ILP problem.

objective function value of the optimal integer solution cannot possibly be greater than $64,306. This information can be important in helping us evaluate the quality of integer solutions we might discover during our search for the optimal solution.

6.5 ROUNDING

As mentioned earlier, the solution to the LP relaxation of an ILP problem might satisfy the ILP problem's integrality conditions and, therefore, represent the optimal integer solution to the problem. But what should we do if this is not the case (as usually happens)? One technique that frequently is applied involves rounding the relaxed LP solution.

When the solution to the LP relaxation of an ILP problem does not result in an integer solution, it is tempting to think that simply rounding this solution will generate the optimal integer solution. Unfortunately, this is not the case. For example, if the values for the decision variables shown in Figure 6.3 are manually rounded up to their closest integer values, as shown in Figure 6.4, the resulting solution is infeasible. The company cannot manufacture 117 Aqua-Spas and 78 Hydro-Luxes because this would involve using more labor and tubing than are available.

Because rounding up does not always work, perhaps we should round down, or truncate, the values for the decision variables identified in the LP relaxation. As shown in Figure 6.5, this results in a feasible solution where 116 Aqua-Spas and 77 Hydro-Luxes are manufactured for a total profit of $63,700. However, this approach presents two possible problems. First, rounding down could also result in an infeasible solution, as shown in Figure 6.6.

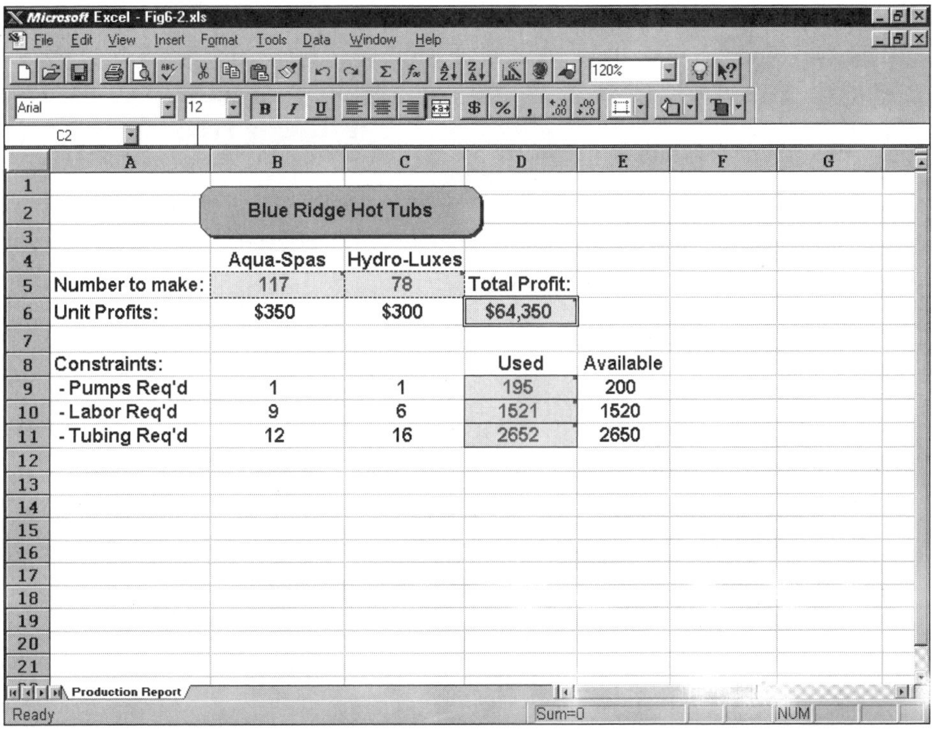

Figure 6.4
Infeasible integer solution obtained by rounding up.

Figure 6.5
Feasible integer
solution
obtained by
rounding down.

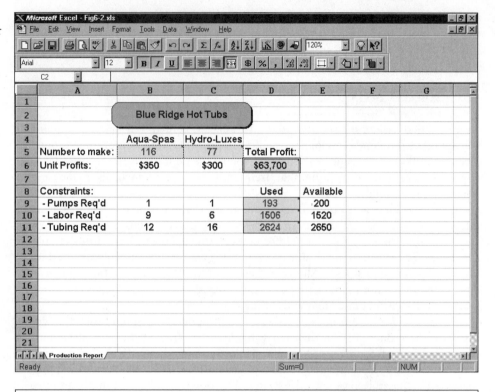

Figure 6.6
How rounding
can result in an
infeasible integer
solution.

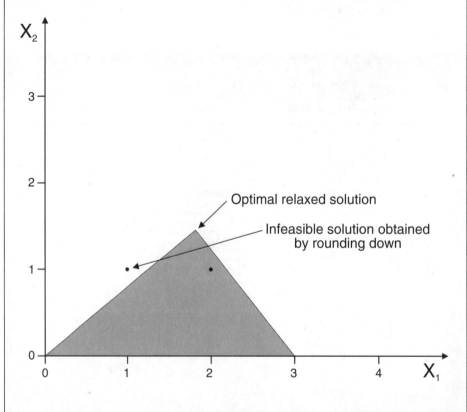

Another problem with rounding down is that even if it results in a feasible integer solution to the problem, there is no guarantee that it is the *optimal* integer solution. For example, the integer solution obtained by rounding down shown in Figure 6.5 produced a total profit of $63,700. However, as shown in Figure 6.7, a better integer solution exists for this problem. If the company produces 118 Aqua-Spas and 76 Hydro-Luxes, it can achieve a total profit of $64,100 (which is the optimal integer solution to this problem). Simply rounding the solution to the LP relaxation of an ILP problem is not guaranteed to provide the optimal integer solution. Although the integer solution obtained in this problem by rounding is very close to the optimal integer solution, rounding does not always work this well.

As we have seen, the solution to the LP relaxation of an ILP is not guaranteed to produce an integer solution, and rounding the solution to the LP relaxation is not guaranteed to produce the optimal integer solution. Therefore, we need another way to find the optimal integer solution to an ILP problem. Various procedures have been developed for this purpose. The most effective and widely used of these procedures is the **branch-and-bound (B&B) algorithm.** The B&B algorithm theoretically allows us to solve any ILP problem by solving a series of LP problems called candidate problems. For those who are interested, a discussion of how the B&B algorithm works is given at the end of this chapter.

6.6   STOPPING RULES

Finding the optimal solution for simple ILP problems can sometimes require the evaluation of hundreds of candidate problems. More complex problems can require

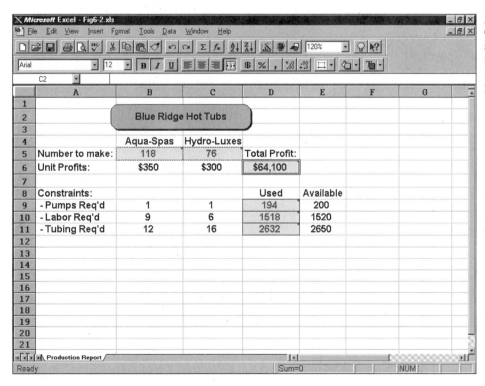

Figure 6.7
Optimal integer solution to the revised Blue Ridge Hot Tubs problem.

the evaluation of thousands of candidate problems, which can be a very time-consuming task even for the fastest computers. For this reason, many ILP packages allow you to specify a suboptimality tolerance of X% (where X is some numeric value), which tells the B&B algorithm to stop when it finds an integer solution that is no more than X% worse than the optimal integer solution. This is another area where obtaining upper or lower bounds on the optimal integer solution can be helpful.

As noted earlier, if we relax all the integrality conditions in an ILP with a maximization objective and solve the resulting LP problem, the objective function value at the optimal solution to the relaxed problem provides an upper bound on the optimal integer solution. For example, when we relaxed the integrality conditions for the revised Blue Ridge Hot Tubs problem and solved it as an LP, we obtained the solution shown in Figure 6.3, which has an objective function value of $64,306. Thus, we know that the optimal integer solution to this problem cannot have an objective function value greater than $64,306. Now, suppose the owners of Blue Ridge Hot Tubs are willing to settle for any integer solution to their problem that is no more than 5% below the optimal integer solution. It is easy to determine that 95% of $64,306 is $61,090 ($0.95 \times \$64,306 = \$61,090$). Therefore, any integer solution with an objective function value of at least $61,090 can be no worse than 5% below the optimal integer solution.

Specifying suboptimality tolerances can be helpful if you are willing to settle for a good but suboptimal solution to a difficult ILP problem. However, most B&B packages employ some sort of default suboptimality tolerance and, therefore, might produce a suboptimal solution to the ILP problem without indicating that a better solution might exist. (We will look at an example where this occurs shortly.) It is important to be aware of suboptimality tolerances because they can determine whether or not the true optimal solution to an ILP problem is found.

6.7   SOLVING ILP PROBLEMS USING SOLVER

Now that you have some understanding of the effort required to solve ILP problems, you can appreciate how using Solver simplifies this process. This section shows how to use Solver with the revised Blue Ridge Hot Tubs problem.

Figure 6.8 (and the file FIG6-8.xls on your data disk) shows the Solver parameters required to solve the revised Blue Ridge Hot Tubs problem as a standard LP problem. However, none of these parameters indicate that the cells representing the decision variables (cells B5 and C5) must assume integer values. To communicate this to Solver, we need to add constraints to the problem by clicking the Add button.

Clicking this button displays the Add Constraint dialog box shown in Figure 6.9. In this dialog box, cells B5 through C5 are specified as the cell references for the additional constraints. Because we want these cells to assume only integer values, we need to select the **int** option from the drop-down menu, as shown in Figure 6.9.

After clicking the OK button, we return to the Solver Parameters dialog box shown in Figure 6.10. This dialog box now indicates that cells B5 and C5 are constrained to assume only integer values. We can now click the Solve button to determine the optimal solution to the problem, shown in Figure 6.11.

The Solver Results dialog box in Figure 6.11 indicates that Solver found a solution that satisfies all constraints and optimality conditions. Thus, we might suspect that the optimal integer solution to this problem involves producing 117 Aqua-Spas and 77 Hydro-Luxes for a total profit of $64,050. However, if you refer back to Figure 6.7, you will recall that an even better integer solution to this problem can be obtained

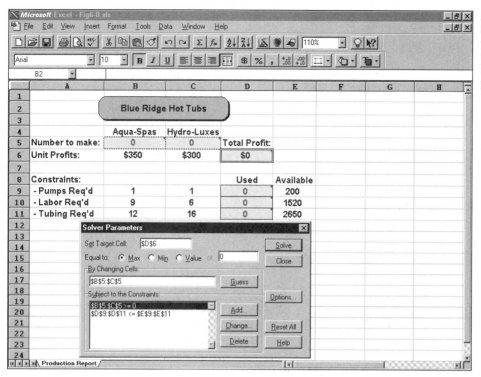

Figure 6.8
Solver
parameters for
the relaxed Blue
Ridge Hot Tubs
problem.

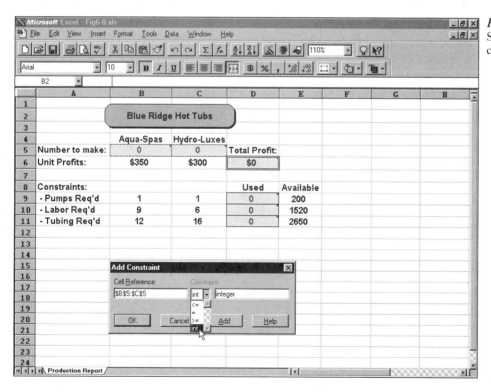

Figure 6.9
Selecting integer
constraints.

Figure 6.10
Solver
parameters
for
the revised Blue
Ridge Hot Tubs
problem with
integer
constraints.

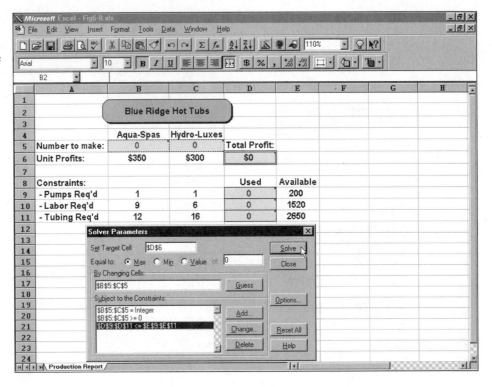

Figure 6.11
Solution to the
revised Blue
Ridge Hot Tubs
problem with
integer
constraints.

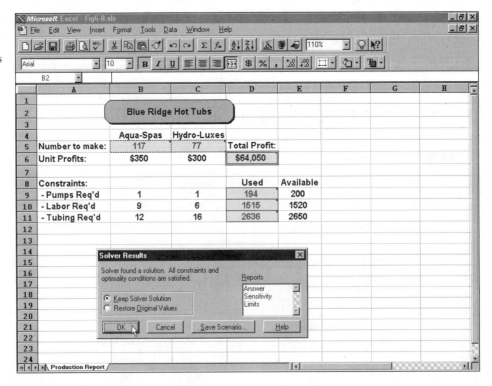

by producing 118 Aqua-Spas and 76 Hydro-Luxes for a total profit of $64,100. So why did Solver select an integer solution with a total profit of $64,050 when a better integer solution exists? The answer lies in Solver's suboptimality tolerance factor.

By default, Solver uses a suboptimality tolerance factor of 5%. So when Solver found the integer solution with the objective function value of $64,050 shown in Figure 6.11, it determined that this solution was within 5% of the optimal integer solution and, therefore, it abandoned its search. To ensure that Solver finds the best possible solution to an ILP problem, we must change its suboptimality tolerance factor by clicking the Options button in the Solver Parameters dialog box. Figure 6.12 shows the resulting Solver Options dialog box.

As shown in Figure 6.12, you can set a number of options to control Solver's operations. The Tolerance option represents Solver's suboptimality tolerance value. To make sure Solver finds the best possible solution to an ILP problem, we must change this setting from its default value of 5% to 0%. If we do this and re-solve the current problem, we obtain the solution shown in Figure 6.13. This solution is the best possible integer solution to the problem.

6.8 OTHER ILP PROBLEMS

Many decision problems encountered in business can be modeled as ILPs. As we have seen from the Blue Ridge Hot Tubs example, some problems that are initially formulated as LP problems might turn into ILP formulations if they require integer solutions. However, the importance of ILP extends beyond simply allowing us to obtain integer solutions to LP problems.

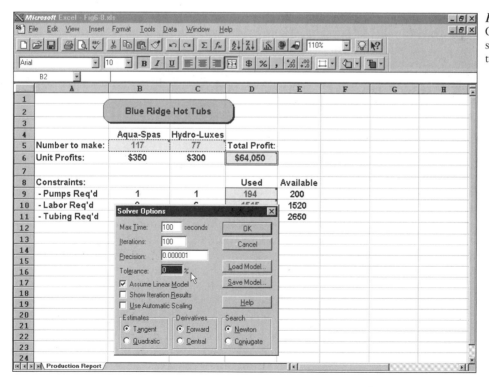

Figure 6.12
Changing the suboptimality tolerance factor.

Figure 6.13
Optimal integer
solution to the
revised Blue
Ridge Hot Tubs
problem.

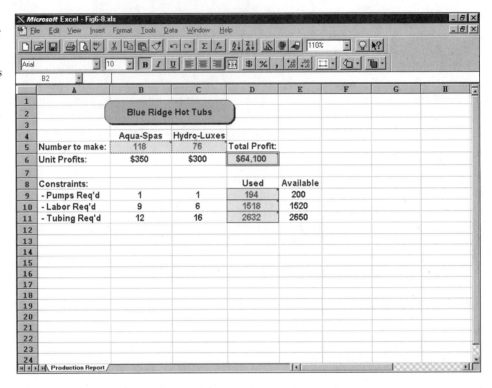

Figure 6.13
Optimal integer
solution to the
revised Blue
Ridge Hot Tubs
problem.

The ability to constrain certain variables to assume only integer values enables us to model a number of important conditions more accurately. For example, up to this point we have not considered the impact of quantity discounts, setup or lump-sum costs, or batch-size restrictions on a given decision problem. Without ILP techniques we could not model these decision issues. We now consider several examples that illustrate the expanded modeling capabilities available through the use of integer variables.

6.9   BINARY VARIABLES

As mentioned earlier, some LP problems naturally evolve into ILP problems when we realize that we need to obtain integer solutions. For example, in the Air-Express problem discussed in Chapter 3, we needed to determine the number of workers to assign to each of seven shifts. Because workers are discrete units, it might be appropriate to impose integrality conditions on the decision variables in this model representing the number of workers scheduled for each shift. To do so, we would change the continuous variables in the model into **general integer variables,** or variables that could assume any integer value (provided that the constraints of the problem are not violated). In many other situations, we might want to use **binary integer variables** (or binary variables), which can assume *only two* integer values: 0 and 1. Binary variables can be useful in a number of practical modeling situations, as illustrated in the following examples.

6.10   A CAPITAL BUDGETING PROBLEM

In a capital budgeting problem, a decision maker is presented with several potential projects or investment alternatives and must determine which projects or investments to choose. The projects or investments typically require different amounts of various resources (for example, money, equipment, personnel) and generate different cash flows to the company. The cash flows for each project or investment are converted to a net present value (NPV). The problem is to determine which set of projects or investments to select in order to achieve the maximum possible NPV. Consider the following example:

> In his position as vice president of research and development (R&D) for CRT Technologies, Mark Schwartz is responsible for evaluating and choosing which R&D projects to support. The company received 18 R&D proposals from its scientists and engineers and identified six projects as being consistent with the company's mission. However, the company does not have the funds available to undertake all six projects. Mark must determine which of the projects to select. The funding requirements for each project are summarized below, along with the NPV the company expects each project to generate.
>
> | | Expected NPV | Capital (in $000s) Required in | | | | |
> | Project | (in $000s) | Year 1 | Year 2 | Year 3 | Year 4 | Year 5 |
> |----------|--------------|--------|--------|--------|--------|--------|
> | 1 | 141 | 75 | 25 | 20 | 15 | 10 |
> | 2 | 187 | 90 | 35 | 0 | 0 | 30 |
> | 3 | 121 | 60 | 15 | 15 | 15 | 15 |
> | 4 | 83 | 30 | 20 | 10 | 5 | 5 |
> | 5 | 265 | 100 | 25 | 20 | 20 | 20 |
> | 6 | 127 | 50 | 20 | 10 | 30 | 40 |
>
> The company currently has $250,000 available to invest in new projects. It has budgeted $75,000 for continued support for these projects in year 2 and $50,000 per year for years 3, 4, and 5.

6.10.1   Defining the Decision Variables

Mark must decide which of the six projects to select. Thus, we need six variables to represent the alternatives under consideration. We will let X_1, X_2, ..., X_6 represent the six decision variables for this problem and assume they operate as:

$$x_i = \begin{cases} 1, \text{ if project } i \text{ is selected} \\ 0, \text{ otherwise} \end{cases} \quad i = 1, 2, ..., 6$$

Each decision variable in this problem is a binary variable that assumes the value 1 if the associated project is selected, or the value 0 if the associated project is not selected. In essence, each variable acts like an "on/off switch" to indicate whether or not a given project has been selected. As we'll see, it takes some effort to ensure that these variables actually operate in this way. For now, just accept that this is possible.

6.10.2   Defining the Objective Function

The objective in this problem is to maximize the total NPV of the selected projects. This is stated mathematically as:

$$\text{MAX: } 141X_1 + 187X_2 + 121X_3 + 83X_4 + 265X_5 + 127X_6$$

Notice that this objective function simply sums the NPV figures for the selected projects.

6.10.3   Defining the Constraints

Several sets of constraints apply to this problem. The most obvious constraints involve the amount of capital available in each year. We need one capital constraint for each year to ensure that the selected projects do not require more capital than is available. This set of constraints is represented by:

$$75X_1 + 90X_2 + 60X_3 + 30X_4 + 100X_5 + 50X_6 \leq 250 \quad \}\text{ year 1 capital constraint}$$
$$25X_1 + 35X_2 + 15X_3 + 20X_4 + 25X_5 + 20X_6 \leq 75 \quad \}\text{ year 2 capital constraint}$$
$$20X_1 + 0X_2 + 15X_3 + 10X_4 + 20X_5 + 10X_6 \leq 50 \quad \}\text{ year 3 capital constraint}$$
$$15X_1 + 0X_2 + 15X_3 + 5X_4 + 20X_5 + 30X_6 \leq 50 \quad \}\text{ year 4 capital constraint}$$
$$10X_1 + 30X_2 + 15X_3 + 5X_4 + 20X_5 + 40X_6 \leq 50 \quad \}\text{ year 5 capital constraint}$$

6.10.4   Setting Up the Binary Variables

In our formulation of this problem, we assume that each decision variable is a binary variable. We must include this assumption in the formal statement of our model by adding the constraints:

$$X_i \leq 1, i = 1, 2, ..., 6$$
$$X_i \geq 0, i = 1, 2, ..., 6$$
$$\text{All } X_i \text{ must be integers}$$

The first set of constraints indicates that all the decision variables must be less than or equal to 1. The next set of constraints are the standard nonnegativity conditions, which indicate that all the decision variables must be greater than or equal to 0. Finally, the last constraint indicates that all the decision variables must assume integer values. Together, these three sets of constraints indicate that the decision variables can assume only integer values in the closed interval from 0 to 1. Therefore, these constraints ensure that the decision variables will operate as binary variables.

6.10.5   Implementing the Model

The ILP model for the CRT Technologies project selection problem is summarized as:

$$\text{MAX:} \qquad 141X_1 + 187X_2 + 121X_3 + 83X_4 + 265X_5 + 127X_6$$
$$\text{Subject to: } 75X_1 + 90X_2 + 60X_3 + 30X_4 + 100X_5 + 50X_6 \leq 250$$
$$25X_1 + 35X_2 + 15X_3 + 20X_4 + 25X_5 + 20X_6 \leq 75$$
$$20X_1 + 0X_2 + 15X_3 + 10X_4 + 20X_5 + 10X_6 \leq 50$$
$$15X_1 + 0X_2 + 15X_3 + 5X_4 + 20X_5 + 30X_6 \leq 50$$

$$10X_1 + 30X_2 + 15X_3 + 5X_4 + 20X_5 + 40X_6 \le 50$$

$$X_i \le 1,\ i = 1, 2, ..., 6$$

$$X_i \ge 0,\ i = 1, 2, ..., 6$$

All X_i must be integers

This model is implemented in the spreadsheet shown in Figure 6.14 (and in the file FIG6-14.xls on your data disk). In this spreadsheet, the data for each project are listed in a separate row.

Cells B6 through B11 contain values of 0 to indicate that they are reserved for representing the six variables in our algebraic model. The LHS formula for the capital constraint is entered in cell D12, then copied to cells E12 through H12, as:

Formula for cell D12: =SUMPRODUCT(D6:D11,$B$6:$B$11)
(Copy to E12 through H12.)

The RHS values for the constraints are listed in cells D13 through H13. Finally, the objective function of the model is implemented in cell D15 as:

Formula for cell D15 =SUMPRODUCT(C6:C11,$B$6:$B$11)

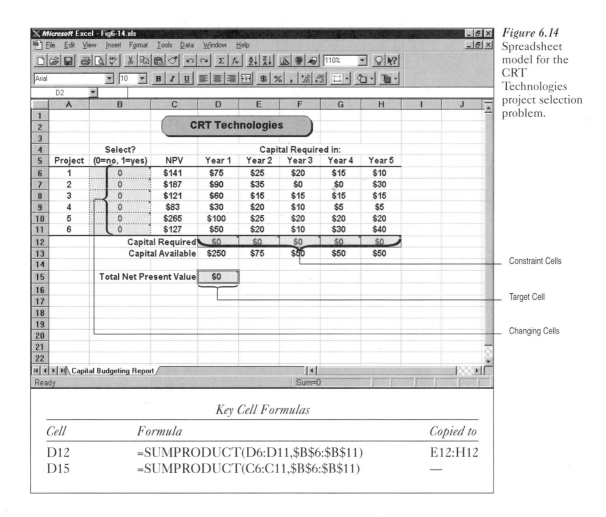

Figure 6.14
Spreadsheet model for the CRT Technologies project selection problem.

Cell	Formula	Copied to
D12	=SUMPRODUCT(D6:D11,$B$6:$B$11)	E12:H12
D15	=SUMPRODUCT(C6:C11,$B$6:$B$11)	—

6.10.6   Solving the Model

To solve this model, we must tell Solver where we have implemented our objective function, decision variables, and constraints. When building the spreadsheet model for this problem, we did not specify that the decision variables must assume only integer values between 0 and 1 (as indicated by the last three constraint sets in our model). However, we can ensure that these conditions are satisfied by the way we describe the problem to Solver.

The Solver Parameters dialog box shown in Figure 6.15 indicates that the objective function is implemented in cell D15 and that the decision variables are represented by cells B6 through B11. Also, notice that four sets of constraints are specified for this problem.

The first three sets of constraints indicate that cells B6 through B11 must assume integer values no greater than 1 and no less than 0. Thus, these constraints ensure that cells B6 through B11 will operate as binary variables. Notice that we implemented these constraints by referring to the cells in the spreadsheet that represent our decision variables—we do not have to set up separate cells in the spreadsheet to implement these constraints. The last set of constraints shown in the dialog box indicates that the values in cells D12 through H12 must be less than or equal to the values in cells D13 through H13 when the problem is solved. These conditions correspond to the capital constraints in the problem.

Because this model contains six decision variables and each variable can assume only one of two values, at most $2^6 = 64$ possible integer solutions exist for this problem. Some of these integer solutions will not fall in the feasible region, so we might suspect that this problem will not be too difficult to solve optimally. If we set the suboptimality tolerance factor to 0 (in the Solver Options dialog box) and solve the problem, we obtain the solution shown in Figure 6.16.

Figure 6.15
Solver parameters for the CRT Technologies project selection problem.

Important Software Note

The Solver in Excel 8.0 has a feature that allows you to indicate that certain changing cells represent binary variables. When you are adding constraints, the dropdown box (see Figure 6.9) used to indicate the type of constraint ("<=", ">=", "=", "int") includes another option labeled "bin" for binary. If you are using Excel 8.0, you can simply select the "bin" option for changing cells that represent binary variables instead of imposing the three different sets of constraints mentioned above. However, if you are using an older version of Excel, you will need to add all three sets of constraints (>=0, <=1, and integer) to any changing cells that you want Solver to treat as binary variables.

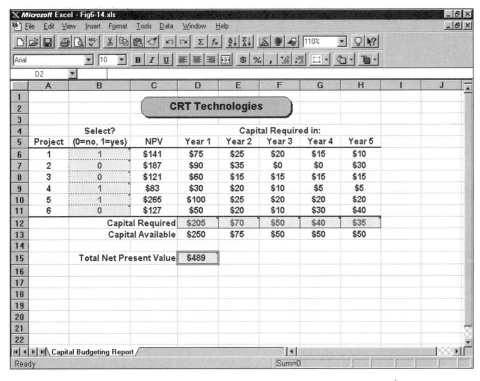

Figure 6.16
Optimal integer solution to the CRT Technologies project selection problem.

6.10.7 Comparing the Optimal Solution to a Heuristic Solution

The optimal solution shown in Figure 6.16 indicates that if CRT Technologies selects projects 1, 4, and 5, it can achieve a total NPV of $489,000. Although this solution does not use all of the capital available in each year, it is still the best possible integer solution to the problem.

Another approach to solving this problem is to create a ranked list of the projects in decreasing order by NPV and then select projects from this list, in order, until the capital is depleted. As shown in Figure 6.17, if we apply this heuristic to the current

Figure 6.17
A suboptimal
heuristic solution
to the CRT
Technologies
project selection
problem.

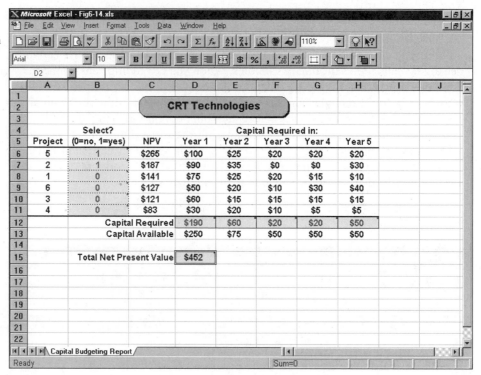

problem, we would select projects 5 and 2, but we could not select any more projects due to a lack of capital in year 5. This solution would generate a total NPV of $452,000. Again, we can see the potential benefit of optimization techniques over heuristic solution techniques.

6.11   BINARY VARIABLES AND LOGICAL CONDITIONS

Binary variables can be used to model a number of logical conditions that might apply in a variety of problems. For example, in the CRT Technologies problem, several of the projects under consideration (for example, projects 1, 3, and 6) might represent alternative approaches for producing a certain part for a product. The company might want to limit the solution to include *no more than one* of these three alternatives. The following type of constraint accomplishes this restriction:

$$X_1 + X_3 + X_6 \le 1$$

Because X_1, X_3, and X_6 represent binary variables, no more than one of them can assume the value 1 and still satisfy the above constraint. If we want to ensure that the solution includes *exactly one* of these alternatives, we could include the following constraint in our model:

$$X_1 + X_3 + X_6 = 1$$

As an example of another type of logical condition, suppose that project 4 involves a microwave communications technology that will not be available to the company unless it undertakes project 5. In other words, the company cannot select project 4 unless it also selects project 5. This type of relationship can be imposed on the solution with the constraint:

$$X_4 - X_5 \leq 0$$

The four possible combinations of values for X_4 and X_5 and their relationships to the previous constraint are summarized as:

Value of X_4	X_5	Meaning	Feasible?
0	0	Do not select either project	yes
1	1	Select both projects	yes
0	1	Select 5, but not 4	yes
1	0	Select 4, but not 5	no

As indicated in this table, the previous constraint prohibits any solution in which project 4 is selected and project 5 is not selected.

As these examples illustrate, you can model certain logical conditions using binary variables. Several problems at the end of this chapter allow you to use binary variables (and your own creativity) to formulate models for decision problems that involve these types of logical conditions.

6.12   THE FIXED-CHARGE PROBLEM

In most of the LP problems discussed in earlier chapters, we formulated objective functions to maximize profits or minimize costs. In each of these cases we associated a per-unit cost or per-unit profit with each decision variable to create the objective function. However, in some situations the decision to produce a product results in a lump-sum, or fixed-charge, cost in addition to a per-unit cost or profit. These types of problems are known as **fixed-charge** or fixed-cost problems. The following are some examples of fixed-costs:

- the cost to lease, rent, or purchase a piece of equipment or a vehicle that will be required if a particular action is taken
- the setup cost required to prepare a machine or production line to produce a different type of product
- the cost to construct a new production line or facility that will be required if a particular decision is made
- the cost of hiring additional personnel that will be required if a particular decision is made

In each of these examples, the fixed costs are *new* costs that will be incurred if a particular action or decision is made. In this respect, fixed costs are different from **sunk costs,** which are costs that will be incurred regardless of what decision is made. Sunk costs are irrelevant for decision-making purposes because, by definition, decisions do not influence these costs. On the other hand, fixed costs are important factors in decision making because the decision determines whether or not these costs will be incurred. The following example illustrates the formulation and solution of a fixed-charge problem.

Remington Manufacturing is planning its next production cycle. The company can produce three products, each of which must undergo machining, grinding, and assembly operations. The table below summarizes the hours of machining, grinding, and assembly required by each unit of each product, and the total hours of capacity available for each operation.

	Hours Required By			
Operation	Product 1	Product 2	Product 3	Total Hours Available
Machining	2	3	6	600
Grinding	6	3	4	300
Assembly	5	6	2	400

The cost accounting department has estimated that each unit of product 1 manufactured and sold will contribute $48 to profit, and each unit of products 2 and 3 contributes $55 and $50, respectively. However, manufacturing a unit of product 1 requires a setup operation on the production line that costs $1,000. Similar setups are required for products 2 and 3 at costs of $800 and $900, respectively. The marketing department believes it can sell all the products produced. Therefore, the management of Remington wants to determine the most profitable mix of products to produce.

6.12.1   Defining the Decision Variables

Although only three products are under consideration in this problem, we need six variables to formulate the problem accurately. We can define these variables as:

$$X_i = \text{the amount of product } i \text{ to be produced, } i = 1, 2, 3$$

$$Y_i = \begin{cases} 1, \text{ if } X_i > 0 \\ 0, \text{ if } X_i = 0 \end{cases} i = 1, 2, 3$$

We need three variables, X_1, X_2, and X_3, to correspond to the amount of products 1, 2, and 3 produced. Each of the X_i variables has a corresponding binary variable, Y_i, that will equal 1 if X_i assumes any positive value, or will equal 0 if X_i is 0. For now, do not be concerned about how this relationship between the X_i and Y_i is enforced. We will explore that soon.

6.12.2   Defining the Objective Function

Given our definition of the decision variables, the objective function for our model is stated as:

$$\text{MAX:} \quad 48X_1 + 55X_2 + 50X_3 - 1000Y_1 - 800Y_2 - 900Y_3$$

The first three terms in this function calculate the marginal profit generated by the number of products 1, 2, and 3 sold. The last three terms in this function subtract the fixed costs for the products produced. For example, if X_1 assumes a positive value, we know from our definition of the Y_1 variables that Y_1 should equal 1. And if $Y_1 = 1$, the value of the objective function will be reduced by $1,000 to reflect payment of the setup cost. On the other hand, if $X_1 = 0$ we know that $Y_1 = 0$. Therefore, if no units of X_1 are produced, the setup cost for product 1 will not be incurred in the objective. Similar relationships exist between X_2 and Y_2 and between X_3 and Y_3.

6.12.3 Defining the Constraints

Several sets of constraints apply to this problem. Capacity constraints are needed to ensure that the number of machining, grinding, and assembly hours used does not exceed the number of hours available for each of these resources. These constraints are stated as:

$$2X_1 + 3X_2 + 6X_3 \leq 600 \quad \text{\} machining constraint}$$
$$6X_1 + 3X_2 + 4X_3 \leq 300 \quad \text{\} grinding constraint}$$
$$5X_1 + 6X_2 + 2X_3 \leq 400 \quad \text{\} assembly constraint}$$

We also need to include nonnegativity conditions on the X_i variables as:

$$X_i \geq 0, i = 1, 2, 3$$

Three sets of constraints on the Y_i variables are needed to ensure that they operate as binary variables. These constraints are represented by:

$$Y_i \leq 1, i = 1, 2, 3$$
$$Y_i \geq 0, i = 1, 2, 3$$
$$\text{All } Y_i \text{ must be integers}$$

As mentioned earlier, we must ensure that the required relationship between the X_i and Y_i variables is enforced. In particular, the value of the Y_i variables can be determined from the X_i variables. Therefore, we need constraints to establish this *link* between the value of the Y_i variables and the X_i variables. These linking constraints are represented by:

$$X_1 \leq M_1 Y_1$$
$$X_2 \leq M_2 Y_2$$
$$X_3 \leq M_3 Y_3$$

In each of these constraints, the M_i is a numeric constant that represents an upper bound on the optimal value of the X_i. Let's assume that all the M_i are arbitrarily large numbers; for example, $M_i = 10,000$. Then each constraint sets up a link between the value of the X_i and the Y_i. For example, if any X_i variables in the above constraints assume a value greater than 0, the corresponding Y_i variable must assume the value 1 or the constraint will be violated. On the other hand, if any of the X_i variables are equal to 0, the corresponding Y_i variables could equal 0 or 1 and still satisfy the constraint. However, if we consider the objective function to this problem, we know that when given a choice, Solver will always set the Y_i equal to 0 (rather than 1) because this results in a better objective function value. Therefore, we can conclude that if any X_i variables are equal to 0, Solver will set the corresponding Y_i variable equal to 0 because this is feasible and results in a better objective function value.

6.12.4 Determining Values for "Big M"

The M_i values used in the linking constraints are sometimes referred to as "Big M" values because they can be assigned arbitrarily large values. However, for reasons that go beyond the scope of this text, these types of problems are much easier to solve if the M_i values are kept as small as possible. As indicated earlier, the M_i values impose upper bounds on the values of the X_i. So, if a problem indicates that a company could manufacture and sell no more than 60 units of X_1, for example, we could let $M_1 = 60$.

However, even if upper bounds for the X_i are not explicitly indicated, it is sometimes easy to derive implicit upper bounds for these variables.

Let's consider the variable X_1 in the Remington problem. What is the maximum number of units of X_1 that can be produced in this problem? Referring back to our capacity constraints, if the company produces 0 units of X_2 and X_3, it would run out of machining capacity after producing $600/2 = 300$ units of X_1. Similarly it would run out of grinding capacity after producing $300/6 = 50$ units of X_1, and it would run out of assembly capacity after producing $400/5 = 80$ units of X_1. Therefore, the maximum number of units of X_1 the company can produce is 50. Using similar logic, we can determine that the maximum units of X_2 the company can produce is MIN(600/3, 300/3, 400/6) = 66.67, and the maximum units of X_3 is MIN(600/6, 300/4, 400/2) = 75. Thus, for this problem, reasonable upper bounds for X_1, X_2, and X_3 are represented by $M_1 = 50$, $M_2 = 67$, and $M_3 = 75$, respectively. (Note that the method illustrated here for obtaining reasonable values for the M_i does not apply if any of the coefficients in the machining, grinding, or assembly constraints are negative. Why is this?) When possible, you should determine reasonable values for the M_i in this type of problem. However, if this is not possible, you can assign arbitrarily large values to the M_i.

6.12.5   Implementing the Model

Using the values for the M_i calculated earlier, our ILP formulation of Remington's production planning model is summarized as:

MAX: $48X_1 + 55X_2 + 50X_3 - 1000Y_1 - 800Y_2 - 900Y_3$

Subject to: $2X_1 + 3X_2 + 6X_3 \leq 600$ } machining constraint

$6X_1 + 3X_2 + 4X_3 \leq 300$ } grinding constraint

$5X_1 + 6X_2 + 2X_3 \leq 400$ } assembly constraint

$X_1 - 50Y_1 \leq 0$

$X_2 - 67Y_2 \leq 0$ } linking constraints

$X_3 - 75Y_3 \leq 0$

$Y_i \leq 1, i = 1, 2, 3$

$Y_i \geq 0, i = 1, 2, 3$ } binary constraints

All Y_i must be integers

$X_i \geq 0, i = 1, 2, 3$ } nonnegativity conditions

This model expresses the linking constraints in a slightly different (but algebraically equivalent) manner in order to follow our convention of having all the variables on the LHS of the inequality and a constant on the RHS. This model is implemented in the spreadsheet shown in Figure 6.18 (and in the file FIG6-18.xls on your data disk).

In the spreadsheet in Figure 6.18, cells B5, C5, and D5 represent the variables X_1, X_2, and X_3, and cells B15, C15, and D15 represent Y_1, Y_2, and Y_3. The coefficients for the objective function are in cells B7 through D8. The objective function is implemented in cell F8 with the formula:

Formula for cell F8:   =SUMPRODUCT(B7:D7,B5:D5) –
                                 SUMPRODUCT(B8:D8,B15:D15)

Cells B11 through D13 contain the coefficients for the machining, grinding, and assembly constraints. The LHS formulas for these constraints are implemented in

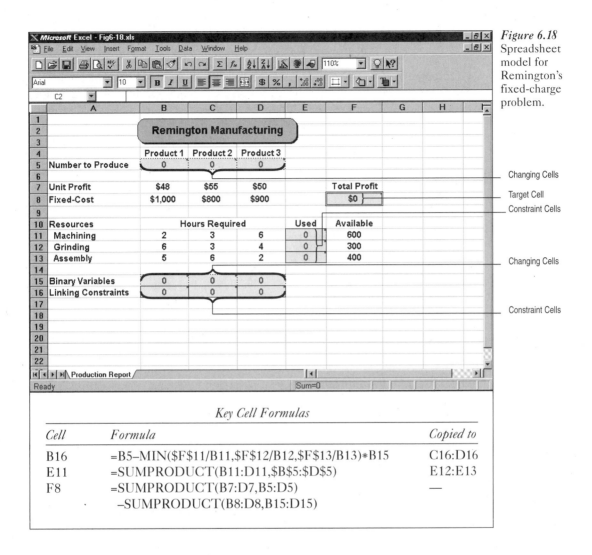

Figure 6.18
Spreadsheet model for Remington's fixed-charge problem.

Key Cell Formulas		
Cell	*Formula*	*Copied to*
B16	=B5−MIN($F$11/B11,$F$12/B12,$F$13/B13)∗B15	C16:D16
E11	=SUMPRODUCT(B11:D11,$B$5:$D$5)	E12:E13
F8	=SUMPRODUCT(B7:D7,B5:D5)	—
	−SUMPRODUCT(B8:D8,B15:D15)	

cells E11 through E13, and cells F11 through F13 contain the RHS values for these constraints. Finally, the LHS formulas for the linking constraints are entered in cells B16 through D16 as:

Formula for cell B16:   =B5−MIN($F$11/B11,$F$12/B12,$F$13/B13)∗B15
(Copy to cells C16 through D16.)

Instead of entering the values for M_i in these constraints, we implemented formulas that would automatically calculate correct M_i values if the user of this spreadsheet changed any of the coefficients or RHS values in the capacity constraints.

6.12.6   Solving the Model

The Solver Parameters dialog box shown in Figure 6.19 indicates the settings required to solve this problem. Notice that the ranges B5 through D5 and B15 through D15, which correspond to the X_i and Y_i variables, are both listed as ranges of cells that can be changed. Also, notice that the necessary constraints have been imposed on cells B15 through D15 to ensure that they assume only binary values.

Potential Pitfall

It is important to note that we are treating cells B15, C15, and D15, which represent the binary variables Y_1, Y_2, and Y_3, just like any other cells representing decision variables. We simply entered values of 0 into these cells to indicate that they represent decision variables. Ultimately, Solver will determine what values should be placed in these cells so that all the constraints are satisfied and the objective function is maximized. Some people try to make Solver's job "easier" by placing IF( ) functions in these cells to determine whether the values should be 0 or 1 depending on the values of cells B5, C5, and D5, which correspond to the variables X_1, X_2, and X_3. Although this approach seems to make sense, it can produce unwanted results. Using IF( ) functions in this way introduces *nonlinearities* in the spreadsheet model that can prevent Solver from finding the optimal solution to the problem. In Chapter 8, Nonlinear Programming, we will see that nonlinear programming problems are very difficult to solve optimally. Thus, it is best to create a model so that it can be solved using linear optimization methods.

Because so few integer variables exist in this problem, we should be able to obtain an optimal integer solution easily. If we set the suboptimality tolerance to 0 in the Solver Options dialog box and instruct Solver to assume a linear model, we obtain the optimal solution to this problem, as shown in Figure 6.20.

6.12.7   Analyzing the Solution

The solution shown in Figure 6.20 indicates that the company should produce 0 units of product 1, 55.55 units of product 2, and 33.33 units of product 3 ($X_1 = 0$, $X_2 = 55.55$,

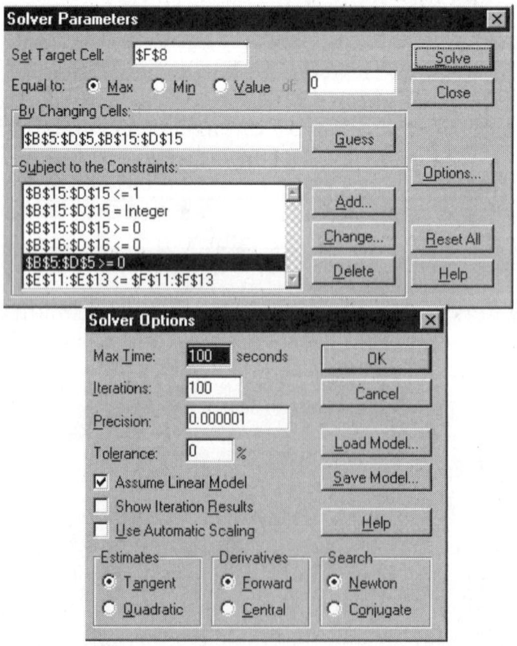

Figure 6.19
Solver parameters for Remington's fixed-charge problem.

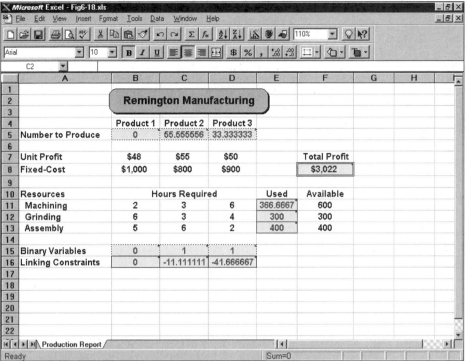

Figure 6.20
Optimal mixed-
integer solution
to Remington's
fixed-charge
problem.

and $X_3 = 33.33$). Solver assigned values of 0, 1, and 1 to cells B15, C15, and D15 ($Y_1 = 0$, $Y_2 = 1$, and $Y_3 = 1$). Thus, Solver maintained the proper relationship between the X_i and Y_i because the linking constraints were specified for this problem.

The values in B16, C16, and D16 to indicate the amounts by which the values for X_1, X_2, and X_3 (in cells B5, C5, and D5) fall below the upper bounds imposed by their respective linking constraints (and calculated in section 6.12.4). Thus, the optimal value of X_2 is approximately 11.11 units below its upper bound of 66.67 and the optimal value of X_3 is approximately 41.67 units below its upper bound of 75. Because the optimal value of Y_1 is zero, the linking constraint for X_1 and Y_1 imposes an upper bound of zero on X_1. Thus, the value in cell B16 indicates that the optimal value of X_1 is zero units below its upper bound of zero.

Because our formulation of this model did not specify that the X_i be integers, we should not be surprised by the fractional values obtained for these variables in this solution. If we round the values of X_2 and X_3 down to 55 and 33, we obtain an integer feasible solution with an objective function value of $2,975. If we want to find the optimal all-integer solution, we can add the appropriate integrality condition for the X_i to the constraint set and then re-solve the problem. This optimal all-integer solution is shown in Figure 6.21.

Note that more computational effort is required to obtain the all-integer solution shown in Figure 6.21 (48 candidate problems) versus the effort required to obtain the mixed-integer solution shown in Figure 6.20 (4 candidate problems). All this additional work resulted in only a $5 improvement in the objective function over the all-integer solution we obtained from rounding down the solution in Figure 6.20. This highlights two important points. First, problems involving binary integer variables are often easier to solve than problems involving general integer variables. Second, good

Figure 6.21
Optimal all-
integer solution
to Remington's
fixed-charge
problem.

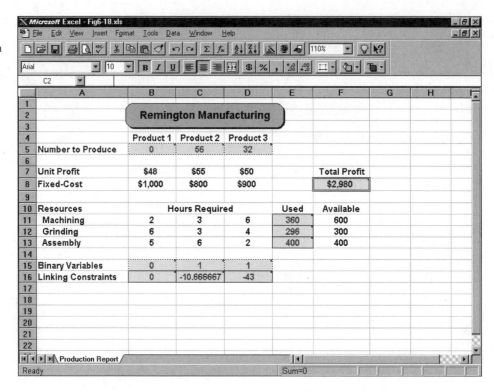

near-optimal solutions often can be obtained by rounding, so this approach is not necessarily ineffective—and could be the only practical solution available for large ILPs
that are difficult to solve.

6.13   MINIMUM ORDER/PURCHASE SIZE

Many investment, production, and distribution problems have minimum purchase
amounts or minimum production lot size requirements that must be met. For example, a particular investment opportunity might require a minimum investment of
$25,000. Or, a supplier of a given part used in a production process might require a
minimum order of 10 units. Similarly, many manufacturing companies have a policy
of not producing any units of a given item unless a certain minimum lot size will be
produced.

To see how these types of minimum order/purchase requirements can be modeled,
suppose that in the previous problem Remington Manufacturing did not want to produce any units of product 3 (X_3) unless it produced at least 40 units of this product.
This type of restriction is modeled as:

$$X_3 \le M_3 Y_3$$
$$X_3 \ge 40 Y_3$$

The first constraint is the same type of linking constraint described earlier, in
which M_3 represents an upper bound on X_3 (or an arbitrarily large number) and Y_3 rep-

resents a binary variable. If X_3 assumes any positive value, Y_3 must equal 1 (if $X_3 > 0$, then $Y_3 = 1$). However, according to the second constraint, if Y_3 equals 1, then X_3 must be greater than or equal to 40 (if $Y_3 = 1$, then $X_3 \geq 40$). On the other hand, if X_3 equals 0, Y_3 must also equal 0 in order to satisfy both constraints. Together, these two constraints ensure that if X_3 assumes any positive value, that value must be at least 40. This example illustrates how binary variables can be used to model a practical condition that is likely to occur in a variety of decision problems.

6.14 QUANTITY DISCOUNTS

In all of the LP problems considered to this point, we have assumed that the profit or cost coefficients in the objective function were constant. For example, consider our revised Blue Ridge Hot Tubs problem, which is represented by:

MAX:	$350X_1 + 300X_2$	} profit
Subject to:	$1X_1 + 1X_2 \leq 200$	} pump constraint
	$9X_1 + 6X_2 \leq 1{,}520$	} labor constraint
	$12X_1 + 16X_2 \leq 2{,}650$	} tubing constraint
	$X_1, X_2 \geq 0$	} nonnegativity conditions
	X_1, X_2 must be integers	} integrality conditions

This model assumes that *every* additional Aqua-Spa (X_1) manufactured and sold results in a $350 increase in profit. It also assumes that every additional Hydro-Lux (X_2) manufactured and sold results in a $300 increase in profit. However, as the production of these products increases, quantity discounts might be obtained on component parts that would cause the profit margin on these items to increase.

For example, suppose that if the company produces more than 75 Aqua-Spas, it will be able to obtain quantity discounts and other economies of scale that would increase the profit margin to $375 per unit for each unit produced in excess of 75. Similarly, suppose that if the company produces more than 50 Hydro-Luxes, it will be able to increase its profit margin to $325 for each unit produced in excess of 50. That is, each of the first 75 units of X_1 and the first 50 units of X_2 would produce profits of $350 and $300 per unit, respectively, and each additional unit of X_1 and X_2 would produce profits of $375 and $325 per unit, respectively. How do we model this type of problem?

6.14.1 Formulating the Model

In order to accommodate the different profit rates that can be generated by producing Aqua-Spas and Hydro-Luxes, we need to define new variables for the problem, where

X_{11} = the number of Aqua-Spas produced at $350 profit per unit

X_{12} = the number of Aqua-Spas produced at $375 profit per unit

X_{21} = the number of Hydro-Luxes produced at $300 profit per unit

X_{22} = the number of Hydro-Luxes produced at $325 profit per unit

Using these variables, we can begin to reformulate our problem as:

MAX: $350X_{11} + 375X_{12} + 300X_{21} + 325X_{22}$

Subject to: $1X_{11} + 1X_{12} + 1X_{21} + 1X_{22} \leq 200$ } pump constraint

                $9X_{11} + 9X_{12} + 6X_{21} + 6X_{22} \leq 1{,}520$ } labor constraint

                $12X_{11} + 12X_{12} + 16X_{21} + 16X_{22} \leq 2{,}650$ } tubing constraint

                All $X_{ij} \geq 0$ } simple lower bounds

                All X_{ij} must be integers   } integrality conditions

This formulation is not complete. Notice that the variable X_{12} would always be preferred over X_{11} because X_{12} requires exactly the same resources as X_{11} and generates a larger per-unit profit. The same relationship holds between X_{22} and X_{21}. Thus, the optimal solution to the problem is $X_{11} = 0$, $X_{12} = 118$, $X_{21} = 0$, and $X_{22} = 76$. However, this solution is not allowable because we cannot produce any units of X_{12} until we have produced 75 units of X_{11}; and we cannot produce any units of X_{22} until we have produced 50 units of X_{21}. Therefore, we must identify some additional constraints to ensure that these conditions are met.

6.14.2   The Missing Constraints

To ensure that the model does not allow any units of X_{12} to be produced unless we have produced 75 units of X_{11}, consider the constraints:

$$X_{12} \leq M_{12}Y_1$$
$$X_{11} \geq 75Y_1$$

In the first constraint, M_{12} represents some arbitrarily large numeric constant and Y_1 represents a binary variable. The first constraint requires that $Y_1 = 1$ if any units of X_{12} are produced (if $X_{12} > 0$, then $Y_1 = 1$). However, if $Y_1 = 1$ then the second constraint would require X_{11} to be at least 75. According to the second constraint, the only way that fewer than 75 units of X_{11} can be produced is if $Y_1 = 0$, which, by the first constraint, implies $X_{12} = 0$. These two constraints do not allow any units of X_{12} to be produced unless at least 75 units of X_{11} have been produced. The following constraints ensure that the model does not allow any units of X_{22} to be produced unless we have produced 50 units of X_{21}:

$$X_{22} \leq M_{22}Y_2$$
$$X_{21} \geq 50Y_2$$

If we include these new constraints in our previous formulation (along with the constraints necessary to make Y_1 and Y_2 operate as binary variables), we would have an accurate formulation of the decision problem. The optimal solution to this problem is $X_{11} = 75$, $X_{12} = 43$, $X_{21} = 50$, $X_{22} = 26$.

6.15   A CONTRACT AWARD PROBLEM

Other conditions often arise in decision problems that can be modeled effectively using binary variables. The following example, which involves awarding contracts, illustrates some of these conditions.

B&G Construction is a commercial building company located in Tampa, Florida. The company has recently signed contracts to construct four buildings in different locations throughout southern Florida. Each building project requires large amounts of cement to be delivered to the building sites. At B&G's request, three cement companies have submitted bids for supplying the cement for these jobs. The following table summarizes the prices the three companies charge per delivered ton of cement and the maximum amount of cement that each company can provide.

Cost per Delivered Ton of Cement

	Project 1	Project 2	Project 3	Project 4	Max. Supply
Company 1	$120	$115	$130	$125	525
Company 2	$100	$150	$110	$105	450
Company 3	$140	$95	$145	$165	550
Total Tons Needed	450	275	300	350	

For example, company 1 can supply a maximum of 525 tons of cement, and each ton delivered to projects 1, 2, 3, and 4 will cost $120, $115, $130, and $125, respectively. The costs vary primarily because of the different distances between the cement plants and the construction sites. The numbers in the last row of the table indicate the total amount of cement (in tons) required for each project.

In addition to the maximum supplies listed, each cement company placed special conditions on its bid. Specifically, company 1 indicated that it will not supply orders of less than 150 tons for any of the construction projects. Company 2 indicated that it can supply more than 200 tons to no more than one of the projects. Company 3 indicated that it will accept only orders that total 200 tons, 400 tons, or 550 tons.

B&G can contract with more than one supplier to meet the cement requirements for a given project. The problem is to determine what amounts to purchase from each supplier to meet the demands for each project at the least total cost.

This problem seems like a transportation problem in which we want to determine how much cement should be shipped from each cement company to each construction project in order to meet the demands of the projects at a minimum cost. However, the special conditions imposed by each supplier require side-constraints, which are not usually found in a standard transportation problem. First, we'll discuss the formulation of the objective function and the transportation constraints. Then, we'll consider how to implement the side-constraints required by the special conditions in the problem.

6.15.1   Formulating the Model: The Objective Function and Transportation Constraints

To begin formulating this problem, we need to define our decision variables as:

X_{ij} = tons of cement purchased from company i for construction project j

The objective function to minimize total cost is represented by:

$$\text{MIN:} \quad 120X_{11} + 115X_{12} + 130X_{13} + 125X_{14}$$
$$+ 100X_{21} + 150X_{22} + 110X_{23} + 105X_{24}$$
$$+ 140X_{31} + 95X_{32} + 145X_{33} + 165X_{34}$$

To ensure that the maximum supply of cement from each company is not exceeded, we need the following constraints:

$$X_{11} + X_{12} + X_{13} + X_{14} \leq 525 \quad \} \text{ supply from company 1}$$
$$X_{21} + X_{22} + X_{23} + X_{24} \leq 450 \quad \} \text{ supply from company 2}$$
$$X_{31} + X_{32} + X_{33} + X_{34} \leq 550 \quad \} \text{ supply from company 3}$$

To ensure that the requirement for cement at each construction project is met, we need the following constraints:

$$X_{11} + X_{21} + X_{31} = 450 \quad\quad \} \text{ demand for cement at project 1}$$
$$X_{12} + X_{22} + X_{32} = 275 \quad\quad \} \text{ demand for cement at project 2}$$
$$X_{13} + X_{23} + X_{33} = 300 \quad\quad \} \text{ demand for cement at project 3}$$
$$X_{14} + X_{24} + X_{34} = 350 \quad\quad \} \text{ demand for cement at project 4}$$

6.15.2   Implementing the Transportation Constraints

The objective function and the constraints of this problem are implemented in the spreadsheet model shown in Figure 6.22 (and in the file FIG6-22.xls on your data disk).

In this spreadsheet, the costs per delivered ton of cement are shown in cells B6 through E8. Cells B12 through E14 represent the decision variables in the model. The objective function is entered in cell G17 as:

Formula for cell G17:   =SUMPRODUCT(B6:E8,B12:E14)

The LHS formulas of the supply constraints are entered in cells F12 through F14 as:

Formula for cell F12:   =SUM(B12:E12)
(Copy to F13 through F14.)

Cells G12 through G14 contain the RHS values for these constraints. The LHS formulas for the demand constraints are entered in cells B15 through E15 as:

Formula for cell B15:   =SUM(B12:B14)
(Copy to C15 through E15.)

Cells B16 through E16 contain the RHS values for these constraints.

6.15.3   Formulating the Model: The Side-Constraints

Company 1 indicated that it will not accept orders for less than 150 tons for any of the construction projects. This minimum order-size restriction is modeled by the following eight constraints, where the Y_{ij} represent binary variables:

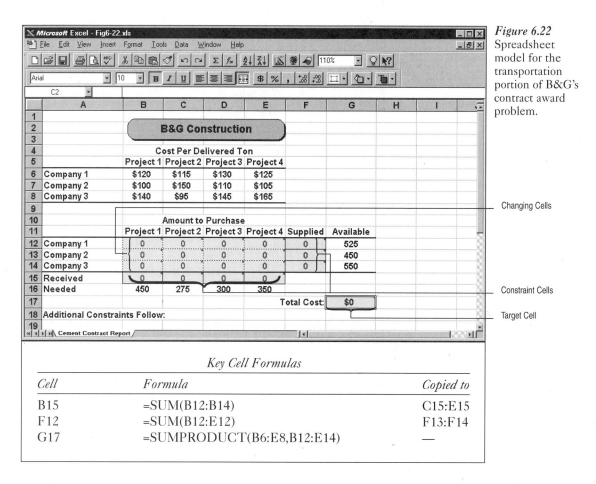

Figure 6.22
Spreadsheet model for the transportation portion of B&G's contract award problem.

Key Cell Formulas

Cell	Formula	Copied to
B15	=SUM(B12:B14)	C15:E15
F12	=SUM(B12:E12)	F13:F14
G17	=SUMPRODUCT(B6:E8,B12:E14)	—

$$X_{11} \leq 525Y_{11} \quad \text{(implement as } X_{11} - 525Y_{11} \leq 0)$$
$$X_{12} \leq 525Y_{12} \quad \text{(implement as } X_{12} - 525Y_{12} \leq 0)$$
$$X_{13} \leq 525Y_{13} \quad \text{(implement as } X_{13} - 525Y_{13} \leq 0)$$
$$X_{14} \leq 525Y_{14} \quad \text{(implement as } X_{14} - 525Y_{14} \leq 0)$$
$$X_{11} \geq 150Y_{11} \quad \text{(implement as } X_{11} - 150Y_{11} \geq 0)$$
$$X_{12} \geq 150Y_{12} \quad \text{(implement as } X_{12} - 150Y_{12} \geq 0)$$
$$X_{13} \geq 150Y_{13} \quad \text{(implement as } X_{13} - 150Y_{13} \geq 0)$$
$$X_{14} \geq 150Y_{14} \quad \text{(implement as } X_{14} - 150Y_{14} \geq 0)$$

Each constraint has an algebraically equivalent constraint, which will ultimately be used in implementing the constraint in the spreadsheet. The first four constraints represent linking constraints that ensure if X_{11}, X_{12}, X_{13}, or X_{14} is greater than 0, then its associated binary variable (Y_{11}, Y_{12}, Y_{13}, or Y_{14}) must equal 1. (These constraints also indicate that 525 is the maximum value that can be assumed by X_{11}, X_{12}, X_{13}, and X_{14}.) The next four constraints ensure that if X_{11}, X_{12}, X_{13}, or X_{14} is greater than 0, it must be at least 150. We include these constraints in the formulation of this model to ensure that any order given to company 1 is for at least 150 tons of cement.

Company 2 indicated that it can supply more than 200 tons to no more than one of the projects. This type of restriction is represented by the following set of constraints where, again, the Y_{ij} represent binary variables:

$$X_{21} \leq 200 + 250Y_{21} \qquad \text{(implement as } X_{21} - 200 - 250Y_{21} \leq 0)$$
$$X_{22} \leq 200 + 250Y_{22} \qquad \text{(implement as } X_{22} - 200 - 250Y_{22} \leq 0)$$
$$X_{23} \leq 200 + 250Y_{23} \qquad \text{(implement as } X_{23} - 200 - 250Y_{23} \leq 0)$$
$$X_{24} \leq 200 + 250Y_{24} \qquad \text{(implement as } X_{24} - 200 - 250Y_{24} \leq 0)$$
$$Y_{21} + Y_{22} + Y_{23} + Y_{24} \leq 1 \quad \text{(implement as is)}$$

The first constraint indicates that the amount supplied from company 2 for project 1 must be less than 200 if $Y_{21} = 0$, or less than 450 (the maximum supply from company 2) if $Y_{21} = 1$. The next three constraints have similar interpretations for the amount supplied from company 2 to projects 2, 3, and 4, respectively. The last constraint indicates that at most one of Y_{21}, Y_{22}, Y_{23}, and Y_{24} can equal 1. Therefore, only one of the projects can receive more than 200 tons of cement from company 2.

The final set of constraints for this problem addresses company 3's stipulation that it will accept only orders totaling 200, 400, or 550 tons. This type of condition is modeled using binary Y_{ij} variables as:

$$X_{31} + X_{32} + X_{33} + X_{34} = 200Y_{31} + 400Y_{32} + 550Y_{33}$$
$$\text{(implement as } X_{31} + X_{32} + X_{33} + X_{34} - 200Y_{31} - 400Y_{32} - 550Y_{33} = 0)$$

$$Y_{31} + Y_{32} + Y_{33} \leq 1 \text{ (implement as is)}$$

These constraints allow for the total amount ordered from company 3 to assume four distinct values. If $Y_{31} = Y_{32} = Y_{33} = 0$, then no cement will be ordered from company 3. If $Y_{31} = 1$, then 200 tons must be ordered. If $Y_{32} = 1$, then 400 tons must be ordered. Finally, if $Y_{33} = 1$, then 550 tons must be ordered from company 3. These two constraints enforce the special condition imposed by company 3.

6.15.4   Implementing the Side-Constraints

Although the side-constraints in this problem allow us to impose important restrictions on the feasible solutions that can be considered, these constraints serve more of a "mechanical" purpose—to make the model work—but are not of primary interest to management. Thus, it is often convenient to implement side-constraints in an out-of-the-way area of the spreadsheet so that they do not detract from the primary purpose of the spreadsheet—in this case, to determine how much cement to order from each potential supplier. Figure 6.23 shows how the side-constraints for the current problem can be implemented in a spreadsheet.

To implement the side-constraints for company 1, we enter the batch-size restriction of 150 in cell B20 and reserve cells B21 through E21 to represent the binary variables Y_{11}, Y_{12}, Y_{13}, and Y_{14}. The LHS formulas for the linking constraints for company 1 are implemented in cells B22 through E22 as:

Formula for cell B22:   =B12–$G$12*B21
(Copy to C22 through E22.)

Cell F22 contains a reminder for us to tell Solver that these cells must be less than or equal to 0. The LHS formulas for the batch-size constraints for company 1 are implemented in cells B23 through E23 as:

Formula for cell B23:   =B12–$B$20*B21
(Copy to C23 through E23.)

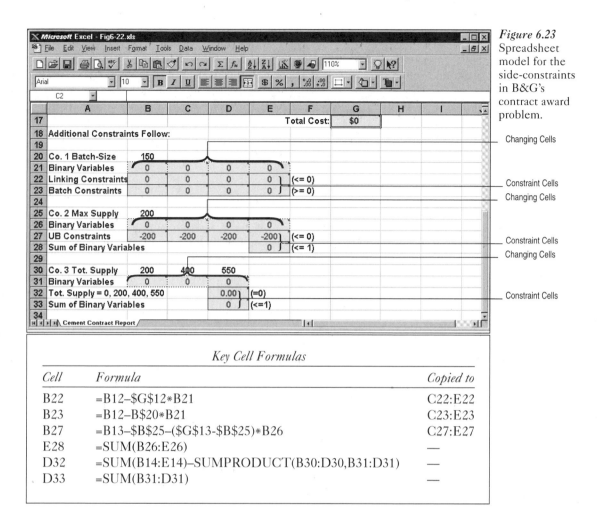

Figure 6.23
Spreadsheet
model for the
side-constraints
in B&G's
contract award
problem.

Key Cell Formulas		
Cell	*Formula*	*Copied to*
B22	=B12-$G$12*B21	C22:E22
B23	=B12-B$20*B21	C23:E23
B27	=B13-$B$25-($G$13-$B$25)*B26	C27:E27
E28	=SUM(B26:E26)	—
D32	=SUM(B14:E14)-SUMPRODUCT(B30:D30,B31:D31)	—
D33	=SUM(B31:D31)	—

Cell F23 contains a reminder for us to tell Solver that these cells must be greater than or equal to 0.

To implement the side-constraints for company 2, we enter the maximum supply value of 200 in cell B25 and reserve cells B26 through E26 to represent the binary variables Y_{21}, Y_{22}, Y_{23}, and Y_{24}. The LHS formulas for the maximum supply constraints are implemented in cells B27 through E27 as:

Formula for cell B27:   =B13-$B$25-($G$13-$B$25)*B26
(Copy to C27 through E27.)

Cell F27 reminds us to tell Solver that these cells must be less than or equal to 0. As discussed earlier, to ensure that no more than one order from company 2 exceeds 200 tons, the sum of the binary variables for company 2 cannot exceed 1. The LHS formula for this constraint is entered in cell E28 as:

Formula for cell E28:   =SUM(B26:E26)

Cell F28 reminds us to tell Solver that this cell must be less than or equal to 1.

To implement the side-constraints for company 3, the three possible total order amounts are entered in cells B30 through D30. Cells B31 through D31 are reserved to represent the binary variables Y_{31}, Y_{32}, and Y_{33}. The LHS formula for company 3's total supply side-constraint is entered in cell D32 as:

Formula for cell D32:   =SUM(B14:E14)–SUMPRODUCT(B30:D30,B31:D31)

Cell E32 reminds us to tell Solver that cell D32 must equal 0. Finally, to ensure that no more than one of the binary variables for company 3 is set equal to 1, we enter the sum of these variables in cell D33 as:

Formula for cell D33:   =SUM(B31:D31)

Cell E33 reminds us to tell Solver that this cell must be less than or equal to 1.

6.15.5 Solving the Model

Due to the large number of variables and constraints in this problem, we summarized the Solver parameters and options required for this problem in Figure 6.24. Note that all of the cells representing binary variables must be identified as changing cells and must be constrained to assume only integer values between 0 and 1.

Figure 6.24
Solver parameters and options for B&G's contract award problem.

Solver Parameters

Set Target Cell: G17
Equal to: Min
By Changing Cells: B12:E14,B21:E21,B26:E26,B31:D31
Subject to the Constraints:

B12:E14 ≥ 0
B21:E21 ≥ 0
B21:E21 ≤ 1
B21:E21 = integer
B26:E26 ≥ 0
B26:E26 ≤ 1
B26:E26 = integer
B31:D31 ≥ 0
B31:D31 ≤ 1
B31:D31 = integer
F12:F14 ≤ G12:G14
B15:E15 = B16:E16
B22:E22 ≤ 0
B23:E23 ≥ 0
B27:E27 ≤ 0
E28 ≤ 1
D32 = 0
D33 ≤ 1

Solver Options

Assume Linear Model   Tolerance = 0%
Use Automatic Scaling Iterations = 100

6.15.6 *Analyzing the Solution*

An optimal solution to this problem is shown in Figure 6.25. (There are alternate optimal solutions to this problem.) In this solution, the amounts of cement required by each construction project are met exactly. Also, each condition imposed by the side-constraints for each company is met. Specifically, the orders awarded to company 1 are for at least 150 tons; only one of the orders awarded to company 2 exceeds 200 tons; and the sum of the orders awarded to company 3 is exactly equal to 400 tons.

6.16 *THE BRANCH-AND-BOUND ALGORITHM (OPTIONAL)*

As mentioned earlier, a special procedure, known as the branch-and-bound (B&B) algorithm is required to solve ILPs. Although we can easily indicate the presence of integer variables in a model, it usually requires quite a bit of effort on Solver's part to actually solve an ILP problem using the B&B algorithm. To better appreciate and understand what is involved in the B&B algorithm, let's consider how it works.

The B&B algorithm starts by relaxing all the integrality conditions in an ILP and solving the resulting LP problem. As noted earlier, if we are lucky, the optimal solution to the relaxed LP problem might happen to satisfy the original integrality conditions. If this occurs, then we are done—the optimal solution to the LP relaxation is also the optimal solution to the ILP. However, it is more likely that the optimal solution to the LP will violate one or more of the original integrality conditions. For example, consider the problem on the next page whose integer and relaxed feasible regions were shown in Figure 6.1 and are repeated in Figure 6.26.

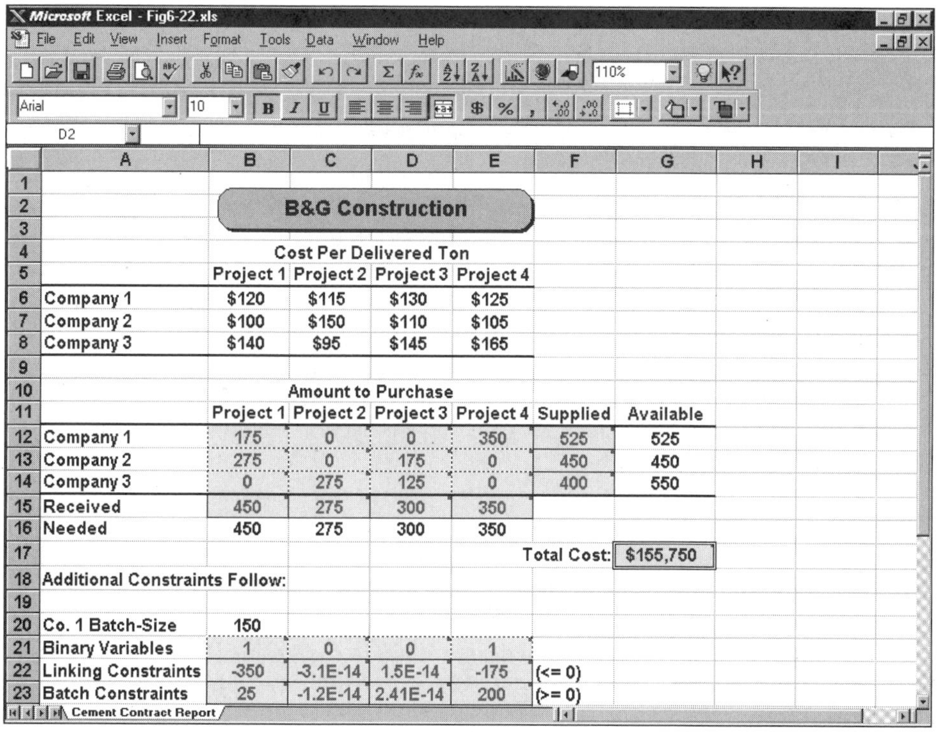

	A	B	C	D	E	F	G
1							
2		B&G Construction					
3							
4		Cost Per Delivered Ton					
5		Project 1	Project 2	Project 3	Project 4		
6	Company 1	$120	$115	$130	$125		
7	Company 2	$100	$150	$110	$105		
8	Company 3	$140	$95	$145	$165		
9							
10		Amount to Purchase					
11		Project 1	Project 2	Project 3	Project 4	Supplied	Available
12	Company 1	175	0	0	350	525	525
13	Company 2	275	0	175	0	450	450
14	Company 3	0	275	125	0	400	550
15	Received	450	275	300	350		
16	Needed	450	275	300	350		
17						Total Cost:	$155,750
18	Additional Constraints Follow:						
19							
20	Co. 1 Batch-Size	150					
21	Binary Variables	1	0	0	1		
22	Linking Constraints	-350	-3.1E-14	1.5E-14	-175	(<= 0)	
23	Batch Constraints	25	-1.2E-14	2.41E-14	200	(>= 0)	

Figure 6.25 Optimal solution to B&G's contract award problem.

Figure 6.26
Solution to LP
relaxation at
noninteger corner
point.

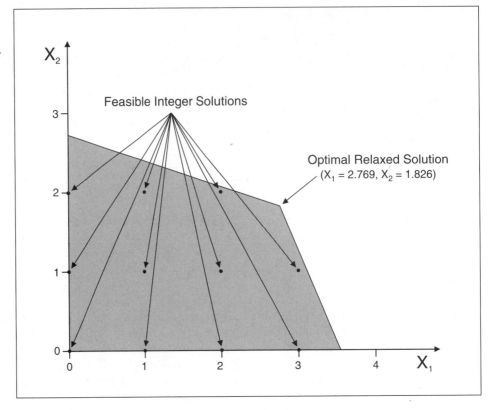

$$\text{MAX:} \qquad 2X_1 + 3X_2$$
$$\text{Subject to:} \quad X_1 + 3X_2 \le 8.25$$
$$2.5X_1 + X_2 \le 8.75$$
$$X_1, X_2 \ge 0$$
$$X_1, X_2 \text{ must be integers}$$

If we relax the integrality conditions in this problem and solve the resulting LP problem, we obtain the solution $X_1 = 2.769$, $X_2 = 1.826$ shown in Figure 6.26. This solution clearly violates the integrality conditions stated in the original problem. Part of the difficulty here is that none of the corner points of the relaxed feasible region are integer feasible (other than the origin). We know that the optimal solution to an LP problem will occur at a corner point of its feasible region but, in this case, none of those corner points (except the origin) correspond to integer solutions. Thus, we need to modify the problem so that the integer feasible solutions to the problem occur at corner points of the relaxed feasible region. This is accomplished by branching.

6.16.1   *Branching*

Any integer variable in an ILP that assumes a fractional value in the optimal solution to the relaxed problem can be designated a **branching variable.** For example, the variables X_1 and X_2 in the previous problem should assume only integer values but were assigned the values $X_1 = 2.769$ and $X_2 = 1.826$ in the optimal solution to the LP relaxation of the problem. Either of these variables could be selected as branching variables.

Let's arbitrarily choose X_1 as our branching variable. Because the current value of X_1 is not integer feasible, we want to eliminate this solution from further consideration. Many other solutions in this same vicinity of the relaxed feasible region can be eliminated as well. That is, X_1 must assume a value less than or equal to 2 ($X_1 \leq 2$) or greater than or equal to 3 ($X_1 \geq 3$) in the optimal integer solution to the ILP. Therefore, all other possible solutions where X_1 assumes values between 2 and 3 (such as the current solution where $X_1 = 2.769$) can be eliminated from consideration. By branching on X_1, our original ILP problem can be subdivided into the following two candidate problems:

Problem I: MAX: $2X_1 + 3X_2$

Subject to: $X_1 + 3X_2 \leq 8.25$

$2.5X_1 + X_2 \leq 8.75$

$X_1 \leq 2$

$X_1, X_2 \geq 0$

X_1, X_2 must be integers

Problem II: MAX: $2X_1 + 3X_2$

Subject to: $X_1 + 3X_2 \leq 8.25$

$2.5X_1 + X_2 \leq 8.75$

$X_1 \geq 3$

$X_1, X_2 \geq 0$

X_1, X_2 must be integers

The integer and relaxed feasible regions for each candidate problem are shown in Figure 6.27. Notice that a portion of the relaxed feasible region shown in Figure 6.26 has been eliminated in Figure 6.27, but none of the feasible integer solutions shown in Figure 6.26 have been eliminated. This is a general property of the branching operation in the B&B algorithm. Also notice that several feasible integer solutions now occur on the boundary lines of the feasible regions shown in Figure 6.27. More importantly, one of these feasible integer solutions occurs at an extreme point of the relaxed feasible region for problem I (at the point $X_1 = 2$, $X_2 = 0$). If we relax the integrality conditions in problem I and solve the resulting LP, we could obtain an integer solution because one of the corner points of the relaxed feasible region corresponds to such a point. (However, this integer feasible extreme point still might not be the optimal solution to the relaxed LP problem.)

6.16.2 Bounding

The next step in the B&B algorithm is to select one of the existing candidate problems for further analysis. Let's arbitrarily select problem I. If we relax the integrality conditions in problem I and solve the resulting LP, we obtain the solution $X_1 = 2$, $X_2 = 2.083$ and an objective function value of 10.25. This value represents an upper bound on the best possible integer solution that can be obtained from problem I. That is, because the relaxed solution to problem I is not integer feasible, we have not yet found the best possible integer solution for this problem. However, we do know that the objective function value of the best possible integer solution that can be obtained from problem I can be no greater than 10.25. As we shall see, this information can be

Figure 6.27
Feasible
solutions to the
candidate
problems after
the first branch.

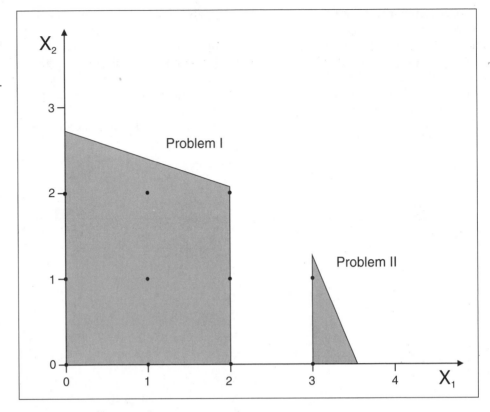

useful in reducing the amount of work required to locate the optimal integer solution
to an ILP problem.

6.16.3   *Branching Again*

Because the relaxed solution to problem I is not entirely integer feasible, the B&B
algorithm proceeds by selecting X_2 as a branching variable and creating two additional candidate problems from problem I. These problems are represented as:

$$\text{Problem III:} \quad \text{MAX:} \qquad 2X_1 + 3X_2$$

Subject to: $X_1 + 3X_2 \leq 8.25$

$2.5X_1 + X_2 \leq 8.75$

$X_1 \leq 2$

$X_2 \leq 2$

$X_1, X_2 \geq 0$

X_1, X_2 must be integers

$$\text{Problem IV:} \quad \text{MAX:} \qquad 2X_1 + 3X_2$$

Subject to: $X_1 + 3X_2 \leq 8.25$

$2.5X_1 + X_2 \leq 8.75$

$X_1 \leq 2$

$$X_2 \geq 3$$
$$X_1, X_2 \geq 0$$
$$X_1, X_2 \text{ must be integers}$$

Problem III is created by adding the constraint $X_2 \leq 2$ to problem I. Problem IV is created by adding the constraint $X_2 \geq 3$ to problem I. Thus, our previous solution to problem I (where $X_2 = 2.083$) will be eliminated from consideration as a possible solution to the LP relaxations of problems III and IV.

Problem IV is infeasible because there are no feasible solutions where $X_2 \geq 3$. The integer and relaxed feasible regions for problems II and III are summarized in Figure 6.28.

All of the corner points to the relaxed feasible region of problem III correspond to integer feasible solutions. Thus, if we relax the integrality conditions in problem III and solve the resulting LP problem, we must obtain an integer feasible solution. The solution to problem III is represented by $X_1 = 2$, $X_2 = 2$ and has an objective function value of 10.

6.16.4   Bounding Again

Although we have obtained an integer feasible solution to our problem, we won't know if it is the *optimal* integer solution until we evaluate the remaining candidate problem (that is, problem II). If we relax the integrality conditions in problem II and solve the resulting LP problem, we obtain the solution $X_1 = 3$, $X_2 = 1.25$ with an objective function value of 9.75.

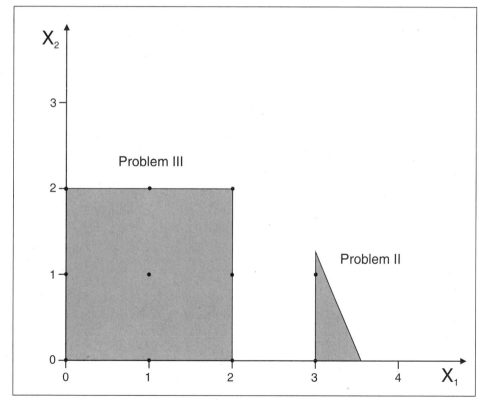

Figure 6.28
Feasible solutions to the candidate problems after the second branch.

Because the solution to problem II is not integer feasible, we might be inclined to branch on X_2 in a further attempt to determine the best possible integer solution for problem II. However, this is not necessary. Earlier we noted that for *maximization* ILP problems, the objective function value at the optimal solution to the LP relaxation of the problem represents an *upper bound* on the optimal objective function value of the original ILP problem. This means that even though we do not yet know the optimal integer solution to problem II, we do know that its objective function value cannot be greater than 9.75. And because 9.75 is worse than the objective function value for the integer solution obtained from problem III, we cannot find a better integer solution by continuing to branch problem II. Therefore, problem II can be eliminated from further consideration. Because we have no more candidate problems to consider, we can conclude that the optimal integer solution to our problem is $X_1 = 2$, $X_2 = 2$ with an optimal objective function value of 10.

6.16.5   Summary of B&B Example

The steps involved in the solution to our example problem can be represented graphically in the form of a **branch-and-bound tree,** as shown in Figure 6.29. Although Figure 6.26 indicates that 11 integer solutions exist for this problem, we do not have to locate all of them in order to prove that the integer solution we found is the optimal solution. The bounding operation of the B&B algorithm eliminated the need to explicitly enumerate all the integer feasible solutions and select the best of those as the optimal solution.

Figure 6.29
Branch-and-bound tree for the example problem.

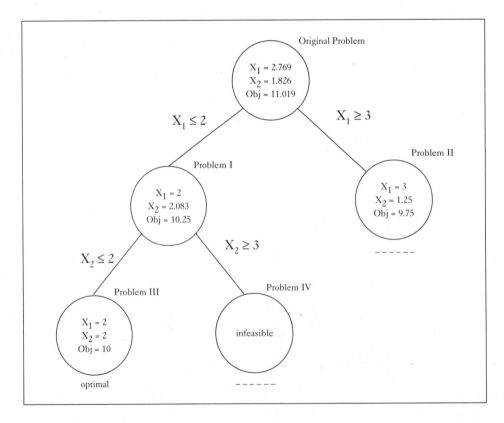

If the relaxed solution to problem II was greater than 10 (say 12.5), then the B&B algorithm would have continued branching from this problem in an attempt to find a better integer solution (an integer solution with an objective function value greater than 10). Similarly, if problem IV had a feasible noninteger solution, we would have needed to perform further branching from that problem if its relaxed objective value was better than that of the best known integer feasible solution. Thus, the first integer solution obtained using B&B will not always be the optimal integer solution. A more detailed description of the operations of the B&B algorithm is given in Figure 6.30.

The Branch-and-Bound Algorithm

1. Relax all the integrality conditions in ILP and solve the resulting LP problem. If the optimal solution to the relaxed LP problem happens to satisfy the original integrality conditions, stop—this is the optimal integer solution. Otherwise, proceed to step 2.

2. If the problem being solved is a maximization problem, let Z_{best} = -infinity. If it is a minimization problem, let Z_{best} = +infinity. (In general Z_{best} represents the objective function value of the best known integer solution as the algorithm proceeds.)

3. Let X_j represent one of the variables that violated the integrality conditions in the solution to the problem that was solved most recently and let b_j represent its noninteger value. Let $INT(b_j)$ represent the largest integer that is less than b_j. Create two new candidate problems: one by appending the constraint $X_j \leq INT(b_j)$ to the most recently solved LP problem, and the other by appending the constraint $X_j \geq INT(b_j)+1$ to the most recently solved LP problem. Place both of these new LP problems in a list of candidate problems to be solved.

4. If the list of candidate problems is empty, proceed to step 9. Otherwise, remove a candidate problem from the list, relax any integrality conditions in the problem, and solve it.

5. If there is not solution to the current candidate problem (that is, it is infeasible), proceed to step 4. Otherwise, let Z_{cp} denote the optimal objective function value for the current candidate problem.

6. If Z_{cp} is not better than Z_{best} (for a maximization problem $Z_{cp} <= Z_{best}$ or for a minimization problem $Z_{cp} >= Z_{best}$), proceed to step 4.

7. If the solution to the current candidate problem *does not* satisfy the original integrality conditions, proceed to step 3.

8. If the solution to the current candidate problem *does* satisfy the original integrality conditions, a better integer solution has been found. Thus, let $Z_{best}=Z_{cp}$ and save the solution obtained for this candidate problem. Then go back to step 4.

9. Stop. The optimal solution has been found and has an objective function value given by the current value of Z_{best}.

Figure 6.30
Detailed description of the B&B algorithm for solving ILP problems.

THE WORLD OF MANAGEMENT SCIENCE

Who Eats the Float?—Maryland National Improves Check Clearing Operations and Cuts Costs

Maryland National Bank (MNB) of Baltimore typically processes about 500,000 checks worth over $250,000,000 each day. Those checks not drawn on MNB or a local bank must be cleared via the Federal Reserve System, a private clearing bank, or a "direct send" by courier service to the bank on which they were drawn.

Because funds are not available until the check clears, banks try to maximize the availability of current funds by reducing the float—the time interval required for a check to clear. Banks publish an availability schedule listing the number of days before funds from a deposited check are available to the customer. If clearing time is longer than the schedule, the bank must "eat the float." If the check is cleared through the Federal Reserve and clearing takes longer than the Federal Reserve availability schedule, then the Federal Reserve "eats the float." If clearing time is actually less than the local bank's availability schedule, the customer "eats the float." The cost of float is related to the daily cost of capital.

MNB uses a system based on binary integer LP to decide the timing and method to be used for each bundle of checks of a certain type (called a cash letter). Total clearing costs (the objective function) include float costs, clearing charges from the Federal Reserve or private clearing banks, and transportation costs for direct sends. Constraints ensure that exactly one method is chosen for each check type and that a method can be used only at a time that method is available. Use of this system saves the bank $100,000 annually.

Source: Markland, Robert E., and Robert M. Nauss, "Improving Transit Check Clearing Operations at Maryland National Bank," *Interfaces*, vol. 13, no. 1, February 1983, pages 1–9.

SUMMARY

This chapter discussed the issues involved in formulating and solving ILP problems. In some cases, acceptable integer solutions to ILP problems can be obtained by rounding the solution to the LP relaxation of the problem. However, this procedure can lead to suboptimal solutions, which might still be viable if you can show that the solution obtained by rounding is within an acceptable distance from the optimal integer solution. This approach might be the only practical way to obtain integer solutions for some ILP problems.

The B&B algorithm is a powerful technique for solving ILP problems. A great deal of skill and creativity are involved in formulating ILPs so that they can be solved efficiently using the B&B technique. Binary variables can be useful in overcoming a number of the simplifying assumptions often made in the formulation of LP models. Here again, quite a bit of creativity might be required on the part of the model builder to identify the constraints to implement various logical conditions in a given problem.

QUESTIONS AND PROBLEMS

1. As shown in Figure 6.1, the feasible region for an ILP consists of a relatively small, *finite* number of points, whereas the feasible region of its LP relaxation consists of an *infinite* number of points. Why, then, are ILPs so much harder to solve than LPs?

2. Identify reasonable values for M_{12} and M_{22} in the example on quantity discounts presented in section 6.14.2 in this chapter.

3. The following questions refer to the CRT Technologies project selection example presented in section 6.10 in this chapter. Formulate a constraint to implement the conditions described in each of the following statements.

    a. Out of projects 1, 2, 4, and 6, CRT's management wants to select exactly two projects.
    b. Project 2 can be selected only if project 3 is selected and vice versa.
    c. Project 5 cannot be undertaken unless both projects 3 and 4 are also undertaken.
    d. If projects 2 and 4 are undertaken, then project 5 must also be undertaken.

4. The following questions refer to the Blue Ridge Hot Tubs example discussed in this chapter.

    a. Suppose Howie Jones has to purchase a single piece of equipment for $1,000 in order to produce any Aqua-Spas or Hydro-Luxes. How will this affect the formulation of the model of his decision problem?
    b. Suppose Howie must buy one piece of equipment that costs $900 in order to produce any Aqua-Spas and a different piece of equipment that costs $800 in order to produce any Hydro-Luxes. How will this affect the formulation of the model for his problem?

5. The following problem was solved as an LP problem in Chapter 3. Now find its optimal integer solution. The manager of the Air-Express hub in Baltimore, Maryland, is concerned about labor costs at the hub and is interested in determining the most effective way to schedule workers. The hub operates seven days a week, and the number of packages it handles each day varies from day to day. Using historical data on the average number of packages received each day, the manager estimates the number of workers needed to handle the packages as:

Day of Week	Workers Required
Sunday	18
Monday	27
Tuesday	22
Wednesday	26
Thursday	25
Friday	21
Saturday	19

The package handlers working for Air-Express are unionized and are guaranteed a five-day work week with two consecutive days off. The base wage for the handlers is $655 per week. Because most workers prefer to have Saturday or Sunday off, the union has negotiated bonuses of $25 per day for its members who work on these days. The possible shifts and salaries for package handlers are:

Shift	Days Off	Wage
1	Sunday and Monday	$680
2	Monday and Tuesday	$705
3	Tuesday and Wednesday	$705
4	Wednesday and Thursday	$705
5	Thursday and Friday	$705
6	Friday and Saturday	$680
7	Saturday and Sunday	$655

How many package handlers should be assigned to each shift if the manager wants to have at least the required number of workers available each day at the least possible cost?

a. Formulate an ILP model for this problem.
b. Create a spreadsheet model for this problem and solve it.
c. What is the optimal solution?

6. Health Care Systems of Florida (HCSF) is planning to build a number of new emergency-care clinics in central Florida. HCSF management has divided a map of the area into seven regions. They want to locate the emergency centers so that all seven regions will be conveniently served by at least one facility. Five possible sites are available for constructing the new facilities. The regions that can be served conveniently by each site are indicated by X in the following table:

Region	Possible Building Sites				
	Sanford	Altamonte	Apopka	Casselberry	Maitland
1	X		X		
2	X	X		X	X
3		X		X	
4			X		X
5	X	X			
6			X		X
7				X	X
Cost ($000s)	$450	$650	$550	$500	$525

a. Formulate an ILP problem to determine which sites should be selected in order to provide convenient service to all locations in the least costly manner.
b. Implement your model in a spreadsheet and solve it.
c. What is the optimal solution?

7. Kentwood Electronics manufactures three components for stereo systems: CD players, tape decks, and stereo tuners. The wholesale price and manufacturing cost of each item are:

Component	Wholesale Price	Manufacturing Cost
CD Player	$150	$75
Tape Deck	$85	$35
Stereo Tuner	$70	$30

Each CD player produced requires three hours of assembly; each tape deck requires two hours of assembly; and each tuner requires one hour of assembly. However, the company manufactures these products only in batches of 150—partial batches are not allowed. The marketing department believes it can sell no more than 150,000 CD players, 100,000 tape decks, and 90,000 stereo tuners. It expects a demand for at least 50,000 units of each item and wants to be able to meet this demand. If Kentwood has 400,000 hours of assembly time available, how many batches of CD players, tape decks, and stereo tuners should it produce in order to maximize profits while meeting the minimum demand figures supplied by marketing?

   a.   Formulate an ILP model for this problem. (Hint: Let your decision variables represent the number of batches of each item to produce.)
   b.   Create a spreadsheet model for this problem and solve it.
   c.   What is the optimal solution?

8.   Radford Castings can produce brake shoes on six different machines. The following table summarizes the manufacturing costs associated with producing the brake shoes on each machine along with the available capacity on each machine. If the company has received an order for 1,800 brake shoes, how should it schedule these machines?

Machine	Fixed Cost	Variable Cost	Capacity
1	$1000	$21	500
2	$950	$23	600
3	$875	$25	750
4	$850	$24	400
5	$800	$20	600
6	$700	$26	800

   a.   Formulate an ILP model for this problem.
   b.   Create a spreadsheet model for this problem and solve it.
   c.   What is the optimal solution?

9.   The teenage daughter of a recently deceased movie star inherited a number of items from her famous father's estate. Rather than convert these assets to cash immediately, her financial advisor has recommended that she let some of these assets appreciate in value before disposing of them. An appraiser has given the following estimates of the assets' worth (in $1,000s) in each of the next five years.

	Year 1	Year 2	Year 3	Year 4	Year 5
Car	$35	$37	$39	$42	$45
Piano	16	17	18	19	20
Necklace	125	130	136	139	144
Desk	25	27	29	30	33
Golf Clubs	40	43	46	50	52
Humidor	5	7	8	10	11

Knowing this teenager's propensity to spend money, her financial advisor would like to develop a plan to dispose of these assets that will maximize the amount of money received and ensure that at least $30,000 of new funds become available each year to pay her college tuition.

    a.   Formulate an ILP model for this problem.

    b.   Create a spreadsheet model for this problem and solve it.

    c.   What is the optimal solution?

10. A developer of video game software has seven proposals for new games. Unfortunately, the company cannot develop all the proposals because its budget for new projects is limited to $950,000 and it has only 20 programmers to assign to new projects. The financial requirements, returns, and the number of programmers required by each project are summarized below. Projects 2 and 6 require specialized programming knowledge that only one of the programmers has. Both of these projects cannot be selected because the programmer with the necessary skills can be assigned to only one of the projects.

Project	Programmers Required	Capital Required	Estimated NPV
1	7	$250	$650
2	6	$175	$550
3	9	$300	$600
4	5	$150	$450
5	6	$145	$375
6	4	$160	$525
7	8	$325	$750

Note: All dollar amounts represent thousands.

    a.   Formulate an ILP model for this problem.

    b.   Create a spreadsheet model for this problem and solve it.

    c.   What is the optimal solution?

11. Tropicsun is a leading grower and distributor of fresh citrus products with three large citrus groves scattered around central Florida in the cities of Mt. Dora, Eustis, and Clermont. Tropicsun currently has 275,000 bushels of citrus at the grove in Mt. Dora, 400,000 bushels at the grove in Eustis, and 300,000 at the grove in Clermont. Tropicsun has citrus processing plants in Ocala, Orlando, and Leesburg with processing capacities to handle 200,000, 600,000, and 225,000 bushels, respectively. Tropicsun contracts with a local trucking company to transport its fruit from the groves to the processing plants. The trucking company charges a flat rate of $8 per mile regardless of how many bushels of fruit are transported. The following table summarizes the distances (in miles) between each grove and processing plant:

Distances (in Miles) Between Groves and Plants

	Processing Plant		
Grove	Ocala	Orlando	Leesburg
Mt. Dora	21	50	40
Eustis	35	30	22
Clermont	55	20	25

Tropicsun wants to determine how many bushels to ship from each grove to each processing plant in order to minimize the total transportation cost.

    a.   Formulate an ILP model for this problem.

    b.   Create a spreadsheet model for this problem and solve it.

    c.   What is the optimal solution?

12. A manufacturer is considering alternatives for building new plants in order to be located closer to three of its primary customers with whom it intends to develop long-term, sole-supplier relationships. The net cost of manufacturing and transporting each unit of the product to its customers will vary depending on where the plant is built and the production capacity of the plant. These costs are summarized in the table below:

Plant	Net Cost Per Unit To Supply Customer		
	X	Y	Z
1	35	30	45
2	45	40	50
3	70	65	50
4	20	45	25
5	65	45	45

The annual demand for products from customers X, Y, and Z is expected to be 40,000, 25,000, and 35,000 units, respectively. The annual production capacity and construction costs for each plant are:

Plant	Production Capacity	Construction Cost (in $000s)
1	40,000	$1,325
2	30,000	$1,100
3	50,000	$1,500
4	20,000	$1,200
5	40,000	$1,400

The company wants to determine which plant to build in order to satisfy customer demand at a minimum total cost.

a. Formulate an ILP model for this problem.
b. Create a spreadsheet model for this problem and solve it.
c. What is the optimal solution?

13. Refer to the previous question. Suppose plants 1 and 2 represent different building alternatives for the same site (that is, only one of these plants can be built). Similarly, suppose plants 4 and 5 represent different building alternatives for another site.

a. What additional constraints are required to model these new conditions?
b. Revise the spreadsheet to reflect these additional constraints and solve the resulting problem.
c. What is the optimal solution?

14. A company manufactures three products: A, B, and C. The company currently has an order for three units of product A, 7 units of product B, and 4 units of product C. There is no inventory for any of these products. All three products require special processing that can be done on one of two machines. The cost of producing each product on each machine is summarized on the next page:

	Cost of Producing a a Unit of Product		
Machine	A	B	C
1	$13	$9	$10
2	$11	$12	$8

The time required to produce each product on each machine is summarized below:

	Time (Hours) Needed to Produce a Unit of Product		
Machine	A	B	C
1	0.4	1.1	0.9
2	0.5	1.2	1.3

Assume machine 1 can be used for eight hours and machine 2 can be used for six hours. Each machine must undergo a special setup operation to prepare it to produce each product. After completing this setup for a product, any number of that product type can be produced. The setup costs for producing each product on each machine are summarized below.

	Setup Costs for Producing		
Machine	A	B	C
1	$55	$93	$60
2	$65	$58	$75

a. Formulate an ILP model to determine how many units of each product to produce on each machine in order to meet demand at a minimum cost.
b. Implement your model in a spreadsheet and solve it.
c. What is the optimal solution?

15. Clampett Oil purchases crude oil products from suppliers in Texas (TX), Oklahoma (OK), Pennsylvania (PA), and Alabama (AL), from which it refines four end-products: gasoline, kerosene, heating oil, and asphalt. Because of differences in the quality and chemical characteristics of the oil from the different suppliers, the amount of each end-product that can be refined from a barrel of crude oil varies depending on the source of the crude. Additionally, the amount of crude available from each source varies, as does the cost of a barrel of crude from each supplier. These values are summarized below. For example, the first line of this table indicates that a barrel of crude from Texas can be refined into 2 barrels of gasoline, 2.8 barrels of kerosene, 1.7 barrels of heating oil, or 2.4 barrels of asphalt. Each supplier requires a minimum purchase of at least 500 barrels.

		Raw Material Characteristics					
		Possible Production Per Barrel					
Crude Oils	Barrels Available	Gas	Kero.	Heat	Asphalt	Cost per Barrel	Trucking Cost
TX	1,500	2.00	2.80	1.70	2.40	$22	$1,500
OK	2,000	1.80	2.30	1.75	1.90	$21	$1,700
PA	1,500	2.30	2.20	1.60	2.60	$22	$1,500
AL	1,800	2.10	2.60	1.90	2.40	$23	$1,400

The company owns a tanker truck that picks up whatever crude oil it purchases. This truck can hold 2,000 barrels of crude. The cost of sending the truck to pick up oil from the various locations is shown in the column labeled "Trucking Cost." The company's plans for its next production cycle specify 750 barrels of gasoline, 800 barrels of kerosene, 1,000 barrels of heating oil, and 300 barrels of asphalt to be produced.

a. Formulate an ILP model that can be solved to determine the purchasing plan that will allow the company to implement its production plan at the least cost.
b. Implement this model in a spreadsheet and solve it.
c. What is the optimal solution?

16. The Clampett Oil Company has a tanker truck that it uses to deliver fuel to customers. The tanker has five different storage compartments with capacities to hold 2,500, 2,000, 1,500, 1,800 and 2,300 gallons, respectively. The company has an order to deliver 2,700 gallons or diesel fuel; 3,500 gallons of regular unleaded gasoline; and 4,200 gallons of premium unleaded gasoline. If each storage compartment can hold only one type of fuel, how should Clampett Oil load the tanker? If it is impossible to load the truck with the full order, the company wants to minimize the total number of gallons by which the order is short. (Hint: Consider using variables to represent shortage amounts.)

a. Formulate an ILP model for this problem.
b. Implement this model in a spreadsheet and solve it.
c. What is the optimal solution?

17. Dan Boyd is a financial planner trying to determine how to invest $100,000 for one of his clients. The cash flows for the investments under consideration are summarized in the following table:

*Summary of Cash In-Flows
and Out-Flows (at beginning of year)*

	A	B	C	D	E
1998	-1.00	0.00	-1.00	0.00	-1.00
1999	+0.45	-1.00	0.00	0.00	0.00
2001	+1.05	0.00	0.00	-1.00	1.25
2001	0.00	+1.30	+1.65	+1.30	0.00

For example, if Dan invests $1 in investment A at the beginning of 1998, he will receive $0.45 at the beginning of 1999 and another $1.05 at the beginning of 2000. Alternatively, he can invest $1 in investment B at the beginning of 1997 and receive $1.30 at the beginning of 2001. Entries of "0.00" in the above table indicate times when no cash in-flows or out-flows can occur. At the beginning of a year, Dan can place any or all of the available money in a money market account that is expected to yield 5% per year. The minimum required investment for each of the possible investments is $50,000.

How should Dan plan his investments if he wants to maximize the amount of money available to his client in 2001?

a. Formulate an ILP model for this problem.
b. Create a spreadsheet model for this problem and solve it using Solver.
c. What is the optimal solution?

18. The Mega-Bucks Corporation is planning its production schedule for the next four weeks and is forecasting the following demand for compound X—a key raw material used in its production process:

Compound X	
Week	Required
1	400 lbs.
2	150 lbs.
3	200 lbs.
4	350 lbs.

The company currently has no compound X on hand. The supplier of this product delivers only in batch sizes that are multiples of 100 pounds (0, 100, 200, 300, and so on). The price of this material is $125 per 100 pounds. Deliveries can be arranged weekly, but there is a delivery charge of $50. Mega-Bucks estimates that it costs $15 for each 100 pounds of compound X held in inventory from one week to the next. Assuming Mega-Bucks does not want more than 50 pounds of compound X in inventory at the end of week 4, how much should it order each week so that the demand for this product will be met in the least costly manner?

a. Formulate an ILP model for this problem.
b. Create a spreadsheet model for this problem and solve it using Solver.
c. What is the optimal solution?

19. An automobile manufacturer is considering mechanical design changes in one of its top-selling cars to reduce the weight of the car by at least 400 pounds to improve its fuel efficiency. Design engineers have identified ten changes that could be made in the car to make it lighter (for example, using composite body pieces rather than metal). The weight saved by each design change and the estimated costs of implementing each change are summarized below:

Design Change	Weight Saved	Cost
1	50 lbs.	$150,000
2	75 lbs.	350,000
3	25 lbs.	50,000
4	150 lbs.	450,000
5	60 lbs.	90,000
6	95 lbs.	35,000
7	200 lbs.	650,000
8	40 lbs.	75,000
9	80 lbs.	110,000
10	30 lbs.	30,000

Changes 4 and 7 represent alternate ways of modifying the engine block and, therefore, only one of these options could be selected. The company wants to determine which changes to make in order to reduce the total weight of the car by at least 400 pounds in the least costly manner.

a. Formulate an ILP model for this problem.
b. Create a spreadsheet model for this problem and solve it.
c. What is the optimal solution?

20. The emergency services coordinator for Clarke County is interested in locating the county's two ambulances to maximize the number of residents that can be reached within four minutes in emergency situations. The county is divided into five regions, and the average times required to travel from one region to the next are summarized below:

From Region	To Region				
	1	2	3	4	5
1	0	4	6	3	2
2	4	0	2	3	6
3	6	2	0	5	3
4	3	3	5	0	7
5	2	6	3	7	0

The population in regions 1, 2, 3, 4, and 5 are estimated as 45,000, 65,000, 28,000, 52,000, and 43,000, respectively. In which two regions should the ambulances be placed?

a. Formulate an ILP model for this problem.
b. Implement your model in a spreadsheet and solve it.
c. What is the optimal solution?

21. The CoolAire Company manufactures air conditioners that are sold to five different retail customers across the United States. The company is evaluating its manufacturing and logistics strategy to ensure that it is operating in the most efficient manner possible. The company can produce air conditioners at six plants across the country and stock these units in any of four different warehouses. The cost of manufacturing and shipping a unit between each plant and warehouse is summarized in the following table along with the monthly capacity and fixed cost of operating each plant.

	Warehouse 1	Warehouse 2	Warehouse 3	Warehouse 4	Fixed Cost	Capacity
Plant 1	$700	$1,000	$900	$1,200	$55,000	300
Plant 2	$800	$500	$600	$700	$40,000	200
Plant 3	$850	$600	$700	$500	$45,000	300
Plant 4	$600	$800	$500	$600	$50,000	250
Plant 5	$500	$600	$450	$700	$42,000	350
Plant 6	$700	$600	$750	$500	$40,000	400

Similarly, the per-unit cost of shipping units from each warehouse to each customer is given below, along with the monthly fixed cost of operating each warehouse.

	Customer 1	Customer 2	Customer 3	Customer 4	Customer 5	Fixed Cost
Warehouse 1	$40	$80	$60	$90	$50	$40,000
Warehouse 2	$60	$50	$75	$40	$35	$50,000
Warehouse 3	$55	$40	$65	$60	$80	$35,000
Warehouse 4	$80	$30	$80	$50	$60	$60,000

The monthly demand from each customer is summarized below.

	Customer 1	Customer 2	Customer 3	Customer 4	Customer 5
Demand	200	300	200	150	250

CoolAire would like to determine which plants and warehouses it should operate to meet demand in the most cost-effective manner.

a. Create a spreadsheet model for this problem and solve it.
b. Which plants and warehouses should CoolAire operate?
c. What is the optimal shipping plan?

22. Solve the following problem manually using the B&B algorithm. You can use the computer to solve the individual problems generated. Create a branch-and-bound tree to display the steps you complete.

$$\text{MAX:} \qquad 6X_1 + 8X_2$$
$$\text{Subject to:} \quad 6X_1 + 3X_2 \le 18$$
$$2X_1 + 3X_2 \le 9$$
$$X_1, X_2 \ge 0$$
$$X_1, X_2 \text{ must be integers}$$

23. During the execution of the B&B algorithm, many candidate problems are likely to be generated and awaiting further analysis. In the B&B example in this chapter, we chose the next candidate problem to analyze in a rather arbitrary way. What other, more structured ways might we use to select the next candidate problem? What are the pros and cons of these techniques?

CASE 6.1   THE MASTERDEBT LOCKBOX PROBLEM

MasterDebt is an national credit card company with thousands of card holders located across the United States. Every day throughout the month, MasterDebt sends out statements to different customers summarizing their charges for the previous month. Customers then have 30 days to remit payment for their bills. MasterDebt includes a pre-addressed envelope with each statement for customers to use in making their payments.

One of the critical problems facing MasterDebt involves determining what address to put on the pre-addressed envelopes sent to various parts of the country. The amount of time that elapses between when a customer writes their check and when MasterDebt receives the cash for the check is referred to as **float.** Checks can spend several days floating in the mail and in processing before being cashed. This float time represents lost revenue to MasterDebt because if they could receive and cash these checks immediately, they could earn additional interest on these funds.

To reduce the interest being lost from floating checks, MasterDebt would like to implement a lockbox system to speed the processing of checks. Under such a system, MasterDebt might have all their customers on the West Coast send their payments to a bank in Sacramento which, for a fee, processes the checks and deposits the proceeds in a MasterDebt account. Similarly, MasterDebt might arrange for a similar service with a bank on the East Coast for their customers there. Such lockbox systems are a common method companies use to improve their cash flows.

MasterDebt has identified six different cities as possible lockbox sites. The annual fixed cost of operating a lockbox in each of the possible locations is given below.

Annual Lockbox Operating Costs (in $1,000s)

Sacramento	Denver	Chicago	Dallas	New York	Atlanta
$25	$30	$35	$35	$30	$35

An analysis was done to determine the average number of days a check floats when sent from seven different regions of the country to each of these six cities. The results of this analysis is summarized below. This table indicates, for instance, that a check sent from the central region of the country to New York spends an average of three days in the mail and in processing before MasterDebt actually receives the cash for the check.

Average Days of Float Between Regions and Possible Lockbox Locations

	Sacramento	Denver	Chicago	Dallas	New York	Atlanta
Central	4	2	2	2	3	3
Mid-Atlantic	6	4	3	4	2	2
Midwest	3	2	3	2	5	4
Northeast	6	4	2	5	2	3
Northwest	2	3	5	4	6	7
Southeast	7	4	3	2	4	2
Southwest	2	3	6	2	7	6

Further analysis was done to determine the average amount of payments being sent from each region of the country. These results are given below.

Average Daily Payments (in $1,000s) by Region

	Payments
Central	$45
Mid-Atlantic	$65
Midwest	$50
Northeast	$90
Northwest	$70
Southeast	$80
Southwest	$60

Thus, if payments from the Central Region are sent to New York, on any given day, there is an average of $135,000 in undeposited checks from the Central Region. Because MasterDebt can earn 15% on cash deposits, it would be losing $20,250 per year in potential interest on these checks alone.

Questions

1. Which of the six potential lockbox locations should MasterDebt use and to which lockbox location should each region be assigned?

2. How would your solution change if a maximum of four regions can be assigned to any lockbox location?

CASE 6.2   REMOVING MORE SNOW IN MONTREAL

Based on: James Campbell and Andre Langevin. "The Snow Disposal Assignment Problem." *Journal of the Operational Research Society*, 1995, pp. 919–929.

Snow removal and disposal are important and expensive activities in Montreal and many northern cities. While snow can be cleared from streets and sidewalks by plowing and shoveling, in prolonged sub-freezing temperatures, the resulting banks of accumulated snow can impede pedestrian and vehicular traffic and must be removed.

To allow timely removal and disposal of snow, a city is divided up into several sectors and snow removal operations are carried out concurrently in each sector. In Montreal, accumulated snow is loaded onto trucks and hauled away to disposal sites (e.g., rivers, quarries, sewer chutes, surface holding areas). For contractual reasons, each sector may be assigned to only a *single* disposal site. (However, each disposal site may receive snow from multiple sectors.) The different types of disposal sites can accommodate different amounts of snow due to either the physical size of the disposal facility or environmental restrictions on the amount of snow (often contaminated by salt and de-icing chemicals) that can be dumped into rivers. The annual capacities for five different snow disposal sites are given below (in 1,000s of cubic meters).

	Disposal Site				
	1	*2*	*3*	*4*	*5*
Capacity	350	250	500	400	200

The cost of removing and disposing of snow depends mainly on the distance it must be trucked. For planning purposes, the city of Montreal uses the straight-line distance between the center of each sector to each of the various disposal sites as an approximation of the cost involved in transporting snow between these locations. The following table summarizes these distances (in kilometers) for ten sectors in the city.

Sector	Disposal Site				
	1	*2*	*3*	*4*	*5*
1	3.4	1.4	4.9	7.4	9.3
2	2.4	2.1	8.3	9.1	8.8
3	1.4	2.9	3.7	9.4	8.6
4	2.6	3.6	4.5	8.2	8.9
5	1.5	3.1	2.1	7.9	8.8
6	4.2	4.9	6.5	7.7	6.1
7	4.8	6.2	9.9	6.2	5.7
8	5.4	6	5.2	7.6	4.9
9	3.1	4.1	6.6	7.5	7.2
10	3.2	6.5	7.1	6	8.3

Using historical snowfall data, the city is able to estimate the annual volume of snow requiring removal in each sector as four times the length of streets in the sectors in meters (i.e., it is assumed each linear meter of street generates four cubic meters of snow to remove over an entire year). The following table estimates the snow removal requirements (in 1,000s of cubic meters) for each sector in the coming year.

Estimated Annual Snow Removal Requirements

1	2	3	4	5	6	7	8	9	10
153	152	154	138	127	129	111	110	130	135

Questions

1. Create a spreadsheet that the City of Montreal could use to determine the most efficient snow removal plan for the coming year. Assume it costs $0.10 to transport one cubic meter of snow one kilometer.

2. Implement your model in a spreadsheet and solve it. What is the optimal solution?

3. How much will it cost Montreal to implement your snow disposal plan?

4. Ignoring the capacity restrictions at the disposal sites, how many different assignments of sectors to disposal sites are possible?

5. Suppose Montreal can increase the capacity of a single disposal site by 100,000 cubic meters. Which disposal site's capacity (if any) should be increased and how much should the city be willing to pay to obtain this extra disposal capacity?

CASE 6.3 PLANNING A TOUR OF NEW YORK CITY

Contributed by Jack Yurkiewicz, Lubin School of Business, Pace University

John Peters kept humming the score from *On the Town*, his favorite Broadway show and movie musical, over and over. *On the Town* is a whimsical lark written by Leonard Bernstein in the 1940s that tells the story of three sailors on a 24-hour shore leave in New York City. The sailors wanted to see as many sights as possible in the short time they have. John remembers seeing the movie version of the musical for the first time and being awed by the sights of the city, particularly the Statue of Liberty, Rockefeller Center, and the many museums. Since seeing the movie, John's great wish has been to visit New York City.

Now John has an opportunity to fulfill his wish. John works as an accountant for a firm in Idaho and is being sent by his company on a business trip to Europe. He must stop in New York City to get his connecting flight, and with some juggling of the airline schedules, John managed to arrange a two-day stopover in New York City. In those two days, John wants to see as much of the city as he can.

What should John see? He has about 20 hours total in which to visit some of the many attractions that the city has to offer. These 20 hours take into account the travel time between sights, time for food and rest, times when the attractions are closed, and so on. There are literally hundreds of places to visit, so John knows that he has to narrow down his choices. He decides to consult the *Michelin Guide*, which is known for its reliable and accurate assessments of the various sights in both foreign and domestic cities. The attractions are rated by stars. A three-star attraction is very highly recommended, a two-star attraction is recommended, a one-star rating indicates the attraction is interesting, and a no-star rating indicates that the attraction is worth seeing only if time allows. Because of the limited time John has, he feels that he should visit only three- and two-star attractions; anything less would not be worth his time on this trip.

The *Michelin Guide* indicates that New York City has almost two dozen three-star attractions and almost three dozen two-star attractions. Because almost all these attractions are on Manhattan Island (New York City), John will ignore sights in the other four boroughs. Based on his interests, John further decides to omit some three-star and two-star attractions, including the Bronx Zoo, Rockefeller Center, and The Cloisters. After reading more about each attraction, he came up with a list of 11 possible attractions he wants to visit. John knows that he cannot do justice to these 11 attractions in just 20 hours. The *Michelin Guide* gives recommendations for the number of hours that a visitor should spend at each attraction. John knows that these are rough time estimates. For example, he could easily spend the entire 20 hours at the Metropolitan Museum of Art, one of the world's great art galleries, instead of just the five hours recommended by the *Michelin Guide*. However, spending one hour there would not be enough either, and if he had to do that, perhaps he would just skip that sight entirely.

John decides that he will not spend more than three hours at any one attraction, no matter how much there is to see or do there. To keep matters simple, he decides to measure the time spent at an attraction in intervals of hours; that is, all visitation times are rounded to the nearest hour. Thus he could spend 1, 2, or 3 hours at a sight, or even 0 hours (which means he will not visit that sight at all). John is more interested in some attractions than others, and visiting these for longer times will be more enjoyable for him than visiting less desirable sights. Thus a three-hour visit to the Frick Collection, described by Michelin as "one of the most beautiful private museums in the world," housing everything from Old Masters to Louis XVI furniture, will give him less enjoyment than a three-hour visit to the Metropolitan Museum of Art. This is not only because the Metropolitan offers more to see, but the Frick Collection requires less time to see everything than the Metropolitan. So a one-hour visit to the Frick Collection will give him more enjoyment than a one-hour visit to the Metropolitan. John must consider the number of sights to see at an attraction, how much time he has to spend there, and how desirable it is for him to visit the attraction.

John put all these factors in the following table. The table shows the attraction, its assigned number of Michelin stars, how much time the *Michelin Guide* recommends a visitor spend there, and how much enjoyment John will get from spending 1, 2, or 3 hours at the attraction. He measures enjoyment on an arbitrary scale of 0 to 100.

| | | | Actual Visit Time | | | |
| | | | 0 hrs | 1 hr | 2 hrs | 3 hrs |
Attraction	Stars	Michelin Guide's Recommended Visit Time	Enjoyment Rating			
Statue of Liberty	***	4	0	10	50	80
World Trade Center	***	2.5	0	50	90	95
Greenwich Village	**	2	0	30	40	60
Empire State Building	***	2	0	25	75	90
United Nations	***	3	0	40	50	75

Attraction	Stars	Michelin Guide's Recommended Visit Time	Actual Visit Time			
			0 hrs	1 hr	2 hrs	3 hrs
			Enjoyment Rating			
Museum of Modern Art	***	2.5	0	35	50	75
Frick Collection	***	2.5	0	40	50	60
Whitney Museum	**	1.5	0	20	45	65
Metropolitan Museum of Art	***	5	0	40	60	100
Guggenheim Museum	**	1.5	0	20	30	65
Museum of Natural History	***	4	0	20	50	90

Question

How much time should John spend visiting each attraction?

REFERENCES

Bean, J., et al. "Selecting Tenants in a Shopping Mall." *Interfaces*, vol. 18, no. 2, 1988.

Calloway, R., M. Cummins, and J. Freeland. "Solving Spreadsheet-Based Integer Programming Models: An Example From the Telecommunications Industry." *Decision Sciences*, vol. 21, 1990.

Nauss, R. and R. Markland. "Theory and Application of an Optimizing Procedure for the Lock Box Location Analysis." *Management Science*, vol. 27, no. 8, 1981.

Nemhauser, G. and L. Wolsey, *Integer and Combinatorial Optimization*. New York: Wiley, 1988.

Peiser, R. and S. Andrus. "Phasing of Income-Producing Real Estate." *Interfaces*, vol. 13, no. 1, 1983.

Stowe, J. "An Integer Programming Solution for the Optimal Credit Investigation/Credit Granting Sequence." *Financial Management*, vol. 14, Summer 1985.

CHAPTER 7

Goal Programming and Multiple Objective Optimization

Chapter 6 discussed the modeling techniques that apply to optimization problems that require integer solutions. This chapter presents two other modeling techniques that are sometimes helpful in solving optimization problems. The first technique—goal programming—involves solving problems containing not one specific objective function, but rather a collection of goals that we would like to achieve. As we'll see, a goal can be viewed as a constraint with a flexible, or soft, RHS value.

The second technique—multiple objective optimization—is closely related to goal programming and applies to problems containing more than one objective function. In business and government, different groups of people frequently pursue different objectives. Therefore, it is quite possible that a variety of objective functions can be proposed for the same optimization problem.

Both techniques require an *iterative solution procedure* in which the decision maker investigates a variety of solutions to find one that is most satisfactory. Thus, unlike the LP and ILP procedures presented earlier, we cannot formulate a multiple objective or goal programming problem and solve one optimization problem to identify the optimal solution. In these problems we might need to solve several variations of the problem before we find an acceptable solution.

We'll begin with the topic of goal programming. Then we'll investigate multiple objective optimization and see how the concepts and techniques of goal programming can be applied to these problems as well.

7.1 GOAL PROGRAMMING

The optimization techniques presented in the preceding chapters have always assumed that the constraints in the model are **hard constraints,** or constraints that *cannot* be violated. For example, labor constraints indicated that the amount of labor used to produce a variety of products could not exceed some fixed amount (such as 1,566 hours). As another example, monetary constraints indicated that the amount of money invested in a number of projects could not exceed some budgeted amount (such as $850,000).

Hard constraints are appropriate in many situations; however, these constraints might be too restrictive in others. For example, when you buy a new car you probably have in mind a maximum purchase price that you do not want to exceed. We might call this your goal. However, you will probably find a way to spend more than this amount if it is impossible to acquire the car you really want for your goal amount. So the goal you have in mind is *not* a hard constraint that cannot be violated. We might view it more accurately as a **soft constraint** representing a target you would like to achieve.

Numerous managerial decision-making problems can be modeled more accurately using goals rather than hard constraints. Often, such problems do not have one explicit objective function to be maximized or minimized over a constraint set but, instead, can be stated as a collection of goals that might also include hard constraints. These types of problems are known as **goal programming** (GP) problems.

7.2   A GOAL PROGRAMMING EXAMPLE

The technique of linear programming can help a decision maker analyze and solve a GP problem. The following example illustrates the concepts and modeling techniques used in GP problems.

Davis McKeown is the owner of a resort hotel and convention center in Myrtle Beach, South Carolina. Although his business is profitable, it is also highly seasonal; the summer months are the most profitable time of year. In order to increase profits during the rest of the year, Davis wants to expand his convention business but, to do so, he needs to expand his conference facilities. Davis hired a marketing research firm to determine the number and sizes of conference rooms that would be required by the conventions he wants to attract. The results of this study indicated that Davis's facilities should include at least 5 small (400 square foot) conference rooms, 10 medium (750 square foot) conference rooms, and 15 large (1,050 square foot) conference rooms. Additionally, the marketing research firm indicated that if the expansion consisted of a total of 25,000 square feet, Davis would have the largest convention center among his competitors—which would be desirable for advertising purposes. While discussing his expansion plans with an architect, Davis learned that he can expect to pay $18,000 for each small conference room in the expansion, $33,000 for each medium conference room, and $45,150 for each large conference room. Davis wants to limit his expenditures on the convention center expansion to approximately $1,000,000.

7.2.1   Defining the Decision Variables

In this problem, the fundamental decision facing the hotel owner is how many small, medium, and large conference rooms to include in the conference center expansion. These quantities are represented by X_1, X_2, and X_3, respectively.

7.2.2   Defining the Goals

This problem is somewhat different from the problems presented earlier in this book. Rather than one specific objective, this problem involves a number of goals, which are stated (in no particular order) as:

Goal 1: The expansion should include approximately 5 small conference rooms.

Goal 2: The expansion should include approximately 10 medium conference rooms.

Goal 3: The expansion should include approximately 15 large conference rooms.

Goal 4: The expansion should consist of approximately 25,000 square feet.

Goal 5: The expansion should cost approximately $1,000,000.

Notice that the word "approximately" appears in each goal. This word underscores the fact that these are soft goals rather than hard constraints. For example, if the first four goals could be achieved at a cost of $1,001,000, it is very likely that the hotel owner would not mind paying an extra $1,000 to achieve such a solution. However, we must determine if we can find a solution that exactly meets all of the goals in this problem and, if not, what trade-offs can be made among the goals to determine an acceptable solution. We can formulate an LP model for this GP problem to help us make this determination.

7.2.3   Defining the Goal Constraints

The first step in formulating an LP model for a GP problem is to create a goal constraint for each goal in the problem. A **goal constraint** allows us to determine how close a given solution comes to achieving the goal. To understand how these constraints should be formulated, let's begin with the three goal constraints associated with the number of small, medium, and large conference rooms in the expansion.

If we wanted to make sure that *exactly* 5 small, 10 medium, and 15 large conference rooms were included in the planned expansion, we would include the following hard constraints in our GP model:

$$X_1 = 5$$
$$X_2 = 10$$
$$X_3 = 15$$

However, the goals stated that the expansion should include *approximately* 5 small conference rooms, *approximately* 10 medium conference rooms, and *approximately* 15 large conference rooms. If it is impossible to achieve all the goals, the hotel owner might consider a solution involving only 14 large conference rooms. The hard constraints would not allow for such a solution; they are too restrictive. However, we can modify them easily to allow for departures from the stated goals, as:

$$X_1 + d_1^- - d_1^+ = 5 \qquad \text{\} small rooms}$$
$$X_2 + d_2^- - d_2^+ = 10 \qquad \text{\} medium rooms}$$
$$X_3 + d_3^- - d_3^+ = 15 \qquad \text{\} large rooms}$$
$$\text{where } d_i^-, d_i^+ \geq 0 \text{ for all } i$$

The RHS value of each goal constraint (the values 5, 10, and 15 in the previous constraints) is the **target value** for the goal because it represents the level of achievement that the decision maker wants to obtain for the goal. The variables d_i^- and d_i^+ are called **deviational variables** because they represent the amount by which each goal deviates from its target value. The d_i^- represent the amount by which each goal's target value is *underachieved*, and the d_i^+ represents the amount by which each goal's target value is *overachieved*.

To illustrate how deviational variables work, suppose that we have a solution where $X_1 = 3$, $X_2 = 13$, and $X_3 = 15$. In order to satisfy the first goal constraint listed above, its deviational variables would assume the values $d_1^- = 2$ and $d_1^+ = 0$ to reflect that the goal of having 5 small conference rooms is *underachieved* by 2. Similarly, in order to satisfy the second goal constraint, its deviational variables would assume the values $d_2^- = 0$ and $d_2^+ = 3$ to reflect that the goal of having 10 medium conference rooms is *overachieved* by 3. Finally, in order to satisfy the third goal constraint, its deviational variables would assume the values $d_3^- = 0$ and $d_3^+ = 0$ to reflect that the goal of having 15 medium conference rooms is *exactly* achieved.

We can formulate the goal constraints for the remaining goals in the problem in a similar manner. Because each small, medium, and large conference room requires 400, 750, and 1,050 square feet, respectively, and the hotel owner wants the total square footage of the expansion to be 25,000, the constraint representing this goal is:

$$400X_1 + 750X_2 + 1{,}050X_3 + d_4^- - d_4^+ = 25{,}000\} \text{ square footage}$$

Because each small, medium, and large conference room results in building costs of $18,000, $33,000, and $45,150, respectively, and the hotel owner wants to keep the cost of the expansion at approximately $1,000,000, the constraint representing this goal is:

$$18{,}000X_1 + 33{,}000X_2 + 45{,}150X_3 + d_5^- - d_5^+ = 1{,}000{,}000\} \text{ building cost}$$

The deviational variables in each of these goal constraints represent the amounts by which the actual values obtained for the goals deviate from their respective target values.

7.2.4 Defining the Hard Constraints

As noted earlier, not all of the constraints in a GP problem have to be goal constraints. A GP problem can also include one or more hard constraints typically found in LP problems. In our example, if $1,000,000 was the absolute maximum amount that the hotel owner was willing to spend on the expansion, this could be included in the model as a hard constraint. (As we'll see, it is also possible to change a soft constraint into a hard constraint during the analysis of a GP problem.)

7.2.5 GP Objective Functions

Although it is fairly easy to formulate the constraints for a GP problem, identifying an appropriate objective function can be quite tricky and usually requires some mental effort. Before formulating the objective function for our sample problem, let's consider some of the issues and options involved in this process.

The objective in a GP problem is to determine a solution that achieves all the goals as closely as possible. The *ideal* solution to any GP problem is one in which each goal is achieved exactly at the level specified by its target value. (In such an ideal solution all the deviational variables in all the goal constraints would equal 0.) Often, it is not possible to achieve the ideal solution because some goals might conflict with others. In such a case, we want to find a solution that deviates as little as possible from the ideal solution. One possible objective for our example GP problem is:

Minimize the sum of the deviations: MIN: $\sum_i (d_i^- + d_i^+)$

With this objective, we attempt to find a solution to the problem where all the deviational variables are 0—or where all the goals are met exactly. But if such a solution is not possible, will this objective always produce a desirable solution? The answer is "probably not."

The previous objective has a number of shortcomings. First, the deviational variables measure entirely different things. In our example problem, d_1^-, d_1^+, d_2^-, d_2^+, d_3^-, and d_3^+ all measure rooms of one size or another, whereas d_4^- and d_4^+ are measures of square footage, and d_5^- and d_5^+ are financial measures of building costs. One obvious criticism of the previous objective is that it is unclear how to interpret any numerical value the objective assumes (7 rooms + 1,500 dollars = 1,507 units of what?).

One solution to this problem is to modify the objective function so that it measures the sum of *percentage deviations* from the various goals. This is accomplished as follows, where t_i represents the target value for goal i:

Minimize the sum of the percentage deviations: MIN: $\sum_i \frac{1}{t_i}(d_i^- + d_i^+)$

In our example problem, if we arrive at a solution where the first goal is underachieved by one room ($d_1^- = 1$) and the fifth goal is overachieved by \$20,000 ($d_5^+ = 20,000$) and all other goals are achieved exactly (all other d_i^- and d_i^+ equal 0). Using the sum of percentage deviations objective, the optimal objective function value is:

$$\frac{1}{t_1}d_1^- + \frac{1}{t_5}d_5^+ = \frac{1}{5} * 1 + \frac{1}{1,000,000} * 20,000 = 20\% + 2\% = 22\%$$

Note that the percentage deviation objective can be used only if all the target values for all the goals are nonzero; otherwise a division by zero error will occur.

Another potential criticism of the previous objective functions concerns how they evaluate deviations. In the previous example, where the objective function value is 22%, the objective function implicitly assumes that having four small conference rooms (rather than five) is 10 times worse than being \$20,000 over the desired building cost budget. That is, the budget overrun of \$20,000 would have to increase 10 times to \$200,000 before the percentage deviation on this goal equaled the 20% deviation caused by being one room below the goal of having five small conference rooms. Is having one fewer conference room really as undesirable as having to pay \$200,000 more than budgeted? Only the decision maker in this problem can answer this question. It would be nice to provide the decision maker a way to evaluate and change the implicit trade-offs among the goals if he or she wanted to do so.

Both of the previous objective functions view a deviation from any goal in any direction as being equally undesirable. For example, according to both of the previous objective functions, a solution resulting in a building cost of \$900,000 (if $X_5 = 900,000$ and $d_5^- = 100,000$) is as undesirable as a solution with a building cost of \$1,100,000 (if $X_5 = 1,100,000$ and $d_5^+ = 100,000$). But, the hotel owner probably would prefer to pay \$900,000 for the expansion rather than \$1,100,000. So, while overachieving the building cost goal is an undesirable occurrence, underachieving this goal is probably desirable or at least neutral. On the other hand, underachieving the goal related to the number of small conference rooms might be viewed as undesirable, whereas overachieving this goal might be viewed as desirable or possibly neutral. Again, it would be nice to provide the decision maker a way to represent which deviations are desirable and undesirable in the objective function.

One solution to the previous criticisms is to allow the decision maker to assign weights to the deviational variables in the objective function of a GP problem to better reflect the importance and desirability of deviations from the various goals. So, a more useful type of objective function for a GP problem is:

Minimize the weighted sum of the deviations: MIN: $\sum_i (w_i^- d_i^- + w_i^+ d_i^+)$

or

Minimize the weighted sum of the percentage deviations: MIN: $\sum_i \frac{1}{t_i}(w_i^- d_i^- + w_i^+ d_i^+)$

In these weighted objective functions, the w_i^- and w_i^+ represent numeric constants that can be assigned values to weight the various deviational variables in the problem. A variable that represents a highly undesirable deviation from a particular goal is assigned a relatively large weight—making it highly undesirable for that variable to assume a value larger than 0. A variable that represents a neutral or desirable deviation from a particular goal is assigned a weight of 0 or some value lower than 0 to reflect that it is acceptable or even desirable for the variable to assume a value greater than 0.

Unfortunately, no standard procedure is available for assigning values to the w_i^- and w_i^+ in a way that guarantees you will find the most desirable solution to a GP problem. Rather, you need to follow an iterative procedure in which you try a particular set of weights, solve the problem, analyze the solution, and then refine the weights and solve the problem again. You might need to repeat this process many times to find a solution that is the most desirable to the decision maker.

7.2.6 Defining the Objective

In our example problem, assume that the decision maker considers it undesirable to underachieve any of the first three goals related to the number of small, medium, and large conference rooms, but is indifferent about overachieving these goals. Also assume that the decision maker considers it undesirable to underachieve the goal of adding 25,000 square feet, but equally undesirable to overachieve this goal. Finally, assume that the decision maker finds it undesirable to spend more than $1,000,000, but is indifferent about spending less than this amount. In this case, if we want to minimize the weighted percentage deviation for our example problem, we use the following objective:

$$\text{MIN: } \frac{w_1^-}{5}d_1^- + \frac{w_2^-}{10}d_2^- + \frac{w_3^-}{15}d_3^- + \frac{w_4^-}{25,000}d_4^- + \frac{w_4^+}{25,000}d_4^+ + \frac{w_5^+}{1,000,000}d_5^+$$

Notice that this objective omits (or assigns weights of 0 to) the deviational variables about which the decision maker is indifferent. Thus, this objective would not penalize a solution where, for example, seven small conference rooms were selected (and therefore $d_1^+ = 2$) because we assume that the decision maker would not view this as an undesirable deviation from the goal of having five small conference rooms. On the other hand, this objective would penalize a solution where three small conference rooms were selected (and therefore $d_1^- = 2$) because this represents an undesirable deviation from the goal of having five small conference rooms. To begin our analysis of this problem we will assume that $w_1^- = w_2^- = w_3^- = w_4^- = w_4^+ = w_5^+ = 1$ and all other weights are 0.

7.2.7 Implementing the Model

To summarize, the LP model for our example GP problem is:

$$\text{MIN: } \frac{w_1^-}{5}d_1^- + \frac{w_2^-}{10}d_2^- + \frac{w_3^-}{15}d_3^- + \frac{w_4^-}{25,000}d_4^- + \frac{w_4^+}{25,000}d_4^+ + \frac{w_5^+}{1,000,000}d_5^+$$

Subject to:

$$X_1 + d_1^- - d_1^+ = 5 \qquad \} \text{ small rooms}$$

$$X_2 + d_2^- - d_2^+ = 10 \qquad \} \text{ medium rooms}$$

$$X_3 + d_3^- - d_3^+ = 15 \qquad \} \text{ large rooms}$$

$$400X_1 + 750X_2 + 1{,}050X_3 + d_4^- - d_4^+ = 25{,}000 \qquad \} \text{ square footage}$$

$$18{,}000X_1 + 33{,}000X_2 + 45{,}150X_3 + d_5^- - d_5^+ = 1{,}000{,}000 \} \text{ building cost}$$

$$d_i^-, d_i^+ \geq 0 \text{ for all } i$$

$$X_i \geq 0 \text{ for all } i$$

$$X_i \text{ must be integers}$$

Because this is an ILP model, it can be implemented in a spreadsheet in the usual way. One approach for doing this is shown in Figure 7.1 (and in the file FIG7-1.xls on your data disk).

Figure 7.1
Spreadsheet implementation of the GP model.

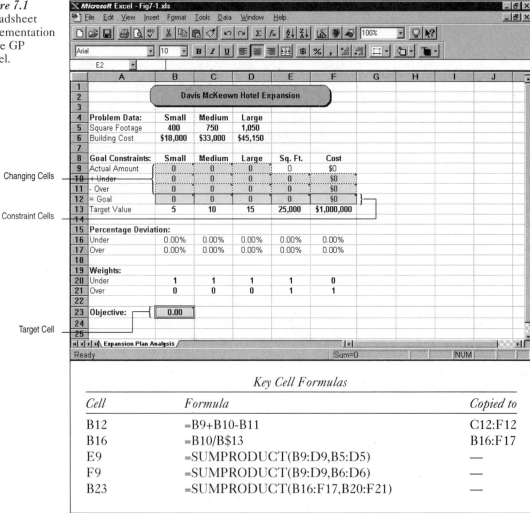

Key Cell Formulas		
Cell	**Formula**	**Copied to**
B12	=B9+B10-B11	C12:F12
B16	=B10/B$13	B16:F17
E9	=SUMPRODUCT(B9:D9,B5:D5)	—
F9	=SUMPRODUCT(B9:D9,B6:D6)	—
B23	=SUMPRODUCT(B16:F17,B20:F21)	—

The first section of the spreadsheet lists basic data about the square footage and costs of the different conference rooms. The next section represents the decision variables, deviational variables, and goal constraints for the problem. Specifically, cells B9 through D9 correspond to X_1, X_2, and X_3—the number of small, medium, and large conference rooms to be included in the expansion. Cells E9 and F9 contain the following formulas, which calculate the total square footage and total building cost for any combination of small, medium, and large conference rooms:

Formula for cell E9:   =SUMPRODUCT(B9:D9,B5:D5)

Formula for cell F9:   =SUMPRODUCT(B9:D9,B6:D6)

Cells B10 through F11 correspond to the deviational variables in our algebraic model. These cells indicate the amount by which each goal is underachieved or overachieved. The LHS formulas for the goal constraints are implemented in cells B12 through F12. Specifically, in cell B12 we enter the following formula, then copy it to cells C12 through F12:

Formula for cell B12:   =B9+B10–B11
(Copy to C12 through F12.)

The target (or RHS) values for the goal constraints are listed in cells B13 through F13.

In order to implement the objective function, we first implemented formulas to convert the values of the deviational variables into percent format by dividing each deviational variable represented in cells B10 through F11 by the appropriate target value. This is done as follows:

Formula for cell B16:   =B10/B$13
(Copy to B16 through F17.)

Next, weights for each of the deviational variables are entered in cells B20 through F21. Because solving a GP problem is an iterative process in which you will probably need to change the weights for the objective, it is best to place the weights in a separate location on the spreadsheet.

Finally, cell B23 contains the following formula, which implements the objective function for the problem:

Formula for cell B23:   =SUMPRODUCT(B16:F17,B20:F21)

7.2.8   Solving the Model

The model can be solved using the Solver parameters and options shown in Figure 7.2. The solution obtained using these settings is shown in Figure 7.3.

7.2.9   Analyzing the Solution

As shown in Figure 7.3, this solution includes exactly 5 small, 10 medium, and 15 large rooms in the expansion. Thus, there is no deviation at all from the target values for the first three goals, which would please the decision maker. However, considering the fourth and fifth goals, the current solution overachieves the targeted square footage level by 250 square feet (or 1%) and is over the building cost goal by $97,250 (or 9.73%).

Figure 7.2
Solver
parameters and
options for the
GP model.

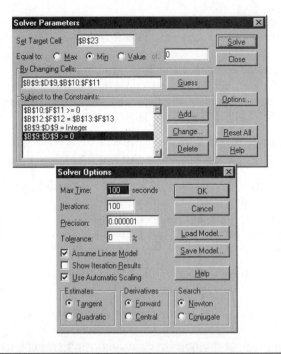

Figure 7.3
First solution to
the GP model.

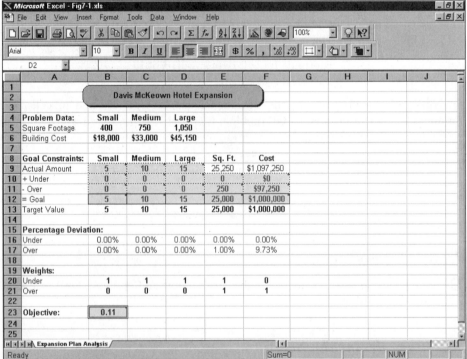

7.2.10   Revising the Model

Although the decision maker might not mind being 1% over the square footage goal,
exceeding the building cost goal by almost $100,000 most likely would be a concern.
The decision maker might want to find another solution that comes closer to achiev-

ing the building cost goal. This can be done by adjusting the weights in the problem so that a larger penalty is assigned to overachieving the building cost goal. That is, we can increase the value in cell F21 representing w_5^+. Again, there is no way to tell exactly how much larger this value should be. As a rule-of-thumb, we might change its value by one order of magnitude, or from 1 to 10. If we make this change in the spreadsheet and re-solve the problem, we obtain the solution shown in Figure 7.4.

In Figure 7.4, notice that increasing the penalty for overachieving the building cost goal from 1 to 10 reduced the overachievement of this goal from $97,250 to $6,950. We are now within 1% of the target value for the building cost goal. However, in order to obtain this improved level of achievement on the building cost goal, we had to give up two large conference rooms, resulting in a 13.33% underachievement for this goal. If the decision maker considers this unacceptable, we can increase the penalty on this deviational variable from 1 to 10 and re-solve the problem. Figure 7.5 shows the resulting solution.

7.2.11   Trade-offs: The Nature of GP

In Figure 7.5, the target number of large conference rooms is met exactly, but the desired number of medium rooms is now underachieved by three. Depending on the preferences of the decision maker, we could continue to fine-tune the weights in the problem until we reach a solution that is most satisfactory to the decision maker. The nature of GP involves making trade-offs among the various goals until a solution is found that gives the decision maker the greatest level of satisfaction. Thus, unlike the other applications of LP presented earlier, the use of LP in GP does not indicate immediately the best possible solution to the problem (unless the decision maker

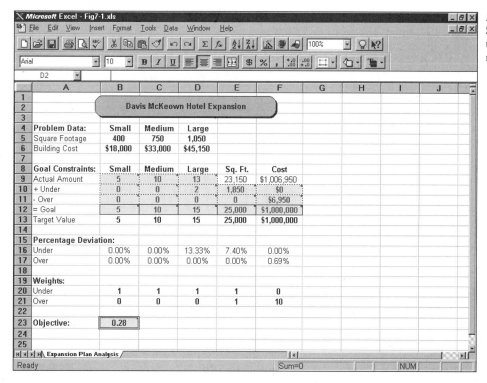

Figure 7.4
Second solution to the GP model.

Figure 7.5
Third solution to
the GP model.

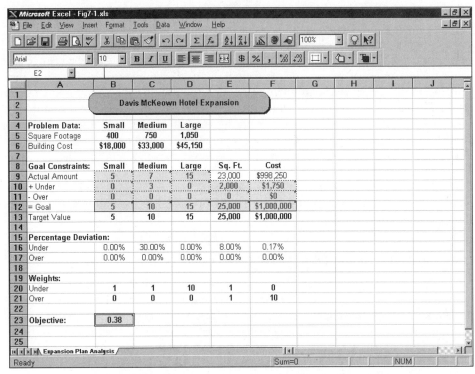

initially specifies an appropriately weighted objective function). Rather, it provides a method by which a decision maker can explore a variety of possible solutions and try to find the solution that comes closest to satisfying the goals under consideration. Figure 7.6 provides a summary of the steps involved in solving a GP problem.

7.3   COMMENTS ABOUT GOAL PROGRAMMING

Some additional comments should be made before we leave the topic of GP. First, it is important to note that different GP solutions cannot be compared simply on the basis of their optimal objective function values. The user changes the weights in the objective functions from iteration to iteration; therefore, comparing their values is not appropriate because they measure different things. The objective function in a GP problem serves more of a mechanical purpose, allowing us to explore possible solutions. Thus, we should compare the solutions that are produced—not the objective function values.

Second, in some GP problems, one or more goals might be viewed as being infinitely more important than the other goals. In this case, we could assign arbitrarily large weights to deviations from these goals to ensure that undesirable deviations from them never occur. This is sometimes referred to as **preemptive GP** because certain goals preempt others in order of importance. If the target values for these goals can be achieved, the use of preemptive weights effectively makes these goals hard constraints that should never be violated.

Third, we can place hard constraints on the amount by which we can deviate from a goal. For example, suppose that the owner of the hotel in our example problem

SUMMARY OF GOAL PROGRAMMING

1. Identify the decision variables in the problem.
2. Identify any hard constraints in the problem and formulate them in the usual way.
3. State the goals of the problem along with their target values.
4. Create constraints using the decision variables that would achieve the goals exactly.
5. Transform the above constraints into goal constraints by including deviational variables.
6. Determine which deviational variables represent undesirable deviations from the goals.
7. Formulate an objective that penalizes the undesirable deviations.
8. Identify appropriate weights for the objective.
9. Solve the problem.
10. Inspect the solution to the problem. If the solution is unacceptable, return to step 8 and revise the weights as needed.

wants to eliminate from consideration any solution that exceeds the target building cost by more than $50,000. We could easily build this requirement into our model with the hard constraint:

$$d_5^+ \leq 50,000$$

Fourth, the concept of deviational variables is not limited to GP. These types of variables can be used in other problems that are quite different from GP problems. So, understanding deviational variables can prove useful in other types of mathematical programming situations.

Finally, another type of objective function, called the **MINIMAX objective**, is sometimes helpful in GP when you want to minimize the maximum deviation from any goal. To implement the MINIMAX objective, we must create one additional constraint for each deviational variable as follows, where Q is the MINIMAX variable:

$$d_1^- \leq Q$$
$$d_1^+ \leq Q$$
$$d_2^- \leq Q$$

and so on ...

The objective is to minimize the value of Q, stated as:

$$\text{MIN: } Q$$

Because the variable Q must be greater than or equal to the values of all the deviational variables, and because we are trying to minimize it, Q will always be set equal to the maximum value of the deviational variables. At the same time, this objective function tries to find a solution where the maximum deviational variable (and the value of Q) is as small as possible. Therefore, this technique allows us to minimize the maximum deviation from all the goals. As we'll see shortly, this type of objective is especially valuable if a GP problem involves hard constraints.

7.4   MULTIPLE OBJECTIVE OPTIMIZATION

We now consider how to solve LP problems involving multiple objective functions. These problems are called **multiple objective linear programming** (MOLP) problems.

Most of the LP and ILP problems discussed in previous chapters involved one objective function. These objective functions typically sought to maximize profits or minimize costs. However, another objective function could be formulated for most of these problems. For example, if a production process creates a toxic pollutant that is dangerous to the environment, a company might want to minimize this toxic by-product. However, this objective is likely to be in direct conflict with the company's other objective of maximizing profits. Problems with multiple objectives require analyzing the trade-offs among the different objectives.

MOLP problems can be viewed as special types of GP problems where, as part of solving the problem, we must also determine target values for each goal or objective. Analyzing these problems effectively also requires that we use the MINIMAX objective described earlier.

7.5   AN MOLP EXAMPLE

The following example illustrates the issues involved in an MOLP problem. Although this example involves only three objectives, the concepts and techniques presented apply to problems involving any number of objectives.

Lee Blackstone is the owner of the Blackstone Mining Company which operates two different coal mines in Wythe and Giles Counties in Southwest Virginia. Due to increased commercial and residential development in the primary areas served by these mines, Lee is anticipating an increase in demand for coal in the coming year. Specifically, her projections indicate a 48 ton increase in the demand for high-grade coal, a 28 ton increase in the demand for medium-grade coal, and a 100 ton increase in the demand for low-grade coal. To handle this increase in demand, Lee must schedule extra shifts of workers at the mines. It costs $40,000 per month to run an extra shift of workers at the Wythe County mine and $32,000 per month at the Giles mine. Only one additional shift can be scheduled each month at each mine. The amount of coal that can be produced in a month's time at each mine by a shift of workers is summarized in the following table.

Type of Coal	Wythe Mine	Giles Mine
High-grade	12 tons	4 tons
Medium-grade	4 tons	4 tons
Low-grade	10 tons	20 tons

Unfortunately, the methods used to extract coal from these mines produce toxic water that enters the local groundwater aquifers. At the Wythe mine, approximately 800 gallons of toxic water per month will be generated by running an extra shift, while the mine in Giles County will generate about 1,250 gallons of toxic water. While these amounts are within EPA guidelines, Lee is concerned about the environment and doesn't want to create any more pollution than is absolutely necessary. Additionally, while the company follows all OSHA safety guidelines, company records indicate that approximately 0.20-life-threatening accidents occur per shift each month at the Wythe mine, while 0.45 accidents occur per shift each month at the Giles mine. Lee knows that mining is a hazardous occupation, but she cares about the health and welfare of her workers and would like to keep the number of life-threatening accidents to a minimum.

7.5.1 Defining the Decision Variables

In this problem, Lee has to determine the number of months to schedule an extra shift at each of the company's mines. Thus, we can define the decision variables as:

X_1 = number of months to schedule an extra shift at the Wythe County mine

X_2 = number of months to schedule an extra shift at the Giles County mine

7.5.2 Defining the Objectives

This problem is different from the other types of LP problems we have considered in that three different objective functions are possible. Lee might be interested in minimizing costs, minimizing the production of toxic waste water, or minimizing the expected number of life-threatening accidents. These three different objectives would be formulated as follows:

Minimize: $\$40X_1 + \$32X_2$ } Production costs (in $1,000s)

Minimize: $800X_1 + 1250X_2$ } Toxic water produced (in gallons)

Minimize: $0.20X_1 + 0.45X_2$ } Life threatening accidents

In an LP model, Lee would be forced to decide which of these three objectives is most important or most appropriate and use that single objective in the model. However, in an MOLP model Lee can consider how all of these objectives (and any others she might want to formulate) can be incorporated into the analysis and solution of the problem.

7.5.3 Defining the Constraints

The constraints for this problem are formulated in the same way as for any LP problem. The following three constraints ensure that required amounts of high-grade, medium-grade, and low-grade coal are produced.

$12X_1 + 4X_2 \geq 48$ } High-grade coal required

$4X_1 + 4X_2 \geq 28$ } Medium-grade coal required

$10X_1 + 20X_2 \geq 100$ } Low-grade coal required

7.5.4 Implementing the Model

To summarize, the MOLP formulation of this problem is represented as:

Minimize:	$\$40X_1 + \$32X_2$	} Production costs (in \$1,000s)
Minimize:	$800X_1 + 1,250X_2$	} Toxic water produced (in gallons)
Minimize:	$0.20X_1 + 0.45X_2$	} Life-threatening accidents
Subject to:		
	$12X_1 + 4X_2 \geq 48$	} High-grade coal required
	$4X_1 + 4X_2 \geq 28$	} Medium-grade coal required
	$10X_1 + 20X_2 \geq 100$	} Low-grade coal required
	$X_1, X_2 \geq 0$	} nonnegativity conditions

This model is implemented in a spreadsheet in the usual way except that three different cells represent the three objective functions. One approach to implementing this model is shown in Figure 7.7 (and in the file FIG7-7.xls on your data disk).

In Figure 7.7, cells B5 and C5 represent the decision variables X_1 and X_2, respectively. The coefficients for the various objective functions are entered in cells B8 through C10. Next, the coefficient for the constraints are entered in cells B13 through C15. The objectives are then implemented in cells D8 through D10 as follows:

Formula for cell D8:   =SUMPRODUCT(B8:C8,$B$5:$C$5)
(Copy to D9 through D10.)

Figure 7.7
Spreadsheet implementation of the MOLP problem.

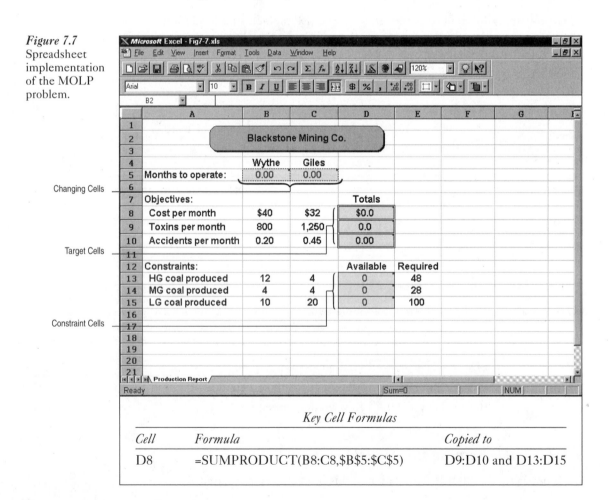

Next, the coefficient for the constraints are entered in cells B13 through C15. The LHS formulas for the constraints are then entered in cells D13 through D15.

Formula for cell D13:   =SUMPRODUCT(B13:C13,$B$5:$C$5)
(Copy to D14 through D15.)

The RHS values for these constraints are given by cells E13 through E15.

7.5.5 Determining Target Values for the Objectives

An LP problem can have only one objective function, so how can we include three objectives in our spreadsheet model? If these objectives had target values, we could treat them the same way as the goals in our example earlier in this chapter. That is, the objectives in this problem can be stated as the following goals if we have appropriate values for t_1, t_2, and t_3:

Goal 1: The total production cost should be approximately t_1.

Goal 2: The gallons of toxic water produced should be approximately t_2.

Goal 3: The number of life-threatening accidents should be approximately t_3.

Unfortunately, the problem did not provide explicit values for t_1, t_2, and t_3. However, if we solve our model to find the solution that minimizes the first objective (total production cost), the optimal value of this objective function would be a reasonable value to use as t_1 in the first goal. Similarly, if we solve the problem two more times minimizing the second and third objectives, respectively, the optimal objective function values for these solutions would provide reasonable values to use as t_2 and t_3 in the second and third goals given above. We could then view our MOLP problem in the format of a GP problem.

Figure 7.8 shows the Solver parameters and options required to determine the minimum production cost that could be realized in this problem. Note that this involves minimizing the value of cell D8. Figure 7.9 shows the optimal solution

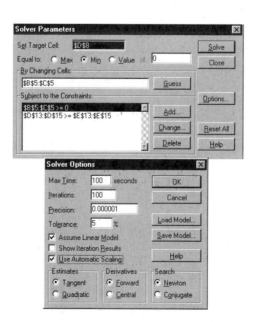

Figure 7.8
Solver
parameters and
options to
minimize
production costs.

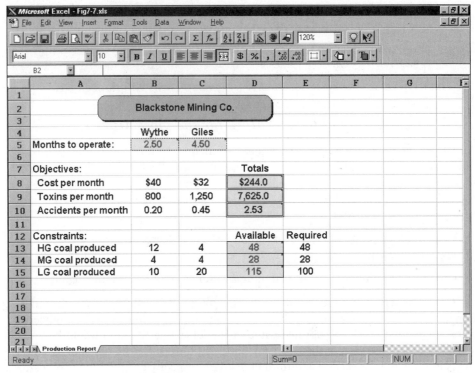

obtained by solving this LP problem. Notice that the best possible (minimum) production cost for this problem is $244 (in $1,000s) and this solution can be obtained by running an extra shift at the Wythe County for 2.5 months and at the Giles County mine for 4.5 months. Thus, a reasonable value for t_1 is $244. It is impossible to obtain a solution to this problem with a production cost lower than this amount.

Figure 7.10 shows the solution obtained if we minimize the generation of toxic groundwater pollutants (obtained by minimizing the value in cell D9). This production schedule requires that we run an extra shift at the Wythe County mine for 4.0 months and at the Giles County mine for 3.0 months and generates a total of 6,950 gallons of toxic water. Thus, a reasonable value for t_2 is 6,950. It is impossible to obtain a solution to this problem that produces less toxic water.

Finally, Figure 7.11 shows the solution obtained if we minimize the expected number of life-threatening accidents (obtained by minimizing the value in cell D10). This production schedule requires that we run an extra shifts at the Wythe County mine for 10 months and not run any extra shifts at the Giles mine. A total of two life-threatening accidents can be expected with this schedule. Thus, a reasonable value for t_3 is 2. It is impossible to obtain a solution to this problem with a lower number of expected life-threatening accidents.

7.5.6   *Summarizing the Target Solutions*

Figure 7.12 summarizes the solutions shown in Figures 7.9, 7.10, and 7.11 and shows where each of the solutions occurs in terms of the feasible region for this problem.

Two important points should be observed here. First, Figure 7.12 clearly shows that the objectives in this problem conflict with one another. Solution 1 has the lowest

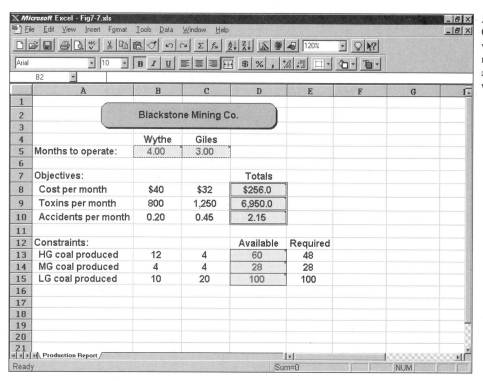

Figure 7.10
Optimal solution when minimizing the amount of toxic water generated.

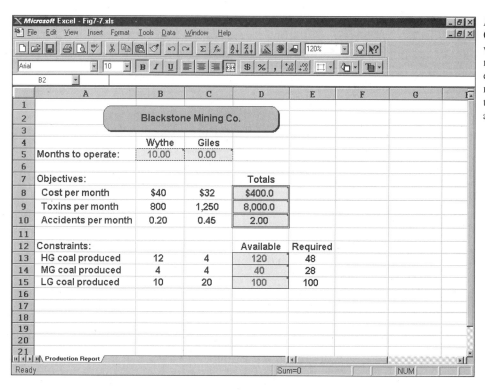

Figure 7.11
Optimal solution when minimizing the expected number of life-threatening accidents.

Figure 7.12
Summary of the solutions minimizing each of the three possible objectives.

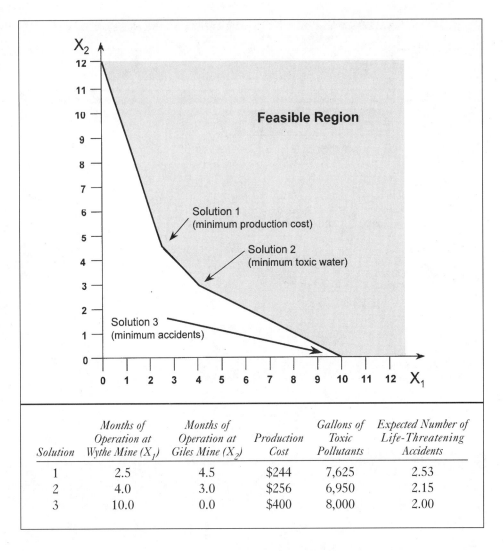

Solution	Months of Operation at Wythe Mine (X_1)	Months of Operation at Giles Mine (X_2)	Production Cost	Gallons of Toxic Pollutants	Expected Number of Life-Threatening Accidents
1	2.5	4.5	$244	7,625	2.53
2	4.0	3.0	$256	6,950	2.15
3	10.0	0.0	$400	8,000	2.00

production cost ($244,000) but also has the highest expected number of accidents (2.53). Conversely, solution 3 has the lowest expected number of accidents (2.0) but generates the highest production costs ($400,000) and also the highest creation of toxic water (8,000 gallons). This is not surprising, but does underscore the fact that this problem involves a trade-off between the three objectives. No single feasible point simultaneously optimizes all of the objective functions. In order to improve the value of one objective, we must sacrifice the value of the others. This characteristic is common to most MOLP problems. Thus, the purpose of MOLP (and of GP) is to study the trade-offs among the objectives in order to find a solution that is the most desirable to the decision maker.

Second, the graph in Figure 7.12 shows the solutions only at three corner points of the feasible region for this problem. Because we have already determined the levels of cost, toxic water production, and expected accident rates offered by these three solutions, if none of these solutions are acceptable, the decision maker may wish to explore some of the other *noncorner-point* feasible solutions shown in Figure 7.12. As we'll see, this poses a tricky problem.

7.5.7 *Determining a GP Objective*

Now that we have target values for the three objectives in our problem, we can formulate a weighted GP objective to allow the decision maker to explore possible solutions. Earlier in this chapter we discussed several GP objectives and illustrated the use of an objective that minimized the weighted percentage deviation from the goals' target values. Let's consider how to formulate this same type of objective for the current problem.

We can restate the objectives of this problem as the goals:

Goal 1: The total production cost should be approximately $244.

Goal 2: The gallons of toxic water produced should be approximately 6,950.

Goal 3: The number of life-threatening accidents should be approximately 2.0.

We now know that the actual total production cost can never be smaller than its target (optimum) value of $244, so the percentage deviation from this goal may be computed as:

$$\frac{\text{actual value} - \text{target value}}{\text{target value}} = \frac{(40X_1 + 32X_2) - 244}{244}$$

Similarly, the actual amount of toxic water generated can never be less than its target (optimum) value of 6,950, so the percentage deviation from this goal is calculated as:

$$\frac{\text{actual value} - \text{target value}}{\text{target value}} = \frac{(800X_1 + 1250X_2) - 6950}{6950}$$

Finally, the actual expected number of life-threatening accidents can never be less than its target (optimum) value of 2 so the percentage deviation from this goal is calculated as:

$$\frac{\text{actual value} - \text{target value}}{\text{target value}} = \frac{(0.20X_1 + 0.45X_2) - 2}{2}$$

These percentage deviation calculations are all linear functions of the decision variables. Thus, if we form an objective function as a weighted combination of these percentage deviation functions, we obtain the following linear objective function:

$$\text{MIN: } w_1 \left(\frac{(40X_1 + 32X_2) - 244}{244} \right) + w_2 \left(\frac{(800X_1 + 1250X_2) - 6950}{6950} \right) + w_3 \left(\frac{(0.20X_1 + 0.45X_2) - 2}{2} \right)$$

Recall from Chapter 2 that the optimal solution to an LP problem (that is, an optimization problem with linear constraints and a linear objective function) *always* occurs at an extreme (Corner) point of the feasible region. So, if we use the preceding objective to solve our example problem as a GP problem, we will *always* obtain one of the four extreme points shown in Figure 7.12 as the optimal solution to the problem, regardless of the weights assigned to w_1, w_2, and w_3. Thus, to explore the nonextreme feasible solutions to this GP problem (or any other GP problem with hard constraints), we need to use a different type of objective function.

7.5.8   The MINIMAX Objective

As it turns out, the MINIMAX objective, described earlier, can be used to explore the points on the edge of the feasible region—in addition to corner points. To illustrate this, let's attempt to minimize the maximum weighted percentage deviation from the target values for the goals in our example problem using the objective:

$$\text{MIN: the maximum of } w_1\left(\frac{(40X_1 + 32X_2) - 244}{244}\right), w_2\left(\frac{(800X_1 + 1250X_2) - 6950}{6950}\right),$$

$$\text{and } w_3\left(\frac{(0.20X_1 + 0.45X_2) - 2}{2}\right)$$

We implement this objective by establishing a MINIMAX variable Q that we minimize with the objective:

MIN: Q

Subject to the additional constraints:

$$w_1\left(\frac{(40X_1 + 32X_2) - 244}{244}\right) \leq Q$$

$$w_2\left(\frac{(800X_1 + 1250X_2) - 6950}{6950}\right) \leq Q$$

$$w_3\left(\frac{(0.20X_1 + 0.45X_2) - 2}{2}\right) \leq Q$$

The first constraint indicates that the weighted percentage deviation from the target production cost must be less than or equal to Q. The second constraint indicates that the weighted percentage deviation from the target level of toxic water production must also be less than or equal to Q. The third constraint indicates that the weighted percentage deviation from the target expected number of life-threatening accidents must also be less than or equal to Q. Thus, as we minimize Q, we are also minimizing the percentage deviations from the target values for each of our goals. In this way, the maximum deviation from any of the goals is minimized—or we have MINImized the MAXimum deviation (hence the term MINIMAX).

7.5.9   Implementing the Revised Model

The revised GP model of our investment problem is summarized as:

MIN: Q

Subject to:

$$
\begin{array}{ll}
12X_1 + 4X_2 \geq 48 & \text{\} High-grade coal required} \\
4X_1 + 4X_2 \geq 28 & \text{\} Medium-grade coal required} \\
10X_1 + 20X_2 \geq 100 & \text{\} Low-grade coal required} \\
w_1(40X_1 + 32X_2 - 244)/244 & \leq Q \text{ \} goal 1 MINIMAX constraint} \\
w_2(800X_1 + 1250X_2 - 6950)/6950 & \leq Q \text{ \} goal 2 MINIMAX constraint} \\
w_3(0.20X_1 + 0.45X_2 - 2)/2 & \leq Q \text{ \} goal 3 MINIMAX constraint} \\
X_1, X_2 \geq 0 & \text{\} nonnegativity conditions}
\end{array}
$$

w_1, w_2, w_3 are positive constants

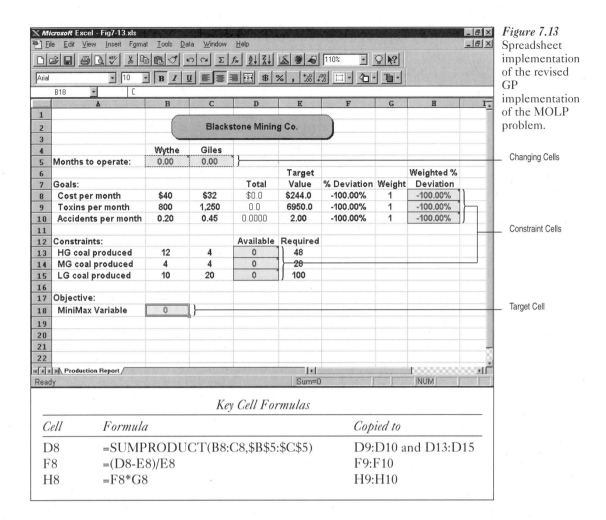

Figure 7.13
Spreadsheet implementation of the revised GP implementation of the MOLP problem.

Changing Cells

Constraint Cells

Target Cell

Key Cell Formulas

Cell	Formula	Copied to
D8	=SUMPRODUCT(B8:C8,$B$5:$C$5)	D9:D10 and D13:D15
F8	=(D8-E8)/E8	F9:F10
H8	=F8*G8	H9:H10

The spreadsheet shown earlier in Figure 7.7 can be modified easily to implement this new model. The revised spreadsheet is shown in Figure 7.13 (and in the file FIG7-13.xls on your data disk).

In Figure 7.13, cells E8 through E10 contain the target values for the goals. The percentage deviations from each goal are calculated in cells F8 through F10 as follows:

Formula for cell F8:   =(D8-E8)/E8
(Copy to cells F9 through F10.)

Arbitrary weights for the deviations from the goals were entered in cells G8 through G10. Cells H8 through H10 contain the following formulas, which calculate the weighted percentage deviation from the goals:

Formula for cell H8:   =F8*G8
(Copy to cells H9 through H10.)

The formulas in cells H8 through H10 are equivalent to the LHS formulas of the MINIMAX constraints for each of the goals in our model. Finally, cell B18 is reserved to represent the MINIMAX variable Q. Notice that this cell is a changing cell (since it represents the variable Q) *and* the target cell (since it also represents the objective to be minimized).

7.5.10   Solving the Model

The Solver parameters and options shown in Figure 7.14 were used to solve the model shown in Figure 7.13. The solution obtained for this model is shown in Figure 7.15.

Figure 7.14
Solver parameters and options for the GP implementation of the MOLP problem.

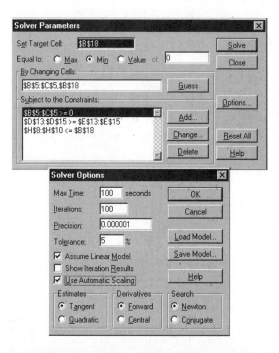

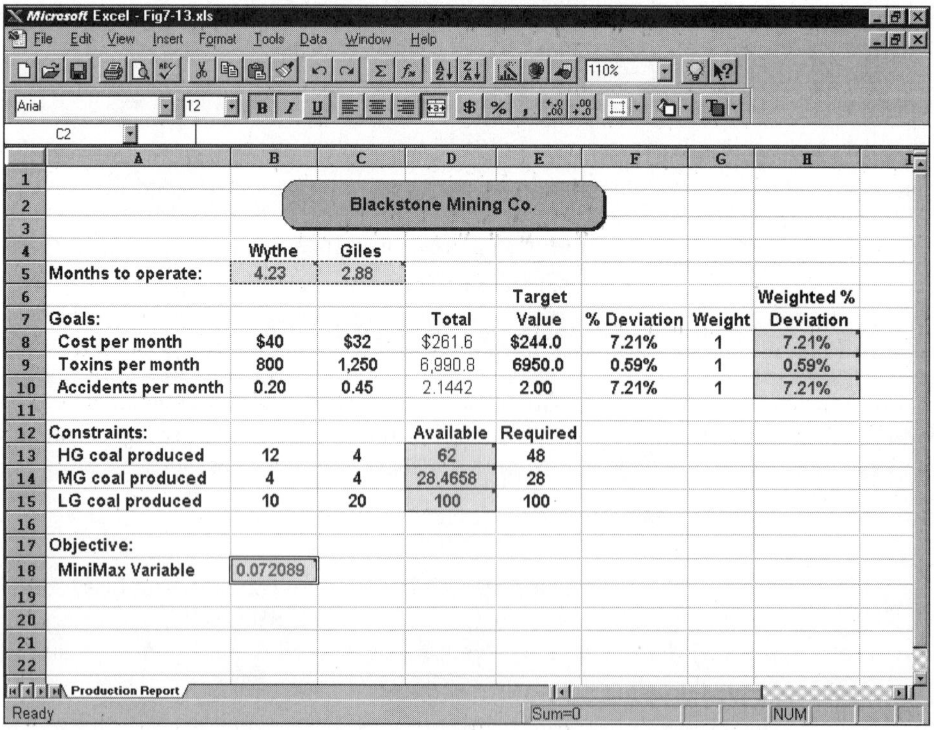

Figure 7.15
Solution to the MOLP problem obtained through GP.

Notice that the solution shown in Figure 7.15 (X_1 = 4.23, X_2 = 2.88) *does not* occur at an extreme point of the feasible region shown earlier in Figure 7.12. Also notice that this solution is within approximately 7.2% of achieving the target solution for goals 1 and 3 and is less than 1% from the target value for goal 2. Thus, the decision maker in this problem might find this solution more appealing than the other solutions occurring at the extreme points of the feasible region. Using other weights would produce different solutions. Figure 7.16 shows a number of representative solutions indicated on the original feasible region for this problem.

Figure 7.16 illustrates that as the relative weight on the first goal (w_1) increases, the solution is driven closer to achieving the target value for this goal (which occurs at the point X_1 = 2.5, X_2 = 4.5, as shown in Figure 7.12). As the relative weight on the second goal (w_2) increases, the solution is driven closer to achieving the target value for this goal (which occurs at the point X_1 = 4.0, X_2 = 3.0). Finally, as the relative weight on the third goal (w_3) increases, the solution is driven closer to achieving the target value for this goal (which occurs at the point X_1 = 10.0, X_2 = 0.0). Thus, by adjusting the weights, the decision maker can explore a variety of solutions that do not necessarily occur at the corner points of the original feasible region to the problem.

7.6 COMMENTS ON MOLP

Figure 7.17 provides a summary of the steps involved in solving an MOLP problem. Although the MOLP example in this chapter was somewhat simple, the same basic process applies in virtually any MOLP problem, regardless of the number of objectives or the complexity of the problem.

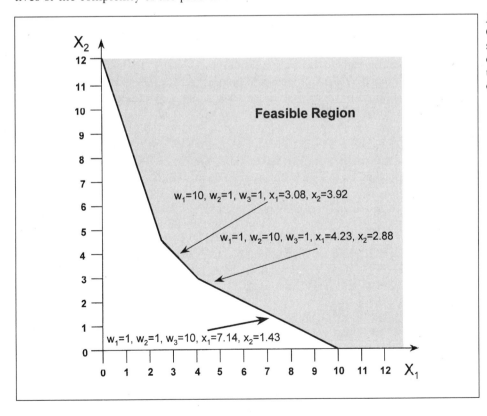

Figure 7.16
Graph of other solutions obtained using the MINIMAX objective.

Figure 7.17
Summary of the
steps involved in
formulating and
solving an
MOLP problem.

SUMMARY OF MULTIPLE OBJECTIVE OPTIMIZATION

1. Identify the decision variables in the problem.
2. Identify the objectives in the problem and formulate them in the usual way.
3. Identify the constraints in the problem and formulate them in the usual way.
4. Solve the problem once for each of the objectives identified in step 2 to determine the optimal value of each objective.
5. Restate the objectives as goals using the optimal objective values identified in step 4 as the target values.
6. For each goal, create a deviation function that measures the amount by which any given solution fails to meet the goal (either as an absolute or a percentage).
7. For each of the deviation functions identified in step 6, assign a weight to the deviation function and create a constraint that requires the value of the weighted deviation function to be less than the MINIMAX variable Q.
8. Solve the resulting problem with the objective of minimizing Q.
9. Inspect the solution to the problem. If the solution is unacceptable, adjust the weights in step 7 and return to step 8.

One advantage of using the MINIMAX objective to analyze MOLP problems is that the solutions generated are always **Pareto optimal**. That is, given any solution generated using this approach we can be certain that no other feasible solution allows an increase in any objective without decreasing at least one other objective. (There are one or two exceptions to this statement, but they go beyond the scope of this text.)

Although the MINIMAX objective is helpful in the analysis of MOLPs, its usefulness is not limited to these problems. Like deviational variables, the MINIMAX technique can prove useful in other types of mathematical programming situations.

In the example MOLP problem presented here, all of the goals were derived from minimization objectives. Because of this, we knew that the actual value for any goal could never be less than its derived target value and we used the following formula to calculate the percentage deviation for each goal constraint:

$$\frac{\text{actual value} - \text{target value}}{\text{target value}}$$

For goals derived from maximization objectives, we know that the actual value of the goal can never be greater than its derived target value and the percentage deviation for such goals should be calculated as:

$$\frac{\text{target value} - \text{actual value}}{\text{target value}}$$

If the target value of a goal is zero, it is not possible to use weighted percentage deviations in the solution to the MOLP (because division by zero is not permissible). In this case, you can simply use weighted deviations.

THE WORLD OF MANAGEMENT SCIENCE
Truck Transport Corporation Controls Costs and Disruptions While Relocating a Terminal

The Truck Transport Corporation, having decided to move its East St. Louis terminal, knew that relationships with customers and suppliers (independent truckers) were critical factors for continued profitable operations. Therefore, evaluating five potential new sites, management considered driver and customer preferences as well as costs in making its final selection.

At Truck Transport Corporation, the traditional approach to evaluating a new site is to include the candidate site in a transportation LP model with the four other terminals and 12 major customers, and find the solution that minimizes total transportation costs. This minimum cost solution is then compared with those for the other candidates to choose the most efficient site. An assignment problem is solved to assign independent truckers to terminals to minimize travel costs from the truckers' homes.

Some of the drivers, however, have strong preferences not to be assigned to particular terminals, usually on the basis of personal relationships with terminal managers. Some customers also have similar preferences. In a competitive market, failure to consider these preferences might cause the drivers or customers to do business elsewhere.

The linear goal programming model used to evaluate the sites combined the transportation problem and the trucker assignment problem. The constraints defined the following deviational variables, in declining order of priority: shortages in number of trips to major customers, shortages in number of trips assigned to each driver, number of driver preferences violated, number of customer preferences violated, increase in transportation costs from drivers' homes, and increase in transportation costs to the customers.

The model was validated by evaluating the East St. Louis site and comparing results to historical costs. The site ultimately selected fully satisfied the requirements for number of shipments and preferences. Total transportation costs for all drivers were projected to increase only $3,200, and customer transportation costs were projected to increase $1,400. The East St. Louis terminal was moved with no changes in the usual patterns of driver turnover or business with customers, and no complaints from drivers about decreased profitability because of the new site.

Source: Schneiderjans, Marc J., N. K. Kwak and Mark C. Helmer, "An Application of Goal Programming to Resolve a Site Location Problem," *Interfaces*, vol. 12, no. 3, June 1982, pages 65–70.

SUMMARY

This chapter presented two separate but closely related issues in optimization—GP and MOLP. GP provides a way of analyzing potential solutions to a decision problem that involves soft constraints. Soft constraints can be stated as goals with target values.

These goals can be translated into constraints through the use of deviational variables, which measure the amount by which a given solution deviates from a particular goal. The objective in GP problems is to minimize some weighted function of the deviational variables. By adjusting the weights on the deviational variables, a variety of potential solutions can be analyzed.

MOLP provides a way to analyze LP problems involving multiple objectives that conflict with one another. Although an MOLP problem is somewhat different from a standard GP problem, the objectives can be restated as goals after identifying appropriate target values for the objectives. The MINIMAX objective is helpful in analyzing the possible solutions to an MOLP problem.

Solving a GP or MOLP problem is not as simple as solving a single LP problem. Rather, a sequence of problems must be solved to allow the decision maker to analyze the trade-offs among the various goals and objectives at different possible solutions. Thus, both of these procedures are highly iterative and interactive.

QUESTIONS AND PROBLEMS

1. What is the difference between an objective function and a goal?

2. Is there an optimal solution to a GP or MOLP problem? Explain.

3. Refer to the MOLP example presented in this chapter.

    a. What weights could be used to generate the solution at $X_1 = 2.5$, $X_2 = 4.5$?
    b. What weights could be used to generate the solution at $X_1 = 4.0$, $X_2 = 3.0$?
    c. What weights could be used to generate the solution at $X_1 = 10.0$, $X_2 = 0.0$?
    d. What weights could be used to generate solutions along the edge of the feasible region that runs from the point $X_1 = 0$, $X_2 = 12.0$ to the point $X_1 = 2.5$, $X_2 = 4.5$?

4. Suppose that the first goal in a GP problem is to make $2X_1 + 5X_2$ approximately equal to 25.

    a. Using the deviational variables d_1^- and d_1^+, what constraint can be used to express this goal?
    b. If we obtain a solution where $X_1 = 4$ and $X_2 = 3$, what values do the deviational variables assume?
    c. Consider a solution where $X_1 = 4$, $X_2 = 3$, $d_1^- = 6$, and $d_1^+ = 4$. Can this solution ever be optimal? Why or why not?

5. Consider the following MOLP:

$$\text{MAX:} \quad 4X_1 + 2X_2$$
$$\text{MIN:} \quad X_1 + 3X_2$$
$$\text{Subject to:} \quad 2X_1 + X_2 \le 18$$
$$X_1 + 4X_2 \le 12$$
$$X_1 + X_2 \ge 4$$
$$X_1, X_2 \ge 0$$

    a. Graph the feasible region for this problem.
    b. Calculate the value of each objective at each extreme point.
    c. What feasible points in this problem are Pareto optimal?

6. It has been suggested that one way to solve MOLP problems is to create a composite objective function as a linear combination of all the objectives in the problem. For example, in the previous problem we might weight the first objective by 0.75 and the second by 0.25 to obtain the composite objective, MAX: $2.75X_1$ + $0.75X_2$. (Note that the second objective in the above problem is equivalent to MAX: $-X_1 - 3X_2$.) We then use this as the objective in an LP model to generate possible solutions. What problem, if any, do you see with this approach?

7. Refer to the MOLP problem presented in this chapter. The solutions shown in Figures 7.9, 7.10, and 7.11 each result in more than the required amount of one or more types of coal being produced, as summarized in the following table:

	Excess production of		
Solution shown in:	High-grade coal	Medium-grade coal	Low-grade coal
Figure 7.9	0 tons	0 tons	15 tons
Figure 7.10	12 tons	0 tons	0 tons
Figure 7.11	72 tons	12 tons	0 tons

a. Formulate an LP model that could be solved to find the solution that minimizes the maximum amount of excess coal produced.
b. Implement your model in a spreadsheet and solve it.
c. What is the optimal solution?
d. Revise your model to find the solution that minimizes the maximum percentage of excess coal produced. What is the optimal solution?

8. Blue Ridge Hot Tubs manufactures and sells two models of hot tubs: the Aqua-Spa and the Hydro-Lux. Howie Jones, the owner and manager of the company, needs to decide how many of each type of hot tub to produce during his next production cycle. Howie buys prefabricated fiberglass hot tub shells from a local supplier and adds the pump and tubing to the shells to create his hot tubs. (This supplier has the capacity to deliver as many hot tub shells as Howie needs.) Howie installs the same type of pump into both hot tubs. He will have only 200 pumps available during his next production cycle. From a manufacturing standpoint, the main difference between the two models of hot tubs is the amount of tubing and labor required. Each Aqua-Spa requires 9 hours of labor and 12 feet of tubing. Each Hydro-Lux requires 6 hours of labor and 16 feet of tubing. Howie expects to have 1,566 production labor hours and 2,880 feet of tubing available during the next production cycle. Howie earns a profit of $350 on each Aqua-Spa he sells and $300 on each Hydro-Lux he sells. He is confident that he can sell all the hot tubs he produces. The production of each Aqua-Spa generates 15 pounds of a toxic resin, while each Hydro-Lux produces 10 pounds of toxic resin. Howie has identified two different objectives that could apply to his problem: he can maximize profit or he can minimize the production of toxic resin. Suppose Howie considers the maximization of profit as half as important as the minimization of toxic resin.

a. Formulate an MOLP model for Howie's decision problem.
b. Implement your model in a spreadsheet and solve it.
c. What is the solution to Howie's MOLP problem?
d. The feasible region for this problem was shown in Figure 2.7. Identify on this graph the Pareto optimal solutions for Howie's MOLP problem.

9. The owner of the Weiner-Meyer meat processing plant wants to determine the best blend of meats to use in the next production run of hamburgers. Three sources of meat can be used. The following table summarizes relevant characteristics of these meats:

	Meat 1	Meat 2	Meat 3
Cost per pound	$0.75	$0.87	$0.98
% Fat	15%	10%	5%
% Protein	70%	75%	80%
% Water	12%	10%	8%
% Filler	3%	5%	7%

A local elementary school has ordered 500 pounds of meat for $1.10 per pound. The only requirement is that the meat consist of at least 75% protein and at most 10% each of water and filler. Ordinarily, the owner would produce the blend of meats that achieved this objective in the least costly manner. However, with the concern of too much fat in school lunches, the owner also wants to produce a blend that minimizes the fat content of the meat produced.

a. Formulate an MOLP for this problem.
b. Implement your formulation in a spreadsheet and individually optimize the two objectives under consideration.
c. How much profit must be forfeited in order to fill this order using the mix that minimizes the fat content?
d. Solve this problem with the objective of minimizing the maximum percentage deviation from the target values of the goals. What solution do you obtain?
e. Assume the owner considers minimizing the fat content twice as important as maximizing profit. What solution does this imply?

10. A new Italian restaurant called the Olive Grove is opening in a number of locations in the Memphis area. The marketing manager for these stores has a budget of $150,000 to use in advertising and promotions for the new stores. The manager can run magazine ads at a cost of $2,000 each that result in 250,000 exposures each. TV ads result in approximately 1,200,000 exposures each, but cost $12,000 each. The manager wants to run at least five TV ads and ten magazine ads, while maximizing the number of exposures generated by the advertising campaign. But the manager also wants to spend no more than $120,000 on magazine and TV advertising so that the remaining $30,000 could be used for other promotional purposes. However, the manager would spend more than $120,000 on advertising if it resulted in a substantial increase in advertising coverage.

a. Formulate a GP model for this problem assuming the marketing manager has the following goals:

Goal 1: Exposures should be maximized.

Goal 2: No more than $120,000 should be spent on advertising.

(Note that you will have to determine an appropriate target value for the first goal.) Assume the marketing manager wants to minimize the maximum percentage deviation from either goal.

b. Implement your model in a spreadsheet and solve it.

c. What is the solution you obtain?

d. What changes do you make to your model if the manager wants to spend less on advertising than your solution suggests?

11. The Royal Seas Company runs three-night cruises to the Caribbean from Port Canaveral. The company wants to run TV ads promoting its cruises to high income men, high income women, and retirees. The company has decided to consider airing ads during prime time, afternoon soap operas, and during the evening news. The number of exposures (in millions) expected to be generated by each type of ad in each of the company's target audiences is summarized below.

	Prime Time	Soap Operas	Evening News
High income men	6	3	6
High income women	3	4	4
Retirees	4	7	3

Ads during prime time, the afternoon soaps, and the news hour cost $120,000, $85,000, and $100,000 respectively. Royal Seas would like to achieve the following goals:

Goal 1: To spend approximately $900,000 of TV advertising.

Goal 2: To generate approximately 45 million exposures among high income men.

Goal 3: To generate approximately 60 million exposures among high income women.

Goal 4: To generate approximately 50 million exposures among retirees.

a. Formulate a GP model for this problem. Assume overachievement of the first goal is equally as undesirable as underachievement of the remaining goals on a percentage deviation basis.

b. Implement your model in a spreadsheet and solve it.

c. What is the optimal solution?

d. What solution allows the company to spend as close to $900,000 as possible without exceeding this amount?

e. Assume that the company can spend no more than $900,000. What solution minimizes the maximum percentage underachievement of all the goals?

f. Which of the two preceding solutions would you most prefer? Why?

12. The Waygate Corporation makes five different types of metal casing for personal computers. The company is in the process of replacing its machinery with three different new models of metal stamping machines: the Robo-I, Robo-II, and Robo-III. The unit costs of each machine are $18,500, $25,000 and $35,000, respectively. Each machine can be programmed to produce any of the five casings. Once the machine is programmed, it produces each type of casing at the following rates:

	Casings per hour				
	Type 1	Type 2	Type 3	Type 4	Type 5
Robo-I	100	130	140	210	80
Robo-II	265	235	170	220	120
Robo-III	200	160	260	180	220

The company has the following goals:

Goal 1: To spend no more than approximately $400,000 on the purchase of new machines.

Goal 2: To have the ability to produce approximately 3,200 units of type 1 casings per hour.

Goal 3: To have the ability to produce approximately 2,500 units of type 2 casings per hour.

Goal 4: To have the ability to produce approximately 3,500 units of type 3 casings per hour.

Goal 5: To have the ability to produce approximately 3,000 units of type 4 casings per hour.

Goal 6: To have the ability to produce approximately 2,500 units of type 5 casings per hour.

a. Formulate a GP model for this problem. Assume all percentage deviations from all goals are equally undesirable.
b. Implement your model in a spreadsheet and solve it.
c. What is the optimal solution?
d. Which solution minimizes the maximum percentage deviation from all the goals?
e. Assume that the company can spend no more than $400,000. Which solution minimizes the maximum percentage deviation from all the remaining goals?

13. The Chick'n-Pick'n fast-food chain is considering how to expand its operations. Three types of retail outlets are possible: a lunch-counter operation designed for office buildings in downtown areas, an eat-in operation designed for shopping malls, and a stand-alone building with drive-through and sit-down facilities. The following table summarizes the number of jobs, start-up costs, and annual returns associated with each type of operation:

	Lunch Counter	Mall	Stand-alone
Jobs	9	17	35
Costs	$150,000	$275,000	$450,000
Returns	$85,000	$125,000	$175,000

The company has $2,000,000 available to pay start-up costs for new operations in the coming year. Additionally, there are five possible sites for lunch-counter operations, seven possible mall locations, and three possible stand-alone locations. The company wants to plan its expansion in a way that maximizes annual returns and the number of jobs created.

a. Formulate an MOLP for this problem.
b. Determine the best possible value for each objective in the problem.
c. Implement your model in a spreadsheet and solve it to determine the solution that minimizes the maximum percentage deviation from the optimal objective function values. What solution do you obtain?
d. Suppose management considers maximizing returns three times as important as maximizing the number of jobs created. What solution does this suggest?

14. A private foundation has offered $3 million to allocate to cities to help fund programs that aid the homeless. Grant proposals were received from cities A, B, and C seeking assistance of $750,000, $1.2 million, and $2.5 million, respectively. In the grant proposals, cities were requested to quantify the number of assistance units that would be provided using the funds (an assistance unit is a night on a bed in a shelter or a free meal). Cities A, B, and C reported they could provide 485,000, 850,000, and 1.5 million assistance units, respectively, with the funds requested during the coming year. The directors of the foundation have two objectives. They want to maximize the number of assistance units obtained with the $3 million. However, they also want to help each of the cities by funding as much of their individual requests as possible (this might be done by maximizing the minimum percentage of funding received by any city).

    a. Formulate an MOLP for this problem.
    b. Determine the best possible value for each objective in the problem.
    c. Implement your model in a spreadsheet and solve it to determine the solution that minimizes the maximum percentage deviation from the optimal objective function values. What solution do you obtain?

15. The marketing manager for Glissen Paint is working on the weekly sales and marketing plan for the firm's industrial and contractor sales staff. Glissen's sales representatives contact two types of customers: existing customers and new customers. Each contact with an existing customer normally takes three hours of the salesperson's time (including travel time) and results in an average sale of $425. Contacts with new customers generally take a bit longer, on average four hours, and result in an average sale of $350. The company's salespeople are required to work 40 hours a week, but often work more to achieve their sales quotas (on which their bonuses are based). The company has a policy limiting the number of hours a salesperson can work to 50 hours per week. The sales manager wants to set customer contact quotas for the salespeople that will achieve the following goals (listed in order of importance):

    Goal 1: Each salesperson should achieve an average weekly sales level of $6,000.

    Goal 2: Each salesperson should contact at least ten existing customers per week.

    Goal 3: Each salesperson should contact at least five new customers per week.

    Goal 4: Each salesperson should limit overtime to no more than five hours per week.

    a. Formulate this problem as a GP with an objective of minimizing the sum of the weighted undesirable percentage deviation from the goals.
    b. Implement your model in a spreadsheet and solve it, assuming equal weights on each goal. What solution do you obtain?

16. A major city in the Northeast wants to establish a central transportation station from which visitors can ride busses to four historic landmarks. The city is arranged in a grid, or block, structure with equally spaced streets running north and south and equally spaced avenues running east and west. The coordinates of any corner of any block in the city can be identified by the street and avenue numbers intersecting at that particular corner. The following table gives the coordinates for the four historic landmarks:

Landmark	Street	Avenue
1	7	3
2	3	1
3	1	6
4	6	9

The transportation planners want to build the transportation station at the location in the city that minimizes the total travel distance (measured rectangularly) to each landmark. For example, if they built the station at 6th Street and 2nd Avenue, the total distance to each landmark will be:

Landmark	Distance
1	$\lvert 7-6 \rvert + \lvert 3-2 \rvert = 1 + 1 = 2$
2	$\lvert 3-6 \rvert + \lvert 1-2 \rvert = 3 + 1 = 4$
3	$\lvert 1-6 \rvert + \lvert 6-2 \rvert = 5 + 4 = 9$
4	$\lvert 6-6 \rvert + \lvert 9-2 \rvert = 0 + 7 = 7$

Total Distance = 22

    a. Plot the locations of the various historical landmarks on a graph where the X-axis represents avenue numbers (starting at 0) and the Y-axis represents street numbers (starting at 0).

    b. Formulate an LP model to determine the corner at which the central transportation station should be located. (Hint: Let the decision variables represent the street location (X_1) and avenue location (X_2) of the station and use deviational variables to measure the absolute street distance and absolute avenue distance from each landmark to X_1 and X_2. Minimize the sum of the deviational variables.)

17. A car dealer specializing in late model used cars collected the following data on the selling price and mileage of five cars of the same make and model year at an auto auction:

Mileage	Price
43,890	$12,500
35,750	$13,350
27,300	$14,600
15,500	$15,750
8,900	$17,500

Because there seems to be a strong relationship between mileage and price, the dealer wants to use this information to predict this type of car's market value on the basis of its mileage. The dealer thinks that the car's selling price can be predicted as:

$$\text{Estimated price} = A + B * \text{mileage}$$

A and B represent numeric constants (which might be positive or negative). Using the data collected at last week's auction, the dealer wants to determine appropriate values for A and B that minimize the following quantity:

$$\text{MIN: } |A+B*43890-12500|+|A+B*35750-13350|+|A+B*27300-14600|$$
$$+|A+B*15500-15750|+|A+B*8900-17500|$$

Notice that this objective seeks to find values of A and B that minimize the sum of the absolute value of the deviations between the actual prices of the cars and the estimated prices.

   a. Create an LP model using deviational variables whose solution provides the best values for A and B using the stated criteria. That is, what values of A and B minimize the sum of the absolute deviations between the actual and estimated selling prices?

   b. Implement your model in a spreadsheet and solve it.

   c. Using the values of A and B determined by your solution, what should the estimated selling price be for each car?

18. Refer to the previous question. Suppose that the car dealer wanted to find values for A and B that minimized the maximum absolute deviation between the actual and estimated selling price for each car. What values of A and B achieve this objective?

19. A job in a machine shop must undergo five operations—A, B, C, D, and E. Each operation can be performed on either of two machines. The following table summarizes the time required for each machine to perform each operation:

	A	B	C	D	E
Machine 1	7	8	4	4	9
Machine 2	5	3	9	6	8

Formulate a model that can be solved to determine the job routing that minimizes the maximum amount of time used on either machine. That is, if t_i is the total time used on machine i, find the solution that minimizes the maximum of t_1 and t_2.

CASE 7.1 PLANNING DIETS FOR THE FOOD STAMP PROGRAM

Based on: Taj S., "A Mathematical Model for Planning Policies for Food Stamps," *Applications of Management Science*, vol. 7, 25–48, 1993.

The United States Department of Agriculture (USDA) is responsible for managing and administering the national food stamp program. This program has the responsibility of providing vouchers to low income families that can be used in place of cash to purchase food at grocery stores. In determining the cash value of the vouchers issued, the USDA must consider how much it costs to obtain a nutritional, well-balanced diet for men and women in various age groups. As a first step in this process, the USDA identified and analyzed 31 different food groups and determined the contributions a serving from each group makes to 24 different nutritional categories. A partial listing of this information is given in Figure 7.18 (and in the file FIG7-18.xls on your data disk).

The last two rows in this spreadsheet indicate the minimum and/or maximum nutrients required per week for men between the ages of 20 and 50. (Maximum values of 9999 indicate that no maximum value applies to that particular nutritional requirement.)

Figure 7.18 Data for the USDA diet planning problem.

Microsoft Excel - Fig7-18.xls

	A	B	C	U	V	W	X	Y	Z	AA	AB	AC
1												
2		Food	Weekly Units	Carbo-hydrates	Total Fat	Saturated Fat	Monosat. Fats	Polysat. Fat	Choles-terol	Sugar	Cost per serving	Pref. Rating
3	1	Potatoes	0	93.80	2.60	1.10	0.80	0.40	2.00	0.00	$0.391	6.68
4	2	High-Nutrient Vegetables	0	30.80	1.00	0.10	0.10	0.40	0.00	4.00	$1.014	17.81
5	3	Other Vegetables	0	37.10	2.00	0.40	0.50	0.80	0.00	16.00	$0.958	13.31
6	4	Mixtures; mostly vegetable	0	174.40	101.00	26.10	21.10	10.80	0.00	256.00	$1.897	24.5
7	5	Vitamin-C-rich fruits	0	81.90	0.70	0.00	0.10	0.10	0.00	4.00	$0.721	15.9
8	6	Other fruit	0	71.40	1.60	0.30	0.30	0.40	0.00	32.00	$0.961	14.88
9	7	Whole-grain/high-fiber breakfast cerea	0	323.60	21.90	4.60	6.90	8.90	0.00	140.00	$2.770	8.22
10	8	Other cereals	0	382.30	6.20	2.50	1.10	1.80	0.00	392.00	$3.327	9.43
11	9	Whole-grain/high-fiber flour, meal, rice	0	328.50	17.90	2.70	4.30	8.80	0.00	8.00	$0.966	4.4
12	10	Other flour, meal, rice, pasta	0	346.00	6.20	1.20	2.30	11.00	52.00	52.00	$0.720	0.28
13	11	Whole grain/high fiber bread	0	217.10	14.90	2.60	3.70	6.40	1.00	4.00	$1.553	5.52
14	12	Other breads	0	225.10	18.60	4.30	7.10	5.20	7.00	16.00	$1.111	4.9
15	13	Bakery products	0	300.40	69.10	21.50	27.20	14.30	112.00	392.00	$2.460	9.03
16	14	Grain mixtures	0	196.80	25.10	9.50	8.60	4.80	61.00	24.00	$1.556	25.67
17	15	Milk, yogurt	0	32.00	14.80	9.30	4.10	0.60	60.00	4.00	$0.362	17.34
18	16	Cheese	0	10.50	134.40	85.15	38.30	4.00	413.00	0.00	$2.811	22.72
19	17	Cream, mixtures mostly milk	0	107.30	60.50	41.80	13.50	2.00	137.00	256.00	$1.223	17.1
20	18	Lower-cost red meats, variety meats	0	1.30	84.90	33.60	37.10	4.50	284.00	0.00	$1.918	44.58
21	19	Higher-cost red meats, variety meats	0	0.60	74.00	28.30	32.50	5.90	278.00	0.00	$2.801	89.24
22	20	Poultry	0	0.40	42.10	12.00	16.90	9.20	271.00	0.00	$1.281	57.53
23	21	Fish, shellfish	0	2.40	12.70	2.70	4.30	3.80	172.00	4.00	$3.471	78.18
24	22	Bacon, sausage, luncheon meats	0	7.60	170.40	63.00	79.10	18.40	287.00	16.00	$2.481	17.83
25	23	Eggs	0	4.90	40.10	12.40	15.24	5.50	1698.00	0.00	$0.838	9.35
26	24	Dry beans, peas, lentils	0	235.60	5.00	1.30	1.00	1.80	5.00	44.00	$1.309	13.08
27	25	Mixtures, mostly meat, poultry, fish, egg	0	58.40	37.70	11.70	14.70	8.00	101.00	20.00	$1.967	46.2
28	26	Nuts, peanut butter	0	88.60	221.70	37.80	102.00	71.10	0.00	56.00	$2.504	21.26
29	27	Fats, oils	0	14.80	370.00	90.40	137.20	125.80	152.00	24.00	$1.198	3.17
30	28	Sugar, sweets	0	406.90	7.30	4.00	2.33	0.50	3.00	1576.00	$1.111	2.39
31	29	Seasonings	0	36.30	5.50	1.80	1.70	1.20	0.00	4.00	$2.077	5.8
32	30	Soft drinks, punches, ades	0	58.40	0.00	0.00	0.00	0.00	0.00	116.00	$0.249	47.42
33	31	Coffee, tea	0	87.70	1.70	0.60	0.10	0.50	0.00	4.00	$6.018	7.7
34		Weekly Total		0	0	0	0	0	0	0	$0.000	0
35		Weekly Lower Limit		0.00	0.00	0.00	0.00	0.00	0.00	0.00		
36		Weekly Upper Limit		9999	676.67	225.56	9999	9999	2100	2436		
37												
38												
39												

Diet Analysis

The USDA used this information to design a diet (or weekly consumption plan) that meets the indicated nutritional requirements. The last two columns in Figure 7.18 represent two different objectives that can be pursued in creating a diet. First, we may wish to identify the diet that meets the nutritional requirements at a minimum cost. While such a diet might be very economical, it might also be very unsatisfactory to the tastes of the people who are expected to eat it. To help address this issue, the USDA conducted a survey to assess people's preferences for different food groups. The last column in Figure 7.18 summarizes these preference ratings, with higher scores indicating more desirable foods and lower scores indicating less desirable foods. Thus, another objective that could be pursued would be that of determining the diet that meets the nutritional requirements and produces the highest total preference rating. However, this solution is likely to be quite expensive. Assume that the USDA has asked you to help them analyze this situation using MOLP.

1. Find the weekly diet that meets the nutritional requirements in the least costly manner. What is the lowest possible minimum cost? What preference rating does this solution have?

2. Find the weekly diet that meets the nutritional requirements with the highest preference rating. What preference rating does this solution have? What cost is associated with this solution?

3. Find the solution that minimizes the maximum percentage deviation from the optimum values for each individual objective. What cost and preference rating is associated with this solution?

4. Suppose that deviations from the optimal cost value are weighted twice as heavily as those from the optimal preference value. Find the solution that minimizes

the maximum weighted percentage deviations. What cost and preference rating is associated with this solution?

5. What other factors or constraints might you want to include in this analysis if you had to eat the resulting diet?

REFERENCES

Gass, S. "A Process for Determining Priorities and Weights for Large-Scale Linear Goal Programs." *Journal of the Operational Research Society*, vol. 37, August 1986.

Ignizio, J. "A Review of Goal Programming: A Tool for Multiobjective Analysis." *Journal of the Operational Research Society*, vol. 29, no. 11, 1978.

Steuer, R. *Multiple Criteria Optimization: Theory, Computation, and Application*. New York: Wiley, 1986.

Taylor, B. and A. Keown. "A Goal Programming Application of Capital Project Selection in the Production Area." *AIIE Transactions*, vol. 10, no. 1, 1978.

CHAPTER 8

Nonlinear Programming

U p to this point in our study of optimization, we have considered only mathematical programming models in which the objective function and constraints are *linear* functions of the decision variables. In many decision problems, the use of such linear functions is appropriate. Other types of optimization problems involve objective functions and constraints that *cannot* be modeled adequately using linear functions of the decision variables. These types of problems are called *nonlinear programming* (NLP) problems.

The process of formulating an NLP problem is virtually the same as formulating an LP problem. In each case you must identify the appropriate decision variables and formulate an appropriate objective function and constraints using these variables. As you'll see, the process of implementing and solving NLP problems in a spreadsheet is also similar to that for LP problems. However, the mechanics (that is, mathematical procedures) involved in solving NLP problems are very different. Although optimization software such as Solver makes this difference somewhat transparent to the user of such systems, it is important to understand these differences so you can understand the difficulties you might encounter when solving an NLP problem. This chapter discusses some of the unique features and challenges involved in solving NLP problems, and presents several examples of managerial decision-making problems that can be modeled as NLP problems.

8.1 THE NATURE OF NLP PROBLEMS

The main difference between an LP and NLP problem is that NLPs can have a nonlinear objective function and/or one or more nonlinear constraints. To understand the differences and difficulties nonlinearities introduce to an optimization problem, consider the various hypothetical NLP problems shown in Figure 8.1.

The first graph in Figure 8.1, labeled (a), illustrates a problem with a linear objective function and a *nonlinear* constraint set. Note that the boundary lines of the feasible region for this problem are not all straight lines. At least one of the constraints in

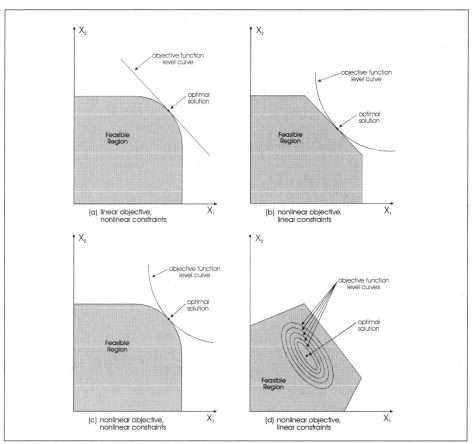

Figure 8.1
Examples of
NLP problems
with optimal
solutions not at a
corner point of
the feasible
region.

this problem must be nonlinear to cause the curve in the boundary line of the feasible region. This curve causes the unique optimal solution to this problem to occur at a solution that is not a corner point of the feasible region.

The second graph in Figure 8.1, labeled (b), shows a problem with a *nonlinear* objective function and a linear constraint set. As indicated in this graph, if an NLP problem has a nonlinear objective function, the level curves associated with the objective are also nonlinear. So from this graph we observe that a nonlinear objective can cause the optimal solution to the NLP problem to occur at a solution that is not a corner point of the feasible region—even if all the constraints are linear.

The third graph in Figure 8.1, labeled (c), shows a problem with a *nonlinear* objective and a *nonlinear* constraint set. Here again, we see that the optimal solution to this NLP problem occurs at a solution that is not a corner point of the feasible region.

Finally, the fourth graph in Figure 8.1, labeled (d), shows another problem with a *nonlinear* objective and a *linear* constraint set. The optimal solution to this problem occurs at a point in the interior of the feasible region.

These graphs illustrate the major difference between LP and NLP problems—an optimal solution to an LP problem always occurs at a corner point of its feasible region, but this is not true of NLP problems. The optimal solution to some NLP problems might not occur on the boundary of the feasible region at all, but at some point in the interior of the feasible region. Therefore, the strategy of searching the corner points of the feasible region employed by the simplex method to solve LP problems will not work with NLP problems. We need another strategy to solve NLP problems.

8.2   SOLUTION STRATEGIES FOR NLP PROBLEMS

The solution procedure Solver uses to solve NLP problems is called the **generalized reduced gradient** (GRG) algorithm. The mathematics involved in this procedure are very complex and go beyond the scope and purpose of this text. However, the following discussion should give you a very basic (if somewhat imprecise) understanding of the ideas behind the GRG and other NLP solution algorithms.

NLP algorithms begin at any feasible solution to the NLP problem. This initial feasible solution is called the **starting point.** The algorithm then attempts to move from the starting point in a direction through the feasible region that causes the objective function value to improve. Some amount of movement (or a **step size**) in the selected feasible direction is then taken, resulting in a new and better feasible solution to the problem. The algorithm next attempts to identify another feasible direction in which to move to obtain further improvements in the objective function value. If such a direction exists, the algorithm determines a new step size and moves in that direction to a new and better feasible solution. This process continues until the algorithm reaches a point where there is no feasible direction in which to move that results in an improvement in the objective function. When no further possibility for improvement exists (or the potential for further improvement becomes arbitrarily small), the algorithm terminates.

Figure 8.2 shows a graphical example of how a crude NLP algorithm might work. In this graph, an initial feasible solution occurs at the origin (point A). The fastest rate of improvement in the objective function valve occurs by moving from point A in the direction that is perpendicular to (or forms a 90-degree angle with) the level curves of

Figure 8.2
Example of an
NLP solution
strategy.

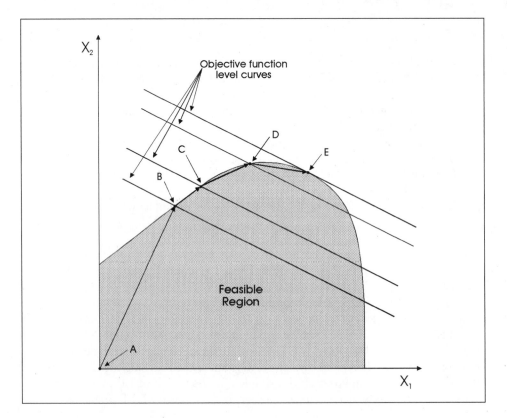

the objective function. Feasible movement in this direction is possible from point A to point B where a boundary of the feasible region is encountered. From point B, moving along the edge of the feasible region to point C further improves the objective function value. At point C the boundary of the feasible region begins to curve; therefore, continued movement in the direction from point B to point C is no longer feasible. From point C, a new direction through the interior of the feasible region allows movement to point D. This process continues from point D until the solution becomes arbitrarily close (or converges) to point E—the optimal solution.

In moving from point A in Figure 8.2, we selected the direction that resulted in the fastest rate of improvement in the objective function. In retrospect, we can see that it would have been better to move from point A in the direction of point E. This direction does not result in the fastest rate of improvement in the objective as we move from point A, but it would have taken us to the optimal solution in a more direct fashion. Thus, it is not always best to move in the direction producing the fastest rate of improvement in the objective, nor it is always best to move as far as possible in that direction. The GRG algorithm used by Solver takes these issues into consideration as it determines the direction and step size of the movements to make. Thus, while the GRG algorithm usually cannot move directly from a starting point to an optimal solution, it does chose the path it takes in a more refined manner than outlined in Figure 8.2.

8.3 LOCAL VS. GLOBAL OPTIMAL SOLUTIONS

NLP solution algorithms terminate whenever they detect that no feasible direction exists in which they can move to produce a better objective function value (or when the amount of potential improvement becomes arbitrarily small). In such a situation, the current solution is a **local optimal** solution—a solution that is better than any other feasible solution in its immediate, or local, vicinity. However, a given local optimal solution might not be the best possible, or **global optimal**, solution to a problem. Another local optimal solution in some other area of the feasible region could be the best possible solution to the problem. This type of anomaly is illustrated in Figure 8.3.

If an NLP algorithm starts at point A in Figure 8.3, it could move immediately to point B and then along the feasible direction from B to C. Because no feasible point in the vicinity of C produces a better objective function value, point C is a local optimal solution and the algorithm terminates at this point. However, this is clearly *not* the best possible solution to this problem. If an NLP algorithm starts at point D in Figure 8.3, it could move immediately to point E, and then follow the feasible direction from E to F and from F to G. Note that point G is both a local and global optimal solution to this problem.

Figure 8.3 highlights two important points about the GRG and all other NLP algorithms:

1. NLP algorithms can terminate at a local optimal solution that might not be the global optimal solution to the problem.
2. The local optimal solution at which an NLP algorithm terminates depends on the initial starting point.

The possibility of terminating at a local optimal solution is undesirable—but we have encountered this type of difficulty before. In our study of integer programming, we noted that suboptimal solutions to ILPs might be acceptable if they are within some allowable tolerance of the global optimal solution. Unfortunately, with NLP

Figure 8.3
Local vs. global
optimal
solutions.

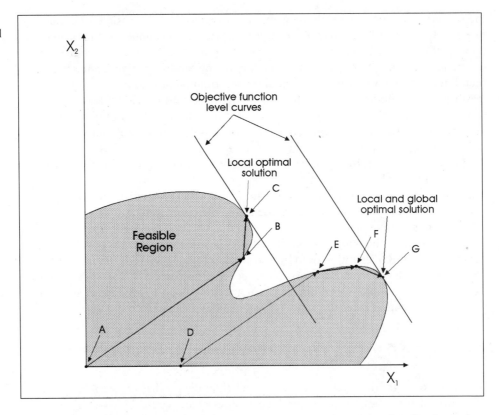

problems we cannot determine easily how much worse a given local optimal solution is than the global optimal solution because there is no general way of obtaining bounds on the optimal objective function values for these problems. However, many NLP problems have a single local optimal solution that, by definition, must also be the global optimal solution. So in many problems, NLP algorithms will locate the global optimal solution. But, as a general rule, we will not know whether the solution obtained for an NLP problem is the global optimal solution. Therefore, it is usually a good idea to try starting NLP algorithms from different points to determine if the problem has different local optimal solutions. This procedure often reveals the global optimal solution. (Two questions at the end of this chapter illustrate this process.)

A Note About Starting Points

Solver sometimes has trouble solving an NLP problem if it starts at the null starting point, where all the decision variables are set equal to 0—even if this solution is feasible. Therefore, when solving an NLP problem, it is best to specify a non-null starting solution whenever possible. It also helps to specify starting values of the same approximate magnitude as the values expected at the optimal solution.

We'll now consider several examples of NLP problems. These examples illustrate some of the differences between LP and NLP problems and provide insight into the broad range of problems that cannot be modeled adequately using LP.

A Note About "Optimal" Solutions

When solving an NLP problem, Solver normally stops when the first of three numerical tests is satisfied, causing one of the following three completion messages to appear:

1. **"Solver found a solution. All constraints and optimality conditions are satisfied."**

   This means Solver found a local optimal solution, but does not guarantee that the solution is the global optimal solution. Unless you know that a problem has only one local optimal solution (which must also be the global optimal), you should run Solver from several different starting points to increase the chances that you find the global optimal solution to your problem.

2. **"Solver has converged to the current solution. All constraints are satisfied."**

   This means the objective function value changed very slowly for the last few iterations. If you suspect the solution is not a local optimal, your problem may be poorly scaled. In Excel 8.0, the convergence option in the Solver Options dialog box can be reduced to avoid convergence at suboptimal solutions.

3. **"Solver cannot improve the current solution. All constraints are satisfied."**

   This rare message means the your model is degenerate and the Solver is cycling. Degeneracy can often be eliminated by removing redundant constraints in a model.

8.4 ECONOMIC ORDER QUANTITY MODELS

The **economic order quantity** (EOQ) problem is one of the most common business problems where nonlinear optimization can be used. This problem is encountered when a manager must determine the optimal number of units of a product to purchase whenever an order is placed. The basic model for an EOQ problem makes the following assumptions:

1. Demand for (or use of) the product is fairly constant throughout the year.
2. Each new order is delivered in full when the inventory level reaches 0.

Figure 8.4 illustrates the type of inventory patterns observed for a product when the preceding conditions are met. In each graph, the inventory levels are depleted at a constant rate, representing constant demand. Also, the inventory levels are replenished instantly whenever the inventory levels reach 0.

The key issue in an EOQ problem is to determine the optimal quantity to order whenever an order is placed for an item. The trade-offs in this decision are evident in Figure 8.4. The graphs indicate two ways of obtaining 150 units of a product during the year. In the first graph, an order for 50 units is received whenever the inventory level drops to 0. This requires that three purchase orders be issued during the year and results in an average inventory level of 25 units. In the second graph, an order for

Figure 8.4
Inventory profiles
of products for
which the EOQ
assumptions are
met.

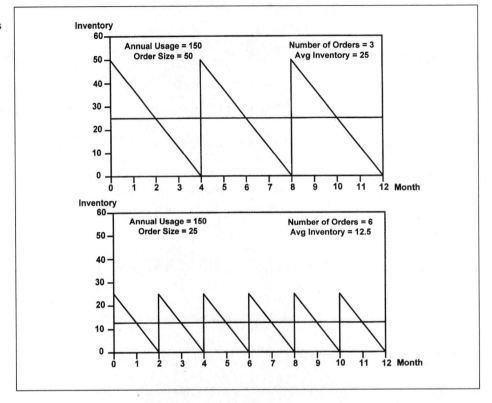

25 units is received whenever the inventory level drops to 0. This requires that six purchase orders be issued throughout the year and results in an average inventory level of 12.5 units. Thus, the first ordering strategy results in fewer purchase orders (and lower ordering costs) but higher inventory levels (and higher carrying costs). The second ordering strategy results in more purchase orders (and higher ordering costs) but lower levels of inventory (and lower carrying costs).

In the basic EOQ model, the total annual cost of stocking a product is computed as the sum of the actual purchase cost of the product, plus the fixed cost of placing orders, plus the cost of holding (or carrying) the product in inventory. Figure 8.5 shows the relationship between order quantity, carrying cost, ordering cost, and total cost. Notice that as the order quantity increases, ordering costs decrease and carrying costs increase. The goal in this type of problem is to find the EOQ that minimizes the total cost.

The total annual cost of acquiring products that meet the stated assumptions is represented by:

$$\text{Total annual cost} = DC + \frac{D}{Q}S + \frac{Q}{2}Ci$$

where:

D = annual demand for the item

C = unit purchase cost for the item

S = fixed cost of placing an order

i = cost of holding one unit in inventory for a year (expressed as a percentage of C)

Q = order quantity, or quantity ordered each time an order is placed

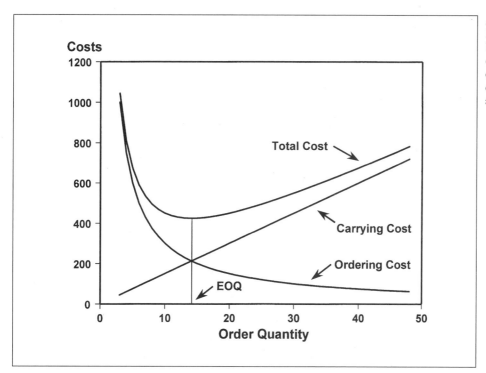

Figure 8.5
Relationship
between order
quantity,
carrying cost,
ordering cost,
and total cost.

The first term in this formula (DC) represents the cost of purchasing a year's worth of the product. The second term $\frac{D}{Q}S$ represents the annual ordering costs. Specifically, $\frac{D}{Q}$ represents the number of orders placed during a year. Multiplying this quantity by S represents the cost of placing these orders. The third term $\frac{Q}{2}Ci$ represents the annual cost of holding inventory. On average, $\frac{Q}{2}$ units are held in inventory throughout the year (see Figure 8.4). Multiplying this term by Ci represents the cost of holding these units. The following example illustrates the use of the EOQ model.

Alan Wang is responsible for purchasing the paper used in all the copy machines and laser printers at the corporate headquarters of MetroBank. Alan projects that in the coming year he will need to purchase a total of 24,000 boxes of paper, which will be used at a fairly steady rate throughout the year. Each box of paper costs $35. Alan estimates that it costs $50 each time an order is placed (this includes the cost of placing the order plus the related costs in shipping and receiving). MetroBank assigns a cost of 18% to funds allocated to supplies and inventories because such funds are the lifeline of the bank and could be lent out to credit card customers who are willing to pay this rate on money borrowed from the bank. Alan has been placing paper orders once a quarter, but he wants to determine if another ordering pattern would be better. He wants to determine the most economical order quantity to use in purchasing the paper.

8.4.1 Implementing the Model

To solve this problem, we first need to create a spreadsheet model of the total cost formula described earlier, substituting the data for Alan's problem for the parameters

D, C, S, and *i*. This spreadsheet implementation is shown in Figure 8.6 (and in the file FIG8-6.xls on your data disk).

In Figure 8.6, cell D4 represents the annual demand (D), cell D5 represents the per-unit cost (C), cell D6 represents the cost of placing an order (S), cell D7 represents the inventory holding cost (*i*) expressed as a percentage of an item's value, and cell D9 represents the order quantity (Q). The data corresponding to Alan's decision problem have been entered into the appropriate cells in this model. Because Alan places orders once a quarter (or 4 times a year), the order quantity in cell D9 is set at 24,000 ÷ 4 = 6,000.

We calculate each of the three pieces part of our total cost function in cells D11, D12, and D13. Cell D11 contains the cost of purchasing a year's worth of paper, cell D12 represents the cost associated with placing orders, and cell D13 is the inventory holding cost that would be incurred. The sum of these costs is calculated in cell D14.

Formula for cell D11: =D5*D4

Formula for cell D12: =D4/D9*D6

Formula for cell D13: =D9/2*D5*D7

Formula for cell D14: =SUM(D11:D13)

Figure 8.6
Spreadsheet
implementation
of MetroBank's
paper purchasing
problem.

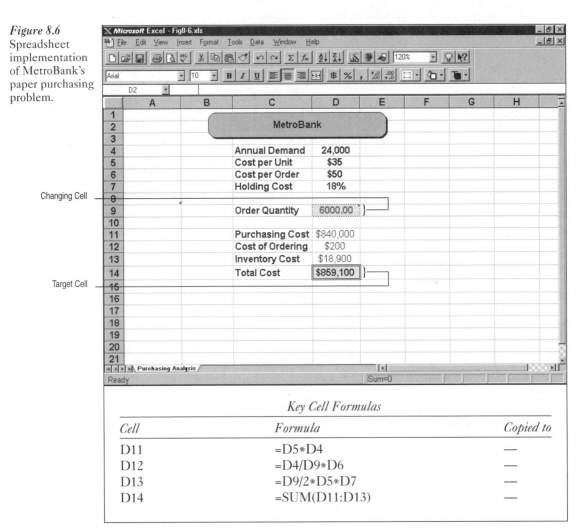

Cell	Formula	Copied to
D11	=D5*D4	—
D12	=D4/D9*D6	—
D13	=D9/2*D5*D7	—
D14	=SUM(D11:D13)	—

8.4.2 Solving the Model

The goal in this problem is to determine the order quantity (the value of Q) that minimizes the total cost. That is, we want Solver to determine the value for cell D9 that minimizes the value in cell D14. Figure 8.7 shows the Solver parameters and options required to solve this problem. Note that a constraint has been placed on cell D9 to prevent the order quantity from becoming 0 or negative. This constraint requires that at least one order must be placed during the year.

A Note About the Assume Linear Model Option

When solving an NLP problem, it is important not to select the Assume Linear Model option because this option causes Solver to attempt to apply the simplex method to the problem. When this option is selected, Solver conducts a number of internal tests to verify that the model is truly linear in the objective and constraints. If this option is selected and Solver's tests indicate that the model is not linear, a dialog box appears indicating that the conditions for linearity are not satisfied.

8.4.3 Analyzing the Solution

The optimal solution to this problem is shown in Figure 8.8. This solution indicates that the optimal number of boxes for Alan to order at any time is approximately 617.

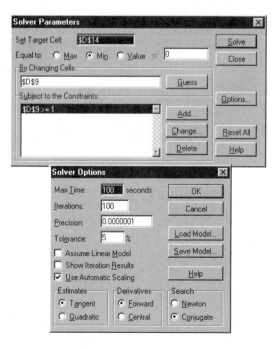

Figure 8.7
Solver parameters and options for MetroBank's paper purchasing problem.

Because the total cost curve in the basic EOQ model has one minimum point, we can be sure that this local optimal solution is also the global optimal solution for this problem. Notice this solution occurs where the total ordering costs are in balance with the total holding costs. Using this order quantity, costs are reduced by approximately $15,211 from the earlier level shown in Figure 8.7 when an order quantity of 6,000 was used.

If Alan orders 617 boxes, he needs to place approximately 39 orders during the year (24,000 ÷ 617 = 38.89), or 1.333 orders per week (52 ÷ 39 = 1.333). As a practical matter, it might be easier for Alan to arrange for one weekly delivery of approximately 461 boxes. This would increase the total cost by only $167 to $844,055 but probably would be easier to manage and still saves the bank over $15,000 per year.

8.4.4   Comments on the EOQ Model

There is another way to determine the optimal order quantity using the simple EOQ model. Using calculus, it can be shown that the optimal value of Q is represented by:

$$Q^* = \sqrt{\frac{2DS}{Ci}}$$

If we apply this formula to our example problem, we obtain:

$$Q^* = \sqrt{\frac{2 \times 24{,}000 \times 50}{35 \times 0.18}} = \sqrt{\frac{2{,}400{,}000}{6.3}} = 617.214$$

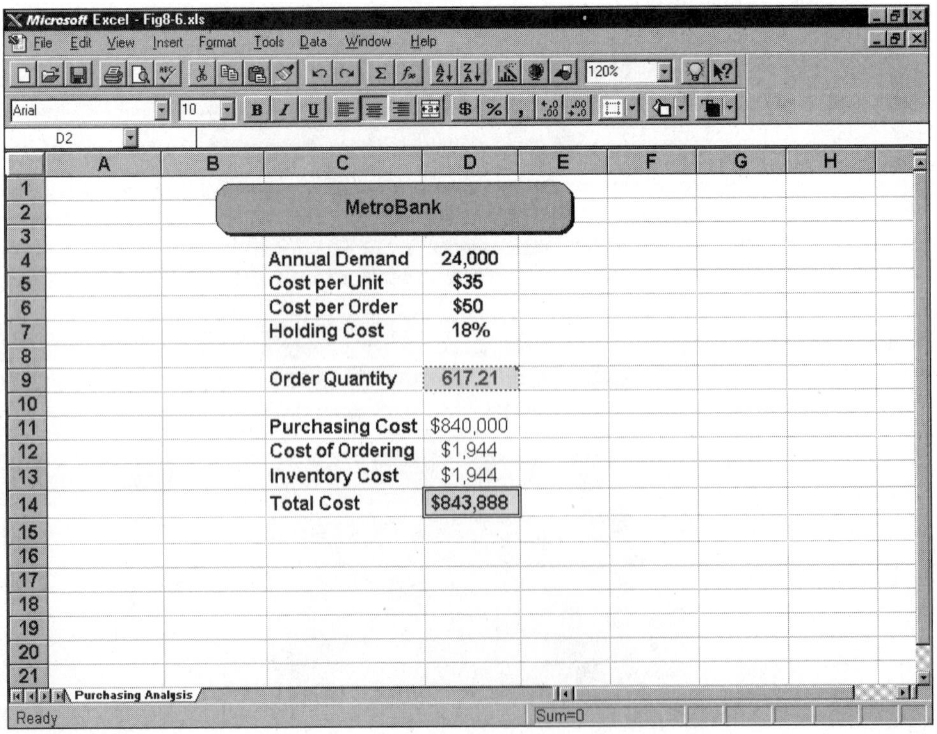

Figure 8.8
Optimal solution to MetroBank's paper purchasing problem.

	A	B	C	D	E	F	G	H
2			MetroBank					
4			Annual Demand	24,000				
5			Cost per Unit	$35				
6			Cost per Order	$50				
7			Holding Cost	18%				
9			Order Quantity	617.21				
11			Purchasing Cost	$840,000				
12			Cost of Ordering	$1,944				
13			Inventory Cost	$1,944				
14			Total Cost	$843,888				

The value obtained using calculus is almost the same value obtained using Solver (see cell B9 in Figure 8.8). The slight difference in the results might be due to rounding, or to Solver stopping just short of converging on the exact solution.

While the above EOQ formula has its uses, we often must impose financial or storage space restrictions when determining optimal order quantities. The above formula does not explicitly allow for such restrictions, but it is easy to impose these types of restrictions using Solver. In some of the problems at the end of this chapter, we will consider how the EOQ model can be adjusted to accommodate these types of restrictions, as well as quantity discounts. A complete discussion of the proper use and role of EOQ models in inventory control is beyond the scope of this text, but can be found in other texts devoted to production and operations management.

8.5   LOCATION PROBLEMS

A number of decision problems involve determining the location of facilities or service center. Examples might include determining the optimal location of manufacturing plants, warehouses, fire stations, or ambulance centers. The objective in these types of problems often is to determine a location that minimizes the distance between two or more service points. You might recall from basic algebra that the straight line (or Euclidean) distance between two points (X_1, Y_1) and (X_2, Y_2) on a standard X-Y graph is defined as:

$$\text{Distance} = \sqrt{(X_1 - X_2)^2 + (Y_1 - Y_2)^2}$$

This type of calculation is likely to be involved in any problem where the decision variables represent possible locations. The distance measure might occur in the objective function (for example, we might want to minimize the distance between two or more points) or it might occur in a constraint (for example, we might want to ensure that some minimum distance exists between two or more locations). Problems involving this type of distance measure are nonlinear. The following example illustrates the use of distance measures in a location problem.

> The Rappaport Communications Company provides cellular telephone services in several mid-western states. The company is planning to expand its customer base by offering cellular service in northeastern Ohio to the cities of Cleveland, Akron, Canton, and Youngstown. The company will install the hardware necessary to service customers in each city on preexisting communications towers in each city. The locations of these towers are summarized in Figure 8.9.
>
> However, the company also needs to construct a new communications tower somewhere between these city to handle inter-city calls. This tower will also allow cellular calls to be routed onto the satellite system for worldwide calling service. The tower the company is planning to build can cover areas within a 40-mile radius. Thus, the tower needs to be located within 40 miles of each of these cities.

It is important to note that we could have overlaid the X- and Y-axes on the map in Figure 8.9 in more than one way. The origin in Figure 8.9 could be located anywhere on the map without affecting the analysis. To establish the X-Y coordinates, we need an absolute reference point for the origin, but virtually any point on the map

Figure 8.9
Map of
Rappaport
Communication's
tower location
problem.

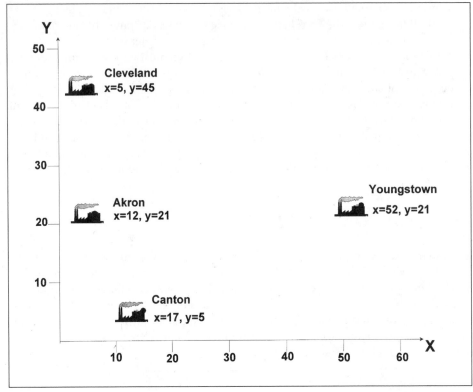

could be selected as the origin. Also we can express the scaling of the X-axis and Y-axis in a number of ways: meters, miles, inches, feet, and so on. For our purposes, we'll assume that each unit along the X- and Y-axes represents one mile.

8.5.1   Defining the Decision Variables

In Figure 8.9, definite X-Y coordinates have been established to describe the locations of the cities. These points are fixed and are not under the decision-maker's control. However, the coordinates of the new communications tower have not been established. We will assume that Rappaport would like to determine the tower location that minimizes the total distance between the new tower and those in each of the four cities. (Note that this is equivalent to minimizing the average distance as well.) Thus, the coordinates of the new tower represent the decision variables in this problem, which are defined as:

X_1 = location of the new tower with respect to the X-axis

Y_1 = location of the new tower with respect to the Y-axis

8.5.2   Defining the Objective

The objective in this problem is to minimize the total distance from the new tower to each of the existing towers, defined as:

$$\text{MIN: } \sqrt{(5 - X_1)^2 + (45 - Y_1)^2} + \sqrt{(12 - X_1)^2 + (21 - Y_1)^2} +$$
$$\sqrt{(17 - X_1)^2 + (5 - Y_1)^2} + \sqrt{(52 - X_1)^2 + (21 - Y_1)^2}$$

The first term in the objective calculates the distance from the tower in Cleveland, at X-Y coordinates (5, 45), to the location of the new tower, whose location is defined by the values X_1 and Y_1. The remaining terms perform similar calculations for the towers in Akron, Canton, and Youngstown.

8.5.3   Defining the Constraints

The problem statement noted that the new tower has a 40-mile transmission radius and therefore must be located within 40 miles of each of the existing towers. The following constraints ensure that the distance from each of the existing towers to the new tower is no larger than 40 miles.

$$\sqrt{(5 - X_1)^2 + (45 - Y_1)^2} \leq 40 \qquad \} \text{ Cleveland distance constraint}$$

$$\sqrt{(12 - X_1)^2 + (21 - Y_1)^2} \leq 40 \qquad \} \text{ Akron distance constraint}$$

$$\sqrt{(17 - X_1)_2 + (5 - Y_1)^2} \leq 40 \qquad \} \text{ Canton distance constraint}$$

$$\sqrt{(52 - X_1)^2 + (21 - Y_1)^2} \leq 40 \qquad \} \text{ Youngstown distance constraint}$$

Graphically, these constraints would be drawn as four circles, each with a 40-mile radius, each centered at one of the of the four existing tower locations. The intersection of these circles would represent the feasible region for the problem.

8.5.4   Implementing the Model

In summary, the problem Rappaport Communications wishes to solve is:

$$\text{MIN: } \sqrt{(5 - X_1)^2 + (45 - Y_1)^2} + \sqrt{(12 - X_1)^2 + (21 - Y_1)^2} +$$
$$\sqrt{(17 - X_1)^2 + (5 - Y_1)^2} + \sqrt{(52 - X_1)^2 + (21 - Y_1)^2}$$

Subject to:

$$\sqrt{(5 - X_1)^2 + (45 - Y_1)^2} \leq 40 \qquad \} \text{ Cleveland distance constraint}$$

$$\sqrt{(12 - X_1)^2 + (21 - Y_1)^2} \leq 40 \qquad \} \text{ Akron distance constraint}$$

$$\sqrt{(17 - X_1)_2 + (5 - Y_1)^2} \leq 40 \qquad \} \text{ Canton distance constraint}$$

$$\sqrt{(52 - X_1)^2 + (21 - Y_1)^2} \leq 40 \qquad \} \text{ Youngstown distance constraint}$$

Note that both the objective and constraints for this problem are nonlinear. One approach to implementing the model for this problem in a spreadsheet is shown in Figure 8.10 (and in the file FIG8-10.xls on your data disk).

In this spreadsheet, cells C6 and D6 are used to represent the decision variables X_1 and Y_1, which correspond to the X-Y coordinates of the location of the new tower. The locations of the existing towers are listed in terms of their X-Y coordinates in

Figure 8.10
Spreadsheet
implementation
of the tower
location
problem.

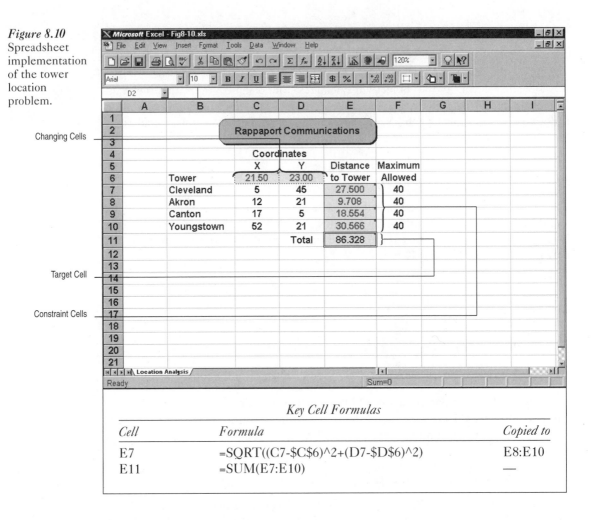

Changing Cells

Target Cell

Constraint Cells

Key Cell Formulas

Cell	Formula	Copied to
E7	=SQRT((C7-$C$6)^2+(D7-$D$6)^2)	E8:E10
E11	=SUM(E7:E10)	—

rows 7 through 10 of columns C and D. Reasonable starting values for X_1 and Y_1 in this problem would be the average values of the X and Y coordinates of the existing tower locations. These averages were computed and entered in cells C6 and D6.

Column E calculates the distance from each existing tower to the selected location for the new tower. Specifically, cell E7 contains the following formula, which is copied to cells E8 through E10:

Formula for cell E7:   =SQRT((C7-$C$6)^2+(D7-$D$6)^2)
(Copy to E8 through E10.)

These cells represent the LHS formulas for the problem. The RHS values for these constraints are given in cells F7 through F10. The objective function for the problem is then implemented easily in cell E11 with the formula:

Formula for cell E11:   =SUM(E7:E10)

8.5.5   *Solving the Model and Analyzing the Solution*

Figure 8.11 shows the Solver parameters and options used to solve this problem, and Figure 8.12 shows the optimal solution.

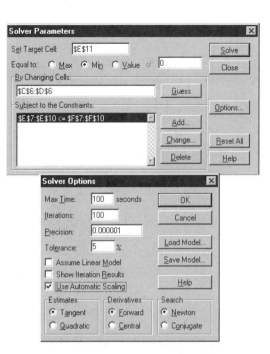

Figure 8.11
Solver parameters and options for the tower location problem.

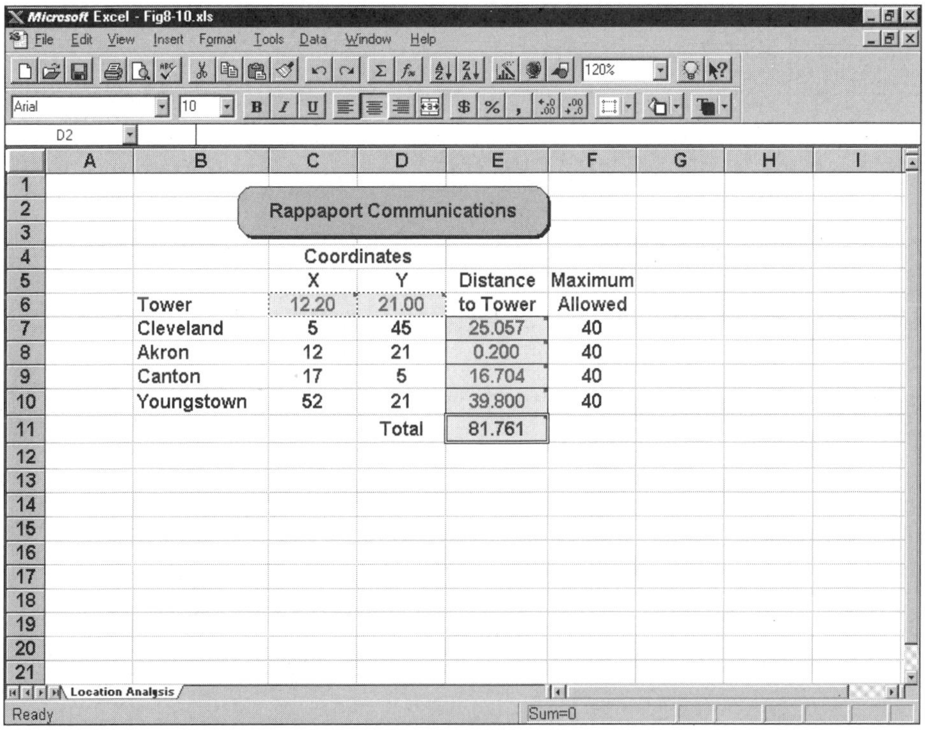

Figure 8.12
Optimal solution to the tower location problem.

The solution in Figure 8.12 indicates that if the new tower plant is located at the coordinates $X_1 = 12.2$ and $Y_1 = 21.0$, the total distance between the towers is 81.76 miles (so the average distance is 20.4 miles). If you try re-solving this problem from a variety of starting points, you can verify that this is the global optimal solution to the problem. Interestingly, the coordinates of this location for the new tower are virtually identical to the coordinates of the existing tower in Akron. So the solution to this problem may not involve building a new tower at all but, instead, Rappaport may want to investigate the feasibility of upgrading or retrofitting the existing Akron tower to play the role of the "new" tower.

8.5.6   Another Solution to the Problem

In the solution shown in Figure 8.12, there is virtually no distance between the new tower and the existing tower in Akron. But the distance from this site to the tower in Youngstown is 39.8 miles—which is nearing the limit of the 40-mile broadcast radius of the new equipment. Thus, Rappaport may prefer a solution that provides more of a safety margin on their broadcast range, to help ensure quality and reliability during inclement weather. Another objective that could be applied to this problem would attempt to minimize the maximum distance from the new tower to each of the existing towers. Figure 8.13 (file FIG8-13.xls on your data disk) shows the solution to this new problem.

Figure 8.13
Another solution to the tower location problem minimizing the maximum distance.

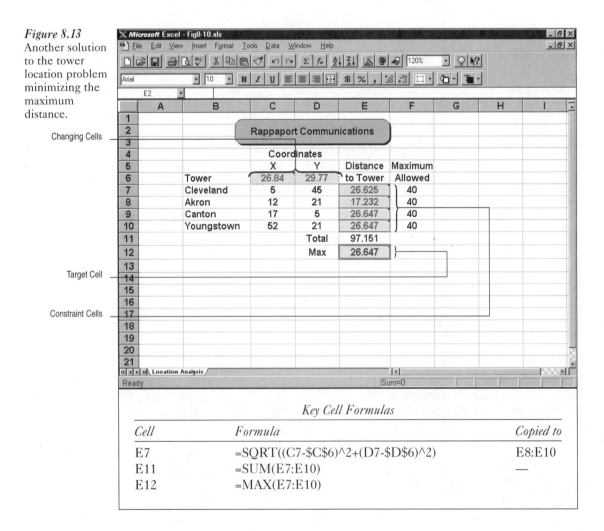

Cell	Formula	Copied to
E7	=SQRT((C7-$C$6)^2+(D7-$D$6)^2)	E8:E10
E11	=SUM(E7:E10)	—
E12	=MAX(E7:E10)	

Key Cell Formulas

To obtain this solution, we implemented a new objective function in cell E12 to compute the maximum of the distances in column E as follows:

Formula for cell E12:   =MAX(E7:E10)

We then instructed Solver to minimize E12 to obtain the solution shown. This solution positions the new tower at the X-Y coordinates (26.84, 29.77). While the total distance associated with this solution increased to 97.15 (or an average of 24.3 miles), the maximum distance was reduced to 26.6 miles. Thus, Rappaport might prefer this solution to the alternative shown in Figure 8.12.

8.5.7 Some Comments About the Solution to Location Problems

When solving location problems, it is possible that the location indicated by the optimal solution may simply not work. For instance, the land at the optimal location may not be for sale, the "land" at this location may be a lake, the land may be zoned for residential purposes only, etc. However, solutions to location problems often give decision makers a good idea about where to start in looking for suitable property to acquire for the problem at hand. It is also be possible to add constraints to location problems that eliminate certain areas from consideration if they are inappropriate or unavailable.

8.6 NONLINEAR NETWORK FLOW PROBLEM

In Chapter 5 we looked at several different types of network flow problems with linear objective functions and linear constraint sets. We noted that the constraints in network flow models have a special structure where the flow into a node must be balanced with the flow out of the same node. Numerous decision problems exist where the balance-of-flow restrictions must be maintained while optimizing a nonlinear objective function. We present one such example here.

SafetyTrans is a trucking company that specializes in transporting extremely valuable and extremely hazardous materials. Due to the nature of its business, the company places great importance of maintaining a clean driving safety record. This not only helps keep their reputation up but it also helps keep their insurance premiums down. The company is also conscious of the fact that when carrying hazardous materials, the environmental consequences of even a minor accident could be disastrous.

While most trucking companies are interested in identifying routes that provide for the quickest or least costly transportation, SafetyTrans likes to ensure that it selects routes that are the least likely to result in an accident. The company is currently trying to identify the safest route for carrying a load of hazardous materials from Los Angeles, California to Amarillo, Texas. The network in Figure 8.14 summarizes the routes under consideration. The numbers on each arc represent the probability of having an accident on each potential leg of the journey. SafetyTrans maintains a national database of such probabilities developed from data they receive from the National Highway Safety Administration and the various Departments of Transportation in each state.

Figure 8.14
Network
representation of
the SafetyTrans
routing problem.

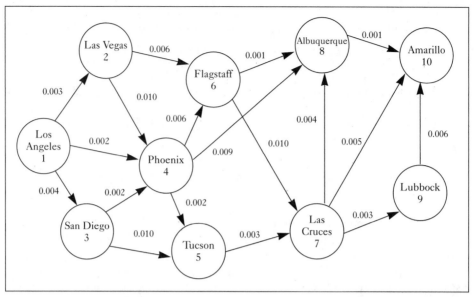

8.6.1   *Defining the Decision Variables*

The problem summarized in Figure 8.14 is very similar to the shortest path problem described in Chapter 5. As in the shortest path problem, here we will need one variable for each of the arcs (or routes) in the problem. Each decision variable will indicate whether or not a particular route is used. We will define these variables as follows:

$$Y_{ij} = \begin{cases} 1, \text{ if the route from node } i \text{ to node } j \text{ is selected} \\ 0, \text{ otherwise} \end{cases}$$

8.6.2   *Defining the Objective*

The objective in this problem is to find the route that minimizes the probability of having an accident, or equivalently, the route that maximizes the probability of not having an accident. Let P_{ij} = the probability of having an accident while traveling from node i to node j. Then the probability of *not* having an accident while traveling from node i to node j is $1 - P_{ij}$. For example, the probability of not having an accident while traveling from Los Angeles to Las Vegas is $1 - P_{12} = 1 - 0.003 = 0.997$. The objective of maximizing the probability of not having an accident is given by:

MAX: $(1 - P_{12}Y_{12})$ $(1 - P_{13}Y_{13})$ $(1 - P_{14}Y_{14})$ $(1 - P_{24}Y_{24})$ $(1 - P_{26}Y_{26})$ ... $(1 - P_{9,10}Y_{9,10})$

The first term in this objective returns the value 1 if $Y_{12} = 0$ and the value $1 - P_{12}$ if $Y_{12} = 1$. Thus, if we take the route from Los Angeles to Las Vegas ($Y_{12} = 1$), the value 0.997 is multiplied by the remaining terms in the objective function. If we do not take the route from Los Angeles to Las Vegas ($Y_{12} = 0$), the value 1 is multiplied by the remaining terms in the objective function. (Of course, multiplying by 1 has no effect.) The remaining terms in the objective have similar interpretations. So, this objective function computes the probabilities of not having accidents on whichever routes are selected and then computes the products of these values. The result is the overall probability of not having an accident on any set of selected routes. This is the value SafetyTrans wants to maximize.

8.6.3 Defining the Constraints

To solve a shortest path network flow problem, we assign the starting node a supply value of -1 and the ending node a demand value of +1 and apply the balance-of-flow rule covered in Chapter 5. This results in the following set of constraints for our example problem.

$$-Y_{12} - Y_{13} - Y_{14} = -1 \qquad \text{\}Balance-of-flow constraint for node 1}$$
$$+Y_{12} - Y_{24} - Y_{26} = 0 \qquad \text{\}Balance-of-flow constraint for node 2}$$
$$+Y_{13} - Y_{34} - Y_{35} = 0 \qquad \text{\}Balance-of-flow constraint for node 3}$$
$$+Y_{14} + Y_{24} + Y_{34} - Y_{45} - Y_{46} - Y_{48} = 0 \text{ \}Balance-of-flow constraint for node 4}$$
$$+Y_{35} + Y_{45} - Y_{57} = 0 \qquad \text{\}Balance-of-flow constraint for node 5}$$
$$+Y_{26} + Y_{46} - Y_{67} - Y_{68} = 0 \qquad \text{\}Balance-of-flow constraint for node 6}$$
$$+Y_{57} + Y_{67} - Y_{78} - Y_{79} - Y_{7,10} = 0 \quad \text{\}Balance-of-flow constraint for node 7}$$
$$+Y_{48} + Y_{68} + Y_{78} - Y_{8,10} = 0 \qquad \text{\}Balance-of-flow constraint for node 8}$$
$$+Y_{79} - Y_{9,10} = 0 \qquad \text{\}Balance-of-flow constraint for node 9}$$
$$+Y_{7,10} + Y_{8,10} + Y_{9,10} = 1 \qquad \text{\}Balance-of-flow constraint for node 10}$$

The first constraint ensures that one unit flows out of node 1 to nodes 2, 3, or 4. The last constraint ensures that one unit flows into node 10 from nodes 7, 8, or 9. The remaining constraints ensure that any flow into nodes 2 through 9 is balanced by an equal amount of flow out of those nodes.

8.6.4 Implementing the Model

In summary, the problem SafetyTrans wants to solve is:

$$\text{MAX: } (1 - 0.003Y_{12})(1 - 0.004Y_{13})(1 - 0.002Y_{14})(1 - 0.010Y_{24})(1 - 0.006Y_{26}) \ldots (1 - 0.006Y_{9,10})$$

Subject to:

$$-Y_{12} - Y_{13} - Y_{14} = -1 \qquad \text{\} Balance-of-flow constraint for node 1}$$
$$+Y_{12} - Y_{24} - Y_{26} = 0 \qquad \text{\} Balance-of-flow constraint for node 2}$$
$$+Y_{13} - Y_{34} - Y_{35} = 0 \qquad \text{\} Balance-of-flow constraint for node 3}$$
$$+Y_{14} + Y_{24} + Y_{34} - Y_{45} - Y_{46} - Y_{48} = 0 \text{ \} Balance-of-flow constraint for node 4}$$
$$+Y_{35} + Y_{45} - Y_{57} = 0 \qquad \text{\} Balance-of-flow constraint for node 5}$$
$$+Y_{26} + Y_{46} - Y_{67} - Y_{68} = 0 \qquad \text{\} Balance-of-flow constraint for node 6}$$
$$+Y_{57} + Y_{67} - Y_{78} - Y_{79} - Y_{7,10} = 0 \quad \text{\}Balance-of-flow constraint for node 7}$$
$$+Y_{48} + Y_{68} + Y_{78} - Y_{8,10} = 0 \qquad \text{\} Balance-of-flow constraint for node 8}$$
$$+Y_{79} - Y_{9,10} = 0 \qquad \text{\} Balance-of-flow constraint for node 9}$$
$$+Y_{7,10} + Y_{8,10} + Y_{9,10} = 1 \qquad \text{\} Balance-of-flow constraint for node 10}$$
$$\text{All } Y_{ij} \text{ binary}$$

One approach to implementing this model is shown in Figure 8.15. In this spreadsheet, cells A6 through A23 represent our decision variables.

The LHS formulas for the constraints in this problem are implemented in cells K6 through K15 using the same technique as described in Chapter 5. The RHS for the constraints are given in cells L6 through L15. Specifically, we enter the following formula in cells K6 and copy down the rest of the column:

Figure 8.15
Spreadsheet
implementation
of the
SafetyTrans
routing problem.

Constraint Cells

Target Cell

Changing Cells

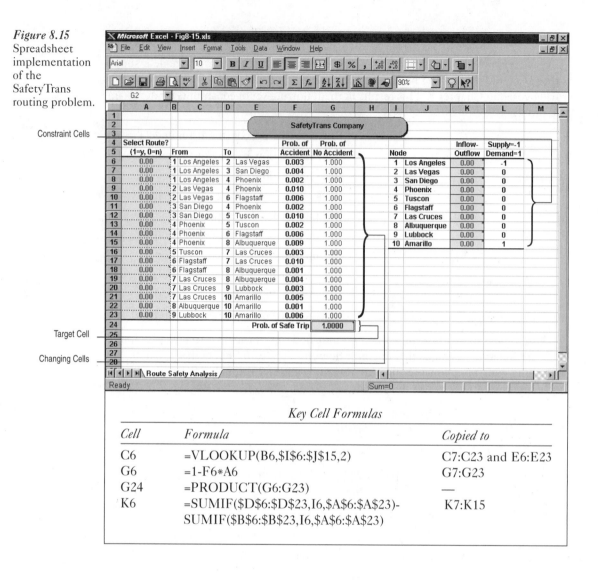

Key Cell Formulas

Cell	Formula	Copied to
C6	=VLOOKUP(B6,$I$6:$J$15,2)	C7:C23 and E6:E23
G6	=1-F6*A6	G7:G23
G24	=PRODUCT(G6:G23)	—
K6	=SUMIF($D$6:$D$23,I6,$A$6:$A$23)-SUMIF($B$6:$B$23,I6,$A$6:$A$23)	K7:K15

Formula for cell K6:   =SUMIF($D$6:$D$23,I6,$A$6:$A$23)
(Copy to cells K7 through K15.)   -SUMIF($B$6:$B$23,I6,$A$6:$A$23)

The probabilities of having an accident on each of the routes are listed in cells F6 through F23. Each of the terms for the objective function were then implemented in cells G6 through G23 as follows:

Formula for cell G6:   = 1-F6*A6
(Copy to cells G7 through G23.)

Note that the formula in G6 corresponds exactly to the first term in the objective $(1 - P_{12}Y_{12})$ as described earlier. Next, the product of the values in cells G6 through G23 is calculated in cell G24 as:

Formula for cell G24:   =PRODUCT(G6:G23)

Figure 8.16 shows the Solver parameters and options used to solve this problem. The optimal solution is shown in Figure 8.17.

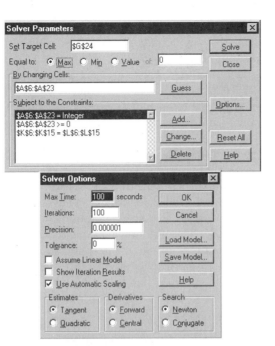

Figure 8.16
Solver
parameters and
options for the
SafetyTrans
problem.

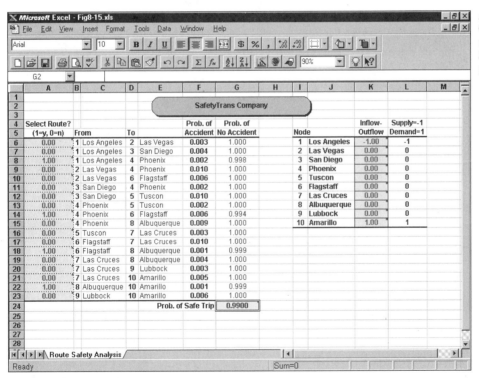

Figure 8.17
Optimal solution
to the
SafetyTrans
problem.

8.6.5   Solving the Model and Analyzing the Solution

The solution to this problem indicates $Y_{14}=Y_{46}=Y_{68}=Y_{8,10}=1$ and all other $Y_{ij}=0$. Thus, the optimal (safest) route is to travel from Los Angeles to Phoenix to Flagstaff to

Albuquerque to Amarillo. Following this route, there is a 0.99 probability of not having an accident. Solving this problem from numerous starting points indicates that this
is the global optimal solution to the problem.

If you solve this model again minimizing the objective, you will discover that the
least-safe route has a 0.9626 probability of not having an accident. This may lead some
to conclude that it doesn't make much difference which route is taken since the differences in the best-case and worst-case probabilities seems minimal. However, if it
costs \$30,000,000 to clean up an accident involving hazardous waste, the expected
cost of taking the safest route is $(1 - 0.99) \times \$30,000,000 = \$300,000$ and the expected
cost of taking the least-safe route is $(1 - 0.9626) \times \$30,000,000 = \$1,122,000$. So while
the differences in probabilities may appear small, the differences in the potential outcomes can be quite significant. Of course, this doesn't even consider the potential loss
of life and environmental damage that no amount of money can fix.

There are a number of other areas to which this type of nonlinear network flow
model can be applied. Analysts are often interested in determining the "weakest
link" in a telecommunications network or production system. The same type of problem described here could be solved to determine the least reliable path through these
types of network.

8.7   PROJECT SELECTION PROBLEMS

In Chapter 6, we looked at a project selection example where we wanted to select the
combination of projects that produced the greatest net present value (NPV) subject
to various resource restrictions. In these types of problems there is often some uncertainty about whether or not a selected project can actually be completed successfully,
and this success might be influenced by the amount of resources devoted to the project. The following example illustrates how nonlinear programming techniques can
be used to help model this uncertainty in a selected project's potential for success.

> The directors of the TMC Corporation are trying to determine how to allocate
> their R&D budget for the coming year. Six different projects are under consid-
> eration. The directors believe that the success of each project depends in part
> on the number of engineers assigned. Each project proposal includes an esti-
> mate of the probability of success as a function of the number of engineers
> assigned. Each probability function is of the form:
>
> $$P_i = \text{probability of success for project } i \text{ if assigned } X_i \text{ engineers} = \frac{X_i}{X_i + \varepsilon_i}$$
>
> where ε_i is a positive constant for project i that determines
> the shape of its probability function.
>
> The probability functions for several of the projects are shown in Figure
> 8.18. The following table summarizes the initial startup funds required for each
> project and the estimated NPV the project would generate if it is a success:
>
> | Project | 1 | 2 | 3 | 4 | 5 | 6 |
> |---|---|---|---|---|---|---|
> | Startup Costs | \$325 | \$200 | \$490 | \$125 | \$710 | \$240 |
> | Net Present Value | \$750 | \$120 | \$900 | \$400 | \$1,110 | \$800 |
> | Probability Parameter ε_i | 3.1 | 2.5 | 4.5 | 5.6 | 8.2 | 8.5 |
> | (Note: All monetary values are in \$1,000s.) | | | | | | |

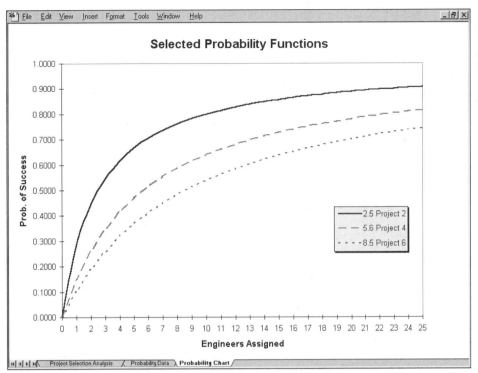

Figure 8.18
Graph showing the probability of success for selected projects in the TMC problem.

TMC's directors have agreed to hire up to 25 engineers to assign to these projects and are willing to allocate $1.7 million of the R&D budget to cover the startup costs for selected projects. They would like to determine the project selection and resource allocation strategy that will maximize the expected NPV.

8.7.1   Defining the Decision Variables

TMC's directors must make two separate but related decision. First, they must determine which projects to select. We will use the following binary variables to model these decisions:

$$Y_i = \begin{cases} 1, \text{ if project } i \text{ is selected} \\ 0, \text{ otherwise} \end{cases}, i = 1, 2, 3, \dots, 6$$

Second, the directors must determine the number of engineers to assign to each project. We will model these decisions with the following variables,

$$X_i = \text{ the number of engineers to assign to project } i, i = 1, 2, 3, \dots, 6$$

8.7.2   Defining the Objective Function

TMC's directors want to maximize the expected NPV of their decision, so our objective function must correspond to this quantity. This requires that we multiply each project's expected return by the probability of the project being successful. This is accomplished as follows:

$$\text{MAX:} \quad \frac{750X_1}{(X_1 + 3.1)} + \frac{120X_2}{(X_2 + 2.5)} + \frac{900X_3}{(X_3 + 4.5)} + \frac{400X_4}{(X_4 + 5.6)} + \frac{1100X_5}{(X_5 + 8.2)} + \frac{800X_6}{(X_6 + 8.5)}$$

8.7.3   Defining the Constraints

There are several constraints that apply to this problem. We must ensure that the projects selected require no more than $1.7 million in startup funds. This is accomplished as follows:

$$325Y_1 + 200Y_2 + 490Y_3 + 125Y_4 + 710Y_5 + 240Y_6 \leq 1700 \quad \} \text{Constraint on} \atop \text{startup funds}$$

Next we must ensure that no more than 25 engineers are assigned to selected projects. This is accomplished by the following constraint:

$$X_1 + X_2 + X_3 + X_4 + X_5 + X_6 \leq 25 \quad \} \text{Constraint on engineers}$$

Finally, we need to make sure that engineers are assigned only to the projects that have been selected. This requires the use of linking constraints which were first presented in Chapter 6 when discussing the fixed-charge problem. The linking constraints for this problem could be stated as:

$$X_i - 25Y_i \leq 0, \, i = 1, 2, 3, \ldots 6 \quad \} \text{Linking constraints}$$

These linking constraints ensure that an X_i variable can be greater than zero if and only if its associated Y_i is one.

Instead of using the previous constraint on the number of engineers and the associated six linking constraints, we could have used the following single nonlinear constraint:

$$X_1Y_1 + X_2Y_2 + X_3Y_3 + X_4Y_4 + X_5Y_5 + X_6Y_6 \leq 25 \quad \} \text{Constraint on engineers}$$

This would sum the number of engineers assigned to selected projects. (Note that if we used this constraint, we would also need to multiply each term in the objective function by its associated Y_i variable. Do you see why?) Using this single nonlinear constraint might appear to be easier than the previous seven constraints. However, when you have a choice between using linear constraints and nonlinear constraints, it is almost always better to use the linear constraints.

8.7.4   Implementing the Model

The model for TMC's project selection problem is summarized as:

$$\text{MAX:} \quad \frac{750X_1}{(X_1 + 3.1)} + \frac{120X_2}{(X_2 + 2.5)} + \frac{900X_3}{(X_3 + 4.5)} + \frac{400X_4}{(X_4 + 5.6)} + \frac{1100X_5}{(X_5 + 8.2)} + \frac{800X_6}{(X_6 + 8.5)}$$

Subject to:

$$325Y_1 + 200Y_2 + 490Y_3 + 125Y_4 + 710Y_5 + 240Y_6 \leq 1700 \quad \} \text{Constraint on startup} \atop \text{funds}$$

$$X_1 + X_2 + X_3 + X_4 + X_5 + X_6 \leq 25 \qquad\qquad\qquad \} \text{Constraint on engineers}$$
$$X_i - 25Y_i \leq 0, \, i = 1, 2, 3, \ldots 6 \qquad\qquad\qquad \} \text{Linking constraints}$$
$$X_i \geq 0 \text{ and integer}$$
$$Y_i \text{ binary}$$

Notice that this problem has a nonlinear objective function and linear constraints. One approach to implementing this model is shown in Figure 8.19 (and in the file FIG8-19.xls on your data disk). In this spreadsheet, cells B7 through B12 will be used to represent our binary Y_i variables indicating whether or not each project is selected. Cells C7 through C12 represent the X_i variables indicating the number of engineers assigned to each project.

We implemented the linking constraints for this problem by entering the LHS formulas in cells D7 through D12 as follows:

$$\text{Formula for cell D7:}\quad \text{=C7-B7*\$C\$14}$$

(Copy to cells D8 through D12.)

We will constrain these values to be less than or equal to zero. The LHS for the constraint on the number of engineers assigned to projects is implemented in cell C13 as follows:

$$\text{Formula for cell C13:}\quad \text{=SUM(C7:C12)}$$

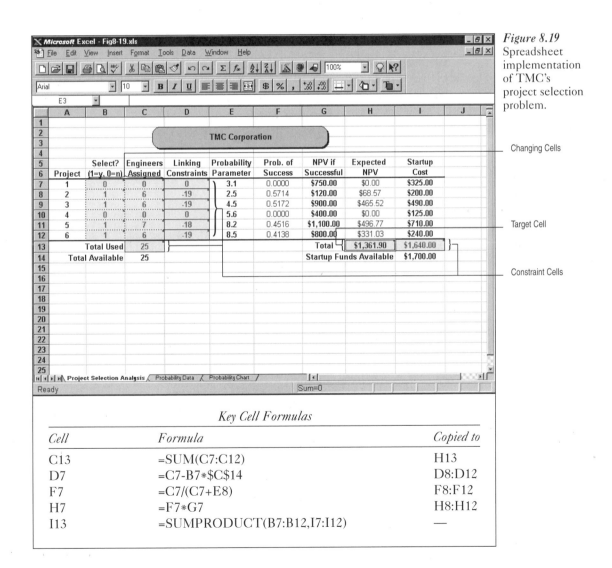

Figure 8.19
Spreadsheet implementation of TMC's project selection problem.

		Key Cell Formulas	
Cell	*Formula*		*Copied to*
C13	=SUM(C7:C12)		H13
D7	=C7-B7*$C$14		D8:D12
F7	=C7/(C7+E8)		F8:F12
H7	=F7*G7		H8:H12
I13	=SUMPRODUCT(B7:B12,I7:I12)		—

The RHS value for this constraint is given in cell C14. Similarly, the LHS for the constraint of the total startup funds is implemented in cell I13 with its RHS value listed in I14.

Formula for cell I13:   =SUMPRODUCT(B7:B12,I7:I12)

To implement the objective function, we first calculate the probability of success for each project. This is done in column F as follows:

Formula for cell F7:   = C7/(C7+E8)

(Copy to cells F8 through F12.)

Next the expected NPV value for each project is computed by multiplying the probability of success for each project by the NPV it should generate if the project is successful. This is done in column H as follows:

Formula for cell H7:   = F7*G7

(Copy to cells H8 through H12.)

Finally, we compute the sum of the expected NPVs for selected projects in cell H13.

Formula for cell H13:   =SUM(H7:H12)

The Solver parameters and settings used to solve this problem are shown in Figure 8.20.

8.7.5   Solving the Model

An arbitrary starting point for this problem was selected as shown in Figure 8.19. From this starting point, Solver located the solution shown in Figure 8.21 which has an expected NPV of approximately $1.538 million.

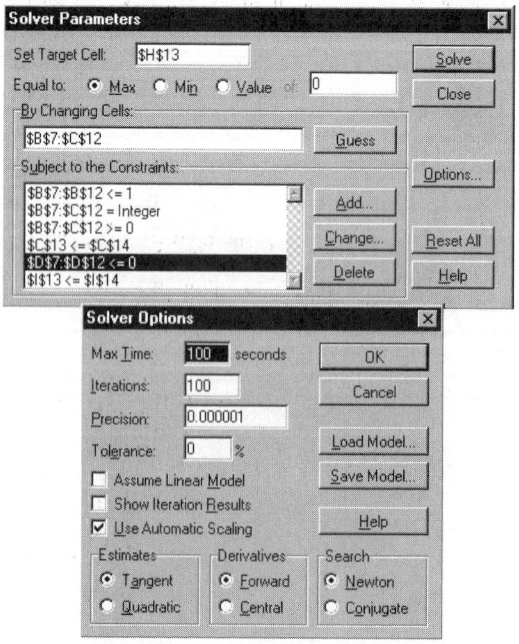

Figure 8.20
Solver
parameters and
options for
TMC's project
selection
problem.

Another starting point for this problem was obtained by selecting projects in descending order based on their expected NPVs in column G. This approach is shown in Figure 8.22 (where the number of engineers assigned to selected projects was

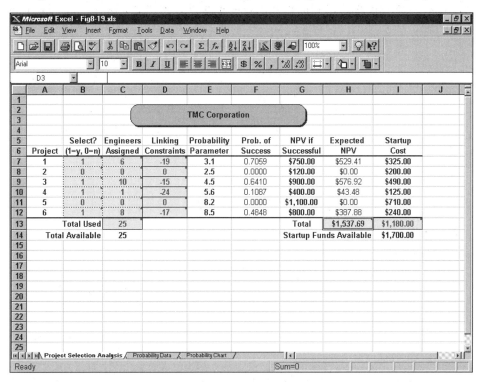

Figure 8.21
First solution to the TMC project selection problem.

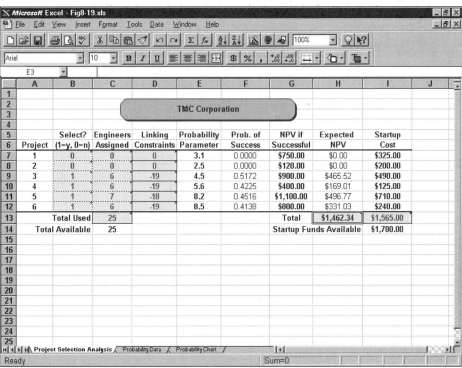

Figure 8.22
A starting point based on maximum NPV.

assigned arbitrarily). From this starting point, Solver located the solution shown in Figure 8.23 which has an expected NPV of approximately $1.583 million.

Another starting point for this problem could be obtained by selecting projects in ascending order based on their startup costs in column I while not violating the constraint on startup funds. Figure 8.24 shows this starting point (where again the number of engineers assigned to selected projects was determined arbitrarily). From this starting point, Solver located the solution shown in Figure 8.25 which has an expected NPV of approximately $1.703 million.

This example should drive home the point that, depending on the starting point you choose, Solver can and will stop at local optimal solutions which are not the global optimal solution. So if you are solving an NLP problem and you are not sure that the problem has a single local and global optimal solution, it is critically important to start Solver from several different initial feasible solutions to guard against obtaining a local optimal solution that may fall far short of the global optimal solution.

8.8   OPTIMIZING EXISTING FINANCIAL SPREADSHEET MODELS

So far in our discussion of optimization, we have always constructed an algebraic model of a decision problem and then implemented this model in a spreadsheet for solution and analysis. However, we can apply optimization techniques to virtually any existing spreadsheet model. Many existing spreadsheets involve financial calculations that are inherently nonlinear. The following is an example of how optimization can be applied to an existing spreadsheet.

Figure 8.23
Second solution to the TMC project selection problem.

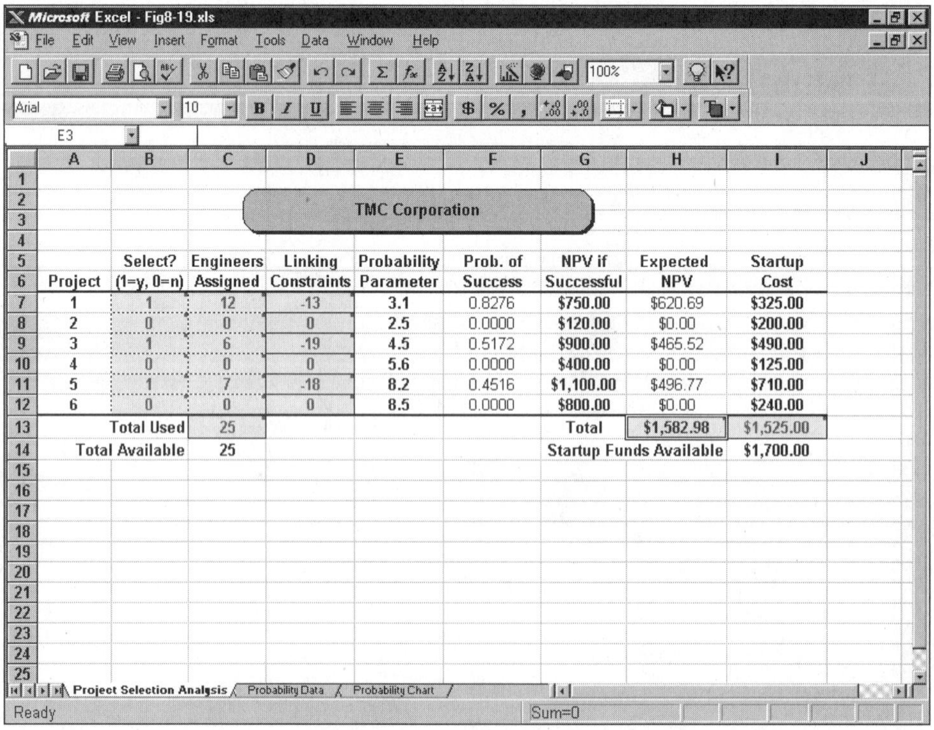

Project	Select? (1=y, 0=n)	Engineers Assigned	Linking Constraints	Probability Parameter	Prob. of Success	NPV if Successful	Expected NPV	Startup Cost
1	1	12	-13	3.1	0.8276	$750.00	$620.69	$325.00
2	0	0	0	2.5	0.0000	$120.00	$0.00	$200.00
3	1	6	-19	4.5	0.5172	$900.00	$465.52	$490.00
4	0	0	0	5.6	0.0000	$400.00	$0.00	$125.00
5	1	7	-18	8.2	0.4516	$1,100.00	$496.77	$710.00
6	0	0	0	8.5	0.0000	$800.00	$0.00	$240.00
Total Used		25				**Total**	$1,582.98	$1,525.00
Total Available		25				**Startup Funds Available**		$1,700.00

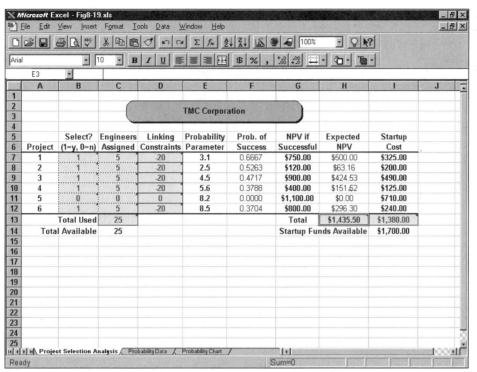

Figure 8.24
A starting point based on minimum startup cost.

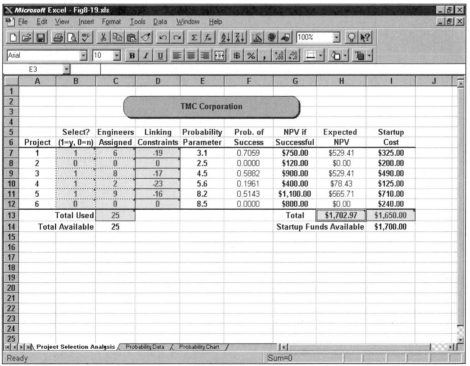

Figure 8.25
Third solution to TMC's project selection problem.

Thom Pearman's life is changing dramatically. He and his wife recently bought a new home and are expecting their second child in a few months. These new responsibilities have prompted Thom to think about some serious issues, including life insurance. Ten years ago, Thom purchased an insurance policy that provides a death benefit of $40,000. This policy is paid for in full and will remain in force for the rest of Thom's life. Alternatively, Thom can surrender this policy and receive an immediate payoff of approximately $6,000 from the insurance company.

Ten years ago, the $40,000 death benefit provided by the insurance policy seemed more than adequate. However, Thom now feels that he needs more coverage to care for his wife and children adequately in the event of his untimely death. Thom is investigating a different kind of insurance that would provide a death benefit of $350,000 but also would require ongoing annual payments to keep the coverage in force. He received the following estimates of the annual premiums for this new policy in each of the next 10 years:

Year	Premium
1	$423
2	$457
3	$489
4	$516
5	$530
6	$558
7	$595
8	$618
9	$660
10	$716

In order to pay the premiums for this new policy, one alternative Thom is considering involves surrendering his existing policy and investing the $6,000 he would receive to generate the after-tax income needed to pay the premiums on his new policy. However, to see if this is possible, he wants to determine the minimum rate of return he would have to earn on his investment to generate after-tax investment earnings that would cover the premium payments for the new policy. Thom likes the idea of keeping the $6,000 in case of an emergency and does not want to use it to pay premiums. Thom's marginal tax rate is 28%.

8.8.1   Implementing the Model

A spreadsheet model for Thom's decision problem is shown in Figure 8.26 (and in the file FIG8-26.xls on your data disk). The strategy in this spreadsheet is to determine how much money would be invested at the beginning of each year, how much money would be earned during the year after taxes, and how much would be left at the end of the year after paying taxes and the insurance premium due for that year.

As shown in Figure 8.26, cells D4 and D5 contain the assumptions about the initial amount invested and Thom's marginal tax rate. Cell D6 represents the expected annual return (which is compounded quarterly). The annual return of 15% was entered in this cell simply for planning purposes. This is the value that we'll attempt to minimize when we optimize the spreadsheet.

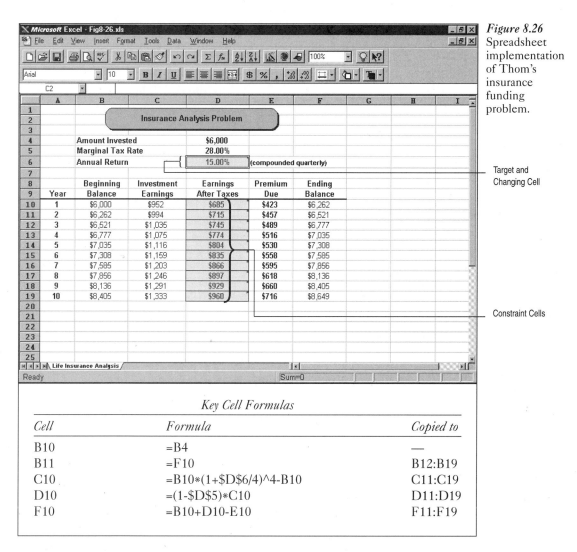

Figure 8.26
Spreadsheet implementation of Thom's insurance funding problem.

Key Cell Formulas

Cell	Formula	Copied to
B10	=B4	—
B11	=F10	B12:B19
C10	=B10*(1+$D$6/4)^4-B10	C11:C19
D10	=(1-$D$5)*C10	D11:D19
F10	=B10+D10-E10	F11:F19

The beginning balance for the first year (cell B10) is equal to the initial amount of money invested. The beginning balance for each of the following years is the ending balance from the previous year. The formula in cell C10 calculates the amount earned for the year given the interest rate in cell D6. This same formula applies to cells C11 through C19.

Formula for cell C10:   = B10*(1+$D$6/4)^4-B10
(Copy to cells C11 through C19.)

Because Thom pays 28% in taxes, the values in the Earnings After Taxes column are 72% of the investment earnings listed in column C (100% – 28% = 72%). The values in the Ending Balance column are the beginning balances plus the earnings after taxes minus the premium due for the year.

8.8.2   Optimizing the Spreadsheet Model

Three elements are involved in any optimization problem: one or more decision variables, an objective function, and constraints. The objective in the current problem is to determine the minimum annual return that will generate after-tax earnings to pay the premiums each year. Thus, the decision variable in this model is the interest rate in cell D6. The value in cell D6 also represents the objective in the problem because we want to minimize its value. For constraints, the after-tax earnings each year should be greater than or equal to the premium due for the year. Thus, we require that the values in cells D10 through D19 be greater than or equal to the values in cells E10 through E19. Figure 8.27 shows the Solver parameters and options required to solve this problem, and Figure 8.28 shows the optimal solution.

8.8.3   Analyzing the Solution

The solution shown in Figure 8.28 indicates that Thom needs to obtain an annual return of at least 13.29% in order for the after-tax earnings from his investment of $6,000 to pay the premiums on his new policy for the next 10 years. This rate of return causes his after-tax earnings in year 10 to equal exactly the premium payment of $716 due that year. Thus, in order for Thom's plan to succeed, he needs to identify an investment that is capable of producing at least a 13.29% annual return each year for the next 10 years. Thom might want to use the technique described in section 8.9 to help design such an investment.

8.8.4   Comments on Optimizing Existing Spreadsheets

One difficulty in optimizing an existing spreadsheet model is determining whether the underlying algebraic model is linear or nonlinear. This is important in determining whether a global optimal solution to the problem has been obtained. As mentioned earlier, if we instruct Solver to assume that the model is linear, it conducts a series of numerical tests to determine whether this assumption is appropriate. If Solver detects that the model is not linear, a message is displayed to that effect and

Figure 8.27
Solver parameters and options for the insurance funding problem.

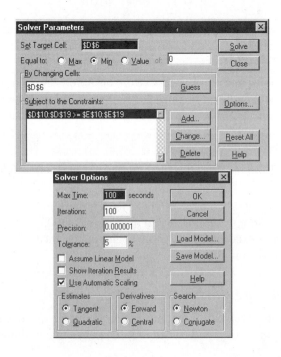

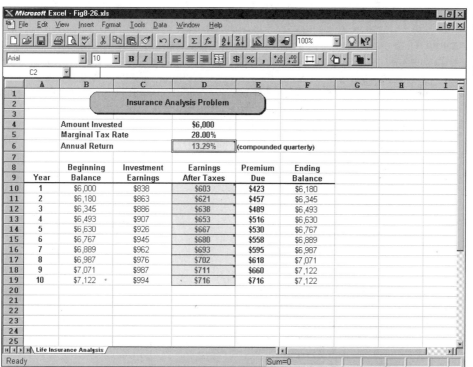

Figure 8.28
Optimal solution
to the insurance
funding
problem.

we need to re-solve the model as an NLP. So when applying optimization techniques to an existing spreadsheet model, it is a good idea to instruct Solver to assume that the model is linear. If Solver can find a solution under this assumption, we can be confident that it is the global optimal solution. If Solver detects that the model is nonlinear, we must be aware that any solution obtained might represent a local optimal solution as opposed to the global optimal solution. In this case, we might re-solve the model several times from different starting points to see if better local optimal solutions exist for the problem. (Note that if a problem is poorly scaled, Solver's linearity tests will sometimes indicate that the model is not linear, when in fact it is.)

As you develop your skills and intuition about spreadsheet optimization, you might be inclined to skip the step of writing out algebraic formulations of your models. For straightforward problems this might be appropriate. However, in more complex problems this can lead to undesirable results. For example, in Chapter 6, Integer Linear Programming, we noted how it can be tempting to implement the binary variables in a fixed-charge problem using an IF( ) function in a spreadsheet. Unfortunately, this causes Solver to view the problem as an NLP rather than as a mixed-integer LP problem. So how you implement the model for a problem can impact whether Solver finds the global optimal solution. As the model builder, you must understand what kind of model you have and implement it in the most appropriate way. Writing out the algebraic formulation of the model often helps to ensure that you thoroughly understand the model you are attempting to solve.

8.9   THE PORTFOLIO SELECTION PROBLEM

One of the most famous applications of NLP involves determining the optimal mix of investments to hold in a portfolio in order to minimize the risk of the portfolio while achieving a desired level of return. One way to measure the risk inherent in an individual investment is the variance (or, alternatively, the standard deviation) of the returns it has generated over a period of time. One of the key objectives in portfolio selection is to smooth out the variation in the return on a portfolio by choosing investments whose returns tend to vary in opposite directions. That is, we'd like to choose investments that have a negative covariance or negative correlation so that when one investment generates a lower-than-average return, another investment in our portfolio offsets this with a higher-than-average return. This tends to make the variance of the return of the portfolio smaller than that of any individual investment. The following example illustrates a portfolio selection problem.

> Ray Dodson is an independent financial advisor. He recently met with a new client, Paula Ribben, who wanted Ray's advice on how best to diversify a portion of her investments. Paula has invested a good portion of her retirement savings in the stock of International Business Corporation (IBC). During the past 12 years, this stock has produced an average annual return of 7.64% with a variance of approximately 0.0026. Paula would like to earn more on her investments, but is very cautious and doesn't like to take risks. Paula has asked Ray to recommend a portfolio of investments that would provide at least a 12% average return with as little additional risk as possible. After some research, Ray identified two additional stocks, from the National Motor Corporation (NMC) and the National Broadcasting System (NBS), that he believes could help meet Paula's investment objectives. Ray's initial research is summarized in Figure 8.29.
>
> As indicated in Figure 8.29, shares of NMC have produced an average rate of return of 13.43% over the past 12 years, while those of NBS have generated an average return of 14.93%. Ray used the COVAR( ) function in Excel to create the covariance matrix in this spreadsheet. The numbers along the main diagonal in this matrix correspond to the variances of the returns for each stock. For example, the covariance matrix indicates that the variances in the annual returns for IBC, NMC, and NBS are approximately 0.0026, 0.0028, and 0.0368, respectively. The entries off the main diagonal represent covariances between different pairs of stocks. For example, the covariance between IBC and NMC is –0.00025, the covariance between IBC and NBS is 0.00440, and the covariance between NMC and NBS is –0.00542.
>
> Ray wants to determine what percentage of Paula's funds should be allocated to each of the stocks in order to achieve an overall expected return of 12% while minimizing the variance of the total return on the portfolio.

8.9.1   Defining the Decision Variables

In this problem we must determine what percentage of the total funds invested should go toward the purchase of each of the three stocks. Thus, to formulate the model for this problem we need the following three decision variables:

$$p_1 = \text{proportion of total funds invested in IBC}$$

$$p_2 = \text{proportion of total funds invested in NMC}$$

$$p_3 = \text{proportion of total funds invested in NBS}$$

Portfolio Data

	Annual Return		
Year	IBC	NMC	NBS
1	11.2%	8.0%	10.9%
2	10.8%	9.2%	22.0%
3	11.6%	6.6%	37.9%
4	-1.6%	18.5%	-11.8%
5	-4.1%	7.4%	12.9%
6	8.6%	13.0%	-7.5%
7	6.8%	22.0%	9.3%
8	11.9%	14.0%	48.7%
9	12.0%	20.5%	-1.9%
10	8.3%	14.0%	19.1%
11	6.0%	19.0%	-3.4%
12	10.2%	9.0%	43.0%
Average	7.64%	13.43%	14.93%

	Covariance Matrix		
	IBC	NMC	NBS
IBC	0.00258	-0.00025	0.00440
NMC	-0.00025	0.00276	-0.00542
NBS	0.00440	-0.00542	0.03677

Portfolio Analysis

Key Cell Formulas

Cell	*Formula*	*Copied to*
B18	=AVERAGE(B6:B17)	C18:D18
G6	=COVAR(B6:B17,$B$6:$B$17)	H6:I6
G7	=COVAR(B6:B17,$C$6:$C$17)	H7:I7
G8	=COVAR(B6:B17,$D$6:$D$17)	H8:I8

Figure 8.29 Data for the portfolio selection problem.

Because these variables represent proportions, we also need to ensure that they assume values no less than 0, and that they sum to 1 (or 100%). We will handle these conditions when we identify the constraints for the problem.

8.9.2 Defining the Objective

The objective in this problem is to minimize the risk of the portfolio as measured by its variance. In general, the variance of a portfolio consisting of n investments is defined in most finance texts as:

$$\text{Portfolio variance} = \sum_{i=1}^{n} \sigma_i^2 p_i^2 + 2\sum_{i=1}^{n-1} \sum_{j=i+1}^{n} \sigma_{ij} p_i p_j$$

where

p_i = the percentage of the portfolio invested in investment i

σ_i^2 = the variance of investment i

$\sigma_{ij} = \sigma_{ji}$ = the covariance between investments i and j

If you are familiar with matrix multiplication, you might realize that the portfolio variance can also be expressed in matrix terms as:

$$\text{Portfolio variance} = \mathbf{p}^T\mathbf{C}\mathbf{p}$$

where

$$\mathbf{p}^T = (p_1, p_2, \ldots, p_n)$$

$$\mathbf{C} = \text{the } n \times n \text{ covariance matrix} = \begin{bmatrix} \sigma_1^2 & \sigma_{12} & \ldots & \sigma_{1n} \\ \sigma_{21} & \sigma_2^2 & \ldots & \sigma_{2n} \\ \vdots & \vdots & \ddots & \vdots \\ \sigma_{n1} & \sigma_{n2} & \ldots & \sigma_n^2 \end{bmatrix}$$

Notice that if 100% of the funds available are placed in a single investment i, then the portfolio variance reduces to σ_i^2 — the variance for that single investment.

In our example problem, we have:

$$\sigma_1^2 = 0.00258, \qquad \sigma_2^2 = 0.00276, \qquad \sigma_3^2 = 0.03677$$
$$\sigma_{12} = -0.00025, \qquad \sigma_{13} = 0.00440, \qquad \sigma_{23} = -0.00542$$

So, using the preceding formula, the objective for our problem is stated as:

$$\text{MIN: } 0.00258\, p_1^2 + 0.00276\, p_2^2 + 0.03677\, p_3^2 +$$
$$2(-0.00025 \times p_1 p_2 + 0.0044 \times p_1 p_3 - 0.00542\, p_2 p_3)$$

This objective function is not a linear combination of the decision variables, so we must solve this problem as an NLP. However, it can be shown that the solution produced when using this objective for a portfolio selection is a global optimal solution.

8.9.3   Defining the Constraints

Only two main constraints apply to this problem. As mentioned earlier, because only three investments are under consideration for this portfolio, and our decision variables represent the percentage of funds invested in each of these investments, we must ensure that our decision variables sum to 100%. This can be accomplished easily as:

$$p_1 + p_2 + p_3 = 1$$

We also need a constraint to ensure that the expected return of the entire portfolio achieves or exceeds the desired return of 12%. This condition is expressed as:

$$0.0764 p_1 + 0.1343 p_2 + 0.1493 p_3 \geq 0.12$$

The LHS of this constraint represents a weighted average of the expected returns from the individual investments. This constraint indicates that the weighted average expected return on the portfolio must be at least 12%.

Finally, because the decision variables must represent proportions, we should also include the following upper and lower bounds:

$$p_1, \ p_2, \ p_3 \geq 0$$
$$p_1, \ p_2, \ p_3 \leq 1$$

The last condition, requiring each of the p_i to be less than or equal to 1, is mathematically redundant because the p_i must also be nonnegative and sum to 1. However, we will include this restriction for completeness.

8.9.4 Implementing the Model

In summary, the algebraic model for this problem is given as:

$$\text{MIN: } 0.00258\, p_1^2 + 0.00276\, p_2^2 + 0.03677\, p_3^2 +$$
$$2(-0.00025 \times p_1 p_2 + 0.0044 \times p_1 p_3 - 0.00542\, p_2 p_3)$$

Subject to:

$$p_1 + p_2 + p_3 = 1$$
$$0.0764 p_1 + 0.1343 p_2 + 0.1493 p_3 \geq 0.12$$
$$p_1, p_2, p_3 \geq 0$$
$$p_1, p_2, p_3 \leq 1$$

One approach to implementing this model in a spreadsheet is shown in Figure 8.30 (and in the file FIG8-30.xls on your data disk). In this spreadsheet, cells G11,

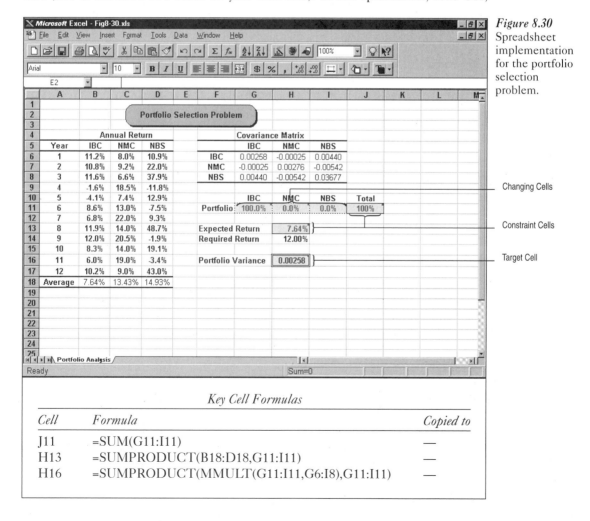

Figure 8.30 Spreadsheet implementation for the portfolio selection problem.

Cell	Formula	Copied to
J11	=SUM(G11:I11)	—
H13	=SUMPRODUCT(B18:D18,G11:I11)	—
H16	=SUMPRODUCT(MMULT(G11:I11,G6:I8),G11:I11)	—

H11, and I11 represent the decision variables p_1, p_2, and p_3, respectively. The initial values in these cells reflect the investor's current portfolio, which consists entirely of stock in IBC.

We can implement the objective function for this problem in a number of ways. The standard approach is to implement a formula that corresponds exactly to the algebraic form of the objective function. This is represented by:

Formula for cell H16:   =G6*G11^2+H7*H11^2+I8*I11^2+
                        2*(H6*G11*H11+I6*G11*I11+H8*H11*I11)

Entering this formula is tedious and prone to error, and would be even more so if this example involved more than three stocks. The following is an alternative, and easier, way of expressing this objective:

Alternative formula for cell H16: =SUMPRODUCT(MMULT(G11:I11,G6:I8),G11:I11)

This alternative formula uses matrix multiplication (the MMULT( ) function) to compute the portfolio variance. Although both formulas generate the same result, the second formula is much easier to enter and can accommodate any number of investments. Notice that the value 0.00258 in cell H16 in Figure 8.30 indicates that when 100% of the funds are invested in IBC stock, the variance of the portfolio is the same as the variance of the IBC stock.

The LHS formulas of the two main constraints are implemented in cells J11 and H13 as:

Formula for cell J11:   =SUM(G11:I11)
Formula for cell H13:   =SUMPRODUCT(B18:D18,G11:I11)

Figure 8.31 shows the Solver parameters and options used to solve this problem, and Figure 8.32 shows the optimal solution.

8.9.5   Analyzing the Solution

In contrast to the original solution shown in Figure 8.30, the optimal solution shown in Figure 8.32 indicates that a better solution would result by placing 27.2% of the investor's money in IBC, 63.4% in NMC, and 9.4% in NBS. Cell H13 indicates that this mix of investments would achieve the desired 12% expected rate of return, and cell H16 indicates that the variance for this portfolio would be only 0.00112.

The solution to this problem indicates that a portfolio exists that produces a *higher* expected return for Paula with *less* risk than was involved in her original portfolio. Paula's original investment would be called inefficient in the terms of portfolio theory. **Portfolio theory** stipulates that for each possible level of investment return, there is a portfolio that minimizes risk, and accepting any greater level of risk at that level of return is inefficient. Alternatively, for each level of investment risk there is a portfolio that maximizes the return, and accepting any lower level of return at this level of risk is also inefficient.

Whether you attempt to minimize risk subject to a certain required rate of return, or maximize the return subject to a given level of risk, the solutions obtained may still be inefficient. For instance, in the solution to our example problem, there may be a different portfolio that produces a higher return for the same level of risk. We could check for this by solving the problem again, maximizing the expected return while holding the minimal level of risk constant.

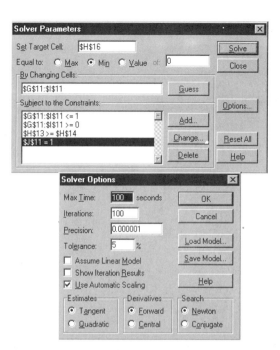

Figure 8.31
Solver parameters and options for the portfolio selection problem.

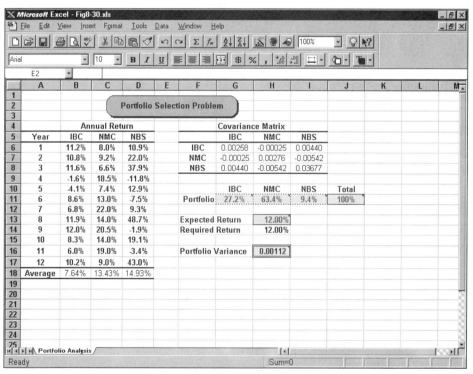

Figure 8.32
Optimal solution to the portfolio selection problem.

The optimal trade-off between risk and return for a given portfolio problem can be summarized by a graph of the **efficient frontier,** which plots the minimal portfolio risk associated with each possible level of return. Figure 8.33 show the efficient frontier for our example problem. This graph is helpful not only in identifying the

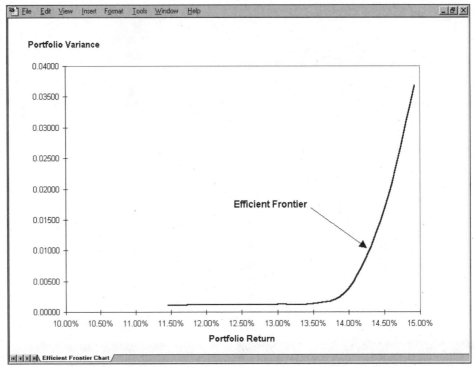

maximum level of risk that should be accepted for each possible level of return, but also in identifying where further increases in expected returns incur much greater amounts of risk.

8.9.6   Handling Conflicting Objectives in Portfolio Problems

As we have seen, there are two different conflicting objectives that can be applied to portfolio selection problems: minimizing risk (portfolio variance) and maximizing expected returns. One way of dealing with these conflicting objectives is to solve the following problem:

MAX: $(1 - r)*($Expected Portfolio Return$) - r*($Portfolio Variance$)$

Subject to: $\Sigma p_i = 1$

$p_i \geq 0$

Here, the p_i again represents the percentages of money we should invest in each stock in the portfolio and r is a constant between 0 and 1 representing the investor's aversion to risk (or the **risk aversion value**). When r = 1 (indicating maximum risk aversion), the objective function attempts to minimize the portfolio variance. Such a solution is shown in Figure 8.34 (file FIG8-34.xls on your data disk) where we have implemented the expected return in cell H13, the portfolio variance in cell H14, the risk aversion factor in cell H15, and the objective function in cell H16. This solution places 36% of the investor's money in IBC, 57% in NMC, and 7.1% in NBS. This results in a portfolio variance of 0.0011. This is the smallest possible portfolio variance for this collection of stocks.

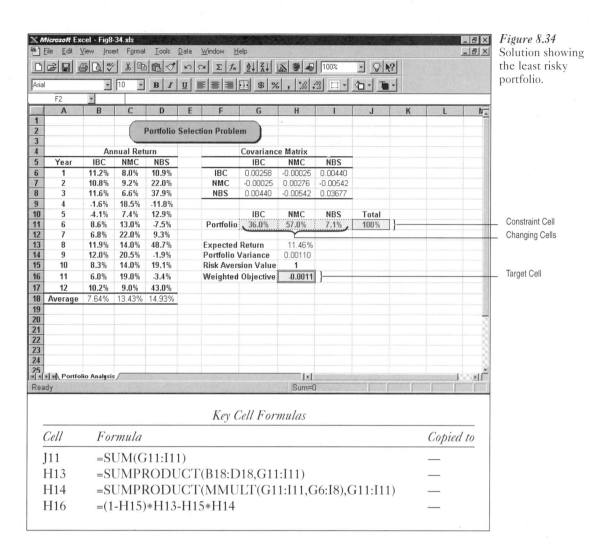

Figure 8.34
Solution showing the least risky portfolio.

Key Cell Formulas

Cell	Formula	Copied to
J11	=SUM(G11:I11)	—
H13	=SUMPRODUCT(B18:D18,G11:I11)	—
H14	=SUMPRODUCT(MMULT(G11:I11,G6:I8),G11:I11)	—
H16	=(1-H15)*H13-H15*H14	—

Conversely, when r = 0 (indicating a total disregard of risk), the objective attempts to maximize the expected portfolio return. This solution is shown in Figure 8.35. This solution places 100% of the investor's money in NBS since this produces the largest return for the portfolio.

For values of r between 0 and 1, Solver will always attempt to keep the expected return as large as possible and the portfolio variance as small as possible (because the objective function in this problem is being maximized). As the value of the parameter r increases, more and more weight is placed on the importance of making the portfolio variance as small as possible (or minimizing risk). Thus, a risk-averse investor should prefer solutions with relatively large values of r. Thus, by solving a series of problems, each time adjusting the value of r, an investor can select a portfolio that provides the greatest utility, or the optimum balance of risk and return for their own attitudes toward risk and return. Alternatively, if an investor feels minimizing risk is twice as important as maximizing returns, we can solve the problem with r = 0.667 (and (1 − r) = 0.333) to reflect the investor's attitude toward risk and return. An r value of 0.99275 will produce the same solution shown in Figure 8.32.

Figure 8.35
Solution showing
the maximum
return portfolio.

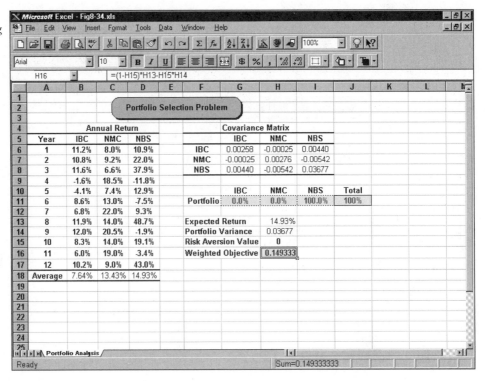

8.10   SENSITIVITY ANALYSIS

In Chapter 4, we analyzed how sensitive the optimal solution to an LP model is to changes in various coefficients in the model. We noted that one advantage of using the simplex method to solve LP problems is that it provides expanded sensitivity information. A certain amount of sensitivity information is also available when using nonlinear optimization methods to solve linear or nonlinear problems.

To understand the sensitivity information available from nonlinear optimization, we'll compare it to what we learned in Chapter 4 about the sensitivity information that results from using the simplex method. In Chapter 4, we solved the following modified version of the Blue Ridge Hot Tubs problem where a third type of hot tub—the Typhoon-Lagoon—was included in the model:

MAX:	$350X_1 + 300X_2 + 320X_3$	} profit
Subject to:	$1X_1 + 1X_2 + 1X_3 \leq 200$	} pump constraint
	$9X_1 + 6X_2 + 8X_3 \leq 1,566$	} labor constraint
	$12X_1 + 16X_2 + 13X_3 \leq 2,880$	} tubing constraint
	$X_1, X_2, X_3 \geq 0$	} nonnegativity conditions

The spreadsheet implementation of this problem is shown in Figure 8.36 (and in the file FIG8-36.xls on your data disk). Figure 8.37 shows the Sensitivity Report generated for this problem after solving it using the simplex method. Figure 8.38 shows the Sensitivity Report for this problem after solving it using Solver's nonlinear optimizer.

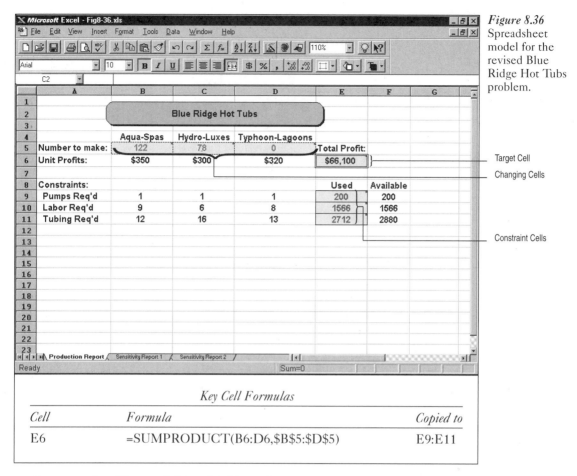

Figure 8.36
Spreadsheet model for the revised Blue Ridge Hot Tubs problem.

	Key Cell Formulas	
Cell	*Formula*	*Copied to*
E6	=SUMPRODUCT(B6:D6,$B$5:$D$5)	E9:E11

In comparing Figures 8.37 and 8.38, notice that the same optimal solution is obtained regardless of whether the problem is solved using the simplex method or the nonlinear optimizer. Both reports indicate that 122 Aqua-Spas, 78 Hydro-Luxes, and 0 Typhoon-Lagoons should be produced. Both reports also indicate that this solution requires 200 pumps, 1,566 labor hours, and 2,712 feet of tubing. The fact that the two optimization techniques found the same optimal solution is not surprising because this problem is known to have a unique optimal solution. However, if an LP problem has alternative optimal solutions, the simplex method and the nonlinear optimizer will not necessarily identify the same optimal solution.

Another similarity between the two Sensitivity Reports is apparent if we compare the values in the Reduced Cost and Shadow Price columns in Figure 8.37 with the values in the Reduced Gradient and Lagrange Multiplier columns in Figure 8.38. The reduced cost for each variable in Figure 8.37 is the same as the reduced gradient for each variable in Figure 8.38. Similarly, the shadow price for each constraint in Figure 8.37 is the same as the Lagrange multiplier for each constraint in Figure 8.38. This is not simply a coincidence.

8.10.1 Lagrange Multipliers

In Chapter 4, we saw that the shadow price of a constraint represents the marginal value of an additional unit of the resource represented by the constraint—or the

Figure 8.37
Sensitivity
Report obtained
after solving the
model using the
simplex method.

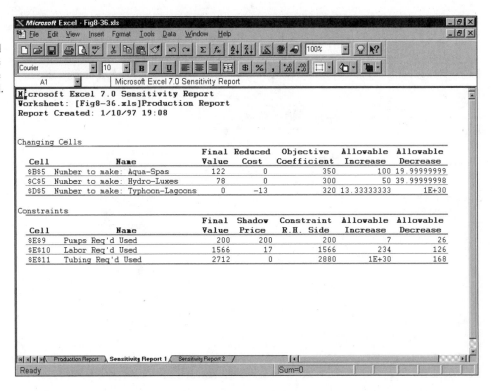

Figure 8.38
Sensitivity
Report obtained
after solving the
model using
Solver's
nonlinear GRG
optimizer.

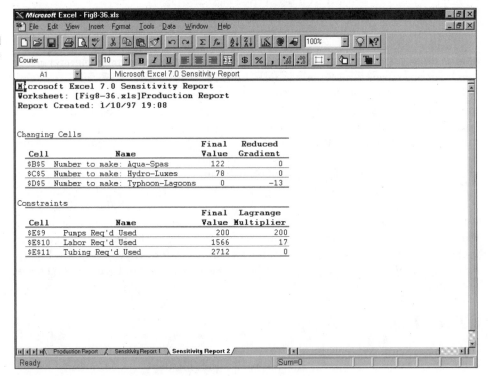

amount by which the objective function would improve if the RHS of the constraint is loosened by one unit. This same interpretation applies in a more approximate sense to Lagrange multipliers. The main difference between shadow prices and Lagrange multipliers involves the range of RHS values over which the shadow price or Lagrange multiplier remains valid.

As discussed in Chapter 4 (and shown in Figure 8.37), after solving an LP problem using the simplex method, we can identify the allowable increase and decrease in a constraint's RHS value over which the shadow price of the constraint remains valid. We can do this because the objective function and constraints in an LP problem are all linear, making the impact of changes in a constraint's RHS value on the objective function value relatively easy to compute. However, in NLP problems we have no general way to determine such ranges for the RHS values of the constraints. So when using Solver's nonlinear optimizer to solve an optimization problem, we cannot easily determine the range of RHS values over which a constraint's Lagrange multiplier will remain valid. The Lagrange multipliers can be used only to estimate the approximate impact on the objective function of changing a constraint's RHS value by small amounts.

8.10.2   *Reduced Gradients*

In Chapter 4 we saw that the reduced cost of a variable that assumes its simple lower (or upper) bound in the optimal solution generally represents the amount by which the objective function would be reduced (or improved) if this variable were allowed to increase by one unit. Again, this same interpretation applies in a more approximate sense to reduced gradient values. In particular, nonzero reduced gradient values indicate the approximate impact on the objective function value of very small changes in the value of a given variable. For example, in Chapter 4 we saw that forcing the production of one Typhoon-Lagoon resulted in a $13.33 reduction in total profit for the problem shown in Figure 8.36. This is reflected by the reduced cost value for Typhoon-Lagoons in Figure 8.37 and the reduced gradient value for Typhoon-Lagoons in Figure 8.38.

Although we used an LP model to discuss the meaning of reduced gradients and Lagrange multipliers, their interpretation is the same for nonlinear problems. As stated earlier, an LP problem can be viewed as a special type of nonlinear programming problem where the objective function and constraints are linear.

8.11   *SOLVER OPTIONS FOR SOLVING NLPS*

Although we can represent an LP problem by a highly structured, and relatively simple, objective function and set of constraints, the objective function and constraints in an NLP problem can be virtually *any* mathematical function. Thus, it is not uncommon to encounter difficulties while trying to solve NLP problems.

Solver provides several options for controlling how it solves NLPs. These options—Estimates, Derivatives, and Search—are located at the bottom of the Solver Options dialog box, as shown in Figure 8.39. The default settings for these options work well for many problems. However, if you have difficulty solving an NLP, you might try changing these options to force Solver to use a different search strategy. A complete description of these options would require an in-depth understanding of calculus, which is not assumed in this book. The following descriptions provide a nontechnical overview of these options.

Figure 8.39
Solver options
for NLP
problems.

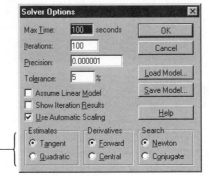

Solver options for
NLP problems

The Estimates option determines how Solver estimates the values of the decision variables while searching for improved solutions. The default setting, Tangent, estimates values using a linear extrapolation technique, whereas the alternate setting, Quadratic, uses a nonlinear extrapolation technique.

The Derivatives option determines how Solver estimates derivatives. When using the default setting, Forward, Solver obtains estimates of first derivatives at a point by perturbing the point once in a forward direction and computing the rise over the run. With the Central setting, Solver obtains estimates of first derivatives by perturbing away from a point in both a backward and forward direction and computes the rise over the run between the two points. The Central setting requires twice as many recalculations as the Forward option but can improve the estimates of the derivatives, yielding better search directions and often fewer iterations. However, the difference in accuracy is usually not worth the extra effort, hence the default is Forward.

The Search option determines how Solver chooses a search direction along which to seek a feasible point with an improved objective value. The default setting, Newton, causes Solver to use the Broyden-Fletcher-Goldfarb-Shanno Quasi-Newton method to identify search directions. The Conjugate setting instructs Solver to use conjugate gradient method. The details of these techniques go beyond the scope of this text but can be found in most texts devoted to NLP.

As mentioned earlier, scaling problems often affect how easily Solver can solve a problem. Thus, selecting the Use Automatic Scaling option is also a possible remedy to try if Solver encounters difficulty in solving an NLP.

Important Software Note

If you are using Excel 8.0, there is another setting labeled **Convergence** in the Solver parameters dialog box. As Solver searches for an optimal solution to an NLP, it terminates if the relative change in the objective function value for several iterations is smaller than the convergence factor. If you think Solver is stopping too quickly as it converges on an optimal solution, you should reduce the convergence setting.

THE WORLD OF MANAGEMENT SCIENCE
Water Spilled Is Energy Lost:
Pacific Gas and Electric Uses Nonlinear
Optimization to Manage Power Generation

The power produced by a hydroelectric generator is a nonlinear function of the flow rate of water through the turbine and the pressure. Pressure, or head, is determined by the difference in water level upstream from the generator.

Pacific Gas and Electric Company (PG&E), the world's largest privately held utility, generates power from fossil fuels, nuclear energy, wind, solar energy, and geothermal steam, as well as hydropower. Its Sierra Nevada Hydro System is a complex network of 15 river basins, 143 reservoirs, and 67 power plants. Streamflow peaks markedly in the spring from snow melting in the mountains, whereas demand for electric power peaks in the summer.

Water spilled from a dam cannot be used to generate power at that dam, although it can increase the head at a dam downstream and contribute to power generation there. If the water spills at a time when all of the downstream reservoirs are full, it will spill from all the dams, and its energy will be lost forever. Hydrologists at PG&E attempt to maximize the useful generation of electricity by strategically timing controlled spills to manage the levels of all reservoirs in the system and minimize wasted flow. If done effectively, this reduces the company's reliance on fossil fuel and reduces the cost of electricity to its customers.

This problem was modeled as a nonlinear program with a nonlinear objective function and linear constraints. Because many of the constraints are network flow constraints, using a network flow algorithm along with the linear terms of the objective function produced a good starting point for the nonlinear programming algorithm. A good starting point can be a critical factor in the successful use of nonlinear programming.

PG&E management confirms that the optimization system saves between $10 and $45 million annually compared to manual systems, and the California Public Utilities Commission has recommended its use to others.

Source: Yoshiro Ikura, George Gross, and Gene Sand Hall, "PG&E's State-of-the-Art Scheduling Tool for Hydro Systems," *Interfaces*, vol. 16, no. 1, January-February 1986, pp. 65-82.

SUMMARY

This chapter introduced some of the basic concepts involved in nonlinear programming and discussed several applications. The steps involved in formulating and solving an NLP problem are not very different from those required to solve an LP problem—the decision variables are identified and an objective function and any constraints are stated in terms of the decision variables. Because the objective function and constraints in an NLP problem might be nonlinear, the calculations involved in solving NLP problems are different from those included in the simplex method, which is used most often to solve LP problems. NLP problems sometimes have several local optimal solutions. Thus, finding the global optimal solution to a difficult

NLP problem might require re-solving the model several times using different initial starting points.

QUESTIONS AND PROBLEMS

1. Can the GRG algorithm be used to solve LP problems? If so, will it always identify a corner point of the feasible region as the optimal solution (as does the simplex method)?

2. In describing the NLP solution strategy summarized in Figure 8.2, we noted that the *fastest* improvement in the objective function is obtained by moving from point A in a direction that is perpendicular to the level curve of the objective function. However, there are other directions that also result in improvements to the objective.

    a. How would you describe or define the set of all directions that result in improvement to the objective?
    b. How would your answer change if the level curve of the objective function at point A was nonlinear?

3. Consider an optimization problem with two variables and the constraints $X_1 \leq 5$, $X_2 \leq 5$ where both X_1 and X_2 are nonnegative.

    a. Sketch the feasible region for this problem.
    b. Sketch level curves of a nonlinear objective for this problem that would have exactly one local optimal solution that is also the global optimal solution.
    c. Redraw the feasible region and sketch level curves of a nonlinear objective for this problem that would have a local optimal solution that is not the global optimal solution.

4. Consider the following function:

    $$Y = -0.865 + 8.454X - 1.696X^2 + 0.132X^3 - 0.00331X^4$$

    a. Plot this function on an X-Y graph for positive values of X from 1 to 20.
    b. How many local maximum solutions are there?
    c. How many local minimum solutions are there?
    d. Use Solver to find the maximum value of Y using a starting value of X = 2. What value of Y do you obtain?
    e. Use Solver to find the maximum value of Y using a starting value of X = 14. What value of Y do you obtain?

5. Consider the following function:

    $$Y = 37.684 - 15.315X + 3.095X^2 - 0.218X^3 + 0.005X^4$$

    a. Plot this function on an X-Y graph for positive values of X from 1 to 20.
    b. How many local maximum solutions are there?
    c. How many local minimum solutions are there?
    d. Use Solver to find the minimum value of Y using a starting value of X = 3. What value of Y do you obtain?
    e. Use Solver to find the minimum value of Y using a starting value of X = 18. What value of Y do you obtain?

6. A car dealership needs to determine how to allocate its $20,000 advertising budget. They have estimated the expected profit from each dollar (X) spent in four different advertising media as follows:

Medium	Expected Profit
Newspaper	$100X^{0.7}$
Radio	$125X^{0.65}$
TV	$180X^{0.6}$
Direct Mail	$250X^{0.5}$

If the company wants to spend at least $500 on each media, how should it allocate its advertising budget in order to maximize profit?

7. The XYZ company produces two products. The total profit achieved from these products is described by the following equation:

$$\text{Total profit} = -0.2X_1^2 - 0.4X_2^2 + 8X_1 + 12X_2 + 1500$$

where

X_1 = thousands of units of product 1

X_2 = thousands of units of product 2

Every 1,000 units of X_1 require one hour of time in the shipping department, and every 1,000 units of X_2 require 30 minutes in the shipping department. Each unit of each product requires two pounds of a special ingredient, of which 64,000 pounds will be available in the next production period. Additionally, 80 hours of shipping labor will be available in the next production period. Demand for X_1 and X_2 is unlimited.

a. Formulate an NLP model for this problem.
b. Implement your model in a spreadsheet and solve it.
c. What is the optimal solution?

8. Refer to the insurance problem faced by Thom Pearman discussed in section 8.8 of this chapter. Let b_i represent the balance in his investment at the beginning of year i and let r represent the annual interest rate.

a. What is the objective function for this problem? Is it linear or nonlinear?
b. Write out the first two constraints for this problem algebraically. Are they linear or nonlinear?

9. In the insurance problem discussed in this chapter, suppose that Thom is confident that he can invest his money to earn a 15% annual rate of return compounded quarterly. Assuming a fixed 15% return, suppose he would now like to determine the minimum amount of money he must invest in order for his after-tax earnings to cover the planned premium payments.

a. Make whatever changes are necessary to the spreadsheet and answer Thom's question.
b. Is the model you solved linear or nonlinear? How can you tell?

10. The yield of a bond is the interest rate that makes the present value of its cash flow equal to its selling price. Assume a bond can be purchased for $975 and generates the following cash flows:

Years from now:	Cash Flow:
1	$100
2	$120
3	$90
4	$100
5	$1,200

Use Solver to determine the yield for this bond. (Hint: In Excel, use the NPV( ) function to compute the present value of the cash flows.) What is the yield on this bond?

11. Suppose a gift shop in Myrtle Beach has an annual demand for 15,000 units for a souvenir kitchen magnet that it buys for $0.50 per unit. Assume it costs $10 to place an order and the inventory carrying cost is 25% of the item's unit cost. Use Solver to determine the optimal order quantity if the company wants to minimize the total cost of procuring this item.

   a. What is the optimal order quantity?
   b. What is the total cost associated with this order quantity?
   c. What are the annual order and annual inventory holding costs for this solution?

12. SuperCity is a large retailer of electronics and appliances. The store sells three different models of TVs that are ordered from different manufacturers. The demands, costs, and storage requirements for each model are summarized in the following table:

	Model 1	Model 2	Model 3
Annual Demand	800	500	1,500
Unit Cost	$300	$1,100	$600
Storage space req'd	9 sq ft	25 sq ft	16 sq ft

It costs $60 to do the administrative work associated with preparing processing and receiving orders, and SuperCity assumes a 25% annual carrying cost for all items it holds in inventory. There is 3,000 square feet of total warehouse space available for storing these items, and the store never wants to have more than $45,000 invested in inventory for these items. The manager of this store would like to determine the optimal order quantity for each model of TV.

   a. Formulate an NLP model for this problem.
   b. Implement your model in a spreadsheet and solve it.
   c. What are the optimal order quantities?
   d. How many orders of each type of TV will be placed each year?
   e. Assuming demand is constant throughout the year, how often should orders be placed?

13. The Radford hardware store expects to sell 1,500 electric garbage disposal units in the coming year. Demand for this product is fairly stable over the year. It costs $20 to place an order for these units and the company assumes a 20% annual holding cost on inventory. The following price structure applies to Radford's purchases of this product:

Order quantity	0 to 499	500 to 999	1,000 and up
Price per unit	$35	$33	$31

So if Radford orders 135 units, they pay $35 per unit; if they order 650, they pay $33 per unit; and if they order 1,200, they pay $31 per unit.

a. What is the most economical order quantity and total cost of this solution? (Hint: Solve a separate EOQ problem for each of the order quantity ranges given and select the solution that yields the lowest total cost.)

b. Suppose the discount policy changed so that Radford had to pay $35 for the first 499 units ordered, $33 for the next 500 units ordered, and $31 for any additional units. What is the most economical order quantity and total cost of this solution?

14. A long-distance telephone company is trying to determine the optimal pricing structure for its daytime and evening long-distance calling rates. It estimates the demand for phone lines as follows:

Daytime Lines (in 1,000s) Demanded per Minute $= 600 - 5,000P_d + 100P_e$

Evening Lines (in 1,000s) Demanded per Minute $= 400 + 3,000P_d - 9500P_e$

where P_d represents the price per minute during the day and P_e represents the price per minute during the evening. Assume it costs $100 per minute to provide every 1,000 lines in long-distance capacity. The company will have to maintain the maximum number of lines demanded throughout the day, even if the demand is greater during the day than during the evening.

a. What prices should the telephone company charge if it wants to maximize profit?

b. How many long distance lines does the company need to maintain?

15. Howie Jones, owner of Blue Ridge Hot Tubs, is facing a new problem. Although sale of the two hot tubs manufactured by his company (Aqua-Spas and Hydro-Luxes) have been brisk, the company is not earning the level of profits that Howie would like to achieve. Having established a reputation for high quality and reliability, Howie believes he can increase profits by increasing the prices of the hot tubs. However, he is concerned that a price increase might have a detrimental effect on demand, so Howie has engaged a marketing research firm to estimate the level of demand for Aqua-Spas and Hydro-Luxes at various prices. The marketing research firm used the technique of regression analysis (discussed in Chapter 9) to develop a model of the relationship between the prices and demand for the hot tubs. After analyzing the situation, the marketing research firm concluded that a reasonable price range for the hot tubs would be between $1,000 and $1,500, and that within this range Howie could expect the demand for hot tubs in the next quarter to vary with price in the following way:

Demand for Aqua-Spas $= 300 - 0.175 \times$ price of Aqua-Spas

Demand for Hydro-Luxes $= 325 - 0.15 \times$ price of Hydro-Luxes

Howie determined that the costs of manufacturing Aqua-Spas and Hydro-Luxes are $850 and $700 per unit, respectively. Ideally, he wants to produce enough hot tubs to meet demand exactly and carry no inventory. Each Aqua-Spa requires 1 pump, 9 hours of labor, and 12 feet of tubing; each Hydro-Lux requires 1 pump, 6 hours of labor, and 16 feet of tubing. Howie's suppliers have committed to supplying him with 200 pumps and 2,800 feet of tubing. Also, 1,566 hours of labor are available for production. Howie wants to determine how much to charge for each type of hot tub and how many of each type to produce.

a. Formulate an NLP model for this problem.
b. Implement your model in a spreadsheet and solve it.
c. What is the optimal solution?
d. Which of the resource constraints are binding at the optimal solution?
e. What values would you expect the Lagrange multipliers to take on for these constraints? (Create a Sensitivity Report for this problem to verify your answer.)

16. Carnival Confections, Inc. produces two popular southern food items, pork-rinds and fried peanuts, which it sells at a local recreation area on weekends. The owners of the business have estimated their profit function on these items to be:

$$0.6p - 0.002p^2 + 0.5f - 0.0009f^2 - 0.001pf$$

Note that p is the number of packages of pork-rinds produced and f is the number of packages of fried peanuts produced. Both of these items require deep frying. The company's fryer has the capacity to produce a total of 600 packages of pork-rinds and/or fried peanuts. One minute of labor is required to dry and package the pork-rinds, and 30 seconds are required to dry and package the peanuts. The company devotes a total of 16 hours of labor to producing these products each week.

a. Formulate an NLP model for this problem.
b. Implement your model in a spreadsheet.
c. What is the optimal solution?

17. A new mother wants to establish a college education fund for her newborn child. She wants this fund to be worth $100,000 in 18 years.

a. If she invests $75 per month, what is the minimum rate of return she would need to earn on her investment? Assume monthly compounding. (Hint: Consider using the future value function FV( ) in your spreadsheet.)
b. Suppose the mother knows of an investment that will guarantee a 12% annual return compounded monthly. What is the minimum amount she should invest each month to achieve her goal?

18. The Arctic Oil Company has recently drilled two new wells in a remote area of Alaska. The company is planning to install a pipeline to carry the oil from the two new wells to a transportation and refining (T&R) center. The locations of the oil wells and the T&R center are summarized below. Assume a unit change in either coordinate represents one mile.

	X coordinate	Y coordinate
Oil well 1	50	150
Oil well 2	30	40
T&R center	230	70

Installing the pipeline is a very expensive undertaking, and the company wants to minimize the amount of pipeline required. Because the shortest distance between two points is a straight line, one of the analysts assigned to the project believes that a separate pipe should be run from each well to the T&R center. Another alternative is to run separate pipes from each well to some intermediate substation where the two lines are joined into a single pipeline that continues on to the T&R center. Arctic Oil's management wants to determine which alternative is best. Furthermore, if using the intermediate substation is best, management wants to determine where this station should be located.

a. Create a spreadsheet model to determine how many miles of pipeline Arctic Oil must install if they run separate pipeline from each oil well to the T&R center. How much pipe will be needed?
b. If Arctic Oil wants to build a substation, where should it be built? How much pipe is needed in this solution?
c. Which alternative is best?
d. Suppose the substation cannot be built within a ten-mile radius of the coordinates X = 80, Y = 95. (Assume the pipeline can run through this area but the substation cannot be built in the area.) What is the optimal location of the substation now and how much pipe will be needed?

19. The Rugger Corporation is a Seattle-based R&D company that recently developed a new type of fiber substrate that is waterproof and resists dirt. Several carpet manufacturers in northeast Georgia would like to use Rugger as their sole supplier for this new fiber. The locations of the carpet manufacturers are summarized below.

Carpet Mill Locations	X coordinate	Y coordinate
Dalton	9	43
Rome	2	28
Canton	51	36
Kennesaw	19	4

Rugger expects to make 130, 75, 90, and 80 deliveries to the carpet producers in Dalton, Rome, Canton, and Kennesaw, respectively. The company would like to build its new plant in the location that would minimize the annual shipping miles. However, Rugger would also like to be within 50 miles of each of its new customers so that it will be easy to provide on-site technical support for any production problems that may occur.

a. Formulate an NLP model for this problem.
b. Implement your model in a spreadsheet and solve it.
c. What is the optimal location for the new plant? How many annual shipping miles is associated with this solution?
d. Suppose the company wants to identify the location that minimizes the average distance to each of its customers. Where is this location and how many annual shipping miles would Rugger incur if the new plant locates there?
e. Suppose the company wants to identify the location that minimizes maximum distance to any of its customers. Where is this location and how many annual shipping miles would Rugger incur if the new plant locates there?

20. An air-ambulance service in Colorado is interested in keeping its helicopter in a central location that would minimize the flight distance to four major ski resorts. An X-Y grid was laid over a map of the area to determine the following latitude and longitude coordinates for the four resorts:

Resort	Longitude	Latitude
Bumpyride	35	57
Keyrock	46	48
Aspirin	37	93
Goldenrod	22	67

a. Formulate an NLP model to determine where the ambulance service should be located in order to minimize the total distance to each resort.
b. Implement your model in a spreadsheet and solve it. Where should the ambulance service be located?
c. What other factors might affect the decision and how might you incorporate them in your model? (Consider, for example, differences in the average number of skiers and accidents at the different resorts, and the topography of the area.)

21. The Heat-Aire Company has two plants that produce identical heat pump units. However, production costs at the two differ due to the technology and labor used at each plant. The total costs of production at the plants depends on the quantity produced, and are described as:

$$\text{Total cost at plant 1:}\quad 2X_1^2 - 1X_1 + 15$$
$$\text{Total cost at plant 2:}\quad X_2^2 + 0.3X_2 + 10$$

Note that X_1 is the number of heat pumps produced at plant 1 and X_2 is the number of heat pumps produced at plant 2. Neither plant can make more than 600 heat pumps.

Heat pumps can be shipped from either plant to satisfy demand from four different customers. The unit shipping costs and demands for each customer are summarized below.

	Customer 1	Customer 2	Customer 3	Customer 4
Plant 1	$23	$30	$32	$26
Plant 2	$33	$27	$25	$24
Demand	300	250	150	400

What is the optimal production and shipping plan if management wants to meet customer demand at the lowest total cost?

a. Formulate an NLP model for this problem.
b. Implement your model in a spreadsheet and solve it.
c. What is the optimal solution?

22. Beth Dale is the Director of Development for a nonprofit organization that depends largely on charitable gifts for its operations. Beth needs to assign four different staff people to make trips to call on four possible donors. Only one staff person can call on each donor and each staff person can make only one call. Beth estimates the probability of each staff person successfully obtaining the donation from each potential giver as follows:

| | *Donor* | | | |
Staff	1	2	3	4
Sam	0.95	0.91	0.90	0.88
Billie	0.92	0.95	0.95	0.82
Sally	0.95	0.93	0.93	0.85
Fred	0.94	0.87	0.92	0.86

a. Formulate an NLP model to determine the assignment of staff persons to donors that maximizes the probability of receiving all donations.

b. Implement your model in a spreadsheet and solve it. What is the optimal solution?

c. Suppose it is estimated that the donations possible from donors 1, 2, 3, and 4 are for $1 million, $2 million, $0.5 million, and $0.75 million, respectively. How should Beth assign her staff if she wants to maximize the expected value of the donations received?

d. All staffers will have the least luck soliciting funds from donor number 4, so no one really wants to be assigned to this donor. Indeed, each staffer will regret not being assigned to the donor with whom they have the highest probability of success. Suppose we define the amount of this regret for each staffer by their maximum probability of success minus the probability of success for their actual assignment. What assignment of staffers to donors will minimize the maximum regret suffered by any staffer?

23. Water is delivered throughout New York City using eight main waterlines which are connected at six pumping stations as shown in Figure 8.40. The number on each of the arcs indicates the maximum allowable flow of water through each waterline (in 1,000s of gallons per minute).

   Because the city's waterlines are aging, breaks have been occurring more frequently and are related to the increasing demands being place on the system. Civil engineers have estimated the probability of a waterline break occurring as follows:

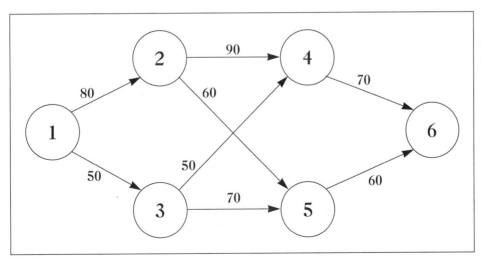

Figure 8.40
Main waterlines and pumping stations in New York.

Probability of failure on the line from station i to station $j = 1 - \text{EXP}(-a_{ij}F_{ij}/1000)$

where F_{ij} is the flow (in 1,000s of gallons per minute) on the line from station i to station j and the values for the parameters a_{ij} are given as follows:

From Station	To Station	a_{ij}
1	2	0.10
1	3 .	0.17
2	4	0.19
2	5	0.15
3	4	0.14
3	5	0.16
4	6	0.11
5	6	0.09

Engineers can use control valves to limit how much water flows through each waterline. During peak demand times, a total of 110,000 gallons of water per minute needs to flow through this system.

a. Create a spreadsheet model to determine the flow pattern that meets the required demand for water in the most reliable way.
b. How much water should flow through each waterline?
c. What is the probability that no waterline will fail while operating in this way?

24. The Wiggly Piggly Grocery Company owns and operates numerous grocery stores throughout the state of Florida. It is developing plans to consolidate warehouse operations so that there will be three different warehouses that supply stores in 10 different regions of the state. The company plans to sell all its existing warehouses and build new, state-of-the-art warehouses. Each warehouse can supply multiple regions; however, all stores in a particular region will be assigned to only one warehouse. The locations of the different regions are summarized below:

	Location	
Region	X	Y
1 Panama City	1.0	14.0
2 Tallahassee	6.1	15.0
3 Jacksonville	13.0	15.0
4 Ocala	12.0	11.0
5 Orlando	13.5	9.0
6 Tampa	11.0	7.5
7 Ft Pierce	17.0	6.0
8 Ft Myers	12.5	3.5
9 West Palm	17.5	4.0
10 Miami	17.0	1.0

a. Create a spreadsheet model to determine approximately where Wiggly Piggly should locate its new warehouses and which regions should be assigned to each of the new warehouses. Assume the company wants to build its warehouses in locations that minimize the distances to each of the regions they serve.
b. What is the optimal solution?

25. An investor wants to determine the safest way to structure a portfolio from several investments. Investment A produces an average annual return of 14% with a variance of 0.025. Investment B produces an average rate of return of 9% with a variance of 0.015. Investment C produces an average rate of return of 8% with a variance of 0.010. Investments A and B have a covariance of 0.00028, and investments A and C have a covariance of -0.006. Investments B and C have a covariance of 0.00125.

    a. Suppose the investor wants to achieve at least a 12% return. What is the least risky way of achieving this goal?
    b. Suppose the investor regards risk minimization as being five times more important than maximizing return. What portfolio would be most appropriate for the investor?

26. Sometimes the historical data on returns and variances may be poor predictors of how investments will perform in the future. In this case, the **scenario approach** to portfolio optimization may be used. Using this technique, we identify several different scenarios of the returns that might occur for each investment during the next year and estimate the probability associated with each scenario. A common set of investment proportions (or weights) is then used to compute a weighted average return r_i for each scenario. The expected return and variance on the portfolio are then estimated as:

$$\text{Expected Portfolio Return} = EPR = \sum r_i s_i$$
$$\text{Variance of Portfolio Return} = VPR = \sum_i (r_i - EPR)^2 s_i$$

    where r_i is the weighted average return under scenario i and s_i is the probability that scenario i will occur. We can use Solver to find the set of investment proportions that generate a desired EPR while minimizing the VPR. Given the following scenarios, find the investment proportions that generate a EPR of 12% while minimizing the VPR.

Scenario	Windsor	Flagship	Templeman	T-Bills	Probability
	Returns				
1	0.14	-0.09	0.10	0.07	0.10
2	-0.11	0.12	0.14	0.06	0.10
3	0.09	0.15	-0.11	0.08	0.10
4	0.25	0.18	0.33	0.07	0.30
5	0.18	0.16	0.15	0.06	0.40

CASE 8.1   ELECTING THE NEXT PRESIDENT

"So it's come down to this," thought Roger Mellichamp as he looked around at the empty Styrofoam coffee cups and papers littering his office. When he accepted the job of campaign manager for his longtime friend's run for the White House, he knew there would be long hours, lots of traveling, and constant media pressure. But the thing he most wanted to avoid was a close race with a final showdown just before the election. Roger knew that making decisions under those circumstances would be agonizing because the success of the campaign and, in many ways, the future of the country would hinge on those very decisions. Unfortunately, that's just where things stand.

With only two weeks before the U.S. presidential election, Roger's friend and the incumbent president are running neck-and-neck in the polls. So Roger's plans for the final two weeks of the campaign will be critical, and he wants to make sure he uses the candidate's time and the campaign's remaining money in the most effective way. While the outcome of the election has been pretty much decided in most states, the electoral votes from the states of Florida, Georgia, California, Texas, Illinois, New York, Virginia, and Michigan are still up for grabs by either candidate. Roger knows they must win as many of these states as possible if his friend is to become the next president.

Several weeks ago, when it became evident that the race was going to be close, Roger hired a statistical consultant to estimate the percentage of votes the campaign will receive in each of the states based on amount of money the campaign spends and the number of times the candidate visits each state during the final two weeks before the election. The results of the consultant's analysis provided the following function:

$$\text{Percentage of votes in state } k = 1 - \text{EXP}(-aV_k - bD_k)$$

where:

V_k = the number of times the candidate visits state k in the last two weeks of the campaign, and

D_k = the dollars (in \$1,000,000s) the campaign spends on advertising in state k in the last two weeks of the campaign.

The following table summarizes the consultant's estimates of the parameters a and b for each state, along with the number of electoral votes at stake in each state:

State	a	b	Electoral Votes
Florida	0.085	0.31	25
Georgia	0.117	0.27	13
California	0.098	0.21	54
Texas	0.125	0.28	32
Illinois	0.128	0.26	22
New York	0.105	0.22	33
Virginia	0.134	0.24	13
Michigan	0.095	0.38	18

Roger believes the candidate can make 21 campaign stops in the next two weeks, and there is \$11 million left in the campaign budget available for advertising. He wants to spend at least \$500,000 in each of these states in the next two weeks. He also wants the candidate to make at least one, but no more than five, campaign stops in each of these states. Within these constraints, Roger would like to allocate these resources to maximize the number of electoral votes his candidate can receive. Assume a candidate needs 51% of the vote to win in each state.

a. Formulate an NLP model for this problem.
b. Implement your model in a spreadsheet and solve it.
c. How much money should Roger spend in each state? How many campaign stops should the candidate make in each state? What is the expected number of electoral votes generated by this solution?

CASE 8.2   WHERE TO PUT THE MONEY

Contributed by Jack Yurkiewicz, Lubin School of Business, Pace University, New York

Barbara Roberts has $30,000 to invest for one year. She received this money as a small inheritance from a distant relative. Barbara wants to buy a notebook computer next year when she enters graduate school. Notebook computer prices are falling steadily, and by next September, one year from now, Barbara believes she can buy a light-weight notebook computer with a passive-matrix color screen for about $900. But Barbara does not want to use any of her $30,000 inheritance to buy the computer because she already earmarked that money to help pay the tuition for the first term. She wants to invest the money wisely so she will have enough money from the interest earned to buy the computer.

Barbara's Uncle Louis, an investment manager, knows of three potential stocks in which she should invest. Barbara agrees with her uncle that the stock market is currently the best place to invest her inheritance. The banks are paying little in dividends and although the stock market is riskier, the returns are greater. The three stocks in Louis's portfolio are Amalgamated Industries, Babbage Computers, and Consolidated Foods. Louis gives Barbara the following chart, which shows these stocks and their returns, in percentages, over the past 10 years.

Year	Amalgamated Industries	Babbage Computers	Consolidated Foods
1985	-3.3	5.92	-2.4
1986	-4.7	-3.8	28.1
1987	11.9	-7	-7.2
1988	9.7	6.6	-2.3
1989	8.6	-4.2	20.4
1990	9.4	11.2	17.4
1991	5.3	3.2	-11.8
1992	-4.9	16.1	-6.6
1993	8.5	10.8	-13.4
1994	-8.3	-8.3	10.9

Barbara wants to maximize the expected return in dollars for the next year. She also wants to minimize her risk. She and Louis agree that the standard measure of risk, the variance of the return of the portfolio, can be used in this situation. That is, Barbara wants to minimize the total variance (which also involves the covariance between the various pairs of stock) of the portfolio. Also, based on her uncle's recommendation, Barbara will diversify her potential holdings, by investing at least $500, but no more than $20,000, in any one stock.

Barbara wants to know if she will have enough money to buy a notebook computer next year. Formulate and solve a nonlinear programming model to determine how much money Barbara should invest in each stock in order to meet her financial goals.

REFERENCES

Bazaraa, M. and C. Shetty. *Nonlinear Programming: Theory and Algorithms.* New York: Wiley, 1993.
DeWitt, et al. "OMEGA: An Improved Gasoline Blending System for Texaco." *Interfaces*, vol. 19, no. 1, 1985.

Kolesar, P. and E. Blum. "Square Roots Law for Fire Engine Response Distances." *Management Science*, vol. 19, 1973.

Lasdon, L. and S. Smith. "Solving Sparse Nonlinear Programs Using GRG." *ORSA Journal on Computing*, vol. 4, no. 1, 1992.

Markowitz, H. *Portfolio Selection, Efficient Diversification of Investments*. New York: Wiley, 1959.

Taylor, B., L. Moore, and E. Clayton. "R&D Project Selection and Manpower Allocation with Integer Nonlinear Programming." *Management Science*, vol. 28, no. 10, 1982.

Vollman, T., W. Berry, and C. Whybark. *Manufacturing Planning and Control Systems*. Homewood, IL: Irwin, 1987.

CHAPTER 9

Regression Analysis

Regression analysis is a modeling technique for analyzing the relationship between a *continuous* (real-valued) dependent variable Y and one or more independent variables X_1, X_2, ..., X_k. The goal in regression analysis is to identify a function that describes, as closely as possible, the relationship between these variables so that we can predict what value the dependent variable will assume given specific values for the independent variables. This chapter shows how to estimate these functions and how to use them to make predictions in a business environment.

9.1 AN EXAMPLE

As a simple example of how regression analysis might be used, consider the relationship between sales for a company and the amount of money it spends on advertising. Few would question that the level of sales for a company will depend on or be influenced by advertising. Thus, we could view sales as the dependent variable Y and advertising as the independent variable X_1. Although some relationship exists between sales and advertising, we might not know the exact functional form of this relationship. Indeed, there probably is not an exact functional relationship between these variables.

We expect that sales for a company depend to some degree on the amount of money the company spends on advertising. But many other factors might also affect a company's sales, such as general economic conditions, the level of competition in the marketplace, product quality, and so on. Nevertheless, we might be interested in studying the relationship between the dependent variable sales (Y) and the independent variable advertising (X_1) and predicting the average level of sales expected for a given level of advertising. Regression analysis provides the tool for making such predictions.

In order to identify a function that describes the relationship between advertising and sales for a company, we first need to collect sample data to analyze. Suppose that we obtain the data shown in Figure 9.1 (and in the file FIG9-1.xls on your data disk) for a company on the level of sales observed for various levels of advertising expenditures in 10 different test markets around the country. We will assume that the different test markets are similar in terms of size and other demographic and economic characteristics. The main difference in each market is the level of advertising expenditure.

The data from Figure 9.1 are displayed graphically in Figure 9.2. This graph suggests a strong linear relationship between advertising expenditures and sales. Note that as advertising expenditures increase, sales increase proportionately. However, the relationship between advertising and sales is not perfect. For example, advertising expenditures of $70,000 were used in three different test markets and resulted in three different levels of sales. Thus, the level of sales that occurs for a given level of advertising is subject to random fluctuation.

Creating a Scatter Plot

To create a scatter plot like the one shown in Figure 9.2:
1. Select cells B4 through C13 shown in Figure 9.1.
2. Click the Insert menu.
3. Click Chart.
4. Click As New Sheet.

Excel's ChartWizard then prompts you to make a number of selections concerning the type of chart you want and how it should be labeled and formatted. After Excel creates a basic chart, you can customize it in many ways. Double-click a chart element to display a dialog box with options for modifying the appearance of the element.

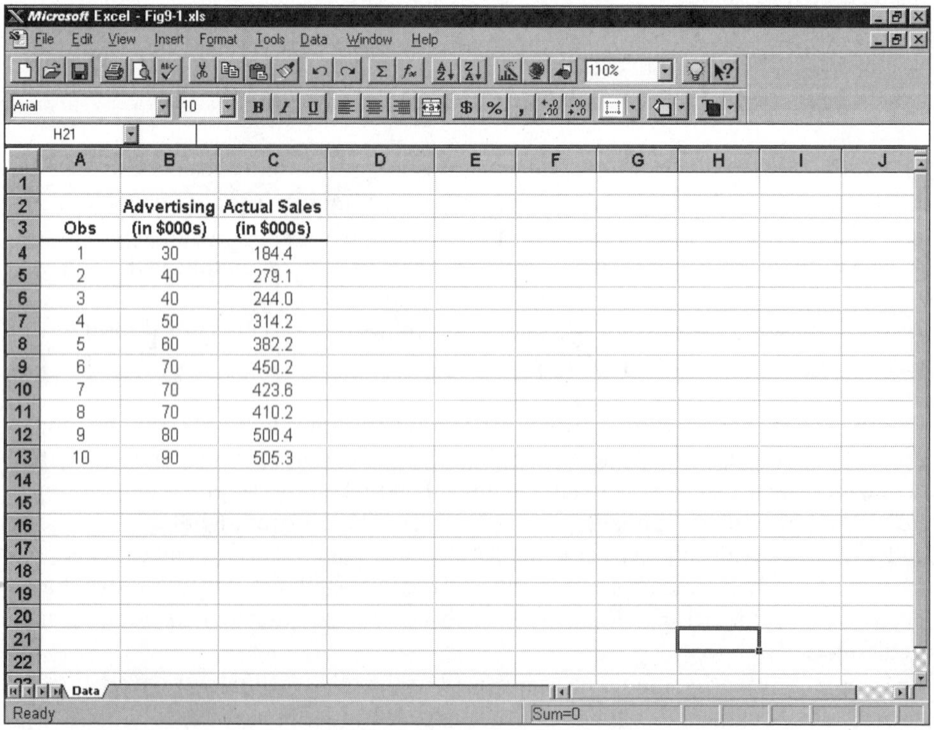

Figure 9.1
Sample data for advertising expenditures and observed sales.

Obs	Advertising (in $000s)	Actual Sales (in $000s)
1	30	184.4
2	40	279.1
3	40	244.0
4	50	314.2
5	60	382.2
6	70	450.2
7	70	423.6
8	70	410.2
9	80	500.4
10	90	505.3

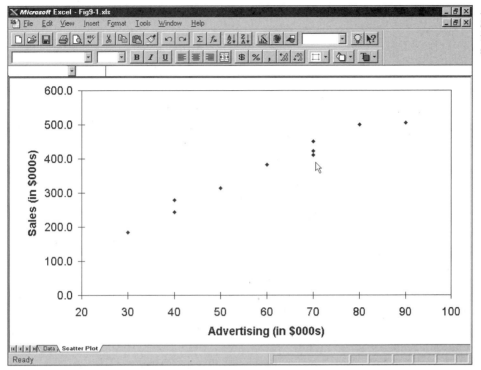

Figure 9.2
Scatter diagram
for sales and
advertising data.

The random fluctuation, or scattering, of the points in Figure 9.2 suggests that some of the variation in sales is not accounted for by advertising expenditures. Because of the scattering of points, this type of graph is called a **scatter diagram** or **scatter plot**. So although there is not a perfect *functional* relationship between sales and advertising (where each level of advertising yields one unique level of sales), there does seem to be a *statistical* relationship between these variables (where each level of sales is associated with a range or distribution of possible sales values).

9.2 REGRESSION MODELS

We will formalize the somewhat imprecise nature of a statistical relationship by adding an *error term* to what is otherwise a functional relationship. That is, in regression analysis we consider models of the form:

$$Y = f(X_1, X_2, ..., X_k) + \varepsilon \qquad \textbf{9.1}$$

where ε represents a random disturbance, or error, term. Equation 9.1 is a **regression model**. The number of independent variables in a regression model differs from one application to another. Similarly, the form of $f(\cdot)$ varies from simple linear functions to more complex polynomial and nonlinear forms. In any case, the model in equation 9.1 conveys the two essential elements of a statistical relationship:

1. A tendency for the dependent variable Y to vary with the independent variable(s) in a systematic way, as expressed by $f(X_1, X_2, ..., X_k)$ in equation 9.1.
2. An element of *unsystematic* or random variation in the dependent variable, as expressed by ε in equation 9.1.

The regression model in equation 9.1 indicates that for any values assumed by the independent variables X_1, ..., X_k there is a probability distribution that describes the possible values that can be assumed by the dependent variable Y. This is portrayed graphically in Figure 9.3 for the case of a single independent variable. The curve drawn in Figure 9.3 represents the regression line (or regression function). It denotes the *systematic* variation between the dependent and independent variables (represented by $f(X_1, X_2, ..., X_k)$ in equation 9.1). The probability distributions in Figure 9.3 denote the *unsystematic* variation in the dependent variable Y at different levels of the independent variable. This represents random variation in the dependent variable (represented by ε in equation 9.1) that cannot be accounted for by the independent variable.

Notice that the regression function in Figure 9.3 passes through the mean, or average, value for each probability distribution. Therefore, the regression function indicates what value, on average, the dependent variable is expected to assume at various levels of the independent variable. If we want to predict what value the dependent variable Y would assume at some level of the independent variable, the best estimate we could make is given by the regression function. That is, our best estimate of the value Y will assume at a certain level of the independent variable X_1 is the mean (or average) of the distribution of values for Y at that level of X_1.

The actual value assumed by the dependent variable is likely to be somewhat different from our estimate because there is some random, unsystematic variation in the dependent variable that cannot be accounted for by our regression function. If we could repeatedly sample and observe actual values of Y at a given level of X_1, sometimes the actual value of Y would be higher than our estimated (mean) value and sometimes it would be lower. So the difference between the actual value of Y and our

Figure 9.3
Diagram of the distribution of Y values at various levels of X.

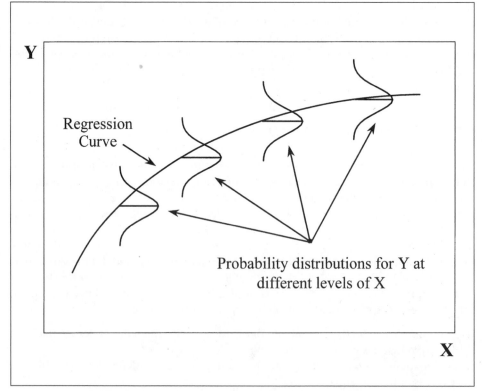

Y

Regression
Curve

Probability distributions for Y at
different levels of X

X

predicted value of Y would, on average, tend toward 0. For this reason, we can assume that the error term ε in equation 9.1 has an average, or expected, value of 0 if the probability distributions for the dependent variable Y at the various levels of the independent variable are normally distributed (bell-shaped) as shown in Figure 9.3.

9.3 SIMPLE LINEAR REGRESSION ANALYSIS

As mentioned earlier, the function $f(\cdot)$ in equation 9.1 can assume many forms. However, the scatter plot in Figure 9.2 suggests that a strong linear relationship exists between the independent variable in our example (advertising expenditures) and the dependent variable (sales). That is, we could draw a straight line through the data in Figure 9.2 that would fit the data fairly well. So the formula of a straight line might account for the systematic variation between advertising and sales. Therefore, the following simple linear regression model might be an appropriate choice for describing the relationship between advertising and sales:

$$Y_i = \beta_0 + \beta_1 X_{1i} + \varepsilon_i \qquad 9.2$$

In equation 9.2, Y_i denotes the *actual* sales value for the ith observation, X_{1i} denotes the advertising expenditures associated with Y_i, and ε_i is an error term indicating that when X_{1i} dollars are spent on advertising, sales might not always equal $\beta_0 + \beta_1 X_{1i}$. The parameter β_0 represents a constant value (sometimes referred to as the Y-intercept because it represents the point where the line goes through the Y-axis) and β_1 represents the slope of the line (that is, the amount by which the line rises or falls per unit increase in X_1). Assuming that a straight line accounts for the systematic variation between Y and X_1, the error terms ε_i represent the amounts by which the actual levels of sales are scattered around the regression line. Again, if the errors are scattered randomly around the regression line, they should average out to 0 or have an expected value of 0.

The model in equation 9.2 is a simple model because it contains only one independent variable. It is linear because none of the parameters (β_0 and β_1) appear as an exponent in the model or are multiplied or divided by one another.

Conceptually, it is important to understand that we are assuming that a large population of Y values occurs at each level of X_1. The parameters β_0 and β_1 represent, respectively, the intercept and slope of the *true* regression line relating these populations. For this reason, β_0 and β_1 are sometimes referred to as **population parameters**. We usually never know the exact numeric values for the population parameters in a given regression problem (we know that these values exist, but we don't know what they are). In order to determine the numeric values of the population parameters, we would have to look at the entire population of Y at each level of X_1—usually an impossible task. However, by taking a sample of Y values at selected levels of X_1 we can estimate the values of the population parameters. We will identify the estimated values of β_0 and β_1 as b_0 and b_1, respectively. The remaining problem is to determine the best values of b_0 and b_1 from our sample data.

9.4 DEFINING "BEST FIT"

An infinite number of values could be assigned to b_0 and b_1. So searching for the exact values for b_0 and b_1 to produce the line that best fits our sample data might seem like searching for a needle in a haystack—and it is certainly not something we want to do manually. To have the computer estimate the values for b_0 and b_1 that produce the line that best fits our data, we must give it some guidance and define what we mean by the best fit.

We will use the symbol $\hat{Y}_i$ to denote our estimated, or fitted, value of Y_i, which is defined as:

$$\hat{Y}_i = b_0 + b_1 X_{1i} \qquad\qquad 9.3$$

We want to the find values for b_0 and b_1 that make all the *estimated* sales values ($\hat{Y}_i$) as close as possible to the *actual* sales values (Y_i). For example, the data in Figure 9.1 indicate that we spent \$30,000 on advertising ($X_{1i} = 30$) and observed sales of \$184,400 ($Y_1 = 184.4$). So in equation 9.3, if we let $X_1 = 30$ we want $\hat{Y}$ to assume a value that is as close as possible to 184.4. Similarly, in the three instances in Figure 9.1 where \$70,000 was spent on advertising ($X_{16} = X_{17} = X_{18} = 70$), we observed sales of \$450,200, \$423,600, and \$410,200 ($Y_6 = 450.2$, $Y_7 = 423.6$, $Y_8 = 410.2$). So in equation 9.3, if we let $X_1 = 70$, we want $\hat{Y}$ to assume a value that is as close as possible to 450.2, 423.6, and 410.2.

If we could find values for b_0 and b_1 so that all the estimated sales values were exactly the same as all the actual sales values ($\hat{Y}_i = Y_i$ for all observations i), we would have the equation of the straight line that passes through each data point—in other words, the line would fit our data perfectly. This is impossible for the data in Figure 9.2 because a straight line could not be drawn to pass through each data point in the graph. In most regression problems it is impossible to find a function that fits the data perfectly because most data sets contain some amount of unsystematic variation.

Although we are unlikely to find values for b_0 and b_1 that will allow us to fit our data perfectly, we will try to find values that make the differences between the estimated values for the dependent variable and the actual values for the dependent variable ($Y_i - \hat{Y}_i$) as small as possible. We refer to the difference $Y_i - \hat{Y}_i$ as the **estimation error** for observation i because it measures how far away the estimated value $\hat{Y}_i$ is from the actual value Y_i. The estimation errors in a regression problem are also referred to as **residuals**.

Although different criteria can be used to determine the best values for b_0 and b_1, the most widely used method determines the values that minimize the sum of squared estimation errors—or **error sum of squares** (ESS) for short. That is, we will attempt to find values for b_0 and b_1 that minimize:

$$\text{ESS} = \sum_{i=1}^{n} (Y_i - \hat{Y}_i)^2 = \sum_{i=1}^{n} [Y_i - (b_0 + b_1 X_{1i})]^2 \qquad\qquad 9.4$$

Several observations should be made concerning ESS. Because each estimation error is squared, the value of ESS will always be nonnegative and, therefore, the smallest value ESS can assume is 0. The only way for ESS to equal 0 is for all the individual estimation errors to be 0 ($Y_i - \hat{Y}_i = 0$ for all observations), in which case the estimated regression line would fit our data perfectly. Thus, minimizing ESS seems to be a good objective to use in searching for the best values of b_0 and b_1. Because regression analysis finds the values of the parameter estimates that minimize the sum of squared estimation errors, it is sometimes referred to as the **method of least squares**.

9.5   *SOLVING THE PROBLEM USING SOLVER*

We can calculate the optimal parameter estimates for a linear regression model in a number of ways. As in earlier chapters, we can use Solver to find the values for b_0 and b_1 that minimize the ESS quantity in equation 9.4.

The problem of finding the optimal values for b_0 and b_1 in equation 9.4 is an unconstrained nonlinear optimization problem. Consider the spreadsheet in Figure 9.4.

In Figure 9.4, cells C15 and C16 represent the values for b_0 and b_1, respectively. These cells are labeled Intercept and Slope because b_0 represents the intercept in equation 9.3 and b_1 represents the slope. Values of 70 and 5 were entered for these cells as rough guesses of their optimal values.

To use Solver to calculate the optimal values of b_0 and b_1, we need to implement a formula in the spreadsheet that corresponds to the ESS calculation in equation 9.4. This formula represents the objective function to be minimized. To calculate the ESS, we first need to calculate the sales values estimated by the regression function in equation 9.3 for each observation in our sample. These estimated sales values ($\hat{Y}_i$) were created in column D as:

Formula for cell D4   =$C$15+$C$16*B4
(Copy to D5 through D13.)

The estimation errors ($Y_i - \hat{Y}_i$) were calculated in column E as:

Formula for cell E4:   =C4–D4
(Copy to E5 through E13.)

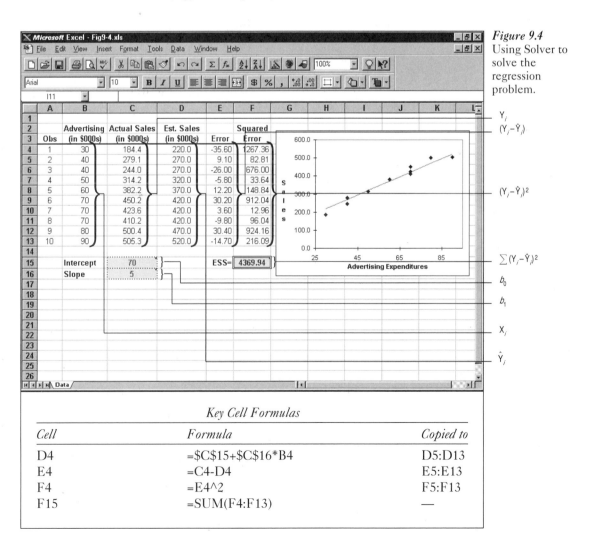

Figure 9.4
Using Solver to solve the regression problem.

			Key Cell Formulas		
Cell		*Formula*			*Copied to*
D4		=$C$15+$C$16*B4			D5:D13
E4		=C4-D4			E5:E13
F4		=E4^2			F5:F13
F15		=SUM(F4:F13)			—

The squared estimation errors $((Y_i - \hat{Y}_i)^2)$ were calculated in column F as:

Formula for cell F4:   =E4^2
(Copy to F5 through F13.)

Finally, the sum of the squared estimation errors (ESS) was calculated in cell F15 as:

Formula for cell F15:   =SUM(F4:F13)

Note that the formula in cell F15 corresponds exactly to equation 9.4.

The graph in Figure 9.4 plots the line connecting the estimated sales values against the actual sales values. The intercept and slope of this line are determined by the values in C15 and C16. Although this line seems to fit our data fairly well, we do not know if this is the line that minimizes the ESS value. However, we can use the Solver parameters and options shown in Figure 9.5 to determine the values for C15 and C16 that minimize the ESS value in F15.

Figure 9.6 shows the optimal solution to this problem. In this spreadsheet the intercept and slope of the line that best fits our data are $b_0 = 36.34235$ and $b_1 = 5.550293$, respectively. The ESS value of 3,336.244 associated with these optimal parameter estimates is better (or smaller) than the ESS value for the parameter estimates shown in Figure 9.4. No other values for b_0 and b_1 would result in an ESS value smaller than the one shown in Figure 9.6. Thus, the equation of the straight line that best fits our data according to the least squares criterion is represented by:

$$\hat{Y}_i = 36.34235 + 5.550293X_{1_i} \qquad\qquad 9.5$$

Figure 9.5
Solver parameters and options for the regression problem.

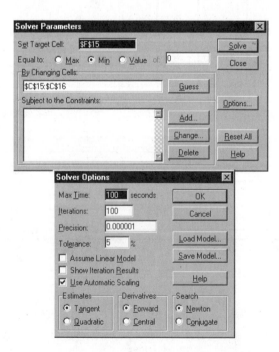

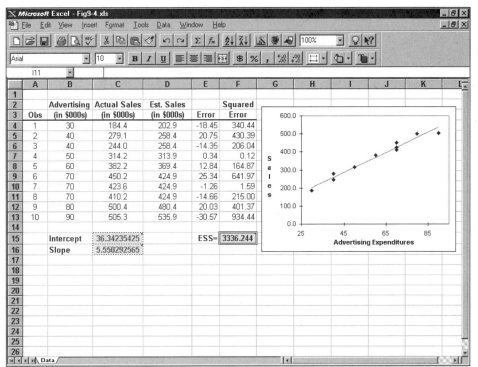

Figure 9.6
Optimal solution to the regression problem.

9.6 SOLVING THE PROBLEM USING THE REGRESSION TOOL

In addition to Solver, Excel provides another tool for solving regression problems that is easier to use and provides more information about a regression problem. We'll demonstrate the use of this regression tool by referring back to the original data for the current problem, shown in Figure 9.1. Before you can use the regression tool in Excel, you need to make sure that the Analysis ToolPak add-in is available. You can do this by completing the following steps:

1. Click the Tools menu.
2. Click Add-Ins.
3. Click Analysis ToolPak. (If Analysis ToolPak is not listed among your available add-ins, exit Excel, double-click the Setup icon in the MSOffice folder, click Add/Remove, select Excel, click Change Option, select Add-Ins, click Change Option, select Analysis ToolPak, and click OK. Then restart Excel and repeat the above instructions.)

After ensuring that the Analysis ToolPak is available, you can access the regression tool by completing the following steps:

1. Click the Tools menu.
2. Click Data Analysis.
3. Click Regression.

After you choose the Regression command, the Regression dialog box appears, as shown in Figure 9.7. This dialog box presents many options and selections; at this point we will focus on only three options: the Y-Range, the X-Range, and the Output-

Figure 9.7
Regression
dialog box.

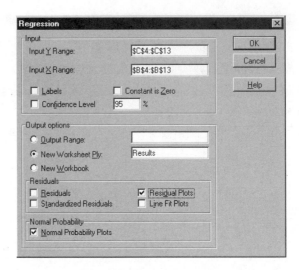

Range. The Y-Range corresponds to the range in the spreadsheet containing the sample observations for the *dependent* variable (C4 through C13 for the example in Figure 9.1). The X-Range corresponds to the range in the spreadsheet containing the sample observations for the *independent* variable (B4 through B13 for the current example). We also need to specify the output range where we want the regression results to be reported. In Figure 9.7, we selected the New Worksheet Ply option to indicate that we want the regression results placed on a new sheet named "Results." With the dialog box selections complete, we can click the OK button and Excel will calculate the least squares values for b_0 and b_1 (along with other summary statistics).

Figure 9.8 shows the Results sheet for our example. For now, we will focus on only a few values in Figure 9.8. Note that the value labeled "Intercept" in cell B17 represents the optimal value for b_0 ($b_0 = 36.342$). The value representing the coefficient for "X Variable 1" in cell B18 represents the optimal value for b_1 ($b_1 = 5.550$). Thus, the estimated regression function is represented by:

$$\hat{Y}_i = b_0 + b_1 X_{1_i} = 36.342 + 5.550 X_{1_i} \qquad 9.6$$

Equation 9.6 is essentially the same result we obtained earlier using Solver (see equation 9.5). Thus, we can calculate the parameter estimates for a regression function using either Solver or the regression tool shown in Figure 9.7. The advantage of the regression tool is that it does not require us to set up any special formulas or cells in the spreadsheet, and it produces additional statistical results about the problem under study.

9.7   EVALUATING THE FIT

Our goal in the example problem is to identify the equation of a straight line that fits our data well. Having calculated the estimated regression line (using either Solver or the regression tool), we might be interested in determining how well the line fits our data. Using equation 9.6 we can compute the estimated or expected level of sales ($\hat{Y}_i$) for each observation in our sample. The $\hat{Y}_i$ values could be calculated in column D of Figure 9.9 as follows:

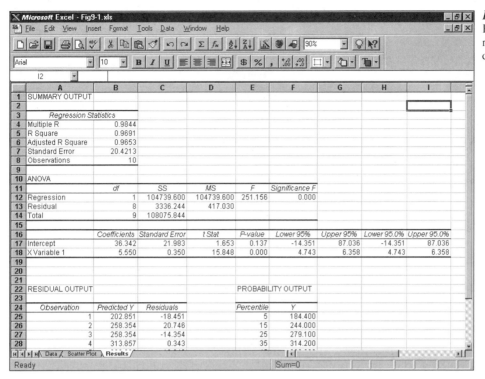

Figure 9.8
Results for the regression calculations.

Formula for cell D4:   =36.342+5.550*B4
(Copy to D5 through D13.)

However, we can also use the TREND( ) function in Excel to compute the $\hat{Y}_i$ values in column D as follows:

Alternate formula for cell D4:   =TREND($C$4:$C$13,$B$4:$B$13,B4)
(Copy to D5 through D13.)

This TREND( ) function computes the least squares linear regression line using a Y-range of C4 through C13 and an X-range of B4 through B13. It then uses this regression function to compute the estimated value of Y using the value of X given in cell B4. Thus, using the TREND( ) function we don't have to worry about typing the wrong values for the estimated intercept or slope. Notice that the resulting estimated sales values shown in Column D in Figure 9.9 match the predicted Y values shown toward the bottom on column B in Figure 9.8.

Figure 9.10 shows a graph of the estimated regression function along with the actual sales data. This function represents the expected amount of sales that would occur for each value of the independent variable (that is, each value in column D of Figure 9.9 falls on this line). To insert this estimated trend line on the existing scatter plot:

1. Click on any of the data points in the scatter plot to select the series of data.
2. Click the Insert menu.
3. Click Trendline.
4. On the Type card, click Linear.
5. On the Options card, select Display Equation on Chart and Display R-squared Value on Chart.
6. Click OK.

Figure 9.9
Estimated sales
values at each
level of
advertising.

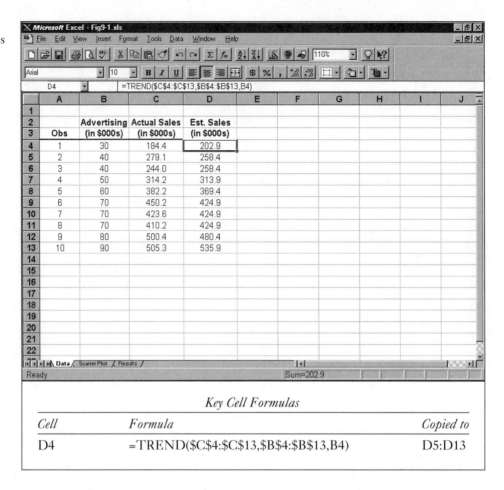

Key Cell Formulas

Cell	Formula	Copied to
D4	=TREND($C$4:$C$13,$B$4:$B$13,B4)	D5:D13

A Note on the TREND( ) Function

The TREND( ) function can be used to calculate the estimated values for linear regression models. The format of the TREND( ) function is as follows:

TREND(Y-range, X-range, X-value for prediction)

where Y-range is the range in the spreadsheet containing the dependent Y variable, X-range is the range in the spreadsheet containing the independent X variable(s), and X-value for prediction is a cell (or cells) containing the values for the independent X variable(s) for which we want an estimated value of Y. The TREND( ) function has an advantage over the regression tool in that it is dynamically updated whenever any inputs to the function change. However, it does not provide the statistical information provided by the regression tool. It is best to use these two different approaches to doing regression in conjunction with one another.

From this graph we see that the regression function seems to fit the data reasonably well in this example. In particular, it seems that the actual sales values fluctuate around this line in a fairly unsystematic, or random, pattern. Thus, it appears that we

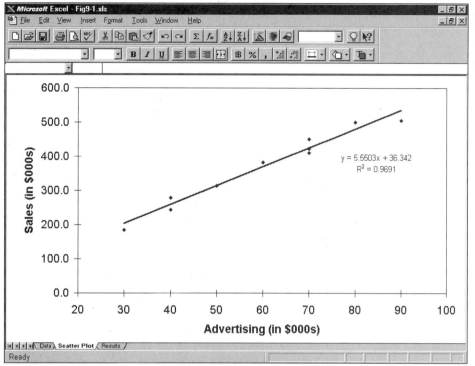

Figure 9.10
Graph of the regression line through the actual sales data.

have achieved our goal of identifying a function that accounts for most, if not all, of the systematic variation between the dependent and independent variables.

9.8 THE R² STATISTIC

In Figures 9.8 and 9.10, the value labeled "R Square" or "R²" provides a goodness-of-fit measure. This value represents the **R² statistic** (also referred to as the **coefficient of determination**). This statistic ranges in value from 0 to 1 ($0 \leq R^2 \leq 1$) and indicates the proportion of the total variation in the dependent variable Y around its mean (average) that is accounted for by the independent variable(s) in the estimated regression function.

The total variation in the dependent variable Y around its mean is described by a measure known as the **total sum of squares** (TSS), which is defined as:

$$\text{TSS} = \sum_{i=1}^{n} (Y_i - \overline{Y})^2 \qquad 9.7$$

The TSS equals the sum of the squared differences between each observation Y_i in the sample and the average value of Y, denoted in equation 9.7 by $\overline{Y}$. The difference between each observed value of Y_i and the average value $\overline{Y}$ can be decomposed into two parts as:

$$Y_i - \overline{Y}_i = (Y_i - \hat{Y}_i) + (\hat{Y}_i - \overline{Y}) \qquad 9.8$$

Figure 9.11 illustrates this decomposition for a hypothetical data point. The value $Y_i - \hat{Y}_i$ in equation 9.8 represents the estimation error, or the amount of the total deviation between Y_i and $\overline{Y}$ that is not accounted for by the regression function. The value

Figure 9.11
Decomposition of
the total deviation
into error and
regression
components.

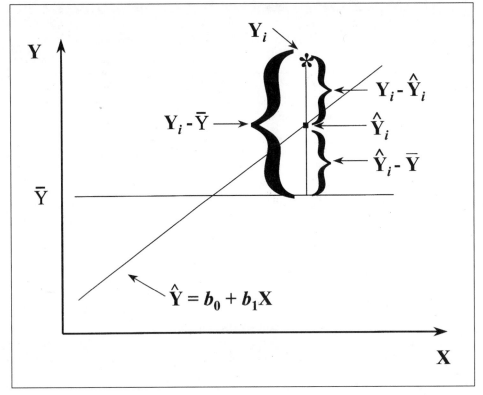

$\hat{Y}_i - \overline{Y}$ in equation 9.8 represents the amount of the total deviation in Y_i from $\overline{Y}$ that is accounted for by the regression function.

The decomposition of the individual deviation in equation 9.8 also applies to the TSS in equation 9.7. That is, the *total sum of squares* (TSS) can be decomposed into the following two parts:

$$\sum_{i=1}^{n} (Y_i - \overline{Y})^2 = \sum_{i=1}^{n} (Y_i - \hat{Y}_i)^2 + \sum_{i=1}^{n} (\hat{Y}_i - \overline{Y})^2 \qquad \textbf{9.9}$$

$$\text{TSS} \quad = \quad \text{ESS} \quad + \quad \text{RSS}$$

ESS is the quantity that is minimized in least squares regression. ESS represents the amount of variation in Y around its mean that the regression function cannot account for, or the amount of variation in the dependent variable that is unexplained by the regression function. Therefore, the **regression sum of squares** (RSS) represents the amount of variation in Y around its mean that the regression function can account for, or the amount of variation in the dependent variable that is explained by the regression function. In Figure 9.8, cells C12, C13, and C14 contain the values for RSS, ESS, and TSS, respectively.

Now consider the following definitions of the R^2 statistic:

$$R^2 = \frac{\text{RSS}}{\text{TSS}} = 1 - \frac{\text{ESS}}{\text{TSS}} \qquad \textbf{9.10}$$

From the previous definition of TSS in equation 9.9, we can see that if ESS = 0 (which can occur only if the regression function fits the data perfectly), then

TSS = RSS and, therefore, $R^2 = 1$. On the other hand, if RSS = 0 (which means that the regression function was unable to explain any of the variation in the behavior of the dependent variable Y), then TSS = ESS and $R^2 = 0$. So, the closer the R^2 statistic is to the value 1, the better the estimated regression function fits the data.

From cell B5 in Figure 9.8 we observe that the value of the R^2 statistic is approximately 0.969. This indicates that approximately 96.9% of the total variation in our dependent variable around its mean has been accounted for by the independent variable in our estimated regression function. Because this value is fairly close to the maximum possible R^2 value (1), this statistic indicates that the regression function we have estimated fits our data well. This is confirmed by the graph in Figure 9.10.

The **multiple R** statistic shown in the regression output in Figure 9.8 represents the strength of the linear relationship between actual and estimated values for the dependent variable. As with the R^2 statistic, the multiple R statistic varies between 0 and 1 with values near 1 indicating a good fit. When a regression model includes only one independent variable, the multiple R statistic is equivalent to the square root of the R^2 statistic. We'll focus on the R^2 statistic because its interpretation is more apparent than that of the multiple R statistic.

9.9   MAKING PREDICTIONS

Using the estimated regression in equation 9.6, we can make predictions about the level of sales expected for different levels of advertising expenditures. For example, suppose the company wants to estimate the level of sales that would occur if $65,000 were spent on advertising in a given market. Assuming the market in question is similar to those used in estimating the regression function, the expected sales level is estimated as:

$$\text{Estimated Sales} = b_0 + b_1 \times 65 = 36.342 + 5.550 \times 65 = 397.092$$
(in $000s)

So if the company spends $65,000 on advertising (in a market similar to those used to estimate the regression function), we would expect to observe sales of approximately $397,092. The *actual* level of sales is likely to differ somewhat from this value due to other random factors influencing sales.

9.9.1   The Standard Error

A measure of the accuracy of the prediction obtained from a regression model is given by the standard deviation of the estimation errors—also known as the standard error, S_e. If we let n denote the number of observations in the data set, and k denote the number of independent variables in the regression model, the formula for the standard error is represented by:

$$S_e = \sqrt{\frac{\sum_{i=1}^{n}(Y_i - \hat{Y}_i)^2}{n - k - 1}}$$

9.11

The **standard error** measures the amount of scatter, or variation, in the actual data around the fitted regression function. Cell B7 in Figure 9.8 indicates that the standard error for our example problem is $S_e = 20.421$.

The standard error is useful in evaluating the level of uncertainty in predictions we make with a regression model. As a *very* rough rule-of-thumb, there is approximately a 68% chance of the actual level of sales falling within ±1 standard error of the predicted value $\hat{Y}_i$. Alternatively, the chance of the actual level of sales falling within ±2 standard errors of the predicted value $\hat{Y}_i$ is approximately 95%. In our example, if the company spends $65,000 on advertising, we could be roughly 95% confident that the actual level of sales observed would fall somewhere in the range from $356,250 to $437,934 ($\hat{Y}_i \pm 2S_e$).

9.9.2   Prediction Intervals for New Values of Y

To calculate a more accurate confidence interval for a prediction, or **prediction interval**, of a new value of Y when $X_1 = X_{1_h}$, we first calculate the estimated value $\hat{Y}_h$ as:

$$\hat{Y}_h = b_0 + b_1 X_{1_h} \qquad\qquad 9.12$$

A $(1 - \alpha)\%$ prediction interval for a new value of Y when $X_1 = X_{1_h}$ is represented by:

$$\hat{Y}_h \pm t_{(1-\alpha/2;\, n-2)} S_p \qquad\qquad 9.13$$

where $t_{(1-\alpha/2;\, n-2)}$ represents the $1 - \alpha/2$ percentile of a t-distribution with $n - 2$ degrees of freedom, and S_p represents the standard prediction error defined by:

$$S_p = S_e \sqrt{1 + \frac{1}{n} + \frac{(X_{1_h} - \overline{X})^2}{\sum\limits_{i=1}^{n} (X_{1_i} - \overline{X})^2}} \qquad\qquad 9.14$$

The rule-of-thumb presented earlier is a generalization of equation 9.13. Notice that S_p is always larger than S_e because the term under the square root symbol is always greater than 1. Also notice that the magnitude of the difference between S_p and S_e increases as the difference between X_{1_h} and $\overline{X}$ increases. Thus, the prediction intervals generated by the rule-of-thumb tend to underestimate the true amount of uncertainty involved in making predictions. This is illustrated in Figure 9.12.

As shown in Figure 9.12, for this example problem there is not a lot of difference between the prediction intervals created using the rule-of-thumb and the more accurate prediction interval given in equation 9.13. In a situation requiring a precise prediction interval, the various quantities needed to construct the prediction interval in equation 9.13 can be computed easily in Excel. Figure 9.13 provides an example of a 95% prediction interval for a new value of sales when $65,000 is spent on advertising.

To create this prediction interval, we first use the TREND( ) function to calculate the estimated sales level ($\hat{Y}_h$) when advertising equals $65,000 ($X_{1_h} = 65$). The value 65 is entered in cell B17 to represent X_{1_h} and the estimated sales level (Y_h) is calculated in cell D17 as:

Formula for cell D17:   =TREND($C$4:$C$13,$B$4:$B$13,B17)

The expected level of sales when $65,000 is spent on advertising is approximately $397,100. The standard error (S_e) shown in cell B19 is extracted from the Results sheet shown in Figure 9.8 as:

Formula for cell B19:   =Results!B7

The standard prediction error (S_p) is calculated in cell B20 as:

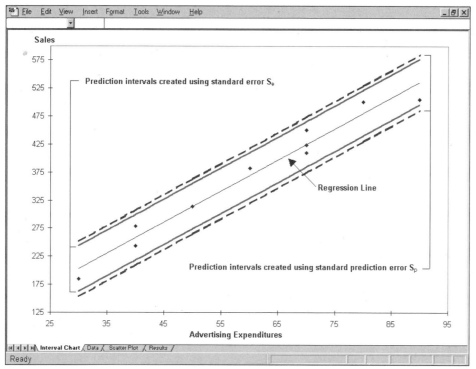

Figure 9.12
Comparison of prediction intervals obtained using the rule-of-thumb and the more accurate statistical calculation.

Formula for cell B20:   =B19*SQRT(1+1/10+
                                 (B17–AVERAGE(B4:B13))^2/(10*VARP(B4:B13)))

The value 10 appearing in the preceding formula corresponds to the sample size n in equation 9.14. The appropriate t-value for a 95% confidence (or prediction) interval is calculated in cell B21 as:

Formula for cell B21:   =TINV(1–0.95,8)

The first argument in the preceding formula corresponds to 1 minus the desired confidence level (or $\alpha = 0.05$). The second argument corresponds to $n - 2$ ($10 - 2 = 8$). Cells E17 and F17 calculate the lower and upper limits of the prediction interval as:

Formula for cell E17:   =D17–B21*B20

Formula for cell F17:   =D17+B21*B20

The results indicate that when $65,000 is spent on advertising we expect to observe sales of approximately $397,100, but realize that the actual sales level is likely to deviate somewhat from this value. However, we can be 95% confident that the actual sales value observed will fall somewhere in the range from $347,556 to $446,666. (Notice that this prediction interval is somewhat wider than the range from $356,250 to $437,934 generated earlier using the rule-of-thumb.)

9.9.3 *Confidence Intervals for Mean Values of Y*

At times you might want to construct a confidence interval for the average, or mean, value of Y when $X_1 = X_{1_h}$. This involves a slightly different procedure from

Figure 9.13
Example of
calculating a
prediction
interval.

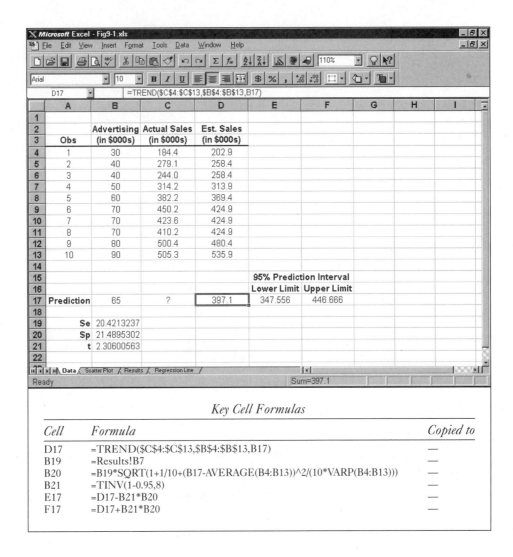

constructing a prediction interval for a new individual value of Y when $X_1 = X_{1_h}$. A $(1 - \alpha)\%$ confidence interval for the average value of Y when $X_1 = X_{1_h}$ is represented by:

$$\hat{Y}_h \pm t_{(1 - \alpha/2;\, n - 2)} S_a \qquad\qquad 9.15$$

where $\hat{Y}_h$ is defined by equation 9.12, $t_{(1 - \alpha/2;\, n - 2)}$ represents the $1 - \alpha/2$ percentile of a *t*-distribution with $n - 2$ degrees of freedom, and S_a is represented by:

$$S_a = S_e \sqrt{\frac{1}{n} + \frac{(X_{1_h} - \overline{X})^2}{\sum\limits_{i=1}^{n} (X_{1_i} - \overline{X})^2}} \qquad\qquad 9.16$$

Comparing the definition of S_a in equation 9.16 with that of S_p in equation 9.14 reveals that S_a will always be smaller than S_p. Therefore, the confidence interval for the average value of Y when $X_1 = X_{1_h}$ will be tighter (or cover a smaller range) than the prediction interval for a new value of Y when $X_1 = X_{1_h}$. This type of confidence interval can be implemented in a similar way to that described earlier for prediction intervals.

9.9.4 A Note About Extrapolation

Predictions made using an estimated regression function might have little or no validity for values of the independent variable that are substantially different from those represented in the sample. For example, the advertising expenditures represented in the sample in Figure 9.1 range from $30,000 to $90,000. Thus, we cannot assume that our model will give accurate estimates of sales levels at advertising expenditures significantly above or below this range of values, because the relationship between sales and advertising might be quite different outside this range.

9.10 STATISTICAL TESTS FOR POPULATION PARAMETERS

Recall that the parameter β_1 in equation 9.2 represents the slope of the *true* regression line (or the amount by which the dependent variable Y is expected to change given a unit change in X_1). If no linear relationship exists between the dependent and independent variables, the true value of β_1 for the model in equation 9.2 should be 0. As mentioned earlier, we cannot calculate or observe the true value of β_1 but instead must estimate its value using the sample statistic b_1. However, because the value of b_1 is based on a sample rather than on the entire population of possible values, its value is probably not exactly equal to the true (but unknown) value of β_1. Thus, we might want to determine how different the true value of β_1 is from its estimated value b_1. The regression results in Figure 9.8 provide a variety of information addressing this issue.

Cell B18 in Figure 9.8 indicates that the estimated value of β_1 is $b_1 = 5.550$. Cells F18 and G18 give the lower and upper limits of a 95% confidence interval for the true value of β_1. That is, we can be 95% confident that $4.74 \leq \beta_1 \leq 6.35$. This indicates that for every $1,000 increase in advertising we would expect to see an increase in sales of approximately $4,740 to $6,350. Notice that this confidence interval does not include the value 0. Thus we can be at least 95% confident that a linear relationship exists between advertising and sales ($\beta_1 \neq 0$). (If we want an interval other than a 95% confidence interval, we can use the Confidence Level option in the Regression dialog box, shown in Figure 9.7, to specify a different interval.)

The *t*-statistic and *P*-value listed in cells D18 and E18 in Figure 9.8 provide another way of testing whether $\beta_1 = 0$. According to statistical theory, if $\beta_1 = 0$ then the ratio of b_1 to its standard error should follow a *t*-distribution with $n - 2$ degrees of freedom. Thus, the *t*-statistic for testing if $\beta_1 = 0$ in cell D18 is:

$$t\text{-statistic in cell D18} = \frac{b_1}{\text{standard error of } b_1} = \frac{5.550}{0.35022} = 15.84789$$

The *P*-value in cell E18 indicates the probability of obtaining an outcome that is more extreme than the observed test statistic value if $\beta_1 = 0$. In this case, the *P*-value is 0, indicating that there is virtually no chance that we will obtain an outcome as large as the observed value for b_1 if the true value of β_1 is 0. Therefore, we conclude that the true value of β_1 is not equal to 0. This is the same conclusion implied earlier by the confidence interval for β_1.

The t-statistic, P-value, and confidence interval for the intercept β_0 are listed in Figure 9.8 in row 17, and would be interpreted in the same way as demonstrated for β_1. Notice that the confidence interval for β_0 straddles the value 0 and, therefore, we cannot be certain that the intercept is significantly different from 0. The P-value for β_0 indicates that we have a 13.689% chance of obtaining an outcome more extreme than the observed value of b_0 if the true value of β_0 is 0. Both of these results indicate a fair chance that $\beta_0 = 0$.

9.10.1   Analysis of Variance

The **analysis of variance** (ANOVA) results, shown in Figure 9.8, provide another way of testing whether or not $\beta_1 = 0$. The values in the MS column in the ANOVA table represent values known as the **mean squared regression** (MSR) and **mean squared error** (MSE), respectively. These values are computed by dividing the RSS and ESS values in C12 and C13 by the corresponding degrees of freedom values in cells B12 and B13.

If $\beta_1 = 0$, then the ratio of MSR to MSE follows an F-distribution. The statistic labeled "F" in cell E12 is:

$$\text{F-statistic in cell E12} = \frac{\text{MSR}}{\text{MSE}} = \frac{104739.600}{417.030} = 251.156$$

The value in F12 labeled "Significance F" is similar to the P-values described earlier, and indicates the probability of obtaining a value in excess of the observed value for the F-statistic if $\beta_1 = 0$. In this case, the significance of F is 0, indicating that there is virtually no chance that we would have obtained the observed value for b_1 if the true value of β_1 is 0. Therefore, we conclude that the true value of β_1 is not equal to 0. This is the same conclusion implied earlier by our previous analysis.

The F-statistic might seem a bit redundant, given that we can use the t-statistic to test whether or not $\beta_1 = 0$. However, the F-statistic serves a different purpose, which becomes apparent in multiple regression models with more than one independent variable. The F-statistic tests whether or not *all* of the β_i for *all* of the independent variables in a regression model are all simultaneously equal to 0. A simple linear regression model contains only one independent variable. In this case, the tests involving the F-statistic and the t-statistic are equivalent.

9.10.2   Assumptions for the Statistical Tests

The methods for constructing confidence intervals are based on important assumptions concerning the simple linear regression model presented in equation 9.2. Throughout this discussion, we assumed that the error terms ε_i are independent, normally distributed random variables with expected (or mean) values of 0 and constant variances. Thus, the statistical procedures for constructing intervals and performing t-tests apply only when these assumptions are true for a given set of data. As long as these assumptions are not seriously violated, the procedures described offer good approximations of the desired confidence intervals and t-tests. Various diagnostic checks can be performed on the residuals $(Y_i - \hat{Y}_i)$ to see whether or not our assumptions concerning the properties of the error terms are valid. These diagnostics are discussed in-depth in most statistics books, but are not repeated in this text. Excel also provides basic diagnostics that can be helpful in determining whether assumptions about the error terms are violated.

The Regression dialog box (shown in Figure 9.7) provides two options for producing graphs that highlight serious violations of the error term assumptions. These options are Residual Plots and Normal Probability Plots. Figure 9.14 shows the graphs produced by these two options for our example problem.

The first graph in Figure 9.14 results from the Residual Plots option. This graph plots the residuals (or estimation errors) versus each independent variable in the regression model. Our example problem involves one independent variable— therefore, we have one residual plot. If the assumptions underlying the regression model are met, the residuals should fall within a horizontal band centered around 0 and should display no systematic tendency to be positive or negative. The residual plot in Figure 9.14 indicates that the residuals for our example problem fall randomly within a range from –30 to +30. Thus, no serious problems are indicated by this graph.

The second graph in Figure 9.14 results from the Normal Probability Plot option. If the error terms in equation 9.2 are normally distributed random variables, the dependent variable in equation 9.2 is a normally distributed random variable prior to sampling. Thus, one way to evaluate whether we can assume that the error terms are normally distributed is to determine if we can assume that the dependent variable is normally distributed. The normal probability plot provides an easy way to evaluate whether the sample values on the dependent variable are consistent with the normality assumption. A plot that is approximately linear (such as the one in Figure 9.14) supports the assumption of normality.

If the residual plot shows a systematic tendency for the residuals to be positive or negative, this indicates that the function chosen to model the systematic variation

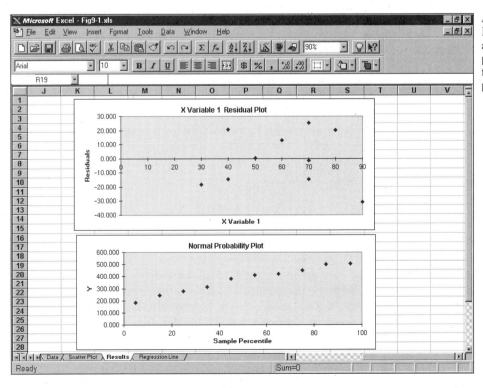

Figure 9.14
Residual plot and normal probability plot for the example problem.

Figure 9.15
Residual plots
indicating that
the fitted
regression model
is not adequate.

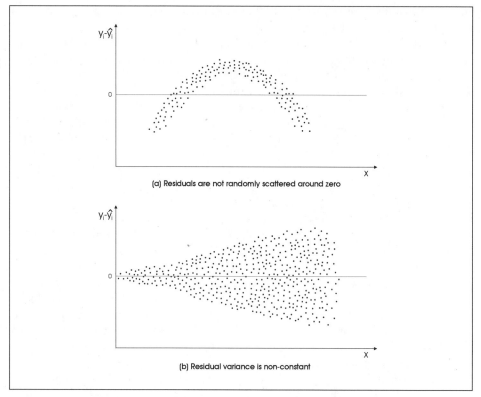

between the dependent and independent variables is inadequate and that another functional form would be more appropriate. An example of this type of residual plot is given in the first graph in Figure 9.15.

If the residual plot indicates that the magnitude of the residuals is increasing (or decreasing) as the value of the independent variable increases, we would question the validity of the assumption of constant error variances. An example of this type of residual plot is given in the second graph in Figure 9.15. (Note that checking for increasing or decreasing magnitude in the residuals requires multiple observations on Y at the same value of X and at various levels of X.) In some cases, a simple transformation of the dependent variable can correct the problem of nonconstant error variances. Such transformations are discussed in more advanced texts on regression analysis.

9.10.3   *A Note About Statistical Tests*

Regardless of the form of the distribution of the error terms, least squares regression can always be used to fit regression curves to data in order to predict the value the dependent variable will assume for a given level of the independent variables. Many decision makers never bother to look at residual plots or to construct confidence intervals for parameters in the regression models for the predictions they make. However, the accuracy of predictions made using regression models depends on how well the regression function fits the data. At the very least, we should always check to see how well a regression function fits a given data set. We can do so using residual plots, graphs of the actual data versus the estimated values, and the R^2 statistic.

9.11 INTRODUCTION TO MULTIPLE REGRESSION

We have seen that regression analysis involves identifying a function that relates the *systematic* changes in a continuous dependent variable to the values of one or more independent variables. That is, our goal in regression analysis is to identify an appropriate representation of the function $f(\cdot)$ in:

$$Y = f(X_1, X_2, ..., X_k) + \varepsilon \qquad \qquad 9.17$$

The previous sections in this chapter introduced some of the basic concepts of regression analysis by considering a special case of equation 9.17 that involves a *single* independent variable. Although such a model might be appropriate in some situations, a business person is far more likely to encounter situations involving more than one (or multiple) independent variables. We'll now consider how *multiple* regression analysis can be applied to these situations.

For the most part, multiple regression analysis is a direct extension of simple linear regression analysis. Although volumes have been written on this topic, we'll focus our attention on the multiple linear regression function represented by:

$$\hat{Y}_i = b_0 + b_1 X_{1_i} + b_2 X_{2_i} + ... + b_k X_{k_i} \qquad \qquad 9.18$$

The regression function in equation 9.18 is similar to the simple linear regression function except that it allows for more than one (or "k") independent variables. Here again, $\hat{Y}_i$ represents the estimated value for the ith observation in our sample whose actual value is Y_i. The symbols $X_{1_i}, X_{2_i}, ..., X_{k_i}$ represent the observed values of the independent variables associated with observation i. Assuming that each of these variables vary in a linear fashion with the dependent variable Y, the function in equation 9.18 might be applied appropriately to a variety of problems.

We can easily visualize the equation of a straight line in our earlier discussion of regression analysis. In multiple regression analysis, the concepts are similar but the results are more difficult to visualize. Figure 9.16 shows an example of the type of regression surface we might fit using equation 9.18 if the regression function involves only two independent variables. With two independent variables, we fit a *plane* to our data. With three or more independent variables, we fit a *hyperplane* to our data. It is difficult to visualize or draw graphs in more than three dimensions, so we cannot actually see what a hyperplane looks like. However, just as a **plane** is a generalization of a straight line into three dimensions, a **hyperplane** is a generalization of a plane into more than three dimensions.

Regardless of the number of independent variables, the goal in multiple regression analysis is the same as the goal in a problem with a single independent variable. That is, we want to find the values for $b_0, b_1, ..., b_k$ in equation 9.18 that minimize the sum of squared estimation errors represented by:

$$\text{ESS} = \sum_{i=1}^{n} (Y_i - \hat{Y}_i)^2$$

We can use the method of least squares to determine the values for $b_0, b_1, ..., b_k$ that minimize ESS. This should allow us to identify the regression function that best fits our data.

Figure 9.16
Example of a
regression
surface for two
independent
variables.

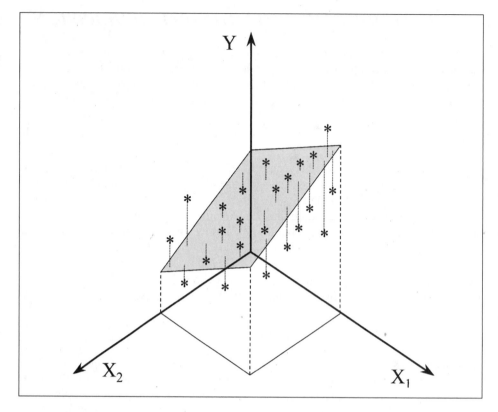

Figure 9.16
Example of a regression surface for two independent variables.

9.12   A MULTIPLE REGRESSION EXAMPLE

The following example illustrates how to perform multiple linear regression.

> A real estate appraiser is interested in developing a regression model to help predict the fair market value of houses in a particular town. She visited the county courthouse and collected the data shown in Figure 9.17 (and in the file FIG9-17.xls on your data disk). The appraiser wants to determine if the selling price of the houses can be accounted for by the total square footage of living area, the size of the garage (as measured by the number of cars that can fit in the garage), and the number of bedrooms in each house. (Note that a garage size of 0 indicates that the house has no garage.)

In this example, the dependent variable Y represents the selling price of a house, and the independent variables X_1, X_2, and X_3 represent the total square footage, the size of the garage, and the number of bedrooms, respectively. To determine if the multiple linear regression function in equation 9.18 is appropriate for these data, we should first construct scatter plots between the dependent variable (selling price) and each independent variable, as shown in Figure 9.18. These graphs seem to indicate a linear relationship between each independent variable and the dependent variable. Thus, we have reason to believe that a multiple linear regression function would be appropriate for these data.

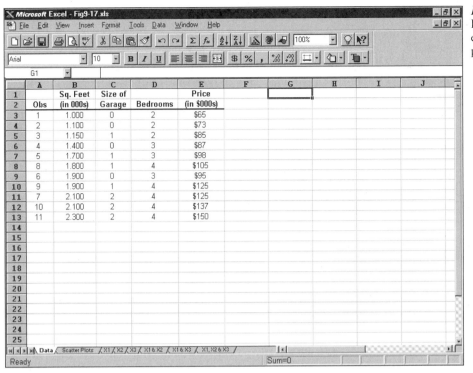

Figure 9.17
Data for the real estate appraisal problem.

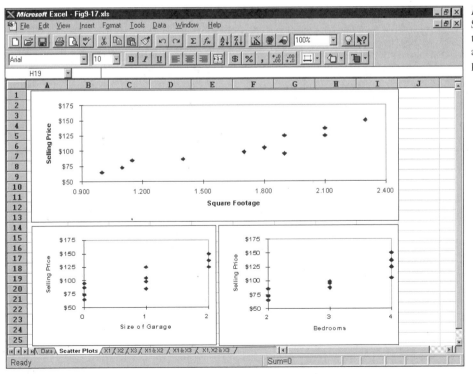

Figure 9.18
Scatter plots of the real estate appraisal problem.

9.13   SELECTING THE MODEL

In our discussion of modeling and problem-solving in Chapter 1, we noted that the best model is often the simplest model that accurately reflects the relevant characteristics of the problem being studied. This is particularly true in multiple regression models. The fact that a particular problem might involve numerous independent variables does not necessarily mean that all of the variables should be included in the regression function. If the data used to build a regression model represents a sample from a larger population of data, it is possible to over-analyze or **overfit** the data in the sample. That is, if we look too closely at a sample of data, we are likely to discover characteristics of the sample that are not representative (or which do not generalize) to the population from which the sample was drawn. This can lead to erroneous conclusions about the population being sampled. To avoid the problem of overfitting when building a multiple regression model, we should attempt to identify the *simplest* regression function that adequately accounts for the behavior of the dependent variable we are studying.

9.13.1   Models with One Independent Variable

With this idea of simplicity in mind, the real estate appraiser in our example problem might begin her analysis by trying to estimate the selling prices of the houses in the sample using a simple regression function with only one independent variable. The appraiser might first try to fit each of the following three simple linear regression functions to the data:

$$\hat{Y}_i = b_0 + b_1 X_{1_i} \qquad\qquad \textbf{9.19}$$

$$\hat{Y}_i = b_0 + b_2 X_{2_i} \qquad\qquad \textbf{9.20}$$

$$\hat{Y}_i = b_0 + b_3 X_{3_i} \qquad\qquad \textbf{9.21}$$

In equations 9.19 through 9.21, $\hat{Y}_i$ represents the estimated or fitted selling price for the ith observation in the sample, and X_{1_i}, X_{2_i}, and X_{3_i} represent the total square footage, size of garage, and number of bedrooms for this same observation i, respectively.

To obtain the optimal values for the b_i in each regression function, the appraiser must perform three separate regressions. She would do so in the same way as described earlier in our example involving the prediction of sales from advertising expenditures. Figure 9.19 summarizes the results of these three regression functions.

Figure 9.19
Regression results for the three simple linear regression models.

Independent Variable in the Model	R^2	Adjusted-R^2	S_e	Parameter Estimates
X_1	0.870	0.855	10.299	$b_0 = 9.503$, $b_1 = 56.394$
X_2	0.759	0.731	14.030	$b_0 = 78.290$, $b_2 = 28.382$
X_3	0.793	0.770	12.982	$b_0 = 16.250$, $b_3 = 27.607$

The values of the R^2 statistic in Figure 9.19 indicate the proportion of the total variation in the dependent variable around its mean accounted for by each of the three simple linear regression functions. (We will comment on the adjusted-R^2 and S_e values shortly.) The model that uses X_1 (square footage) as the independent variable accounts for 87% of the variation in Y (selling price). The model using X_2 (garage size) accounts for roughly 76% of the variation in Y, and the model that uses X_3 (number of bedrooms) as the independent variable accounts for about 79% of the variation in the selling price.

If the appraiser wants to use only one of the available independent variables in a simple linear regression model to predict the selling price of a house, it seems that X_1 would be the best choice because, according to the R^2 statistics, it accounts for more of the variation in selling price than either of the other two variables. In particular, X_1 accounts for about 87% of the variation in the dependent variable. This leaves approximately 13% of the variation in Y unaccounted for. Thus, the best linear regression function with one independent variable is represented by:

$$\hat{Y}_i = b_0 + b_1 X_{1_i} = 9.503 + 56.394 X_{1_i} \qquad 9.22$$

9.13.2 Models with Two Independent Variables

Next, the appraiser might want to determine if one of the other two variables could be combined with X_1 in a *multiple* regression model to account for a significant portion of the remaining 13% variation in Y that was not accounted for by X_1. To do this, the appraiser could fit each of the following multiple regression functions to the data:

$$\hat{Y}_i = b_0 + b_1 X_{1_i} + b_2 X_{2_i} \qquad 9.23$$

$$\hat{Y}_i = b_0 + b_1 X_{1_i} + b_3 X_{3_i} \qquad 9.24$$

To determine the optimal values for the b_i in the regression model in equation 9.23, we would use the settings shown in the Regression dialog box in Figure 9.20. The Input X-Range in this dialog box is the range in Figure 9.17 that corresponds to the values for X_1 (total square footage) and X_2 (garage size). After we click the OK button, Excel performs the appropriate calculations and displays the regression results shown in Figure 9.21.

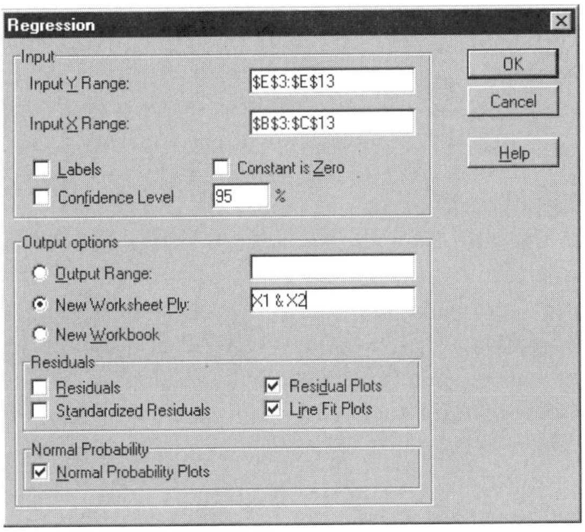

Figure 9.20
Regression dialog box settings for the multiple regression model using square footage and garage size as independent variables.

Figure 9.21
Results of the multiple regression model using square footage and garage size as independent variables.

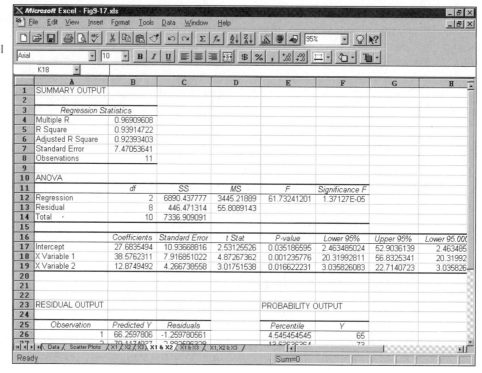

Figure 9.21 lists *three* numbers in the Coefficients column. These numbers correspond to the parameter estimates b_0, b_1, and b_2. Note that the value listed for X Variable 1 is the coefficient for the first variable in the X-Range (which, in some cases, might be X_2 or X_3, depending on how the data are arranged in the spreadsheet). The value for X Variable 2 corresponds to the second variable in the X-Range (which might be X_3 or X_1, depending on the arrangement of the data).

From the regression results in Figure 9.21, we know that when using X_1 (square footage) and X_2 (garage size) as independent variables the estimated regression function is:

$$\hat{Y}_i = b_0 + b_1 X_{1_i} + b_2 X_{2_i} = 27.684 + 38.576 X_{1_i} + 12.875 X_{2_i} \qquad \textbf{9.25}$$

Notice that adding the second independent variable caused the values of b_0 and b_1 to change from their earlier values shown in equation 9.22. Thus, the values assumed by the parameters in a regression model might vary depending on the number (and combination) of variables in the model.

We could obtain the values for the parameters in the second multiple regression model (in equation 9.24) in the same way. Note, however, that before issuing the Regression command again we would need to rearrange the data in the spreadsheet so that the values for X_1 (total square footage) and X_3 (number of bedrooms) are located next to each other in one contiguous block. The regression tool in Excel (and in most other spreadsheet software packages) requires that the X-Range be represented by one contiguous block of cells.

Figure 9.22 compares the regression results for the model in equation 9.24 and the results for the model in equation 9.23 versus the earlier results of the best simple

---

Important Software Note

When using the regression tool, the values for the independent variables *must* be listed in *adjacent* columns in the spreadsheet and cannot be separated by any intervening columns. That is, the Input X-Range option in the Regression dialog box must always specify a contiguous block of numbers.

---

linear regression model in equation 9.22, where X_1 was the only independent variable in the model.

These results indicate that when using X_1 (square footage) and X_3 (number of bedrooms) as independent variables, the estimated regression function is:

$$\hat{Y}_i = b_0 + b_1 X_{1_i} + b_3 X_{3_i} = 8.311 + 44.313 X_{1_i} + 6.743 X_{3_i} \qquad \textbf{9.26}$$

The appraiser was hoping that the inclusion of a second independent variable in the models in equation 9.23 and equation 9.24 might help to explain a significant portion of the remaining 13% of the variation in the dependent that was not accounted for by the simple linear regression function in equation 9.22. How can we tell if this happened?

9.13.3   Inflating R^2

Figure 9.22 indicates that adding either X_2 or X_3 to the simple linear regression model caused the R^2 statistic to increase. This should not be surprising. As it turns out, the value of R^2 can never decrease as a result of adding an independent variable to a regression function. The reason for this is easy to see. Recall that $R^2 = 1 - \frac{\text{ESS}}{\text{TSS}}$. Thus, the only way R^2 could decrease as the result of adding an independent variable (X_n) to the model would be if ESS *increased*. However, because the method of least squares attempts to minimize ESS, a new independent variable cannot cause ESS to increase because this variable could simply be ignored by setting $b_n = 0$. In other words, if adding the new independent variable does not help to reduce ESS, least squares regression would simply ignore the new variable.

When you add *any* independent variable to a regression function, the value of the R^2 statistic can never decrease and will usually increase at least a little. Therefore, we can make the R^2 statistic arbitrarily large simply by including enough independent variables in the regression function—regardless of whether or not the new independent variables are related at all to the dependent variable. For example, the real estate

Independent Variable in the Model	R^2	Adjusted-R^2	S_e	Parameter Estimates
X_1	0.870	0.855	10.299	$b_0 = 9.503, b_1 = 56.394$
X_1 and X_2	0.939	0.924	7.471	$b_0 = 27.684, b_1 = 38.576, b_2 = 12.875$
X_1 and X_3	0.877	0.847	10.609	$b_0 = 8.311, b_1 = 44.313, b_3 = 6.743$

Figure 9.22
Comparison of regression results for models with two independent variables versus the best model with one independent variable.

appraiser could probably increase the value R^2 to some degree by including another independent variable in the model that represents the height of the mailbox at each house—which probably has little to do with the selling price of a house. This results in a model that overfits our data and may not generalize well to other data not included in the sample being analyzed.

9.13.4   The Adjusted-R^2 Statistic

The value of the R^2 statistic can be inflated artificially by including independent variables in a regression function that have little or no logical connection with the dependent variable. Thus, another goodness-of-fit measure, known as the **adjusted-R^2 statistic** (denoted by R_a^2), has been suggested which accounts for the number of independent variables included in a regression model. The adjusted-R^2 statistic is defined as:

$$R_a^2 = 1 - \left(\frac{\text{ESS}}{\text{TSS}} \right) \left(\frac{n-1}{n-k-1} \right) \qquad\qquad 9.27$$

where n represents the number of observations in the sample, and k represents the number of independent variables in the model. As variables are added to a regression model, the ratio of ESS to TSS in equation 9.27 will decrease (because ESS decreases and TSS remains constant), but the ratio of $n-1$ to $n-k-1$ will increase (because $n-1$ remains constant and $n-k-1$ decreases). Thus, if we add a variable to the model that does not reduce ESS enough to compensate for the increase in k, the adjusted-R^2 value will decrease.

The adjusted-R^2 value can be used as a **"rule-of-thumb"** to help us decide if an additional independent variable enhances the predictive ability of a model or if it simply inflates the R^2 statistic artificially. However, using the adjusted-R^2 statistic in this way is not foolproof and requires a good bit of judgment on the part of the person performing the analysis.

9.13.5   The Best Model with Two Independent Variables

As shown in Figure 9.22, when X_2 (garage size) is introduced to the model, the adjusted-R^2 *increases* from 0.855 to 0.924. We can conclude from this increase that the addition of X_2 to the regression model helps to account for a significant portion of the remaining variation in Y that was not accounted for by X_1. On the other hand, when X_3 is introduced as an independent variable in the regression model, the adjusted-R^2 statistic in Figure 9.22 *decreases* (from 0.855 to 0.847). This indicates that adding this variable to the model does not help account for a significant portion of the remaining variation in Y if X_1 is already in the model. The best model with two independent variables is given in equation 9.25, which uses X_1 (total square footage) and X_2 (garage size) as predictors of selling price. According to the R^2 statistic in Figure 9.22, this model accounts for about 94% of the total variation in Y around its mean. This model leaves roughly 6% of the variation in Y unaccounted for.

9.13.6   Multicollinearity

We should not be too surprised that no significant improvement was observed when X_3 (number of bedrooms) was added to the model containing X_1 (total square footage), because both of these variables represent similar factors. That is, the number of bedrooms in a house is closely related (or correlated) to the total square footage in the house. Thus, if we have already used total square footage to help explain variations in the selling prices of houses (as in the first regression function), adding information about the number of bedrooms would be somewhat redundant. Our analysis confirms this.

The term **multicollinearity** is used to describe the situation when the independent variables in a regression model are correlated among themselves. Multicollinearity tends to increase the uncertainty associated with the parameters estimates (b_i) in a regression model and should be avoided whenever possible. Specialized procedures for detecting and correcting multicollinearity can be found in advanced texts on regression analysis.

9.13.7 *The Model with Three Independent Variables*

As a final test, the appraiser might want to see if X_3 (number of bedrooms) helps to explain a significant portion of the remaining 6% variation in Y that was not accounted for by the model using X_1 and X_2 as independent variables. This involves fitting the following multiple regression function to the data:

$$\hat{Y}_i = b_0 + b_1X_{1_i} + b_2X_{2_i} + b_3X_{3_i} \qquad \textbf{9.28}$$

Figure 9.23 shows the regression results for this model. The results of this model are also summarized for comparison purposes in Figure 9.24, along with the earlier results for the best model with one independent variable and the best model with two independent variables.

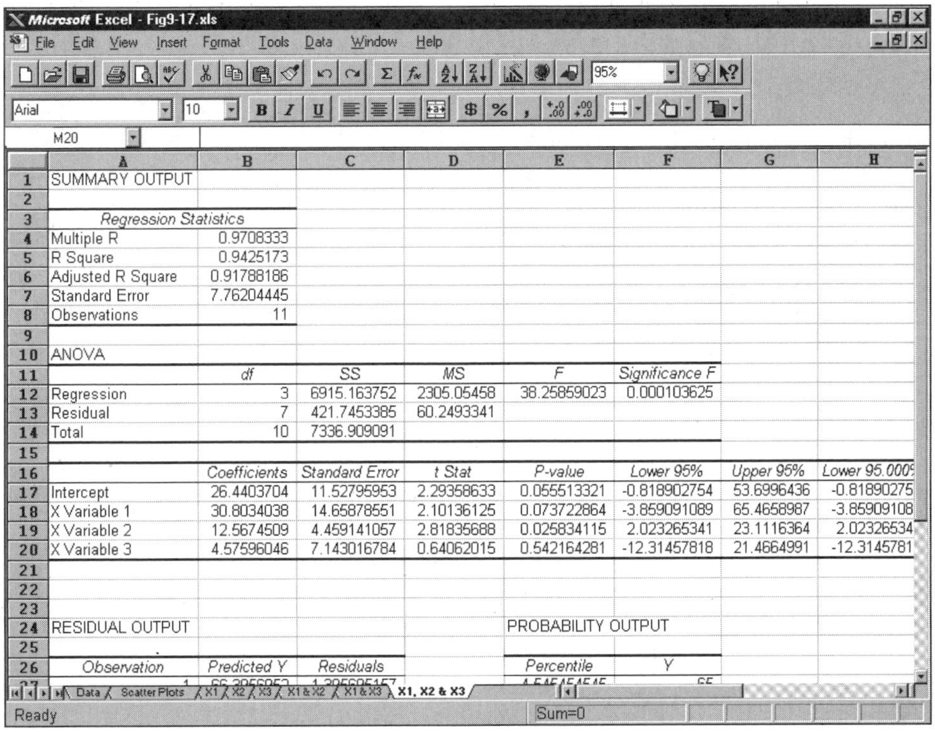

	A	B	C	D	E	F	G	H
1	SUMMARY OUTPUT							
2								
3	*Regression Statistics*							
4	Multiple R	0.9708333						
5	R Square	0.9425173						
6	Adjusted R Square	0.91788186						
7	Standard Error	7.76204445						
8	Observations	11						
9								
10	ANOVA							
11		*df*	*SS*	*MS*	*F*	*Significance F*		
12	Regression	3	6915.163752	2305.05458	38.25859023	0.000103625		
13	Residual	7	421.7453385	60.2493341				
14	Total	10	7336.909091					
15								
16		*Coefficients*	*Standard Error*	*t Stat*	*P-value*	*Lower 95%*	*Upper 95%*	*Lower 95.000*
17	Intercept	26.4403704	11.52795953	2.29358633	0.055513321	-0.818902754	53.6996436	-0.81890275
18	X Variable 1	30.8034038	14.65878551	2.10136125	0.073722864	-3.859091089	65.4658987	-3.85909108
19	X Variable 2	12.5674509	4.459141057	2.81835688	0.025834115	2.023265341	23.1116364	2.02326534
20	X Variable 3	4.57596046	7.143016784	0.64062015	0.542164281	-12.31457818	21.4664991	-12.3145781
21								
22								
23								
24	RESIDUAL OUTPUT				PROBABILITY OUTPUT			
25								
26	*Observation*	*Predicted Y*	*Residuals*		*Percentile*	*Y*		

Figure 9.23
Results of regression model using all three independent variables.

Figure 9.24
Comparison of regression results for the model with three independent variables versus the best models with one and two independent variables.

Independent Variable in the Model	R^2	Adjusted-R^2	S_e	Parameter Estimates
X_1	0.870	0.855	10.299	$b_0 = 9.503$, $b_1 = 56.394$
X_1 and X_2	0.939	0.924	7.471	$b_0 = 27.684$, $b_1 = 38.576$, $b_2 = 12.875$
X_1, X_2, and X_3	0.943	0.918	7.762	$b_0 = 26.440$, $b_1 = 30.803$, $b_2 = 12.567$, $b_3 = 4.576$

Figure 9.24 indicates that when X_3 is added to the model that contains X_1 and X_2, the R^2 statistic increases slightly (from 0.939 to 0.943). However, the adjusted-R^2 drops from 0.924 to 0.918. Thus, it does not appear that adding information about X_3 (number of bedrooms) helps to explain selling prices in any significant way when X_1 (total square footage) and X_2 (size of garage) are already in the model.

It is also interesting to note that the best model with two independent variables also has the smallest standard error S_e. This means that the confidence intervals around any predictions made with this model will be narrower (or more precise) than those of the other models. It can be shown that the model with the highest adjusted-R^2 always has the smallest standard error. For this reason, the adjusted-R^2 statistic is sometimes the sole criterion used to select which multiple regression model to use in a given problem. However, other procedures for selecting regression models exist and are discussed in advanced texts on regression analysis.

9.14   MAKING PREDICTIONS

On the basis of this analysis, the appraiser most likely would choose to use the estimated regression model in equation 9.25, which includes X_1 (total square footage) and X_2 (garage size) as independent variables. For a house with X_{1_i} total square feet and space for X_{2_i} cars in its garage, the estimated selling price $\hat{Y}_i$ is:

$$\hat{Y}_i = 27.684 + 38.576X_{1_i} + 12.875X_{2_i}$$

For example, the expected selling price (or average market value) of a house with 2,100 square feet and a two-car garage is estimated as:

$$\hat{Y}_i = 27.684 + 38.576 \times 2.1 + 12.875 \times 2 = 134.444$$

or approximately $134,444. Note that in making this prediction we expressed the square footage of the house in the same units in which X_1 (total square footage variable) was expressed in the sample used to estimate the model. This should be done for all independent variables when making predictions.

The standard error of the estimation errors for this model is 7.471. Therefore, we should not be surprised to see prices for houses with 2,100 square feet and two-car garages varying within roughly ±2 standard errors (or ±$14,942) of our estimate. That is, we expect prices on this type of house to be as low as $119,500 or as high as $149,400 depending on other factors not included in our analysis (such as age or condition of the roof, presence of a swimming pool, and so on).

As demonstrated earlier in the case of simple linear regression models, more accurate techniques exist for constructing prediction intervals using multiple regression models. In the case of a multiple regression model, the techniques used to construct prediction intervals require a basic knowledge of matrix algebra, which is not assumed in this text. The interested reader should consult advanced texts on multiple regression analysis for a description of how to construct more accurate prediction intervals using multiple regression models. Keep in mind that the simple rule-of-thumb described earlier gives an underestimated (narrower) approximation of the more accurate prediction interval.

9.15   BINARY INDEPENDENT VARIABLES

As just mentioned, the appraiser might want to include other independent variables in her analysis. Some of these, such as age of the roof, could be measured numerically and be included as an independent variable. But how would we create variables to represent the presence of a swimming pool or the condition of the roof?

The presence of a swimming pool can be included in the analysis with a binary independent variable coded as:

$$X_{p_i} = \begin{cases} 1, \text{ if house } i \text{ has a pool} \\ 0, \text{ otherwise} \end{cases}$$

The condition of the roof could also be modeled with binary variables. Here, however, we might need more than one binary variable to model all the possible conditions. If some qualitative variable can assume p possible values, we need $p - 1$ binary variables to model the possible outcomes. For example, suppose that the condition of the roof could be rated as good, average, or poor. There are three possible values for the variable representing the condition of the roof; therefore, we need two binary variables to model these outcomes. These binary variables are coded as:

$$X_{r_i} = \begin{cases} 1, \text{ if the roof of house } i \text{ is in good condition} \\ 0, \text{ otherwise} \end{cases}$$

$$X_{r+1_i} = \begin{cases} 1, \text{ if the roof of house } i \text{ is in average condition} \\ 0, \text{ otherwise} \end{cases}$$

It might appear that we left out a coding for a roof in poor condition. However, note that this condition is implied when $X_{r_i} = 0$ and $X_{r+1_i} = 0$. That is, if the roof is *not* in good condition (as implied by $X_{r_i} = 0$) *and* the roof is *not* in average condition (as implied by $X_{r+1_i} = 0$), then the roof must be in poor condition. Thus, we need only two binary variables to represent three possible roof conditions. For reasons that go beyond the scope of this text, the computer could not perform the least squares calculations if we included a third binary variable to indicate houses with roofs in poor condition. Also, it would be inappropriate to model the condition of the roof with a single variable coded as 1 for good, 2 for average, and 3 for poor because this implies that the average condition is twice as bad as the good condition, and that the poor condition is three times as bad as the good condition and 1.5 times as bad as the average condition.

As this example illustrates, we can use binary variables as independent variables in regression analysis to model a variety of conditions that are likely to occur. In each case, the binary variables would be placed in the X-Range of the spreadsheet and appropriate b_i values would be calculated by the regression tool.

9.16   *STATISTICAL TESTS FOR THE POPULATION PARAMETERS*

Statistical tests for the population parameters in a multiple regression model are performed in much the same way as for the simple regression model. As described earlier, the F-statistic tests whether or not *all* of the β_i for *all* of the independent variables are *all* simultaneously equal to 0 ($\beta_1 = \beta_2 = \ldots = \beta_k = 0$). The value in the regression results labeled Significance of F indicates the probability of this condition being true for the data under consideration.

In the case of a multiple regression model, the *t*-statistics for each independent variable require a slightly different interpretation due to the possible presence of multicollinearity. Each *t*-statistic can be used to test whether or not the associated population parameter $\beta_i = 0$ *given all the other independent variables in the model*. For example, consider the *t*-statistics and *P*-values associated with the variable X_1 shown in Figures 9.21 and 9.23. The *P*-value for X_1 in cell E18 of Figure 9.21 indicates only a 0.1% chance that $\beta_1 = 0$ when X_2 is the only other independent variable in the model. The *P*-value for X_1 in cell E18 of Figure 9.23 indicates a 7.4% chance that $\beta_1 = 0$ when X_2 and X_3 are also in the model. This illustrates one of the potential problems caused by multicollinearity. Because X_1 and X_3 are highly correlated, it is less certain that X_1 plays a significant (nonzero) role in accounting for the behavior of the dependent variable Y when X_3 is also in the model.

In Figure 9.23 the *P*-value associated with X_3 indicates a 54.2% chance that $\beta_3 = 0$ given the other variables in the model. Thus, if we had started our analysis by including all three independent variables in the model, the *P*-value for X_3 in Figure 9.23 suggests that it might be wise to drop X_3 from the model because there is a fairly good chance that it contributes 0 ($\beta_3 = 0$) to explaining the behavior of the dependent variable, given the other variables in the model. In this case, if we drop X_3 from the model, we end up with the same model selected using the adjusted-R^2 criterion.

The statistical tests considered here are valid only when the underlying errors around the regression function are normally distributed random variables with constant means and variances. The graphical diagnostics described earlier apply equally to the case of multiple regression. However, the various statistics presented give reasonably accurate results if the assumptions about the distribution of the error terms are not violated too seriously. Furthermore, the R^2 and adjusted-R^2 statistics are purely descriptive in nature and do not depend in any way on the assumptions about the distribution of the error terms.

9.17   *POLYNOMIAL REGRESSION*

When introducing the multiple linear regression function in equation 9.18, we noted that this type of model might be appropriate when the independent variables vary in a linear fashion with the dependent variable. Business problems exist where there is *not* a linear relationship between the dependent and independent variables. For example, suppose that the real estate appraiser in our earlier example had collected the data in Figure 9.25 (and in the file FIG9-25.xls on your data disk) showing the total square footage and selling price for a number of houses. Figure 9.26 shows a scatter plot of these data.

Figure 9.26 indicates a very strong relationship between total square footage and the selling price of the houses in this sample. However, this relationship is *not* linear.

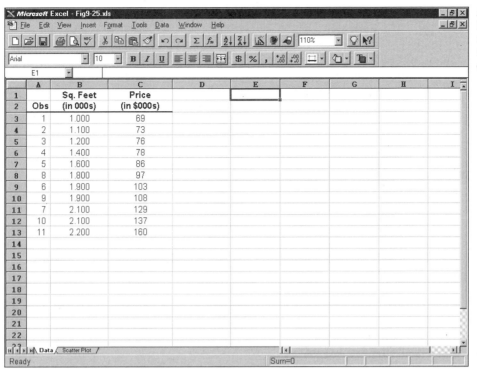

Figure 9.25
Data for
nonlinear
regression
example.

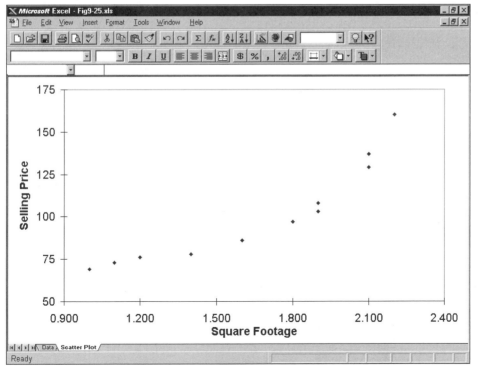

Figure 9.26
Scatter plot of
data showing
relationship
between total
square footage
and selling price.

Rather, more of a *curvilinear* relationship exists between these variables. Does this mean that linear regression analysis cannot be used with these data? Not at all.

The data in Figure 9.25 (plotted in Figure 9.26) indicate a *quadratic* relationship between square footage and selling price. So, to account adequately for the variation in the selling price of houses, we need to use the following type of regression function:

$$\hat{Y}_i = b_0 + b_1 X_{1_i} + b_2 X_{1_i}^2 \qquad\qquad 9.29$$

where $\hat{Y}_i$ represents the estimated selling price of the *i*th house in our sample, and X_{1_i} represents the total square footage in the house. Notice that the second independent variable in equation 9.29 is the first independent variable squared (X_1^2).

9.17.1   *Expressing Nonlinear Relationships Using Linear Models*

Equation 9.29 is not a linear function because it contains the nonlinear variable $X_{1_i}^2$. It *is* linear with respect to the parameters the computer must estimate—namely, b_0, b_1, and b_2. That is, none of the parameters in the regression function appear as an exponent or are multiplied together. Thus, we can use least squares regression to estimate the optimal values for b_0, b_1, and b_2. Note that if we define a new independent variable as $X_{2_i} = X_{1_i}^2$, then the regression function in equation 9.29 is equivalent to:

$$\hat{Y}_i = b_0 + b_1 X_{1_i} + b_2 X_{2_i} \qquad\qquad 9.30$$

Equation 9.30 is equivalent to the multiple linear regression function in equation 9.29. As long as a regression function is linear with respect to its parameters, we can use Excel's regression analysis tool use to find the least squares estimates for the parameters.

To fit the regression function in equation 9.30 to our data, we must create a second independent variable to represent the values of X_{2_i}, as shown in Figure 9.27.

Because the X-Range for the Regression command must be represented as one contiguous block, we inserted a new column between the square footage and selling price columns and placed the values of X_{2_i} in this column. Note that $X_{2_i} = X_{1_i}^2$ in column C in Figure 9.27:

> Formula for cell C3:   =B3^2
> (Copy to C4 through C13.)

The regression results are generated with a Y-Range of D3:D13 and an X-Range of B3:C13. Figure 9.28 shows the regression results.

In Figure 9.28 the estimated regression function is represented by:

$$\hat{Y}_i = b_0 + b_1 X_{1_i} + b_2 X_{2_i} = 194.9714 - 203.3812 X_{1_i} + 83.4063 X_{2_i} \qquad 9.31$$

According to the R^2 statistic, this function accounts for 97.0% of the total variation in selling prices, so we expect that this function fits our data well. We can verify this by plotting the prices that would be estimated by the regression function in equation 9.31 for each observation in our sample against the actual selling prices.

To calculate the estimated selling prices, we applied the formula in equation 9.31 to each observation in the sample, as shown in Figure 9.29 where the following formula was entered in cell E3, then copied to cells E4 through E20:

> Formula for cell E3:   =TREND($D$3:$D$13,$B$3:$C$13,B3:C3)
> (Copy to E4 through E13.)

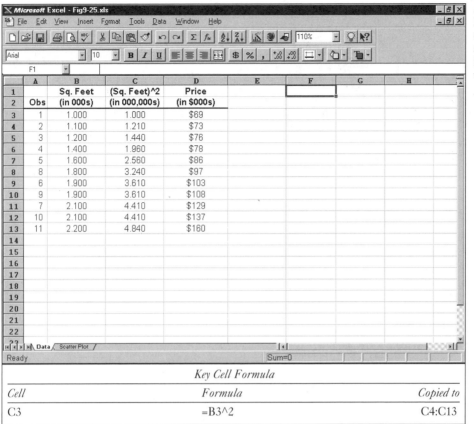

Figure 9.27
Modification of data to include squared independent variable.

Key Cell Formula

Cell	Formula	Copied to
C3	=B3^2	C4:C13

Figure 9.28
Regression results for nonlinear example problem.

Figure 9.29
Estimated
selling prices
using a second
order polynomial
model.

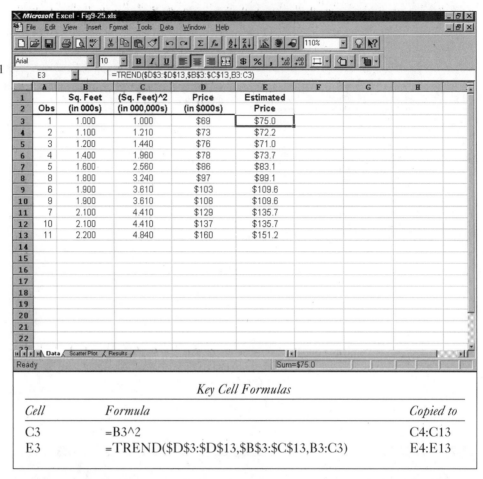

Key Cell Formulas

Cell	Formula	Copied to
C3	=B3^2	C4:C13
E3	=TREND($D$3:$D$13,$B$3:$C$13,B3:C3)	E4:E13

Figure 9.30 shows a curve representing the estimated prices calculated in column E of Figure 9.29. This curve was added to our previous scatter plot as follows:

1. Click on any of the data points in the scatter plot to select the series of data.
2. Click the Insert menu.
3. Click Trendline.
4. On the Type card, click Polynomial and use an Order value of 2.
5. On the Options card, select Display Equation on Chart and Display R-squared Value on Chart.
6. Click OK.

This graph indicates that our regression model accounts for the nonlinear, quadratic relationship between the square footage and selling price of a house in a reasonably accurate manner.

Figure 9.31 shows the result obtained by fitting a third-order polynomial model to our data of the form.

$$\hat{Y}_i = b_0 + b_1 X_{1_i} + b_2 X_{1_i}^2 + b_3 X_{1_i}^3 \qquad 9.32$$

This model appears to provide an even better fit than the model shown in Figure 9.30. We could continue to add higher order terms to the model and further increase the value of the R^2 statistic. Here again, the adjusted-R^2 statistic could help us select a model that provides a good fit to our data without overfitting the data.

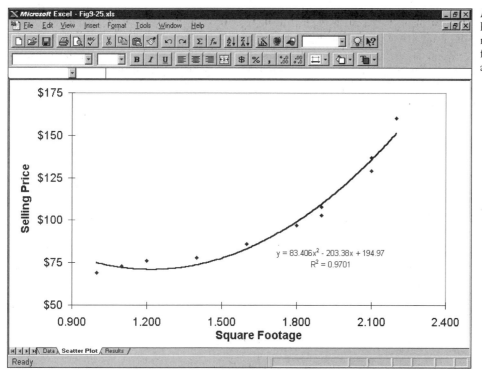

Figure 9.30
Plot of estimated regression function versus actual data.

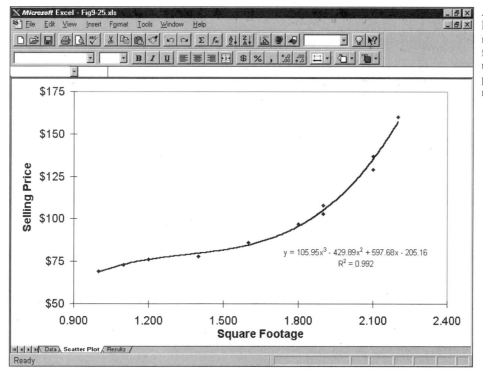

Figure 9.31
Plot of estimated regression function using a third-order polynomial model.

9.17.2   Summary of Nonlinear Regression

This brief example of a polynomial regression problem highlights the fact that regression analysis can be used not only in fitting straight lines or hyperplanes to linear data, but also in fitting other types of curved surfaces to nonlinear data. An in-depth discussion of nonlinear regression is beyond the intended scope of this book, but a wealth of information is available on this topic in numerous texts devoted solely to regression analysis.

This example should help you appreciate the importance of preparing scatter plots of each independent variable against the dependent variable in a regression problem to see if the relationship between the variables is linear or nonlinear. Relatively simple nonlinear relationships, such as the one described in the previous example, can often be accounted for by including squared or cubed terms in the model. In more complicated cases, sophisticated transformations of the dependent or independent variables might be required.

THE WORLD OF MANAGEMENT SCIENCE
Better Predictions Create
Cost Savings for Ohio National Bank

The Ohio National Bank in Columbus must process checks for clearing in a timely manner in order to minimize float. This had been difficult because of wide and seemingly unpredictable variations in the volume of checks received.

As checks pass through the processing center, they are encoded with the dollar amount in magnetic ink at the bottom of the check. This operation requires a staff of clerks, whose work schedules must be planned so that staffing is adequate during peak times. Because the bank couldn't accurately predict these peaks, deadlines often were missed and the clerks often were required to work overtime.

The variations in check volume seemed to be caused by changes in business activity brought about by the calendar—that is, volume was influenced by certain months, days of the week, days of the month, and proximity to certain holidays. A linear regression model was developed to predict staffing needs using a set of binary (dummy) independent variables representing these calendar effects. The regression study was very successful. The resulting model had a coefficient of determination (R^2) of 0.94 and a mean absolute percentage error of 6%. The bank then used these predictions as input to an LP shift-scheduling model that minimized the number of clerks needed to cover the predicted check volumes.

The planning process required data on check volumes and productivity estimates from the line supervisors in the encoding department. Initial reluctance of the supervisors to supply this information presented an obstacle to the implementation of the system. Eventually this was overcome by taking time to explain the reasons for the data collection to the supervisors.

The new system provides estimated savings of $700,000 in float costs and $300,000 in labor costs. The close-out time of 10 P.M. is now met 98% of the time; previously, it was rarely met. Management has performed sensitivity analysis with the model to study the effects of productivity improvements associated with employing experienced full-time encoding clerks instead of part-time clerks.

Source: L. J. Krajewski, and L. P. Ritzman, "Shift Scheduling in Banking Operations: A Case Application," *Interfaces*, vol. 10, no. 2, April 1980, pp. 1–6.

SUMMARY

Regression analysis is a statistical technique that can be used to identify and analyze the relationship between one or more independent variables and a continuous dependent variable. This chapter presented an overview of some key issues involved in performing regression analysis and demonstrated some of the tools and methods available in Excel to assist managers in performing regression analysis.

The goal in regression analysis is to identify a function of the independent variables that adequately accounts for the behavior of the dependent variable. The method of least squares provides a way to determine the best values for the parameters in a regression model for a given sample of data. After identifying such a function, it can be used to predict what value the dependent variable will assume given specific values for the independent variables. Various statistical techniques are available for evaluating how well a given regression function fits a data set and for determining which independent variables are most helpful in explaining the behavior of the dependent variable. Although regression functions can assume a variety of forms, this chapter focused on linear regression models where a linear combination of the independent variables is used to model the dependent variable. Simple transformations of the independent variables can allow this type of model to fit both linear and nonlinear data sets.

QUESTIONS AND PROBLEMS

1. Members of the Roanoke Health and Fitness Club pay an annual membership fee of $250 plus $3 each time they use the facility. Let X denote the number of times a person visits the club during the year. Let Y denote the total annual cost for membership in the club.

    a. What is the mathematical relationship between X and Y?
    b. Is this a functional or statistical relationship? Explain your answer.

2. In comparing two different regression modes that were developed using the same data, we might say that the model with the higher R^2 value will provide the most accurate predictions. Is this true? Why or why not?

3. Show how R_a^2 and S_e are related algebraically (identify the function $f(\cdot)$ such that $R_a^2 = f(S_e)$).

4. Least squares regression finds the estimated values for the parameters in a regression model to minimize ESS $\sum_{i=1}^{n}(Y_i - \hat{Y}_i)^2$. Why is it necessary to square the estima-

tion errors? What problem might be encountered if we attempt to minimize just the sum of the estimation errors?

5. An accounting firm that specializes in auditing mining companies collected the following data on the long-term assets and long-term debt of 12 clients:

Long-Term Assets	Long-Term Debt
26	16
39	20
45	24
47	26
47	30
48	36
54	38
56	43
60	46
62	42
64	38
69	48

Note: All figures are in $1,000,000s.

   a. Prepare a scatter plot of the data. Does there appear to be a linear relationship between these variables?
   b. Develop a simple linear regression model that can be used to predict long-term debt from long-term assets. What is the estimated regression equation?
   c. Interpret the value of R^2.
   d. Suppose that the accounting firm has a client with total assets of $50,000,000. Construct an approximate 95% confidence interval for the amount of long-term debt the firm expects this client to have.

6. The IRS wants to develop a method for detecting whether or not individuals have overstated their deductions for charitable contributions on their tax returns. To assist in this effort, the IRS supplied the following data listing the adjusted gross income (AGI) and charitable contributions for 11 taxpayers whose returns were audited and found to be correct.

AGI (in $1,000s)	Charitable Contributions
$55	$4,200
$58	$4,800
$63	$6,329
$67	$8,017
$74	$7,400
$78	$8,600
$83	$12,290
$88	$10,406
$92	$11,820
$98	$12,090
$105	$14,675

   a. Prepare a scatter plot of the data. Does there appear to be a linear relationship between these variables?

b. Develop a simple linear regression model that can be used to predict the level of charitable contributions from a return's AGI. What is the estimated regression equation?

c. Interpret the value of R^2.

d. How might the IRS use the regression results to identify returns with unusually high charitable contributions?

7. Roger Gallagher owns a used car lot that deals solely in used Corvettes. He would like to develop a regression model to help predict the price he can expect to receive for the cars he owns. He collected the following data concerning a number of cars he has sold in recent months:

Mileage (in 1,000s)	Model Year	T-Top	Price
115	1968	y	$13,875
95	1970	n	$11,000
125	1972	n	$8,000
85	1974	y	$14,950
77	1976	y	$15,625
105	1978	n	$11,300
88	1979	n	$13,250
73	1981	y	$16,500
55	1983	n	$16,500
65	1987	y	$19,500
45	1988	n	$22,300
15	1988	n	$25,500
23	1991	y	$31,900

Let Y = selling price, X_1 = mileage, X_2 = model year, and X_3 = whether or not the car had a T-top.

a. If Roger wants to use a simple linear regression function to estimate the selling price of a car, which X variable do you recommend he use?

b. Determine the parameter estimates for the regression function represented by:

$$\hat{Y}_i = b_0 + b_1 X_{1i} + b_2 X_{2i}$$

What is the estimated regression function? Does X_2 help to explain the selling price of the cars if X_1 is also in the model? What might be the reason for this?

c. Set up a binary variable (X_{3i}) to indicate whether or not each car in the sample has a T-top. Determine the parameter estimates for the regression function represented by:

$$\hat{Y}_i = b_0 + b_1 X_{1i} + b_3 X_{3i}$$

Does X_3 help to explain the selling price of the cars if X_1 is also in the model? Explain.

d. According to the previous model, on average, how much does a T-top add to the value of a car?

e. Determine the parameter estimates for the regression function represented by:

$$\hat{Y}_i = b_0 + b_1 X_{1i} + b_2 X_{2i} + b_3 X_{3i}$$

What is the estimated regression function?

f. Of all the regression functions considered here, which do you recommend Roger use?

8. Refer to question 7. Prepare scatter plots of the values of X_1 and X_2 against Y.

   a. Do these relationships seem to be linear or nonlinear?

   b. Determine the parameter estimates for the regression function represented by:

$$\hat{Y}_i = b_0 + b_1 X_{1i} + b_2 X_{2i} + b_3 X_{3i} + b_4 X_{4i}$$

   where $X_{4i} = X_{2i}^2$. What is the estimated regression function?

   c. Consider the P-values for each β_i in this model. Do these values indicate that any of the independent variables should be dropped from the model?

9. The O-rings in the booster rockets on the space shuttle are designed to expand when heated to seal different chambers of the rocket so that solid rocket fuel is not ignited prematurely. According to engineering specifications, the O-rings expand by some amount, say at least 5%, in order to ensure a safe launch. Hypothetical data on the amount of O-ring expansion and the atmospheric temperature in Fahrenheit at the time of several different launches are given below:

Temperature	% O-ring Expansion
93	22.3
88	21.0
87	20.6
81	19.7
73	18.7
72	19.0
68	17.3
64	16.2
55	15.5

   a. Prepare a scatter plot of the data. Does there appear to be a linear relationship between these variables?

   b. Obtain a simple linear regression model to estimate the amount of O-ring expansion as a function of atmospheric temperature. What is the estimated regression function?

   c. Interpret the R^2 statistic for the model you obtained.

   d. Suppose that NASA officials are considering launching a space shuttle when the temperature is 29 degrees. What amount of O-ring expansion should they expect at this temperature according to your model?

   e. On the basis of your analysis of these data, would you recommend that the shuttle be launched if the temperature is 29 degrees? Why or why not?

10. An analyst for Phidelity Investments wants to develop a regression model to predict the annual rate of return for a stock based on the price-earnings ratio of the stock and a measure of the stock's risk. The following data were collected for a random sample of stocks:

PE Ratio	Risk	Return
7.4	1.0	7.6
11.1	1.3	13.0
8.7	1.1	8.9
11.2	1.2	10.9
11.6	1.7	12.1
12.2	1.3	12.8
12.5	1.2	11.3
12.5	1.3	14.1
13.0	1.6	14.8
13.4	1.4	16.7

a. Prepare scatter plots for each independent variable versus the dependent variable. What type of model do these scatter plots suggest might be appropriate for the data?

b. Let Y = Return, X_1 = PE Ratio, and X_2 = Risk. Obtain the regression results for the following regression model:

$$\hat{Y}_i = b_0 + b_1 X_{1i} + b_2 X_{2i}$$

Interpret the value of R^2 for this model.

c. Obtain the regression results for the following regression model:

$$\hat{Y}_i = b_0 + b_1 X_{1i} + b_2 X_{2i} + b_3 X_{3i} + b_4 X_{4i}$$

where $X_{3i} = X_{1i}^2$ and $X_{4i} = X_{2i}^2$. Interpret the value of R^2 for this model.

d. Which of the previous two models would you recommend that the analyst use?

11. AutoReports is a consumer magazine that reports on the cost of maintaining various types of automobiles. The magazine collected the following data on the annual maintenance cost of a certain type of luxury imported automobile along with the age of the car:

Age	Maintenance Cost
1	$100
2	$375
2	$325
3	$455
3	$520
4	$485
4	$530
5	$595
5	$515
6	$700
6	$800
7	$1,000
7	$950

a. Prepare a scatter plot of these data.

b. Fit the following regression model to the data:

$$\hat{Y}_i = b_0 + b_1 X_{1i}$$

Plot the maintenance costs that are estimated by this model along with the actual costs in the sample. How well does this model fit the data?

c. Fit the following regression model to the data:

$$\hat{Y}_i = b_0 + b_1 X_{1i} + b_2 X_{2i}$$

where $X_{2i} = X_{1i}^2$. Plot the maintenance costs that are estimated by this model along with the actual costs in the sample. How well does this model fit the data?

d. Fit the following regression model to this data:

$$\hat{Y}_i = b_0 + b_1 X_{1i} + b_2 X_{2i} + b_3 X_{3i}$$

where $X_{2i} = X_{1i}^2$ and $X_{3i} = X_{1i}^3$. Plot the maintenance costs that are estimated by this model along with the actual costs in the sample. How well does this model fit the data?

12. Throughout our discussion of regression analysis, we used the Regression command to obtain the parameter estimates that minimize the sum of squared estimation errors. Suppose that we want to obtain parameter estimates that minimize the sum of the absolute value of the estimation errors, or:

$$\text{MIN:} \sum_{i=1}^{n} |Y_i - \hat{Y}_i|$$

a. Use Solver to obtain the parameter estimates for a simple linear regression function that minimizes the sum of the absolute value of the estimation errors for the data in question 9.

b. What advantages, if any, do you see in using this alternate objective to solve a regression problem?

c. What disadvantages, if any, do you see in using this alternate objective to solve a regression problem?

13. Throughout our discussion of regression analysis, we used the Regression command to obtain the parameter estimates that minimize the sum of squared estimation errors. Suppose that we want to obtain parameter estimates that minimize the absolute value of the maximum estimation error or:

$$\text{MIN: MAX} \left(|Y_1 - \hat{Y}_i|, |Y_2 - \hat{Y}_2|, ..., |Y_n - \hat{Y}_n| \right)$$

a. Use Solver to obtain the parameter estimates for a simple linear regression function that minimizes the absolute value of the maximum estimation error for the data in question 9.

b. What advantages, if any, do you see in using this alternate objective to solve a regression problem?

c. What disadvantages, if any, do you see in using this alternate objective to solve a regression problem?

CASE 9.1 THE GEORGIA PUBLIC SERVICE COMMISSION

Nolan Banks is an auditor for the Public Service Commission for the state of Georgia. The Public Service Commission is a government agency responsible for ensuring that utility companies throughout the state manage their operations efficiently so that they can provide quality services to the public at fair prices.

Georgia is the largest state east of the Mississippi River, and various communities and regions throughout the state have different companies that provide water, power, and phone service. These companies have a monopoly in the areas they serve and, therefore, could take unfair advantage of the public. One of Nolan's jobs is to visit the companies and audit their financial records to detect whether or not any abuse is occurring.

A major problem Nolan faces in his job is determining whether or not the expenses reported by the utility companies are reasonable. For example, when he reviews a financial report for a phone company, he might see line maintenance costs of $1,345,948, and he needs to determine if this amount is reasonable. This determination is complicated by the fact that the companies differ in size—so he cannot compare the costs of one company directly to another. Similarly, he cannot come up with a simple ratio to determine costs (such as 2% for the ratio of line maintenance costs to total revenue) because a single ratio might not be appropriate for companies of different sizes.

To help solve this problem, Nolan wants you to build a regression model to estimate what level of line maintenance expense would be expected for companies of different sizes. One measure of size for a phone company is the number of customers it has. Nolan collected the following data on the number of customers and line maintenance expenses of 12 companies he audited in the past year and determined were being run in a reasonably efficient manner.

Customers (in 1,000s)	Line Maintenance Expense (in $1,000s)
25.3	484.6
36.4	672.3
37.9	839.4
45.9	694.9
53.4	836.4
66.8	681.9
78.4	1,037.0
82.6	1,095.6
93.8	1,563.1
97.5	1,377.9
105.7	1,711.7
124.3	2,138.6

1. Enter the data in a spreadsheet.

2. Create a scatter diagram of these data.

3. Use regression to estimate the parameters for the following linear equation for the data.

$$\hat{Y} = b_0 + b_1 X_1$$

What is the estimated regression equation?

4. Interpret the value for R^2 obtained using the equation from question 3.

5. According to the equation in question 3, what level of line maintenance expense would be expected for a phone company with 75,000 customers? Show how you arrive at this value.

6. Suppose that a phone company with 75,000 customers reports a line maintenance expense of $1,500,000. Based on the results of the linear model, should Nolan view this amount as reasonable or excessive?

7. In your spreadsheet, calculate the estimated line maintenance expense that would be predicted by the regression function for each company in the sample. Plot the predicted values you calculate on your graph (connected with a line) along with the original data. Does it appear that a linear regression model is appropriate?

8. Use regression to estimate the parameters for the following quadratic equation for the data:

$$\hat{Y} = b_0 + b_1 X_1 + b_2 X_1^2$$

To do this, you must insert a new column in your spreadsheet next to the original X values. In this new column, calculate the values X_1^2. What is the new estimated regression equation for this model?

9. Interpret the value for R^2 obtained using the equation in question 8.

10. What is the value for the adjusted-R^2 statistic? What does this statistic tell you?

11. What level of line maintenance expense would be expected for a phone company with 75,000 customers according to this new estimated regression function? Show how you arrive at this value.

12. In your spreadsheet, calculate the estimated line maintenance expense that would be predicted by the quadratic regression function for each company in the sample. Plot these values on your graph (connected with a line) along with the original data and the original regression line.

13. Suppose that a phone company with 75,000 customers reports a line maintenance expense of $1,500,000. Based on the results of the quadratic model, should Nolan view this amount as reasonable or excessive?

14. Which of the two regression functions would you suggest Nolan use for prediction purposes?

REFERENCES

Montgomery D. and E. Peck. *Introduction to Linear Regression Analysis.* New York: Wiley, 1991.
Neter, J., W. Wasserman, and M. Kutner. *Applied Linear Statistical Models.* Homewood, IL: Irwin, 1990.
Younger, M. *A First Course in Linear Regression.* Boston: Duxbury Press, 1985.

CHAPTER 10

Discriminant Analysis

$\mathbf{D}$iscriminant analysis (DA) is a statistical technique that uses the information available in a set of independent variables to predict the value of a *discrete*, or *categorical*, dependent variable. Typically, the dependent variable in a DA problem is coded as a series of integer values representing various groups to which the observations in a sample belong. The goal of DA is to develop a rule for predicting to what group a new observation is most likely to belong based on the values the independent variables assume. To gain an understanding of the purpose and value of DA, consider the following business situations where DA could be useful.

Credit Scoring.   The credit manager of a mortgage company classifies the loans it has made into two groups: those resulting in default and those that are current. For each loan, the manager has data describing the income, assets, liabilities, credit history, and employment history of the person who received the loan. The manager wants to use this information to develop a rule for predicting whether or not a new loan applicant will default if granted a loan.

Insurance Rating.   An automotive insurance company uses claims data from the past five years to classify its current policyholders into three categories: high risk, moderate risk, and low risk. The company has data describing each policyholder's age, marital status, number of children, educational level, employment record, and number of traffic citations received during the past five years. The company wants to analyze how the three groups differ with regard to these characteristics and use this information to predict into which risk category a new insurance applicant is likely to fall.

DA differs from most other predictive statistical methods (for example, regression analysis) because the dependent variable is *discrete*, or *categorical*, rather than *continuous*. For instance, in the first example given above, the credit manager wants to predict whether a loan applicant will: (1) default or (2) repay the loan. Similarly, in the second example, the company wants to predict into which risk category a new client is most likely to fall: (1) high risk, (2) moderate risk, or (3) low risk. In each example we can arbitrarily assign a number (1, 2, 3, ...) to each group represented in the problem, and our goal is to predict to which group (1, 2, 3, ...) a new observation is most likely to belong.

It might seem that we could handle these types of problems with least squares regression by using the independent variables to predict the value of a discrete dependent variable coded to indicate the group membership (1, 2, 3, ...) of each observation in the sample. This is true for problems involving only two groups, such as the credit scoring example given earlier. However, the regression approach does not work in problems involving more than two groups, such as the insurance rating example. Because many DA problems involve the analysis of only two groups, we will split our discussion of DA into two parts. The first introduces the concepts of DA and covers the regression approach to the two-group problem. The second presents the more general k-group problem in DA (where $k \geq 2$).

10.1   THE TWO-GROUP DA PROBLEM

The following personnel selection example illustrates the regression approach to two-group DA. Later, we'll extend this example to illustrate the more general k-group approach to DA.

> In her role as personnel director for ACME Manufacturing, Marie Becker is responsible for interviewing and hiring new hourly employees for the factory. As part of the preemployment screening process, each prospective hourly employee is required to take an exam that measures mechanical and verbal aptitudes. Marie has access to historical data on the test scores received by all of ACME's current employees. As part of an annual performance evaluation, each factory employee is rated as performing at either a satisfactory or unsatisfactory level. Marie also has access to these data. Marie wants to analyze the data about current employees to see if there are differences between the preemployment test scores for the satisfactory and unsatisfactory workers. If so, she wants to use this information to develop a rule for predicting whether or not a new potential employee will be a satisfactory or unsatisfactory worker on the basis of the test scores.

This example is somewhat oversimplified because it involves only two independent, or explanatory, variables—the mechanical and verbal aptitude test scores. The personnel director probably has access to many more variables that are likely to be important determinants of satisfactory and unsatisfactory job performance. However, this example is restricted to two independent variables for convenience in illustrating how DA works. The approach to DA described here can be applied to problems involving any number of independent variables.

The two groups of interest in this example—satisfactory and unsatisfactory employees—will be labeled group 1 and group 2, respectively. The mechanical and verbal aptitude test scores for the current ACME employees are listed in Figure 10.1 (and in the file FIG10-1.xls on your data disk) in the Mechanical and Verbal columns. We will refer to this group of observations as the "analysis sample" because we will analyze this data set to develop a rule for classifying new job applicants. The Group column in the spreadsheet contains the value 1 for observations representing satisfactory employees, and the value 2 for unsatisfactory employees.

10.1.1   Group Locations and Centroids

Because this data set includes only two independent variables, we can display these data graphically, as shown in Figure 10.2. The ovals drawn in Figure 10.2 outline the

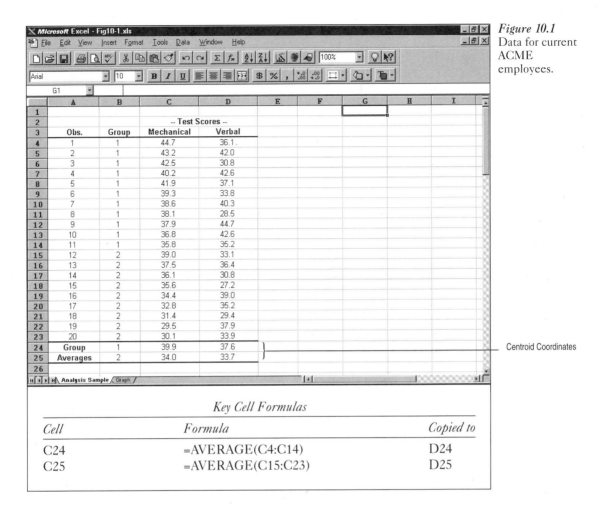

Figure 10.1
Data for current
ACME
employees.

Centroid Coordinates

Key Cell Formulas

Cell	Formula	Copied to
C24	=AVERAGE(C4:C14)	D24
C25	=AVERAGE(C15:C23)	D25

---

typical observations for group 1 and group 2. The points in Figure 10.2 labeled "C_1" and "C_2" represent the centroids for group 1 and group 2, respectively. A group's **centroid** is the set of averages for the independent variables for the group. The centroid indicates where a group is centered, or located. The coordinates of the group centroids are calculated in Figure 10.1 in the rows labeled "Group Averages" as:

> Formula for cell C24: =AVERAGE(C4:C14)
> (Copy to D24.)

> Formula for cell C25: =AVERAGE(C15:C23)
> (Copy to D25.)

The centroid for group 1 is (39.9, 37.6) and the centroid for group 2 is (34.0, 33.7).

We might expect that the more the centroids for the groups in a DA problem differ, the easier it is to distinguish between the groups. In general, this is true. For example, because the group centroids in Figure 10.2 are well separated, it is easy to see that the unsatisfactory employees tend to have lower mechanical and verbal aptitudes than the satisfactory employees. However, if the two groups' centroids were both located at the same point, it would be difficult to tell which group an observation belonged to based on only its location, because all observations would be scattered around the same centroid point.

Figure 10.2
Graph of data for
current
employees.

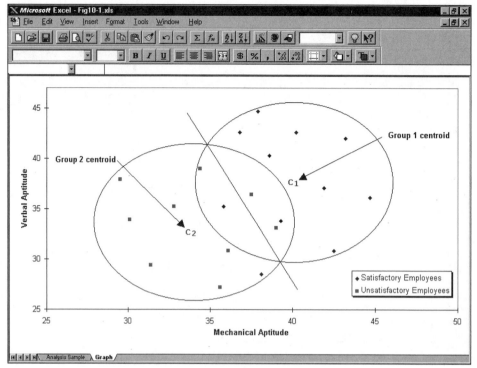

Although the groups in Figure 10.2 are well separated, the two groups overlap. This overlapping area makes it difficult to establish a rule or boundary line for separating the satisfactory employees from the unsatisfactory ones. One such boundary line has been drawn arbitrarily in Figure 10.2. DA provides an objective means for determining the best straight line for separating or distinguishing between groups.

10.1.2   Calculating Discriminant Scores

Viewing the data in Figure 10.1 from a regression perspective, we want to model the behavior of the Group variable using the mechanical and verbal aptitude test scores. In the following regression equation, the dependent variable $\hat{Y}$ represents the estimated value of the Group variable, and X_1 and X_2 correspond to values for the independent variables representing the mechanical and verbal test scores, respectively:

$$\hat{Y}_i = b_0 + b_1X_{1i} + b_2X_{2i} \qquad \textbf{10.1}$$

Note that we can expand equation 10.1 easily to include any number of independent variables. But regardless of the number of independent variables in a problem, the purpose of the regression equation is to combine the information available in the variables into a single-valued estimate of the Group variable. This estimated value of the Group variable is referred to as a **discriminant score** and is denoted by $\hat{Y}$. But what are the values of b_0, b_1, and b_2 that will result in the best discriminant scores for our data? We can use the regression tool in Excel to estimate these values.

The Regression dialog box in Figure 10.3 shows the settings required for the current problem. Notice that the Input Y-Range entry corresponds to the Group values shown in Figure 10.1, and the Input X-Range entry corresponds to the values of the mechanical and verbal aptitude test scores. Figure 10.4 shows the regression results.

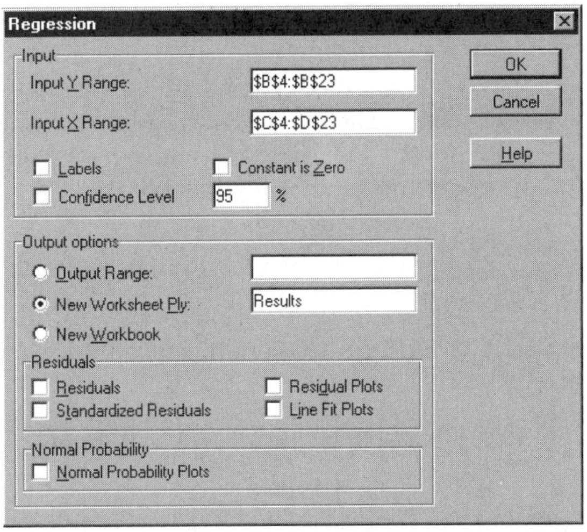

Figure 10.3 Regression dialog box for the personnel selection example.

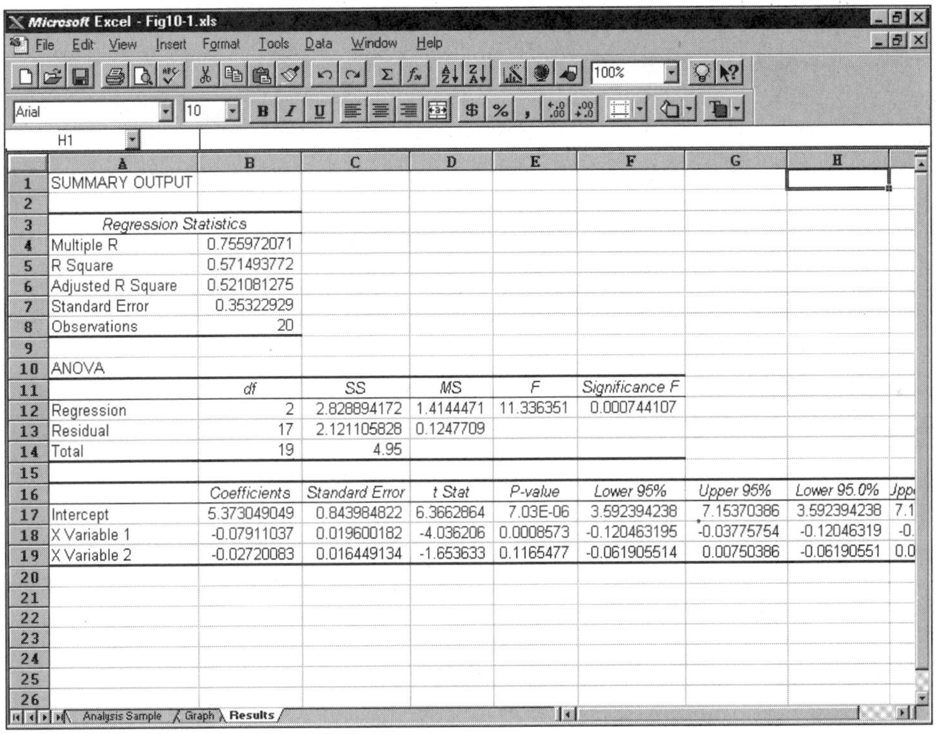

	A	B	C	D	E	F	G	H
1	SUMMARY OUTPUT							
2								
3	*Regression Statistics*							
4	Multiple R	0.755972071						
5	R Square	0.571493772						
6	Adjusted R Square	0.521081275						
7	Standard Error	0.35322929						
8	Observations	20						
9								
10	ANOVA							
11		*df*	*SS*	*MS*	*F*	*Significance F*		
12	Regression	2	2.828894172	1.4144471	11.336351	0.000744107		
13	Residual	17	2.121105828	0.1247709				
14	Total	19	4.95					
15								
16		*Coefficients*	*Standard Error*	*t Stat*	*P-value*	*Lower 95%*	*Upper 95%*	*Lower 95.0%*
17	Intercept	5.373049049	0.843984822	6.3662864	7.03E-06	3.592394238	7.15370386	3.592394238
18	X Variable 1	-0.07911037	0.019600182	-4.036206	0.0008573	-0.120463195	-0.03775754	-0.12046319
19	X Variable 2	-0.02720083	0.016449134	-1.653633	0.1165477	-0.061905514	0.00750386	-0.06190551

Figure 10.4 Regression results for the personnel selection example.

The estimated value for b_0 is represented by the Intercept value in cell B17 of Figure 10.4, and the estimated values for b_1 and b_2 are shown in cells B18 and B19, respectively. Thus, our estimated regression function is:

$$\hat{Y}_i = 5.373 - 0.0791X_{1_i} - 0.0272X_{2_i} \qquad \textbf{10.2}$$

(Note that because the dependent variable in a two-group DA problem assumes only two possible values, it cannot be a normally distributed variable. Thus, virtually all of the statistical results in the regression output for a two-group DA problem are not subject to their usual interpretation. Even the R^2 statistic is not a particularly meaningful goodness-of-fit measure for these types of problems. Later, we'll discuss another way to assess how well a given regression function performs on a DA problem.)

Equation 10.2 is applied to the data in our example to generate the discriminant score values for each observation. These values are listed in the Discriminant Score column in Figure 10.5 (and in the file FIG10-5.xls on your data disk).

For example, the discriminant score for the first observation could be calculated in cell E4 as:

Formula for cell E4:   =5.373–0.0791*C4–0.0272*D4   **10.3**
(Copy to E5 through E23.)

Alternatively, we could calculate the discriminant scores using the TREND( ) function as follows:

Formula for cell E4:   =TREND($B$4:$B$23,$C$4:$D$23,C4:D4)   **10.3a**
(Copy to E5 through E23.)

Figure 10.5
Discriminant scores for the personnel selection example.

	A	B	C	D	E	F
1						
2			-- Test Scores --		Discriminant	Predicted
3	Obs.	Group	Mechanical	Verbal	Score	Group
4	1	1	44.7	36.1	0.855	1
5	2	1	43.2	42.0	0.813	1
6	3	1	42.5	30.8	1.173	1
7	4	1	40.2	42.6	1.034	1
8	5	1	41.9	37.1	1.049	1
9	6	1	39.3	33.8	1.345	1
10	7	1	38.6	40.3	1.223	1
11	8	1	38.1	28.5	1.584	2 **
12	9	1	37.9	44.7	1.159	1
13	10	1	36.8	42.6	1.303	1
14	11	1	35.8	35.2	1.583	2 **
15	12	2	39.0	33.1	1.387	1 **
16	13	2	37.5	36.4	1.416	1 **
17	14	2	36.1	30.8	1.679	2
18	15	2	35.6	27.2	1.817	2
19	16	2	34.4	39.0	1.591	2
20	17	2	32.8	35.2	1.821	2
21	18	2	31.4	29.4	2.089	2
22	19	2	29.5	37.9	2.008	2
23	20	2	30.1	33.9	2.070	2
24	Group	1	39.9	37.6	1.193	
25	Averages	2	34.0	33.7	1.764	
26				Cut-off Value:	1.479	

Analysis Sample / Graph / Results /

Key Cell Formulas

Cell	Formula	Copied to
E4	=TREND($B$4:$B$23,$C$4:$D$23,C4:D4)	E5:E23
E24	=AVERAGE(E4:E14)	—
E25	=AVERAGE(E15:E23)	—
E26	=(E24+E25)/2	—
F4	=IF(E4<=$E$26,1,2)	F5:F23
G4	=IF(F4<>B4,"**","")	G5:G23

Using either equation 10.3 or 10.3a in cell E4 should give approximately the same result, though those obtained using the TREND( ) function should be more accurate (due to less rounding error).

The formula in cell E4 is copied to cells E5 through E23 to calculate the discriminant scores for each of the remaining observations. Cells E24 and E25 calculate the average discriminant score for each group using the following formulas:

> Formula for cell E24:   =AVERAGE(E4:E14)
>
> Formula for cell E25:   =AVERAGE(E15:E23)

We will refer to these average discriminant scores for groups 1 and 2 as $\hat{\bar{Y}}_1$ and $\hat{\bar{Y}}_2$, respectively.

10.1.3   The Classification Rule

Because the discriminant scores are not equal to our group values of 1 and 2, we need a method for translating these scores into group membership predictions. The following classification rule can be used for this purpose:

Classification Rule: If an observation's discriminant score is less than or equal to some cutoff value, then assign it to group 1; otherwise, assign it to group 2.

The remaining problem is to determine an appropriate cutoff value. We can do so in a number of ways. One possibility is to select the cutoff value that minimizes the *number* of misclassifications in the analysis sample. However, this approach might not be best if our goal is to classify new observations correctly. Consider the situation that would occur if the independent variables were normally distributed with equal variances and covariances equal to 0. The resulting distributions of discriminant scores would be similar to those shown in Figure 10.6.

Notice that the distributions of discriminant scores for group 1 and group 2 are centered at $\hat{\bar{Y}}_1$ and $\hat{\bar{Y}}_2$, respectively. The area in Figure 10.6 where the tails of the distributions overlap corresponds to observations that are most likely to be classified incorrectly. Generally, DA attempts to minimize this area of overlap. With these data conditions, it is easy to see that the midpoint between the average discriminant score for each group is likely to be the best choice for a cutoff value because this point minimizes the *probability* of misclassification for future observations. Even if the independent variables violate the normality assumption, this midpoint value often provides good classification results for new observations. The cutoff value listed in cell E26 of Figure 10.5 is the average of the estimates of $\hat{\bar{Y}}_1$ and $\hat{\bar{Y}}_2$:

$$\text{Cutoff value} = \frac{\hat{\bar{Y}}_1 + \hat{\bar{Y}}_2}{2} = \frac{1.193 + 1.764}{2} = 1.479 \qquad \textbf{10.4}$$

Note, however, that the midpoint cutoff value is not always optimal and, in some cases, might lead to poor classification results.

10.1.4   Refining the Cutoff Value

Because the tails of the distributions in Figure 10.6 overlap, we can be fairly certain that some observations will be classified incorrectly using the classification rule stated earlier. For example, our classification rule might predict that certain job applicants will be satisfactory employees when, in fact, they will be unsatisfactory. Hiring such

Figure 10.6
Possible
distributions of
discriminant
scores.

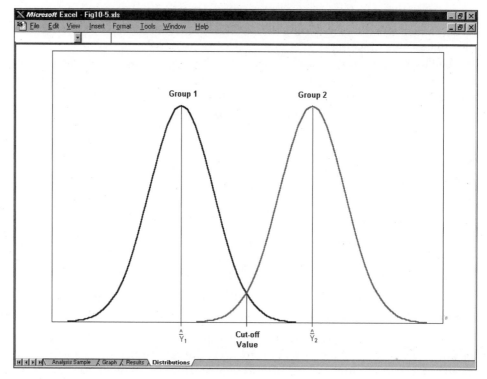

employees could be a costly mistake. Alternatively, our classification rule might predict incorrectly that certain applicants will be unsatisfactory when, in fact, they would be very good employees. Not hiring these applicants would represent a lost opportunity (or opportunity cost) for the company. However, these *costs of misclassification* are not taken into account by the midpoint cutoff value in equation 10.4.

To illustrate another potential problem with the midpoint cutoff value, suppose that the personnel director knows from experience that the majority of applicants to the company are unqualified and would be unsatisfactory workers. In this case, the population of unqualified (potentially unsatisfactory) applicants is larger than the population of qualified (potentially satisfactory) applicants. Thus, a higher probability exists that a given applicant will be an unsatisfactory worker rather than a satisfactory worker. It would be helpful if we could incorporate these pre-existing, or prior, probabilities in our classification rule. However, the midpoint cutoff value in equation 10.4 assumes that new observations are equally likely to come from either group.

We can use an alternative method for specifying what cutoff value to use in our classification rule. This method considers the costs of misclassification and prior probabilities. Suppose that we define the costs of misclassification and prior probabilities as:

$C(1 \mid 2)$= the cost of classifying an observation into group 1 when it belongs to group 2

$C(2 \mid 1)$= the cost of classifying an observation into group 2 when it belongs to group 1

p_1 = the prior probability that a new observation belongs to group 1

p_2 = the prior probability that a new observation belongs to group 2

A general method for determining the cutoff value for the classification rule is represented by:

$$\text{Cutoff value} = \frac{\hat{\bar{Y}}_1 + \hat{\bar{Y}}_1}{2} + \frac{S^2_{\hat{Y}_p}}{\hat{\bar{Y}}_1 - \hat{\bar{Y}}_2} \times LN\left(\frac{p_2 C(1\,|\,2)}{p_1 C(2\,|\,1)}\right) \qquad \textbf{10.5}$$

where LN(.) represents the natural logarithm, and

$$S^2_{\hat{Y}_p} = \frac{(n_1 - 1)\,S^2_{\hat{Y}_1} + (n_2 - 1)\,S^2_{\hat{Y}_1}}{n_1 + n_2 - 2}$$

where n_i represents the number of observations in group i and $S^2_{\hat{Y}_i}$ represents the sample variance of the discriminant scores for group i. Notice that if the costs of misclassification are equal ($C(1\,|\,2) = C(2\,|\,1)$) and the prior probabilities are equal ($p_1 = p_2$), the cutoff value in equation 10.5 reduces to the midpoint cutoff value in equation 10.4 because $LN(1) = 0$.

To illustrate this refined cutoff value, suppose that the personnel director in our example believes there is a 40% chance that a given applicant would be a satisfactory employee ($p_1 = 0.40$) and a 60% chance that a given applicant would be an unsatisfactory employee ($p_2 = 0.60$). Furthermore, suppose that the company considers it twice as costly to hire a person who turns out to be an unsatisfactory worker as it is to not hire a person who would have been a satisfactory worker. This implies that $C(1\,|\,2) = 2 \times C(2|1)$.

To calculate the refined cutoff value obtained using equation 10.5, we first calculate $S^2_{\hat{Y}_1}$ and $S^2_{\hat{Y}_2}$ using Excel's VAR( ) function to obtain:

$$S^2_{\hat{Y}_1} = VAR(E4:E14) = 0.0648$$

$$S^2_{\hat{Y}_2} = VAR(E15:E23) = 0.0705$$

Because $n_1 = 11$ and $n_2 = 9$, $S^2_{\hat{Y}_p}$ is computed as:

$$S^2_{\hat{Y}_p} = \frac{(11 - 1)(0.0648) + (9 - 1)(0.0705)}{(11 + 9 - 2)} = 0.06733$$

We can then use equation 10.5 to compute the refined cutoff value as:

$$\text{Refined cutoff value} = \frac{1.193 + 1.764}{2} + \frac{0.06733}{1.193 - 1.764} LN\left(\frac{2(0.6)}{(0.4)}\right) = 1.349$$

This refined cutoff value reduces the chance of an observation from group 2 being misclassified into group 1 (which is the more costly mistake) and increases the chance of an observation from group 1 being misclassified into group 2 (which is the less costly mistake).

10.1.5 Classification Accuracy

Our ultimate goal in DA is to predict to which group a new observation (or job applicant) belongs. Because we already know which group each observation in our analysis sample belongs to, it might seem pointless to try to classify these observations. Yet, by doing so we can get some idea of how accurate our classification rule is likely to be with other new observations whose true group memberships are unknown. For our example, if we use the midpoint cutoff value technique, our classification rule is:

Classification Rule: If an observation's discriminant score is less than or equal to 1.479, then assign it to group 1; otherwise, assign it to group 2.

The Predicted Group column in Figure 10.5 contains the results of applying this classification rule. This rule is implemented by placing the following formula in cell F4 and copying it to cells F5 through F23:

Formula for cell F4:   =IF(E4<=$E$26,1,2)
(Copy to F5 through F23.)

Comparing the values in the Predicted Group column to the values in the Group column indicates that a number of observations in the analysis sample were misclassified using the preceding classification rule. Misclassified observations can be identified easily by implementing the following formula in cell G4 and copying it to cells G5 through G23:

Formula for cell G4:   =IF(F4<>B4,"**","")
(Copy to G5 through G23.)

This marks the misclassified observations with asterisks (**) in Figure 10.5. Figure 10.7 summarizes these classification results.

Figure 10.7 shows that nine of the eleven observations (81.8%) that belong to group 1 were classified correctly in this group, and the other two observations (18.2%) belonging to group 1 were misclassified into group 2. Similarly, seven of the nine observations (77.8%) that belong to group 2 were classified correctly in this group, and the other two observations (22.2%) belonging to group 2 were misclassified into group 1. Overall, sixteen out of twenty observations (80.0%) in our analysis sample were classified correctly, and a total of four observations (20.0%) were misclassified. The matrix shown in Figure 10.7 is sometimes referred to as a **confusion matrix** because it indicates how much confusion exists regarding the group memberships of the observations in the analysis sample.

From these results, we might expect that our classification rule will provide correct classifications approximately 80% of the time if we use it to predict the group membership of new applicants. Actually, the figure of 80% is probably somewhat favorably biased. That is, the observations in our analysis sample influenced the development of the classification rule; therefore, we expect that this rule might be successful in classifying these same observations. However, we should not expect the procedure to duplicate this level of accuracy when classifying new observations that did not influence the development of the classification rule.

Figure 10.7
Summary of
classification
results on the
analysis sample
for the two
groups.

		Predicted Group		
		1	2	Total
Actual Group	1	9	2	11
	2	2	7	9
	Total	11	9	20

10.1.6 Classifying New Employees

As mentioned previously, the ultimate goal in DA is to predict into which group a new observation (or potential employee) is most likely to fall. In our example, this involves predicting whether or not a new job applicant will be a satisfactory or unsatisfactory employee. Figure 10.8 shows a new worksheet named Classification Sample. This worksheet is similar to the one in Figure 10.1, but here all the observations represent new job applicants being considered for employment. Because we do not know whether these applicants will be satisfactory or unsatisfactory employees, question marks (?) have been entered in the Group column. The values in the Mechanical and Verbal columns represent the applicants' scores on the two aptitude tests.

We can use the regression results and classification rule developed for our analysis sample to calculate discriminant scores and predict whether each new observation (or applicant) would fall into group 1 or group 2. To calculate these scores, the following formula is implemented in cell E4 and copied to cells E5 through E9:

Formula for cell E4   =TREND('Analysis Sample'!$B$4:$B$23,'Analysis
(Copy to E5 through E9.)   Sample'!$C$4:$D$23,C4:D4)

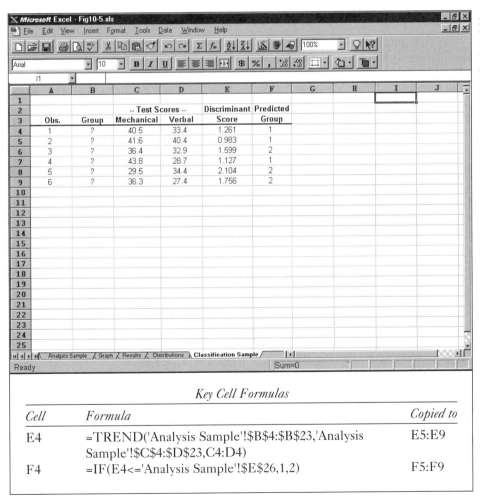

Figure 10.8
Predicted group memberships of the new job applicants.

Key Cell Formulas

Cell	Formula	Copied to
E4	=TREND('Analysis Sample'!$B$4:$B$23,'Analysis Sample'!$C$4:$D$23,C4:D4)	E5:E9
F4	=IF(E4<='Analysis Sample'!$E$26,1,2)	F5:F9

The classification rule is implemented by entering the following formula in cell F4 and copying it to cells F5 through F9:

Formula for cell F4:   =IF(E4<='Analysis Sample'!$E$26,1,2)
(Copy to F5 through F9.)

The Predicted Group column shows an *estimate*, or *forecast*, of which group each new job applicant would fall into if hired. For example, we are predicting that the applicants listed as observations 1, 2, and 4 in Figure 10.8 would be satisfactory employees (belonging to group 1) and the other applicants would be unsatisfactory (belonging to group 2).

Only time will tell how accurate these predictions are for the applicants hired, and we will never know if the predictions are correct for applicants that are not hired. But the DA technique has provided the personnel director with an objective way of incorporating the mechanical and verbal aptitude test scores in the hiring decision. As with any statistical tool, these results should be used in conjunction with other information available and with the decision maker's professional judgment of each applicant's potential value to the company.

10.2   THE k-GROUP DA PROBLEM

It might seem as if the regression approach for two-group DA could be extended easily to problems with more than two groups. For example, suppose that we have a problem with three groups (labeled A, B, and C) and one independent variable X. We could set up a dependent variable Y and assign it a value of 1, 2, or 3 to indicate observations belonging to group A, B, or C, respectively. We might attempt to model the behavior of this dependent variable as:

$$\hat{Y}_i = b_0 + b_1 X_i \qquad\qquad \textbf{10.6}$$

We could then apply regression analysis to estimate values for b_0 and b_1 so that we could calculate the discriminant scores $\hat{Y}_i$. Figure 10.9 (and file FIG10-9.xls on your data disk, displays hypothetical data for such a problem.

Having obtained the discriminant scores, we might use the following rule to classify observations:

If the discriminant score is	Assign observation to group
$\hat{Y} < 1.5$	A
$1.5 \le \hat{Y} \le 2.5$	B
$\hat{Y} > 2.5$	C

Although such an approach might seem reasonable, it has a major flaw. Note that the linear relationship between the dependent and independent variables in Figure 10.9 is due solely to the manner in which the dependent variable numbers were assigned to the groups. That is, if we assign the number 2 to group A and the number 1 to group B, the linear relationship between the variables is destroyed, as illustrated in Figure 10.10.

In general, the regression function in equation 10.6 cannot be used for DA problems with more than two groups because the relationship between the dependent and independent variables might not be linear. Even if we could make the relationship

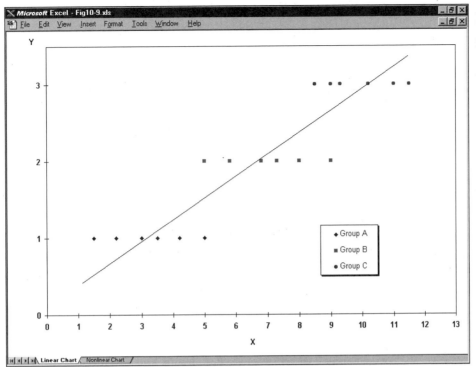

Figure 10.9
Graph of three-group example with one independent variable showing a linear relationship,

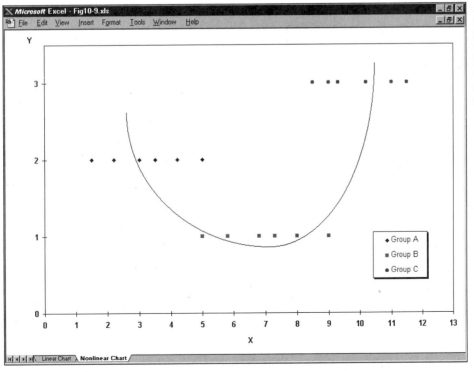

Figure 10.10
Graph of three-group example with one independent variable showing a nonlinear relationship.

linear with some appropriate coding for the dependent variable, it can be very difficult to discern what this coding should be if the problem involves more than one independent variable. In this section, we will discuss another approach to DA that can be used when the problem involves more than two groups.

10.2.1   Multiple Discriminant Analysis

To distinguish this approach from the two-group regression approach, we refer to it as **multiple discriminant analysis** (MDA). The following modified personnel selection example illustrates the MDA approach.

> Suppose that instead of being rated as either satisfactory or unsatisfactory in their annual performance reviews, the employees for ACME Manufacturing are rated as performing in either a superior, average, or inferior manner. Marie wants to analyze the differences in pre-employment screening test scores for these three groups of employees and develop a rule for predicting to which group a new potential employee would belong. Her plan is to hire any applicant classified in the superior group and reject applicants in the inferior group. Applicants in the average group will be screened more closely with additional interviews and reference checking before Marie makes a hiring decision.

In this example, the personnel director is interested in discriminating among *three* groups: (1) superior employees, (2) average employees, and (3) inferior employees. We cannot apply the regression-based technique described earlier to this example because it involves more than two groups. We are using three groups in this example for convenience in illustrating the MDA approach. This approach can be applied to problems involving any number of groups. The MDA approach also can accommodate more than two independent variables.

The data for this example are displayed in Figure 10.11 (and in the file FIG10-11.xls on your data disk). The Analysis Sample worksheet contains data for the company's current employees, whom the personnel director has classified into one of the three groups: (1) superior, (2) average, and (3) inferior. These group assignments are indicated by the numbers in the Group column. Each employee's mechanical and verbal scores on the aptitude test are displayed in the adjacent columns.

Although the MDA approach is different from the regression technique described earlier for the two-group example, the basic idea is the same. Figure 10.12 shows the plot of all the scores on the aptitude tests for each group along with the centroids. Note that most of the observations in each group cluster around the group's centroid. If we don't already know to which group an observation belongs, we could classify the observation based on its proximity to the centroids. That is, to determine to which group a new observation belongs, we could plot it on this graph and visually judge the distance between it and each of the centroids. A logical classification rule is to assign observations to the group represented by the closest centroid. This is the approach taken in MDA, although at a somewhat more sophisticated level.

10.2.2   Distance Measures

The problem with the visual approach is that some observations might be "too close to call," appearing to be equally close to several centroids. For example, in Figure 10.12 several points fall midway between two of the centroids and might be difficult

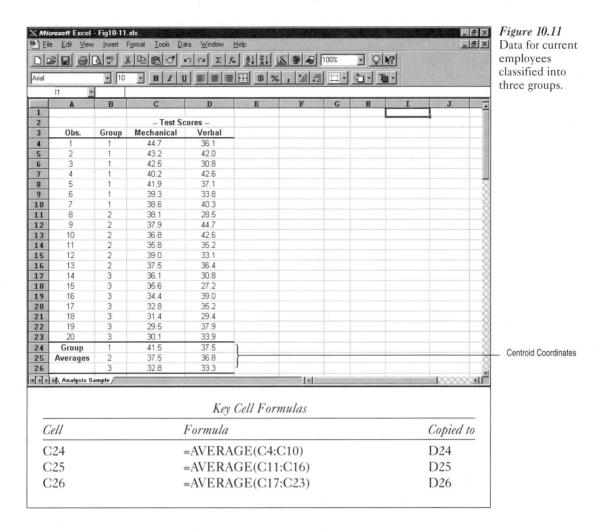

Figure 10.11
Data for current
employees
classified into
three groups.

Centroid Coordinates

Key Cell Formulas

Cell	Formula	Copied to
C24	=AVERAGE(C4:C10)	D24
C25	=AVERAGE(C11:C16)	D25
C26	=AVERAGE(C17:C23)	D26

to classify visually. Also, if the problem involves more than two independent variables, the graph displaying the data must be drawn in three or more dimensions, making a visual inspection of the data difficult or impossible. Rather than just "eyeballing" it, we need a more formal measure of the distance between each observation and each centroid.

You might recall from high school algebra (or Chapter 8) that the Euclidean (straight-line) distance between two points (A_1, B_1) and (A_2, B_2) in two dimensions can be measured by:

$$\text{Distance} = \sqrt{(A_1 - A_2)^2 + (B_1 - B_2)^2} \qquad \textbf{10.7}$$

For example, the distance between two arbitrary points (3, 7) and (9, 5) is:

$$\sqrt{(3 - 9)^2 + (7 - 5)^2} = \sqrt{40} = 6.324$$

This distance formula generalizes easily to any number of dimensions. We can use this formula in MDA to measure the distance from a given observation to the centroid of each group, and then assign the observation to the group it is closest to. From a statistical viewpoint, this distance measure in equation 10.7 is somewhat weak because it ignores the variances of the independent variables. To see this, suppose that X_1

Figure 10.12
Graph of data for
the three-group
example.

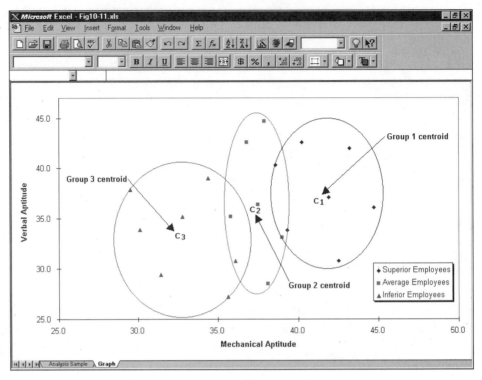

represents one of the independent variables and X_2 the other. If X_2 has a much larger variance than X_1, the effects of *small but important* differences in X_1 could be masked or dwarfed in equation 10.7 by *large but unimportant* differences in X_2. Figure 10.13 illustrates this problem, where the ellipses represent regions containing 99% of the values belonging to each group.

Consider the observation labeled P_1 in Figure 10.13. This observation appears to be closest to C_2 and, indeed, if we used the standard distance measure in equation 10.7, we would assign it to group 2 because its distance from C_1 with respect to the X_2-axis is relatively large. However, it is extremely unlikely that this observation belongs to group 2 because its location with respect to the X_1-axis exceeds the typical values for group 2. Thus, it would be helpful to refine our distance measure in equation 10.7 to account for possible differences in the variances of the independent variables.

If we let D_{ij} represent the distance from observation i to the centroid for group j, we can define this distance as:

$$D_{ij} = \sqrt{\sum_k \frac{(x_{ik} - \bar{x}_{jk})^2}{s_{jk}^2}} \qquad\qquad \textbf{10.8}$$

where x_{ik} represents the value of observation i on the kth independent variable, $\bar{x}_{jk}$ represents the average value of group j on the kth independent variable, and s_{jk}^2 represents the sample variance of group j on the kth independent variable.

10.2.3   MDA Classification

There are numerous variations on the distance measure in equation 10.8. One of the most popular variations—known as the **Mahalanobis distance measure**—refines

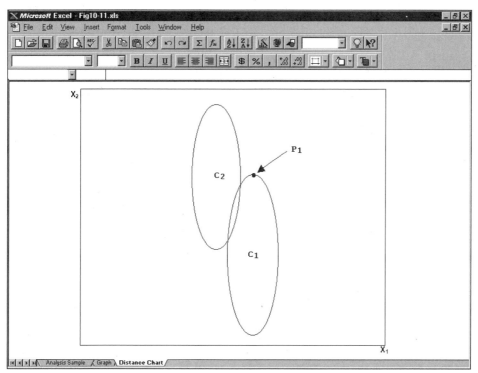

Figure 10.13
Regions
containing 99%
of the
observations in
each group.

the calculation in equation 10.8 to account for differences in the covariances between the independent variables. An add-in called DA.xla was written to make it easy to perform MDA in Excel using Mahalanobis distance measures. (See the box titled Installing and Using the DA.xla Add-In.) This add-in calculates the Mahalanobis distance from each observation to the centroid for each of the possible groups. It then assigns each observation to the group it is closest to based on these distance measures.

Installing and Using the DA.xla Add-In

To use the DA.xla add-in, simply open the file called DA.xla found on your data disk. This automatically adds a new option labeled Discriminant Analysis to your Tools menu. This new option remains on the Tools menu until you exit Excel. If you want to make the DA.xla add-in a more permanent addition to your Tools menu:

1. Click the Tools menu.
2. Select Add-Ins.
3. Click the Browse button.
4. Locate the file DA.xla and click OK.
5. Click OK on the Add-Ins dialog box.

The Discriminant Analysis option will now be listed on your Tools menu whenever you start Excel. You can eliminate this option by de-selecting it in the Add-Ins dialog box.

After the DA.xla add-in is installed, the dialog box in Figure 10.14 may be invoked as follows:

1. Click the Tools menu.
2. Select Discriminant Analysis.

This dialog box is similar to that of the regression tool in Excel. We must indicate the Y-Range and X-Range for the analysis sample, as well as the X-Range for the classification sample. We must also indicate the name we want assigned to the sheet containing the output of the analysis. An optional check box on the Discriminant Analysis dialog box can be selected to instruct the add-in to use a pooled covariance matrix in computing the distances. This box should be checked if there is reason to believe that the variances and covariances of the independent (X-Range) variables are the same in each group. (With the Use Pooled Covariance Matrix box selected, the DA.xla add-in should produce the same results as the regression approach to DA for two-group problems.) Figure 10.15 displays the results of the Discriminant Analysis add-in for our example problem.

As shown in Figure 10.15, the Discriminant Analysis add-in first computes the centroids for each group. Next, the Mahalanobis distance from each observation in the analysis sample to the centroid of each group is computed. These distances are displayed in cells B11 through D30. The column labeled Predicted Group indicates which group each observation in closest to based on these distance measures, while the adjacent column, labeled Actual Group, indicates what group each observation in the analysis sample actually belongs to.

In rows 33 through 40, a confusion matrix is shown summarizing the results from the analysis sample. This matrix indicates that six of the seven observations actually

Figure 10.14
Dialog box for the DA.xla add-in.

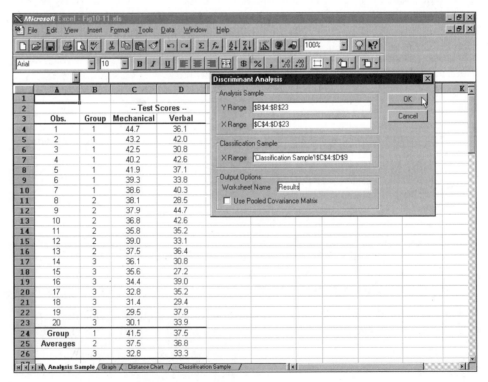

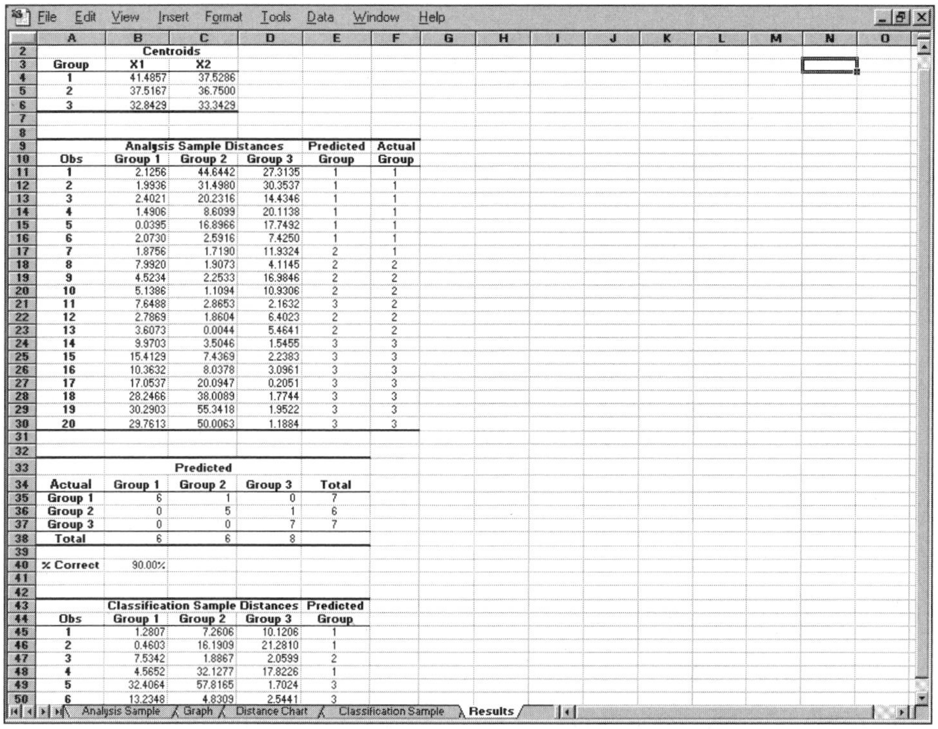

Group	X1	X2
Centroids		
1	41.4857	37.5286
2	37.5167	36.7500
3	32.8429	33.3429

	Analysis Sample Distances			Predicted	Actual
Obs	Group 1	Group 2	Group 3	Group	Group
1	2.1256	44.6442	27.3135	1	1
2	1.9936	31.4980	30.3537	1	1
3	2.4021	20.2316	14.4346	1	1
4	1.4906	8.6099	20.1138	1	1
5	0.0395	16.8966	17.7492	1	1
6	2.0730	2.5916	7.4250	1	1
7	1.8756	1.7190	11.9324	2	1
8	7.9920	1.9073	4.1145	2	2
9	4.5234	2.2533	16.9846	2	2
10	5.1386	1.1094	10.9306	2	2
11	7.6488	2.8653	2.1632	3	2
12	2.7869	1.8604	6.4023	2	2
13	3.6073	0.0044	5.4641	2	2
14	9.9703	3.5046	1.5455	3	3
15	15.4129	7.4369	2.2383	3	3
16	10.3632	8.0378	3.0961	3	3
17	17.0537	20.0947	0.2051	3	3
18	28.2466	38.0089	1.7744	3	3
19	30.2903	55.3418	1.9522	3	3
20	29.7613	50.0063	1.1884	3	3

	Predicted			
Actual	Group 1	Group 2	Group 3	Total
Group 1	6	1	0	7
Group 2	0	5	1	6
Group 3	0	0	7	7
Total	6	6	8	
% Correct	90.00%			

	Classification Sample Distances			Predicted
Obs	Group 1	Group 2	Group 3	Group
1	1.2807	7.2606	10.1206	1
2	0.4603	16.1909	21.2810	1
3	7.5342	1.8867	2.0599	2
4	4.5652	32.1277	17.8226	1
5	32.4064	57.8165	1.7024	3
6	13.2348	4.8309	2.5441	3

Figure 10.15 Results obtained using the DA.xla add-in.

belong to group 1 were correctly classified as belonging to group 1, while one observation (number 7) from group 1 was erroneously classified as coming from group 2. Similarly, five of the six observations belonging to group 2 were correctly classified, while one observation (number 11) from group 2 was misclassified into group 3. Finally, all seven observations from group 3 in the analysis sample were correctly classified. Thus, cell B40 indicates that a total of 18 out of 20 observations (or 90%) were correctly classified.

Rows 43 through 50 of Figure 10.15 show the classification results for the same six new applicants that were classified using the two-group approach to DA in Figure 10.8. It is interesting to compare the results of these analyses. Recall that the personnel director's plan is to classify applicants into three groups and hire any applicant in the superior group (group 1), reject any applicant in the inferior group (group 3), and conduct a follow-up interview and check the references on applicants in the average group (group 2). In Figure 10.15, note that applicants 1, 2, and 4, who were classified earlier as satisfactory, are now identified as superior candidates. Applicants 5 and 6, who were classified earlier as unsatisfactory, are now identified as inferior candidates. However, applicant 3, who was classified earlier as unsatisfactory, is now identified as average and requires additional screening by the personnel director before a hiring decision is made.

SUMMARY

DA is a statistical technique that can be used to develop a rule for predicting in which of two or more groups an observation belongs. DA is similar to regression analysis in

THE WORLD OF MANAGEMENT SCIENCE
La Quinta Motor Inns Predicts
Successful Sites with Discriminant Analysis

Management at La Quinta Motor Inns wanted a fast, reliable method for predicting whether potential sites for new inns would be successful. One of the first issues to be resolved in designing a regression model was to define a measure of success that would be useful in making predictions. After considering several alternatives, operating margin—defined as profit plus depreciation and interest expenses as a percentage of total revenue—was chosen. Total revenue and total profit were unsuitable measures because they are too highly correlated with the size of the inn. Occupancy was also considered unsuitable because it is too sensitive to the economic cycle.

Data were collected on all 151 existing inns operated by La Quinta at the time of the study. The regression model was developed using 57 inns, and the other 94 were set aside for validation. During the selection of independent variables, care was taken to measure collinearity and keep it under control. A coefficient of determination (R^2) of 0.51 was obtained for a model showing that operating margin is positively influenced by the price of the inn (a measure of the competitive room rate of the market area) and the location of nearby colleges. Negative influences were distance to the nearest La Quinta Inn (a reverse measure of market penetration) and median income in the market area (suggesting an industrial economic base). After careful analysis, one outlier was deleted from the data, substantially improving the model.

The regression model itself was not the tool that management had in mind, however. Management needed a criterion to use for either choosing or rejecting potential sites. After specifying an acceptable risk of choosing a bad site, classification tables were used to develop a decision rule for discriminating between "good" sites and "bad" sites. The cutoff value was a predicted operating margin of 35%.

The model was then tested on the 94 inns set aside for validation, and the error rates were as expected. Set up as a spreadsheet, the model is now used to screen potential sites for possible development, with the final decision made by the president of the company.

Source: Sheryl E. Kimes, and James A. Fitzsimmons, "Selecting Profitable Hotel Sites at La Quinta Motor Inns," *Interfaces*, vol. 20, no. 2, March-April 1990, pages 12–20.

that it uses a set of independent variables to predict the value of a dependent variable. However, in DA the dependent variable is coded in a discrete, or categorical, manner to represent the different groups under consideration.

This chapter presented two approaches to DA. When the problem involves only two groups, regression analysis can be used to develop a classification rule. However, when the problem involves more than two groups, the regression approach is no longer appropriate and the more general k-group approach to DA is required. The k-group DA approach can be used with problems involving two or more groups.

DA is a powerful technique with a deep and rich theoretical basis. Our discussion of DA has only scratched the surface, but it should give you a good understanding of the issues involved in DA and some of the methods for solving classification problems. Other techniques exist for performing DA and MDA and these might be more appropriate for a particular data set than the procedures described in this chapter.

QUESTIONS AND PROBLEMS

1. What is a centroid?

2. It can be argued that regression analysis and DA both use a set of independent variables to predict the value of a dependent variable. What, then, is the difference between regression analysis and DA?

3. In discussing the approach to DA using distance measures, we calculated the distance from an observation to the centroid of each group. We then assigned the observation to the group it was closest to based on the distance measures. Can you think of another way distance measures might be used to classify observations? What classification rule is used under this method?

4. This chapter noted that the R^2 statistic cannot be relied upon as a goodness-of-fit measure in the regression approach to two-group DA. What was the value of the R^2 statistic for the two-group DA example in this chapter? How does it compare with the percentage of correctly classified observations in this same example?

5. The director of the MBA program at Salterdine University wants to use DA to determine which applicants to admit to the MBA program. The director believes that an applicant's undergraduate grade-point average (GPA) and score on the GMAT exam are helpful in predicting which applicants will be good students. To assist in this endeavor, the director asked a committee of faculty members to classify 30 of the current students in the MBA program into two groups: (1) good students and (2) weak students. The following data summarize these ratings, along with the GPA and GMAT scores for the 30 students.

   a. What are the coordinates of the centroids for the good students and the weak students?
   b. Use the regression approach to two-group DA to develop a classification rule for predicting to which group a new student will belong. State your classification rule.
   c. Create a confusion matrix that summarizes the accuracy of your classification rule on the current students. Overall, how accurate does your classification rule appear to be?

Student	Faculty Rating	GPA	GMAT
1	1	2.96	596
2	1	3.14	473
3	1	3.22	482
4	1	3.29	527
5	1	3.69	505
6	1	3.46	693
7	1	3.03	626

Student	Faculty Rating	GPA	GMAT
8	1	3.19	663
9	1	3.63	447
10	1	3.59	588
11	1	2.86	494
12	1	2.85	496
13	1	3.14	419
14	1	3.28	371
15	1	2.89	447
16	2	3.15	313
17	2	3.50	402
18	2	2.89	485
19	2	2.80	444
20	2	3.13	416
21	2	2.54	446
22	2	2.43	425
23	2	2.20	474
24	2	2.36	531
25	2	2.57	542
26	2	2.35	406
27	2	2.72	412
28	2	2.51	458
29	2	2.36	399
30	2	2.19	482

d. Suppose that the MBA director receives applications for admission to the MBA program from the following individuals. According to DA, which of these individuals do you expect to be good students and which do you expect to be weak?

Name	GPA	GMAT
Mike Dimoupolous	3.02	450
Scott Frazier	2.97	587
Paula Curry	3.95	551
Terry Freeman	2.45	484
Dana Simmons	3.26	524

6. Refer to question 5. The MBA director could make two types of admission mistakes using DA. One mistake is to classify a student into the weak category (and, therefore, not admit the student) when, in fact, the student belongs in the good category. We will call this a type I error. The other type of error (which we will call a type II error) is to classify a student into the good category (and, therefore, admit the student) when, in fact, the student is a weak student. Suppose that the MBA director considers a type I error to be twice as costly as a type II error. How does the classification rule change to accommodate these unequal costs of misclassification? What is the new classification rule?

7. Refer to question 5 and answer the following questions:

a. Use the Mahalanobis distance measure approach to DA to classify each of the current students.

b. Create a confusion matrix that summarizes the accuracy of the distance measure approach on the data for the current students. Overall, how accurate does the distance measure approach to DA appear to be on these data?

c. Classify each of the five new applicants from question 5 using the distance measure approach. Whom do you expect to be good students and whom do you expect to be weak?

d. If the two approaches to DA reach the same conclusion about a given applicant, what effect should this have on the MBA director's opinion of that applicant? What action might the director take if the two approaches to DA suggest conflicting classifications?

8. The manager of the commercial loan department for a bank wants to develop a rule to use in determining whether or not to approve various requests for loans. The manager believes that three key characteristics of a company's performance are important in making this decision: liquidity, profitability, and activity. The manager measures liquidity as the ratio of current assets to current liabilities. Profitability is measured as the ratio of net profit to sales. Activity is measured as the ratio of sales to fixed assets. The manager has collected the following data for a sample of 18 loans that the bank has made in the past five years. These loans have been classified into two groups: (1) those that were acceptable and (2) those that should have been rejected.

Observation	Category	Liquidity	Profitability	Activity
1	1	0.90	0.34	1.53
2	1	0.88	0.23	1.67
3	1	0.92	0.28	1.43
4	1	0.89	0.14	1.24
5	1	0.78	0.35	1.80
6	1	0.81	0.26	2.01
7	1	0.72	0.18	1.75
8	1	0.93	0.22	0.99
9	1	0.82	0.26	1.40
10	2	0.78	0.26	1.34
11	2	0.78	0.27	1.67
12	2	0.72	0.18	1.53
13	2	0.69	0.16	1.20
14	2	0.63	0.15	0.88
15	2	0.58	0.22	1.42
16	2	0.81	0.18	1.59
17	2	0.67	0.21	1.21
18	2	0.65	0.16	1.37

a. What are the coordinates of the centroids for the two groups?

b. Use the regression approach to two-group DA to develop a classification rule for predicting whether or not a given loan applicant will repay the loan, if approved. State your classification rule.

c. Create a confusion matrix that summarizes the accuracy of your classification rule on the data for the current loans. Overall, how accurate does your classification rule seem?

d. Suppose that the manager receives loan applications from companies with the following financial information. According to DA, which of these companies do you expect to be acceptable credit risks?

Company	Liquidity	Profitability	Activity
A	0.78	0.27	1.58
B	0.91	0.23	1.67
C	0.68	0.33	1.43
D	0.78	0.23	1.23
E	0.67	0.26	1.78

9. Refer to question 8. Suppose that the manager wants to classify loan applicants into one of three groups: (1) acceptable loan applications, (2) loan applications requiring further scrutiny, and (3) unacceptable loan applications. Assume that the first six observations given in question 8 correspond to group 1, the next six correspond to group 2, and the final six correspond to group 3.

a. Use the distance measure approach to DA to classify each loan.
b. Create a confusion matrix that summarizes the accuracy of the distance measure approach on the data for the current loans. Overall, how accurate does the distance measure approach to DA appear to be on these data?
c. Classify each of the five new applicants from question 8 using the distance measure approach. Into which of the three groups do you expect each loan applicant to fall?

10. Consider the two-group personnel selection example discussed in this chapter. Some might argue that the best classification rule for this problem is the one that minimizes the number of misclassifications in the analysis sample. Formulate a mixed-integer programming model that could be solved to determine the linear classification rule that minimizes the number of misclassifications in the analysis sample. (Hint: Create one constraint for each observation. Include a unique binary variable in each constraint to indicate whether or not the observation is misclassified.)

CASE 10.1   PREDICTING BANK FAILURE

Based on K.Y. Tam and M.Y. Kiang, "Managerial Applications of Neural Networks: The Case of Bank Failure Prediction," *Management Science*, 1992, vol. 38, no. 7, 926–947.

The number of bankruptcies in the banking industry recently reached an historic high unparalleled since the Great Depression. In 1984, fewer than 50 bankruptcy cases were filed with the Federal Deposit Insurance Corporation (FDIC), whereas in 1991, more than 400 were filed. To monitor the member banks and to assure their proper compliance with federal regulations, the FDIC commits substantial efforts to both on-site examinations and off-site surveillance activities. To facilitate this process, the FDIC is developing an early warning system that will alert the agency to banks that might be approaching or entering financial distress. Using the technique of DA, you'll help the FDIC develop such an early warning system.

Specifically, the FDIC wants to develop a procedure to help predict if a bank will enter financial distress in the coming year. The following financial ratios are helpful in making such predictions:

$$\text{Ratio 1} = \frac{\text{Total Capital}}{\text{Total Assets}}$$

$$\text{Ratio 2} = \frac{\text{Total Expenses}}{\text{Total Assets}}$$

$$\text{Ratio 3} = \frac{\text{Total Loans and Leases}}{\text{Total Deposits}}$$

The FDIC supplied you with data on these ratios collected one year ago for a sample of banks. It also indicated which banks are currently in financial distress. These data are summarized in the table below (and in the file BankData.xls on your data disk).

		Analysis Sample		
Obs	*Group*	*Ratio 1*	*Ratio 2*	*Ratio 3*
1	1	8.1	0.13	0.64
2	1	6.6	0.10	1.04
3	1	5.8	0.11	0.66
4	1	12.3	0.09	0.80
5	1	4.5	0.11	0.69
6	1	9.1	0.14	0.74
7	1	1.1	0.12	0.63
8	1	8.9	0.12	0.75
9	1	0.7	0.16	0.56
10	1	9.8	0.12	0.65
11	2	7.3	0.10	0.55
12	2	14.0	0.08	0.46
13	2	9.6	0.08	0.72
14	2	12.4	0.08	0.43
15	2	18.4	0.07	0.52
16	2	8.0	0.08	0.54
17	2	12.6	0.09	0.30
18	2	9.8	0.07	0.67
19	2	8.3	0.09	0.51
20	2	20.6	0.13	0.79

Note: Group 1 = financially distressed banks
Group 2 = financially strong banks

1. Calculate the centroids for each group in the analysis sample. What do these values indicate?

2. Use the regression approach to two-group DA to develop a rule for predicting whether or not a bank will enter financial distress. State the classification rule you identify.

3. Use the classification rule you identify in question 2 to classify each observation in the analysis sample. Create a confusion matrix summarizing the classification results. Overall, how accurate does this classification rule seem to be?

4. Suppose that the FDIC also gave you the data below on six new banks. Based on the classification rule you developed using regression, which (if any) of the six new banks would you expect to enter financial distress?

Obs	Group	Ratio 1	Ratio 2	Ratio 3
1	?	3.3	0.13	0.63
2	?	9.2	0.08	0.26
3	?	9.3	0.09	0.59
4	?	3.2	0.16	0.57
5	?	11.4	0.09	0.69
6	?	8.1	0.14	0.72

5. The FDIC also wants you to analyze the data using the Mahalanobis distance measure approach discussed in this chapter. Carry out this analysis. Which of the two methods would you recommend that the FDIC use?

REFERENCES

Altman, E. I., R. B. Avery, R. A. Eisenbeis, and J. F. Sinkey. *Application of Classification Techniques in Business, Banking and Finance.* Greenwich, CT: JAI Press, 1981.

Booth, D. E., A. Pervaiz, S. N. Ahkam, and B. Osyk. "A Robust Multivariate Procedure for the Identification of Problem Savings and Loan Institutions." *Decision Sciences,* 1989, 20, 320–333.

Campbell, T. S. and J. K. Dietrich. "The Determinants of Default on Insured Conventional Residential Mortgage Loans." *Journal of Finance,* 38, 1983, 1569–1581.

Flury, B. and H. Riedwyl. *Multivariate Statistics: A Practical Approach.* New York: Chapman and Hall, 1988.

Hand, D. J. *Discrimination and Classification.* New York: Wiley, 1981.

Labe, R. "Database Marketing Increases Prospecting Effectiveness at Merrill Lynch." *Interfaces,* vol. 24, no. 5, 1994.

Morrison, D. F. *Multivariate Statistical Methods,* Third Edition. New York: McGraw-Hill, 1990.

Welker, R. B. "Discriminant and Classification Analysis as an Aid to Employee Selection." *Accounting Review,* 49, 1974, 514–523.

CHAPTER 11

Time Series Analysis

A time series is a set of observations on a quantitative variable collected over time. For example, every night the evening news reports the closing value of the Dow Jones Industrial Average. These closing values represent a series of values for a quantitative variable over time—or a time series. Most businesses keep track of a number of time series variables. Examples might include daily, weekly, monthly, or quarterly figures on sales, costs, profits, inventory, back-orders, customer counts, and so on.

Businesses often are interested in forecasting future values of a time series variable. For example, if we could accurately predict future closing values of the Dow Jones Industrial Average, we could become very wealthy investing in the stock market by "buying low and selling high." In constructing business plans, most companies make some attempt to forecast the expected levels of sales, costs, profits, inventory, back-orders, customer counts, and so on. These types of forecasts often are required inputs to the other types of modeling techniques discussed throughout this text.

In Chapter 9, we investigated how to build and use regression models to predict the behavior of a dependent variable using one or more independent variables that are believed to be related to the dependent variable in a *causal* fashion. That is, when building a regression model, we often select independent variables that are believed to cause the observed behavior of the dependent variable. Although we can sometimes use this same approach to build a causal regression model for a time series variable, we cannot always do so.

For example, we might not know which causal independent variables are influencing a particular time series variable. And even if we do have some idea of which causal variables are affecting a time series, there might not be any data available for those variables. If data on the causal variables are available, the best regression function estimated from these data might not fit the data well. Finally, even if the estimated regression function fits the data well, we might have to forecast the values of the causal independent variables in order to estimate future values of the dependent (time series) variable. Forecasting the causal independent variables might be more difficult than forecasting the original time series variable.

435

11.1   TIME SERIES METHODS

In some situations, it might be difficult, undesirable, or even impossible to forecast time series data using a causal regression model. In these cases, the only alternative might be to use a time series forecasting method in which we analyze the past behavior of the time series variable in order to predict its future behavior. If we discover some sort of systematic behavior in the time series variable, we might attempt to construct a model of this behavior to help us forecast its future behavior. For example, we might find a long-term upward (or downward) trend in the time series that might be expected to continue in the future. Or, we might discover some predictable seasonal fluctuations in the data that could help us make estimates about the future.

This chapter presents a variety of methods for analyzing time series data. We'll first discuss several techniques that are appropriate for *stationary* time series, where there is no significant upward or downward trend in the data over time. Then, we'll discuss techniques for handling *nonstationary* time series, where there is some upward or downward trend in the data over time. Finally, we'll discuss techniques for modeling seasonal patterns in time series data.

11.2   MEASURING ACCURACY

Many methods are available for modeling time series data. In most cases, it is impossible to know in advance which method will be the most effective for a given data set. Thus, a common approach to time series analysis involves trying several modeling techniques on a given data set and evaluating how well they explain the past behavior of the time series variable. We can evaluate these techniques by constructing line graphs that show the actual data versus the values predicted by the various modeling techniques. More formal quantitative measures of the accuracy of time series modeling techniques also exist. Two common accuracy measures are the **mean absolute deviation** (MAD) and the **mean square forecast error** (MSE). These two quantities are defined as:

$$\text{MAD} = \sum_i \frac{|Y_i - \hat{Y}_i|}{n}$$

$$\text{MSE} = \sum_i \frac{(Y_i - \hat{Y}_i)^2}{n}$$

In each of these formulas, Y_i represents the *actual* value for the ith observation in the time series and $\hat{Y}_i$ is the *forecasted* value for this observation. Both of these quantities measure the differences between the actual values in the time series and the predicted, or fitted, values generated by the forecasting technique. The MSE measure is closely related to the sum of square estimation errors criterion introduced in our discussion of regression analysis. Although both the MAD and the MSE measures are commonly used in time series modeling, we will focus on the MSE measure because it is somewhat easier to calculate.

11.3   EXTRAPOLATION MODELS

Extrapolation techniques for time series analysis involve building models that account for the past behavior of a time series variable in an effort to predict the future behavior of the variable. The general form of an extrapolation model is:

$$\hat{Y}_{t+1} = f(Y_t, Y_{t-1}, Y_{t-2}, \ldots), \qquad \qquad \textbf{11.1}$$

where $\hat{Y}_{t+1}$ represents the predicted value for the time series variable in time period $t + 1$, Y_t represents the value of the time series variable in time period t, Y_{t-1} represents the value of the time series variable in time period $t - 1$, and so on. The goal of an extrapolation model is to identify a function $f(\cdot)$ that produces accurate forecasts of future values of the time series variable.

11.3.1 An Example

The following example demonstrates several of the most common extrapolation techniques used in time series forecasting.

> Electra-City is a retail store that sells audio and video equipment for the home and car. Each month the manager of the store must order merchandise from a distant warehouse. Currently, the manager is trying to estimate how many VCRs the store is likely to sell in the next month. To assist in this process, he has collected the data shown in Figure 11.1 (and in the file FIG11-1.xls on your data disk) on the number of VCRs sold in each of the previous 24 months. He wants to use these data in making his prediction.

After collecting the data for a time series variable, the next step in building a time series model is to inspect the data plotted over time. Figure 11.1 includes a plot of the VCR data. Notice that this plot does not suggest a strong upward or downward trend in the data. This plot suggests that the number of VCRs sold each month fell somewhere between 30 and 40 units over the past two years with no apparent pattern or

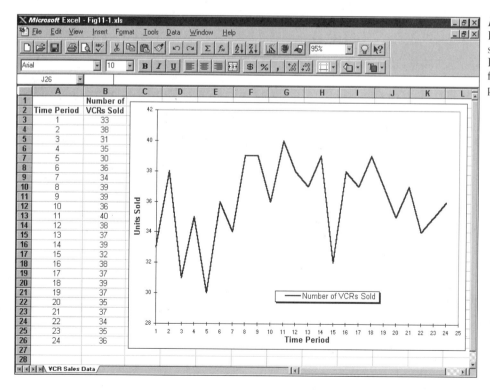

Figure 11.1
Historical VCR sales data for the Electra-City forecasting problem.

> ### · *Creating a Line Graph*
>
> To create a scatter plot like the one shown in Figure 11.1:
>
> 1. Select cells A1 through B26.
> 2. Click the Insert menu.
> 3. Click Chart.
> 4. Click On This Sheet.
> 5. Drag in the spreadsheet to indicate where you want the chart located.
>
> Excel's ChartWizard then prompts you to make a number of selections concerning the type of chart you want and how it should be labeled and formatted. After Excel creates a basic chart, you can customize it in many ways. Double-clicking a chart element displays a dialog box with options for modifying the appearance of the element.

regularity from month to month. Thus, we expect that one of the extrapolation techniques discussed in the following sections would be an appropriate method for modeling these data.

11.4   MOVING AVERAGES

The **moving average** technique is probably the easiest extrapolation method to use and understand. With this technique, the predicted value of the time series in period $t + 1$ (denoted by $\hat{Y}_{t+1}$) is simply the average of the k previous observations in the series; that is:

$$\hat{Y}_{t+1} = \frac{Y_t + Y_{t-1} + Y_{t-k+1}}{k} \qquad\qquad \textbf{11.2}$$

The value k in equation 11.2 determines how many previous observations will be included in the moving average. No general method exists for determining what value of k will be best for a particular time series. Therefore, we must try several values of k to see which gives the best results. This is illustrated in Figure 11.2 (and in the file FIG11-2.xls on your data disk) where the monthly number of VCRs sold for Electra-City is fit using moving average models with k values of 2 and 4.

We generated the moving average forecasts in Figure 11.2 using the AVERAGE( ) function. For example, the two-month moving average forecasts are generated by implementing the following formula in cell C5 and copying it to cells C6 through C26:

> Formula for cell C5:   =AVERAGE(B3:B4)
> (Copy to C6 through C26.)

The four-month moving average forecasts are generated by implementing the following formula in cell D7 and copying it to cells D8 through D26:

> Formula for cell D7:   =AVERAGE(B3:B6)
> (Copy to D8 through D26.)

The actual VCR sales data are plotted in Figure 11.3 along with the predicted values from the two moving average models. This graph shows that the predicted values

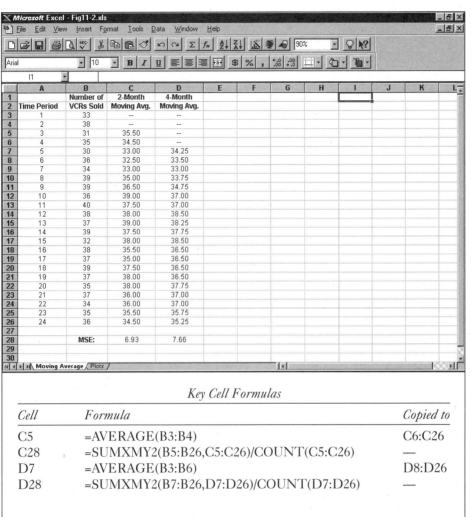

Figure 11.2
Moving average
forecasts for the
VCR sales data.

Key Cell Formulas

Cell	Formula	Copied to
C5	=AVERAGE(B3:B4)	C6:C26
C28	=SUMXMY2(B5:B26,C5:C26)/COUNT(C5:C26)	—
D7	=AVERAGE(B3:B6)	D8:D26
D28	=SUMXMY2(B7:B26,D7:D26)/COUNT(D7:D26)	—

tend to be less volatile, or smoother, than the actual data. This should not be surprising because the moving average technique tends to average out the peaks and valleys occurring in the original data. Thus, the moving average technique is sometimes referred to as a *smoothing* method. The larger the value of k (or the more past data points are averaged together), the smoother the moving average prediction will be.

We can evaluate the relative accuracy of the two moving average forecasting functions by comparing the MSE values for these two techniques shown in cells C28 and D28 in Figure 11.2. The following formulas calculate these MSE values:

Formula for cell C28: =SUMXMY2(B5:B26,C5:C26)/COUNT(C5:C26)

Formula for cell D28: =SUMXMY2(B7:B26,D7:D26)/COUNT(D7:D26)

(Note that the SUMXMY2( ) function calculates the sum of squared differences between corresponding values in two different ranges. The COUNT( ) function returns the number of values in a range.)

The MSE value describes the overall fit of the forecasting technique to the historical data. By comparing the MSE values for the two moving averages, we might

Figure 11.3
Plot of moving
average
predictions
versus actual
VCR sales data.

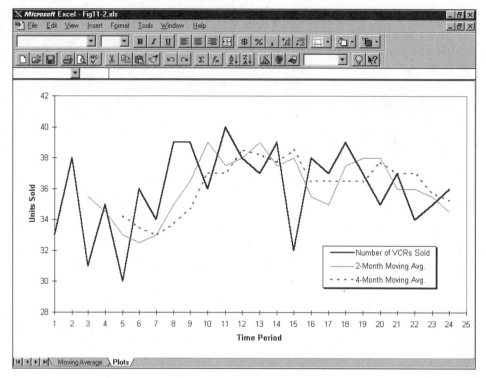

conclude that the two-month moving average (with an MSE of 6.93) provides more accurate forecasts than the four-month moving average (with an MSE of 7.66). Note, however, that the MSE includes and weighs relatively old data with the same importance as the most recent data. Thus, selecting a forecast based on the total MSE of the forecasting functions might not be wise because a forecasting function might have achieved a lower total MSE by fitting older data points very well while being relatively inaccurate on more recent data.

Because we want to *forecast* future observations, we might be interested in how well the forecasting function performed on the most recent data. We can determine this by calculating other MSE values using only the most recent data. For example, if we calculate MSE values using only the two most recent time periods (periods 23 and 24), the four-month moving average produces an MSE of 1.125/2 = 0.5625 and the two-month moving average produces an MSE of 2.50/2 = 1.25. (You should verify these figures on your own.) Thus, we might conclude that the four-month moving average model should be used to predict the future because it produced the most accurate predictions of the actual values observed during the past two time periods.

11.4.1   Forecasting with the Moving Average Model

Assuming that the manager of Electra-City is satisfied with the accuracy of the two-month moving average model, the prediction of the number of VCRs to be sold in the next month (time period 25) is calculated as:

$$\hat{Y}_{25} = \frac{Y_{24} + Y_{23}}{2} = \frac{36 + 35}{2} = 35.5$$

To forecast *more* than one period into the future using the moving average technique, we must substitute forecasted values for unobserved actual values. For example, suppose that at the end of time period 24 we want to forecast the number of VCRs to be sold in time periods 25 *and* 26. Using a two-period moving average, the forecast for time period 26 is represented by:

$$\hat{Y}_{26} = \frac{Y_{25} + Y_{24}}{2}$$

However, at time period 24 we don't know the actual value for Y_{25}. We have to substitute $\hat{Y}_{25}$ for Y_{25} in the previous equation to generate the forecast for time period 26. Therefore, at time period 24 our estimate of the number of VCRs to be sold in time period 26 is:

$$\hat{Y}_{26} = \frac{\hat{Y}_{25} + Y_{24}}{2} = \frac{35.5 + 36}{2} = 35.75$$

11.5   WEIGHTED MOVING AVERAGES

One drawback of the moving average technique is that all the past data used in calculating the average are weighted equally. However, we can often obtain a more accurate forecast by assigning different weights to the data. The **weighted moving average** extrapolation technique is a simple variation on the moving average technique that allows for weights to be assigned to the data being averaged. In the weighted moving average technique, the forecasting function is represented by:

$$\hat{Y}_{t+1} = w_1 Y_t + w_2 Y_{t-1} + \ldots + w_k Y_{t-k+1} \qquad \textbf{11.3}$$

where $0 \leq w_i \leq 1$ and $\sum_{i=1}^{k} w_i = 1$. Note that the simple moving average forecast in equation 11.2 is a special case of equation 11.3 where $w_1 = w_2 = \ldots = w_k = \frac{1}{k}$.

Although the weighted moving average offers greater flexibility than the moving average, it is also a bit more complicated. In addition to determining a value for k, we must also determine values for the weights w_i in equation 11.3. However, for a given value of k, we can use Solver to determine the values for w_i that minimize the MSE (or MAD). The spreadsheet implementation of a two-month weighted moving average model for the Electra-City example is shown in Figure 11.4 (and in the file FIG11-4.xls on your data disk).

Cells F3 and F4 represent the weights w_1 and w_2, respectively. Cell F5 is the sum of cells F3 and F4. The weighted average forecasting function is implemented in cell C5 with the following formula, which is copied to cells C6 through C26:

Formula for cell C5:   =$F$3*B4+$F$4*B3
(Copy to C6 through C26.)

Notice that with $w_1 = w_2 = 0.5$ the weighted average predictions are identical to those of the simple moving average method shown in Figure 11.2. The formula for the MSE value in C28 is the same as the formula for the two-month moving average described earlier.

We can use the Solver parameters and options shown in Figure 11.5 to identify the values for the weights in cells F3 and F4 that minimize the MSE. Notice that this is a nonlinear optimization problem because MSE represents a nonlinear objective function. Figure 11.6 shows the solution to this problem.

Notice that the optimal weights of $w_1 = 0.291$ and $w_2 = 0.709$ reduce the value of the MSE only slightly, from 6.93 to 6.29.

Figure 11.4
Spreadsheet
implementation
of the weighted
moving average
model.

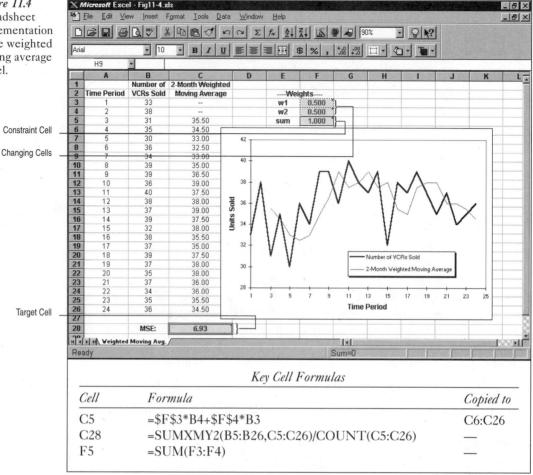

Key Cell Formulas		
Cell	*Formula*	*Copied to*
C5	=$F$3*B4+$F$4*B3	C6:C26
C28	=SUMXMY2(B5:B26,C5:C26)/COUNT(C5:C26)	—
F5	=SUM(F3:F4)	—

11.5.1   Forecasting with the Weighted Moving Average Model

Using the weighted moving average technique, the predicted number of VCRs to be sold at Electra-City in the next month (time period 25) is calculated as:

$$\hat{Y}_{25} = w_1 Y_{24} + w_2 Y_{23} = 0.291 \times 36 + 0.709 \times 35 = 35.3$$

We can also use the weighted moving average technique to forecast more than one time period into the future. However, as with the moving average technique, we must substitute forecasted values for unobserved actual values where needed. For example, suppose that at the end of time period 24 we want to forecast the number of VCRs to be sold in time periods 25 *and* 26. The weighted moving average forecast for time period 26 is represented by:

$$\hat{Y}_{26} = w_1 Y_{25} + w_2 Y_{24}$$

However, at time period 24 we don't know the actual value for Y_{25}. We have to substitute $\hat{Y}_{25}$ for Y_{25} in the previous equation to generate the forecast for time period 26. Therefore, at time period 24 our estimate of the number of VCRs to be sold in time period 26 is:

$$\hat{Y}_{26} = w_1 \hat{Y}_{25} + w_2 Y_{24} = 0.291 \times 35.3 + 0.709 \times 36 = 35.80$$

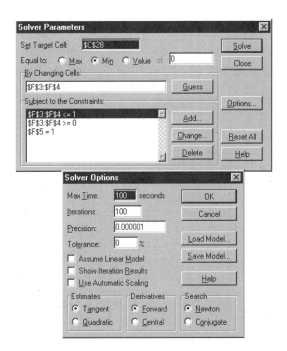

Figure 11.5
Solver parameters and options for the weighted moving average model.

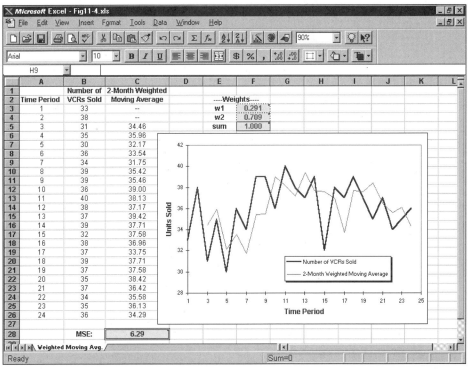

Figure 11.6
Optimal solution for the weighted moving average model.

11.6 EXPONENTIAL SMOOTHING

Exponential smoothing is another averaging technique that allows weights to be assigned to past data. Exponential smoothing models assume the following form:

$$\hat{Y}_{t+1} = \hat{Y}_t + \alpha(Y_t - \hat{Y}_t) \qquad \qquad \textbf{11.4}$$

Equation 11.4 indicates that the predicted value for time period $t + 1$ ($\hat{Y}_{t+1}$) is equal to the predicted value for the previous period ($\hat{Y}_t$) plus an adjustment for the error made in predicting the previous period's value ($\alpha(Y_t - \hat{Y}_t)$). The parameter (alpha) in equation 11.4 can assume any value between 0 and 1 ($0 \leq \alpha \leq 1$).

It can be shown that the exponential smoothing formula in equation 11.4 is equivalent to:

$$\hat{Y}_{t+1} = \alpha Y_t + \alpha(1 - \alpha)Y_{t-1} + \alpha(1 - \alpha)^2 Y_{t-2} + \ldots + \alpha(1 - \alpha)^n Y_{t-n} + \ldots$$

As shown in the previous equation, the forecast $\hat{Y}_{t+1}$ in exponential smoothing is a weighted combination of all previous values in the time series where the most recent observation Y_t receives the heaviest weight (α), the next most recent observation Y_{t-1} receives the next heaviest weight ($\alpha(1 - \alpha)$), and so on.

In an exponential smoothing model, small values of α tend to produce sluggish forecasts that do not react quickly to changes in the data. A value of α close to 1 produces a forecast that reacts more quickly to changes in the data. Figure 11.7 (file FIG11-7.xls on your data disk) illustrates these relationships, showing the results of two exponential smoothing models for the VCR sales data with α-values of 0.1 and 0.9.

We can use Solver to determine the optimal value for α when building an exponential smoothing forecasting model for a particular data set. The spreadsheet implementation of the exponential smoothing forecasting model for the Electra-City example is shown in Figure 11.8 (and in the file FIG11-8.xls on your data disk).

Figure 11.7
Two exponential smoothing models of the VCR sales data.

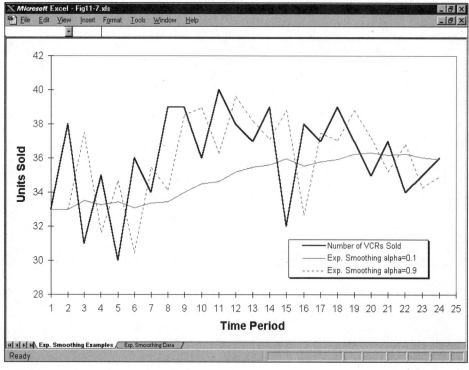

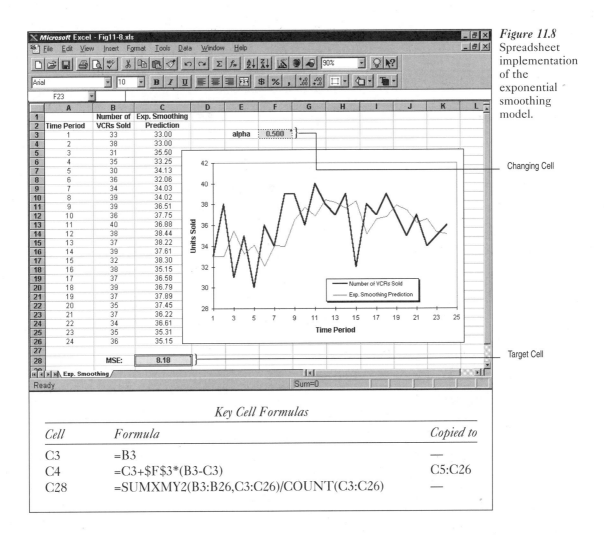

Figure 11.8
Spreadsheet implementation of the exponential smoothing model.

Key Cell Formulas

Cell	Formula	Copied to
C3	=B3	—
C4	=C3+$F$3*(B3-C3)	C5:C26
C28	=SUMXMY2(B3:B26,C3:C26)/COUNT(C3:C26)	—

In Figure 11.8, cell F3 represents α. In an exponential smoothing forecasting model, it is customary to assume that $\hat{Y}_1 = Y_1$. Thus, in Figure 11.8, cell C3 contains the following formula:

Formula for cell C3:   =B3

The forecasting function in equation 11.4 begins for time period $t = 2$ with the following formula, which is implemented in cell C4 and copied to cells C5 through C26:

Formula for cell C4:   =C3+$F$3*(B3–C3)
(Copy to C5 through C26.)

The formula in cell C28 calculates the MSE value as:

Formula for cell C28:   =SUMXMY2(B3:B26,C3:C26)/COUNT(C3:C26)

We can use the Solver parameters and options shown in Figure 11.9 to identify the value for α that minimizes the MSE. Again, this is a nonlinear optimization problem because the MSE represents a nonlinear objective function. Figure 11.10 shows the solution to this problem. Notice that the optimal value for α is given in cell F3 as 0.268.

Figure 11.9
Solver
parameters and
options for the
exponential
smoothing
model.

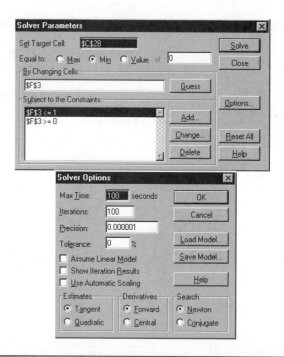

Figure 11.10
Optimal solution
for the
exponential
smoothing
model.

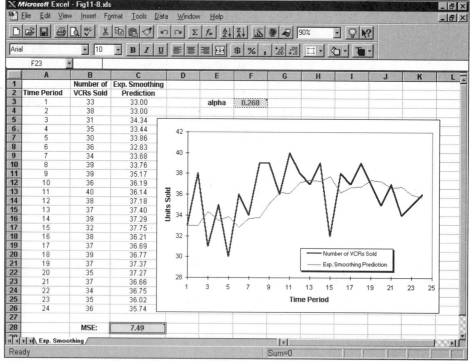

11.6.1   Forecasting with the Exponential Smoothing Model

Using the exponential smoothing model, the predicted number of VCRs to be sold at
Electra-City in the next month (time period 25) is calculated as:

$$\hat{Y}_{25} = \hat{Y}_{24} + \alpha(Y_{24} - \hat{Y}_{24}) = 35.74 + 0.268 \times (36 - 35.74) = 35.81$$

An interesting property of the exponential smoothing technique becomes apparent when we try to use it to forecast more than one time period into the future. For example, suppose that at time period 24 we want to forecast the number of VCRs to be sold in time periods 25 *and* 26. The forecast for time period 26 is represented by:

$$\hat{Y}_{26} = \hat{Y}_{25} + \alpha(Y_{25} - \hat{Y}_{25})$$

Because Y_{25} is unknown at time period 24, we must substitute $\hat{Y}_{25}$ for Y_{25} in the previous equation. However, in that case we obtain $\hat{Y}_{26} = \hat{Y}_{25}$. In fact, the forecast for all future time periods would equal $\hat{Y}_{25}$. So when using exponential smoothing, the forecast for *all* future time periods equal the same value. This is consistent with the underlying idea of a stationary time series. If a time series is stationary (or has no trend), it is reasonable to assume that the forecast of the next time period and all future time periods should equal the same value. Thus, the exponential smoothing forecasting model for all future time periods (t = 25, 26, 27, ...) in the Electra-City example is represented by:

$$\hat{Y}_t = 35.81$$

11.7 TREND MODELS

The forecasting techniques presented so far are appropriate for stationary time series data in which there is no significant trend in the data over time. However, it is not unusual for time series data to exhibit some type of upward or downward trend over time. **Trend** is the long-term sweep or general direction of movement in a time series. It reflects the net influence of long-term factors that affect the time series in a fairly consistent and gradual way over time. In other words, the trend reflects changes in the data that occur with the passage of time.

Because the moving average, weighted moving average, and exponential smoothing techniques involve some average of previous values to forecast future values, they consistently *underestimate* the actual values if there is an upward trend in the data. For example, consider the time series data given by 2, 4, 6, 8, 10, 12, 14, 16, and 18. These data show a clear upward trend leading us to expect that the next value in the time series should be 20. However, the forecasting techniques discussed up to this point would forecast that the next value in the series is less than or equal to 18 because no weighted average of the given data could exceed 18. Similarly, if there is a downward trend in the data over time, all of the methods discussed so far would produce predictions that *overestimate* the actual values in the time series. In the following sections we'll consider several techniques that are appropriate for nonstationary time series involving an upward or downward trend in the data over time.

11.7.1 An Example

The following example will be used to illustrate a variety of techniques for modeling trends in time series data.

WaterCraft Inc. is a manufacturer of personal water crafts (also known as jet skis). Throughout its first five years of operation, the company has enjoyed a fairly steady growth in sales of its products. The officers of the company are preparing sales and manufacturing plans for the coming year. A critical input to these plans involves a forecast of the level of sales that the company expects to achieve. Quarterly sales data for the company during the past five years are given in Figure 11.11 (and in the file FIG11-11.xls on your data disk).

The plot of the data in Figure 11.11 suggests a fairly strong upward trend in the data over time. Thus, to forecast the value of this time series variable, we can use one of the forecasting techniques discussed in the following sections. These techniques account for a trend in the data.

11.8   HOLT'S METHOD

Holt's method is often an effective forecasting tool for time series data that exhibit a linear trend. After observing the value of the time series at period t (Y_t), Holt's method computes an estimate of the base, or expected, level of the time series (E_t), and the expected rate of increase or decrease (trend) per period (T_t). The forecasting function in Holt's method is represented by:

$$\hat{Y}_{t+k} = E_t + kT_t \qquad\qquad 11.5$$

where

$$E_t = \alpha Y_t + (1 - \alpha)(E_{t-1} + T_{t-1}) \qquad\qquad 11.6$$

$$T_t = \beta(E_t - E_{t-1}) + (1 - \beta)T_{t-1} \qquad\qquad 11.7$$

Figure 11.11
Historical sales data for the WaterCraft sales forecasting problem.

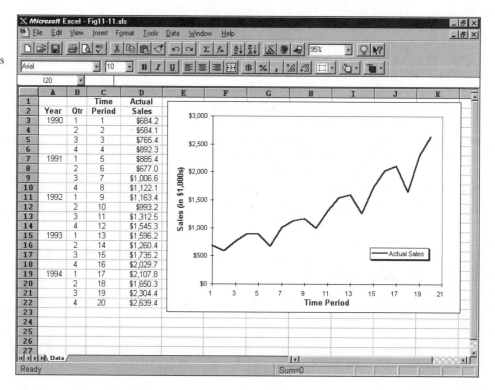

We can use the forecasting function in equation 11.5 to obtain forecasts k time periods into the future where $k = 1, 2, 3$, and so on. The forecast for time period $t + k$ (or $\hat{Y}_{t+k}$) is the base level at time period t (given by E_t) plus the expected influence of the trend during the next k time periods (given by kT_t).

The smoothing parameters α and β (beta) in equations 11.6 and equation 11.7 can assume any value between 0 and 1 ($0 \le \alpha \le 1$, $0 \le \beta \le 1$). If there is an upward trend in the data, E_t tends to be larger than E_{t-1}, making the quantity $E_t - E_{t-1}$ in equation 11.7 positive. This tends to increase the value of the trend adjustment factor T_t. Alternatively, if there is a downward trend in the data, E_t tends to be smaller than E_{t-1}, making the quantity $E_t - E_{t-1}$ in equation 11.7 negative. This tends to decrease the value of the trend adjustment factor T_t.

Although Holt's method might appear to be more complicated than the techniques discussed earlier, it is a simple three-step process:

1. Compute the base level E_t for time period t using equation 11.6.
2. Compute the expected trend value T_t for time period t using equation 11.7.
3. Compute the final forecast $\hat{Y}_{t+k}$ for time period $t + k$ using equation 11.5.

The spreadsheet implementation of Holt's method for the WaterCraft problem is shown in Figure 11.12 (and in the file FIG11-12.xls on your data disk).

Cells J3 and J4 represent the values of α and β, respectively. Column E implements the base levels for each time period as required in step 1 (that is, this column contains the E_t values). Equation 11.6 assumes that for any time period t the base level for the previous time period (E_{t-1}) is known. It is customary to assume that $E_1 = Y_1$, as reflected by the formula in cell E3:

Formula for cell E3:   =D3

The remaining E_t values are calculated using equation 11.6 in cells E4 through E22 as:

Formula for cell E4:   =$J$3*D4+(1–$J$3)*(E3+F3)
(Copy to E5 through E22.)

Column F implements the expected trend values for each time period as required in step 2 (that is, this column contains the T_t values). Equation 11.7 assumes that for any time period t the expected trend value at the previous time period (T_{t-1}) is known. So we assume as an initial trend estimate that $T_t = 0$ (although any other initial trend estimate could be used), as reflected by the formula in cell F3:

Formula for cell F3:   =0

The remaining T_t values are calculated using equation 11.7 in cells F4 through F22 as:

Formula for cell F4:   =$J$4*(E4–E3)+(1–$J$4)*F3
(Copy to F5 through F22.)

According to equation 11.5, at any time period t the forecast for time period $t + 1$ is represented by:

$$\hat{Y}_{t+1} = E_t + 1 \times T_t$$

At time period $t = 1$ shown in Figure 11.12, the forecast for time period $t = 2$ (shown in cell G4) is obtained by summing the values in cells E3 and F3, which correspond to E_1 and T_1, respectively. Thus, the forecast for time period $t = 2$ is implemented in cell G4 as:

Figure 11.12
Spreadsheet
implementation
of Holt's
method.

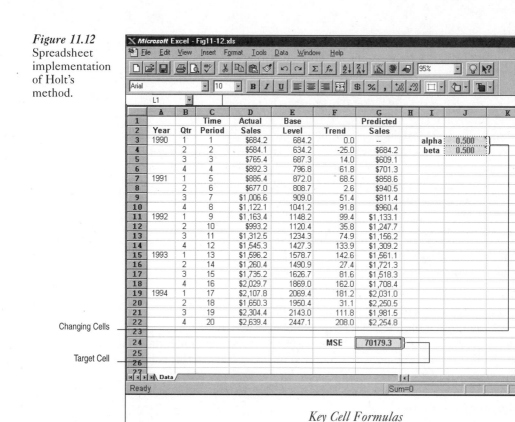

Key Cell Formulas

Cell	Formula	Copied to
E3	=D3	—
E4	=$J$3*D4+(1-$J$3)*(E3+F3)	E5:E22
F3	=0	—
F4	=$J$4*(E4-E3)+(1-$J$4)*F3	F5:F22
G4	=SUM(E3:F3)	G5:G22
G24	=SUMXMY2(D4:D22,G4:G22)/COUNT(G4:G22)	—

Formula for cell G4:   =SUM(E3:F3)
(Copy to G5 through G22.)

This formula is copied to cells G5 through G22 to compute the predictions made using Holt's method for the remaining time periods.

Before making predictions using Holt's method, we want to identify optimal values for α and β. We can use Solver to determine the values for α and β that minimize the MSE (or the MAD). The MSE for the predicted values is calculated in cell G24 as:

Formula for cell G24:   =SUMXMY2(D4:D22,G4:G22)/COUNT(G4:G22)

We can use the Solver parameters and options shown in Figure 11.13 to identify the values for α and β that minimize the nonlinear MSE objective. Figure 11.14 shows the solution to this problem. The graph in Figure 11.14 indicates that the predictions obtained using Holt's method follow the trend in the data quite well.

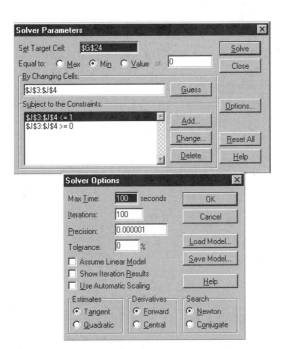

Figure 11.13
Solver
parameters and
options for
Holt's method.

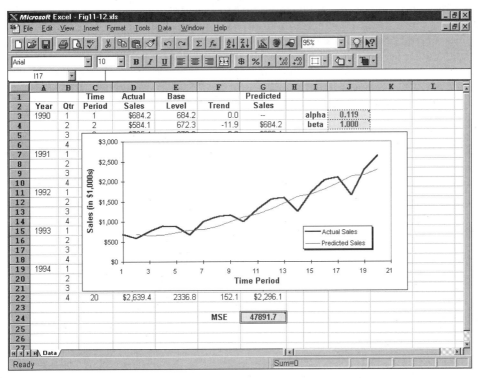

Figure 11.14
Optimal solution
using Holt's
method.

11.8.1   Forecasting with Holt's Method

We can use the results in Figure 11.14 to compute forecasts for any future time period. According to equation 11.5, at time period 20 the forecast for time period 20 + *k* is
represented by:

$$\hat{Y}_{20+k} = E_{20} + kT_{20}$$

The values of E_{20} and T_{20} are given in Figure 11.14 in cells E22 and F22, respectively ($E_{20} = 2336.8$ and $T_{20} = 152.1$). So at time period 20, forecasts for time periods 21, 22, 23, and 24 are computed as:

$$\hat{Y}_{21} = E_{20} + 1 \times T_{20} = 2336.8 + 1 \times 152.1 = 2,488.9$$

$$\hat{Y}_{22} = E_{20} + 2 \times T_{20} = 2336.8 + 2 \times 152.1 = 2,641.0$$

$$\hat{Y}_{23} = E_{20} + 3 \times T_{20} = 2336.8 + 3 \times 152.1 = 2,793.1$$

$$\hat{Y}_{24} = E_{20} + 4 \times T_{20} = 2336.8 + 4 \times 152.1 = 2,945.2$$

Although we can use Holt's method to forecast a value for any future time period (or any value of $k \geq 1$), as the forecast horizon lengthens, our confidence in the accuracy of the forecast diminishes because there is no guarantee that the historical trends on which the model is based will continue indefinitely into the future.

11.9   MODELING TIME SERIES TRENDS USING REGRESSION

We can build a regression model of a time series if data are available for one or more independent variables that account for the systematic movements in the time series. Even if no independent variables have a causal relationship with the time series, some independent variables might have a *predictive* relationship with the time series. A predictor variable does not have a cause-and-effect relationship with the time series. Yet the behavior of a predictor variable might be correlated to that of the time series in a way that helps us forecast future values of the time series. In the following sections we'll consider how to use predictor variables as independent variables in regression models for time series data.

As mentioned earlier, trend is the long-term sweep or general direction of movement in a time series that reflects changes in the data over time. The mere passage of time does not cause the trend in the time series. But like the consistent passage of time, the trend of a time series reflects the steady upward or downward movement in the general direction of the series. Thus, time itself might represent a predictor variable that could be useful in accounting for the trend in a time series.

11.10   LINEAR TREND MODEL

To see how we might use time as an independent variable, consider the following linear regression model:

$$Y_t = \beta_0 + \beta_1 X_{1_t} + \varepsilon_t \qquad\qquad \textbf{11.8}$$

where $X_{1_t} = t$. That is, the independent variable X_{1_t} represents the time period t ($X_{1_1} = 1$, $X_{1_2} = 2$, $X_{1_3} = 3$, and so on). The regression model in equation 11.8 assumes that the *systematic* variation in the time series (Y_t) can be described by the regression function $\beta_0 + \beta_1 X_{1_t}$ (which is a linear function of time). The error term ε_t in equation 11.8 represents the *unsystematic*, or random, variation in the time series not accounted for by our model. Because the values of Y_t are assumed to vary randomly around (above and below) the regression function $\beta_0 + \beta_1 X_{1_t}$, the average (or expected) value of ϵ_t is 0. Thus, if we use ordinary least squares to estimate the parameters in equation 11.8, our best estimate of Y_t for any time period t is:

$$\hat{Y}_t = b_0 + b_1 X_{1_t} \qquad \qquad 11.9$$

In equation 11.9, the estimated value of the time series at time period t ($\hat{Y}_t$) is a linear function of the independent variable, which is coded to represent time. Thus, equation 11.9 represents the equation of the line passing through the time series that minimizes the sum of squared differences between the actual values (Y_t) and the estimated values ($\hat{Y}_t$). We might interpret this line to represent the linear trend in the data.

An example of this technique is shown in Figure 11.15 (and in the file FIG11-15.xls on your data disk) for the quarterly sales data for WaterCraft. We can use the Time Period values in column C as the values for the independent variable X_1 in our regression model. Thus, we can use the Regression command settings shown in Figure 11.16 to obtain the values for b_0 and b_1 required for the estimated regression function for these data.

Figure 11.17 shows the results of the Regression command, which indicate that the estimated regression function is:

$$\hat{Y}_t = 375.17 + 92.6255 X_{1_t} \qquad \qquad 11.10$$

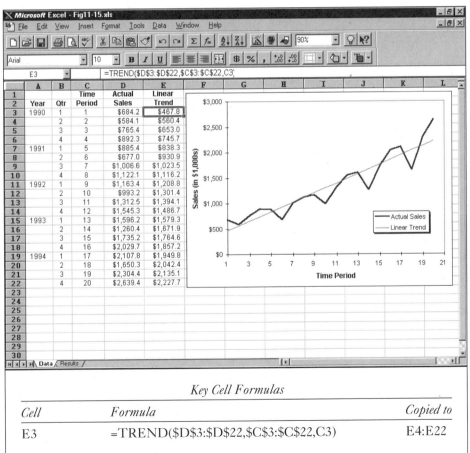

Figure 11.15
Spreadsheet implementation of the linear trend model.

				Key Cell Formulas	
Cell		*Formula*			*Copied to*
E3		=TREND($D$3:$D$22,$C$3:$C$22,C3)			E4:E22

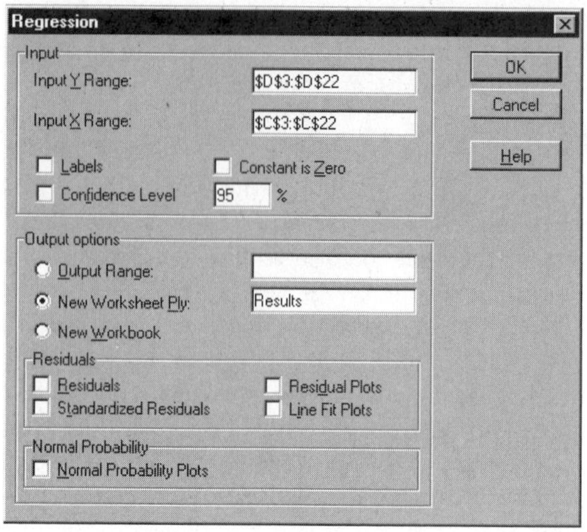

Figure 11.16 Regression command settings for the linear trend model.

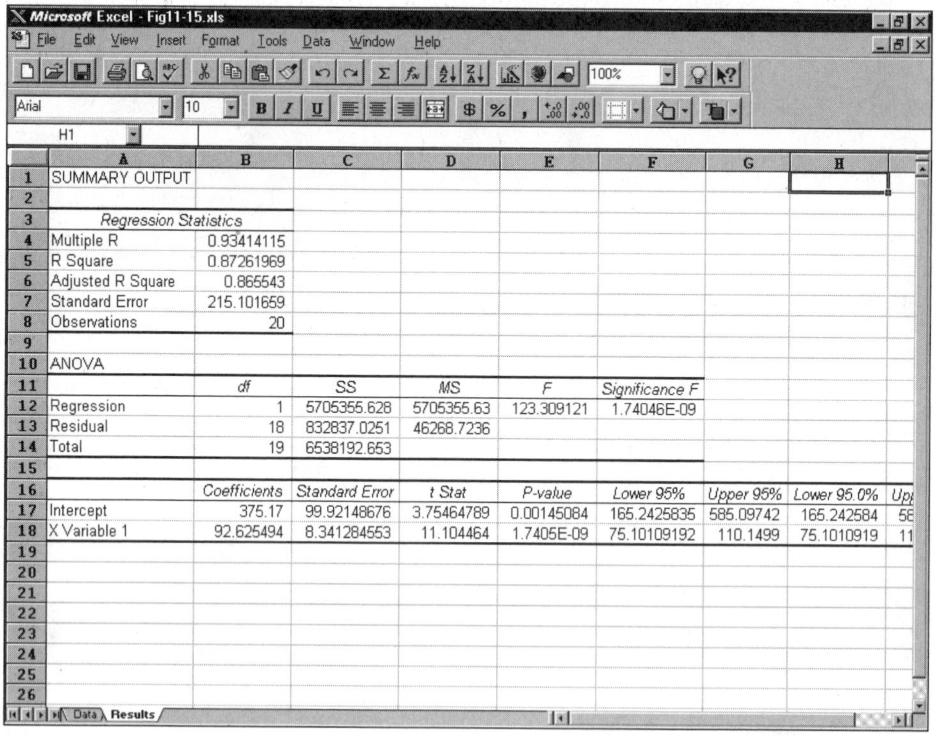

	A	B	C	D	E	F	G	H	I
1	SUMMARY OUTPUT								
2									
3	*Regression Statistics*								
4	Multiple R	0.93414115							
5	R Square	0.87261969							
6	Adjusted R Square	0.865543							
7	Standard Error	215.101659							
8	Observations	20							
9									
10	ANOVA								
11		*df*	*SS*	*MS*	*F*	*Significance F*			
12	Regression	1	5705355.628	5705355.63	123.309121	1.74046E-09			
13	Residual	18	832837.0251	46268.7236					
14	Total	19	6538192.653						
15									
16		*Coefficients*	*Standard Error*	*t Stat*	*P-value*	*Lower 95%*	*Upper 95%*	*Lower 95.0%*	*Up*
17	Intercept	375.17	99.92148676	3.75464789	0.00145084	165.2425835	585.09742	165.242584	58
18	X Variable 1	92.625494	8.341284553	11.104464	1.7405E-09	75.10109192	110.1499	75.1010919	11

Figure 11.17 Regression results for the linear trend model.

Figure 11.15 shows the predicted sales level for each time period in column E (labeled "Linear Trend") where the following formula is entered in cell E3 and copied to cells E4 through E22:

Formula for cell E3: =TREND($D$3:$D$22,$C$3:$C$22,C3)
(Copy to E4 through E22.)

11.10.1   *Forecasting with the Linear Trend Model*

We can use equation 11.10 to generate forecasts of sales for any future time period t by setting $X_{1_t} = t$. For example, forecasts for time periods 21, 22, 23, and 24 are computed as:

$$\hat{Y}_{21} = 375.17 + 92.6255 \times 21 = 2{,}320.3$$

$$\hat{Y}_{22} = 375.17 + 92.6255 \times 22 = 2{,}412.9$$

$$\hat{Y}_{23} = 375.17 + 92.6255 \times 23 = 2{,}505.6$$

$$\hat{Y}_{24} = 375.17 + 92.6255 \times 24 = 2{,}598.2$$

Again, as the forecast horizon lengthens, our confidence in the accuracy of the forecasts diminishes because there is no guarantee that the historical trends on which the model is based will continue indefinitely into the future.

A Note on the TREND( ) Function

The TREND( ) function can be used to calculate the estimated values for linear regression models. The format of the TREND( ) function is as follows:

TREND(Y-range, X-range, X-value for prediction)

where Y-range is the range in the spreadsheet containing the dependent Y variable, X-range is the range in the spreadsheet containing the independent X variable(s), and X-value for prediction is a cell (or cells) containing the values for the independent X variable(s) for which we want an estimated value of Y. The TREND( ) function has an advantage over the regression tool in that it is dynamically updated whenever any inputs to the function change. However, it does not provide the statistical information provided by the regression tool. It is best to use these two different approaches to doing regression in conjunction with one another.

11.11   QUADRATIC TREND MODEL

Although the graph of the estimated linear regression function shown in Figure 11.15 accounts for the upward trend in the data, the actual values do not appear to be scattered randomly around the trend line, as was assumed by our regression model in equation 11.8. An observation is more likely to be substantially below the line or only slightly above the line. This suggests that the linear trend model might not be appropriate for this data.

As an alternative, we might try fitting a curved trend line to the data using the following quadratic model:

$$Y_t = \beta_0 + \beta_1 X_{1_t} + \beta_2 X_{2_t} + \varepsilon_t \qquad\qquad \textbf{11.11}$$

where $X_{1_t} = t$ and $X_{2_t} = t^2$. The resulting *estimated* regression function for this model is:

$$\hat{Y}_t = b_0 + b_1 X_{1_t} + b_2 X_{2_t} \qquad\qquad \textbf{11.12}$$

To estimate the quadratic trend function, we must add a column to the spreadsheet to represent the additional independent variable $X_{2_t} = t^2$. This can be accomplished as shown in Figure 11.18 (and in the file FIG11-18.xls on your data disk) by inserting a new column D and placing the values t^2 in this column. Thus, the following formula is entered in cell D3 and copied to cells D4 through D22:

Formula for cell D3:   =C3^2

(Copy to D4 through D22.)

We can obtain the values of b_0, b_1, and b_2 required for the estimated regression function for these data using the Regression command settings shown in Figure 11.19.

Figure 11.20 shows the results of the Regression command, which indicate that the estimated regression function is:

$$\hat{Y}_t = 653.67 + 16.671X_{1_t} + 3.617X_{2_t} \qquad \textbf{11.13}$$

Figure 11.18 shows the estimated sales level for each time period in column F (labeled "Quadratic Trend") where the following formula is entered in cell F3 and copied to cells F4 through F22:

Formula for cell F3:   =TREND($E$3:$E$22,$C$3:$D$22,C3:D3)

(Copy to F4 through F22.)

Figure 11.18
Spreadsheet implementation of the quadratic trend model.

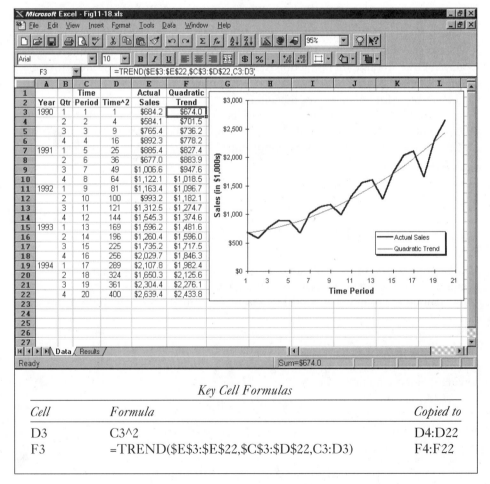

	Key Cell Formulas	
Cell	*Formula*	*Copied to*
D3	C3^2	D4:D22
F3	=TREND($E$3:$E$22,$C$3:$D$22,C3:D3)	F4:F22

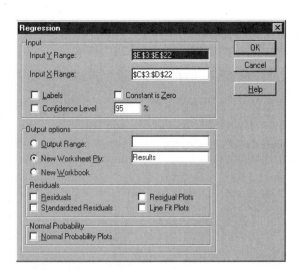

Figure 11.19
Regression
command
settings for the
quadratic trend
model.

Figure 11.20
Regression
results for the
quadratic trend
model.

	A	B	C	D	E	F	G	H
1	SUMMARY OUTPUT							
2								
3	*Regression Statistics*							
4	Multiple R	0.9527572						
5	R Square	0.90774627						
6	Adjusted R Square	0.89689289						
7	Standard Error	188.363328						
8	Observations	20						
9								
10	ANOVA							
11		*df*	*SS*	*MS*	*F*	*Significance F*		
12	Regression	2	5935020.018	2967510.01	83.6371997	1.59354E-09		
13	Residual	17	603172.6355	35480.7433				
14	Total	19	6538192.653					
15								
16		*Coefficients*	*Standard Error*	*t Stat*	*P-value*	*Lower 95%*	*Upper 95%*	*Lower 95.0%*
17	Intercept	653.669724	140.1388691	4.66444269	0.00022238	358.0021422	949.337306	358.0021422
18	X Variable 1	16.6710238	30.73462528	0.54241832	0.59457035	-48.17345798	81.5155055	-48.173458
19	X Variable 2	3.61687954	1.421620143	2.54419548	0.02095861	0.617519025	6.61624005	0.617519025

Figure 11.18 also shows a graph of the sales levels predicted by the quadratic trend model versus the actual data. Notice that the quadratic trend curve fits the data better than the straight trend line shown in Figure 11.15. In particular, the deviations of the actual values above and below this curve are now more balanced.

11.11.1   *Forecasting with the Quadratic Trend Model*

We can use equation 11.13 to generate forecasts of sales for any future time period t by setting $X_{1_t} = t$ and $X_{2_t} = t^2$. For example, forecasts for time periods 21, 22, 23, and 24 are computed as:

$$\hat{Y}_{21} = 653.67 + 16.671 \times 21 + 3.617 \times (21)^2 = 2{,}598.9$$

$$\hat{Y}_{22} = 653.67 + 16.671 \times 22 + 3.617 \times (22)^2 = 2{,}771.1$$

$$\hat{Y}_{23} = 653.67 + 16.671 \times 23 + 3.617 \times (23)^2 = 2{,}950.5$$

$$\hat{Y}_{24} = 653.67 + 16.671 \times 24 + 3.617 \times (24)^2 = 3{,}137.2$$

As with earlier models, as the forecast horizon lengthens, our confidence in the accuracy of the forecasts diminishes because there is no guarantee that the historical trends on which the model is based will continue indefinitely into the future.

11.12 SEASONALITY

The goal of any forecasting procedure is to develop a model that accounts for as much of the systematic variation in the past behavior of a time series as possible. The assumption is that a model that accurately explains what happened in the past will be useful in predicting what will happen in the future. Do the trend models shown in Figures 11.14, 11.15, and 11.18 adequately account for all the systematic variation in the time series data?

All these graphs show a fairly regular pattern of fluctuation around the trend line. Notice that each point below the trend line is followed by three points at or above the trend line. This suggests some additional *systematic* (or predictable) variation in the time series exists that is not accounted for by these models.

Although trend reflects the long-term direction or sweep in a time series, a time series can also include a strong seasonal component. This seasonal component, or *seasonality*, appears as a regular, repeating pattern in the data around the trend line. For example, in time series data for monthly fuel oil sales, we would expect to see regular jumps in the data during the winter months each year. Similarly, monthly or quarterly sales data for suntan lotion would likely show consistent peaks during the summer and valleys during the winter.

Figures 11.14, 11.15, and 11.18 suggest that the data in the graphs include seasonal effects. In the second quarter of each year, sales drop well below the trend lines, whereas sales in the remaining quarters are at or above the trend line. Forecasts of future values for this time series would be more accurate if they reflected these systematic seasonal effects. The following sections discuss several techniques for modeling seasonal effects in time series data.

11.13 ADJUSTING TREND PREDICTIONS WITH SEASONAL INDICES

A simple and effective way of modeling seasonal effects in a time series is to develop seasonal indices that reflect the average percentage by which observations in each season differ from their projected trend values. In the WaterCraft example, observations occurring in the second quarter fall below the values predicted using a trend model. Similarly, observations in the first, third, and fourth quarters are at or above the values predicted using a trend model. Thus, if we can determine seasonal indices representing the average amount by which the observations in a given quarter fall above or below the trend line, we could adjust our trend projections by these amounts and increase the accuracy of our forecasts.

We will demonstrate the calculation of seasonal indices for the quadratic trend model developed earlier. However, we could complete this process using any of the other trend models discussed in this chapter. In Figure 11.21 (and in the file FIG11-21.xls on your data disk), columns A through F repeat the calculations for the quadratic trend model discussed earlier.

11.13.1 Computing Seasonal Indices

The goal in developing seasonal indices is to determine the average percentage by which observations in each season differ from the values projected for them using the trend model. To accomplish this, in column G of Figure 11.21 we calculated the ratio of each actual value in column E to its corresponding projected trend value shown in column F, as:

Formula for cell G3:   =E3/F3

(Copy to G4 through G22.)

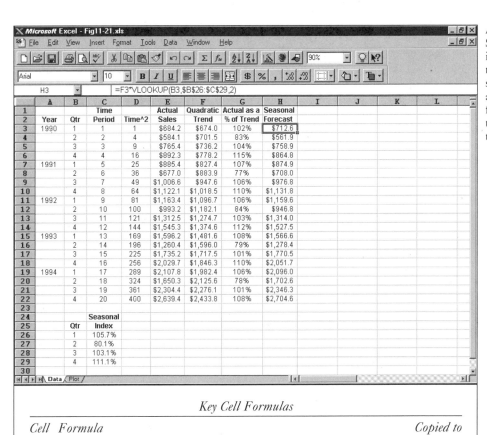

Figure 11.21
Spreadsheet implementation to calculate seasonal indices and seasonal forecasts using the quadratic trend mode.

Key Cell Formulas

Cell	Formula	Copied to
D3	=C3^2	D4:D22
F3	=TREND($E$3:$E$22,$C$3:$D$22,C3:D3)	F4:F22
G3	=E3/F3	G4:G22
C26	=SUMIF($B$3:$B$22,B26,$G$3:$G$22)/COUNTIF($B$3:$B$22,B26)	C27:C29
H3	=F3*VLOOKUP(B3,$B$26:$C$29,2)	H4:H22

The value in cell G3 indicates that the actual value in time period 1 was 102% of (or approximately 2% larger than) its estimated trend value. The value in cell G4 indicates that the actual value in time period 2 was 83% of (or approximately 17% smaller than) its estimated trend value. The remaining values in column G have similar interpretations.

We obtain the seasonal index for each quarter by computing the average of the values in column G on a quarter-by-quarter basis. For example, the seasonal index for quarter 1 equals the average of the values in cells G3, G7, G11, G15, and G19. The seasonal index for quarter 2 equals the average of the values in cells G4, G8, G12, G16, and G20. Similar computations are required to calculate seasonal indices for quarters 3 and 4. We can use separate AVERAGE( ) functions for each quarter to compute these averages. However, for large data sets, such an approach would be tedious and prone to error. Thus, the averages shown in cells C26 through C29 are calculated as:

Formula for cell C26:   =SUMIF($B$3:$B$22,B26,$G$3:$G$22)/
(Copy to C27 through C29.)   COUNTIF($B$3:$B$22,B26)

The SUMIF( ) and COUNTIF( ) functions perform conditional sums and counts. The SUMIF( ) function in the previous formula sums the values in cells G3 through G22 for which the corresponding value in cells B3 through B22 equals the value in cell B26. This corresponds to the sum of the values in column G that occur in quarter 1. The COUNTIF( ) function in the previous equation counts the number of elements in cells B3 through B22 that equal the value in cell B26—or the number of quarter 1 observations.

The seasonal index for quarter 1 shown in cell C26 indicates that, on average, the actual sales value in the first quarter of any given year will be 105.7% of (or 5.7% larger than) the estimated trend value for the same time period. Similarly, the seasonal index for quarter 2 shown in cell C27 indicates that, on average, the actual sales value in the second quarter of any given year will be 80.1% of (or approximately 20% less than) the estimated trend value for the same time period. The seasonal indices for the third and fourth quarters have similar interpretations.

We can use the calculated seasonal indices to refine or adjust the trend estimates. This is accomplished in column H of Figure 11.21 as:

Formula for cell H3:   =F3*VLOOKUP(B3,$B$26:$C$29,2)
(Copy to H4 through H22.)

This formula takes the estimated trend value for each time period and multiplies it by the appropriate seasonal index for the quarter in which the time period occurs. The trend estimates for quarter 1 observations are multiplied by 105.7%, the trend estimates for quarter 2 observations are multiplied by 80.1%, and so on for quarters 3 and 4 observations.

Figure 11.22 shows a graph of the actual sales data versus the seasonal forecast calculated in column H of Figure 11.21. As this graph illustrates, the use of seasonal indices is very effective on this particular data set.

11.13.2   Forecasting with Seasonal Indices

We can use the seasonal indices to adjust trend projections of future time periods for the expected effects of seasonality. Earlier, we used the quadratic trend model to obtain the following forecasts of the expected level of sales in time periods 21, 22, 23, and 24:

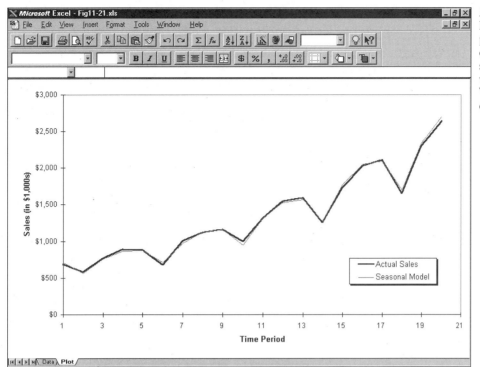

Figure 11.22
Plots of the
predictions
obtained using
seasonal indices
versus the actual
WaterCraft sales
data.

$$\hat{Y}_{21} = 653.67 + 16.671 \times 21 + 3.617 \times (21)^2 = 2{,}598.9$$

$$\hat{Y}_{22} = 653.67 + 16.671 \times 22 + 3.617 \times (22)^2 = 2{,}771.1$$

$$\hat{Y}_{23} = 653.67 + 16.671 \times 23 + 3.617 \times (23)^2 = 2{,}950.5$$

$$\hat{Y}_{24} = 653.67 + 16.671 \times 24 + 3.617 \times (24)^2 = 3{,}137.2$$

To adjust these trend forecasts for the expected effects of seasonality, we multiply each of them by the appropriate seasonal index. Because time periods 21, 22, 23, and 24 occur in quarters 1, 2, 3, and 4, respectively, the seasonal forecasts are computed as:

Seasonal forecast for time period 21	=	$2{,}598.9 \times 105.7\%$	=	$2{,}747.03$
Seasonal forecast for time period 22	=	$2{,}771.1 \times 80.1\%$	=	$2{,}219.65$
Seasonal forecast for time period 23	=	$2{,}950.5 \times 103.1\%$	=	$3{,}041.97$
Seasonal forecast for time period 24	=	$3{,}137.2 \times 111.1\%$	=	$3{,}485.43$

11.14   WINTER'S METHOD

Winter's method is another forecasting technique that we can apply to time series exhibiting trend and seasonality. This method is similar to Holt's method (discussed earlier) but incorporates a number of adjustments for the possible effects of seasonality.

Summary of the Calculation and Use of Seasonal Indices

1. Create a trend model and calculate the estimated value ($\hat{Y}_t$) for each observation in the sample.
2. For each observation, calculate the ratio of the actual value to the predicted trend value ($Y_t / \hat{Y}_t$).
3. For each season, compute the average of the ratios calculated in step 2. These are the seasonal indices.
4. Multiply any forecast produced by the trend model by the appropriate seasonal index calculated in step 3.

To demonstrate this method, we let p represent the number of seasons in the time series (for quarterly data, $p = 4$; for monthly data, $p = 12$). The forecasting function in Winter's method is represented by:

$$\hat{Y}_{t+k} = (E_t + kT_t)S_{t+k-p} \qquad \qquad \textbf{11.14}$$

where

$$E_t = \alpha \frac{Y_t}{S_{t-p}} + (1 - \alpha)(E_{t-1} + T_{t-1}) \qquad \qquad \textbf{11.15}$$

$$T_t = \beta(E_t - E_{t-1}) + (1 - \beta)T_{t-1} \qquad \qquad \textbf{11.16}$$

$$S_t = \gamma \frac{Y_t}{E_t} + (1 - \gamma)S_{t-p} \qquad \qquad \textbf{11.17}$$

We can use the forecasting function in equation 11.14 to obtain forecasts k time periods into the future where $k = 1, 2, ..., p$. The forecast for time period $t + k$ ($\hat{Y}_{t+k}$) is obtained in equation 11.14 by multiplying the expected base level at time period $t + k$ (given by $E_t + kT_t$) by the most recent estimate of the seasonality associated with this time period (given by S_{t+k-p}). The smoothing parameters α, β, and γ (gamma) in equations 11.15, 11.16, and 11.17 can assume any value between 0 and 1 ($0 \le \alpha \le 1$, $0 \le \beta \le 1$, $0 \le \gamma \le 1$).

The expected base level of the time series in time period t (E_t) is updated in equation 11.15, which takes a weighted average of the following two values:

* $E_{t-1} + T_{t-1}$, which represents the expected base level of the time series at time period t before observing the actual value at time period t (given by Y_t)

* $\dfrac{Y_t}{S_{t-p}}$, which represents the deseasonalized estimate of the base level of the time series at time period t after observing Y_t.

The estimated per-period trend factor T_t is updated using equation 11.16, which is identical to the procedure in equation 11.7 used in Holt's method. The estimated seasonal adjustment factor for each time period is calculated using equation 11.17, which takes a weighted average of the following two quantities:

- S_{t-p}, which represents the most recent seasonal index for the season in which time period t occurs.

- $\dfrac{Y_t}{E_t}$, which represents an estimate of the seasonality associated with time period t after observing Y_t.

Winter's method is somewhat more complicated than the process of calculating seasonal indices described earlier, but it is basically a four-step process:

1. Compute the base level E_t for time period t using equation 11.15.
2. Compute the estimated trend value T_t for time period t using equation 11.16.
3. Compute the estimated seasonal index S_t for time period t using equation 11.17.
4. Compute the final forecast $\hat{Y}_{t+k}$ for time period $t + k$ using equation 11.14.

The spreadsheet implementation of Winter's method for the WaterCraft data is shown in Figure 11.23 (and in the file FIG11-23.xls on your data disk). Cells D24, D25, and D26 represent the values of α, β, and γ, respectively.

Equations 11.15 and 11.17 assume that at time period t an estimate of the seasonal index from time period $t - p$ exists or that there is a value for S_{t-p}. Thus, our first task in implementing Winter's method is to estimate values for $S_1, S_2, ..., S_p$ (or, in this case, S_1, S_2, S_3, and S_4). One easy way to make these initial estimates is to let:

$$S_t = \frac{1}{p} \frac{Y_t}{(Y_1 + Y_2 + ... + Y_p)}, \ t = 1, 2, ..., p \qquad \textbf{11.18}$$

Equation 11.18 indicates that the initial seasonal estimate S_t for each of the first p time periods is the ratio of the observed value in time period Y_t divided by the average value observed during the first p periods. In our example, the first four seasonal factors shown in column G in Figure 11.23 are calculated using equation 11.18 as:

Formula for cell G3:   =D3/AVERAGE($D$3:$D$6)
(Copy to G4 through G6.)

The first E_t value that can be computed using equation 11.15 occurs at time period $p + 1$ (in our example, time period 5) because this is the first time period for which S_{t-p} is known. However, to compute E_5 using equation 11.15, we also need to know E_4 (which cannot be computed using equation 11.15 because S_0 is undefined) and T_4 (which cannot be computed using equation 11.16 because E_4 and E_3 are undefined). Thus, we assume $E_4 = Y_4/S_4$ (so that $E_4 \times S_4 = Y_4$) and $T_4 = 0$, as reflected by placing the following formulas in cells E6 and F6:

Formula for cell E6:   =D6/G6

Formula for cell F6:   =0

A Note on Initializing Winter's Method

It is important to note that the other methods can be used to initialize the seasonality (S_t), base level (E_t), and trend (T_t) values when using Winter's method. When the data set being modeled is large, the initial values are likely to have little impact on your forecasts. However, as the size of the data set decreases, the impact of the initial values becomes more pronounced.

Figure 11.23
Spreadsheet
implementation
of Winter's
method.

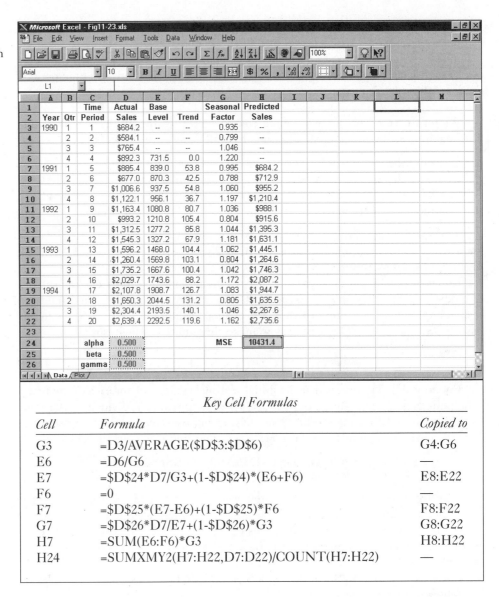

	A	B	C	D	E	F	G	H
1			Time	Actual	Base		Seasonal	Predicted
2	Year	Qtr	Period	Sales	Level	Trend	Factor	Sales
3	1990	1	1	$684.2	--	--	0.935	--
4		2	2	$584.1	--	--	0.799	--
5		3	3	$765.4	--	--	1.046	--
6		4	4	$892.3	731.5	0.0	1.220	--
7	1991	1	5	$885.4	839.0	53.8	0.995	$684.2
8		2	6	$677.0	870.3	42.5	0.788	$712.9
9		3	7	$1,006.6	937.5	54.8	1.060	$955.2
10		4	8	$1,122.1	956.1	36.7	1.197	$1,210.4
11	1992	1	9	$1,163.4	1080.8	80.7	1.036	$988.1
12		2	10	$993.2	1210.8	105.4	0.804	$915.6
13		3	11	$1,312.5	1277.2	85.8	1.044	$1,395.3
14		4	12	$1,545.3	1327.2	67.9	1.181	$1,631.1
15	1993	1	13	$1,596.2	1468.0	104.4	1.062	$1,445.1
16		2	14	$1,260.4	1569.8	103.1	0.804	$1,264.6
17		3	15	$1,735.2	1667.6	100.4	1.042	$1,746.3
18		4	16	$2,029.7	1743.6	88.2	1.172	$2,087.2
19	1994	1	17	$2,107.8	1908.7	126.7	1.083	$1,944.7
20		2	18	$1,650.3	2044.5	131.2	0.805	$1,635.5
21		3	19	$2,304.4	2193.5	140.1	1.046	$2,267.6
22		4	20	$2,639.4	2292.5	119.6	1.162	$2,735.6
23								
24			alpha	0.500			MSE	10431.4
25			beta	0.500				
26			gamma	0.500				

Key Cell Formulas

Cell	Formula	Copied to
G3	=D3/AVERAGE($D$3:$D$6)	G4:G6
E6	=D6/G6	—
E7	=$D$24*D7/G3+(1-$D$24)*(E6+F6)	E8:E22
F6	=0	—
F7	=$D$25*(E7-E6)+(1-$D$25)*F6	F8:F22
G7	=$D$26*D7/E7+(1-$D$26)*G3	G8:G22
H7	=SUM(E6:F6)*G3	H8:H22
H24	=SUMXMY2(H7:H22,D7:D22)/COUNT(H7:H22)	—

We generated the remaining E_t values using equation 11.15, which is implemented in Figure 11.23 as:

Formula for cell E7:   =$D$24*D7/G3+(1–$D$24)*(E6+F6)
(Copy to E8 through E22.)

We generated the remaining T_t values using equation 11.16, which is implemented in Figure 11.23 as:

Formula for cell F7:   =$D$25*(E7–E6)+(1–$D$25)*F6
(Copy to F8 through F22.)

We used equation 11.17 to generate the remaining S_t values in Figure 11.23 as:

Formula for cell G7:   =$D$26*D7/E7+(1–$D$26)*G3
(Copy to G8 through G22.)

Finally, at time period 4, we can use the forecasting function in equation 11.14 to predict one period ahead for time period 5. This is implemented in Figure 11.23 as:

Formula for cell H7:   =SUM(E6:F6)*G3
(Copy to H8 through H22.)

Before making predictions using Winter's method, we want to identify optimal values for α, β, and γ. We can use Solver to determine the values for α, β, and γ that minimize the MSE (or the MAD). The MSE for the predicted values is calculated in cell H24 as:

Formula for cell H24:   =SUMXMY2(H7:H22,D7:D22,)/COUNT(H7:H22)

We can use the Solver parameters and options shown in Figure 11.24 to identify the values for α, β, and γ that minimize the nonlinear MSE objective. Figure 11.25 shows the solution to this problem.

Figure 11.26 displays a graph of the predictions obtained using Winter's method against the actual data. This graph indicates that although Winter's method got off to a rocky start, it provides a forecasting function that fits the recent data in this problem reasonably well. The rocky start shown in the graph is common with Winter's method and can be attributed to the simple estimates we provided for the initial seasonal factors and for E_4 and T_4.

11.14.1   Forecasting with Winter's Method

We can use the results in Figure 11.25 to compute forecasts for any future time period. According to equation 11.14, at time period 20 the forecast for time period $20 + k$ is represented by:

$$\hat{Y}_{20+k} = (E_{20} + kT_{20})S_{20+k-p}$$

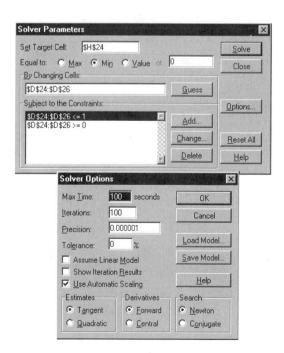

Figure 11.24
Solver parameters and options for Winter's method.

Figure 11.25
Optimal solution
for Winter's
method.

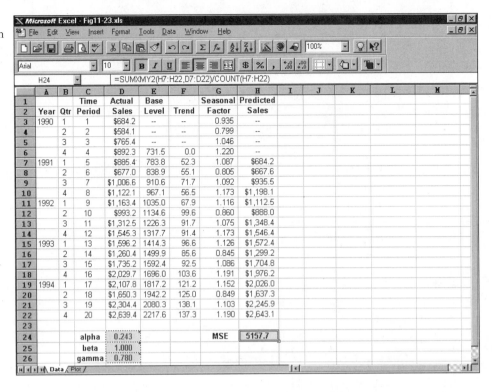

Figure 11.26
Plot of the
predictions
obtained using
Winter's method
versus the actual
WaterCraft sales
data.

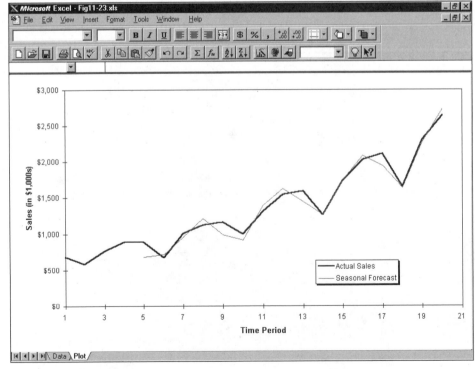

Figure 11.25 shows the values of E_{20} and T_{20} in cells E22 and F22, respectively ($E_{20} = 2217.6$ and $T_{20} = 137.3$). At time period 20, forecasts for time periods 21, 22, 23, and 24 are computed as:

$$\hat{Y}_{21} = (E_{20} + 1 \times T_{20})S_{17} = (2217.6 + 1 \times 137.3)1.152 = 2{,}712.8$$

$$\hat{Y}_{22} = (E_{20} + 2 \times T_{20})S_{18} = (2217.6 + 2 \times 137.3)0.849 = 2{,}115.9$$

$$\hat{Y}_{23} = (E_{20} + 3 \times T_{20})S_{19} = (2217.6 + 3 \times 137.3)1.103 = 2{,}900.3$$

$$\hat{Y}_{24} = (E_{20} + 4 \times T_{20})S_{20} = (2217.6 + 4 \times 137.3)1.190 = 3{,}292.5$$

11.15   SEASONAL REGRESSION MODELS

As discussed in Chapter 9, Regression Analysis, an indicator variable is a binary variable that assumes a value of 0 or 1 to indicate whether or not a certain condition is true. To model seasonality in a time series, we might set up several indicator variables to indicate which season each observation represents. In general, if there are p seasons, we need $p - 1$ indicator variables in our model. For example, the WaterCraft sales data were collected on a quarterly basis. Because we have four seasons to model ($p = 4$), we need three indicator variables, which we define as:

$$X_{3_t} = \begin{cases} 1, \text{ if } Y_t \text{ is an observation from quarter 1} \\ 0, \text{ otherwise} \end{cases}$$

$$X_{4_t} = \begin{cases} 1, \text{ if } Y_t \text{ is an observation from quarter 2} \\ 0, \text{ otherwise} \end{cases}$$

$$X_{5_t} = \begin{cases} 1, \text{ if } Y_t \text{ is an observation from quarter 3} \\ 0, \text{ otherwise} \end{cases}$$

Notice that the definitions of X_{3_t}, X_{4_t}, and X_{5_t} assign a unique coding for the variables to each quarter in our data. These codings are summarized as:

Quarter	Value of X_{3_t}	X_{4_t}	X_{5_t}
1	1	0	0
2	0	1	0
3	0	0	1
4	0	0	0

Together, the values of X_{3_t}, X_{4_t}, and X_{5_t} indicate in which quarter observation Y_t occurs.

11.15.1   The Seasonal Model

We might expect that the following regression function would be appropriate for the time series data in our example:

$$Y_t = \beta_0 + \beta_1 X_{1_t} + \beta_2 X_{2_t} + \beta_3 X_{3_t} + \beta_4 X_{4_t} + \beta_5 X_{5_t} + \varepsilon_t \qquad \textbf{11.19}$$

where, $X_{1_t} = t$ and $X_{2_t} = t^2$. This regression model combines the variables that account for a quadratic trend in the data with additional indicator variables discussed earlier to account for any systematic seasonal differences.

To better understand the effect of the indicator variables, notice that for observations occurring in the fourth quarter, the model in equation 11.19 reduces to:

$$Y_t = \beta_0 + \beta_1 X_{1_t} + \beta_2 X_{2_t} + \varepsilon_t \qquad \textbf{11.20}$$

because in the fourth quarter $X_{3_t} = X_{4_t} = X_{5_t} = 0$. For observations occurring in the first quarter, we can express equation 11.19 as:

$$Y_t = (\beta_0 + \beta_3) + \beta_1 X_{1_t} + \beta_2 X_{2_t} + \varepsilon_t \qquad \textbf{11.21}$$

because, by definition, in the first quarter $X_{3_t} = 1$ and $X_{4_t} = X_{5_t} = 0$. Similarly, for observations in the second and third quarters the model in equation 11.19 reduces to:

For the second quarter: $Y_t = (\beta_0 + \beta_4) + \beta_1 X_{1_t} + \beta_2 X_{2_t} + \varepsilon_t$ **11.22**

For the third quarter: $Y_t = (\beta_0 + \beta_5) + \beta_1 X_{1_t} + \beta_2 X_{2_t} + \varepsilon_t$ **11.23**

Equations 11.20 through 11.23 show that the values β_3, β_4, and β_5 in equation 11.19 indicate the average amounts by which the values of observations in the first, second, and third quarters are expected to differ from observations in the fourth quarter. That is, β_3, β_4, and β_5 indicate the expected effects of seasonality in the first, second, and third quarters, respectively, relative to the fourth quarter.

An example of the seasonal regression function in equation 11.19 is given in Figure 11.27 (and in the file FIG11-27.xls on your data disk).

The major difference between Figures 11.18 and 11.27 is the addition of the data in columns E, F, and G in Figure 11.27. These columns represent the indicator values for the independent variables X_{3_t}, X_{4_t}, and X_{5_t}, respectively. We created these values by entering the following formula in cell E3 and copying it to E4 through G22:

Formula for cell E3:   =IF($B3=E$2,1,0)
(Copy to E4 through G22.)

In Figure 11.27, column I (labeled "Seasonal Model") shows the predicted sales level for each time period where the following formula is entered in cell I3 and copied to cells I4 through I22:

Formula for cell I3:   =TREND($H$3:$H$22,$C$3:$G$22,C3:G3)
(Copy to I4 through I22.)

We obtain the values of b_0, b_1, b_2, b_3, b_4, and b_5 required for the estimated regression function using the Regression command settings shown in Figure 11.28. Figure 11.29 shows the results of this command, which indicate that the estimated regression function is:

$$\hat{Y}_t = 824.472 + 17.319 X_{1_t} + 3.485 X_{2_t} - 86.805 X_{3_t} - 424.736 X_{4_t} - 123.453 X_{5_t} \qquad \textbf{11.24}$$

The coefficients for the indicator variables are given by $b_3 = -86.805$, $b_4 = -424.736$, and $b_5 = -123.453$. Because X_{3_t} is the indicator variable for quarter 1 observations, the value of b_3 indicates that, on average, the sales level in quarter 1 of any year is expected to be approximately \$86,805 lower than the level expected for quarter 4. The value of b_4 indicates that the typical sales value in quarter 2 of any given year is expected to be approximately \$424,736 less than the level expected in quarter 4. Finally, the

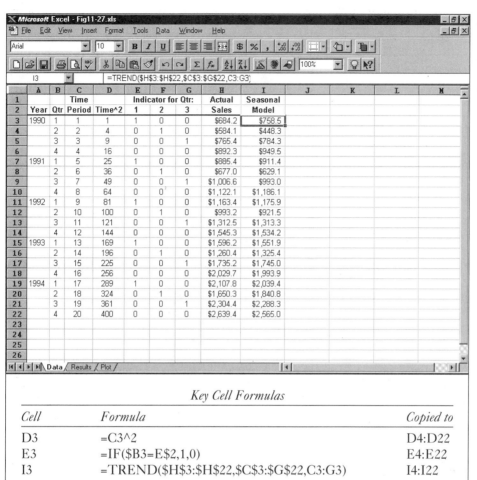

Figure 11.27
Spreadsheet implementation of the seasonal regression model.

Key Cell Formulas

Cell	Formula	Copied to
D3	=C3^2	D4:D22
E3	=IF($B3=E$2,1,0)	E4:E22
I3	=TREND($H$3:$H$22,$C$3:$G$22,C3:G3)	I4:I22

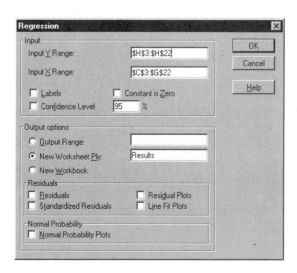

Figure 11.28
Regression command settings for the seasonal regression model.

value of b_5 indicates that the typical sales value in quarter 3 is expected to be approximately \$123,453 less than the level expected in quarter 4.

In Figure 11.29, notice that $R^2 = 0.986$, suggesting that the estimated regression function fits the data very well. This is also evident from the graph in Figure 11.30, which shows the actual data versus the predictions of the seasonal forecasting model.

11.15.2 Forecasting with the Seasonal Regression Model

We can use the estimated regression function in equation 11.24 to forecast an expected level of sales for any future time period by assigning appropriate values to the independent variables. For example, forecasts of WaterCraft's sales in the next four quarters are represented by:

$$\hat{Y}_{21} = 824.472 + 17.319(21) + 3.485(21\text{^}2) - 86.805(1) - 424.736(0) - 123.453(0) = 2{,}638.7$$

$$\hat{Y}_{22} = 824.472 + 17.319(22) + 3.485(22\text{^}2) - 86.805(0) - 424.736(1) - 123.453(0) = 2{,}468.0$$

$$\hat{Y}_{23} = 824.472 + 17.319(23) + 3.485(23\text{^}2) - 86.805(0) - 424.736(0) - 123.453(1) = 2{,}943.4$$

$$\hat{Y}_{24} = 824.472 + 17.319(24) + 3.485(24\text{^}2) - 86.805(0) - 424.736(0) - 123.453(0) = 3{,}248.1$$

11.16 COMBINING FORECASTS

Given the number and variety of forecasting techniques available, it can be difficult to select a *single* method to use in predicting future values of a time series variable. Indeed, the state-of-the-art research in time series forecasting suggests that we should

Figure 11.29 Regression results for the seasonal regression model.

Microsoft Excel - Fig11-27.xls

	A	B	C	D	E	F	G	H
1	SUMMARY OUTPUT							
2								
3	*Regression Statistics*							
4	Multiple R	0.992740856						
5	R Square	0.985534407						
6	Adjusted R Square	0.980368124						
7	Standard Error	82.19264615						
8	Observations	20						
9								
10	ANOVA							
11		*df*	*SS*	*MS*	*F*	*Significance F*		
12	Regression	5	6443613.818	1288722.764	190.76275	2.31527E-12		
13	Residual	14	94578.83513	6755.631081				
14	Total	19	6538192.653					
15								
16		*Coefficients*	*Standard Error*	*t Stat*	*P-value*	*Lower 95%*	*Upper 95%*	*Lower 95.0%*
17	Intercept	824.4727144	71.38844455	11.54910601	1.5268E-08	671.3595927	977.5858361	671.3595927
18	X Variable 1	17.3188557	13.43309658	1.289267563	0.21819982	-11.49229666	46.13000806	-11.4922967
19	X Variable 2	3.48547572	0.620679918	5.615576755	6.3681E-05	2.154248511	4.81670293	2.154248511
20	X Variable 3	-86.8050143	52.88906781	-1.64126573	0.12300747	-200.2408838	26.63085515	-200.240884
21	X Variable 4	-424.73674	52.40244365	-8.105285	1.1757E-06	-537.1289039	-312.344577	-537.128904
22	X Variable 5	-123.453356	52.09941535	-2.36957278	0.03271855	-235.1955882	-11.7111244	-235.19558E
23								
24								
25								
26								

Data / Results / Plot

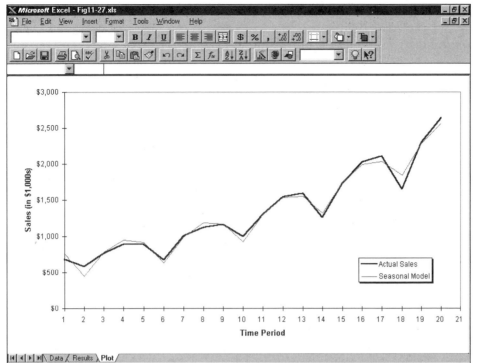

Figure 11.30
Plot of seasonal regression model predictions versus actual WaterCraft sales data.

not use a single forecasting method. Rather, we can obtain more accurate forecasts by combining the forecasts from several methods into a composite forecast.

For example, suppose that we used three methods to build forecasting models of the same time series variable. We denote the predicted value for time period t using each of these methods as F_{1_t}, F_{2_t}, and F_{3_t}, respectively. One simple approach to combining these forecasts into a composite forecast $\hat{Y}_t$ might involve taking a linear combination of the individual forecasts as:

$$\hat{Y}_t = b_0 + b_1 F_{1_t} + b_2 F_{2_t} + b_3 F_{3_t} \qquad \textbf{11.25}$$

We could determine the values for the b_i using Solver or least squares regression to minimize the MSE between the combined forecast $\hat{Y}_t$ and the actual data. The combined forecast $\hat{Y}_t$ in equation 11.25 will be at least as accurate as any of the individual forecasting techniques. To see this, suppose that F_{1_t} is the most accurate of the individual forecasting techniques. If $b_1 = 1$ and $b_0 = b_2 = b_3 = 0$, then our combined forecast would be $\hat{Y}_t = F_{1_t}$. Thus, b_0, b_2, and b_3 would be assigned nonzero values only if this helps to reduce the MSE and produce more accurate predictions.

In Chapter 9, Regression Analysis, we noted that adding independent variables to a regression model can never decrease the value of the R^2 statistic. Therefore, it is important to ensure that each independent variable in a multiple regression model accounts for a significant portion of the variation in the dependent variable and does not simply inflate the value of R^2. Similarly, combining forecasts can never increase the value of the MSE. Thus, when combining forecasts, we must ensure that each forecasting technique plays a significant role in accounting for the behavior of the dependent time series variable. Using the adjusted-R^2 statistic in building multiple regression models, as described in Chapter 9, can also be applied to the problem of selecting forecasting techniques to combine in time series analysis.

THE WORLD OF MANAGEMENT SCIENCE
Check Processing Revisited—The Chemical Bank Experience

Chemical Bank of New York employs more than 500 people to process checks averaging $2 billion per day. Scheduling shifts for these employees requires accurate predictions of check flows. This is done with a regression model that forecasts daily check volume using independent variables that represent calendar effects. The regression model used by Ohio National Bank (see "Better Predictions Create Cost Savings for Ohio National Bank" in Chapter 9) is based on this Chemical Bank model.

The binary independent variables in the regression model represent months, days of the month, weekdays, and holidays. Of 54 possible variables, 29 were used in the model to yield a coefficient of determination (R^2) of 0.83 and a standard deviation of 142.6.

The forecast errors, or residuals, were examined for patterns that would suggest the possibility of improving the model. Analysts noticed a tendency for overpredictions to follow one another and underpredictions to follow one another, implying that check volumes could be predicted not only by calendar effects but also by the recent history of prediction errors.

An exponential smoothing model was used to forecast the residuals. The regression model combined with the exponential smoothing model then became the complete model for predicting check volumes. Fine-tuning was accomplished by investigating different values of the smoothing constant (α) from 0.05 to 0.50. A smoothing constant of 0.2 produced the best results, reducing the standard deviation from 142.6 to 131.8. Examination of the residuals for the complete model showed nothing but random variations, indicating that the exponential smoothing procedure was working as well as could be expected.

Although the complete model provides better forecasts on the average, it occasionally overreacts and increases the error for some periods. Nevertheless, the complete model is considered to be preferable to regression alone.

Source: Kevin Boyd and Vincent A. Mabert, "A Two Stage Forecasting Approach at Chemical Bank of New York for Check Processing," *Journal of Bank Research*, vol. 8, no. 2, Summer 1977, pages 101–107.

SUMMARY

This chapter presented several methods for forecasting future values of a time series variable. The chapter discussed time series methods for stationary data (without a strong upward or downward trend), nonstationary data (with a strong upward or downward linear or nonlinear trend), and data with repeating seasonal patterns. In each case, the goal is to fit models to the past behavior of a time series and use the models to project future values.

Because time series vary in nature (for example, with and without trend, with and without seasonality), it is helpful to be aware of the different forecasting techniques and the types of problems for which they are intended. There are many other time series modeling techniques besides those discussed in this chapter. Descriptions of these other techniques can be found in texts devoted to time series analysis.

In modeling time series data, it is often useful to try several techniques and then compare them based on measures of forecast accuracy, including a graphical inspection of how well the model fits the historical data. If no one procedure is clearly better than the others, it might be wise to combine the forecasts from the different procedures using a weighted average or some other method.

QUESTIONS AND PROBLEMS

1. What is the result of using regression analysis to estimate a linear trend model for a stationary time series?

2. A manufacturing company uses a certain type of steel rod in one of its products. The design specifications for this rod indicate that it must be between 0.353 to 0.357 inches in diameter. The machine that manufactures these rods is set up to produce them at 0.355 inches in diameter, but there is some variation in its output. Provided that the machine is producing rods within 0.353 to 0.357 inches in diameter, its output is considered acceptable or within control limits. Management uses a control chart to track the diameter of the rods being produced by the machine over time so that remedial measures can be taken if the machine begins to produce unacceptable rods. Figure 11.31 shows an example of this type of chart.

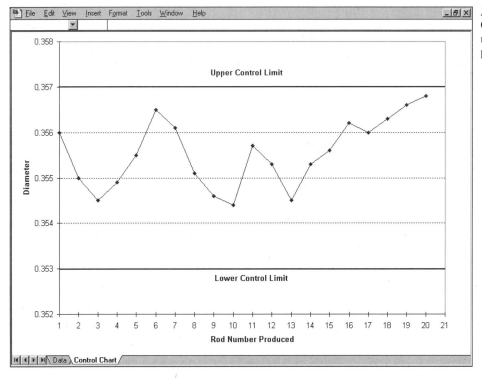

Figure 11.31
Graph for rod manufacturing problem.

Unacceptable rods represent waste. Thus, management wants to develop a procedure to predict when the machine will start producing rods that are outside the control limits, so that appropriate actions can be taken to prevent the production of rods that must be scrapped. Of the time series models discussed in this chapter, which is the most appropriate tool for this problem? Explain your answer.

3. Each month, Joe's Auto Parts uses exponential smoothing (with $\alpha = 0.25$) to predict the number of cans of brake fluid that will be sold during the next month. In June, Joe forecast that he would sell 37 cans of brake fluid during July. Joe actually sold 43 cans in July.

    a. What is Joe's forecast for brake fluid sales in August and September?
    b. Suppose that Joe sells 32 cans of brake fluid in August. What is the revised forecast for September?

Questions 4 through 9 refer to the following data set representing annual sales (in $1,000s) for a small business.

Year	Sales	Year	Sales
1975	283	1985	462
1976	288	1986	452
1977	336	1987	474
1978	388	1988	476
1979	406	1989	497
1980	412	1990	487
1981	416	1991	523
1982	435	1992	528
1983	428	1993	532
1984	435	1994	552

4. Prepare a line graph of these data. Do the data appear to be stationary or nonstationary?

5. Compute the two-period and four-period moving average predictions for the data set.

    a. Prepare a line graph comparing the moving average predictions against the original data.
    b. Do the moving averages tend to overestimate or underestimate the actual data? Why?
    c. Compute forecasts for 1995 and 1996 using the two-period and four-period moving average techniques.

6. Use Solver to determine the weights for a three-period weighted moving average that minimizes the MSE for the data set.

    a. What are the optimal values for the weights?
    b. Prepare a line graph comparing the weighted moving average predictions against the original data.
    c. What are the forecasts for 1995 and 1996 using this technique?

7. Create an exponential smoothing model that minimizes the MSE for the data set. Use Solver to determine the optimal value of α.

   a. What is the optimal value of α?
   b. Prepare a line graph comparing the exponential smoothing predictions against the original data.
   c. What are the forecasts for 1995 and 1996 using this technique?

8. Use Holt's method to create a model that minimizes the MSE for the data set. Use Solver to determine the optimal values of α and β.

   a. What are the optimal values of α and β?
   b. Prepare a line graph comparing the predictions from Holt's method versus the original data.
   c. What are the forecasts for 1995 and 1996 using this technique?

9. Use regression analysis to fit a linear trend model to the data set.

   a. What is the estimated regression function?
   b. Interpret the R^2 value for your model.
   c. Prepare a line graph comparing the linear trend predictions against the original data.
   d. What are the forecasts for 1995 and 1996 using this technique?
   e. Fit a quadratic trend model to these data. What is the estimated regression function?
   f. Compare the adjusted-R^2 value for this model to that of the linear trend model. What is implied by this comparison?
   g. Prepare a line graph comparing the quadratic trend predictions against the original data.
   h. What are the forecasts for 1995 and 1996 using this technique?
   i. If you had to choose between the linear and quadratic trend models, which would you use? Why?

Questions 10 through 14 refer to the following data set representing the number of four-wheel drive utility vehicles sold by a local car dealer during the past three years.

Year	Quarter	Units Sold
1992	1	23
	2	25
	3	36
	4	31
1993	1	26
	2	28
	3	48
	4	36
1994	1	31
	2	42
	3	53
	4	43

10. Use regression analysis to fit a linear trend model to the data set.

    a. What is the estimated regression function?
    b. Interpret the R^2 value for your model.

    c. Prepare a line graph comparing the linear trend predictions against the original data.

    d. What are the forecasts for each quarter in 1995 using this technique?

    e. Calculate seasonal indices for each quarter using the results of the linear trend model.

    f. Use these seasonal indices to compute seasonal forecasts for each quarter in 1995.

11. Use regression analysis to fit a quadratic trend model to the data set.

    a. What is the estimated regression function?

    b. Compare the adjusted-R^2 value for this model to that of the linear trend model. What is implied by this comparison?

    c. Prepare a line graph comparing the quadratic trend predictions against the original data.

    d. What are the forecasts for each quarter in 1995 using this technique?

    e. Calculate seasonal indices for each quarter using the results of the quadratic trend model.

    f. Use these seasonal indices to compute seasonal forecasts for each quarter in 1995.

12. Use Holt's method to create a model that minimizes the MSE for the data set. Use Solver to determine the optimal values of α and β.

    a. What are the optimal values of α and β?

    b. Prepare a line graph comparing the predictions from Holt's method against the original data.

    c. What are the forecasts for each quarter in 1995 using this technique?

    d. Calculate seasonal indices for each quarter using the results of Holt's method.

    e. Use these seasonal indices to compute seasonal forecasts for each quarter in 1995.

13. Use Winter's method to create a seasonal model that minimizes the MSE for the data set. Use Solver to determine the optimal values of α, β, and γ.

    a. What are the optimal value of α, β, and γ?

    b. Prepare a line graph comparing the predictions from Winter's method against the original data.

    c. What are the forecasts for each quarter in 1995 using this technique?

14. Use regression analysis to fit a seasonal model with linear trend to the data set.

    a. What is the estimated regression function?

    b. Interpret the R^2 value for your model.

    c. Interpret the parameter estimates corresponding to the indicator variables in your model.

    d. Prepare a line graph comparing the linear trend predictions against the original data.

    e. What are the forecasts for each quarter in 1995 using this technique?

Questions 15 through 19 refer to the following data set representing the selling price of three-month old calves at a livestock auction during the past 22 weeks.

Week	Price	Week	Price
1	$176	12	$172
2	$172	13	$174
3	$174	14	$177
4	$177	15	$180
5	$173	16	$178
6	$171	17	$176
7	$172	18	$179
8	$173	19	$175
9	$174	20	$176
10	$173	21	$174
11	$171	22	$175

15. Prepare a line graph of these data. Do the data appear to be stationary or nonstationary?

16. Compute the two-period and four-period moving average predictions for the data set.

   a. Prepare a line graph comparing the moving average predictions against the original data.
   b. Compute the MSE for each of the two moving averages. Which appears to provide the best fit for this data set?
   c. Compute forecasts for the next two weeks using the two-period and four-period moving average techniques.

17. Use Solver to determine the weights for a four-period weighted moving average on the data set that minimizes the MSE.

   a. What are the optimal values for the weights?
   b. Prepare a line graph comparing the weighted moving average predictions against the original data.
   c. What are the forecasts for weeks 23 and 24 using this technique?

18. Create an exponential smoothing model that minimizes the MSE for the data set. Use Solver to estimate the optimal value of α.

   a. What is the optimal value of α?
   b. Prepare a line graph comparing the exponential smoothing predictions against the original data.
   c. What are the forecasts for weeks 23 and 24 using this technique?

19. Use Holt's method to create a model that minimizes the MSE for the data set. Use Solver to estimate the optimal values of α and β.

   a. What are the optimal values of α and β?
   b. Are these values surprising? Why or why not?

Questions 20 through 23 refer to the following data set representing two years of monthly health insurance claims for a self-insured company.

Year	Month	Claims	Year	Month	Claims
1993	1	$10,159	1994	1	$12,300
1993	2	$11,175	1994	2	$13,224
1993	3	$12,310	1994	3	$13,606
1993	4	$12,446	1994	4	$13,659
1993	5	$13,213	1994	5	$16,442
1993	6	$16,412	1994	6	$17,334
1993	7	$17,405	1994	7	$19,605
1993	8	$14,233	1994	8	$18,997
1993	9	$14,606	1994	9	$15,971
1993	10	$12,969	1994	10	$15,740
1993	11	$13,980	1994	11	$16,919
1993	12	$14,755	1994	12	$18,931

20. Use regression analysis to fit a linear trend model to the data set.

    a. What is the estimated regression function?
    b. Interpret the R^2 value for your model.
    c. Prepare a line graph comparing the linear trend predictions against the original data.
    d. What are the forecasts for each of the first six months in 1995 using this technique?
    e. Calculate seasonal indices for each month using the results of the linear trend model.
    f. Use these seasonal indices to compute seasonal forecasts for the first six months in 1995.

21. Use regression analysis to fit a quadratic trend model to the data set.

    a. What is the estimated regression function?
    b. Compare the adjusted-R^2 value for this model to that of the linear trend model. What is implied by this comparison?
    c. Prepare a line graph comparing the quadratic trend predictions against the original data.
    d. What are the forecasts for each of the first six months in 1995 using this technique?
    e. Calculate seasonal indices for each month using the results of the quadratic trend model.
    f. Use these seasonal indices to compute seasonal forecasts for each of the first six months in 1995.

22. Use Holt's method to create a model that minimizes the MSE for the data set. Use Solver to determine the optimal values of α and β.

    a. What are the optimal values of α and β?
    b. Prepare a line graph comparing the predictions from Holt's method against the original data.
    c. What are the forecasts for each of the first six months in 1995 using this technique?
    d. Calculate seasonal indices for each month using the results of Holt's method.
    e. Use these seasonal indices to compute seasonal forecasts for each of the first six months in 1995.

23. Use Winter's method to create a seasonal model that minimizes the MSE for the data set. Use Solver to determine the optimal values of α, β, and γ.

   a. What are the optimal values of α, β, and γ?
   b. Prepare a line graph comparing the predictions from Winter's method against the original data.
   c. What are the forecasts for each of the first six months in 1995 using this technique?

CASE 11.1   FORECASTING COLAS

Tarrows, Pearson, Foster and Zuligar (TPF&Z), is one of the largest actuarial consulting firms in the United States. In addition to providing its clients with expert advice on executive compensation programs and employee benefits programs, TPF&Z also helps its clients determine the amounts of money they must contribute annually to defined benefit retirement programs.

Most companies offer two different types of retirement programs to their employees: defined contribution plans and defined benefit plans. Under a **defined contribution plan,** the company contributes a fixed percentage of an employee's earning to fund the employee's retirement. Individual employees covered by this type of plan determine how their money is to be invested (e.g., stocks, bonds, or fixed-income securities) and whatever the employees are able to accumulate over the years constitutes their retirement fund. In a **defined benefit plan,** the company provides covered employees with retirement benefits that are usually calculated as a percentage of the employee's final salary (or sometimes an average of the employee's highest five years of earnings). Thus, under a defined benefit plan the company is obligated to make payments to retired employees, but the company must determine how much of its earnings to set aside each year to cover these future obligations. Actuarial firms like TPF&Z assist companies in making this determination.

Several of TPF&Z's clients offer employees defined benefit retirement plans that allow for cost of living adjustments (COLAs). Here, an employee's retirement benefit is still based on some measure of their final earnings, but these benefits are increased over time as the cost of living rises. These COLAs are often tied to the national consumer price index (CPI) which tracks the cost of a fixed market basket of items over time. Each month the Federal government calculates and publishes the CPI. Monthly CPI data from January 1980 through September 1996 is given in the following table (and in the file CPIData.xls on your data disk).

In order to assist their clients in determining the amount of money to accrue during a year for their annual contribution to their defined benefit programs, TPF&Z must forecast the value of the CPI one year into the future. Pension assets represent the largest single source of investment funds in the world. As a result, small changes or differences in TPF&Z's CPI forecast translate into hundreds of millions of dollars in corporate earnings being diverted from the bottom line into pension reserves. Needless to say, the partners of TPF&Z want their CPI forecasts to be as accurate as possible.

Consumer Price Index Data 1980–1996

Month	1980	1981	1982	1983	1984	1985	1986	1987	1988	1989	1990	1991	1992	1993	1994	1995	1996
Jan	77.8	87.0	94.3	97.8	101.9	105.5	109.6	111.2	115.7	121.1	127.4	134.6	138.1	142.6	146.2	150.3	154.4
Feb	78.9	87.9	94.6	97.9	102.4	106.0	109.3	111.6	116.0	121.6	128.0	134.8	138.6	143.1	146.7	150.9	154.9
Mar	80.1	88.5	94.5	97.9	102.6	106.4	108.8	112.1	116.5	122.3	128.7	135.0	139.3	143.6	147.2	151.4	155.7
Apr	81.0	89.1	94.9	98.6	103.1	106.9	108.6	112.7	117.1	123.1	128.9	135.2	139.5	144.0	147.4	151.9	156.3
May	81.8	89.8	95.8	99.2	103.4	107.3	108.9	113.1	117.5	123.8	129.2	135.6	139.7	144.2	147.5	152.2	156.6
Jun	82.7	90.6	97.0	99.5	103.7	107.6	109.5	113.5	118.0	124.1	129.9	136.0	140.2	144.4	148.0	152.5	156.7
Jul	82.7	91.6	97.5	99.9	104.1	107.8	109.5	113.8	118.5	124.4	130.4	136.2	140.5	144.4	148.4	152.5	157.0
Aug	83.3	92.3	97.7	100.2	104.5	108.0	109.7	114.4	119.0	124.6	131.6	136.6	140.9	144.8	149.0	152.9	157.3
Sep	84.0	93.2	97.9	100.7	105.0	108.3	110.2	115.0	119.8	125.0	132.7	137.2	141.3	145.1	149.4	153.2	157.8
Oct	84.8	93.4	98.2	101.0	105.3	108.7	110.3	115.3	120.2	125.6	133.5	137.4	141.8	145.7	149.5	153.7	—
Nov	86.5	93.7	98.0	101.2	105.3	109.0	110.4	115.4	120.3	125.9	133.8	137.8	142.0	145.8	149.7	153.6	—
Dec	86.3	94.0	97.6	101.3	105.3	109.3	110.5	115.4	120.5	126.1	133.8	137.9	141.9	145.8	149.7	153.5	—

1. Prepare a plot of the CPI data. Based on this plot, which of the time-series forecasting techniques covered in this chapter would *not* be appropriate for forecasting this time series?

2. Apply Holt's method to this data set and use Solver to find the values of α (alpha) and β (beta) which minimize the MSE between the actual and predicted CPI values. What is the MSE using this technique? What is the forecasted CPI value for September 1997 using this technique?

3. Apply linear regression to model the CPI as a function of time. What is the MSE using this technique? What is the forecasted CPI value for September 1997 using this technique?

4. Create a graph showing the actual CPI values plotted along with the predicted values obtained using Holt's method and the linear regression model. Which forecasting technique seems to fit the actual CPI data the best?

   Based on this graph, do you think it is appropriate to use linear regression on this data set? Explain your answer.

5. A partner of the firm has looked at your graph and asked you to repeat your analysis excluding the data prior to 1991. What MSE do you obtain using Holt's method? What MSE do you obtain using linear regression? What is the forecasted CPI value for September 1997 using each technique?

6. Graph your results again. Which forecasting technique seems to fit the actual CPI data the best?

   Based on this graph, do you think it is appropriate to use linear regression on this data set? Explain your answer.

7. The same partner is pleased with your new results but has one final request. She would like to consider if it is possible to combine the predictions obtained using Holt's method and linear regression to obtain a composite forecast that is more accurate than either technique used in isolation. The partner wants you to combine the predictions in the following manner:

$$\text{Combined Prediction} = w \times H + (1 - w) \times R$$

where H represents the predictions from Holt's method, R represents the predictions obtained using the linear regression model, and w is a weighting parameter between 0 and 1. Use Solver to determine the value of w that minimizes the MSE between the actual CPI values and the combined predictions. What is the optimal value of w and what is the associated MSE? What is the forecasted CPI value for September 1997 using this technique?

8. What CPI forecast for September of 1997 would you recommend TPF&Z actually use?

CASE 11.2   FORECASTING BOX-OFFICE RETURNS

Contributed by Jack Yurkiewicz, Lubin School of Business, Pace University, New York.

For years, people in the motion picture industry—critics, film historians, and others—have eagerly awaited the second issue in January of *Variety*. Long considered the show business bible, *Variety* is a weekly trade newspaper that reports on all aspects of the entertainment industry: movies, television, recordings, concert tours, and so on. The second issue in January, called the Anniversary Edition, summarizes how the entertainment industry fared in the previous year, both artistically and commercially.

In this issue, *Variety* publishes its list of All Time Film Rental Champs. This list indicates, in descending order, motion pictures and the amount of money they returned to the studio. Because a movie theater rents a film from a studio for a limited time, the money paid for admission by ticket buyers is split between the studio and the theater owner. For example, if a ticket buyer pays $8 to see a particular movie, the theater owner keeps about $4, and the studio receives the other $4. The longer a movie plays in a theater, the greater the percentage of the admission price returned to the studio. A film playing for an entire summer could eventually return as much as 90% of the $8 to the studio. The theater owner also benefits from such a success because although the owner's percentage of the admission price is small, the sales of concessions (candy, soda, and so on) provide greater profits. Thus, both the studio and the theater owner win when a film continues to draw audiences for a long time. *Variety* lists the rental figures (the actual dollar amounts returned to the studios) that the films have accrued in their domestic releases (United States and Canada).

In addition, *Variety* provides a monthly Box-Office Barometer of the film industry, which is a profile of the month's domestic box-office returns. This profile is not measured in dollars, but scaled according to some standard. By the late 1980s, for example, the scale was based on numbers around 100, with 100 representing the average box-office return of 1980. The figures from 1987 through 1996 are given in the table (and in the file BXOffice.xls on your data disk).

All the figures are scaled around 1980's box-office returns, but instead of dollars, artificial numbers are used. Film executives can get a relative indication of box-office figures compared to the arbitrary 1980 scale. For example, in January 1987 the box-office returns to the film industry were 95% of the average that year, whereas in January 1988 the returns were 104% of the average of 1980 (or, they were 4% above the average of 1980's figure).

Month	1987	1988	1989	1990	1991	1992	1993	1994	1995	1996
January	95	104	101	88	132	125	111	127	119	147
February	94	100	96	110	109	118	123	129	147	146
March	98	99	82	129	101	121	121	132	164	133
April	96	88	84	113	111	140	139	108	135	148
May	95	89	85	114	140	141	119	115	124	141
June	115	108	124	169	179	201	156	149	168	191
July	107	109	134	131	145	152	154	155	159	178
August	104	101	109	139	140	138	136	129	137	156
September	96	106	121	120	120	137	105	117	149	119
October	112	102	111	115	129	138	132	166	159	138
November	98	78	101	116	118	144	123	152	175	175
December	102	111	112	128	139	148	164	173	195	188

From the time series given in the table, you will make a forecast for the 12 months of the next year, 1997.

1. Produce a line graph of the data over time. From this graph, do you see a pattern? Can you detect any seasonality in the data?

2. Use exponential smoothing. Comment on the appropriateness of exponential smoothing on this data set. Use Solver to find the optimal (minimal MSE) smoothing constant. Plot the predictions from this model on the graph with the original data. How well does this technique fit the data? Make forecasts for the 12 months of 1997.

3. Use Holt's method. Comment on the appropriateness of Holt's method on this data set. Use Solver to find the optimal (minimal MSE) smoothing constants. Plot the predictions from this model on the graph with the original data. How well does this technique fit the data? What are your forecasts for the 12 months of 1997?

4. Use regression to build a linear trend model. Comment on the goodness-of-fit of this model to the data. Plot the predictions from this model on the graph with the original data. How well does this technique fit the data?

5. Use Winter's method. Comment on the appropriateness of Winter's method on this data set. Use Solver to find the optimal (minimal MSE) smoothing constants. Plot the predictions from this model on the graph with the original data. How well does this technique fit the data? What are your forecasts for the 12 months of 1997?

6. Develop seasonal indices for the linear trend model developed in question 4. Use these indices to adjust predictions from the linear trend model for seasonal effects. Plot the predictions from this model on the graph with the original data. How well does this technique fit the data? Make forecasts for the 12 months of 1997 using this technique.

7. Using mean squared error as your criterion, in which forecasting method of those you tried do you have the most confidence for making accurate forecasts for 1997?

REFERENCES

Clemen, R. T. "Combining Forecasts: A Review and Annotated Bibliography." *International Journal of Forecasting*, vol. 5, 1989.

Clements, D. and R. Reid. "Analytical MS/OR Tools Applied to a Plant Closure." *Interfaces*, vol. 24, no. 2, 1994.

Gardner, E. "Exponential Smoothing: The State of the Art." *Journal of Forecasting*, vol. 4, no. 1, 1985.

Georgoff, D. and R. Murdick. "Managers Guide to Forecasting." *Harvard Business Review*, vol. 64, no. 1, 1986.

Makridakis, S. and S. Wheelwright. *Forecasting: Methods and Applications*. New York: Wiley, 1986.

Pindyck, R. and D. Rubinfeld. *Econometric Models and Economic Forecasts*. New York: McGraw-Hill, 1989.

CHAPTER 12

Simulation

Chapter 1 discussed how the calculations in a spreadsheet can be viewed as a mathematical model that defines a functional relationship between various input variables (or independent variables) and one or more bottom-line performance measures (or dependent variables). The following equation expresses this relationship:

$$Y = f(X_1, X_2, ..., X_k)$$

In many spreadsheets, the values of various input cells are determined by the person using the spreadsheet. These input cells correspond to the independent variables $X_1, X_2, ..., X_k$ in the above equation. Various formulas (represented by $f(\cdot)$ above) are entered in other cells of the spreadsheet to transform the values of the input cells into some bottom-line output (denoted by Y above). Simulation is a technique that is helpful in analyzing models where the value to be assumed by one or more independent variables is uncertain.

12.1 RANDOM VARIABLES AND RISK

In order to compute a value for the bottom-line performance measure of a spreadsheet model, each input cell must be assigned a specific value so that all the related calculations can be performed. However, some uncertainty often exists regarding the value that should be assumed by one or more independent variables (or input cells) in the spreadsheet. This is particularly true in spreadsheet models that represent future conditions. A **random variable** is any variable whose value cannot be predicted or set with certainty. Thus, many input variables in a spreadsheet model represent random variables whose actual values cannot be predicted with certainty.

For example, projections of the cost of raw materials, future interest rates, future numbers of employees, and expected product demand are random variables because their true values are unknown and will be determined in the future. If we cannot say with certainty what value one or more input variables in a model will assume, we also cannot say with certainty what value the dependent variable will assume. This uncertainty associated with the value of the dependent variable introduces an element of risk to the decision-making problem. Specifically, if the dependent variable represents some bottom-line performance measure that managers use to make decisions, and its value is uncertain, any decisions made on the basis of this value are based on uncertain (or incomplete) information. When such a decision is made, some chance exists that the decision will not produce the intended results. This chance, or uncertainty, represents an element of **risk** in the decision-making problem.

The term "risk" also implies the *potential* for loss. The fact that a decision's outcome is uncertain does not mean that the decision is particularly risky. For example, whenever we put money into a soft drink machine, there is a chance that the machine will take our money and not deliver the product. However, most of us would not consider this risk to be particularly great. From past experience, we know that the chance of not receiving the product is small. But even if the machine takes our money and does not deliver the product, most of us would not consider this to be a tremendous loss. Thus, the amount of risk involved in a given decision-making situation is a function of the uncertainty in the outcome of the decision and the magnitude of the potential loss. A proper assessment of the risk present in a decision-making situation should address both of these issues, as the examples in this chapter will demonstrate.

12.2   WHY ANALYZE RISK?

Many spreadsheets built by business people contain *estimated* values for the uncertain input variables in their models. If a manager cannot say with certainty what value a particular cell in a spreadsheet will assume, this cell most likely represents a random variable. Ordinarily, the manager will attempt to make an informed guess about the values such cells will assume. The manager hopes that inserting the expected, or most likely, values for all the uncertain cells in a spreadsheet will provide the most likely value for the cell containing the bottom-line performance measure (Y). The problem with this type of analysis is that it tells the decision maker nothing about the *variability* of the performance measure.

For example, in analyzing a particular investment opportunity, we might determine that the expected return on a $1,000 investment is $10,000 within two years. But how much variability exists in the possible outcomes? If all the potential outcomes are scattered closely around $10,000 (say from $9,000 to $11,000), then the investment opportunity might still be attractive. If, on the other hand, the potential outcomes are scattered widely around $10,000 (say from –$30,000 to +$50,000), then the investment opportunity might be unattractive. Although these two scenarios might have the same expected or average value, the risks involved are quite different. Thus, even if we can determine the expected outcome of a decision using a spreadsheet, it is just as important, if not more so, to consider the risk involved in the decision.

12.3   METHODS OF RISK ANALYSIS

Several techniques are available to help managers analyze risk. Three of the most common are best-case/worst-case analysis, what-if analysis, and simulation. Of these methods, simulation is the most powerful and, therefore, is the technique we will focus on in this chapter. Although the other techniques might not be effective in risk analysis, they are probably used more often than simulation by most managers in business today. This is largely due to the fact that most managers are unaware of the spreadsheet's ability to perform simulation and of the benefits provided by this technique. Before discussing simulation, let's first briefly look at the other methods of risk analysis to understand their strengths and weaknesses.

12.3.1   Best-Case/Worst-Case Analysis

If we don't know what value a particular cell in a spreadsheet will assume, we could enter a number that we think is the most likely value for the uncertain cell. If we enter such numbers for all the uncertain cells in the spreadsheet, we can easily calculate the most likely value of the bottom-line performance measure. (This is also called the **base-case** scenario.) However, this scenario gives us no information about how far away the actual outcome might be from this expected or most likely value.

One simple solution to this problem is to calculate the value of the bottom-line performance measure using the **best-case,** or most optimistic, and **worst-case,** or most pessimistic, values for the uncertain input cells. These additional scenarios show the range of possible values that might be assumed by the bottom-line performance measure. As indicated in the earlier example about the $1,000 investment, knowing the range of possible outcomes is very helpful in assessing the risk involved in different alternatives. However, simply knowing the best-case and worst-case outcomes tells us nothing about the distribution of possible values within this range, nor does it tell us the probability of either scenario occurring.

Figure 12.1 displays several probability distributions that might be associated with the value of a bottom-line performance measure within a given range. Each of these distributions describe variables that have identical ranges and similar average values. But each distribution is very different in terms of the risk it represents to the decision maker. The appeal of best-case/worst-case analysis is that it is easy to do. Its weakness is that it tells us nothing about the shape of the distribution associated with the bottom-line performance measure. As we'll see later, knowing the shape of the distribution of the bottom-line performance measure can be critically important in helping us answer a number of managerial questions.

12.3.2   What-If Analysis

Prior to the introduction of electronic spreadsheets in the early 1980s, the use of best-case/worst-case analysis was often the only feasible way for a manager to analyze the risk associated with a decision. This process was extremely time consuming, error prone, and tedious, using only a piece of paper, pencil, and calculator to recalculate the performance measure of a model using different values for the uncertain inputs. The arrival of personal computers and electronic spreadsheets made it much easier for a manager to play out a large number of scenarios in addition to the best and worst cases—which is the essence of what-if analysis.

In **what-if analysis**, a manager changes the values of the uncertain input variables to see what happens to the bottom-line performance measure. By making a series of such changes, a manager can gain some insight into how sensitive the performance measure is to changes to the input variables. Although many managers perform this type of manual what-if analysis, it has three major flaws.

First, if the values selected for the independent variables are based on only the manager's judgment, the resulting sample values of the performance measure are

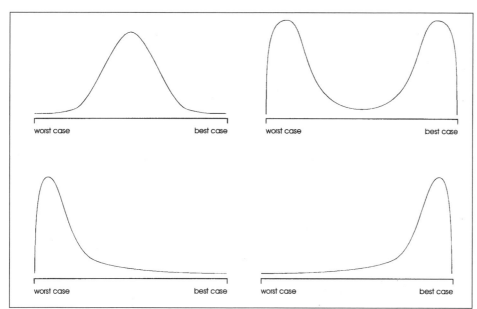

Figure 12.1
Possible distributions of performance measure values within a given range.

likely to be biased. That is, if several uncertain variables can each assume some range of values, it would be difficult to ensure that the manager tests a fair, or representative, sample of all possible combinations of these values. To select values for the uncertain variables that correctly reflect their random variations, the values must be randomly selected from a distribution, or pool, of values that reflects the appropriate range of possible values as well as the appropriate relative frequencies of these variables.

Second, hundreds or thousands of what-if scenarios might be required to create a valid representation of the underlying variability in the bottom-line performance measure. No one would want to perform these scenarios manually nor would anyone be able to make sense of the resulting stream of numbers that would flash by on the screen.

The third problem with what-if analysis is that the insight the manager might gain from playing out various scenarios is of little value when recommending a decision to top management. What-if analysis simply does not supply the manager with the tangible evidence (facts and figures) needed to justify why a given decision was made or recommended. Additionally, what-if analysis does not address the problem identified in our earlier discussion of best-case/worst-case analysis—it does not allow us to estimate the distribution of the performance measure in a formal enough manner. Thus, what-if analysis is a step in the right direction, but it's not quite a large enough step to allow managers to analyze risk effectively in the decisions they face.

12.3.3   Simulation

Simulation is a technique that measures and describes various characteristics of the bottom-line performance measure of a model when one or more values for the independent variables are uncertain. If any independent variables in a model are random variables, the dependent variable (Y) also represents a random variable. The objective in simulation is to *describe* the distribution and characteristics of the possible values of the bottom-line performance measure Y, given the possible values and behavior of the independent variables X_1, X_2, ..., X_k.

The idea behind simulation is similar to the notion of playing out many what-if scenarios. The difference is that the process of assigning values to the cells in the spreadsheet that represent random variables is automated so that: (1) the values are assigned in a nonbiased way, and (2) the spreadsheet user is relieved of the burden of determining these values. With simulation, we repeatedly and randomly generate sample values for each uncertain input variable (X_1, X_2, ..., X_k) in our model and then compute the resulting value of our bottom-line performance measure (Y). We can then use the sample values of Y to estimate the true distribution and other characteristics of the performance measure Y. For example, we can use the sample observations to construct a frequency distribution of the performance measure, to estimate the range of values over which the performance measure might vary, to estimate the performance measure mean and variance, and to estimate the probability that the actual value of the performance measure will be greater than (or less than) a particular value. All these measures provide greater insight into the risk associated with a given decision than a single value calculated based on the expected values for the uncertain independent variables.

12.4   A CORPORATE HEALTH INSURANCE EXAMPLE

The following example demonstrates the mechanics of preparing a spreadsheet model for risk analysis using simulation. The example presents a fairly simple model to illustrate the process and provide a sense of the amount of effort involved. However, the process for performing simulation is basically the same regardless of the size of the model.

Lisa Pon has just been hired as an analyst in the corporate planning department of Hungry Dawg Restaurants. Her first assignment is to determine how much money the company needs to accrue in the coming year to pay for its employees' health insurance claims. Hungry Dawg is a large, growing chain of restaurants that specializes in traditional southern foods. The company has become large enough that it no longer buys insurance from a private insurance company. The company is now self-insured, meaning that it pays health insurance claims with its own money (although it contracts with an outside company to handle the administrative details of processing claims and writing checks).

The money the company uses to pay claims comes from two sources: employee contributions (or premiums deducted from employees' paychecks) and company funds (the company must pay whatever costs are not covered by employee contributions). Each employee covered by the health plan contributes $125 per month. However, the number of employees covered by the plan changes from month to month as employees are hired and fired, quit, or simply add or drop health insurance coverage. A total of 18,533 employees were covered by the plan last month. The average monthly health claim per covered employee was $250 last month.

An example of how most analysts would model this problem is shown in Figure 12.2 (and in the file FIG12-2.xls on your data disk). The spreadsheet begins with a listing of the initial conditions and assumptions for the problem. For example, cell D5 indicates that 18,533 employees are covered currently by the health plan, and cell D6 indicates that the average monthly claim per covered employee is $250. The average monthly contribution per employee is $125, as shown in cell D7. The values in cells D5 and D6 are unlikely to stay the same for the entire year. Thus, we need to make some assumptions about the rate at which these values are likely to increase during the year. For example, we might assume that the number of covered employees will increase by about 2% per month, and that the average claim per employee will increase at a rate of 1% per month. These assumptions are reflected in cells F5 and F6. The average contribution per employee is assumed to be constant over the coming year.

Using the assumed rate of increase in the number of covered employees (cell F5), we can create formulas for cells B11 through B22 that cause the number of covered employees to increase by the assumed amount each month. (The details of these formulas are covered later.) The expected monthly employee contributions shown in column C are calculated as $125 times the number of employees in each month. We can use the assumed rate of increase in average monthly claims (cell F6) to create formulas for cells D11 through D22 that cause the average claim per employee to increase at the assumed rate. The total claims for each month (shown in column E) are calculated as the average claim figures in column D times the number of employees for each month in column B. Because the company must pay for any claims that are not covered by the employee contributions, the company cost figures in column G are calculated as the total claims minus the employee contributions (column E minus column C). Finally, cell G23 sums the company cost figures listed in column G,

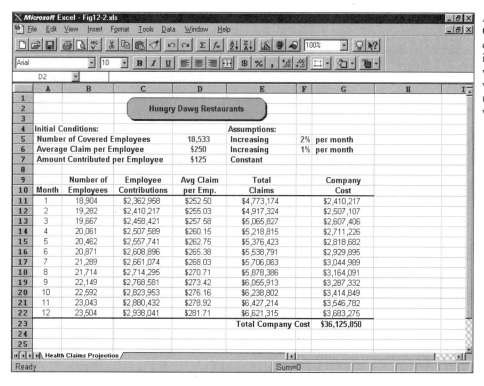

Figure 12.2
Original corporate health insurance model with expected values for uncertain variables.

and shows that the company can expect to contribute $36,125,850 of its revenues toward paying the health insurance claims of its employees in the coming year.

12.4.1   A Critique of the Base-Case Model

Now let's consider the model we just described. The example model assumes that the number of covered employees will increase by *exactly* 2% each month and that the average claim per covered employee will increase by *exactly* 1% each month. Although these values might be reasonable approximations of what might happen, they are unlikely to reflect exactly what will happen. In fact, the number of employees covered by the health plan each month is likely to vary randomly around the average increase per month—that is, the number might decrease in some months and increase by more than 2% in others. Similarly, the average claim per covered employee might be lower than expected in certain months and higher than expected in others.

Both of these figures are likely to exhibit some uncertainty or random behavior, even if they do move in the general upward direction assumed throughout the year. So we cannot say with certainty that the total cost figure of $36,125,850 is exactly what the company will have to contribute toward health claims in the coming year. It is simply a prediction of what might happen. The actual outcome could be smaller or larger than this estimate. Using the original model, we have no idea how much larger or smaller the actual result could be—nor do we have any idea how the actual values are distributed around this estimate. We do not know if there is a 10%, 50%, or 90% chance of the actual total costs exceeding this estimate. To determine the variability or risk inherent in the bottom-line performance measure of total company costs, we'll apply the technique of simulation to our model.

12.5   RANDOM NUMBER GENERATORS

To perform simulation in an electronic spreadsheet, we must first place a **random number generator** (RNG) formula in each cell that represents a random, or uncertain, independent variable. Each RNG provides a sample observation from an appropriate distribution that represents the range and frequency of possible values for the variable. Once the RNGs are in place, new sample values are provided automatically by the RNGs each time the spreadsheet is recalculated. We can recalculate the spreadsheet *n* times, where *n* is the desired number of replications or scenarios, and the value of the bottom-line performance measure will be stored after each replication. We can analyze these stored observations to gain insight into the behavior and characteristics of the performance measure.

The process of simulation involves a lot of work, but, fortunately, the spreadsheet can do most of the work for us fairly easily. As mentioned earlier, the first step is to place an RNG formula in each cell that contains an uncertain value. Each formula will generate (or return) a number that represents a randomly selected value from a distribution, or pool, of values. The distributions from which these samples are taken should be representative of the underlying pool of values expected to occur in each uncertain cell.

12.5.1   The RAND( ) Function

Excel, like most other spreadsheet packages, includes a built-in function called RAND( ) that provides the foundation for creating various RNGs. The **RAND( )**

function returns a uniformly distributed random number between 0.0 and 1.0 whenever the spreadsheet is recalculated (technically, $0 \leq$ RAND( ) $< 0.99\overline{9}$). If you enter the RAND( ) formula in some cell in a spreadsheet, and press the recalculate key (function key [F9]) repeatedly, a series of random numbers between 0.0 and 1.0 appears in the cell.

The RAND( ) function enables us to do some interesting modeling. As a simple example, suppose that we want to simulate the toss of a fair coin in a spreadsheet. When tossing a fair coin, there are two possible outcomes: heads or tails. If the coin is fair (that is, not weighted or biased toward one outcome over the other), we expect that each outcome has an equal probability of occurring each time we toss the coin. That is, the probability of heads is 0.5 and the probability of tails is 0.5 on any toss. However, before any given toss we cannot say with certainty whether the observed outcome will be heads or tails.

Using the RAND( ) function, we can create a formula that simulates the process of tossing the coin. Suppose that the value 1 represents the occurrence of heads and the value 0 represents the occurrence of tails. Now consider the following formula:

IF(RAND( )<0.5,1,0)

Whenever the spreadsheet is recalculated, the RAND( ) function will return a random value between 0 and 1. If the value returned by RAND( ) is less than 0.5, the previous IF( ) function will return the value 1 (representing heads); otherwise, it will return the value 0 (representing tails). Because the RAND( ) function has a 0.5 probability of returning a value less than 0.5, there is a 50% chance that the IF( ) function will generate the heads value, and a 50% chance that it will generate the tails value each time the spreadsheet is recalculated.

As another example, suppose that we want to simulate rolling a fair, six-sided die using a spreadsheet. In this case, each roll of the die can produce one of six possible outcomes (the value 1, 2, 3, 4, 5, or 6). We need an RNG that randomly generates the integer numbers from 1 to 6 with each value having a 1/6 chance of occurring. Because RAND( ) generates uniformly distributed random numbers between 0.0 and 1.0, 6*RAND( ) would generate uniformly distributed random numbers between 0.0 and 6.0 (technically, $0 \leq$ 6*RAND( ) $\leq 5.99\overline{9}$).

Now suppose that we took this interval from 0.0 to 6.0 and divided it into six equal pieces as follows:

	Lower Limit	Upper Limit
1	0.0	0.99$\overline{9}$
2	1.0	1.99$\overline{9}$
3	2.0	2.99$\overline{9}$
4	3.0	3.99$\overline{9}$
5	4.0	4.99$\overline{9}$
6	5.0	5.99$\overline{9}$

Because each of the six intervals is exactly the same size, the value of 6*RAND( ) is equally likely to fall in each of them. If the value generated by 6*RAND( ) falls between 0.0 and 0.99$\overline{9}$, we could associate this with the outcome of rolling a 1 on the die; if 6*RAND( ) falls between 1.0 and 1.99$\overline{9}$, we could associate this with rolling a 2 on the die, and so forth. This makes sense, but what mathematical function makes this association happen? Consider the following formula:

$$INT(6*RAND(\ ))+1$$

The INT( ) function returns the integer portion of the value inside its parentheses (for example, INT(4.85) = 4, INT(2.13) = 2). The following table summarizes the different outcomes generated using this formula:

If 6*RAND( ) falls in the interval	INT(6*RAND( ))+1 returns the value
0.0 to 0.99$\overline{9}$	1
1.0 to 1.99$\overline{9}$	2
2.0 to 2.99$\overline{9}$	3
3.0 to 3.99$\overline{9}$	4
4.0 to 4.99$\overline{9}$	5
5.0 to 5.99$\overline{9}$	6

Again, because each interval in the table is exactly the same size, the value of 6*RAND( ) is equally likely to fall in each interval. Therefore, each value generated by the formula INT(6*RAND( ))+1 also is equally likely to occur. Thus, the formula INT(6*RAND( ))+1 accurately simulates the act of rolling a fair, six-sided die.

12.5.2   RNG Functions

The two previous examples represent random variables that follow the **discrete uniform distribution,** which is appropriate for modeling random variables with n distinct possible outcomes, each outcome being equally likely (or having a $1/n$ probability of occurring). The following formula can be used to randomly generate the integers $a, a + 1, a + 2, ..., a + n - 1$ with equal probability of occurrence:

RNG for the discrete uniform distribution: INT(n*RAND( ))+a **12.2**

This formula is equivalent to the formula used in the die rolling example, where $a = 1$ and $n = 6$. Also, we could have used this same formula with $a = 0$ and $n = 2$ to simulate the toss of a fair coin.

Figure 12.3 (and the file FIG12-3.xls on your data disk) gives an example of the RNG for the discrete uniform distribution and several other formulas that utilize the RAND( ) function to generate random numbers from several other probability distributions. Notice that the numbers shown in column D of this spreadsheet will change each time the spreadsheet is recalculated (by pressing the [F9] function key).

While it is possible to use the formulas shown in Figure 12.3 to generate random numbers in Excel, it is more convenient (and less error prone) to use the Visual Basic for Applications (VBA) macro language to create user defined functions that implement various RNGs. A VBA add-in file named RNG.xla (found on your data disk) was created to simplify the process of using RNGs in Excel. Refer to the box titled "Installing and Using the RNG.xla Add-In" for instructions on installing this add-in on your computer. Figure 12.4 describes the RNG functions implemented in the RNG.xla add-in.

The functions listed in Figure 12.4 allows us to generate a variety of random numbers easily. For example, if we think that the behavior of an uncertain cell could be modeled as a normally distributed random variable with a mean of 125 and standard deviation of 10, then according to Figure 12.4 we could enter the formula =RNGNormal(125,10) in this cell. (The arguments in this function could also be formulas and could refer to

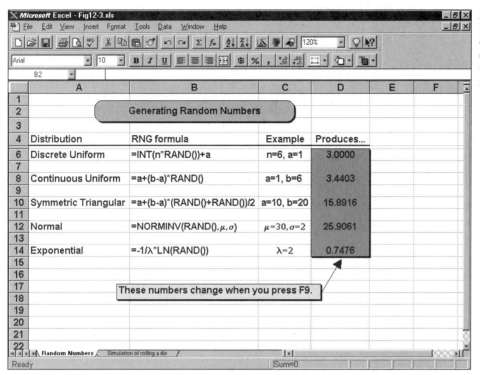

Figure 12.3
Examples of common RNGs constructed with the RAND( ) function.

Installing and Using the RNG.XLA Add-In

In order to access the functions shown in Figure 12.4, you must first install the RNG.xla add-in on your computer. To do this:

1. Copy the RNG.xla file to your hard drive (preferably to the directory C:\MSOffice\Excel\Library).
2. In Excel, select Tools, Add-Ins, click the Browse button, locate the RNG.xla file, and click OK.

This instructs your computer to always open the RNG.xla add-in whenever you start Excel. You can deselect the RNG.xla at any time by using the Tools, Add-Ins command again. Excel will not be able to properly interpret files that make use of the functions in Figure 12.4 unless the RNG.xla add-in is installed on your computer in the manner outlined above.

---

other cells in the spreadsheet.) Whenever the spreadsheet is recalculated, this function would return a randomly selected value from a normal distribution with a mean of 125 and standard deviation of 10.

Similarly, a cell in our spreadsheet might have a 30% chance of assuming the value 10, a 50% chance of assuming the value 20, and a 20% chance of assuming the value 30. As noted in Figure 12.4, we could use the formula =RNGDiscrete({10,20,30},{0.3,0.5,0.2}) to model this random behavior. (Alternatively, if the values 10, 20, and 30 were entered in cells A1 through A3 and the values 0.3, 0.5, and 0.2 were entered in B1 through B3, we could use the formula =RNGDiscrete(A1:A3,B1:B3).) If we recalculated the

Figure 12.4
Random number functions available in the RNG.xla add-in file.

Distribution	RNG Function	Description
Binomial	RNGBinomial(n,p)	Returns the number of "successes" in a sample of size n where each trial has a probability p of "success."
Discrete Uniform	RNGDuniform(min,max)	Returns one of the integers between min and max, inclusive. Each value is equally likely to occur.
General Discrete	RNGDiscrete({x_1,x_2,...x_n}, {p_1,p_2,...p_n})	Returns one of the *n values* represented by the x_i. The value x_i occurs with probability p_i.
Poisson	RNGPoisson(λ)	Returns a random number of events occurring per some unit of measure (for example, arrivals per hour, defects per yard, and so on). The parameter λ represents the average number of events occurring per unit of measure.
Continuous Uniform	RNGUniform(min,max)	Returns a value in the range from a minimum (*min*) to a maximum (*max*). Each value in this range is equally likely to occur.
Chi-square	RNGChisq(λ)	Returns a value from a chi-square distribution with mean λ.
Exponential	RNGExponential(λ)	Returns a value from an exponential distribution with mean λ. Often used to model the time between events or the lifetime of a device with a constant probability of failure.
Normal	RNGNormal(μ,σ)	Returns a value from a normal distribution with mean μ and standard deviation σ.
Truncated Normal	RNGTnormal(μ,σ,min,max)	Same as RNGNormal except the distribution is truncated to the range specified by a minimum (*min*) and a maximum (*max*).
Triangular	RNGTriang(min,most likely,max)	Returns a value from a triangular distribution covering the range specified by a minimum (*min*) and a maximum (*max*). The shape of the distribution is then determined by the size of the most likely value relative to *min* and *max*.

spreadsheet many times, this formula would return the value 10 approximately 30% of the time, the value 20 approximately 50% of the time, and the value 30 approximately 20% of the time.

The arguments required by the RNG functions allow us to generate random numbers from distributions with a wide variety of shapes. Figures 12.5 and 12.6 illustrate some of these distributions.

Troubleshooting

If you install the RNG.xla add-in in the directory C:\MSOffice\Excel\Library, any spreadsheet you create that uses these functions will expect to find the RNG.xla add-in in the same directory on any other computer on which this file is used. If you try to open a file that uses these functions on a computer that does not have RNG.xla installed in the same directory, Excel will display a dialog box saying,

"This document contains links. Reestablish links?"

Answer NO to this question. The file will then be opened, but the cells containing references to RNG functions will all return the "#REF!" error code. To fix this, first make sure the RNG.xla file is installed and loaded (select Tools, Add-Ins and make sure the box labeled RNG is selected.) If the problem still persists, click Edit, Links, Change Source, then locate the RNG.xla file on the computer you are using and click OK. The functions should then work correctly on that computer. Note: If you install the RNG.xla file in the same directory on every computer you use, you should never have this problem.

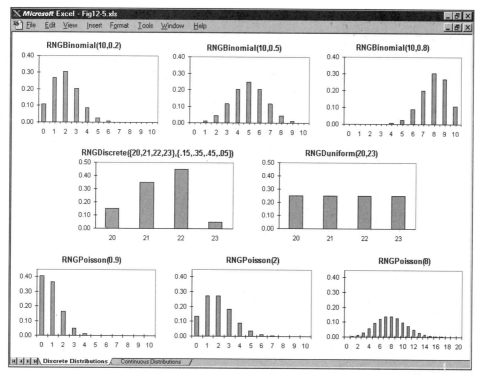

Figure 12.5
Examples of some discrete probability distributions.

Figure 12.6
Examples of
some continuous
probability
distributions.

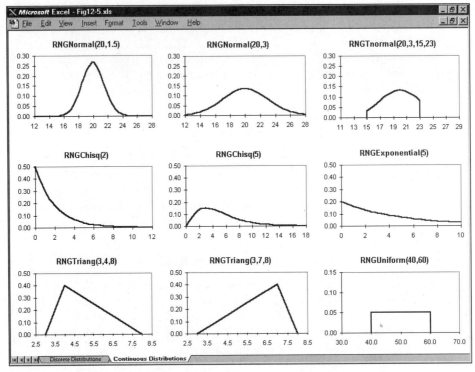

12.5.3   Discrete vs. Continuous Random Variables

An important distinction exists between the random variables in Figure 12.5 and 12.6. In particular, the RNGs depicted in Figure 12.5 generate *discrete* outcomes, whereas those represented in Figure 12.6 generate *continuous* outcomes. The distinction between discrete and continuous random variables is very important.

For example, the number of defective tires on a new car is a discrete random variable because it can assume only one of five distinct values: 0, 1, 2, 3, or 4. On the other hand, the amount of fuel in a new car is a continuous random variable because it can assume any value between 0 and the maximum capacity of the fuel tank. Thus, when selecting an RNG for an uncertain variable in a model, it is important to consider whether the variable can assume discrete or continuous values.

12.6   PREPARING THE MODEL FOR SIMULATION

To simulate the model for Hungry Dawg Restaurants described earlier, we must first select appropriate RNGs for the uncertain variables in the model. If available, historical data on the uncertain variables could be analyzed to determine appropriate RNGs for these variables. If past data are not available, or if we have reason to expect the future behavior of a variable to be significantly different from the past, then we must use judgment in selecting appropriate RNGs to model the random behavior of the uncertain variables.

For our example problem, let's assume that by analyzing historical data, we determined that the change in the number of covered employees from one month to the next is expected to vary uniformly between a 3% decrease and a 7% increase. (Note that this should cause the *average* change in the number of employees to be a 2% increase, because 0.02 is the midpoint between –0.03 and +0.07.) Further, assume that we can model the average monthly claim per covered employee as a normally distributed random variable with the mean increasing by 1% per month and a standard deviation of approximately $3. (Note that this will cause the average increase in claims per covered employee from one month to the next to be approximately 1%.) These assumptions are reflected in cells F5 through H6 at the top of Figure 12.7 (and in the file FIG12-7.xls on your data disk).

To implement the formula to generate a random number of employees covered by the health plan, we'll use the RNGUniform( ) function shown in Figure 12.4 to sample from a continuous uniform distribution. The RNGUniform( ) function generates random numbers between the minimum and maximum values that we supply.

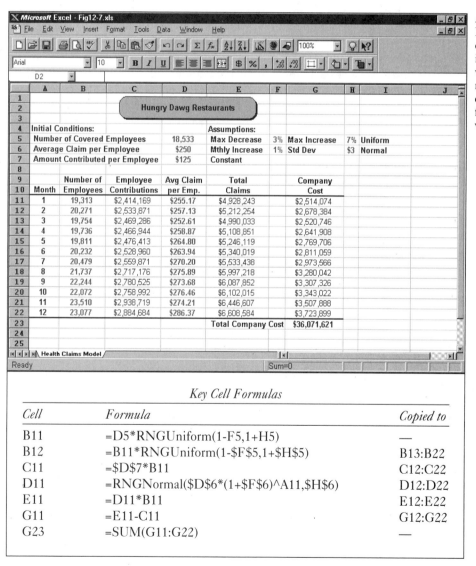

Figure 12.7
Modified corporate health insurance model with RNGs replacing expected values for uncertain variables.

Key Cell Formulas

Cell	Formula	Copied to
B11	=D5*RNGUniform(1-F5,1+H5)	—
B12	=B11*RNGUniform(1-$F$5,1+$H$5)	B13:B22
C11	=$D$7*B11	C12:C22
D11	=RNGNormal($D$6*(1+$F$6)^A11,$H$6)	D12:D22
E11	=D11*B11	E12:E22
G11	=E11-C11	G12:G22
G23	=SUM(G11:G22)	—

Important Notice

You should install the RNG.xla add-in before opening FIG12-7.xls. Also, once you open the spreadsheet in FIG12-7.xls, the numbers on your screen will not match those shown in Figure 12.7 because these numbers are generated randomly.

In our example problem, the number of employees in any given month should equal the number of employees in the previous month multiplied by a random number between 97% and 107%; that is:

Number of employees in current month = Number of employees in previous month $\times$ RNGUniform(0.97,1.07)

Notice that if the RNGUniform( ) function in this equation returns the value 0.97, this formula causes the number of employees in the current month to equal 97% of the number in the previous month (for a 3% decrease). Alternatively, if RNGUniform( ) function returns the value 1.07, this causes the number of employees in the current month to equal 107% of the number in the previous month (for a 7% increase). All the values between these two extremes (between 97% and 107%) are also possible and equally likely to occur. Thus, in Figure 12.7 the following formulas were used to randomly generate the number of employees covered by the health insurance plan each month:

Formula for cell B11:   =D5*RNGUniform(1-F5,1+H5)

Formula for cell B12:   =B11*RNGUniform(1-$F$5,1+$H$5)
(Copy to B13 through B22.)

To implement the formula to generate the average claims per covered employee in each month, we'll use the RNGNormal( ) function described in Figure 12.4. This formula requires that we supply the value of the mean (μ) and standard deviation (σ) of the distribution from which we want to sample. The assumed $3 standard deviation ($\sigma$) for the average monthly claim, shown in cell H6 of Figure 12.7, is constant from month to month. Thus, the only remaining problem is to figure out the proper mean value (μ) for each month.

In this case, the mean for any given month should be 1% larger than the mean in the previous month. For example, the mean for month 1 is:

Mean in month 1 = (original mean) $\times$ 1.01

and the mean for month 2 is:

Mean in month 2 = (mean in month 1) $\times$ 1.01

If we substitute the previous definition of the mean in month 1 into the above equation, we obtain

Mean in month 2 = (original mean) $\times$ $(1.01)^2$

Similarly, the mean in month 3 is:

Mean in month 3 = (mean month 2) $\times$ 1.01 = (original mean) $\times$ $(1.01)^3$

So, in general, the mean (μ) for month n is:

$$\text{Mean in month } n = (\text{original mean}) \times (1.01)^n$$

Thus, to generate the average claim per covered employee in each month, we'll use the following formula:

Formula for cell D11:   =RNGNormal($D$6*(1+$F$6)^A11,$H$6)
(Copy to D12 through D22.)

Note that the term "$D$6*(1+$F$6)^A11" in this formula implements the general definition of the mean (μ) in month n.

At this point, the modifications to the model are complete. Each time the recalculate key (the function key [F9]) is pressed, the RNGs will automatically select new values for all the cells in the spreadsheet that represent uncertain (or random) variables. With each recalculation, a new value for the bottom-line performance measure (total company cost) will appear in cell G23. By pressing the recalculate key several times, we can observe representative values of the company's total cost for health claims.

12.7 REPLICATING THE MODEL

The next step in the simulation process involves recalculating the model several hundred times and recording the resulting values generated for the output cell, or bottom-line performance measure. Suppose that we want to perform 300 replications of the model and store the resulting observations of the dependent variable on a new worksheet named Simulation. To create and name this new worksheet:

1. Click the Insert menu.
2. Select Worksheet. Excel inserts a new worksheet in your workbook.
3. Click the Format menu.
4. Click Worksheet.
5. Click Rename.
6. Type Simulation.
7. Click OK.

Because we want to perform 300 replications of our model, we entered the numbers 1, 2, 3, ..., 300 starting in cell A3, as shown in Figure 12.8. This is done as follows:

1. Type the starting value (1) in cell A3 and press [Enter].
2. Click cell A3.
3. Click the Edit menu, click Fill, then click Series.
4. Select the Series in Columns option and enter a Stop value of 300.
5. Click OK.

Excel automatically fills the column below the selected cell (A3) with values increasing by 1 (the Step value) until it reaches the Stop value of 300. Because we want to track the company cost value in cell G23 of the Health Claims Model worksheet, we entered the following formula in cell B3:

Formula for cell B3:   ='Health Claims Model'!G23

Cell B2 contains the label Company Cost to identify the values that will ultimately appear in column B.

Figure 12.8
Worksheet
prepared to
simulate the
corporate health
insurance model.

Cell	Formula	Copied to
B3	='Health Claims Model'!G23	—

We can now use the Data Table command to fill in the remainder of column B. Keep in mind that the Data Table command is designed for a purpose other than what we are using it for here. However, we can use this command to "trick" Excel into performing the replications needed in our simulation.

By using the Data Table command, we're instructing Excel to substitute each value in column A into some cell of the spreadsheet, recalculate the spreadsheet, and record in column B the associated value for the output cell (cell B3 in this case). Ordinarily, the values listed in the first column of a data table (column A) represent values that we want Excel to enter into some input cell of the spreadsheet. The resulting data table then shows what happens to the output cell given each of the input cell values. However, for our purposes we'll instruct Excel to enter each value in column A into an input cell that has no impact on the value of the output cell. For example, we might use cell A1 in Figure 12.8 as the input cell. In this way, we can "trick" Excel into recalculating the spreadsheet 300 times while storing the values of the output cell (cell G23 on the Health Claims Model sheet) in column B.

To execute the Data Table command:

1. Select the range A3 through B302. (An easy way to do this is to select cells A3 and B3, then while pressing the shift key, double click on the selection border at the bottom of cell A3.)
2. Click the Data menu.

3. Click Table.
4. In the Table dialog box, enter cell A1 for the Column input cell.
5. Click OK.

Excel substitutes each value in the range A4 through A302 into cell A1, recalculates the workbook, and stores the resulting company cost figures in the adjacent cells in column B. Depending on your computer's speed, this recalculation might take 20 to 30 seconds, or possibly a couple of minutes.

Software Tip

The Data Table command will execute more quickly if you use a separate workbook for each model you are simulating and have only one workbook open while you are doing simulation. So create a separate workbook for each homework problem you do and make sure you close each workbook when you complete each problem. Also, before running a large number of replications, it is a good idea to first verify your model by replicating it a small number of times (say 20 to 50 times). Once you are convinced your model is working correctly, you may increase the size of the data table to the desired sample size.

After running the Data Table command, you should have a list of values in column B representing 300 possible company cost outcomes, similar to those shown in Figure 12.9. The numbers you generate on your computer will *not* match those in Figure 12.9. The procedure demonstrated here generates a *random* sample of 300 observations from an infinite number of possible values. Again, the random sample you generate will be different from the one shown in Figure 12.9, but the characteristics of your sample should be very similar to those of the sample shown in Figure 12.9.

Each new entry Excel created, starting in cell B4, contains the array formula {=TABLE(,A1)}. This is how the Data Table command performs the repeated substitution and recalculation we just described. If we don't change the formulas in column B into values, every time the spreadsheet is recalculated we'll have to wait for this process to reexecute and we'll get a new sample of 300 replications. This wastes time and prevents us from focusing on the results of one batch of 300 observations in order to make decisions. To convert the formulas in column B to values:

1. Select the range B3 through B302.
2. Click the Edit menu.
3. Click Copy.
4. Click the Edit menu.
5. Click Paste Special.
6. Click Values.
7. Click OK.
8. Press [Enter].

The values in column B are now numeric constants that will not change even if the spreadsheet is recalculated.

12.7.1 Determining the Sample Size

You might wonder why we elected to perform 300 replications. Why not 200 or 800? Unfortunately, there is no easy answer to this question. Remember that the goal in

Figure 12.9
Results of the
Data Table
command for the
corporate health
insurance
problem.

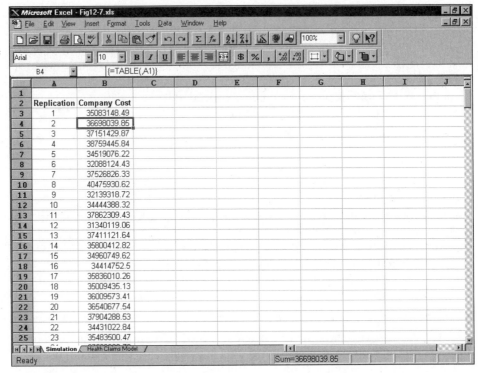

Important Software Note

Instead of converting data table to values, another way to prevent the data table from recalculating is to do the following:

1. Click the Tools menu.
2. Click Options.
3. Click the Calculation tab.
4. Click Automatic Except Tables.
5. Click OK.

This tells Excel to recalculate the data tables only when you manually recalculate the spreadsheet by pressing the F9 function key. This can be helpful if you want to run several different simulations under a variety of input conditions.

---

simulation is to use a sample of observations on a bottom-line performance measure to estimate various characteristics about its behavior. For example, we might want to estimate the mean value of the performance measure and the shape of its probability distribution. However, we saw earlier that different values of the bottom-line performance measure occurred each time we manually recalculated the model in Figure 12.7. Thus, there is an infinite number of possibilities—or an **infinite population**—of total company cost values associated with this model.

We cannot analyze all of these infinite possibilities. But by taking a large enough sample from this infinite population, we can make reasonably accurate estimates about the characteristics of the underlying population of values. The larger the sample we take (that is, the more replications we do), the more accurate our final results will be. But performing many replications takes time and computer resources, so we must make a trade-off in terms of estimation accuracy versus convenience. There is no simple answer to the question of how many replications to perform, but as a minimum, you should always perform at least 100 replications, and more as time and resources permit or accuracy demands.

12.8 DATA ANALYSIS

As mentioned earlier, the objective of performing a simulation is to estimate various characteristics of the performance measure resulting from uncertainty in some or all of the input variables. After performing the replications, we must summarize and analyze the data in order to draw conclusions.

Most spreadsheet packages have built-in functions for performing statistical calculations. Excel also provides a data analysis tool we can use to generate numerous descriptive statistics automatically. To use the data analysis tool:

1. Click the Tools menu.
2. Click Data Analysis.
3. Click Descriptive Statistics.
4. Complete the Descriptive Statistics dialog box, as shown in Figure 12.10.
5. Click OK.

(If the Data Analysis option is not available on your Tools menu, select the Add-Ins option from the Tools menu, then select the Analysis ToolPak option. The Data Analysis option should then appear on your Tools menu. If Analysis ToolPak is not listed among your available add-ins, you must exit Excel, rerun the MSOffice setup program and add the Analysis ToolPak add-in to your installation of Excel.)

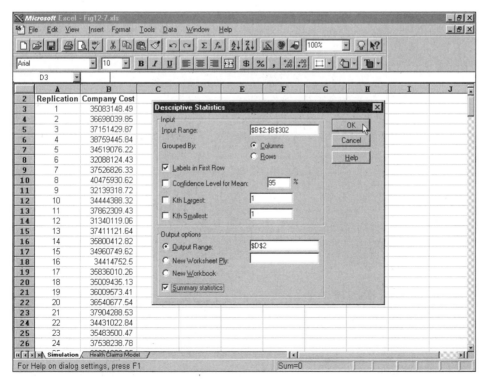

Figure 12.10 Descriptive Statistics dialog box for the corporate health insurance problem.

Figure 12.11 shows the resulting descriptive summary statistics for our sample of company cost data. We could have generated these values using a variety of Excel's built-in statistical functions. For example, we could have calculated the mean value shown in cell E4 using the formula =AVERAGE(B3:B302). However, the Descriptive Statistics command simplifies this process. Note that we can edit the results produced by this command to delete any unnecessary information.

12.8.1   The Best Case and the Worst Case

Decision makers usually want to know the best-case and worst-case scenarios to get an idea of the range of possible outcomes they might face. This information is available from the simulation results, as shown by the Minimum and Maximum values listed in Figure 12.11. Although cell E4 indicates that the average value observed in this sample of 300 observations is approximately $36.0 million, cell E13 indicates that the smallest cost observed is about $30.0 million (representing the best case) and cell E14 indicates the largest cost is approximately $42.8 million (representing the worst case). (Note that if you generate your own sample of 300 observations, the statistics you calculate will *not* match those shown in Figure 12.11.) These figures should give the decision maker a good idea about the range of possible cost values that might occur. Note that these values might be difficult to determine manually in a complex model with many uncertain independent variables.

12.8.2   Determining the Distribution of Outcomes

Although the data in Figure 12.11 offer some insight into the best and worst possible outcomes of a decision, other factors should also be considered. The best- and worst-case scenarios are the most extreme outcomes, and might not be likely to occur.

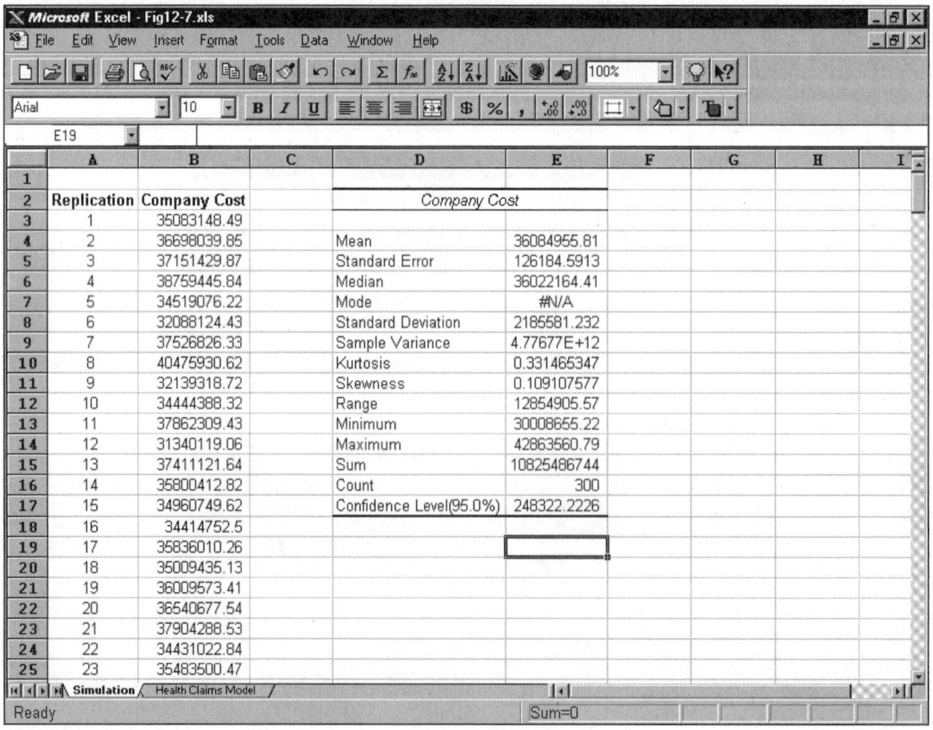

Figure 12.11
Statistical results of the simulation data for the corporate health insurance model.

	A	B	C	D	E
2	Replication	Company Cost		Company Cost	
3	1	35083148.49			
4	2	36698039.85		Mean	36084955.81
5	3	37151429.87		Standard Error	126184.5913
6	4	38759445.84		Median	36022164.41
7	5	34519076.22		Mode	#N/A
8	6	32088124.43		Standard Deviation	2185581.232
9	7	37526826.33		Sample Variance	4.77677E+12
10	8	40475930.62		Kurtosis	0.331465347
11	9	32139318.72		Skewness	0.109107577
12	10	34444388.32		Range	12854905.57
13	11	37862309.43		Minimum	30008655.22
14	12	31340119.06		Maximum	42863560.79
15	13	37411121.64		Sum	10825486744
16	14	35800412.82		Count	300
17	15	34960749.62		Confidence Level(95.0%)	248322.2226
18	16	34414752.5			
19	17	35836010.26			
20	18	35009435.13			
21	19	36009573.41			
22	20	36540677.54			
23	21	37904288.53			
24	22	34431022.84			
25	23	35483500.47			

Determining the likelihood of these outcomes requires that we know something about the shape of the distribution of our bottom-line performance measure. Thus, we might also want to construct a frequency distribution and histogram for the 300 observations generated for our performance measure. To construct a frequency distribution and histogram:

1. Click the Tools menu.
2. Click Data Analysis.
3. Click Histogram.
4. Complete the Histogram dialog box, as shown in Figure 12.12.
5. Click OK.

The resulting new worksheet, named Histogram, contains a frequency distribution and histogram of our data which, after some simple formatting, appear as shown in Figure 12.13.

The Frequency column in Figure 12.13 indicates the number of observations from our simulation results that fall into the bins defined in column A. For example, the value in cell B2 indicates that one of the 300 replications resulted in a value that is less than or equal to $30,008,655. The value in cell B3 indicates that two of the 300 observations assumed values greater than $30,008,655 and less than or equal to $30,764,826. Similarly, cell B18 indicates that three observations have values between $41,351,219 and $42,107,390, and cell B19 indicates that two observations were greater than $42,107,390. In cell B9, we see that the most frequently occurring values are in the range $34,545,681 to $35,301,852. (Again, your results will *not* match those shown in Figure 12.13.)

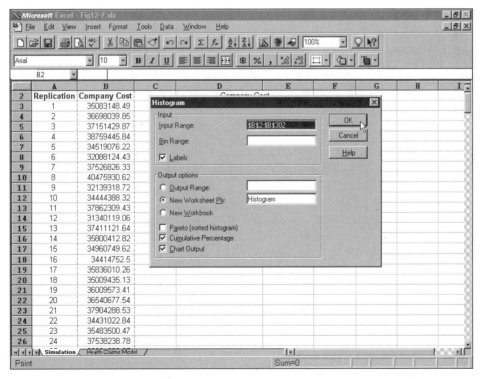

Figure 12.12
Histogram dialog box.

Figure 12.13
Frequency
distribution and
Histogram for
the corporate
health insurance
model.

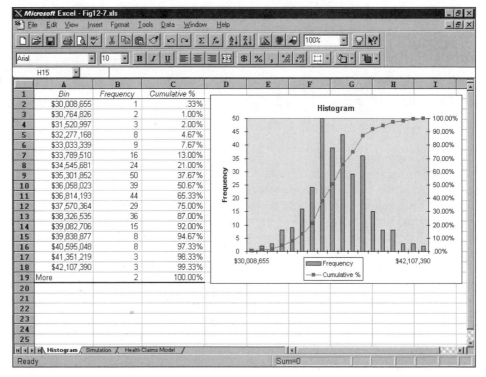

The histogram in Figure 12.13 gives a visual representation of the frequency distribution values. This graph shows that the distribution of the total health claims the company must pay is somewhat bell-shaped.

12.8.3   The Cumulative Distribution of the Output Cell

The Cumulative % column in Figure 12.13 shows the percentage of observations in the sample that are less than or equal to the values listed in column A. For example, cell C2 indicates that 0.33% of the 300 observations are less than $30,008,655, cell C3 indicates that 1% of the 300 observations are less than or equal to $30,764,826, and so on. These cumulative frequencies are also plotted on the graph shown in Figure 12.13.

Cumulative frequencies are helpful in answering a number of questions that might arise. For example, suppose that the chief financial officer (CFO) for Hungry Dawg Restaurants would rather accrue an excess of money to pay health claims than not accrue enough money. The CFO might want to know what amount the company should accrue so that there is only about a 10% chance of coming up short of funds at the end of the year. The value in cell C13 of Figure 12.13 indicates that 87% of the 300 observations are less than or equal to $38,326,535 and the value in cell C14 indicates that 92% of the observations are less than or equal to $39,082,706. Thus, assuming that our sample is representative of the actual distribution of total health costs the company might incur, we could tell the CFO that if Hungry Dawg budgets $39 million for health claims, there is roughly a 10% chance of the company not accruing enough funds.

Another way of answering the CFO's question is to sort the 300 observations in our sample in ascending order. (This can be done easily by selecting the range B3 through B302 in the Simulation worksheet and clicking the Ascending Sort button [A to Z] on the toolbar.) The 270th largest number represents the 90th percentile of the distribution because 90% of the values in the sample are less than this value (and only 10% are greater than this value). For the 300 values represented in Figure 12.13, the 270th largest number in the sample is $38,747,460, which is fairly close to the recommendation of $39 million suggested by our previous analysis.

One final point underscores the value of simulation. How could we answer the CFO's question using best-case/worst-case analysis or what-if analysis? The fact is, we could not answer the question with any degree of accuracy without using simulation to obtain the cumulative frequencies shown in Figure 12.13.

Software Tip

The **COUNTIF( )**function is often very useful in estimating probabilities from simulation results. For example, the proportion of sample observations in Figure 12.13 which are less than $39 million can be computed as =COUNTIF(B3:B302,"<$39,000,000")/300.

12.9   THE UNCERTAINTY OF SAMPLING

To this point, we have used simulation to generate 300 observations on our bottom-line performance measure and then calculated various statistics to describe the characteristics and behavior of the performance measure. For example, Figure 12.11 indicates that the mean of our sample is approximately $36.0 million. Using the results in Figure 12.13, we estimate that approximately a 90% chance exists for the performance measure assuming a value less than $39 million. But what if we repeat this process and generate another 300 observations? Would the sample mean for the new 300 observations also be $36.0 million? Or would exactly 90% of the observations in the new sample be less than $39 million?

The answer to both of these questions is "probably not." The sample of 300 observations used in our analysis was taken from a population of values that is theoretically infinite in size. That is, if we had enough time and our computer had enough memory, we could generate an infinite number of values for our bottom-line performance measure. Theoretically, we could then analyze this infinite population of values to determine its true mean value, its true standard deviation, and the true probability of the performance measure being less than $39 million. Unfortunately, we do not have the time or computer resources to determine these true characteristics (or parameters) of the population. The best we can do is take a sample from this population and, based on our sample, make estimates about the true characteristics of the underlying population. Our estimates will differ depending on the sample we choose and the size of the sample.

The mean of the sample we take is probably not equal to the true mean we would observe if we could analyze the entire population of values for our performance measure. The sample mean we calculate is just an estimate of the true population mean. In our example problem, we estimated that a 90% chance exists for our output variable to assume a value less than $39 million. However, this most likely is not equal to the true probability we would calculate if we could analyze the entire population. Thus, there is some element of uncertainty surrounding the statistical estimates resulting from simulation because we are using a sample to make inferences about the population. Fortunately, there are ways of measuring and describing the amount of uncertainty present in some of the estimates we make about the population under study. This is typically done by constructing confidence intervals for the population parameters being estimated.

12.9.1   *Constructing a Confidence Interval for the True Population Mean*

Constructing a confidence interval for the true population mean is a simple process. If $\bar{y}$ and s represent, respectively, the mean and standard deviation of a sample size n from any population, then assuming n is sufficiently large ($n \geq 30$), the Central Limit Theorem tells us that the lower and upper limits of a 95% confidence interval for the true mean of the population are represented by:

$$95\% \text{ Lower Confidence Limit} = \bar{y} - 1.96 \times \frac{s}{\sqrt{n}}$$

$$95\% \text{ Upper Confidence Limit} = \bar{y} + 1.96 \times \frac{s}{\sqrt{n}}$$

Although we can be fairly certain that the sample mean $\bar{y}$ we calculate from our sample data is not equal to the true population mean, we can be 95% confident that the true mean of the population falls somewhere between the lower and upper limits given above. If we want a 90% or 99% confidence interval, we must change the value 1.96 in the above equations to 1.645 or 2.575, respectively. (The values 1.645 and 2.575 represent the 95 and 99.5 percentiles of the standard normal distribution, respectively.)

For our example, the lower and upper limits of a 95% confidence interval for the true mean of the population of total company cost values can be calculated easily, as shown in cells E20 and E21 in Figure 12.14. The formulas for these cells are:

Formula for cell E20:   =E4–1.96*E8/SQRT(E16)

Formula for cell E21:   =E4+1.96*E8/SQRT(E16)

Thus, we can be 95% confident that the true mean of the population of total company cost values falls somewhere in the interval from $35,837,634 to $36,332,278.

Software Tip

In Figure 12.14, the value in cell E17 labeled Confidence Level (95%) corresponds to the half-width of a 95% confidence interval for the true population mean (that is, E17 ≈ 1.96*E8/SQRT(E16)).

12.9.2   *Constructing a Confidence Interval for a Population Proportion*

In our example we estimated that 90% of the population of total company cost values fall below $39 million based on our sample of 300 observations. However, if we could evaluate the entire population of total cost values, we might find that only 80% of these values fall below $39 million. Or we might find that 99% of the entire population fall below this mark. It would be helpful to determine how accurate the 90%

Figure 12.14
Confidence
intervals for the
population mean
and population
proportion.

Key Cell Formulas		
Cell	Formula	Copied to
E20	=E4-1.96*E8/SQRT(E16)	—
E21	=E4+1.96*E8/SQRT(E16)	—
E24	=E23-1.96*SQRT(E23*(1-E23)/E16)	—
E25	=E23+1.96*SQRT(E23*(1-E23)/E16)	—

value is. So, at times we might want to construct a confidence interval for the true proportion of a population that falls below (or above) some value, say Y_p.

To see how this is done, let $\bar{p}$ denote the proportion of observations in a sample of size n that falls below some value Y_p. Assuming that n is sufficiently large ($n \geq 30$), the Central Limit Theorem tells us that the lower and upper limits of a 95% confidence interval for the true proportion of the population falling below Y_p are represented by:

$$95\% \text{ Lower Confidence Limit} = \bar{p} - 1.96 \times \sqrt{\frac{\bar{p}(1-\bar{p})}{n}}$$

$$95\% \text{ Upper Confidence Limit} = \bar{p} + 1.96 \times \sqrt{\frac{\bar{p}(1-\bar{p})}{n}}$$

Although we can be fairly certain that the proportion of observations falling below Y_p in our sample is not equal to the true proportion of the population falling below Y_p, we can be 95% confident that the true proportion of the population falling below Y_p is contained within the lower and upper limits given by the previous equations. Again, if we want a 90% or 99% confidence interval, we must change the value 1.96 in the above equation to 1.645 or 2.575, respectively.

Using these formulas, we can calculate the lower and upper limits of a 95% confidence interval for the true proportion of the population falling below $39 million. From our simulation results, we know that approximately 90% of the observations in our sample are less than $39 million. Thus, our estimated value of $\bar{p}$ is 0.90. This value was entered into cell E23 in Figure 12.14. The upper and lower limits of a 95% confidence interval for the true proportion of the population falling below $39 million are calculated in cells E24 and E25 of Figure 12.14 using the following formulas:

Formula for cell E24:   =E23–1.96*SQRT(E23*(1–E23)/E16)

Formula for cell E25:   =E23+1.96*SQRT(E23*(1–E23)/E16)

We can be 95% confident that the true proportion of the population of total cost values falling below $39 million is between 0.866 and 0.934. Because this interval is fairly tight around the value 0.90, we can be reasonably certain that the $39 million figure quoted to the CFO has approximately only a 10% chance of being exceeded.

12.9.3   Sample Sizes and Confidence Interval Widths

The formulas for the confidence intervals in the previous section depend directly on the number of replications (n) in the simulation. As the number of replications (n) increases, the width of the confidence interval decreases (or becomes more precise). Thus, for a given level of confidence (for example, 95%), the only way to make the upper and lower limits of the interval closer together (or tighter) is to make n larger— that is, use a larger sample size. A larger sample should provide more information about the population and, therefore, allow us to be more accurate in estimating the true parameters of the population.

12.10   THE BENEFITS OF SIMULATION

What have we accomplished through simulation? Are we really better off than if we had just used the results of the original model proposed in Figure 12.2? The estimated value for the expected total cost to the company in Figure 12.2 is comparable to that obtained through simulation (although this will not always be the case). But remember that the goal of modeling is to give us greater insight into a problem to help us make more informed decisions.

The results of our simulation analysis do give us greater insight into the example problem. In particular, we now have some idea of the best- and worst-case total cost outcomes for the company. We have a better idea of the distribution and variability of the possible outcomes and a more precise idea about where the mean of the distribution is located. We also now have a way of determining how likely it is for the actual outcome to fall above or below some value. Thus, in addition to our greater insight and understanding of the problem, we also have solid empirical evidence (the facts and figures) to support our recommendations.

12.11 ADDITIONAL USES OF SIMULATION

Earlier we indicated that simulation is a technique that *describes* the behavior or characteristics of a bottom-line performance measure. The next two examples show how describing the behavior of a performance measure gives a manager a useful tool in determining the optimal value for one or more controllable parameters in a decision problem. These examples reinforce the mechanics of using simulation and also demonstrate some additional simulation modeling techniques.

12.12 AN INVENTORY CONTROL EXAMPLE

According to *The Wall Street Journal* (7/18/94), U.S. businesses had a combined inventory worth $884.77 billion dollars as of the end of May 1994. Because so much money is tied up in inventories, businesses face many important decisions regarding the management of these assets. Frequently asked questions regarding inventory include:

- What's the best level of inventory for a business to maintain?
- When should goods be reordered (or manufactured)?
- How much safety stock should be held in inventory?

The study of inventory control principles is split into two distinct areas—one assumes that demand is known (or deterministic), and the other assumes that demand is random (or stochastic). If demand is known, various formulas can be derived that provide answers to the previous questions. (An example of one such formula is given in the discussion of the EOQ model in Chapter 8.) However, when demand for a product is uncertain or random, answers to the previous questions cannot be expressed in terms of a simple formula. In these situations, the technique of simulation proves to be a useful tool, as illustrated in the following example.

Laura Tanner is the owner of Computers of Tomorrow (COT), a retail computer store in Austin, Texas. Competition in retail computer sales is fierce—both in terms of price and service. Laura is concerned about the number of stockouts occurring on a popular type of computer monitor. This monitor is priced competitively and generates a marginal profit of $45 per unit sold. Stockouts are very costly to the business because when customers cannot buy this item at COT, they simply buy it from a competing store and COT loses the sale (there are no back-orders). Laura measures the effects of stockouts on her business in terms of service level, or the percentage of total demand that can be satisfied from inventory.

Laura has been following the policy of ordering 50 monitors whenever her daily ending inventory position (defined as ending inventory on hand plus outstanding orders) falls below her reorder point of 28 units. Laura places the order at the beginning of the next day. Orders are delivered at the beginning of the day and, therefore, can be used to satisfy demand on that day. For example, if the ending inventory position on day 2 is less than 28, Laura places the order at the beginning of day 3. If the actual time between order and delivery, or lead time, turns out to be four days, then the order arrives at the start of day 7. The current level of on-hand inventory is 50 units and no orders are pending.

COT sells an average of six monitors per day. However, the actual number sold on any given day can vary. By reviewing her sales records for the past several months, Laura determined that the daily demand for this monitor is a random variable that can be described by the following probability distribution:

Units Demanded:	0	1	2	3	4	5	6	7	8	9	10
Probability:	0.01	0.02	0.04	0.06	0.09	0.14	0.18	0.22	0.16	0.06	0.02

The manufacturer of this computer monitor is located in California. Although it takes an average of four days for COT to receive an order from this company, Laura has determined that the lead time of a shipment of monitors is also a random variable that can be described by the following probability distribution:

Lead Time (days):	3	4	5
Probability:	0.2	0.6	0.2

One way to guard against stockouts and improve the service level is to increase the reorder point for the item so that more inventory is on hand to meet the demand occurring during the lead time. Laura wants to determine the reorder point that results in an average service level of 99%.

12.12.1   Creating the RNGs

To solve this problem, we need to build a model to represent the inventory of computer monitors during an average month of 30 days. This model must account for the random daily demands that can occur and the random lead times encountered when orders are placed. Both variables are examples of *general, discrete* random variables because the possible outcomes they assume consist solely of integers, and the probabilities associated with each outcome are not equal (or not uniform). Thus, we will use the RNGDiscrete( ) function described in Figure 12.4 to model these variables.

To ensure that we understand what the RNGDiscrete( ) functions does, let's consider how we'd simulate the random order lead times in this problem using the RAND( ) function. Here, we need an RNG that returns the value 3 with probability 0.2, the value 4 with probability 0.6, and the value 5 with probability 0.2. Recall that RAND( ) returns a uniformly distributed random number between 0 and 1. If we subdivide the interval from 0 to 1 into three mutually exclusive and exhaustive pieces with widths corresponding to the probabilities associated with each possible lead time, we get:

Lower Limit	Upper Limit	Lead Time
0.0	0.19$\overline{9}$	3
0.2	0.79$\overline{9}$	4
0.8	0.99$\overline{9}$	5

The numbers generated by the RAND( ) function fall in the first interval (from 0 to 0.19$\overline{9}$) approximately 20% of the time, the second interval (from 0.2 to 0.79$\overline{9}$) approximately 60% of the time, and the third interval (from 0.8 to 0.99$\overline{9}$) approximately 20% of the time. The width of each of these intervals corresponds directly to the desired probability of each lead time value. So if we associate each interval with the indicated lead times, a lead time of three days has a 20% chance of occurring, a four-day lead time has a 60% chance of occurring, and a five-day lead time has a 20% chance of occurring. (We could use similar logic to break the interval from 0 to 1 into 11 mutually exclusive and exhaustive intervals to correspond to the different random demands that might occur.) The RNGDiscrete( ) function uses this same logic to generate general discrete random numbers.

The data describing the distributions of both of the random variables in this problem are entered in Excel as shown in Figure 12.15 (and in the file FIG12-15.xls on your data disk).

Given the data in Figure 12.15, we can use the following formulas to generate random order lead times and random daily demands that follow the appropriate probability distributions:

RNG for order lead time: =RNGDiscrete(B6:B8,C6:C8)

RNG for daily demand: =RNGDiscrete(E6:E16,F6:F16)

12.12.2 Implementing the Model

Now that we have a way of generating the random numbers needed in this problem, we can consider how the model should be built. As shown in Figure 12.16, we begin by creating a worksheet that lists the basic parameters for the model (or variables that are under the decision maker's control).

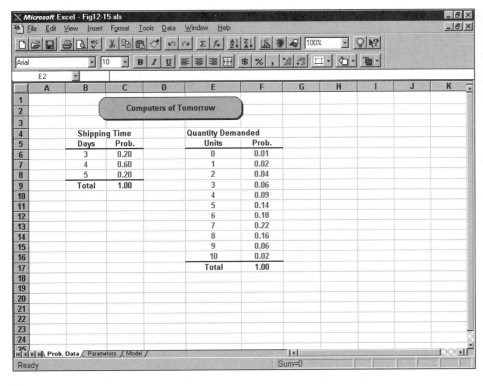

Figure 12.15
Probability distributions for shipping times and demand for COT's inventory problem.

Figure 12.16
Parameters
worksheet for
COT's inventory
problem.

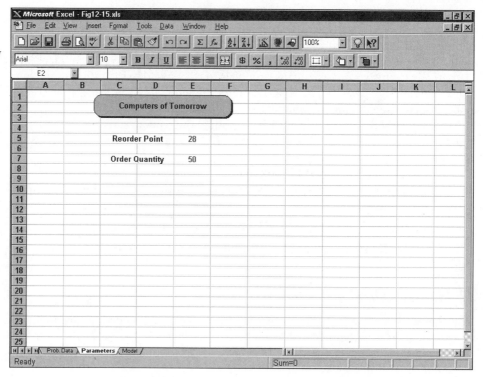

Laura wants to determine the reorder point that results in an average service level of 99%. Cell E5 in Figure 12.16 is used to represent the reorder point. The order quantity for the problem is given in cell E7 so that Laura could also use this model to investigate the impact of changes in order quantity.

Figure 12.17 shows the model representing 30 days of inventory activity. In this spreadsheet, column B represents the inventory on hand at the beginning of each day, which is simply the ending inventory from the previous day. The formulas in column B are:

Formula in cell B6:   =50

Formula in cell B7:   =F6
(Copy to B8 through B35.)

Column C represents the number of units scheduled to be received each day. We'll discuss the formulas in column C after we discuss columns H, I, and J, which relate to ordering and order lead times.

In column D, we use the technique described earlier to generate random daily demands, as:

Formula for cell D6:=RNGDiscrete('Prob. Data'!$E$6:$E$16,'Prob. Data'!$F$6:$F$16)
(Copy to D7 through D35.)

Because it is possible for demand to exceed the available supply, column E indicates how much of the daily demand can be met. If the beginning inventory (in column B) plus the ordered units received (in column C) is greater than or equal to the actual demand, then all the demand can be satisfied; otherwise, COT can sell only as many units as are available. This condition is modeled as:

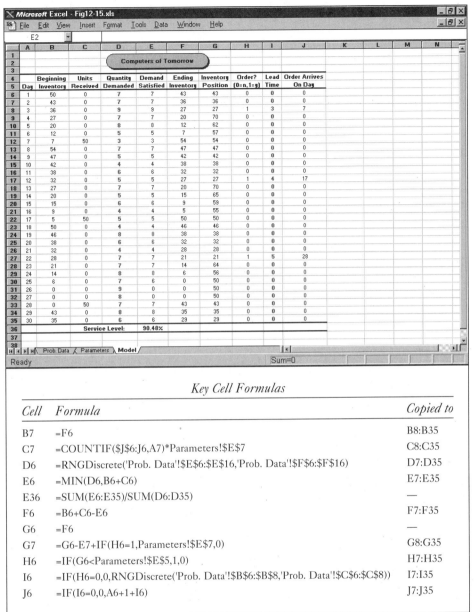

Figure 12.17
Spreadsheet representing a random month of inventory data.

Key Cell Formulas

Cell	Formula	Copied to
B7	=F6	B8:B35
C7	=COUNTIF($J$6:J6,A7)*Parameters!$E$7	C8:C35
D6	=RNGDiscrete('Prob. Data'!$E$6:$E$16,'Prob. Data'!$F$6:$F$16)	D7:D35
E6	=MIN(D6,B6+C6)	E7:E35
E36	=SUM(E6:E35)/SUM(D6:D35)	—
F6	=B6+C6-E6	F7:F35
G6	=F6	—
G7	=G6-E7+IF(H6=1,Parameters!$E$7,0)	G8:G35
H6	=IF(G6<Parameters!$E$5,1,0)	H7:H35
I6	=IF(H6=0,0,RNGDiscrete('Prob. Data'!$B$6:$B$8,'Prob. Data'!$C$6:$C$8))	I7:I35
J6	=IF(I6=0,0,A6+1+I6)	J7:J35

Formula for cell E6:   =MIN(D6,B6+C6)
(Copy to E7 through E35.)

The values in column F represent the on-hand inventory at the end of each day, and are calculated as:

Formula for cell F6:   =B6+C6-E6
(Copy to F7 through F35.)

To determine whether or not to place an order, we first must calculate the inventory position, which was defined earlier as the ending inventory plus any outstanding orders. This is implemented in column G as follows:

Formula for cell G6:   =F6
Formula for cell G7:   =G6-E7+IF(H6=1,Parameters!$E$7,0)
(Copy to G8 through G35.)

Column H indicates if an order should be placed based on inventory position and the reorder point, as:

Formula for cell H6:   =IF(G6<Parameters!$E$5,1,0)
(Copy to H7 through H35.)

If an order is placed, we must generate the random lead time required to receive the order. This is done in column I as:

Formula for cell I6:=IF(H6=0,0,RNGDiscrete('Prob. Data'!$B$6:$B$8,'Prob. Data'!$C$6:$C$8))
(Copy to I7 through I35.)

This formula returns the value 0 if no order was placed (if H6 = 0); otherwise, it returns a random lead time value (if H6 = 1).

If an order is placed, column J indicates the day on which the order will be received based on its random lead time in column I. This is done as:

Formula for cell J6:   =IF(I6=0,0,A6+1+I6)
(Copy to J7 through J35.)

The values in column C are coordinated with those in column J. The nonzero values in column J indicate the days on which orders will be received. For example, cell J8 indicates that an order will be received on day 7. The actual receipt of this order is reflected by the value of 50 in cell C12, which represents the receipt of an order at the beginning of day 7. The formula in cell C12 that achieves this is:

Formula for cell C12:   =COUNTIF($J$6:J11,A12)*Parameters!$E$7

This formula counts how many times the value in cell A12 (representing day 7) appears as a scheduled receipt day between days 1 through 6 in column J. This represents the number of orders scheduled to be received on day 7. We then multiply this by the order quantity (50), given in cell E7 on the Parameters worksheet, to determine the total units to be received on day 7. So the values in column C are generated as:

Formula for cell C6:   =0

Formula for cell C7:   =COUNTIF($J$6:J6,A7)*Parameters!$E$7
(Copy to C8 through C35.)

The service level for the model is calculated in cell E36 using the values in columns D and E as:

Formula for cell E36:   =SUM(E6:E35)/SUM(D6:D35)

Again, the service level represents the proportion of total demand that can be satisfied from inventory.

12.12.3   Replicating the Model

The model in Figure 12.17 indicates one possible scenario that could occur if Laura uses a reorder point of 28 units for the computer monitor. In the scenario shown, the value in cell E36 indicates that 90.48% of the total demand is satisfied. By replicating this model over and over, Laura could keep track of the service level occurring in each replication and average these values to determine the expected service level obtained with a reorder point of 28.

Using the simulation techniques described earlier, Laura could repeat this process with reorder points of 30 units, 32 units, and so on, until she finds the reorder point that achieved her goal of an average service level of 99%. However, there is another, easier way that Laura can perform the replications, as shown in Figure 12.18.

We prepared the spreadsheet in Figure 12.18 to replicate our model using a two-input (or two-way) data table. In cell B11 we entered the value 1 and used the Edit, Fill, Series command to fill the remainder of this column with the values 2, 3, and so on, up to 200. Cells C10 through G10 contain the values 28, 30, 32, 34, and 36, respectively, to represent a variety of reorder points that Laura might want to investigate to determine which reorder point will produce the desired service level. To track the service level associated with each replication of the model, the following formula is entered in cell B10:

Formula in cell B10:   =Model!E36

We can now use the Data Table command to instruct Excel to substitute each value in the range C10 through G10 into cell E5 and recalculate the workbook 200 times, keeping track of the value that results in cell B10 for each replication. This is done as shown in the steps on page 518.

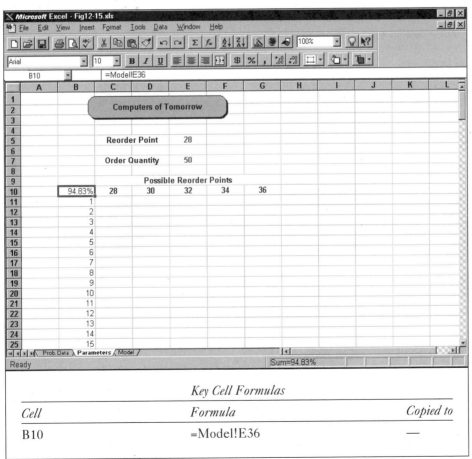

Figure 12.18
Spreadsheet prepared to simulate the service level at various reorder points using a two-way data table.

	Key Cell Formulas	
Cell	*Formula*	*Copied to*
B10	=Model!E36	—

> ### Important Software Note
>
> When using a two-way data table, the formula whose value you want to track must be placed in the upper-left corner of the data table range.

1. Select the range B10 through G210.
2. Click the Data menu.
3. Click Table.
4. In the Table dialog box, enter cell E5 for the Row input cell and enter cell A1 for the Column input cell.
5. Click OK. (This operation might take a minute or two if your computer is slow.)

Excel substitutes each value in the range C10 through G10 into cell E5. For each value substituted into cell E5, each value in the range B11 through B210 is substituted into cell A1 and the workbook is recalculated. The resulting value in cell B10 (representing the service level occurring in that replication) is then recorded in the appropriate cell in the data table. So for each reorder point value entered into cell E5, the workbook is replicated 200 times and the service level observed in each replication is recorded in the appropriate column of the data table. Because the model being recalculated here is fairly large, this could take several minutes depending on the speed of your computer. The results of this operation (after some simple formatting) are shown in Figure 12.19. (The random numbers you generate will *not* match those shown in Figure 12.19.)

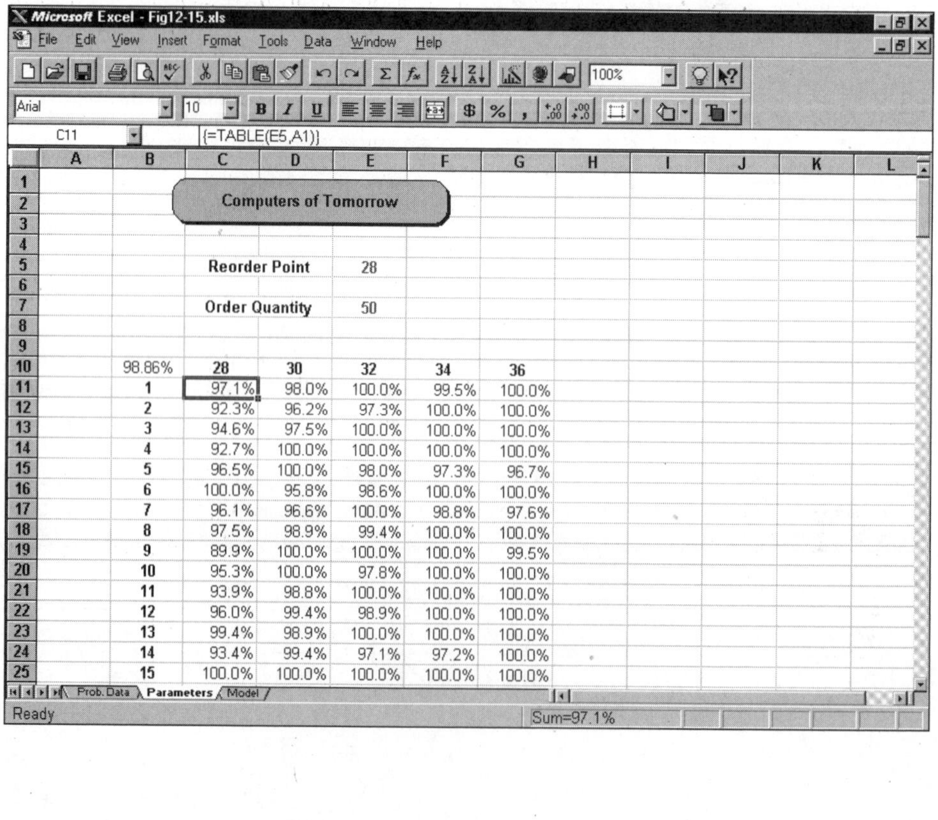

Figure 12.19
Results of the Data Table command for COT's inventory problem.

	A	B	C	D	E	F	G
5			Reorder Point		28		
7			Order Quantity		50		
10		98.86%	28	30	32	34	36
11		1	97.1%	98.0%	100.0%	99.5%	100.0%
12		2	92.3%	96.2%	97.3%	100.0%	100.0%
13		3	94.6%	97.5%	100.0%	100.0%	100.0%
14		4	92.7%	100.0%	100.0%	100.0%	100.0%
15		5	96.5%	100.0%	98.0%	97.3%	96.7%
16		6	100.0%	95.8%	98.6%	100.0%	100.0%
17		7	96.1%	96.6%	100.0%	98.8%	97.6%
18		8	97.5%	98.9%	99.4%	100.0%	100.0%
19		9	89.9%	100.0%	100.0%	100.0%	99.5%
20		10	95.3%	100.0%	97.8%	100.0%	100.0%
21		11	93.9%	98.8%	100.0%	100.0%	100.0%
22		12	96.0%	99.4%	98.9%	100.0%	100.0%
23		13	99.4%	98.9%	100.0%	100.0%	100.0%
24		14	93.4%	99.4%	97.1%	97.2%	100.0%
25		15	100.0%	100.0%	100.0%	100.0%	100.0%

Each new entry Excel created starting in cell C11 contains the array formula {=TABLE(E5,A1)}. This is how the Data Table command performs the repeated substitution and recalculation. If we don't change these formulas into values, every time the spreadsheet is recalculated we'll have to wait (and wait) for this process to re-execute and we'll get a new sample of 200 replications for each reorder point listed at the top of the data table. To convert the contents of the data table into values:

1. Select the range C11 through G210.
2. Click the Edit menu.
3. Click Copy.
4. Click the Edit menu.
5. Click Paste Special.
6. Click Values.
7. Click OK.
8. Press [Enter].

The values in the data table are now numeric constants that will not change even if the spreadsheet is recalculated.

12.12.4 Data Analysis

The results of the simulation can be summarized easily using the Descriptive Statistics command described earlier. To do this:

1. Click the Tools menu.
2. Click Data Analysis.
3. Click Descriptive Statistics.
4. Complete the Descriptive Statistics dialog box, as shown in Figure 12.20.
5. Click OK. (This operation might take a minute or two if your computer is slow.)

The descriptive statistics about the sample data are placed on a new worksheet named Results. After deleting some of the extraneous information produced by the Descriptive Statistics command, and after some simple formatting, the results appear as shown in Figure 12.21.

Figure 12.21 indicates that COT's current reorder point of 28 units results in an average service level of approximately 95.92%. This implies that COT is unable to satisfy approximately 4.08% of the total demand using this reorder point. Cell C9 translates this into dollars as:

Formula for cell C9:　　=(1–C4)*6*30*45
(Copy to D9 through G9.)

Because the average daily demand for the monitor is for six units, and each monitor sold generates a marginal profit of $45, cell C9 indicates that in an average month COT loses about $330.55 in profit due to stockouts on this item.

However, our simulation results indicate that as the reorder point increases, the service level also increases and the percentage of lost sales decreases. Thus, if Laura increases the reorder point to 36, COT's average service level for the monitor would increase to 99.68% and the average monthly profit lost due to stockouts would decrease to approximately $25.75.

Figure 12.20
Descriptive
Statistics dialog
box for COT's
inventory
problem.

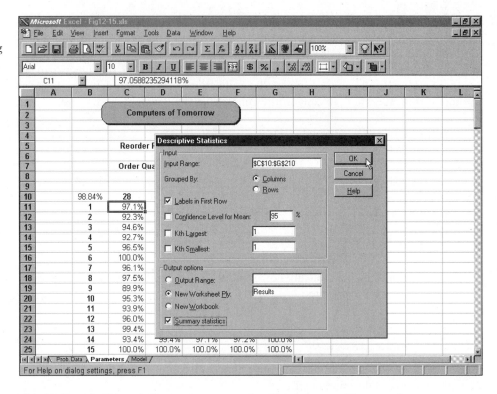

12.12.5   A Final Comment on the Inventory Example

Although increasing the reorder point decreases the percentage of lost sales, it also increases the average level of inventory held. Thus, another objective that might be considered in this problem involves weighing the costs of holding more inventory against the benefits of having fewer lost sales. We'll consider such an objective further in one of the problems at the end of this chapter.

12.13   AN OVERBOOKING EXAMPLE

Businesses that allow customers to make reservations for services (such as airlines, hotels, and car rental companies) know that some percentage of the reservations made will not be used for one reason or another, leaving these companies with a difficult decision problem. If they accept reservations for only the number of customers that can actually be served, then a portion of the company's assets will be underutilized when some customers with reservations fail to arrive. This results in an opportunity loss for the company. On the other hand, if they overbook (or accept more reservations than can be handled), then at times more customers will arrive than can actually be served. This typically results in additional financial costs to the company and often generates ill will among those customers who cannot be served. The following example illustrates how simulation might be used to help a company determine the optimal number of reservations to accept.

Marty Ford is an operations analyst for Piedmont Commuter Airlines (PCA). Recently, Marty was asked to make a recommendation on how many reservations

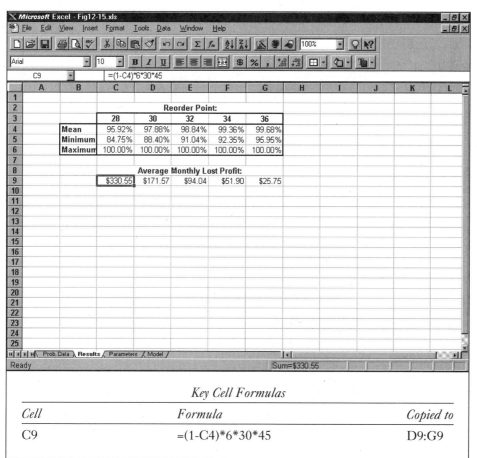

Figure 12.21 Simulation results for COT's inventory problem.

PCA should book on Flight 343—a flight in high demand from a small regional airport to a major hub airport. Historical data show that PCA frequently has seats left on Flight 343 if it accepts only 19 reservations (the plane's capacity). Industry statistics show that for every ticket sold for a commuter flight, a 0.10 probability exists that the ticket holder will not be on the flight. PCA sells non-refundable tickets for Flight 343 for $85 per seat. Thus, every empty seat on this flight represents an opportunity cost—even if a no-show customer had purchased a ticket for the seat—because the seat could be filled by another passenger paying $85. On the other hand, if PCA overbooks this flight and more than 19 passengers show up, some of them will have to be bumped to a later flight. To compensate for the inconvenience of being bumped, PCA gives these passengers vouchers for a free meal, a free flight at a later date, and sometimes also pays for them to stay overnight in a hotel near the airport. PCA pays an average of $155 for each passenger who gets bumped. Marty wants to determine if PCA can increase profits by overbooking this flight and, if so, how many reservations should be accepted to produce the maximum average profit. Marty wants to set up a model that allows him to investigate the consequences of accepting up to 24 reservations.

12.13.1 Implementing the Model

A spreadsheet model for this problem is shown in Figure 12.22 (and in the file FIG12-22.xls on your data disk).

This spreadsheet begins by listing the relevant data from the problem, including the number of seats available on the plane, the price PCA charges for each seat, the probability of a no-show (or a ticketed passenger not arriving in time for the flight), the cost of bumping passengers, and the number of reservations that will be accepted.

The uncertain, or random, element of this problem is the number of passengers arriving to board the plane, represented in cell C10 in Figure 12.22. If n tickets are sold and each ticket holder has a $p = 0.1$ probability of not showing up (or $1 - p = 0.9$ probability of showing up), then the number of passengers arriving to board the flight is a random variable that follows the binomial probability distribution—or a binomial random variable. Thus, the following formula for cell C10 generates the random number of ticketed passengers who arrive for each flight:

Figure 12.22
Spreadsheet model for PCA's overbooking problem.

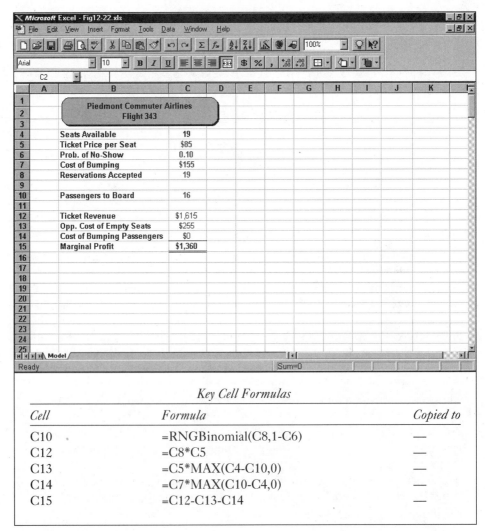

Key Cell Formulas		
Cell	Formula	Copied to
C10	=RNGBinomial(C8,1-C6)	—
C12	=C8*C5	—
C13	=C5*MAX(C4-C10,0)	—
C14	=C7*MAX(C10-C4,0)	—
C15	=C12-C13-C14	—

Formula for cell C10:   =RNGBinomial(C8,1-C6)

Cell C12 represents the ticket revenue PCA earns based on the number of tickets they sell for each flight. The formula for this cell is:

Formula for cell C12:   =C8*C5

Cell C13 computes the opportunity loss PCA incurs on each empty seat on a flight.

Formula for cell C13:   =C5*MAX(C4-C10,0)

Cell C14 computes the costs PCA incurs when passengers must be bumped (i.e., when the number of passengers wanting to board exceeds the number of available seats).

Formula for cell C14:   =C7*MAX(C10-C4,0)

Finally, cell C15 computes the marginal profit PCA earns on each flight.

Formula for cell C15:   =C12-C13-C14

12.13.2   Replicating the Model

Marty wants to determine the number of reservations to accept that, on average, will result in the highest marginal profit. Figure 12.23 shows the spreadsheet in the format of a two-way data table.

In cell F5, we entered the value 1 and used the Edit, Fill, Series command to fill the remainder of this column with the values 2, 3, and so on, up to 200. Cells G4 through L4 contain the values 19, 20, 21, 22, 23, and 24, respectively, to represent different numbers of reservations that PCA might accept. The formula in cell F4 refers back to the marginal profit in cell C15 because this is the bottom-line performance measure we want to track in this model.

Formula for cell F4:   =C15

We can now use the Data Table command to instruct Excel to substitute each value in the range G4 through L4 into cell C8 and recalculate the spreadsheet 200 times, keeping track of the value that results in cell F4 for each replication. This is done as follows:

1. Select the range F4 through L204.
2. Click the Data menu.
3. Click Table.
4. In the Table dialog box, enter cell C8 for the Row input cell and enter cell A1 for the Column input cell.
5. Click OK.

Excel substitutes each value in the range G4 through L4 into cell C8. For each value substituted into cell C8, each value in the range F5 through F204 is substituted into cell A1 and the workbook is recalculated. The resulting value in cell F4 (representing the marginal profit earned in that replication) is then recorded in the appropriate cell in the data table. So for each possible number of reservations entered into cell C8, the spreadsheet is replicated 200 times and the marginal profit observed in each replication is recorded in the appropriate column of the data table. Again, this could take several seconds to several minutes depending on the speed of your computer.

Figure 12.23
Spreadsheet prepared to simulate the average profit achieved by accepting different numbers of reservations using a two-way data table.

	Key Cell Formulas	
Cell	Formula	Copied to
F4	=C15	—

When Excel is finished running the replications, we need to convert the formula entries in the data table into values by completing the following:

1. Select the range F5 through L204.
2. Click the Edit menu.
3. Click Copy.
4. Click the Edit menu.
5. Click Paste Special.
6. Click Values.
7. Click OK.
8. Press [Enter].

Figure 12.24 shows the results of the simulation and the average profit associated with each number of reservations accepted. (Your results will *not* match those shown in Figure 12.24.) These averages are calculated as:

Formula for cell G2:   =AVERAGE(G5:G204)
(Copy to H2 through L2.)

The averages in Figure 12.24 indicate that if PCA accepts only 19 reservations, its average marginal profit on this flight will be approximately $1,460 (assuming vacant seats are counted as an opportunity cost at $85 per seat). As the number of reservations

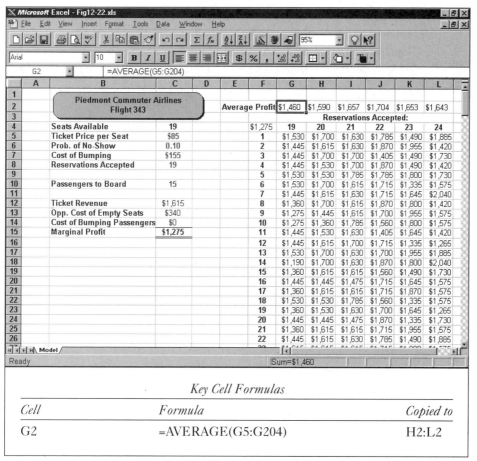

Figure 12.24
Simulation results for PCA's overbooking problem.

accepted increases, the average profit also increases and reaches a maximum of $1,704 at 22 reservations. Thus, it appears that the optimal number of reservations for PCA to accept is 22.

12.13.3   A Final Comment on the Overbooking Example

This problem assumed that all the reservations available for Flight 343 would always be taken—or that there would never be unused reservations. However, if PCA accepts up to 22 reservations, there might be times when only 16 or 17 seats would be demanded. Thus, the demand for seats on this flight could be modeled more accurately as a random variable. We'll explore this issue more fully in one of the problems at the end of this chapter.

SUMMARY

This chapter introduced the concept of risk analysis and simulation. Many of the input cells in a spreadsheet represent random variables whose values cannot be determined with certainty. Any uncertainty in the input cells flows through the spreadsheet model to create a related uncertainty in the value of the output cell(s). Decisions made on the basis of these uncertain values involve some degree of risk.

THE WORLD OF MANAGEMENT SCIENCE
The U.S. Postal Service
Moves to the Fast Lane

Mail flows into the U.S. Postal Service at the rate of 500 million pieces per day, and it comes in many forms. There are standard-sized letters with nine-digit ZIP codes (with or without imprinted bar codes), five-digit ZIP codes, typed addresses that can be read by optical character readers, handwritten addresses that are barely decipherable. Christmas cards in red envelopes addressed in red ink and so on. The enormous task of sorting all these pieces at the sending post office and at the destination has caused postal management to consider and adopt many new forms of technology. These include operator-assisted mechanized sorters, optical character readers (last-line and multiple-line), and bar code sorters. Implementation of new technology brings with it associated policy decisions, such as rate discounts for bar coding by the customer, finer sorting at the origin, and so on.

A simulation model called META (model for evaluating technology alternatives) assists management in evaluating new technologies, configurations, and operating plans. Using distributions based on experience or projections of the effects of new policies, META simulates a random stream of mail of different types, routes the mail through the system configuration being tested, and prints reports detailing total pieces handled, capacity utilization, work hours required, space requirements, and cost.

META has been used on several projects associated with the Postal Service corporate automation plan. These include facilities planning, benefits of alternate sorting plans, justification of efforts to enhance address readability, planning studies for reducing the time carriers spend sorting vs. delivering, and identification of mail types that offer the greatest potential for cost savings.

According to the Associate Postmaster General, "... META became the vehicle to help steer our organization on an entirely new course at a speed we had never before experienced."

Source: Michael E. Cebry, Anura H. deSilva and Fred J. DiLisio, "Management Science in Automating Postal Operations: Facility and Equipment Planning in the United States Postal Service," *Interfaces*, vol. 22, no. 1, January–February 1992, pages 110–130.

Various methods of risk analysis are available, including best-case/worst-case analysis, what-if analysis, and simulation. Of these three methods, simulation is the only technique that provides hard evidence (facts and figures) that can be used objectively in making decisions. To simulate a model, RNGs are used to select representative values for each uncertain independent variable in the model. This process is repeated over and over to generate a sample of representative values for the dependent variable(s) in the model. The variability and distribution of the sample values for the dependent variable(s) can then be analyzed to gain insight into the possible outcomes that might occur. This technique can also be used to test different configurations of controllable parameters in the model in an attempt to determine the optimal values for these parameters.

QUESTIONS AND PROBLEMS

1. Under what condition(s) is it appropriate to use simulation to analyze a model? That is, what characteristics should a model possess in order for simulation to be used?

2. The graph of the probability distribution of a normally distributed random variable with a mean of 20 and standard deviation of 3 is shown in Figure 12.6.

   a. Use the RNGNormal( ) function to generate 100 sample values from this distribution.
   b. Produce a histogram of the 100 sample values you generated. Does your histogram look like the graph for this distribution in Figure 12.6?
   c. Repeat this experiment, only this time sample 1,000 values.
   d. Produce a histogram for the 1,000 sample values you generated. Does the histogram now more closely resemble the graph in Figure 12.6 for this distribution?
   e. Why does your second histogram look more "normal" than the first one?

3. Refer to the Hungry Dawg Restaurant example presented in section 12.4 of this chapter. Health claim costs actually tend to be seasonal, with higher levels of claims occurring during the summer months (when kids are out of school and more likely to injure themselves) and during December (when people schedule elective procedures before the next year's deductible must be paid). The following table summarizes the seasonal adjustment factors that apply to RNGs for average claims in the Hungry Dawg problem. For instance, the average claim for month 6 should be multiplied by 115% and those for month 1 should be multiplied by 80%.

Month:	1	2	3	4	5	6	7	8	9	10	11	12
Seasonal Factor:	0.80	0.85	0.87	0.92	0.93	1.15	1.20	1.18	1.03	0.95	0.98	1.14

   Suppose the company maintains an account from which it pays health insurance claims. Assume there is $2.5 million in the account at the beginning of month 1. Each month, employee contributions are deposited into this account and claims are paid from the account.

   a. Modify the spreadsheet shown in Figure 12.7 to include the cash flows in this account. If the company deposits $3 million in this account every month, what is the probability that the account will have insufficient funds to pay claims at some point during the year? Use 300 replications. (HINT: You can use the COUNTIF( ) function to count the number of months in a year where the ending balance in the account is below 0.)
   b. If the company wants to deposit an equal amount of money in this account each month, what should this amount be if it wants there to only be a 5% chance of having insufficient funds?

4. One of the examples in section 12.11 of this chapter dealt with determining the optimal reorder point for a computer monitor sold by Computers of Tomorrow (COT) in Austin, Texas. In this example we found that increasing the reorder point decreased the number of lost sales. However, this also increased the average amount of inventory carried. Suppose that it costs COT $0.30 per day in holding

costs for each monitor in beginning inventory, and it costs $20 to place an order. Each monitor sold generates a profit of $45, and each lost sale results in an opportunity cost of $65 (including the lost profit of $45 and $20 in lost goodwill). Modify the spreadsheet shown in Figure 12.15 to determine the reorder point that maximizes the average monthly profit associated with this monitor.

5. One of the examples in section 12.13 of this chapter dealt with determining the optimal number of reservations for Piedmont Commuter Airlines (PCA) to accept for one of its flights that uses a plane with 19 seats. The model discussed in the chapter assumes that all the reservations would be used, but some customers would not show up for the flight. It is probably more realistic to assume that the demand for these reservations is somewhat random. For example, suppose that the demand for reservations on this flight is given by the following discrete probability distribution:

Reservations Demanded:	12	13	14	15	16	17	18	19	20	21	22	23	24
Probability:	0.01	0.03	0.04	0.07	0.09	0.11	0.15	0.18	0.14	0.08	0.05	0.03	0.02

The number of passengers receiving reservations depends on the number of reservations PCA accepts and the demand for these reservations. For each passenger receiving a reservation, a 0.10 probability exists that he will not arrive at the gate to board the plane. Modify the spreadsheet shown in Figure 12.22 to determine the number of reservations PCA should accept to maximize the average profit associated with this flight.

6. A debate recently erupted about the optimal strategy for playing a game on the TV show called "Let's Make a Deal." In one of the games on this show, the contestant would be given the choice of prizes behind three closed doors. A valuable prize was behind one door and worthless prizes were behind the other two doors. After the contestant selected a door, the host would open one of the two remaining doors to reveal one of the worthless prizes. Then, before opening the selected door, the host would give the contestant the opportunity to switch his or her selection to the other door that had not been opened. The question is, should the contestant switch?

    a. Suppose a contestant is allowed to play this game 500 times, always picks door number 1, and never switches when given the option. If the valuable prize is equally likely to be behind each door at the beginning of each play, how many times would the contestant win the valuable prize? Use simulation to answer this question.

    b. Now suppose the contestant is allowed to play this game another 500 times. This time the player always selects door number 1 initially and switches when given the option. Using simulation, how many times would the contestant win the valuable prize?

    c. If you were a contestant on this show, what would you do if given the option of switching doors?

7. The monthly demand for the latest computer at Newland Computers follows a normal distribution with a mean of 350 and standard deviation of 75. Newland purchases these computers for $1,200 and sells them for $2,300. It costs the company $100 to place an order and $12 for every computer held in inventory at the end of each month. Currently the company places an order for 1,000 computers

whenever the inventory at the end of a month falls below 100 units. Assume unmet demand in any month is lost to competitors and that orders placed at the end of one month arrive at the beginning of the next month.

a. Create a spreadsheet model to simulate the profit the company will earn on this product over the next two years. Use 200 replications. What is the average level of profit the company will earn?

b. Suppose the company wants to determine the optimum reorder point and order quantity. Specifically, for every 100-unit increase in the reorder point, they will reduce the order quantity by 100. Which combination of reorder point and order quantity will provide the highest average profit over the next two years?

8. The manager of Moore's Catalog Showroom is trying to predict how much revenue will be generated by each major department in the store during 1998. The manager has estimated the minimum and maximum growth rates possible for revenues in each department. The manager believes that any of the possible growth rates between the minimum and maximum values are equally likely to occur. These estimates are summarized in the following table:

Department	1997 Revenues	Growth Rates	
		Minimum	Maximum
Electronics	$6,342,213	2%	10%
Garden Supplies	$1,203,231	–4%	5%
Jewelry	$4,367,342	–2%	6%
Sporting Goods	$3,543,532	–1%	8%
Toys	$4,342,132	4%	15%

Create a spreadsheet to simulate the total revenues that could occur in the coming year. Run 500 replications of the model and do the following:

a. Construct a 95% confidence interval for the average level of revenues the manager could expect for 1998.

b. According to your model, what are the chances that total revenues in 1998 will be more than 5% larger than those in 1997?

9. The Harriet Hotel in downtown Boston has 100 rooms that rent for $125 per night. It costs the hotel $30 per room in variable costs (cleaning, bathroom items, etc.) each night a room is occupied. For each reservation accepted, there is a 5% chance that the guest will not arrive. If the hotel overbooks, it costs $200 to compensate guests whose reservations cannot be honored.

How many reservations should the hotel accept if it wishes to maximize the average daily profit? Use 500 simulations for each reservation level you consider.

10. Lynn Price recently completed her MBA and accepted a job with an electronics manufacturing company. Although she likes her job, she is also looking forward to retiring one day. To ensure that her retirement is comfortable, Lynn intends to invest $3,000 of her salary into a tax-sheltered retirement fund at the end of each year. Lynn is not certain what rate of return this investment will earn each year, but she expects each year's rate of return could be modeled appropriately as a normally distributed random variable with a mean of 12% and standard deviation of 2%.

a. If Lynn is 30 years old, how much money should she expect to have in her retirement fund at age 60? (Use 500 replications.)

b. Construct a 95% confidence interval for the average amount Lynn will have at age 60.

c. What is the probability that Lynn will have more than $1 million in her retirement fund when she reaches age 60?

d. How much should Lynn invest each year if she wants there to be a 90% chance of having at least $1 million in her retirement fund at age 60?

11. Employees of Georgia-Atlantic are permitted to contribute a portion of their earnings (in increments of $500) to a flexible spending account from which they can pay medical expenses not covered by the company's health insurance program. Contributions to an employee's "flex" account are not subject to income taxes. However, the employee forfeits any amount contributed to the "flex" account that is not spent during the year. Suppose Greg Davis makes $60,000 per year from Georgia-Atlantic and pays a marginal tax rate of 28%. Greg and his wife estimate that in the coming year their normal medical expenses not covered by the health insurance program could be as small as $500, as large as $5,000 and most likely about $1,300. However, Greg also believes there is a 5% change that an abnormal medical event could occur which might add $10,000 to the normal expenses paid from their flex account. If their uncovered medical claims exceed their contribution to their "flex" account, they will have to cover these expenses with the after-tax money Greg brings home.

   Use simulation to determine the amount of money Greg should contribute to his flexible spending account in the coming year if he wants to maximize his disposable income (after taxes and all medical expenses are paid). Use 500 replications for each level of "flex" account contribution you consider.

12. Acme Equipment Company is considering the development of a new machine that would be marketed to tire manufacturers. Research and development costs for the project are expected to be about $4 million but could vary between $3 and $6 million. The market life for the product is estimated to be three to eight years with all intervening possibilities being equally likely. The company thinks it will sell 250 units per year, but acknowledges that this figure could be as low as 50 or as high as 350. The company will sell the machine for about $23,000. Finally, the cost of manufacturing the machine is expected to be $14,000 but could be as low as $12,000 or as high as $18,000. The company's cost of capital is 15%.

   a. Use appropriate RNGs to create a spreadsheet to calculate the possible net present values (NPVs) that could result from taking on this project.

   b. Replicate the model 500 times. What is the expected NPV for this project?

   c. What is the probability of this project generating a positive NPV for the company?

13. Representatives from the American Heart Association are planning to go door-to-door throughout a community, soliciting contributions. From past experience they know that when someone answers the door, 80% of the time it is a female and 20% of the time it is a male. They also know that 70% of the females who answer the door make a donation, whereas only 40% of the males who answer the door make donations. The amount of money that females contribute follows a normal distribution with a mean of $20 and standard deviation of $3. The amount of money males contribute follows a normal distribution with a mean of $10 and standard deviation of $2.

a. Create a spreadsheet model that simulates what might happen whenever a representative of the American Heart Association knocks on a door and someone answers.

b. Replicate your model 500 times. What is the average contribution the Heart Association can expect to receive when someone answers the door?

c. Suppose that the Heart Association plans to visit 300 homes on a given Saturday. If no one is home at 25% of the residences, what is the total amount that the Heart Association can expect to receive in donations?

14. After spending 10 years as an assistant manager for a large restaurant chain, Ray Clark has decided to become his own boss. The owner of a local submarine sandwich store wants to sell the store to Ray for $65,000 to be paid in installments of $13,000 in each of the next five years. According to the current owner, the store brings in revenue of about $110,000 per year and incurs operating costs of about 63% of sales. Thus, once the store is paid for, Ray should make about $35,000–$40,000 per year before taxes. Until the store is paid for, he will make substantially less—but he will be his own boss. Realizing that some uncertainty is involved in this decision, Ray wants to simulate what level of net income he can expect to earn during the next five years as he operates and pays for the store. In particular, he wants to see what could happen if sales are allowed to vary uniformly between $90,000 and $120,000, and if operating costs are allowed to vary uniformly between 60% and 65% of sales. Assume that Ray's payments for the store are not deductible for tax purposes and that he is in the 28% tax bracket.

a. Create a spreadsheet model to simulate the annual net income Ray would receive during each of the next five years if he decides to buy the store.

b. Given the money he has in savings, Ray thinks he can get by for the next five years if he can make at least $12,000 from the store each year. Replicate the model 500 times and track: 1) the minimum amount of money Ray makes over the five-year period represented by each replication, and 2) the total amount Ray makes during the five-year period represented by each replication.

c. What is the probability that Ray will make at least $12,000 in each of the next five years?

d. What is the probability that Ray will make at least $60,000 total over the next five years?

15. Bob Davidson owns a newsstand outside the Waterstone office building complex in Atlanta, near Hartsfield International Airport. He buys his papers wholesale at $0.50 per paper and sells them for $0.75. Bob wonders what is the optimal number of papers to order each day. Based on history, he has found that demand (even though it is discrete) can be modeled by a normal distribution with a mean of 50 and standard deviation of 5. When he has more papers than customers, he can recycle all the extra papers the next day and receive $0.05 per paper. On the other hand, if he has more customers than papers, he loses some goodwill in addition to the lost profit on the potential sale of $0.25. Bob estimates the incremental lost goodwill costs five day's worth of business (that is, dissatisfied customers will go to a competitor the next week, but come back to him the week after that).

a. Create a spreadsheet model to determine the optimal number of papers to order each day. Use 250 replications and round the demand values generated by the normal RNG to the closest integer value.

b. Construct a 95% confidence interval for the expected payoff from the optimal decision.

16. Vinton Auto Insurance is trying to decide how much money to keep in liquid assets to cover insurance claims. In the past, the company held some of the premiums it received in interest-bearing checking accounts and put the rest into investments that are not quite as liquid, but tend to generate a higher investment return. The company wants to study cash flows to determine how much money it should keep in liquid assets to pay claims. After reviewing historical data, the company determined that the average repair bill per claim is normally distributed with a mean of $1,700 and standard deviation of $400. It also determined that the number of repair claims filed each week is a random variable that follows the probability distribution given below:

Number of Repair Claims	Probability
1	0.05
2	0.06
3	0.10
4	0.17
5	0.28
6	0.14
7	0.08
8	0.07
9	0.05

In addition to repair claims, the company also receives claims for cars that have been "totaled" and cannot be repaired. A 20% chance of receiving this type of claim exists in any week. These claims for "totaled" cars typically cost anywhere from $2,000 to $35,000, with $13,000 being the most common cost.

a. Create a spreadsheet model of the total claims cost incurred by the company in any week.
b. Replicate the model 500 times and create a histogram of the distribution of total cost values that were generated.
c. What is the average cost the company should expect to pay each week?
d. Suppose that the company decides to keep $20,000 cash on hand to pay claims. What is the probability that this amount would not be adequate to cover claims in any week?
e. Create a 95% confidence interval for the true probability of claims exceeding $20,000 in a given week.

17. The owner of a local car dealership has just received a call from a regional distributor stating that a $5,000 bonus will be awarded if the owner's dealership sells at least 10 new cars next Saturday. On an average Saturday, this dealership has 75 potential customers look at new cars, but there is no way to determine exactly how many customers will come this particular Saturday. The owner is fairly certain that the number would not be less than 40, but also thinks it would be unrealistic to expect more than 120 (which is the largest number of customers to ever show up in one day).

   The owner determined that, on average, about 1 out of 10 customers who look at cars at the dealership actually purchase a car—or, a 0.10 probability (or 10% chance) exists that any given customer will buy a new car.

a. Create a spreadsheet model for this problem and generate 1,000 random outcomes for the number of cars the dealership might sell next Saturday.

b. What is the probability that the dealership will earn the $5,000 bonus?

c. If you were this dealer, what is the maximum amount of money you'd be willing to spend on sales incentives to try to earn this bonus?

18. Dr. Sarah Benson is an ophthalmologist who, in addition to prescribing glasses and contact lenses, performs optical laser surgery to correct nearsightedness. This surgery is fairly easy and inexpensive to perform. Thus, it represents a potential gold mine for her practice. To inform the public about this procedure, Dr. Benson advertises in the local paper and holds information sessions in her office one night a week at which she shows a videotape about the procedure and answers any questions potential patients might have. The room where these meetings are held can seat 10 people, and reservations are required. The number of people attending each session varies from week to week. Dr. Benson cancels the meeting if two or fewer people have made reservations. Using data from the previous year, Dr. Benson determined that the distribution of reservations is as follows:

Number of Reservations:	0	1	2	3	4	5	6	7	8	9	10
Probability:	0.02	0.05	0.08	0.16	0.26	0.18	0.11	0.07	0.05	0.01	0.01

Using data from the past year, Dr. Benson determined that each person who attends an information has a 0.25 probability of electing to have the surgery. Of those who do not, most cite the cost of the procedure—$2,000—as their major concern.

a. On average, how much revenue does Dr. Benson's practice in laser surgery generate each week? (Use 500 replications.)

b. On average, how much revenue would the laser surgery generate each week if Dr. Benson did not cancel sessions with two or fewer reservations?

c. Dr. Benson believes that 40% of the people attending the information sessions would have the surgery if she reduced the price to $1,500. Under this scenario, how much revenue could Dr. Benson expect to realize per week from laser surgery?

19. Michael Abrams runs a specialty clothing store that sells collegiate sports apparel. One of his primary business opportunities involves selling custom screen-printed sweatshirts for college football bowl games. He is trying to determine how many sweatshirts to produce for the upcoming Tangerine Bowl game. During the month before the game, Michael plans to sell his sweatshirts for $25 a piece. At this price, he believes the demand for sweatshirts will be triangularly distributed with a minimum demand of 10,000, maximum demand of 30,000, and a most likely demand of 18,000. During the month after the game, Michael plans to sell any remaining sweatshirts for $12 a piece. At this price, he believes the demand for sweatshirts will be triangularly distributed with a minimum demand of 2,000, maximum demand of 7,000, and a most likely demand of 5,000. Two months after the game, Michael plans to sell any remaining sweatshirts to a surplus store which has agreed to buy up to 2,000 sweatshirts for a price of $3 per shirt. Michael can order custom screen-printed sweatshirts for $8 a piece in lot sizes of 3,000.

a. On average, how much profit would Michael earn if he orders 18,000 sweatshirts? Use 500 replications.

b. How many sweatshirts should he order if he wants to maximize his expected profit? Again use 500 replications in each simulation you perform.

20. The Major Motors Corporation is trying to decide whether or not to introduce a new midsize car. The directors of the company want to produce the car only if it has at least an 80% chance of generating a positive net present value over the next 10 years. If the company decides to produce the car, it will have to pay an uncertain initial start-up cost that is estimated to follow a triangular distribution with a minimum value of $300 million, maximum value of $600 million, and a most likely value of $450 million. In the first year the company would produce 100,000 units. Demand during the first year is uncertain but expected to be normally distributed with a mean of 95,000 and standard deviation of 7,000. For any year in which the demand exceeds production, production will be increased by 5% in the following year. For any year in which the production exceeds demand, production will be decreased by 5% in the next year and the excess cars will be sold to a rental car company at a 20% discount. After the first year, the demand in any year will be modeled as a normally distributed random variable with a mean equal to the actual demand in the previous year and standard deviation of 7,000. In the first year, the sales price of the car will be $13,000 and the total variable cost per car is expected to be $7,500. Both the selling price and variable cost is expected to increase each year at the rate of inflation which is assumed to be uniformly distributed between 2% and 7%. The company uses a discount rate of 9% to discount future cash flows.

    a. Create a spreadsheet model for this problem and replicate it 300 times. What is the minimum, average, and maximum NPV Major Motors can expect if they decide to produce this car? (HINT: Consider using the NPV( ) function to discount the profits Major Motors would earn each year.)
    b. What is the probability of Major Motors earning a positive NPV over the next 10 years?
    c. Should they produce this car?

21. Each year, the Schriber Corporation must determine how much to contribute to the company's pension plan. The company uses a 10-year planning horizon to determine the contribution which, if made annually in each of the next 10 years, would allow for only a 10% chance of the fund running short of money. The company then makes that contribution in the current year (year 1) and repeats this process in each subsequent year to determine the specific amount to contribute each year. (Last year the company contributed $43 million to the plan.) The pension plan covers two types of employees: hourly and salaried. In the current year, there will be 6,000 former hourly employees and 3,000 former salaried employees receiving benefits from the plan. The change in the number of retired hourly employees from one year to the next is expected to vary according to a normal distribution with mean of 4% and standard deviation of 1%. The change in the number of retired salaried employees from one year to the next is expected to vary between 1% and 4% according to a truncated normal distribution with mean of 2% and standard deviation of 1%. Currently, hourly retirees receive an average benefit of $15,000 per year, while salaried retirees receive an average annual benefit of $40,000. Both of these averages are expected to increase annually with the rate of inflation, which is assumed to vary annually between 2% and 7% according to a triangular distribution with a most likely value of 3.5%. The current balance in the company's pension fund is $1.5 billion. Investments in this fund earn an annual return that is assumed to be normally distributed with a mean of 12% and standard deviation of 2% each year. Create a spreadsheet model for this problem and use

simulation to determine the pension fund contribution the company should make in the current year. Assume benefits are paid throughout the year and the company contribution is made at the end of the year. What is your recommendation?

CASE 12.1   THE SOUND'S ALIVE COMPANY

Contributed by Jack Yurkiewicz, Lubin School of Business, Pace University.

Marissa Jones is the president and CEO of Sound's Alive, a company that manufactures and sells a line of speakers, CD players, receivers, high-definition televisions, and other items geared for the home entertainment market. Respected throughout the industry for bringing many high-quality, innovative products to market, Marissa is considering adding a speaker system to her product line.

The speaker market has changed dramatically during the last several years. Originally, high-fidelity aficionados knew that to reproduce sound covering the fullest range of frequencies—from the lowest kettle drum to the highest violin—a speaker system had to be large and heavy. The speaker had various drivers: a woofer to reproduce the low notes, a tweeter for the high notes, and a midrange driver for the broad spectrum of frequencies in between. Many speaker systems had a minimum of three drivers, but some had even more. The trouble was that such a system was too large for anything but the biggest rooms, and consumers were reluctant to spend thousands of dollars and give up valuable wall space to get the excellent sound these speakers could reproduce.

The trend has changed during the past several years. Consumers still want good sound, but they want it from smaller boxes. Therefore, the satellite system became popular. Consisting of two small boxes that house either one driver (to cover the midrange and high frequencies) or two (a midrange and tweeter), a satellite system can easily be mounted on walls or shelves. To reproduce the low notes, a separate subwoofer that is approximately the size of a cube 18 inches on a side is also needed. This subwoofer can be placed anywhere in the room. Taking up less space than a typical large speaker system and sounding almost as good, yet costing hundreds of dollars less, these satellite systems are hot items in the high-fidelity market.

Recently the separate wings of home entertainment—high-fidelity (receivers, speakers, CD players, CDs, cassettes, and so on), television (large-screen monitors, video cassette recorders, laser players), and computers (games with sounds, virtual reality software, and so on)—have merged into the home theater concept. To simulate the movie environment, a home theater system requires the traditional stereo speaker system plus additional speakers placed in the rear of the room so that viewers are literally surrounded with sound. Although the rear speakers do not have to match the high quality of the front speakers and, therefore, can be less expensive, most consumers choose a system in which the front and rear speakers are of equal quality, reproducing the full range of frequencies with equal fidelity.

It is this speaker market that Marissa wants to enter. She is considering having Sound's Alive manufacture and sell a home theater system that consists of seven speakers. Three small speakers—each with one dome tweeter that could reproduce the frequency range of 200 Hertz to 20,000 Hertz (upper-low frequencies to the highest frequencies)—would be placed in front, and three similar speakers would be placed strategically around the sides and back of the room. To reproduce the lowest frequencies (from 35 Hertz to 200 Hertz), a single subwoofer would also be part of the system. This sub-woofer is revolutionary because it is smaller than the ordinary sub-woofer, only 10 inches per side, and it has a built-in amplifier to power it. Consumer and critics are thrilled with the music from early prototype systems, claiming that these speakers have the best balance of sound and size. Marissa is extremely encouraged by these early reviews, and although her company has never produced a product with its house label on it (having always sold systems from established high-fidelity companies), she believes that Sound's Alive should enter the home theater market with this product.

Phase One: Projecting Profits

Marissa decides to create a spreadsheet that will project profits over the next several years. After consulting with economists, market analysts, employees in her own company, and employees from other companies that sell house brand components. Marissa is confident that the gross revenues for these speakers in 1998 would be around $6 million. She must also figure that a small percentage of speakers will be damaged in transit, or some will be returned by dissatisfied customers shortly after the sales. These returns and allowances (R&As) are usually calculated as 2% of the gross revenues. Hence, the net revenues are simply the gross revenues minus the R&As. Marissa believes that the 1998 labor costs for these speakers will be $995,100. The cost of materials (including boxes to ship the speakers) should be $915,350 for 1998. Finally, her overhead costs (rent, lighting, heating in winter, air conditioning in summer, security, and so on) for 1998 should be $1,536,120. Thus, the cost of goods sold is the sum of labor, material, and overhead costs. Marissa figures the gross profit as the difference between the net revenues and the cost of goods sold. In addition, she must consider the selling, general, and administrative (SG&A) expenses. These expenses are more difficult to estimate, but the standard industry practice is to use 18% of the net revenues as the nominal percentage value for these expenses. Therefore, Marissa's profit *before taxes* is the gross profit minus the SG&A value. To calculate taxes, Marissa multiplies her profits before taxes times the tax rate, currently 30%. If her company is operating at a loss, however, no taxes would have to be paid. Finally, Marissa's net (or after tax) profit is simply the difference between the profit before taxes and the actual taxes paid.

To determine the numbers for 1999 through 2001, Marissa assumes that gross revenues, labor costs, material costs, and overhead costs will increase over the years. Although the rates of increase for these items are difficult to estimate, Marissa figures that gross revenues will increase by 9% per year, labor costs will increase by 4% per year, material costs will increase by 6% per year, and overhead costs will increase by 3% per year. She figures that the tax rate will not change from the 30% mark, and she assumes that the SG&A value will remain at 18%.

The basic layout of the spreadsheet that Marissa creates is shown in the following figure (and in the file FIG12-25.xls on your data disk). (Ignore the Competitive Assumptions section for now; we'll consider it later.) Construct the spreadsheet and determine the values for the years 1998 through 2001, then determine the totals for the four years.

Marissa not only wants to determine her net profits for 1998 through 2001, she also must justify her decisions to the company's Board of Trustees. Should she even consider entering this market, from a financial point of view? One way to answer this question is to find the net present value (NPV) of the net profits for 1998 through

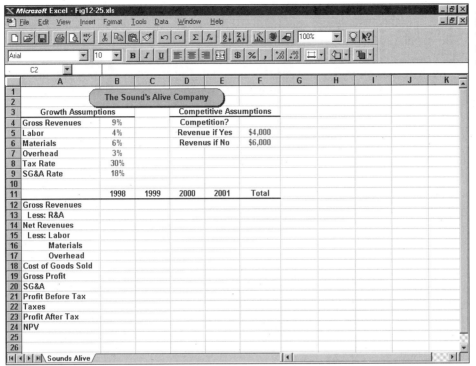

Figure 12.25
Spreadsheet template for the Sound's Alive case.

2001. Use Excel's NPV capability to find the NPV, at the current interest rate of 5%, of the profit values for 1998 through 2001.

To avoid large values in the spreadsheet, enter all dollar calculations in thousands. For example, enter labor costs as 995.10 and overhead costs as 1536.12.

Phase Two: Bringing Competition Into the Model

With her spreadsheet complete, Marissa is confident that entering the home theater speaker market would be lucrative for Sound's Alive. However, she has not considered one factor in her calculations—competition. The current market leader and company she is most concerned about is the Bose Corporation. Bose pioneered the concept of a satellite speaker system, and its AMT series is very successful. Marissa is concerned that Bose will enter the home market, cutting into her gross revenues. If Bose does enter the market, Marissa believes that Sound's Alive would still make money; however, she would have to revise her gross revenues estimate from $6 million to $4 million for 1998.

To account for the competition factor, Marissa revises her spreadsheet by adding a Competition Assumptions section. Cell F4 will contain either a 0 (no competition) or a 1 (if Bose enters the market). Cells F5 and F6 provide the gross revenue estimates (in thousands of dollars) for the two possibilities. Modify your spreadsheet to take these options into account. Use the IF( ) function for the gross revenues for 1998 (cell B12). If Bose does enter the market, not only would Marissa's gross revenues be lower, but the labor, materials, and overhead costs would also be lower because Sound's Alive would be making and selling fewer speakers. Marissa thinks that if Bose enters the market, her 1998 labor costs would be $859,170, 1998 material costs would be

$702,950, and 1998 overhead costs would be $1,288,750. She believes that her growth rate assumptions would stay the same whether or not Bose enters the market. Add these possible values to your spreadsheet using the IF( ) function in the appropriate cells.

Look at the net profits for 1998 through 2001. In particular, examine the NPV for the two scenarios: Bose does or does not enter the home theater speaker market.

Phase Three: Bringing Uncertainty Into the Model

Jim Allison, the chief of operations at Sound's Alive and a quantitative methods specialist, plays a key role in providing Marissa with estimates for the various revenues and costs. He is uneasy about the basic estimates for the growth rates. For example, although market research indicates that a 9% gross revenue increase per year is reasonable, Jim knows that if this value is 7%, for example, the profit values and the NPV would be quite different. Even more troublesome is a potential tax increase, which would hit Sound's Alive hard. Jim believes that the tax rate could vary around the expected 30% figure. Finally, Jim is uncomfortable with the industry's standard estimate of 18% for the SG&A rate. Jim thinks that this value could be higher or even lower.

The Sound's Alive problem is too complicated for solving with what-if analysis because seven assumed values could change: the growth rates for gross revenues, labor, materials, overhead costs, tax rate, SG&A percent, and whether or not Bose enters the market. Jim believes that a Monte Carlo simulation would be a better approach. Jim thinks that the behavior of these variables can be modeled as follows:

Gross Revenues (%): normally distributed, mean = 9.9, std dev = 1.4
Labor Growth (%): normally distributed, mean = 3.45, std dev = 1.0

Materials (%)	Probability
4	0.10
5	0.15
6	0.15
7	0.25
8	0.25
9	0.10

Overhead (%)	Probability
2	0.20
3	0.35
4	0.25
5	0.20

Tax Rate (%)	Probability
30	0.15
32	0.30
34	0.30
36	0.25

SG&A (%)	Probability
15	0.05
16	0.10
17	0.20
18	0.25
19	0.20
20	0.20

Finally, Jim and Marissa agree that there is a 50/50 chance that Bose will enter the market.

Use simulation to analyze the Sound's Alive problem. Based on your results, what is the expected net profit for the years 1998 through 2001, and what is the expected NPV for this business venture?

The Board of Trustees told Marissa that the stockholders would feel comfortable with this business venture if its NPV is at least $5 million. What are the chances that Sound's Alive home theater venture will result in an NPV of $5 million or more?

CASE 12.2   THE FOXRIDGE INVESTMENT GROUP

Inspired by a case written by MBA students Fred Hirsch and Ray Rogers for Professor Larry Weatherford at the University of Wyoming.

The Foxridge Investment Group buys and sells rental income properties in Southwest Virginia. Bill Hunter, president of Foxridge, has asked for your assistance in analyzing a small apartment building the group is interested in purchasing.

The property in question is a small two-story structure with three rental units on each floor. The purchase price of the property is $170,000, representing $30,000 in land value and $140,000 in buildings and improvements. Foxridge will depreciate the buildings and improvements value on a straight-line basis over 27.5 years. The Foxridge Group will make a down payment of $40,000 to acquire the property and finance the remainder of the purchase price over 20 years with an 11% fixed-rate loan with payments due annually. Figure 12.26 (and the file FIG12-26.xls on your data disk) summarizes this and other pertinent information.

If all units are fully occupied, Mr. Hunter expects the property to generate rental income of $35,000 in the first year and expects to increase the rent at the rate of inflation (currently 4%). Because vacancies occur and some residents may not always be able to pay their rent, Mr. Hunter factors in a 3% vacancy & collection (V&C) allowance against rental income. Operating expenses are expected to be approximately 45% of rental income. The group's marginal tax rate is 28%.

If the group decides to purchase this property, their plan is to hold it for five years and then sell it to another investor. Presently, property values in this area are increasing at a rate of approximately 2.5% per year. The group will have to pay a sales commission of 5% of the gross selling price when they sell the property.

Figure 12.27 shows a spreadsheet model Mr. Hunter developed to analyze this problem. This model first uses the data and assumptions given in Figure 12.26 to generate the expected net cash flows in each of the next five years. It then provides a final summary of the proceeds expected from selling the property at the end of five years. The total net present value (NPV) of the project is then calculated in cell I18 using the discount rate of 12% in cell C24 of Figure 12.26. Thus, after discounting all the

Figure 12.26
Assumptions for
the Foxridge
Investment
Group case.

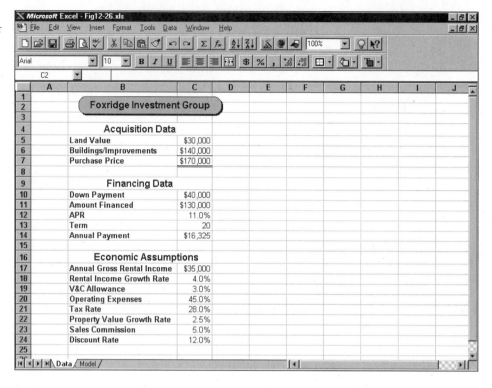

Figure 12.27
Cash flow and
financial
summary for the
Foxridge
Investment
Group case.

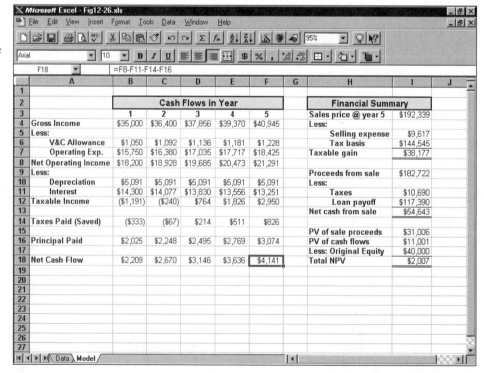

future cash flows associated with this investment by 12% per year, the investment still generates an NPV of $2,007.

While the group has been using this type of analysis for many years to make investment decisions, one of Mr. Hunter's investment partners recently read an article in *The Wall Street Journal* about risk analysis and simulation using spreadsheets. As a result, the partner realizes there is quite a bit of uncertainty associated with many of the economic assumptions shown in Figure 12.26. After explaining the potential problem to Mr. Hunter, the two have decided to apply simulation to this model before making a decision. Since neither of them know how to do simulation, they have asked for your assistance.

To model the uncertainty in this decision problem, Mr. Hunter and his partner have decided that the growth in rental income from one year to the next could vary uniformly from 2% to 6% years 2 through 5. Similarly, they believe the V&C allowance in any year could be as low as 1% in any year and as high as 5%, with 3% being the most likely outcome. They think the operating expenses in each year should be normally distributed with a mean of 45% and standard deviation of 2% but should never be less than 40% and never greater than 50% of gross income. Finally, they believe the property value growth rate could be as small as 1% or as large as 5%, with 2.5% being the most likely outcome.

1. Revise the spreadsheets shown in Figures 12.26 and 12.27 to reflect the uncertainty outlined above.
2. Construct a 95% confidence interval for the average total NPV the Foxridge Investment Group can expect if they undertake this project. (Use 500 replications.) Interpret this confidence interval.
3. Based on your analysis, what is the probability of this project generating a positive total NPV if the group uses a 12% discount rate?
4. Suppose the investors are willing to buy the property if the expected total NPV is greater then zero. Based on your analysis, should they buy this property?
5. Assume the investors decide to increase the discount rate to 14% and repeat questions 2, 3, and 4.

REFERENCES

Banks, J. and J. Carson. *Discrete-Event Simulation*. Englewood Cliffs, NJ: Prentice Hall, 1984.

Hamzawi, S. "Management and Planning of Airport Gate Capacity: A Microcomputer-Based Gate Assignment Simulation Model." *Transportation Planning and Technology*, vol. 11, 1986.

Kaplan, A. and S. Frazza. "Empirical Inventory Simulation: A Case Study." *Decision Sciences*, vol. 14, January 1983.

Khoshnevis, B. *Discrete Systems Simulation*. New York: McGraw-Hill, 1994.

Law, A. and W. Kelton. *Simulation Modeling and Analysis*. New York: McGraw-Hill, 1990.

Marcus, A. "The Magellan Fund and Market Efficiency." *Journal of Portfolio Management*, Fall 1990.

Russell, R. and R. Hickle. "Simulation of a CD Portfolio." *Interfaces*, vol. 16, no. 3, 1986.

Vollman, T., W. Berry and C. Whybark. *Manufacturing Planning and Control Systems*. Homewood, IL: Irwin, 1987.

Watson, H. *Computer Simulation in Business*. New York: Wiley, 1981.

CHAPTER 13

Simulation Using @Risk

Chapter 1 discussed how the calculations in a spreadsheet can be viewed as a mathematical model that defines a functional relationship between various input variables (or independent variables) and one or more bottom-line performance measures (or dependent variables). The following equation expresses this relationship:

$$Y = f(X_1, X_2, ..., X_k)$$

In many spreadsheets, the values of various input cells are determined by the person using the spreadsheet. These input cells correspond to the independent variables $X_1, X_2, ..., X_k$ in the above equation. Various formulas (represented by $f(\cdot)$ above) are entered in other cells of the spreadsheet to transform the values of the input cells into some bottom-line output (denoted by Y above). Simulation is a technique that is helpful in analyzing models where the value to be assumed by one or more independent variables is uncertain.

Chapter 12 described how to perform simulation using the inherent capabilities of Excel. This chapter discusses how to perform the same type of analysis using a popular commercial spreadsheet add-in called @RISK (pronounced "at risk"). If you do not have access to a copy of @Risk, you will not be able to do the things described in this chapter. You can find information about @Risk on the World Wide Web at http://www.palisade.com.

13.1 RANDOM VARIABLES AND RISK

In order to compute a value for the bottom-line performance measure of a spreadsheet model, each input cell must be assigned a specific value so that all the related calculations can be performed. However, some uncertainty often exists regarding the value that should be assumed by one or more independent variables (or input cells) in the spreadsheet. This is particularly true in spreadsheet models that represent future conditions. A **random variable** is any variable whose value cannot be predicted or set with certainty. Thus, many input variables in a spreadsheet model represent random variables whose actual values cannot be predicted with certainty.

For example, projections of the cost of raw materials, future interest rates, future numbers of employees, and expected product demand are random variables because their true values are unknown and will be determined in the future. If we cannot say with certainty what value one or more input variables in a model will assume, we also cannot say with certainty what value the dependent variable will assume. This uncertainty associated with the value of the dependent variable introduces an element of risk to the decision-making problem. Specifically, if the dependent variable represents some bottom-line performance measure that managers use to make decisions, and its value is uncertain, any decisions made on the basis of this value are based on uncertain (or incomplete) information. When such a decision is made, some chance exists that the decision will not produce the intended results. This chance, or uncertainty, represents an element of **risk** in the decision-making problem.

The term "risk" also implies the *potential* for loss. The fact that a decision's outcome is uncertain does not mean that the decision is particularly risky. For example, whenever we put money into a soft drink machine, there is a chance that the machine will take our money and not deliver the product. However, most of us would not consider this risk to be particularly great. From past experience, we know that the chance of not receiving the product is small. But even if the machine takes our money and does not deliver the product, most of us would not consider this to be a tremendous loss. Thus, the amount of risk involved in a given decision-making situation is a function of the uncertainty in the outcome of the decision and the magnitude of the potential loss. A proper assessment of the risk present in a decision-making situation should address both of these issues, as the examples in this chapter will demonstrate.

13.2   WHY ANALYZE RISK?

Many spreadsheets built by business people contain *estimated* values for the uncertain input variables in their models. If a manager cannot say with certainty what value a particular cell in a spreadsheet will assume, this cell most likely represents a random variable. Ordinarily, the manager will attempt to make an informed guess about the values such cells will assume. The manager hopes that inserting the expected, or most likely, values for all the uncertain cells in a spreadsheet will provide the most likely value for the cell containing the bottom-line performance measure (Y). The problem with this type of analysis is that it tells the decision maker nothing about the variability of the performance measure.

For example, in analyzing a particular investment opportunity, we might determine that the expected return on a $1,000 investment is $10,000 within two years. But how much variability exists in the possible outcomes? If all the potential outcomes are scattered closely around $10,000 (say from $9,000 to $11,000), then the investment opportunity might still be attractive. If, on the other hand, the potential outcomes are scattered widely around $10,000 (say from −$30,000 up to +$50,000), then the investment opportunity might be unattractive. Although these two scenarios might have the same expected or average value, the risks involved are quite different. Thus, even if we can determine the expected outcome of a decision using a spreadsheet, it is just as important, if not more so, to consider the risk involved in the decision.

13.3   METHODS OF RISK ANALYSIS

Several techniques are available to help managers analyze risk. Three of the most common are best-case/worst-case analysis, what-if analysis, and simulation. Of these methods, simulation is the most powerful and, therefore, is the technique that we'll focus on in this chapter. Although the other techniques might not be completely effective in risk analysis, they are probably used more often than simulation by most managers in business today. This is largely due to the fact that most managers are unaware of the spreadsheet's ability to perform simulation and of the benefits provided by this technique. So before discussing simulation, let's first briefly look at the other methods of risk analysis to understand their strengths and weaknesses.

13.3.1   Best-Case/Worst-Case Analysis

If we don't know what value a particular cell in a spreadsheet will assume, we could enter a number that we think is the most likely value for the uncertain cell. If we enter such numbers for all the uncertain cells in the spreadsheet, we can easily calculate the most likely value of the bottom-line performance measure. This is also called the **base-case** scenario. However, this scenario gives us no information about how far away the actual outcome might be from this expected, or most likely, value.

One simple solution to this problem is to calculate the value of the bottom-line performance measure using the **best-case,** or most optimistic, and **worst-case,** or most pessimistic, values for the uncertain input cells. These additional scenarios show the range of possible values that might be assumed by the bottom-line performance measure. As indicated in the earlier example about the $1,000 investment, knowing the range of possible outcomes is very helpful in assessing the risk involved in different alternatives. However, simply knowing the best-case and worst-case outcomes tells us nothing about the distribution of possible values within this range, nor does it tell us the probability of either scenario occurring.

Figure 13.1 displays several probability distributions that might be associated with the value of a bottom-line performance measure within a given range. Each of these distributions describes variables that have identical ranges and similar average values. But each distribution is very different in terms of the risk it represents to the decision maker. The appeal of best-case/worst-case analysis is that it is easy to do. Its weakness is that it tells us nothing about the shape of the distribution associated with the bottom-line performance measure. As we'll see later, knowing the shape of the distribution of the bottom-line performance measure can be critically important in helping us answer a number of managerial questions.

13.3.2   What-If Analysis

Prior to the introduction of electronic spreadsheets in the early 1980s, the use of best-case/worst-case analysis was often the only feasible way for a manager to analyze the risk associated with a decision. This process was extremely time consuming, error prone, and tedious, using only a piece of paper, pencil, and calculator to recalculate the performance measure of a model using different values for the uncertain inputs. The arrival of personal computers and electronic spreadsheets made it much easier for a manager to play out a large number of scenarios in addition to the best and worst cases—which is the essence of what-if analysis.

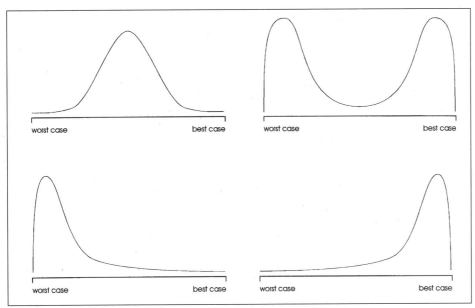

Figure 13.1
Possible distributions of performance measure values within a given range.

In **what-if analysis,** a manager changes the values of the uncertain input variables to see what happens to the bottom-line performance measure. By making a series of such changes, a manager can gain some insight into how sensitive the performance measure is to changes to the input variables. Although many managers perform this type of manual what-if analysis, it has three major flaws.

First, if the values selected for the independent variables are based only on the manager's judgment, the resulting sample values of the performance measure are likely to be biased. That is, if several uncertain variables can each assume some range of values, it would be difficult to ensure that the manager tests a fair, or representative, sample of all possible combinations of these values. To select values for the uncertain variables that correctly reflect their random variations, the values must be randomly selected from a distribution, or pool, of values that reflects the appropriate range of possible values, as well as the appropriate relative frequencies of these variables.

Second, hundreds or thousands of what-if scenarios might be required to create a valid representation of the underlying variability in the bottom-line performance measure. No one would want to perform these scenarios manually nor would anyone be able to make sense of the resulting stream of numbers that would flash by on the screen.

The third problem with what-if analysis is that the insight the manager might gain from playing out various scenarios is of little value when recommending a decision to top management. What-if analysis simply does not supply the manager with the tangible evidence (facts and figures) needed to justify why a given decision was made or recommended. Additionally, what-if analysis does not address the problem identified in our earlier discussion of best-case/worst-case analysis—it does not allow us to estimate the distribution of the performance measure in a formal enough manner. Thus, what-if analysis is a step in the right direction, but it is not quite a large enough step to allow managers to analyze risk effectively in the decisions they face.

13.3.3   Simulation

Simulation is a technique that measures and describes various characteristics of the bottom-line performance measure of a model when one or more values for the independent variables are uncertain. If any independent variables in a model are random variables, the dependent variable (Y) also represents a random variable. The objective in simulation is to describe the distribution and characteristics of the possible values of the bottom-line performance measure Y, given the possible values and behavior of the independent variables $X_1, X_2, ..., X_k$.

The idea behind simulation is similar to the notion of playing out many what-if scenarios. The difference is that the process of assigning values to the cells in the spreadsheet that represent random variables is automated so that: (1) the values are assigned in a nonbiased way, and (2) the spreadsheet user is relieved of the burden of determining these values. With simulation we repeatedly and randomly generate sample values for each uncertain input variable ($X_1, X_2, ..., X_k$) in our model and then compute the resulting value of our bottom-line performance measure (Y). We can then use the sample values of Y to estimate the true distribution and other characteristics of the performance measure Y. For example, we can use the sample observations to construct a frequency distribution of the performance measure, to estimate the range of values over which the performance measure might vary, to estimate its mean and variance, and to estimate the probability that the actual value of the performance measure will be greater than (or less than) a particular value. All these measures provide greater insight into the risk associated with a given decision than a single value calculated based on the expected values for the uncertain independent variables.

13.4   A CORPORATE HEALTH INSURANCE EXAMPLE

The following example demonstrates the mechanics of preparing a spreadsheet model for risk analysis using simulation. The example presents a fairly simple model to illustrate the process and give a sense of the amount of effort involved. However, the process for performing simulation is basically the same regardless of the size of the model.

Lisa Pon has just been hired as an analyst in the corporate planning department of Hungry Dawg Restaurants. Her first assignment is to determine how much money the company needs to accrue in the coming year to pay for its employees' health insurance claims. Hungry Dawg is a large, growing chain of restaurants that specializes in traditional southern foods. The company has become large enough that it no longer buys insurance from a private insurance company. The company is now self-insured, meaning that it pays health insurance claims with its own money (although it contracts with an outside company to handle the administrative details of processing claims and writing checks).

The money the company uses to pay claims comes from two sources: employee contributions (or premiums deducted from employees' paychecks) and company funds (the company must pay whatever costs are not covered by employee contributions). Each employee covered by the health plan contributes $125 per month. However, the number of employees covered by the plan changes from month to month as employees are hired and fired, quit, or simply add or drop health insurance coverage. A total of 18,533 employees were covered by the plan last month. The average monthly health claim per covered employee was $250 last month.

An example of how most analysts would model this problem is shown in Figure 13.2 (and in the file FIG13-2.xls on your data disk). The spreadsheet begins with a listing of the initial conditions and assumptions for the problem. For example, cell D5 indicates that 18,533 employees are currently covered by the health plan, and cell D6 indicates that the average monthly claim per covered employee is $250. The average monthly contribution per employee is $125, as shown in cell D7. The values in cells D5 and D6 are unlikely to stay the same for the entire year. Thus, we need to make some assumptions about the rate at which these values are likely to increase during the year. For example, we might assume that the number of covered employees will increase by about 2% per month, and that the average claim per employee will increase at a rate of 1% per month. These assumptions are reflected in cells F5 and F6. The average contribution per employee is assumed to be constant over the coming year.

Using the assumed rate of increase in the number of covered employees (cell F5), we can create formulas for cells B11 through B22 that cause the number of covered employees to increase by the assumed amount each month. (The details of these formulas are covered later.) The expected monthly employee contributions shown in column C are calculated as $125 times the number of employees in each month. We can use the assumed rate of increase in average monthly claims (cell F6) to create formulas for cells D11 through D22 that cause the average claim per employee to increase at the assumed rate. The total claims for each month (shown in column E)

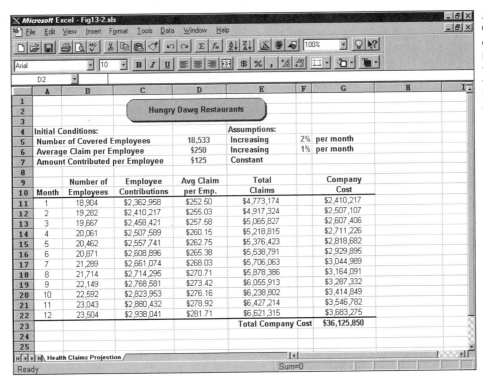

Figure 13.2
Original corporate health insurance model with expected values for uncertain variables.

are calculated as the average claim figures in column D times the number of employees for each month in column B. Because the company must pay for any claims that are not covered by the employee contributions, the company cost figures in column G are calculated as the total claims minus the employee contributions (column E minus column C). Finally, cell G23 sums the company cost figures listed in column G and shows that the company can expect to contribute $36,125,850 of its revenues toward paying the health insurance claims of its employees in the coming year.

13.4.1   A Critique of the Base-Case Model

Now let's consider the model we just described. The example model assumes that the number of covered employees will increase by *exactly* 2% each month and that the average claim per covered employee will increase by *exactly* 1% each month. Although these values might be reasonable approximations of what might happen, they are unlikely to reflect exactly what will happen. In fact, the number of employees covered by the health plan each month is likely to vary randomly around the average increase per month—that is, the number might decrease in some months and increase by more than 2% in others. Similarly, the average claim per covered employee might be lower than expected in certain months and higher than expected in others.

Both of these figures are likely to exhibit some uncertainty or random behavior, even if they do move in the general upward direction assumed throughout the year. So we cannot say with certainty that the total cost figure of $36,125,850 is exactly what the company will have to contribute toward health claims in the coming year. It is simply a prediction of what might happen. The actual outcome could be smaller or larger than this estimate. Using the original model, we have no idea how much larger or smaller the actual result could be—nor do we have any idea of how the actual values are distributed around this estimate. We do not know if there is a 10%, 50%, or 90% chance of the actual total costs exceeding this estimate. To determine the variability or risk inherent in the bottom-line performance measure of total company costs, we'll apply the technique of simulation to our model.

13.5   SPREADSHEET SIMULATION USING @RISK

To perform simulation in a spreadsheet, we must first place a **random number generator** (RNG) formula in each cell that represents a random, or uncertain, independent variable. Each RNG provides a sample observation from an appropriate distribution that represents the range and frequency of possible values for the variable. Once the RNGs are in place, new sample values are provided automatically each time the spreadsheet is recalculated. We can recalculate the spreadsheet n times, where n is the desired number of replications or scenarios, and the value of the bottom-line performance measure will be stored after each replication. We can analyze these stored observations to gain insights into the behavior and characteristics of the performance measure.

The process of simulation involves a lot of work but, fortunately, the spreadsheet can do most of the work for us fairly easily. In particular, the spreadsheet add-in package @RISK is designed specifically to make spreadsheet simulation a simple process. The @RISK software provides the following capabilities, which are not otherwise available while working in Excel: additional functions that are helpful in generating the random numbers needed in simulation; additional commands that are helpful in setting up and running the simulation; and graphical and statistical summaries of the simulation data. As we'll see, these capabilities make simulation a relatively easy technique to apply in spreadsheets.

13.5.1 Starting @RISK

If you are running @RISK from a local area network (LAN) or in a computer lab, your instructor or LAN coordinator should give you directions on how to access this software. If you are running @RISK on your own computer, you can access @RISK by locating and double-clicking the @RISK icon shown in Figure 13.3. This loads the memory resident portion of @RISK and automatically takes you into Excel, where you see the @RISK toolbar shown in Figure 13.4. Shortly, we'll discuss the purpose of the buttons on this toolbar.

13.6 RANDOM NUMBER GENERATORS

As mentioned earlier, the first step in spreadsheet simulation is to place an RNG formula in each cell that contains an uncertain value. Each of these formulas will generate (or return) a number that represents a randomly selected value from a distribution,

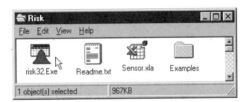

Figure 13.3
The @RISK program icon.

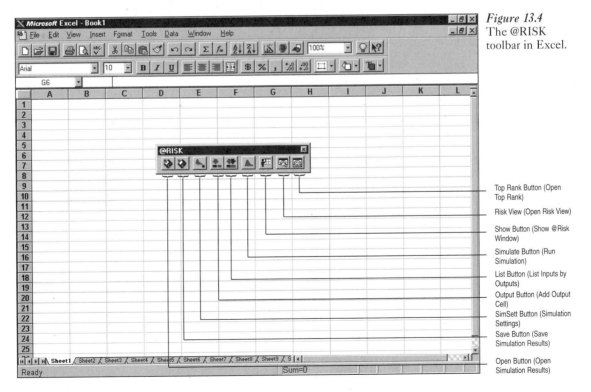

Figure 13.4
The @RISK toolbar in Excel.

Top Rank Button (Open Top Rank)

Risk View (Open Risk View)

Show Button (Show @Risk Window)

Simulate Button (Run Simulation)

List Button (List Inputs by Outputs)

Output Button (Add Output Cell)

SimSett Button (Simulation Settings)

Save Button (Save Simulation Results)

Open Button (Open Simulation Results)

or pool, of values. The distributions that these samples are taken from should be representative of the underlying pool of values expected to occur in each uncertain cell.

@RISK provides several functions that can be used to create the RNGs required for simulating a model. Figure 13.5 describes some of the RNGs that will be most useful to you.

Figure 13.5
Commonly used RNGs supplied with @RISK.

Distribution	RNG Function	Description
Binomial	RiskBinomial(n,p)	Returns the number of "successes" in a sample of size n where each trial has a probability p of "success."
Discrete	RiskDiscrete($\{x_1,x_2,...x_n\}$, $\{p_1,p_2,...p_n\}$)	Returns one of the n values represented by the x_i. The value x_i occurs with probability p_i.
Discrete	RiskDuniform($\{x_1,x_2,...,x_n\}$)	Returns one of the n values represented by the x_i. Each value x_i is equally likely to occur.
Poisson	RiskPoisson(λ)	Returns a random number of events occurring per some unit of measure (for example, arrivals per hour, defects per yard, and so on). The parameter λ represents the average number of events occurring per unit of measure.
Chi-square	RiskChisq(λ)	Returns a value from a chi-square distribution with mean λ.
Continuous	RiskUniform(min,max)	Returns a value in the range from a minimum (*min*) to a maximum (*max*). Each value in this range is equally likely to occur.
Exponential	RiskExpon(λ)	Returns a value from an exponential distribution with mean λ. Often used to model the time between events or the lifetime of a device with a constant probability of failure.
Normal	RiskNormal(μ,σ)	Returns a value from a normal distribution with mean μ and standard deviation σ.
Truncated	RiskTnormal(μ,σ,min,max)	Same as RiskNormal except the distribution is truncated to the range specified by a minimum (*min*) and a maximum (*max*).
Triangular	RiskTriang(min,most likely,max)	Returns a value from a triangular distribution covering the range specified by a minimum (*min*) and a maximum (*max*). The shape of the distribution is then determined by the size of the most likely value relative to *min* and *max*.

The functions listed in Figure 13.5 allow us to generate a variety of random numbers easily. For example, if we think that the behavior of an uncertain cell could be modeled as a normally distributed random variable with a mean of 125 and standard deviation of 10, then according to Figure 13.5 we could enter the formula =RiskNormal(125,10) in this cell. (The arguments in this function could also be formulas and could refer to other cells in the spreadsheet.) Using appropriate settings in @RISK (to be described shortly), we can instruct the spreadsheet to return a randomly selected value from a normal distribution with a mean of 125 and standard deviation of 10 for this cell whenever the spreadsheet is recalculated.

Similarly, a cell in our spreadsheet might have a 30% chance of assuming the value 10, a 50% chance of assuming the value 20, and a 20% chance of assuming the value 30. As noted in Figure 13.5, we could use the formula =RiskDiscrete({10,20,30},{0.3,0.5,0.2}) to model this random behavior. If we recalculated the spreadsheet many times, this formula would return the value 10 approximately 30% of the time, the value 20 approximately 50% of the time, and the value 30 approximately 20% of the time.

The arguments, or parameters, required by the RNG functions allow us to generate random numbers from distributions with a wide variety of shapes. Figures 13.6 and 13.7 illustrate some examples of the distributions. Additional information about these and other RNGs provided by @RISK is available in Appendix A of the @RISK manual and in the on-line Help facility in @RISK.

13.6.1 *Discrete vs. Continuous Random Variables*

An important distinction exists between the graphs in Figures 13.6 and 13.7. In particular, the RNGs depicted in Figure 13.6 generate *discrete* outcomes, whereas those

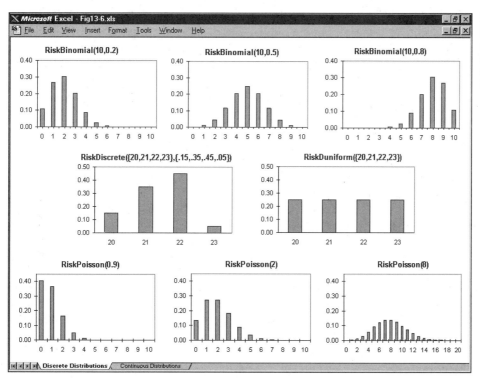

Figure 13.6
Examples of distributions associated with selected discrete RNGs.

Figure 13.7
Examples of
distributions
associated with
selected
continuous
RNGs.

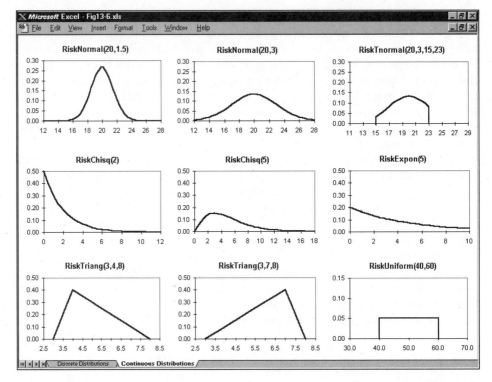

Figure 13.7
Examples of
distributions
associated with
selected
continuous
RNGs.

represented in Figure 13.7 generate *continuous* outcomes. That is, the first four RNGs listed in Figure 13.5 can return only a distinct set of individual values, whereas the other RNGs can return any value from an infinite set of values. The distinction between discrete and continuous random variables is very important.

For example, the number of defective tires on a new car is a discrete random variable because it can assume only one of five distinct values: 0, 1, 2, 3, or 4. On the other hand, the amount of fuel in a new car is a continuous random variable because it can assume any value between 0 and the maximum capacity of the fuel tank. Thus, when selecting an RNG for an uncertain variable in a model, it is important to consider whether the variable can assume discrete or continuous values.

13.7   PREPARING THE MODEL FOR SIMULATION

To apply simulation to the model for Hungry Dawg Restaurants described earlier, we must first select appropriate RNGs for the uncertain variables in the model. If available, historical data on the uncertain variables could be analyzed to determine appropriate RNGs for these variables. If past data are not available, or if we have some reason to expect the future behavior of a variable to be significantly different from the past, then we must use judgment in selecting appropriate RNGs to model the random behavior of the uncertain variables.

For our example problem, let's assume that by analyzing historical data, we determined that the change in the number of covered employees from one month to the next is expected to vary uniformly between a 3% decrease and a 7% increase. (Note that this should cause the average change in the number of employees to be a 2%

increase, because 0.02 is the midpoint between –0.03 and +0.07.) Further, assume that we can model the average monthly claim per covered employee as a normally distributed random variable with the mean (μ) increasing by 1% per month and a standard deviation (σ) of approximately 3%. (Note that this will cause the *average* increase in claims per covered employee from one month to the next to be approximately 1%.) These assumptions are reflected in cells F5 through H6 at the top of Figure 13.8 (and in the file FIG13-8.xls on your data disk).

To implement the formula to generate a random number of employees covered by the health plan, we'll use the RiskUniform( ) function described in Figure 13.5. Because the change in the number of employees from one month to the next can vary between a 3% decrease and a 7% increase, the number of employees in the current month is equal to the number of employees in the previous month multiplied by the sum of 1 plus the percentage change. Applying this logic, we obtain the following equation for the number of employees in a given month:

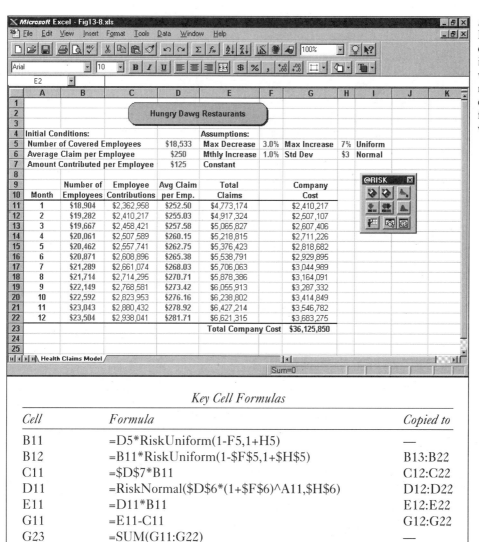

Figure 13.8
Modified corporate health insurance model with RNGs replacing expected values for uncertain variables.

Key Cell Formulas

Cell	Formula	Copied to
B11	=D5*RiskUniform(1-F5,1+H5)	—
B12	=B11*RiskUniform(1-$F$5,1+$H$5)	B13:B22
C11	=$D$7*B11	C12:C22
D11	=RiskNormal($D$6*(1+$F$6)^A11,$H$6)	D12:D22
E11	=D11*B11	E12:E22
G11	=E11-C11	G12:G22
G23	=SUM(G11:G22)	—

$$\text{Number of employees in current month} = \text{Number of employees in previous month} \times \text{RiskUniform}(0.97, 1.07)$$

If the RiskUniform( ) function returns the value 0.97, this formula causes the number of employees in the current month to equal 97% of the number in the previous month (a 3% decrease). Alternatively, if the RiskUniform( ) function returns the value 1.07, this formula causes the number of employees in the current month to equal 107% of the number in the previous month (a 7% increase). All the values between these two extremes (between 0.97 and 1.07) are also possible and equally likely to occur. The following formulas were used to create formulas that randomly generate the number of employees in each month in Figure 13.8:

Formula for cell B11:   =D5*RiskUniform(1−F5,1+H5)

Formula for cell B12:   =B11*RiskUniform(1−$F$5,1+$H$5)
(Copy to B13 through B22.)

Note that the terms "1−$F$5" and "1+$H$5" in the above formulas generate the values 0.97 and 1.07, respectively.

To implement the formula to generate the average claims per covered employee in each month, we'll use the RiskNormal( ) function described in Figure 13.5. This formula requires that we supply the value of the mean (μ) and standard deviation (σ) of the distribution from which we want to sample. The assumed $3 standard deviation ($\sigma$) for the average monthly claim, shown in cell H6 in Figure 13.8, is constant from month to month. Thus, the only remaining problem is to figure out the proper mean value (μ) for each month.

In this case, the mean for any given month should be 1% larger than the mean in the previous month. For example, the mean for month 1 is:

$$\text{Mean in month 1} = (\text{original mean}) \times 1.01$$

and the mean for month 2 is:

$$\text{Mean in month 2} = (\text{mean in month 1}) \times 1.01$$

If we substitute the previous definition of the mean in month 1 into the previous equation, we obtain,

$$\text{Mean in month 2} = (\text{original mean}) \times (1.01)^2$$

Similarly, the mean in month 3 is:

$$\text{Mean in month 3} = (\text{mean in month 2}) \times 1.01 = (\text{original mean}) \times (1.01)^3$$

So in general, the mean (μ) for month n is:

$$\text{Mean in month } n = (\text{original mean}) \times (1.01)^n$$

Thus, to generate the average claim per covered employee in each month, we use the following formula:

Formula for cell D11:   =RiskNormal($D$6*(1+$F$6)^A11,$H$6)
(Copy to D12 through D22.)

The term "$D$6*(1+$F$6)^A11" in this formula implements the general definition of the mean (μ) in month n.

13.7.1 Expected Values vs. Sample Values

If we click the SimSett button on the @RISK toolbar shown in Figure 13.8, the Simulation Settings dialog box shown in Figure 13.9 appears.

The Standard Recalc option on the Sampling card in Figure 13.9 has three radio button selections: Expected Value, Monte Carlo, and True EV. This option determines whether the RNGs return random samples or expected values.

Every RNG has an average, or expected, value associated with its probability distribution. @RISK provides two options—Expected Value and True EV—that return the expected value of each RNG rather than random sample values. The only difference between these two options is that the Expected Value option (the default) rounds the expected value of a discrete RNG to its nearest integer value, whereas the True EV option does not. These options are helpful if we want to see what value the bottom-line performance measure would assume if all the uncertain cells in the spreadsheet assumed their expected values. However, to have the RNGs in our spreadsheet return random sample values, we must select the Monte Carlo option.

After selecting the Monte Carlo option, each time we press the recalculate key (the function key [F9]), the RNGs automatically select new values for all the cells in the spreadsheet that represent uncertain (or random) variables. Similarly, with each recalculation, a new value for the bottom-line performance measure (total company cost) appears in cell G23. Thus, by pressing the recalculate key several times, we can observe representative values of the company's total cost for health claims. This also helps to verify that we implemented the RNGs correctly and that they are generating appropriate values for each uncertain cell.

13.8 RUNNING THE SIMULATION

The next step in performing the simulation involves recalculating the spreadsheet several hundred or several thousand times and recording the resulting values generated for the output cell, or bottom-line performance measure. Fortunately, @RISK can do this for us if we indicate how many times we want it to recalculate (or replicate) the model and which cell(s) in the spreadsheet we want to track.

13.8.1 Selecting the Output Cells to Track

We can use the +Output button on the @RISK toolbar (see Figure 13.4) to indicate the output cell (or cells) that we want @RISK to track during the simulation. In the current example, cell G23 represents the output cell we want @RISK to track. To indicate this:

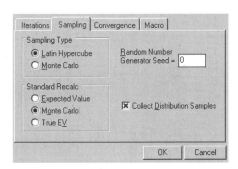

Figure 13.9
Sampling options in the Simulation Settings dialog box.

1. Click cell G23.
2. Click the +Output button on the @RISK toolbar.

In some simulations, we might want to analyze several performance measures. In such a case, we can follow the preceding procedure repeatedly to select additional output cells to track.

13.8.2   Selecting the Number of Iterations

Figure 13.10 shows the Iterations card in the Simulation Settings dialog box for @RISK. The "# Iterations =" option in this dialog box allows us to specify the number of iterations (or replications) to include in our simulation. Thus, to indicate that we want to perform 300 replications of our model:

1. Click the SimSett button to display the Simulation Settings dialog box.
2. Type 300 in the box labeled "# Iterations =".
3. Click OK.

13.8.3   Determining the Sample Size

You might wonder why we selected 300 replications. Why not 200, or 1,000? Unfortunately, there is no easy answer to this question. Remember that the goal in simulation is to estimate various characteristics about the bottom-line performance measure(s) under consideration. For example, we might want to estimate the mean value of the performance measure and the shape of its probability distribution. However, a different value of the bottom-line performance measure occurs each time we manually recalculate the model in Figure 13.8. Thus, there is an infinite number of possibilities—or an **infinite population**—of total company cost values associated with this model.

We cannot analyze all of these infinite possibilities. But by taking a large enough sample from this infinite population, we can make reasonably accurate estimates about the characteristics of the underlying infinite population of values. The larger the sample we take (that is, the more replications we do), the more accurate our final results will be. But, performing many replications takes time, so we must make a trade-off in terms of estimation accuracy versus convenience. Thus, there is no simple answer to the question of how many replications to perform, but, as a bare minimum you should always perform at least 100 replications, and more as time permits or accuracy demands.

Figure 13.10
Iterations options in the Simulation Settings dialog box.

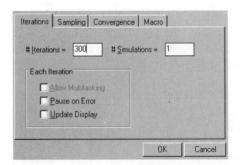

13.8.4 Running the Simulation

Having identified the output cells to track and the number of replications to perform, we now need to instruct @RISK to perform the simulation by clicking the Simulate button on the @RISK toolbar (see Figure 13.4). @RISK then begins to perform the specified number of replications. Depending on the number of iterations selected, the size of the model, and the speed of your computer, it could take anywhere from several seconds to several minutes for these computations to be carried out.

For our example problem, @RISK performs 300 recalculations of the model, keeping track of the value in cell G23 for each replication. By default, @RISK updates the computer screen after each replication, which is very time-consuming. If you deselect the Update Display option shown in Figure 13.10, @RISK will not update the screen after each replication and will perform the replications much faster.

13.9 DATA ANALYSIS

As mentioned earlier, the objective of performing simulation is to estimate various characteristics of the performance measure resulting from uncertainty in some or all of the input variables. After performing the replications, @RISK summarizes the output data, as shown in Figure 13.11.

As shown in the Summary of Results area, the average (or mean) value for cell G23 is approximately $36.1 million. (Note that the Mean value of 3.613679E+07 shown in Figure 13.11 is in scientific notation. The "E+07" at the end of this notation indicates that the decimal point in the number should be shifted 7 places to the right to produce 36,136,790.) Additional information about the simulation results is available by clicking

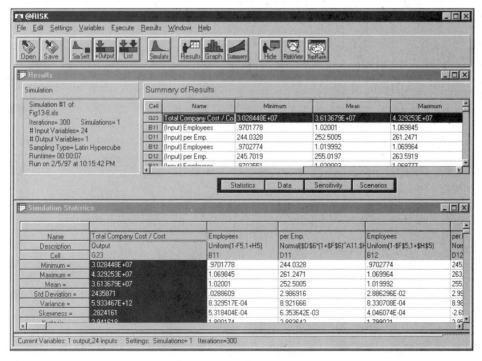

Figure 13.11
Summary of results provided by @RISK for the corporate health insurance model.

the Statistics button in the Results window, or by clicking the Graph button on the toolbar. (If you are working through this example on a computer, the graphs and statistics you generate will probably be somewhat different from the results shown here because you are working with a different sample of 300 observations.)

13.9.1 The Best Case and the Worst Case

Decision makers usually want to know the best-case and worst-case scenarios to get an idea of the range of possible outcomes they might face. This information is available from the simulation results, as shown by the Minimum and Maximum values listed in Figure 13.11.

Although the average total cost value observed in the 300 replications is $36.1 million, in one case the total cost is approximately $30.3 million (representing the best case) and in another case the total cost is approximately $43.3 million (representing the worst case). These figures should give the decision maker a good idea about the range of possible cost values that might occur. Note that these values might be difficult to determine manually in a complex model with many uncertain independent variables.

13.9.2 Viewing the Distribution of the Output Cells

The best- and worst-case scenarios are the most extreme outcomes, and might not be likely to occur. To determine the likelihood of these outcomes requires that we know something about the shape of the distribution of our bottom-line performance measure. To view a graph of the distribution of the results of the 300 replications generated for the output cell in our model:

1. In the Results window, select the row representing cell G23 in the Summary of Results area.
2. Click the Graph button on the toolbar (see Figure 13.11).

A histogram of the simulation data for cell G23 appears. This graph, shown in Figure 13.12, provides a visual summary of the approximate shape of the probability distribution associated with the output cell tracked by @RISK during the simulation.

We can use the Graph, Format options available on the Results menu to adjust the scale of the graph and change the minimum and maximum values displayed along the X- or Y-axis of the histogram.

As shown in Figure 13.12, the shape of the distribution associated with the total cost variable is somewhat bell-shaped, with a maximum value around $43 million and a minimum value around $30 million. Thus, we now have a clear idea of the shape of the distribution associated with our bottom-line performance measure—one of the goals in simulation.

If we tracked more than one output cell during the simulation, we could display histograms of the values occurring in these other cells by highlighting the appropriate cell in the Summary of Results area of the Results window, then clicking the Graph button. We could perform the same procedure to view the distributions of the input cells.

13.9.3 Viewing the Cumulative Distribution of the Output Cells

At times we might want to view a graph of the cumulative probability distribution associated with one of the output cells tracked during a simulation. For example, suppose that the chief financial officer (CFO) for Hungry Dawg would rather accrue an excess of

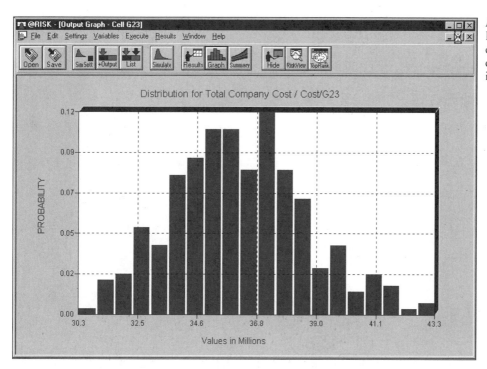

Figure 13.12
Histogram of
costs for the
corporate health
insurance model.

money to pay health claims than not accrue enough money. The CFO might want to know what amount the company should accrue so that there is only a 10% chance of coming up short of funds at the end of the year. How much money would you recommend be accrued?

Figure 13.13 shows a graph of the cumulative probability distribution of the values that occurred in cell G23 during the simulation. This graph could help us answer the preceding question. To change the graph shown in Figure 13.12 to the cumulative distribution graph shown in Figure 13.13:

1. Click the Results menu.
2. Click Graph.
3. Click Format.
4. On the Type card, click Cumulative ascending.
5. Click Area graph.
6. Click OK.

This graph displays the probability of the selected output cell taking on a value smaller than each value on the X-axis. For example, this graph indicates that approximately a 10% chance exists of the output cell (Total Company Cost) assuming a value smaller than approximately $33 million. Similarly, this graph indicates that roughly an 80% chance exists of total costs being less than approximately $38 million (or a 20% chance of total costs exceeding approximately $38 million). Thus, from this graph we would estimate that roughly a 10% chance exists of the company's costs exceeding approximately $39 million.

13.9.4   Obtaining Exact Cumulative Probabilities

We can obtain a more exact answer to the CFO's question from information in the Simulation Statistics window shown in Figure 13.11. The maximized version of this window is shown in Figure 13.14.

Figure 13.13
Ascending
cumulative
frequency
distribution of
costs for the
corporate health
insurance model.

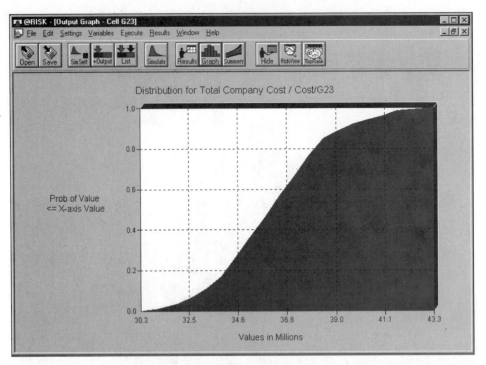

Figure 13.14
Percentiles for
the distribution
of costs.

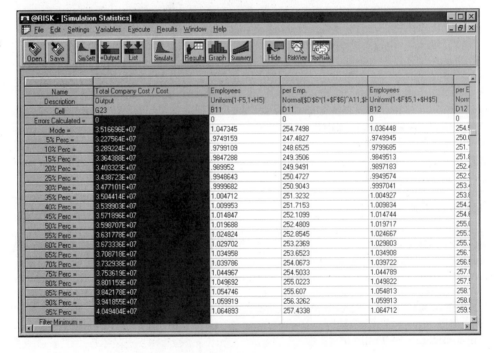

Scrolling down the Simulation Statistics window reveals a number of percentile values for the output cell G23. For example, the 10th percentile of the values generated for the output cell is $32,892,240. That is, 10% of the 300 values generated for cell G23 are less than or equal to $32,892,240. Similarly, the 90th percentile of the distribution of values is $39,418,550. That is, 90% of the 300 values generated for cell

G23 are less than or equal to $39,418,550. Thus, based on these results, if the company accrues $39.4 million, we would expect that only a 10% chance exists of the actual company costs exceeding this amount.

In this case, the percentile value we want to find is given in the Simulation Statistics window. But what happens if we're interested in a percentile value that's not a multiple of 5? For example, what if we need to find the 88th percentile of the distribution? To do this:

1. Click Target #1 (Perc%)= in the Output G23 column shown in Figure 13.15.
2. Type 88 and then press [Enter]. The value 88% appears in the box.

The value for the 88th percentile (39,001,864) appears in the box labeled "Target #1 (Value)=" as shown in Figure 13.15.

This indicates that roughly a 12% chance exists of total costs exceeding $39.0 million. We can obtain other percentiles in a similar manner.

The ability to perform this type of analysis highlights the power and value of simulation and @RISK. For example, how could we have answered the CFO's question about how much money to accrue using best-case/worst-case analysis or what-if analysis? The fact is, we could not answer the question with any degree of accuracy without using simulation.

13.10   INCORPORATING GRAPHS AND STATISTICS INTO A SPREADSHEET

At times you will want to save some of the graphs or statistics created by @RISK. You can do so by selecting the Reports to Worksheet option from the Results menu. This option displays the Reports to Worksheet dialog box shown in Figure 13.16.

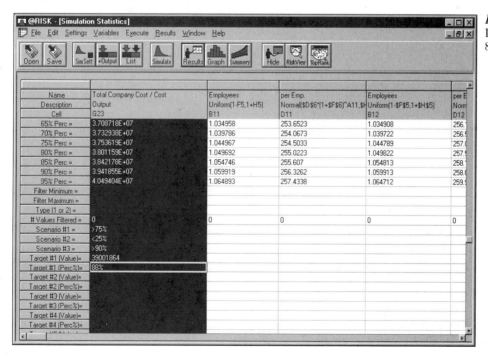

Figure 13.15
Determining the 88th percentile.

Figure 13.16
Reports to
Worksheet
dialog box.

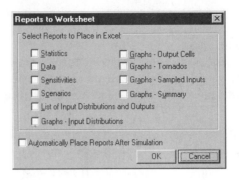

This dialog box provides options for saving different results to Excel. Excel automatically saves all the selected graphs and statistics in several worksheets of a new workbook.

13.10.1   Saving Graphs to Separate Files

Sometimes, you might want to save a particular graph in its own graph file (either bitmap or metafile) rather than saving it as a worksheet file. To do this:
1. With the graph displayed, click File, then click Save.
2. Click the type of file you want to save (either bitmap or metafile).
3. Enter a graph filename.
4. Click OK.

13.10.2   The List Button

The List button on the @RISK toolbar displays the Inputs By Output window shown in Figure 13.17.

This window helps us to verify that our model is implemented correctly. The Outputs section shows information about all the cells selected for tracking as Outputs. The Delete Output button below this listing allows us to remove unwanted output cells so that @RISK will not track their values during the simulation runs. The Inputs

Figure 13.17
Inputs By
Output window.

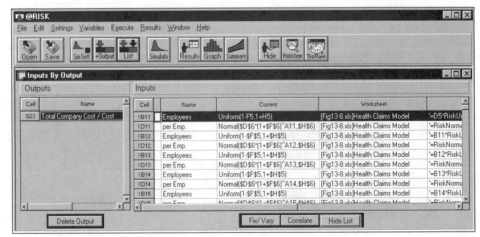

section displays information about all the cells that contain RNGs (which @RISK refers to as Inputs). The buttons below this listing provide additional modeling features that are beyond the scope of this text.

13.10.3 The Open and Save Buttons

The Save button on the @RISK toolbar allows you to save the simulation results and graphs you create so that you can refer to them later without having to rerun the entire simulation. Then you can use the Open button on the @RISK toolbar to retrieve the saved simulation results. Whenever you quit @RISK, a dialog box appears asking if you want to save the current simulation data. If you click Yes, a summary file is created for the current simulation results. Later you can open this summary file in @RISK by clicking the Open button on the @RISK toolbar.

13.11 THE UNCERTAINTY OF SAMPLING

To this point, we have used simulation to generate 300 observations on our bottom-line performance measure and then calculated various statistics to describe the characteristics and behavior of the performance measure. For example, Figure 13.11 indicates that the mean company cost value in our sample is $36,136,790, and Figure 13.14 shows that a 90% chance exists of this performance measure assuming a value less than $39,418,550. But what if we repeat this process and generate another 300 observations? Would the sample mean for the new 300 observations also be exactly $36,136,790? Or would exactly 90% of the observations in the new sample be less than $39,418,550?

The answer to both these questions is "probably not." The sample of 300 observations used in our analysis was taken from a population of values that is theoretically infinite in size. That is, if we had enough time and our computer had enough memory, we could generate an infinite number of values for our bottom-line performance measure. Theoretically, we could then analyze this infinite population of values to determine its true mean value, its true standard deviation, and the true probability of the performance measure being less than $39,418,550. Unfortunately, we do not have the time or computer resources to determine these true characteristics (or parameters) of the population. The best we can do is take a sample from this population and, based on our sample, make estimates about the true characteristics of the underlying population. Our estimates will differ depending on the sample we choose and the size of the sample.

So, the mean of the sample we take is probably not equal to the true mean we would observe if we could analyze the entire population of values for our performance measure. The sample mean we calculate is just an estimate of the true population mean. In our example problem, we estimated that a 90% chance exists for our output variable to assume a value less than $39,418,550. However, this most likely is not equal to the true probability we would calculate if we could analyze the entire population. Thus, there is some element of uncertainty surrounding the statistical estimates resulting from simulation because we are using a sample to make inferences about the population. Fortunately, there are ways of measuring and describing the amount of uncertainty present in some of the estimates we make about the population under study. This is typically done by constructing confidence intervals for the population parameters being estimated.

13.11.1   Constructing a Confidence Interval for the True Population Mean

Constructing a confidence interval for the true population mean is a simple process. If $\bar{y}$ and s represent, respectively, the mean and standard deviation of a sample of size n from any population, then assuming n is sufficiently large ($n \geq 30$), the Central Limit Theorem tells us that the lower and upper limits of a 95% confidence interval for the true mean of the population are represented by:

$$95\% \text{ Lower Confidence Limit} = \bar{y} - 1.96 \times \frac{s}{\sqrt{n}}$$

$$95\% \text{ Upper Confidence Limit} = \bar{y} + 1.96 \times \frac{s}{\sqrt{n}}$$

Although we can be fairly certain that the sample mean we calculate from our sample data is not equal to the true population mean, we can be 95% confident that the true mean of the population falls somewhere between the lower and upper limits given above. If we want a 90% or 99% confidence interval, we must change the value 1.96 in the above equation to 1.645 or 2.575, respectively. The values 1.645 and 2.575 represent the 95 and 99.5 percentiles of the standard normal distribution, respectively.

For our example, the lower and upper limits of a 95% confidence interval for the true mean of the population of total company cost values can be calculated easily, as shown in cells B7 and B8 in Figure 13.18. (The sample mean and standard deviation shown in Figure 13.18 were obtained from Figure 13.11.) The formulas for these cells are:

Formula for cell B7: =B4–1.96*B5/SQRT(B2)

Formula for cell B8: =B4+1.96*B5/SQRT(B2)

Thus, we can be 95% confident that the true mean of the population of total company cost values falls somewhere in the interval from \$35,861,145 to \$36,412,435.

13.11.2   Constructing a Confidence Interval for a Population Proportion

In our example we estimated that 90% of the population of total company cost values fall below \$39,418,550, based on our sample of 300 observations. However, if we could evaluate the entire population of total cost values, we might find that only 80% of these values fall below \$39,418,550. Or we might find that 99% of the entire population falls below this mark. It would be helpful to determine how accurate the 90% value is. So, at times we might want to construct a confidence interval for the true proportion of a population that falls below (or above) some value, say Y_p.

To see how this is done, let $\bar{p}$ denote the proportion of observations in a sample of size n that falls below some value Y_p. Assuming that n is sufficiently large ($n \geq 30$), the Central Limit Theorem tells us that the lower and upper limits of a 95% confidence interval for the true proportion of the population falling below Y_p are represented by:

$$95\% \text{ Lower Confidence Limit} = \bar{p} - 1.96 \times \sqrt{\frac{\bar{p}(1 - \bar{p})}{n}}$$

$$95\% \text{ Upper Confidence Limit} = \bar{p} + 1.96 \times \sqrt{\frac{\bar{p}(1 - \bar{p})}{n}}$$

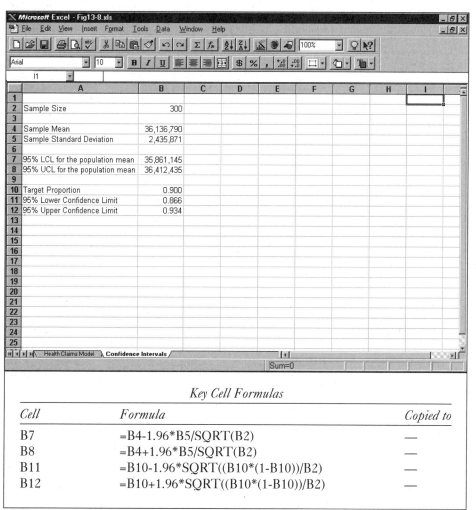

Figure 13.18
95% Confidence
intervals for the
corporate health
insurance model.

Cell	Formula	Copied to
	Key Cell Formulas	
B7	=B4-1.96*B5/SQRT(B2)	—
B8	=B4+1.96*B5/SQRT(B2)	—
B11	=B10-1.96*SQRT((B10*(1-B10))/B2)	—
B12	=B10+1.96*SQRT((B10*(1-B10))/B2)	—

Although we can be fairly certain that the proportion of observations falling below Y_p in our sample is not equal to the true proportion of the population falling below Y_p, we can be 95% confident that the true proportion of the population falling below Y_p is contained within the lower and upper limits given above. Again, if we want a 90% or 99% confidence interval, we must change the value 1.96 in the above equations to 1.645 or 2.575, respectively.

Using these formulas, we can calculate the lower and upper limits of a 95% confidence interval for the true proportion of the population falling below $39,418,550. From our simulation results, we know that 90% of the observations in our sample are less than $39,418,550. Thus, our estimated value of $\bar{p}$ is 0.90. This value was entered into cell B10 in Figure 13.18. The upper and lower limits of a 95% confidence interval for the true proportion of the population falling below $39,418,550 are calculated in cells B11 and B12 of Figure 13.18 using the following formulas:

Formula for cell B11: =B10–1.96*SQRT(B10*(1–B10)/B2)

Formula for cell B12: =B10+1.96*SQRT(B10*(1–B10)/B2)

We can be 95% confident that the true proportion of the population of total cost values falling below $39,418,550 is between 0.866 and 0.934. Because this interval is fairly tight around the value 0.90, we can be reasonably certain that the $39,418,550 figure quoted to the CFO has approximately a 10% chance of being exceeded.

13.11.3   Sample Sizes and Confidence Interval Widths

The formulas for the confidence intervals in the previous section depend directly on the number of replications (n) in the simulation. As the number of replications (n) increases, the width of the confidence interval decreases (or becomes more precise). Thus, for a given level of confidence (for example, 95%), the only way to make the upper and lower limits of the interval closer together (or tighter) is to make n larger—that is, use a larger sample size. A larger sample should provide more information about the population and, therefore, allow us to be more accurate in estimating the true parameters of the population.

13.12   THE BENEFITS OF SIMULATION

What have we accomplished through simulation? Are we really better off than if we had just used the results of the original model proposed in Figure 13.2? The estimated value for the expected total cost to the company in Figure 13.2 is comparable to that obtained through simulation (although this might not always be the case). But remember that the goal of modeling is to give us greater insight into a problem to help us make more informed decisions.

The results of our simulation analysis do give us greater insight into the example problem. In particular, we now have some idea of the best- and worst-case total cost outcomes for the company. We have a better idea of the distribution and variability of the possible outcomes, and a more precise idea about where the mean of the distribution is located. We also now have a way of determining how likely it is for the actual outcome to fall above or below some value. Thus, in addition to our greater insight and understanding of the problem, we also have solid empirical evidence (the facts and figures) to support our recommendations.

13.13   ADDITIONAL USES OF SIMULATION

Earlier we indicated that simulation is a technique that *describes* the behavior or characteristics of a bottom-line performance measure. The next two examples show how describing the behavior of a performance measure gives a manager a useful tool in determining the optimal value for one or more controllable parameters in a decision problem. These examples reinforce the mechanics of using simulation and also demonstrate some additional simulation modeling techniques.

13.14   AN INVENTORY CONTROL EXAMPLE

According to *The Wall Street Journal* (7/18/94), U.S. businesses had a combined inventory worth $884.77 billion dollars as of the end of May 1994. Because so much money is tied up in inventories, businesses face many important decisions regarding the management of these assets. Frequently asked questions regarding inventory include:

- What's the best level of inventory for a business to maintain?
- When should goods be reordered (or manufactured)?
- How much safety stock should be held in inventory?

The study of inventory control principles is split into two distinct areas—one assumes that demand is known (or deterministic), and the other assumes that demand is random (or stochastic). If demand is known, various formulas can be derived that provide answers to the previous questions (an example of one such formula is given in the discussion of the EOQ model in chapter 8.) However, when demand for a product is uncertain or random, answers to previous questions cannot be expressed in terms of a simple formula. In these situations, the technique of simulation proves to be a useful tool, as illustrated in the following example.

Laura Tanner is the owner of Computers of Tomorrow (COT), a retail computer store in Austin, Texas. Competition in retail computer sales is fierce—both in terms of price and service. Laura is concerned about the number of stockouts occurring on a popular type of computer monitor. This monitor is priced competitively and generates a marginal profit of $45 per unit sold. Stockouts are very costly to the business because when customers cannot buy this item at COT, they simply buy it from a competing store and COT loses the sale (there are no backorders). Laura measures the effects of stockouts on her business in terms of service level, or the percentage of total demand that can be satisfied from inventory.

Laura has been following the policy of ordering 50 monitors whenever her daily ending inventory position (defined as ending inventory on hand plus outstanding orders) falls below her reorder point of 28 units. Laura places the order at the beginning of the next day. Orders are delivered at the beginning of the day and, therefore, can be used to satisfy demand on that day. For example, if the ending inventory position on day 2 is less than 28, Laura places the order at the beginning of day 3. If the actual time between order and delivery, or lead time, turns out to be four days, then the order arrives at the start of day 7. The current level of on-hand inventory is 50 units and no orders are pending.

COT sells an average of six monitors per day. However, the actual number sold on any given day can vary. By reviewing her sales records for the past several months, Laura determined that the actual daily demand for this monitor is a random variable that can be described by the following probability distribution:

Units Demanded:	0	1	2	3	4	5	6	7	8	9	10
Probability:	0.01	0.02	0.04	0.06	0.09	0.14	0.18	0.22	0.16	0.06	0.02

The manufacturer of this computer monitor is located in California. Although it takes an average of four days for COT to receive an order from this company, Laura has determined that the lead time of a shipment of monitors is also a random variable that can be described by the following probability distribution:

Lead Time (days):	3	4	5
Probability:	0.2	0.6	0.2

One way to guard against stockouts and improve the service level is to increase the reorder point for the item so that more inventory is on hand to meet the demand occurring during the lead time. Laura wants to determine the reorder point that results in an average service level of 99%.

13.14.1   Creating the RNGs

To solve this problem, we need to build a model to represent the inventory of computer monitors during an average month of 30 days. This model must account for the random daily demands that can occur and the random lead times encountered when orders are placed. First we'll consider how to create RNGs to model the daily demands and order lead times. The data for these variables are entered in the spreadsheet as shown in Figure 13.19 (and in the file FIG13-19.xls on your data disk).

The order lead time and daily demand variables are both examples of *general, discrete* random variables because the possible outcomes they assume consist solely of integers, and the probabilities associated with each outcome are not equal (or not uniform). Thus, using the RiskDiscrete( ) function described in Figure 13.5, the RNGs for each variable are:

RNG for order lead time: =RiskDiscrete(Data!$B$6:$B$8,Data!$C$6:$C$8)

RNG for daily demand: =RiskDiscrete(Data!$E$6:$E$16,Data!$F$6:$F$16)

13.14.2   Implementing the Model

Now that we have a way of generating the random numbers needed in this problem, we can consider how the model should be built. Figure 13.20 shows the model representing 30 days of inventory activity.

Because Laura wants to determine the reorder point that results in an average service level of 99%, cell D6 in Figure 13.20 is used to represent the reorder point. The order quantity is given in cell D7 so that Laura could also investigate the impact of changes in this value.

Figure 13.19
RNG data for COT's inventory problem.

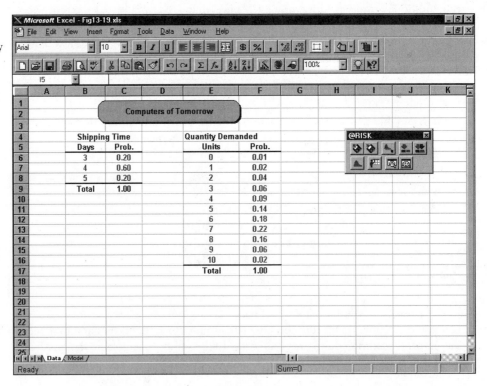

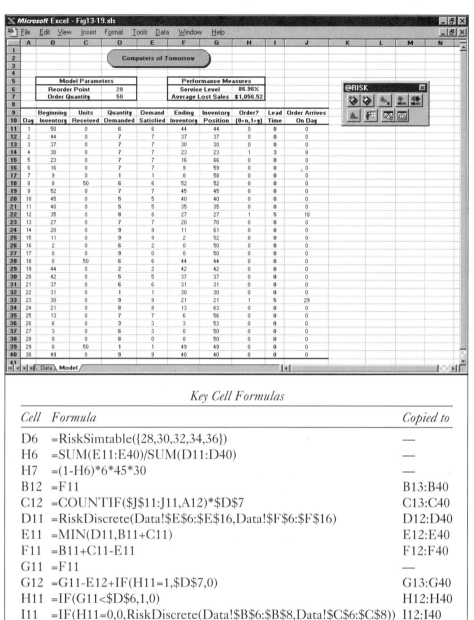

Figure 13.20
Spreadsheet model for COT's inventory problem.

Key Cell Formulas

Cell	Formula	Copied to
D6	=RiskSimtable({28,30,32,34,36})	—
H6	=SUM(E11:E40)/SUM(D11:D40)	—
H7	=(1-H6)*6*45*30	—
B12	=F11	B13:B40
C12	=COUNTIF($J$11:J11,A12)*$D$7	C13:C40
D11	=RiskDiscrete(Data!$E$6:$E$16,Data!$F$6:$F$16)	D12:D40
E11	=MIN(D11,B11+C11)	E12:E40
F11	=B11+C11-E11	F12:F40
G11	=F11	—
G12	=G11-E12+IF(H11=1,$D$7,0)	G13:G40
H11	=IF(G11<$D$6,1,0)	H12:H40
I11	=IF(H11=0,0,RiskDiscrete(Data!$B$6:$B$8,Data!$C$6:$C$8))	I12:I40
J11	=IF(H11=0,0,A11+1+I11)	J12:J40

The inventory on hand at the beginning of each day is calculated in column B in Figure 13.20. The beginning inventory for each day is simply the ending inventory from the previous day. The formulas in column B are:

Formula for cell B11:   =50

Formula for cell B12:   =F11
(Copy to B13 through B40.)

Column C represents the number of units scheduled to be received each day. We'll discuss the formulas in column C after we discuss columns H, I, and J, which relate to ordering and order lead times.

In column D, we use the technique described earlier to generate random daily demands, as:

Formula for cell D11:   =RiskDiscrete(Data!$E$6:$E$16,Data!$F$6:$F$16)
(Copy to D12 through D40.)

Because it is possible for demand to exceed the available supply, column E indicates how much of the daily demand can be met. If the beginning inventory (in column B) plus the ordered units received (in column C) is greater than or equal to the actual demand, then all the demand can be satisfied; otherwise, COT can sell only as many units as are available. This condition is modeled as:

Formula for cell E11:   =MIN(D11,B11+C11)
(Copy to E12 through E40.)

The values in column F represent the on-hand inventory at the end of each day and are calculated as:

Formula for cell F11:   =B11+C11–E11
(Copy to F12 through F40.)

To determine whether or not to place an order, we first must calculate the inventory position, which was defined earlier as the ending inventory plus any outstanding orders. This is implemented in column G as:

Formula for cell G11:   =F11

Formula for cell G12:   =G11-E12+IF(H11=1,$D$7,0)
(Copy to G13 through G40.)

Column H indicates if an order should be placed based on inventory position and the reorder point, as:

Formula for cell H11:   =IF(G11<$D$6,1,0)
(Copy to H12 through H40.)

If an order is placed, then we must generate the random lead time required to receive the order. This is done in column I as:

Formula for cell I11: =IF(H11=0,0,RiskDiscrete(Data!$B$6:$B$8,Data!$C$6:$C$8))
(Copy to I12 through I40.)

This formula returns the value 0 if no order was placed (if H11=0); otherwise, it returns a random lead time value (if H11=1).

If an order is placed, column J indicates the day on which the order will be received based on its random lead time in column I. This is done as:

Formula for cell J11:   =IF(H11=0,0,A11+1+I11)
(Copy to J12 through J40.)

The values in column C are coordinated with those in column J. The nonzero values in column J indicate the days on which orders will be received. For example, cell J14 indicates that an order will be received on day 8. The actual receipt of this order is reflected by the value of 50 in cell C18, which represents the receipt of an order at the beginning of day 8. The formula in cell C18 that achieves this is:

Formula for cell C18:   =COUNTIF($J$11:J17,A18)*$D$7

This formula counts how many times the value in cell A18 (representing day 8) appears as a scheduled receipt day between days 1 through 7 in column J. This represents the number of orders scheduled to be received on day 8. We then multiply this by the order quantity (50), given in cell D7 to determine the total units to be received on day 8. Thus, the values in column C are generated as:

Formula for cell C11:   =0

Formula for cell C12:   =COUNTIF($J$11:J11,A12)*$D$7
(Copy to C13 through C40.)

The service level for the model is calculated in cell H6 using the values in columns D and E as:

Formula for cell H6:   =SUM(E11:E40)/SUM(D11:D40)

Again, the service level represents the proportion of total demand that can be satisfied from inventory. The value in cell H6 indicates that in the scenario shown, 86.96% of the total demand is satisfied. Cell H7 translates this service level into dollars as:

Formula for cell H7:   =(1–H6)*6*45*30

Because the average daily demand for this monitor is for six units, and each monitor sold generates a marginal profit of $45, cell H7 indicates that in the scenario for this month, COT would lose about $1,057 in profits per month if their service level is 86.96%.

13.14.3 Replicating the Model

The model in Figure 13.20 indicates one possible scenario that could occur if Laura uses a reorder point of 28 units for the computer monitor. By replicating this model over and over, Laura could keep track of the service level occurring in each replication and average these values to determine the expected service level obtained with a reorder point of 28.

Using the simulation techniques described earlier, Laura could repeat this process with reorder points of 30 units, 32 units, and so on, until she finds the reorder point that achieves her goal of an average service level of 99%. However, there is another, easier way that Laura can perform the replications.

Suppose that we want to run five different simulations using reorder points of 28, 30, 32, 34, and 36, respectively. We can instruct @RISK to do this for us by entering the following formula in cell D6:

Formula for cell D6:   =RiskSimtable({28,30,32,34,36})

In this case, @RISK sets the value of D6 to each number listed in the RiskSimtable( ) function. For each value, @RISK performs n replications of the model and summarizes the results. Before running the replications, we need to indicate the output cells we want to track by completing the following steps:

1. Select cells H6 and H7.
2. Click the +Outputs button on the @RISK toolbar.

Suppose that we want to run 200 replications of the model for each possible reorder point value. To do this:

1. Click the SimSett button on the @RISK toolbar.
2. Enter 200 in the box labeled "# Iterations =".
3. Enter 5 in the box labeled "# Simulations =" (because there are 5 values in the RiskSimtable( ) function in cell D6).
4. Click the Update Display option to deselect this option (to make the simulation run faster).
5. Click OK.
6. Click the Simulate button on the @RISK toolbar to start the simulation.

Completing the simulation could take several minutes depending on the speed of your computer. After performing the replications, @RISK summarizes the output data. Figure 13.21 shows the maximized Results window for the first simulation, which used a reorder point of 28.

13.14.4   Data Analysis

Figure 13.21 indicates that COT's current reorder point of 28 units results in an average service level of approximately 96.1%, with a minimum value of 84.5% and a maximum value of 100%. This implies that, on average, COT is unable to satisfy approximately 3.9% of the total demand using this reorder point. The results of tracking output cell H7 indicate that in an average month, COT loses about $314 in profits each month due to stockouts on the monitor.

By default, @RISK lists the results of one simulation at a time. To see the results of all five simulations at once, click the Merge Sim#'s button at the bottom of the Results window. Figure 13.22 shows the result of all five simulations.

By comparing the expected service levels of all five simulations shown in Figure 13.22, we see that as the reorder point increases, the service level also increases (or

Figure 13.21
Summary of results from first simulation of COT's inventory problem.

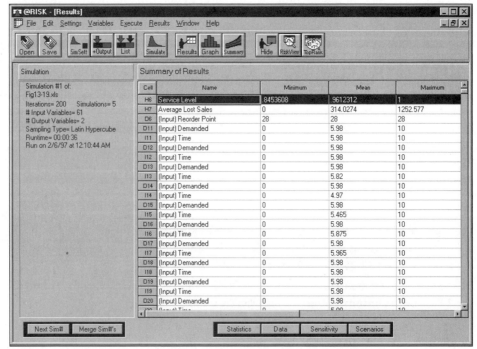

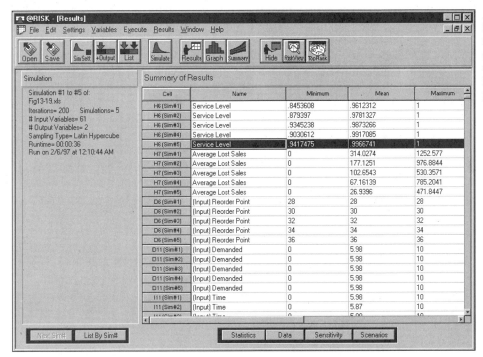

Figure 13.22
Summary of results from all five simulations of COT's inventory problem.

the percentage of lost sales decreases). So if Laura increases the reorder point to 36, COT's average service level for the monitor would increase to 99.67%, and the average monthly profit lost due to stockouts would decrease to approximately $27.

13.14.5 A Final Comment on the Inventory Example

Although increasing the reorder point decreases the percentage of lost sales, it also increases the average level of inventory held. Thus, another objective that might be considered in this problem involves weighing the costs of holding more inventory and placing more orders against the benefits of having fewer lost sales. We'll consider such an objective further in one of the problems at the end of this chapter.

13.15 AN OVERBOOKING EXAMPLE

Businesses that allow customers to make reservations for services (such as airlines, hotels, and car rental companies) know that some percentage of the reservations made will not be used for one reason or another, leaving these companies with a difficult decision problem. If they accept reservations for only the number of customers that can actually be served, then a portion of the company's assets will be underutilized when some customers with reservations fail to arrive. This results in an opportunity loss for the company. On the other hand, if they overbook (or accept more reservations than can be handled), then at times more customers will arrive than can actually be served. This typically results in additional financial costs to the company and often generates ill will among those customers who cannot be served. The following example illustrates how simulation might be used to help a company determine the optimal number of reservations to accept.

Marty Ford is an operations analyst for Piedmont Commuter Airlines (PCA). Recently, Marty was asked to make a recommendation on how many reservations PCA should book on Flight 343—a flight in high demand from a small regional airport to a major hub airport. Historical data show that PCA frequently has seats left on Flight 343 if it accepts only 19 reservations (the plane's capacity). Industry statistics show that for every ticket sold for a commuter flight, a 0.10 probability exists that the ticket holder will not be on the flight. PCA sells nonrefundable tickets for Flight 343 for $85 per seat. Thus, every empty seat on this flight represents an opportunity cost—even if a no-show customer had purchased a ticket for the seat—because the seat could be filled by another passenger paying $85. On the other hand, if PCA overbooks this flight and more than 19 passengers show up, some of them will have to be bumped to a later flight.

To compensate for the inconvenience of being bumped, PCA gives these passengers vouchers for a free meal, a free flight at a later date, and sometimes also pays for them to stay overnight in a hotel near the airport. PCA pays an average of $155 for each passenger that gets bumped. Marty wants to determine if PCA can increase profits by overbooking this flight and, if so, how many reservations should be accepted to produce the maximum average profit. Marty wants to set up a model that allows him to investigate the consequences of accepting up to 24 reservations.

13.15.1 Implementing the Model

A spreadsheet model for this problem is shown in Figure 13.23 (and in the file FIG13-23.xls on your data disk).

The spreadsheet begins by listing the relevant data from the problem, including the number of seats available on the plane, the price PCA charges for each seat, the probability of a no-show (a ticketed passenger not arriving in time for the flight), the cost of bumping passengers, and the number of reservations that will be accepted.

The random element in this problem is the number of passengers arriving to board the plane, represented in cell C10 in Figure 13.23. Because each ticketed passenger has a 0.10 probability of being a no-show, a 0.9 probability exists that each ticketed passenger will arrive in time to board the flight. Thus, the RiskBinomial( ) function (described in Figure 13.5) is used in cell C10 to model the number of ticketed passengers that actually arrive for a flight:

Formula for cell C10:   =RiskBinomial(C8,1–C6)

Cell C12 represents the ticket revenue PCA earns based on the number of tickets they sell for each flight. The formula for this cell is:

Formula for cell C12:   =C8*C5

Cell C13 computes the opportunity loss PCA incurs on each empty seat on a flight.

Formula for cell C13:   =C5*MAX(C4-C10,0)

Cell C14 computes the costs PCA incurs when passengers must be bumped (i.e., when the number of passengers wanting to board exceeds the number of available seats).

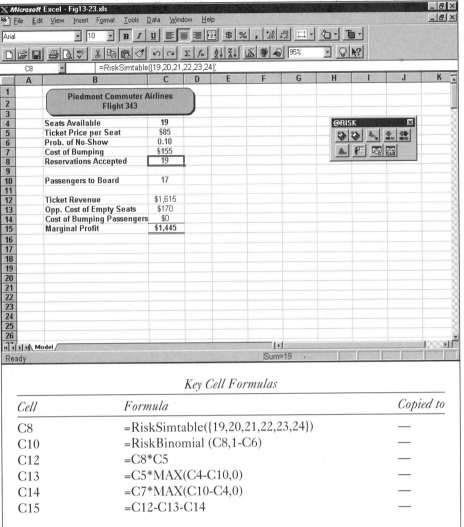

Figure 13.23
PCA model with RNGs for uncertain cells.

Key Cell Formulas

Cell	Formula	Copied to
C8	=RiskSimtable({19,20,21,22,23,24})	—
C10	=RiskBinomial (C8,1-C6)	—
C12	=C8*C5	—
C13	=C5*MAX(C4-C10,0)	—
C14	=C7*MAX(C10-C4,0)	—
C15	=C12-C13-C14	—

Formula for cell C14:   =C7*MAX(C10-C4,0)

Finally, cell C15 computes the marginal profit PCA earns on each flight.

Formula for cell C15:   =C12–C13–C14

13.15.2 Replicating the Model

Marty wants to determine the number of reservations to accept that, on average, will result in the highest marginal profit. To do so, he needs to use the RiskSimtable( ) function to simulate what would happen if 19, 20, 21, 22, 23, and 24 reservations are accepted. Cell C8 contains the following formula:

Formula for cell C8:   =RiskSimtable({19,20,21,22,23,24})

This formula instructs @RISK to use six different values in cell C8 and simulate what will happen with each value.

Before starting the simulation, we must indicate the output cell(s) we want to track. To do so for our example problem:

1. Click cell C12.
2. Click the +Output button on the @RISK toolbar.

Next, we must indicate the number of simulations and the number of replications per simulation. To do so:

1. Click the SimSett button on the @RISK toolbar.
2. Enter 200 in the box labeled "# Iterations =".
3. Enter 6 in the box labeled "# Simulations =" (because there are 6 values in the RiskSimtable( ) function in cell C8).
4. Click the Update Display option to deselect this option (to make the simulation run faster).
5. Click OK.
6. Click the Simulate button on the @RISK toolbar to start the simulation.

@RISK places the different values in cell C8, beginning with the value 19 and ending with the value 24, and runs a simulation consisting of 200 replications for each value. Depending on the speed of your computer, this could take several minutes.

After performing the replications, @RISK summarizes the output data. Figure 13.24 shows the maximized Results window for the first simulation, in which 19 reservations were accepted.

13.15.3   Data Analysis

Figure 13.24 indicates that PCA can, on average, expect to earn a marginal profit of approximately $1,453 when 19 reservations are accepted for Flight 343. The minimum

Figure 13.24
Summary of
results from first
simulation of the
PCA model.

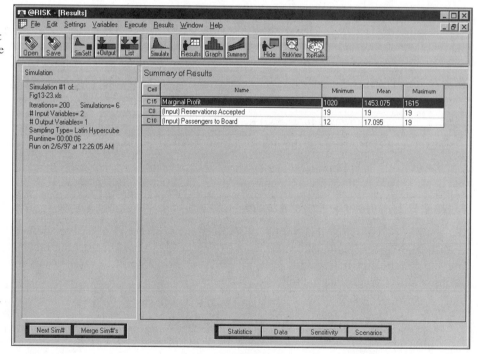

and maximum marginal profit levels occurring in the 200 replications with 19 reservations are $1,020 and $1,615, respectively.

By default, @RISK lists the results of one simulation at a time. To see the results of all six simulations at once, click the Merge Sim#'s button at the bottom of the Results window. Figure 13.25 shows the results of all six simulations.

By comparing the expected profits of all six simulations, we see that they range from a low of $1,453 (when 19 reservations are accepted) to a high of $1,683 (when 22 reservations are accepted). Thus, if PCA wants to maximize the expected profit for Flight 343, it should accept 22 reservations for this flight.

13.15.4   A Final Comment on the Overbooking Example

This problem assumed that all the reservations available for Flight 343 would always be taken—or that there would never be unused reservations. However, if PCA accepts up to 22 reservations, there might be times when only 16 or 17 seats would be demanded. Thus, the demand for seats on this flight could be modeled more accurately as a random variable. We'll explore this issue more fully in one of the problems at the end of this chapter.

SUMMARY

This chapter introduced the concept of risk analysis and simulation. Many of the input cells in a spreadsheet represent random variables whose values cannot be determined with certainty. Any uncertainty in the input cells flows through the spreadsheet model to create a related uncertainty in the value of the output cell(s). Decisions made on the basis of these uncertain values involve some degree of risk.

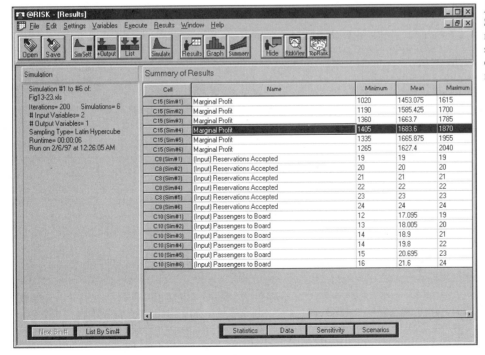

Figure 13.25 Summary of results from all six simulations of the PCA model.

Cell	Name	Minimum	Mean	Maximum
C15 (Sim#1)	Marginal Profit	1020	1453.075	1615
C15 (Sim#2)	Marginal Profit	1190	1585.425	1700
C15 (Sim#3)	Marginal Profit	1360	1663.7	1785
C15 (Sim#4)	Marginal Profit	1405	1683.6	1870
C15 (Sim#5)	Marginal Profit	1335	1665.875	1955
C15 (Sim#6)	Marginal Profit	1265	1627.4	2040
C8 (Sim#1)	(Input) Reservations Accepted	19	19	19
C8 (Sim#2)	(Input) Reservations Accepted	20	20	20
C8 (Sim#3)	(Input) Reservations Accepted	21	21	21
C8 (Sim#4)	(Input) Reservations Accepted	22	22	22
C8 (Sim#5)	(Input) Reservations Accepted	23	23	23
C8 (Sim#6)	(Input) Reservations Accepted	24	24	24
C10 (Sim#1)	(Input) Passengers to Board	12	17.095	19
C10 (Sim#2)	(Input) Passengers to Board	13	18.005	20
C10 (Sim#3)	(Input) Passengers to Board	14	18.9	21
C10 (Sim#4)	(Input) Passengers to Board	14	19.8	22
C10 (Sim#5)	(Input) Passengers to Board	15	20.695	23
C10 (Sim#6)	(Input) Passengers to Board	16	21.6	24

THE WORLD OF MANAGEMENT SCIENCE
The U.S. Postal Service
Moves to the Fast Lane

Mail flows into the U.S. Postal Service at the rate of 500 million pieces per day, and it comes in many forms. There are standard-sized letters with nine-digit ZIP codes (with or without imprinted bar codes), five-digit ZIP codes, typed addresses that can be read by optical character readers, handwritten addresses that are barely decipherable. Christmas cards in red envelopes addressed in red ink and so on. The enormous task of sorting all these pieces at the sending post office and at the destination has caused postal management to consider and adopt many new forms of technology. These include operator-assisted mechanized sorters, optical character readers (last-line and multiple-line), and bar code sorters. Implementation of new technology brings with it associated policy decisions, such as rate discounts for bar coding by the customer, finer sorting at the origin, and so on.

A simulation model called META (model for evaluating technology alternatives) assists management in evaluating new technologies, configurations, and operating plans. Using distributions based on experience or projections of the effects of new policies, META simulates a random stream of mail of different types, routes the mail through the system configuration being tested, and prints reports detailing total pieces handled, capacity utilization, work hours required, space requirements, and cost.

META has been used on several projects associated with the Postal Service corporate automation plan. These include facilities planning, benefits of alternate sorting plans, justification of efforts to enhance address readability, planning studies for reducing the time carriers spend sorting vs. delivering, and identification of mail types that offer the greatest potential for cost savings.

According to the Associate Postmaster General, "... META became the vehicle to help steer our organization on an entirely new course at a speed we had never before experienced."

Source: Michael E. Cebry, Anura H. deSilva and Fred J. DiLisio, "Management Science in Automating Postal Operations: Facility and Equipment Planning in the United States Postal Service," *Interfaces*, vol. 22, no. 1, January-February 1992, pages 110-130.

Various methods of risk analysis are available, including best-case/worst-case analysis, what-if analysis, and simulation. Of these three methods, simulation is the only technique that provides hard evidence (facts and figures) that can be used objectively in making decisions. To simulate a model, RNGs are used to select representative values for each uncertain independent variable in the model. This process is repeated over and over to generate a sample of representative values for the dependent variable(s) in the model. The variability and distribution of the sample values for the dependent variable(s) can then be analyzed to gain insight into the possible outcomes that might occur. This chapter highlighted the use of the @RISK add-in to perform spreadsheet simulation.

QUESTIONS AND PROBLEMS

1. Under what condition(s) is it appropriate to use simulation to analyze a model? That is, what characteristics should a model possess in order for simulation to be used?

2. The graph of the probability distribution of a normally distributed random variable with a mean of 20 and standard deviation of 3 is shown in Figure 13.7.

   a. Use the RNGNormal( ) function to generate 100 sample values from this distribution.
   b. Produce a histogram of the 100 sample values you generated. Does your histogram look like the graph for this distribution in Figure 13.7?
   c. Repeat this experiment, only this time sample 1,000 values.
   d. Produce a histogram for the 1,000 sample values you generated. Does the histogram now more closely resemble the graph in Figure 13.7 for this distribution?
   e. Why does your second histogram look more "normal" than the first one?

3. Refer to the Hungry Dawg Restaurant example presented in section 13.4 of this chapter. Health claim costs actually tend to be seasonal, with higher levels of claims occurring during the summer months (when kids are out of school and more likely to injure themselves) and during December (when people schedule elective procedures before the next year's deductible must be paid). The following table summarizes the seasonal adjustment factors that apply to RNGs for average claims in the Hungry Dawg problem. For instance, the average claim for month 6 should be multiplied by 115% and those for month 1 should be multiplied by 80%.

Month:	1	2	3	4	5	6	7	8	9	10	11	12
Seasonal Factor:	0.80	0.85	0.87	0.92	0.93	1.15	1.20	1.18	1.03	0.95	0.98	1.14

Suppose the company maintains an account from which it pays health insurance claims. Assume there is $2.5 million in the account at the beginning of month 1. Each month, employee contributions are deposited into this account and claims are paid from the account.

   a. Modify the spreadsheet shown in Figure 13.8 to include the cash flows in this account. If the company deposits $3 million in this account every month, what is the probability that the account will have insufficient funds to pay claims at some point during the year? Use 300 replications. (HINT: You can use the COUNTIF( ) function to count the number of months in a year where the ending balance in the account is below 0.)
   b. If the company wants to deposit an equal amount of money in this account each month, what should this amount be if they want there to only be a 5% chance of having insufficient funds?

4. One of the examples in section 13.14 of this chapter dealt with determining the optimal reorder point for a computer monitor sold by Computers of Tomorrow (COT) in Austin, Texas. In this example we found that increasing the reorder point decreased the number of lost sales. However, this also increased the average amount of inventory carried. Suppose that it costs COT $0.30 per day in holding costs for each monitor in beginning inventory, and it costs $20 to place an order.

Each monitor sold generates a profit of $45, and each lost sale results in an opportunity cost of $65 (including the lost profit of $45 and $20 in lost goodwill). Modify the spreadsheet shown in Figure 13.19 to determine the reorder point that maximizes the average monthly profit associated with this monitor.

5. One of the examples in section 13.15 of this chapter dealt with determining the optimal number of reservations for Piedmont Commuter Airlines (PCA) to accept for one of its flights that uses a plane with 19 seats. The model discussed in the chapter assumes that all the reservations would be used, but some customers would not show up for the flight. It is probably more realistic to assume that the demand for these reservations is somewhat random. For example, suppose that the demand for reservations on this flight is given by the following discrete probability distribution:

Reservations Demanded:	12	13	14	15	16	17	18	19	20	21	22	23	24
Probability:	0.01	0.03	0.04	0.07	0.09	0.11	0.15	0.18	0.14	0.08	0.05	0.03	0.02

The number of passengers receiving reservations depends on the number of reservations PCA accepts and the demand for these reservations. For each passenger receiving a reservation, a 0.10 probability exists that he will not arrive at the gate to board the plane. Modify the spreadsheet shown in Figure 13.23 to determine the number of reservations PCA should accept to maximize the average profit associated with this flight.

6. A debate recently erupted about the optimal strategy for playing a game on the TV show called "Let's Make a Deal." In one of the games on this show, the contestant would be given the choice of prizes behind three closed doors. A valuable prize was behind one door and worthless prizes were behind the other two doors. After the contestant selected a door, the host would open one of the two remaining doors to reveal one of the worthless prizes. Then, before opening the selected door, the host would give the contestant the opportunity to switch his or her selection to the other door that had not been opened. The question is, should the contestant switch?

    a. Suppose a contestant is allowed to play this game 500 times, always picks door number 1, and never switches when given the option. If the valuable prize is equally likely to be behind each door at the beginning of each play, how many times would the contestant win the valuable prize? Use simulation to answer this question.

    b. Now suppose the contestant is allowed to play this game another 500 times. This time the player always selects door number 1 initially and switches when given the option. Using simulation, how many times would the contestant win the valuable prize?

    c. If you were a contestant on this show, what would you do if given the option of switching doors?

7. The monthly demand for the latest computer at Newland Computers follows a normal distribution with a mean of 350 and standard deviation of 75. Newland purchases these computers for $1,200 and sells them for $2,300. It costs the company $100 to place an order and $12 for every computer held in inventory at the end of each month. Currently the company places an order for 1,000 computers whenever the inventory at the end of a month falls below 100 units. Assume

unmet demand in any month is lost to competitors and that orders placed at the end of one month arrive at the beginning of the next month.

a. Create a spreadsheet model to simulate the profit the company will earn on this product over the next two years. Use 200 replications. What is the average level of profit the company will earn?

b. Suppose the company wants to determine the optimum reorder point and order quantity. Specifically, for every 100-unit increase in the reorder point, they will reduce the order quantity by 100. Which combination of reorder point and order quantity will provide the highest average profit over the next two years?

8. The manager of Moore's Catalog Showroom is trying to predict how much revenue will be generated by each major department in the store during 1998. The manager has estimated the minimum and maximum growth rates possible for revenues in each department. The manager believes that any of the possible growth rates between the minimum and maximum values are equally likely to occur. These estimates are summarized in the following table:

		Growth Rates	
Department	1997 Revenues	Minimum	Maximum
Electronics	$6,342,213	2%	10%
Garden Supplies	$1,203,231	–4%	5%
Jewelry	$4,367,342	–2%	6%
Sporting Goods	$3,543,532	–1%	8%
Toys	$4,342,132	4%	15%

Create a spreadsheet to simulate the total revenues that could occur in the coming year. Run 500 replications of the model and do the following:

a. Construct a 95% confidence interval for the average level of revenues the manager could expect for 1998.

b. According to your model, what are the chances that total revenues in 1998 will be more than 5% larger than those in 1997?

9. The Harriet Hotel in downtown Boston has 100 rooms that rent for $125 per night. It costs the hotel $30 per room in variable costs (cleaning, bathroom items, etc.) each night a room is occupied. For each reservation accepted, there is a 5% chance that the guest will not arrive. If the hotel overbooks, it costs $200 to compensate guests whose reservations cannot be honored.

How many reservations should the hotel accept if it wishes to maximize the average daily profit? Use 500 simulations for each reservation level you consider.

10. Lynn Price recently completed her MBA and accepted a job with an electronics manufacturing company. Although she likes her job, she is also looking forward to retiring one day. To ensure that her retirement is comfortable, Lynn intends to invest $3,000 of her salary into a tax-sheltered retirement fund at the end of each year. Lynn is not certain what rate of return this investment will earn each year, but she expects each year's rate of return could be modeled appropriately as a normally distributed random variable with a mean of 12% and standard deviation of 2%.

    a. If Lynn is 30 years old, how much money should she expect to have in her retirement fund at age 60? (Use 500 replications.)

    b. Construct a 95% confidence interval for the average amount Lynn will have at age 60.

    c. What is the probability that Lynn will have more than $1 million in her retirement fund when she reaches age 60?

    d. How much should Lynn invest each year if she wants there to be a 90% chance of having at least $1 million in her retirement fund at age 60?

11. Employees of Georgia-Atlantic are permitted to contribute a portion of their earnings (in increments of $500) to a flexible spending account from which they can pay medical expenses not covered by the company's health insurance program. Contributions to an employee's "flex" account are not subject to income taxes. However, the employee forfeits any amount contributed to the "flex" account that is not spent during the year. Suppose Greg Davis makes $60,000 per year from Georgia-Atlantic and pays a marginal tax rate of 28%. Greg and his wife estimate that in the coming year their normal medical expenses not covered by the health insurance program could be as small as $500, as large as $5,000 and most likely about $1,300. However, Greg also believes there is a 5% change that an abnormal medical event could occur which might add $10,000 to the normal expenses paid from their flex account. If their uncovered medical claims exceed their contribution to their "flex" account, they will have to cover these expenses with the after-tax money Greg brings home.

    Use simulation to determine the amount of money Greg should contribute to his flexible spending account in the coming year if he wants to maximize his disposable income (after taxes and all medical expenses are paid). Use 500 replications for each level of "flex" account contribution you consider.

12. Acme Equipment Company is considering the development of a new machine that would be marketed to tire manufacturers. Research and development costs for the project are expected to be about $4 million but could vary between $3 and $6 million. The market life for the product is estimated to be three to eight years with all intervening possibilities being equally likely. The company thinks it will sell 250 units per year, but acknowledges that this figure could be as low as 50 or as high as 350. The company will sell the machine for about $23,000. Finally, the cost of manufacturing the machine is expected to be $14,000 but could be as low as $12,000 or as high as $18,000. The company's cost of capital is 15%.

    a. Use appropriate RNGs to create a spreadsheet to calculate the possible net present values (NPVs) that could result from taking on this project.

    b. Replicate the model 500 times. What is the expected NPV for this project?

    c. What is the probability of this project generating a positive NPV for the company?

13. Representatives from the American Heart Association are planning to go door-to-door throughout a community, soliciting contributions. From past experience they know that when someone answers the door, 80% of the time it is a female and 20% of the time it is a male. They also know that 70% of the females who answer the door make a donation, whereas only 40% of the males who answer the door make donations. The amount of money that females contribute follows a normal distribution with a mean of $20 and standard deviation of $3. The amount of money males contribute follows a normal distribution with a mean of $10 and standard deviation of $2.

a. Create a spreadsheet model that simulates what might happen whenever a representative of the American Heart Association knocks on a door and someone answers.

b. Replicate your model 500 times. What is the average contribution the Heart Association can expect to receive when someone answers the door?

c. Suppose that the Heart Association plans to visit 300 homes on a given Saturday. If no one is home at 25% of the residences, what is the total amount that the Heart Association can expect to receive in donations?

14. After spending 10 years as an assistant manager for a large restaurant chain, Ray Clark has decided to become his own boss. The owner of a local submarine sandwich store wants to sell the store to Ray for $65,000 to be paid in installments of $13,000 in each of the next five years. According to the current owner, the store brings in revenue of about $110,000 per year and incurs operating costs of about 63% of sales. Thus, once the store is paid for, Ray should make about $35,000–$40,000 per year before taxes. Until the store is paid for, he will make substantially less—but he will be his own boss. Realizing that some uncertainty is involved in this decision, Ray wants to simulate what level of net income he can expect to earn during the next five years as he operates and pays for the store. In particular, he wants to see what could happen if sales are allowed to vary uniformly between $90,000 and $120,000, and if operating costs are allowed to vary uniformly between 60% and 65% of sales. Assume that Ray's payments for the store are not deductible for tax purposes and that he is in the 28% tax bracket.

a. Create a spreadsheet model to simulate the annual net income Ray would receive during each of the next five years if he decides to buy the store.

b. Given the money he has in savings, Ray thinks he can get by for the next five years if he can make at least $12,000 from the store each year. Replicate the model 500 times and track: 1) the minimum amount of money Ray makes over the five-year period represented by each replication, and 2) the total amount Ray makes during the five-year period represented by each replication.

c. What is the probability that Ray will make at least $12,000 in each of the next five years?

d. What is the probability that Ray will make at least $60,000 total over the next five years?

15. Bob Davidson owns a newsstand outside the Waterstone office building complex in Atlanta, near Hartsfield International Airport. He buys his papers wholesale at $0.50 per paper and sells them for $0.75. Bob wonders what is the optimal number of papers to order each day. Based on history, he has found that demand (even though it is discrete) can be modeled by a normal distribution with a mean of 50 and standard deviation of 5. When he has more papers than customers, he can recycle all the extra papers the next day and receive $0.05 per paper. On the other hand, if he has more customers than papers, he loses some goodwill in addition to the lost profit on the potential sale of $0.25. Bob estimates the incremental lost goodwill costs five day's worth of business (that is, dissatisfied customers will go to a competitor the next week, but come back to him the week after that).

a. Create a spreadsheet model to determine the optimal number of papers to order each day. Use 250 replications and round the demand values generated by the normal RNG to the closest integer value.

b. Construct a 95% confidence interval for the expected payoff from the optimal decision.

16. Vinton Auto Insurance is trying to decide how much money to keep in liquid assets to cover insurance claims. In the past, the company held some of the premiums it received in interest-bearing checking accounts and put the rest into investments that are not quite as liquid, but tend to generate a higher investment return. The company wants to study cash flows to determine how much money it should keep in liquid assets to pay claims. After reviewing historical data, the company determined that the average repair bill per claim is normally distributed with a mean of $1,700 and standard deviation of $400. It also determined that the number of repair claims filed each week is a random variable that follows the probability distribution given below:

Number of Repair Claims	Probability
1	0.05
2	0.06
3	0.10
4	0.17
5	0.28
6	0.14
7	0.08
8	0.07
9	0.05

In addition to repair claims, the company also receives claims for cars that have been "totaled" and cannot be repaired. A 20% chance of receiving this type of claim exists in any week. These claims for "totaled" cars typically cost anywhere from $2,000 to $35,000, with $13,000 being the most common cost.

a. Create a spreadsheet model of the total claims cost incurred by the company in any week.
b. Replicate the model 500 times and create a histogram of the distribution of total cost values that were generated.
c. What is the average cost the company should expect to pay each week?
d. Suppose that the company decides to keep $20,000 cash on hand to pay claims. What is the probability that this amount would not be adequate to cover claims in any week?
e. Create a 95% confidence interval for the true probability of claims exceeding $20,000 in a given week.

17. The owner of a local car dealership has just received a call from a regional distributor stating that a $5,000 bonus will be awarded if the owner's dealership sells at least 10 new cars next Saturday. On an average Saturday, this dealership has 75 potential customers look at new cars, but there is no way to determine exactly how many customers will come this particular Saturday. The owner is fairly certain that the number would not be less than 40, but also thinks it would be unrealistic to expect more than 120 (which is the largest number of customers to ever show up in one day).

The owner determined that, on average, about 1 out of 10 customers who look at cars at the dealership actually purchase a car—or, a 0.10 probability (or 10% chance) exists that any given customer will buy a new car.

a. Create a spreadsheet model for this problem and generate 1,000 random outcomes for the number of cars the dealership might sell next Saturday.

b. What is the probability that the dealership will earn the $5,000 bonus?

c. If you were this dealer, what is the maximum amount of money you'd be willing to spend on sales incentives to try to earn this bonus?

18. Dr. Sarah Benson is an ophthalmologist who, in addition to prescribing glasses and contact lenses, performs optical laser surgery to correct nearsightedness. This surgery is fairly easy and inexpensive to perform. Thus, it represents a potential gold mine for her practice. To inform the public about this procedure, Dr. Benson advertises in the local paper and holds information sessions in her office one night a week at which she shows a videotape about the procedure and answers any questions potential patients might have. The room where these meetings are held can seat 10 people, and reservations are required. The number of people attending each session varies from week to week. Dr. Benson cancels the meeting if two or fewer people have made reservations. Using data from the previous year, Dr. Benson determined that the distribution of reservations is as follows:

Number of Reservations:	0	1	2	3	4	5	6	7	8	9	10
Probability:	0.02	0.05	0.08	0.16	0.26	0.18	0.11	0.07	0.05	0.01	0.01

Using data from the past year, Dr. Benson determined that each person who attends an information has a 0.25 probability of electing to have the surgery. Of those who do not, most cite the cost of the procedure—$2,000—as their major concern.

a. On average, how much revenue does Dr. Benson's practice in laser surgery generate each week? (Use 500 replications.)

b. On average, how much revenue would the laser surgery generate each week if Dr. Benson did not cancel sessions with two or fewer reservations?

c. Dr. Benson believes that 40% of the people attending the information sessions would have the surgery if she reduced the price to $1,500. Under this scenario, how much revenue could Dr. Benson expect to realize per week from laser surgery?

19. Michael Abrams runs a specialty clothing store that sells collegiate sports apparel. One of his primary business opportunities involves selling custom screen-printed sweatshirts for college football bowl games. He is trying to determine how many sweatshirts to produce for the upcoming Tangerine Bowl game. During the month before the game, Michael plans to sell his sweatshirts for $25 a piece. At this price, he believes the demand for sweatshirts will be triangularly distributed with a minimum demand of 10,000, maximum demand of 30,000, and a most likely demand of 18,000. During the month after the game, Michael plans to sell any remaining sweatshirts for $12 a piece. At this price, he believes the demand for sweatshirts will be triangularly distributed with a minimum demand of 2,000, maximum demand of 7,000, and a most likely demand of 5,000. Two months after the game, Michael plans to sell any remaining sweatshirts to a surplus store which has agreed to buy up to 2,000 sweatshirts for a price of $3 per shirt. Michael can order custom screen-printed sweatshirts for $8 a piece in lot sizes of 3,000.

a. On average, how much profit would Michael earn if he orders 18,000 sweatshirts? Use 500 replications.

b. How many sweatshirts should he order if he wants to maximize his expected profit? Again use 500 replications in each simulation you perform.

20. The Major Motors Corporation is trying to decide whether or not to introduce a new midsize car. The directors of the company want to produce the car only if it has at least an 80% chance of generating a positive net present value over the next 10 years. If the company decides to produce the car, it will have to pay an uncertain initial start-up cost that is estimated to follow a triangular distribution with a minimum value of $300 million, maximum value of $600 million, and a most likely value of $450 million. In the first year the company would produce 100,000 units. Demand during the first year is uncertain but expected to be normally distributed with a mean of 95,000 and standard deviation of 7,000. For any year in which the demand exceeds production, production will be increased by 5% in the following year. For any year in which the production exceeds demand, production will be decreased by 5% in the next year and the excess cars will be sold to a rental car company at a 20% discount. After the first year, the demand in any year will be modeled as a normally distributed random variable with a mean equal to the actual demand in the previous year and standard deviation of 7,000. In the first year, the sales price of the car will be $13,000 and the total variable cost per car is expected to be $7,500. Both the selling price and variable cost is expected to increase each year at the rate of inflation which is assumed to be uniformly distributed between 2% and 7%. The company uses a discount rate of 9% to discount future cash flows.

    a. Create a spreadsheet model for this problem and replicate it 300 times. What is the minimum, average, and maximum NPV Major Motors can expect if they decide to produce this car? (HINT: Consider using the NPV( ) function to discount the profits Major Motors would earn each year.)

    b. What is the probability of Major Motors earning a positive NPV over the next 10 years?

    c. Should they produce this car?

21. Each year, the Schriber Corporation must determine how much to contribute to the company's pension plan. The company uses a 10-year planning horizon to determine the contribution which, if made annually in each of the next 10 years, would allow for only a 10% chance of the fund running short of money. The company then makes that contribution in the current year (year 1) and repeats this process in each subsequent year to determine the specific amount to contribute each year. (Last year the company contributed $43 million to the plan.) The pension plan covers two types of employees: hourly and salaried. In the current year, there will be 6,000 former hourly employees and 3,000 former salaried employees receiving benefits from the plan. The change in the number of retired hourly employees from one year to the next is expected to vary according to a normal distribution with mean of 4% and standard deviation of 1%. The change in the number of retired salaried employees from one year to the next is expected to vary between 1% and 4% according to a truncated normal distribution with mean of 2% and standard deviation of 1%. Currently, hourly retirees receive an average benefit of $15,000 per year, while salaried retirees receive an average annual benefit of $40,000. Both of these averages are expected to increase annually with the rate of inflation, which is assumed to vary annually between 2% and 7% according to a triangular distribution with a most likely value of 3.5%. The current balance in the company's pension fund is $1.5 billion. Investments in this fund earn an annual return that is assumed to be normally distributed with a mean of 12% and standard deviation of 2% each year. Create a spreadsheet model for this problem and use

simulation to determine the pension fund contribution the company should make in the current year. Assume benefits are paid throughout the year and the company contribution is made at the end of the year. What is your recommendation?

CASE 13.1 THE SOUND'S ALIVE COMPANY

Contributed by Jack Yurkiewicz, Lubin School of Business, Pace University

Marissa Jones is the president and CEO of Sound's Alive, a company that manufactures and sells a line of speakers, CD players, receivers, high-definition televisions, and other items geared for the home entertainment market. Respected throughout the industry for bringing many high-quality, innovative products to market, Marissa is considering adding a speaker system to her product line.

The speaker market has changed dramatically during the last several years. Originally, high-fidelity aficionados knew that to reproduce sound covering the fullest range of frequencies—from the lowest kettle drum to the highest violin—a speaker system had to be large and heavy. The speaker had various drivers: a woofer to reproduce the low notes, a tweeter for the high notes, and a midrange driver for the broad spectrum of frequencies in between. Many speaker systems had a minimum of three drivers, but some had even more. The trouble was that such a system was too large for anything but the biggest rooms, and consumers were reluctant to spend thousands of dollars and give up valuable wall space to get the excellent sound these speakers could reproduce.

The trend has changed during the past several years. Consumers still want good sound, but they want it from smaller boxes. Therefore, the satellite system became popular. Consisting of two small boxes that house either one driver (to cover the midrange and high frequencies) or two (a midrange and tweeter), a satellite system can easily be mounted on walls or shelves. To reproduce the low notes, a separate subwoofer that is approximately the size of a cube 18 inches on a side is also needed. This subwoofer can be placed anywhere in the room. Taking up less space than a typical large speaker system and sounding almost as good, yet costing hundreds of dollars less, these satellite systems are hot items in the high-fidelity market.

Recently the separate wings of home entertainment—high-fidelity (receivers, speakers, CD players, CDs, cassettes, and so on), television (large-screen monitors, video cassette recorders, laser players), and computers (games with sounds, virtual reality software, and so on)—have merged into the home theater concept. To simulate the movie environment, a home theater system requires the traditional stereo speaker system plus additional speakers placed in the rear of the room so that viewers are literally surrounded with sound. Although the rear speakers do not have to match the high quality of the front speakers and, therefore, can be less expensive, most consumers choose a system in which the front and rear speakers are of equal quality, reproducing the full range of frequencies with equal fidelity.

It is this speaker market that Marissa wants to enter. She is considering having Sound's Alive manufacture and sell a home theater system that consists of seven speakers. Three small speakers—each with one dome tweeter that could reproduce the frequency range of 200 Hertz to 20,000 Hertz (upper-low frequencies to the highest frequencies)—would be placed in front, and three similar speakers would be placed strategically around the sides and back of the room. To reproduce the lowest frequencies (from 35 Hertz to 200 Hertz), a single sub-woofer would also be part of the system.

This subwoofer is revolutionary because it is smaller than the ordinary subwoofer, only 10 inches per side, and it has a built-in amplifier to power it. Consumer and critics are thrilled with the music from early prototype systems, claiming that these speakers have the best balance of sound and size. Marissa is extremely encouraged by these early reviews, and although her company has never produced a product with its house label on it (having always sold systems from established high-fidelity companies), she believes that Sound's Alive should enter the home theater market with this product.

Phase One: Projecting Profits

Marissa decides to create a spreadsheet that will project profits over the next several years. After consulting with economists, market analysts, employees in her own company, and employees from other companies that sell house brand components. Marissa is confident that the gross revenues for these speakers in 1998 would be around $6 million. She must also figure that a small percentage of speakers will be damaged in transit, or some will be returned by dissatisfied customers shortly after the sales. These returns and allowances (R&As) are usually calculated as 2% of the gross revenues. Hence, the net revenues are simply the gross revenues minus the R&As. Marissa believes that the 1998 labor costs for these speakers will be $995,100. The cost of materials (including boxes to ship the speakers) should be $915,350 for 1998. Finally, her overhead costs (rent, lighting, heating in winter, air conditioning in summer, security, and so on) for 1998 should be $1,536,120. Thus, the cost of goods sold is the sum of labor, material, and overhead costs. Marissa figures the gross profit as the difference between the net revenues and the cost of goods sold. In addition, she must consider the selling, general, and administrative (SG&A) expenses. These expenses are more difficult to estimate, but the standard industry practice is to use 18% of the net revenues as the nominal percentage value for these expenses. Therefore, Marissa's profit *before taxes* is the gross profit minus the SG&A value. To calculate taxes, Marissa multiplies her profits before taxes times the tax rate, currently 30%. If her company is operating at a loss, however, no taxes would have to be paid. Finally, Marissa's net (or after tax) profit is simply the difference between the profit before taxes and the actual taxes paid.

To determine the numbers for 1999 through 2001, Marissa assumes that gross revenues, labor costs, material costs, and overhead costs will increase over the years. Although the rates of increase for these items are difficult to estimate, Marissa figures that gross revenues will increase by 9% per year, labor costs will increase by 4% per year, material costs will increase by 6% per year, and overhead costs will increase by 3% per year. She figures that the tax rate will not change from the 30% mark, and she assumes that the SG&A value will remain at 18%.

The basic layout of the spreadsheet that Marissa creates is shown in the following figure (and in the file FIG13-26.xls on your data disk). (Ignore the Competitive Assumptions section for now; we'll consider it later.) Construct the spreadsheet and determine the values for the years 1998 through 2001, then determine the totals for the four years.

Marissa not only wants to determine her net profits for 1998 through 2001, she also must justify her decisions to the company's Board of Trustees. Should she even consider entering this market, from a financial point of view? One way to answer this question is to find the net present value (NPV) of the net profits for 1998 through 2001. Use Excel's NPV capability to find the NPV, at the current interest rate of 5%, of the profit values for 1998 through 2001.

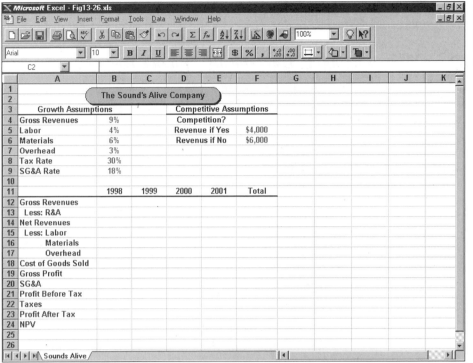

Figure 13.26
Spreadsheet
template for the
Sound's Alive
case.

To avoid large values in the spreadsheet, enter all dollar calculations in thousands. For example, enter labor costs as 995.10 and overhead costs as 1536.12.

Phase 2: Bringing Competition Into the Model

With her spreadsheet complete, Marissa is confident that entering the home theater speaker market would be lucrative for Sound's Alive. However, she has not considered one factor in her calculations—competition. The current market leader and company she is most concerned about is the Bose Corporation. Bose pioneered the concept of a satellite speaker system, and its AMT series is very successful. Marissa is concerned that Bose will enter the home market, cutting into her gross revenues. If Bose does enter the market, Marissa believes that Sound's Alive would still make money; however, she would have to revise her gross revenues estimate from $6 million to $4 million for 1998.

To account for the competition factor, Marissa revises her spreadsheet by adding a Competition Assumptions section. Cell F4 will contain either a 0 (no competition) or a 1 (if Bose enters the market). Cells F5 and F6 provide the gross revenue estimates (in thousands of dollars) for the two possibilities. Modify your spreadsheet to take these options into account. Use the IF( ) function for the gross revenues for 1998 (cell B12). If Bose does enter the market, not only would Marissa's gross revenues be lower, but the labor, materials, and overhead costs would also be lower because Sound's Alive would be making and selling fewer speakers. Marissa thinks that if Bose enters the market, her 1998 labor costs would be $859,170, 1998 material costs would be $702,950, and 1998 overhead costs would be $1,288,750. She believes that her growth rate assumptions would stay the same whether or not Bose enters the market. Add these possible values to your spreadsheet using the IF( ) function in the appropriate cells.

Look at the net profits for 1998 through 2001. In particular, examine the NPV for the two scenarios: Bose does or does not enter the home theater speaker market.

Phase Three: Bringing Uncertainty Into the Model

Jim Allison, the chief of operations at Sound's Alive and a quantitative methods specialist, plays a key role in providing Marissa with estimates for the various revenues and costs. He is uneasy about the basic estimates for the growth rates. For example, although market research indicates that a 9% gross revenue increase per year is reasonable, Jim knows that if this value is 7%, for example, the profit values and the NPV would be quite different. Even more troublesome is a potential tax increase, which would hit Sound's Alive hard. Jim believes that the tax rate could vary around the expected 30% figure. Finally, Jim is uncomfortable with the industry's standard estimate of 18% for the SG&A rate. Jim thinks that this value could be higher or even lower.

The Sound's Alive problem is too complicated for solving with what-if analysis because seven assumed values could change: the growth rates for gross revenues, labor, materials, overhead costs, tax rate, SG&A percent, and whether or not Bose enters the market. Jim believes that a Monte Carlo simulation would be a better approach. Jim thinks that the behavior of these variables can be modeled as follows:

Gross Revenues (%): normally distributed, mean = 9.9, std dev = 1.4
Labor Growth (%): normally distributed, mean = 3.45, std dev = 1.0

Materials (%)	Probability
4	0.10
5	0.15
6	0.15
7	0.25
8	0.25
9	0.10

Overhead (%)	Probability
2	0.20
3	0.35
4	0.25
5	0.20

Tax Rate (%)	Probability
30	0.15
32	0.30
34	0.30
36	0.25

SG&A (%)	Probability
15	0.05
16	0.10
17	0.20
18	0.25
19	0.20
20	0.20

Finally, Jim and Marissa agree that there is a 50/50 chance that Bose will enter the market.

Use simulation to analyze the Sound's Alive problem. Based on your results, what is the expected net profit for the years 1998 through 2001, and what is the expected NPV for this business venture?

The Board of Trustees told Marissa that the stockholders would feel comfortable with this business venture if its NPV is at least $5 million. What are the chances that Sound's Alive home theater venture will result in an NPV of $5 million or more?

CASE 13.2   FOXRIDGE INVESTMENT GROUP

Inspired by a case written by MBA students Fred Hirsch and Ray Rogers for Professor Larry Weatherford at the University of Wyoming.

The Foxridge Investment Group buys and sells rental income properties in Southwest Virginia. Bill Hunter, president of Foxridge, has asked for your assistance in analyzing a small apartment building the group is interested in purchasing.

The property in question is a small two-story structure with three rental units on each floor. The purchase price of the property is $170,000, representing $30,000 in land value and $140,000 in buildings and improvements. Foxridge will depreciate the buildings and improvements value on a straight-line basis over 27.5 years. The Foxridge Group will make a down payment of $40,000 to acquire the property and finance the remainder of the purchase price over 20 years with an 11% fixed-rate loan with payments due annually. Figure 13.27 (and the file FIG13-27.xls on your data disk) summarizes this and other pertinent information.

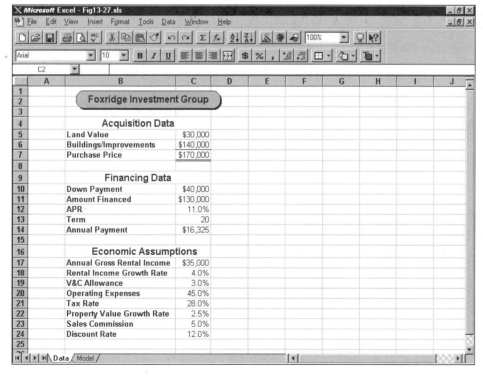

Figure 13.27
Assumptions for the Foxridge Investment Group case.

If all units are fully occupied, Mr. Hunter expects the property to generate rental income of $35,000 in the first year and expects to increase the rent at rate the of inflation (currently 4%). Because vacancies occur and some residents may not always be able to pay their rent, Mr. Hunter factors in a 3% vacancy & collection (V&C) allowance against rental income. Operating expenses are expected to be approximately 45% of rental income. The group's marginal tax rate is 28%.

If the group decides to purchase this property, their plan is to hold it for five years and then sell it to another investor. Presently, property values in this area are increasing at a rate of approximately 2.5% per year. The group will have to pay a sales commission of 5% of the gross selling price when they sell the property.

Figure 13.28 shows a spreadsheet model Mr. Hunter developed to analyze this problem. This model first uses the data and assumptions given in Figure 13.27 to generate the expected net cash flows in each of the next five years. It then provides a final summary of the proceeds expected from selling the property at the end of five years. The total net present value (NPV) of the project is then calculated in cell I18 using the discount rate of 12% in cell C24 of Figure 13.27. Thus, after discounting all the future cash flows associated with this investment by 12% per year, the investment still generates an NPV of $2,007.

While the group has been using this type of analysis for many years to make investment decisions, one of Mr. Hunter's investment partners recently read an article in *The Wall Street Journal* about risk analysis and simulation using spreadsheets. As a result, the partner realizes there is quite a bit of uncertainty associated with many of the economic assumptions shown in Figure 13.27. After explaining the potential problem to Mr. Hunter, the two have decided to apply simulation to this model before making a decision. Since neither of them know how to do simulation, they have asked for your assistance.

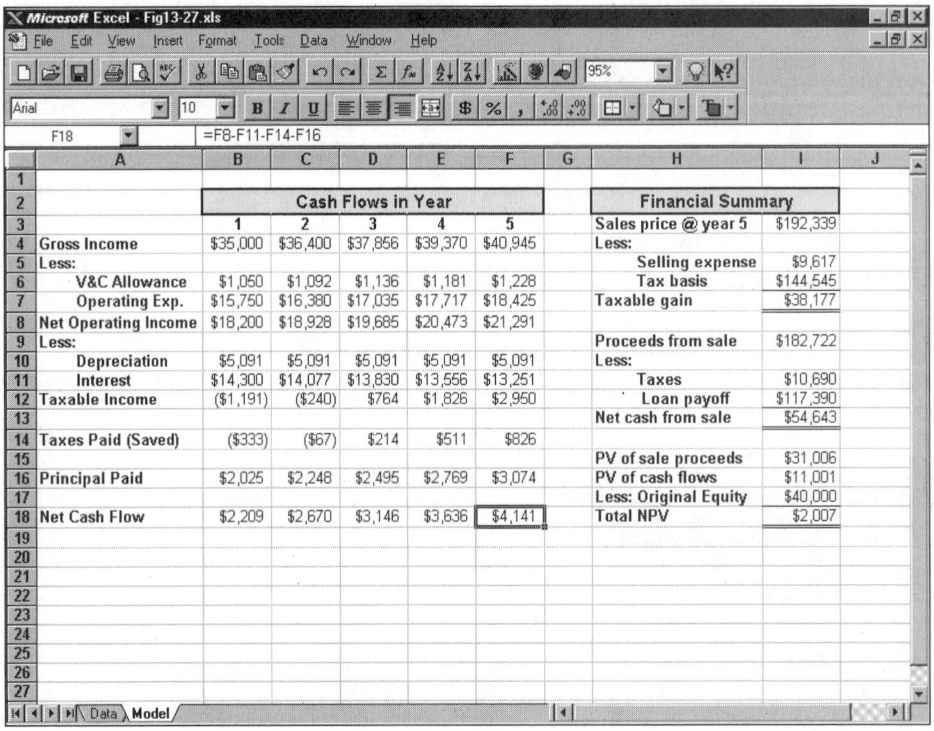

Figure 13.28
Cash flow and financial summary for the Foxridge Investment Group case.

	A	B	C	D	E	F	G	H	I	J
	F18			=F8-F11-F14-F16						
2			**Cash Flows in Year**					**Financial Summary**		
3		1	2	3	4	5		Sales price @ year 5	$192,339	
4	Gross Income	$35,000	$36,400	$37,856	$39,370	$40,945		Less:		
5	Less:							Selling expense	$9,617	
6	V&C Allowance	$1,050	$1,092	$1,136	$1,181	$1,228		Tax basis	$144,545	
7	Operating Exp.	$15,750	$16,380	$17,035	$17,717	$18,425		Taxable gain	$38,177	
8	Net Operating Income	$18,200	$18,928	$19,685	$20,473	$21,291				
9	Less:							Proceeds from sale	$182,722	
10	Depreciation	$5,091	$5,091	$5,091	$5,091	$5,091		Less:		
11	Interest	$14,300	$14,077	$13,830	$13,556	$13,251		Taxes	$10,690	
12	Taxable Income	($1,191)	($240)	$764	$1,826	$2,950		Loan payoff	$117,390	
13								Net cash from sale	$54,643	
14	Taxes Paid (Saved)	($333)	($67)	$214	$511	$826				
15								PV of sale proceeds	$31,006	
16	Principal Paid	$2,025	$2,248	$2,495	$2,769	$3,074		PV of cash flows	$11,001	
17								Less: Original Equity	$40,000	
18	Net Cash Flow	$2,209	$2,670	$3,146	$3,636	$4,141		Total NPV	$2,007	

To model the uncertainty in this decision problem, Mr. Hunter and his partner have decided that the growth in rental income from one year to the next could vary uniformly from 2% to 6% years 2 through 5. Similarly, they believe the V&C allowance in any year could be as low as 1% in any year and as high as 5%, with 3% being the most likely outcome. They think the operating expenses in each year should be normally distributed with a mean of 45% and standard deviation of 2% but should never be less than 40% and never greater than 50% of gross income. Finally, they believe the property value growth rate could be as small as 1% or as large as 5%, with 2.5% being the most likely outcome.

1. Revise the spreadsheets shown in Figures 13.27 and 13.28 to reflect the uncertainty outlined above.

2. Construct a 95% confidence interval for the average total NPV the Foxridge Investment Group can expect if they undertake this project. (Use 500 replications.) Interpret this confidence interval.

3. Based on your analysis, what is the probability of this project generating a positive total NPV if the group uses a 12% discount rate?

4. Suppose the investors are willing to buy the property if the expected total NPV is greater then zero. Based on your analysis, should they buy this property?

5. Assume the investors decide to increase the discount rate to 14% and repeat questions 2, 3, and 4.

REFERENCES

Banks, J. and J. Carson. *Discrete-Event Simulation.* Englewood Cliffs, NJ: Prentice Hall, 1984.

Hamzawi, S. "Management and Planning of Airport Gate Capacity: A Microcomputer-Based Gate Assignment Simulation Model." *Transportation Planning and Technology,* vol. 11, 1986.

Kaplan, A. and S. Frazza. "Empirical Inventory Simulation: A Case Study." *Decision Sciences,* vol. 14, January 1983.

Khoshnevis, B. *Discrete Systems Simulation.* New York: McGraw-Hill, 1994.

Law, A. and W. Kelton. *Simulation Modeling and Analysis.* New York: McGraw-Hill, 1990.

Marcus, A. "The Magellan Fund and Market Efficiency." *Journal of Portfolio Management,* Fall 1990.

Russell, R. and R. Hickle. "Simulation of a CD Portfolio." *Interfaces,* vol. 16, no. 3, 1986.

Vollman, T., W. Berry and C. Whybark. *Manufacturing Planning and Control Systems.* Homewood, IL: Irwin, 1987.

Watson, H. *Computer Simulation in Business.* New York: Wiley, 1981.

CHAPTER 14

Queuing Theory

Sometimes it seems as if we spend most of our lives waiting in lines. We wait in lines at grocery stores, banks, airports, hotels, restaurants, theaters, theme parks, post offices, and traffic lights. At home we are likely to spend time waiting in an "electronic line" if we use the telephone to order merchandise from mail-order firms, or to call the customer service number of most computer hardware or software companies.

Some reports indicate that Americans spend 37 *billion* hours a year waiting in lines. Much of this time represents a loss of a limited resource (time) that can never be recovered. Add the frustration and irritation many people experience while waiting in lines and it is easy to see why businesses should be interested in reducing or eliminating the amount of time their customers spend waiting in lines.

Waiting lines do not always contain people. In a manufacturing company, for example, subassemblies often wait in a line at machining centers to have the next operation performed on them. At a video rental store, returned videos often wait to be placed on shelves so they can be rented again. Electronic messages on the Internet sometimes wait at intermediate computing centers before they are sent to their final destinations. Costs could be reduced, or customer service improved, by reducing the amount of time that the subassemblies, videos, or electronic messages spend waiting in line.

In management science terminology, the term **queuing theory** represents the body of knowledge dealing with waiting lines. Queuing theory was conceived in the early 1900s when a Danish telephone engineer named A. K. Erlang began studying the congestion and waiting times occurring in the completion of telephone calls. Since then, a number of quantitative models have been developed to help business people understand waiting lines and make better decisions about how to manage them. This chapter introduces some of these models and discusses other issues involved in queuing theory.

14.1 THE PURPOSE OF QUEUING MODELS

Most queuing problems focus on determining the level of service that a company should provide. For example, grocery stores must determine how many cash registers to operate at a given time of day so that customers do not have to wait too long to check out. Banks must determine how many tellers to schedule at various times of day to maintain an acceptable level of service. Companies that lease copying machines must determine the number of technicians to employ so that repairs can be made in a timely manner.

In many queuing problems, management has some control over the level of service provided. In the examples just mentioned, customer waiting times could be kept to a minimum by employing a large number of servers (in the form of cashiers, tellers, and technicians). However, this can be expensive, or actually wasteful, if an excessive number of idle servers is maintained. On the other hand, employing a small number of servers keeps the cost of providing service low, but is likely to result in longer customer waiting times and greater customer dissatisfaction. Thus, a trade-off exists between the cost of providing service and the cost of having dissatisfied customers if service is lacking. The nature of this trade-off is illustrated in Figure 14.1.

Figure 14.1 indicates that as service levels increase, the cost of providing service also increases, but the cost of customer dissatisfaction decreases (as does the length of time customers must wait for service). As service levels decrease, the cost of providing service also decreases, but the cost of customer dissatisfaction increases. The objective in many queuing problems is to find the optimal service level that achieves an acceptable balance between the cost of providing service and customer satisfaction.

14.2   QUEUING SYSTEM CONFIGURATIONS

The queuing systems we encounter in everyday life are configured in a variety of ways. Three typical configurations are illustrated in Figure 14.2.

The first configuration in Figure 14.2 represents a single-queue, single-server system. In this configuration, customers enter the system and wait in line on a first-in,

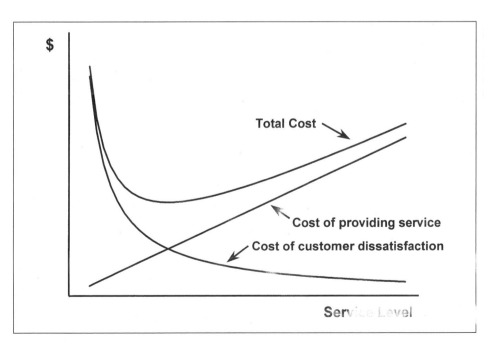

Figure 14.1
Trade-off between costs of providing service and customer satisfaction.

Figure 14.2
Examples of
different queuing
system
configurations.

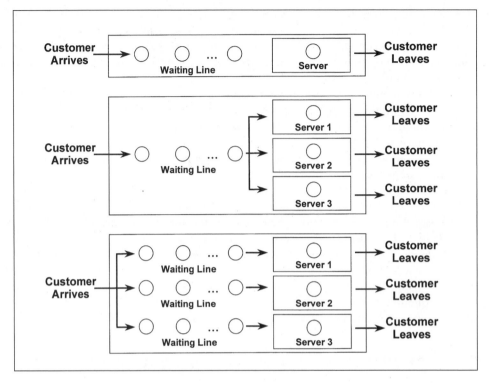

first-out (FIFO) basis until they receive service, then they exit the system. This type of queuing system is employed at most Wendy's and Taco Bell restaurants. You might also encounter this type of queuing system at some automatic teller machines (ATMs).

The second configuration in Figure 14.2 represents a single-queue, multi-server system. Here again, customers enter the system and join a FIFO queue. Upon reaching the front of the line, a customer is serviced by the next available server. The example shows three servers, but there could be more or fewer servers depending on the problem at hand. This type of queuing system is found at most airport check-in counters, post offices, and banks.

The third configuration in Figure 14.2 represents a collection of single-queue, single-server systems. In this type of arrangement, when customers arrive they must choose one of the queues and then wait in that line to receive service. This type of system is found at most grocery stores and most Burger King and McDonald's restaurants.

This chapter discusses queuing models that can be used to analyze the first two types of configurations shown in Figure 14.2. In some cases, the individual queues in the third configuration in Figure 14.2 can be analyzed as independent, single-queue, single-server systems. Thus, the results presented for the first type of configuration can sometimes be generalized to analyze the third configuration also.

14.3   CHARACTERISTICS OF QUEUING SYSTEMS

To create and analyze mathematical models of the queuing configurations shown in Figure 14.2, we must make some assumptions about the way in which customers arrive to the system and the amount of time it takes for them to receive service.

14.3.1 Arrival Rate

In most queuing systems, customers (or jobs in a manufacturing environment) arrive in a somewhat random fashion. That is, the number of arrivals that occurs in a given time period represents a random variable. It is often appropriate to model the arrival process in a queuing system as a Poisson random variable. To use the Poisson probability distribution, we must specify a value for the **arrival rate,** denoted as λ, representing the average number of arrivals per time period. (For a Poisson random variable, the variance of the number of arrivals per time period is also λ.) The probability of x arrivals in a specific time period is represented by:

$$P(x) = \lambda^x e^{-\lambda}/x! \quad \text{for } x = 0, 1, 2, \dots \qquad \textbf{14.1}$$

where e represents the base of the natural logarithm ($e = 2.71828$) and $x! = (x)(x-1)(x-2)\dots(2)(1)$. ($x!$ is referred to as x factorial and can be calculated using the FACT( ) function in Excel.)

For example, suppose that calls to the customer service hotline of a computer retailer occur at a rate of five per hour and follow a Poisson probability distribution ($\lambda = 5$). The probability distribution associated with the number of calls arriving in a given hour is illustrated in Figure 14.3 (and in the file FIG14-3.xls on your data disk).

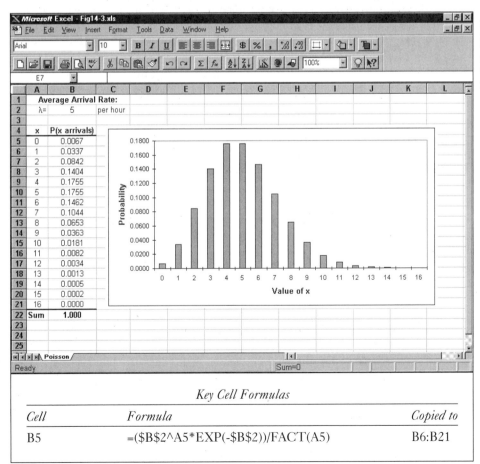

Figure 14.3
Example of a Poisson probability distribution with mean $\lambda=5$.

Key Cell Formulas		
Cell	*Formula*	*Copied to*
B5	=($B$2^A5*EXP(-$B$2))/FACT(A5)	B6:B21

In Figure 14.3, the values in column B represent the probabilities associated with each value in column A. For example, the value in cell B5 indicates that a 0.0067 probability exists of 0 calls arriving in a given hour; cell B6 indicates that a 0.0337 probability exists of 1 call arriving, and so on. The histogram of the probability distribution indicates that, on average, we can expect approximately five calls to arrive in one hour. However, because the Poisson distribution is skewed to the right, a significantly larger number of calls (in this case, 13 or more) could arrive in some one-hour time periods.

Figure 14.3 indicates that the probability of six calls occurring in a given hour is 0.1462. However, the six calls probably will not occur at the same time. Some random amount of time is likely to transpire between arriving calls. This time between arrivals is known as the **interarrival time.** If the number of arrivals in a given period of time follows a Poisson distribution with mean λ, it can be shown that the interarrival times follow an exponential probability distribution with mean $1/\lambda$.

For example, if calls to the computer retailer's hotline follow a Poisson distribution and occur at an average rate of $\lambda = 5$ per hour, the interarrival times follow an exponential distribution with an average interarrival time of $1/5 = 0.2$ hours. That is, calls occur once every 12 minutes, on average (because there are 60 minutes in an hour and $0.2*60$ minutes $= 12$ minutes).

The exponential distribution plays a key role in queuing models. It is one of the few probability distributions that exhibit the memoryless (or lack of memory) property. An arrival process is **memoryless** if the time until the next arrival occurs does not depend on how much time has elapsed since the last arrival. The Russian mathematician Markov was the first to recognize the memoryless property of certain random variables. Therefore, the memoryless property is also sometimes referred to as the **Markov** or **Markovian property.**

All the queuing models presented in this chapter assume that arrivals follow a Poisson distribution (or, equivalently, that interarrival times follow an exponential distribution). To use these models, it is important to verify that this assumption is valid for the queuing system being modeled. One way to verify that arrivals can be approximated by the Poisson distribution is to collect data on the number of arrivals occurring per time period for several hours, days, or weeks. The average number of arrivals per time period can be calculated from these data and used as an estimate of λ. A histogram of the actual data can be constructed and compared to a histogram of the actual probabilities expected of a Poisson random variable with mean λ. If the histograms are similar, it is reasonable to assume that the arrival process is approximately Poisson. (Additional goodness-of-fit tests can be found in most texts on queuing and simulation.)

14.3.2   Service Rate

A customer who arrives at a service facility spends some amount of time (possibly 0) waiting in line for service to begin. We refer to this time as **queue time. Service time** is the amount of time a customer spends at a service facility once the actual performance of service begins. (So service time *does not* include queue time.)

It is often appropriate to model the service times in a queuing system as an exponential random variable. To use the exponential probability distribution for this purpose, we must specify a value for the **service rate,** denoted by μ, representing the average number of customers (or jobs) that can be served per time period. The average service time per customer is $1/\mu$ time periods (and the variance of the service time per customer is $(1/\mu)^2$ time periods). Because the exponential distribution is continuous, the probability of an exponential random variable equaling any specific value is zero. Thus, probabilities associated with an exponential random variable must be defined in terms of intervals. If the distribution of service times follows an exponential distribution, the probability that the service time T of a given customer will be between t_1 and t_2 time periods is defined by:

$$P(t_1 \leq T \leq t_2) = \int_{t_1}^{t_2} \mu e^{-\mu x}\,dx = e^{-\mu t_1} - e^{-\mu t_2}, \text{ for } t_1 \leq t_2 \qquad \textbf{14.2}$$

For example, suppose that the operator on the customer service hotline can service calls at a rate of seven per hour, on average, and that the service times follow an exponential distribution ($\mu = 7$). Figure 14.4 (and the file FIG14-4.xls on your data disk) shows the probability of the service time falling within several time intervals.

In Figure 14.4, the value in cell D5 indicates that a 0.295 probability exists that it will take from 0 to 0.05 hours (or 3 minutes) to service any call. Similarly, the value in cell D9 indicates that a 0.073 probability exists that it will take between 0.2 and 0.25 hours (or from 12 to 15 minutes) to service any call.

The data and graph in Figure 14.4 indicate that for exponential distributions, shorter service times have the largest relative probability of occurring. In reality, some minimal amount of time is usually required to provide most services. This might lead us to believe that the exponential distribution would tend to underestimate the actual service time required by most customers. However, the exponential distribution

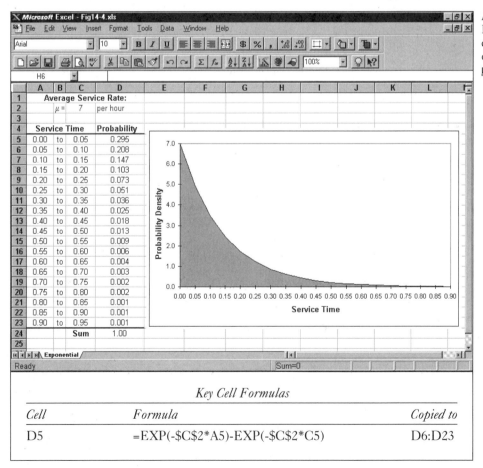

Figure 14.4
Example of an exponential distribution with $\mu=7$.

<table>
<thead>
<tr><th colspan="3">Key Cell Formulas</th></tr>
<tr><th>Cell</th><th>Formula</th><th>Copied to</th></tr>
</thead>
<tbody>
<tr><td>D5</td><td>=EXP(-$C$2*A5)-EXP(-$C$2*C5)</td><td>D6:D23</td></tr>
</tbody>
</table>

also assumes that some very long service times will occur (though very infrequently). The possibility of these very long (but infrequent) service times provides a balance to the very short (but frequent) service times so that, on average, the exponential distribution provides a reasonably accurate description of the behavior of service times in many real-world problems. But keep in mind that the exponential distribution is not an adequate model of service times in all applications.

One way to verify that the service rate can be modeled using the exponential distribution is to collect data on the service times occurring per time period for several hours, days, or weeks. The average number of customers serviced per time period can be calculated from these data and used as an estimate of the service rate μ. Using actual data, a relative frequency distribution of the service times falling within various intervals can be constructed and compared to the distribution of the actual probabilities expected for each interval for an exponential random variable with a service rate of μ (like the one shown in Figure 14.4). If the distributions are similar, it is reasonable to assume that the distribution of service times is approximately exponential. (Again, additional goodness-of-fit tests can be found in most texts on queuing and simulation.)

14.4   KENDALL NOTATION

Given the variety of queuing models that exist, a system known as **Kendall notation** was developed to allow the key characteristics of a specific queuing model to be described in an efficient manner. With Kendall notation, simple queuing models can be described by three characteristics in the following general format:

$$1/2/3$$

The first characteristic identifies the nature of the arrival process using the following standard abbreviations:

> M = Markovian interarrival times (following an exponential distribution)
> D = deterministic interarrival times (not random)

The second characteristic identifies the nature of the service times using the following standard abbreviations:

> M = Markovian service times (following an exponential distribution)
> G = general service times (following a nonexponential distribution)
> D = deterministic service times (not random)

Finally, the third characteristic indicates the number of servers available. So, using Kendall notation, an M/M/1 queue refers to a queuing model in which the time between arrivals follows an exponential distribution, the service times follow an exponential distribution, and there is one server. An M/G/3 queue refers to a model in which the interarrival times are assumed to be exponential, the service times follow some general distribution, and three servers are present.

An expanded version of Kendall notation involves specifying six (rather than three) queue characteristics. A more complete description of this notation can be found in advanced management science or queuing texts.

14.5   QUEUING MODELS

Numerous queuing models are available to evaluate different combinations of arrival distributions, service time distributions, and other queuing characteristics. This chapter discusses only a few of these models. Typical operating characteristics of interest include:

Characteristic	Description
U	Utilization factor, or the percentage of time that all servers are busy
P_0	Probability that there are no units in the system
L_q	Average number of units in line waiting for service
L	Average number of units in the system (in line and being served)
W_q	Average time a unit spends in line waiting for service
W	Average time a unit spends in the system (in line and being served)
P_w	Probability that an arriving unit has to wait for service
P_n	Probability of n units in the system

Information about these operating characteristics can be helpful to managers who need to make decisions about the trade-offs between the costs of providing different levels of service and the associated impact on customers' experiences in the queuing system. Where possible, researchers have derived closed-form equations to calculate various operating characteristics of a particular queuing model. For instance, for the M/M/1 queuing model it can be shown that:

$$W = \frac{1}{\mu - \lambda}$$

$$L = \lambda W$$

$$W_q = W - \frac{1}{\mu}$$

$$L_q = \lambda W_q$$

This chapter does not show the derivation of the equations used to calculate operating characteristics. Rather, it simply states the equations for several common queuing models and shows how they can be used. The equations for the queuing models we'll consider are implemented in spreadsheet templates in the file Q.xls on your data disk. Figure 14.5 shows the introduction screen for these templates.

As Figure 14.5 indicates, the templates in this file can be used to analyze four types of queuing models: the M/M/s model, the M/M/s model with finite queue length, the M/M/s model with finite arrival population, and the M/G/1 model.

14.6   THE M/M/S MODEL

The M/M/s model is appropriate for analyzing queuing problems where the following assumptions are met:

- There are s servers, where s is a positive integer.
- Arrivals follow a Poisson distribution and occur at an average rate of λ per time period.

Figure 14.5
Introductory
screen for Q.xls
queuing
template file.

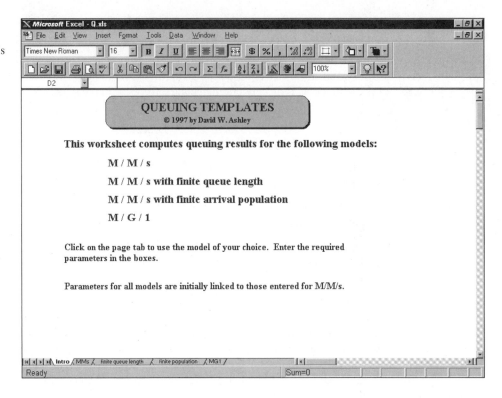

- Each server provides service at an average rate of μ per time period, and actual service times follow an exponential distribution.
- Arrivals wait in a single FIFO queue and are serviced by the first available server.
- $\lambda < s\mu$.

The final assumption indicates that the total service capacity of the system, $s\mu$, must be strictly greater than the rate at which arrivals occur λ. If the arrival rate exceeds the system's total service capacity, the system would fill up over time and the queue would become infinitely long. In fact, the queue becomes infinitely long even if the average arrival rate λ is equal to the average service rate $s\mu$. To see why, note that individual arrival times and service times vary in an unpredictable manner (even though their averages may be constant). So there will be times when the servers are idle. This idle time is lost forever and the servers will not be able to make up for this at other times when the demand for service is heavy. (Note that demand is never lost forever but is assumed to wait patiently in the queue.) This causes the servers to fall hopelessly behind if $\lambda \geq s\mu$.

The formulas describing the operating characteristics of the M/M/s model are given in Figure 14.6. Although these formulas might seem somewhat daunting, they are easy to use when implemented in a spreadsheet template.

14.6.1   An Example

The following example illustrates how the M/M/s model might be used.

The customer support hotline for Bitway Computers is currently staffed by a single technician. Calls arrive randomly at a rate of five per hour and follow a

$$U = \lambda/(s\mu)$$

$$P_0 = \left(\sum_{n=0}^{s-1} \frac{(\lambda/\mu)^n}{n!} + \frac{(\lambda/\mu)^s}{s!} \left(\frac{s\mu}{s\mu - \lambda} \right) \right)^{-1}$$

$$L_q = \frac{P_0(\lambda/\mu)^{s+1}}{(s-1)!(s - \lambda/\mu)^2}$$

$$L = L_q + \frac{\lambda}{\mu}$$

$$W_q = \frac{L_q}{\lambda}$$

$$W = W_q + \frac{1}{\mu}$$

$$P_w = \frac{1}{s!} \left(\frac{\lambda}{\mu} \right)^s \left(\frac{s\mu}{s\mu - \lambda} \right) P_0$$

$$P_n = \frac{(\lambda/\mu)^n}{n!} P_0, \text{ for } n \leq s$$

$$P_n = \frac{(\lambda/\mu)^n}{s!s^{(n-s)}} P_0, \text{ for } n > s$$

Figure 14.6
Formulas describing the operating characteristics of an M/M/s queue.

Poisson distribution. The technician can service calls at an average rate of seven per hour, but the actual time required to handle a given call is an exponential random variable. The president of Bitway, Rod Taylor, has received numerous complaints from customers about the length of time they must wait "on hold" for service when calling the hotline. Rod wants to determine the average length of time customers currently wait before the technician answers their calls. If the average waiting time is more than five minutes, he wants to determine how many technicians would be required to reduce the average waiting time to two minutes or less.

14.6.2 The Current Situation

Because only one technician (or server) currently staffs Bitway's customer service hotline, we can calculate the operating characteristics for the hotline using an M/M/1 queuing model. Figure 14.7 shows the results of this model for Bitway's current configuration.

Cells E2, E3, and E4 contain the values for the arrival rate, service rate, and number of servers in our example problem, respectively. (Note that this template is designed to accommodate a maximum of 40 servers.) The various operating characteristics of this model are calculated automatically in column F.

Figure 14.7
Results of the
M/M/1 model for
Bitway's
customer service
model.

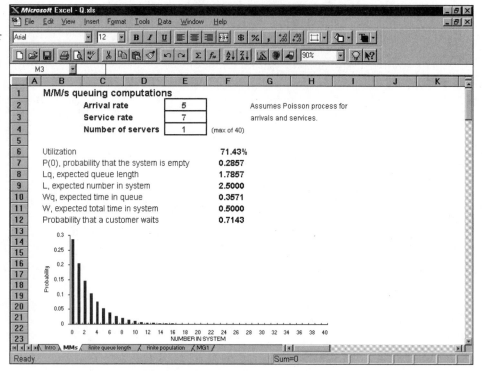

The value in cell F12 indicates that a 0.7143 probability exists that callers to Bitway's customer service hotline must wait on hold before receiving service from the technician. The value in cell F10 indicates that the average length of this wait is 0.3571 hours (or approximately 21.42 minutes). The value in cell F11 indicates that, on average, a caller spends a total of 0.5 hours (or 30 minutes) waiting for service and being served under Bitway's current hotline configuration. Thus, it appears that the customer complaints to Bitway's president are justifiable.

14.6.3   Adding a Server

To improve the level of service on the hotline, Bitway could investigate how the operating characteristics of the system would change if two technicians were assigned to answer calls. That is, incoming calls could be handled by either one of two equally capable technicians. We can calculate the operating characteristics for this configuration using an M/M/2 queuing model, as shown in Figure 14.8.

The value in cell F12 indicates that, with two servers, the probability that a caller must wait before receiving service drops significantly from 0.7143 to 0.1880. Similarly, cell F10 indicates that the average amount of time a caller must wait before service begins drops to 0.0209 hours (or approximately 1.25 minutes). Thus, it seems that adding a second technician to the customer service hotline would achieve the two-minute average waiting time objective Rod wants.

Although the addition of a second server greatly reduces the average time hotline callers spend waiting for service to begin, it does not reduce the expected *service time*. For the M/M/1 model in Figure 14.7, which includes only one server, the expected total time in the system is 0.5 hours and the expected queue time is 0.3571 hours.

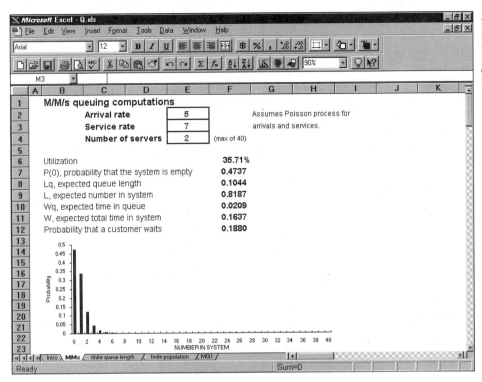

Figure 14.8
Results of the
M/M/2 model for
Bitway's
customer service
hotline.

This implies that the expected service time is 0.5 − 0.3571 = 0.1429 hours. For the M/M/2 model in Figure 14.8, which includes two servers, the expected total time in the system is 0.1637 hours and the expected queue time is 0.0209 hours. This implies an expected service time of 0.1637 − 0.0209 = 0.1429 hours (allowing for a slight rounding error). The M/M/2 model assumes that both servers can provide service at the same rate—in this case, an average of seven calls per hour. Therefore, the average service time per call should be 1/7 = 0.1429 hours, which is consistent with the observed results.

14.6.4   Economic Analysis

Bitway will undoubtedly incur some additional costs in going from one to two customer support technicians. This might include the cost of salary and benefits for the additional technician and perhaps an additional telephone line. However, the improved service level provided by the two-server system should reduce the number of customer complaints and perhaps lead to favorable word-of-mouth advertising and increased business for the company. Rod could attempt to quantify these benefits and compare them to the cost of adding a customer support technician. Alternatively, Rod may simply view the addition of the customer support technician as a competitive necessity.

14.7   THE M/M/s MODEL WITH FINITE QUEUE LENGTH

The results for the M/M/s models in Figures 14.7 and 14.8 assume that the size or capacity of the waiting area is infinite, so that all arrivals to the system join the queue and wait for service. In some situations, however, the size or capacity of the waiting area might be restricted—in other words, there might be a finite queue length. The formulas describing the operating characteristics of an M/M/s queue with a finite queue length of K are summarized in Figure 14.9.

To see how this queuing model might be used, suppose that Bitway's telephone system can keep a maximum of five calls on hold at any point in time. If a new call is made to the hotline when five calls are already in the queue, the new call receives a busy signal. One way to reduce the number of calls encountering busy signals is to increase the number of calls that can be put on hold. However, if a call is answered only to be put on hold for a long time, the caller might find this more annoying than receiving a busy signal. Thus, Rod might want to investigate what effect adding a second technician to answer hotline calls would have on the number of calls receiving busy signals and on the average time callers must wait before receiving service.

14.7.1   The Current Situation

Because only one technician (or server) currently staffs Bitway's customer service hotline, we can calculate the current operating characteristics for the hotline using an M/M/1 queuing model with a finite queue length of five. Figure 14.10 shows the results of this model for Bitway's current configuration.

Figure 14.9
Formulas describing the operating characteristics of an M/M/s queue with a finite queue length of K.

$$U = (L - L_q)/s$$

$$P_0 = \left(1 + \sum_{n=1}^{s} \frac{(\lambda/\mu)^n}{n!} + \frac{(\lambda/\mu)^s}{s!} \sum_{n=s+1}^{K} \left(\frac{\lambda}{s\mu}\right)^{n-s}\right)^{-1}$$

$$P_n = \frac{(\lambda/\mu)^n}{n!} P_0, \text{ for } n = 1, 2, \ldots, s$$

$$P_n = \frac{(\lambda/\mu)^n}{s!\,s^{n-s}} P_0, \text{ for } n = s + 1, s + 2, \ldots, K$$

$$P_n = 0, \text{ for } n > K$$

$$L_q = \frac{P_0(\lambda/\mu)^s \rho}{s!(1 - \rho)^2} \left(1 - \rho^{K-s} - (K-s)\rho^{K-s}(1-\rho)\right), \text{ where } \rho = \lambda/(s\mu)$$

$$L = \sum_{n=0}^{s-1} nP_n + L_q + s\left(1 - \sum_{n=0}^{s-1} P_n\right)$$

$$W_q = \frac{L_q}{\lambda(1 - P_K)}$$

$$W = \frac{L}{\lambda(1 - P_K)}$$

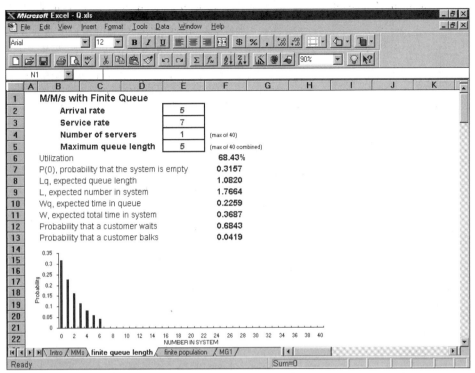

Figure 14.10
Results of the
M/M/1 model
with a finite
queue length of
five for Bitway's
customer service
hotline.

Cells E2, E3, and E4 contain the values for the arrival rate, service rate, and number of servers in our example problem, respectively. Cell E5 contains the maximum queue length of five. Note that the template in Figure 14.10 is designed to accommodate a maximum of 40 servers and also requires that the sum of the values E4 and E5 not exceed 40.

The value in cell F13 indicates that a 0.0419 probability exists that callers to Bitway's customer service hotline will balk (or, in this case, receive a busy signal). A **balk** refers to an arrival that does not join the queue because the queue is full or too long. The value in cell F10 indicates that the average length of this wait is 0.2259 hours (or approximately 13.55 minutes). The value in cell F11 indicates that, on average, a caller spends a total of 0.3687 hours (or 22.12 minutes) either waiting for service or being served under Bitway's current hotline configuration.

14.7.2 Adding a Server

To improve the level of service on the hotline, Bitway could investigate how the operating characteristics of the system would change if two technicians were assigned to answer calls. We can calculate the operating characteristics for this configuration using an M/M/2 queuing model with a finite queue length of five, as shown in Figure 14.11.

The value in cell F13 indicates that, with two servers, the probability that a caller receives a busy signal drops to 0.0007. Similarly, cell F10 indicates that the average amount of time a caller must wait before service begins drops to 0.0204 hours (or approximately 1.22 minutes). Thus, it seems that adding a second technician to the customer service hotline would achieve the two-minute average waiting time objective Rod wants and would virtually eliminate any chance of a customer receiving a

Figure 14.11
Results of the
M/M/2 model
with a finite
queue length of
five for Bitway's
customer service
hotline.

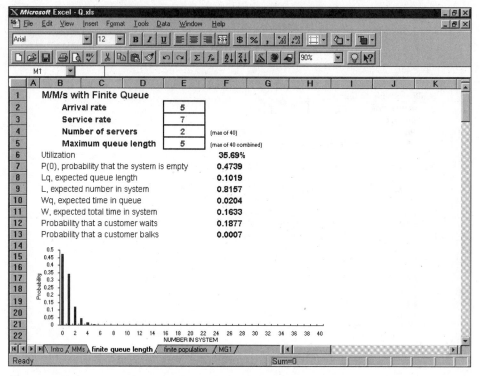

busy signal. Here again, Rod should consider weigh the costs of adding the additional support technician against the benefits of eliminating the chances of customers receiving busy signals when they call the customer support hotline.

14.8   THE M/M/s MODEL WITH FINITE POPULATION

The previous queuing models assume that the customers (or calls) arriving at the queuing system come from a population of potential customers that is infinite, or extremely large. Under this assumption, the mean arrival rate, λ, remains constant regardless of the number of calls in the system.

In some queuing problems, however, the possible number of arriving customers is finite. In other words, these queuing models have a finite arrival (or calling) population. In such a model, the average arrival rate for the system changes depending on the number of customers in the queue. The M/M/s model for finite arrival populations is appropriate for analyzing queuing problems where the following assumptions are met:

- There are s servers, where s is a positive integer.
- There are N potential customers in the arrival population.
- The arrival pattern of *each customer* follows a Poisson distribution with a mean arrival rate of λ per time period.
- Each server provides service at an average rate of μ per time period, and actual service times follow an exponential distribution.
- Arrivals wait in a single FIFO queue and are serviced by the first available server.

Note that the average arrival rate for this model (λ) is defined in terms of the rate at which *each customer* arrives. The formulas describing the operating characteristics for an M/M/s queue with a finite arrival population of size N are summarized in Figure 14.12.

14.8.1 An Example

One of the most common applications for the M/M/s model with a finite arrival population is the machine repair problem, as illustrated in the following example.

The Miller Manufacturing Company owns 10 identical machines that it uses in the production of colored nylon thread for the textile industry. Machine breakdowns occur following a Poisson distribution with an average of 0.01 breakdowns occurring per operating hour per machine. The company loses $100 each hour a machine is inoperable. The company employs one technician to fix these machines when they break down. Service times to repair the machines are exponentially distributed with an average of eight hours per repair. Thus, service is performed at a rate of 1/8 machines per hour. Management wants to analyze what impact adding another service technician would have on the average length of time required to fix a machine when it breaks down. Service technicians are paid $20 per hour.

$$P_0 = \left(\sum_{n=0}^{s-1} \frac{N!}{(N-n)!n!} \left(\frac{\lambda}{\mu}\right)^n + \sum_{n=s}^{N} \frac{N!}{(N-n)!s!s^{n-s}} \left(\frac{\lambda}{\mu}\right)^n \right)^{-1}$$

$$P_n = \frac{N!}{(N-n)!n!} \left(\frac{\lambda}{\mu}\right)^n P_0, \text{ if } 0 \le n \le s$$

$$P_n = \frac{N!}{(N-n)!s!s^{n-s}} \left(\frac{\lambda}{\mu}\right)^n P_0, \text{ if } s < n \le N$$

$$P_n = 0, \text{ if } n > N$$

$$L_q = \sum_{n=s}^{N} (n-s)P_n$$

$$L = \sum_{n=0}^{s-1} nP_n + L_q + s\left(1 - \sum_{n=0}^{s-1} P_n\right)$$

$$W_q = \frac{L_q}{\lambda(N-L)}$$

$$W = \frac{L}{\lambda(N-L)}$$

Figure 14.12
Formulas describing the operating characteristics of an M/M/s queue with a finite arrival population of size N.

14.8.2   The Current Situation

The 10 machines in this problem represent a finite set of objects that can break down. Therefore, the M/M/s model for a finite calling operation is appropriate to use for analyzing this problem. The current operating characteristics for Miller Manufacturing's machine repair problem are summarized in Figure 14.13.

Because the individual machines break down at a rate of 0.01 per hour, this is the rate at which individual machines "arrive" for repair. Thus, cell E2 contains the value 0.01 to represent the arrival rate per customer (machine). The technician can service broken machines at an average rate of 1/8 = 0.125 machines per hour, as indicated in cell E3. The number of servers (or technicians) is shown in cell E4. Because there are 10 machines that can break down, cell E5 contains a population size of 10. The spreadsheet calculates the overall arrival rate shown in cell H2. Because there are 10 machines, each with a 0.01 probability of breaking down each hour, the overall arrival rate of broken machines is 10*0.01 = 0.1, as indicated in cell H2.

The operating characteristics for this system are calculated in cells F6 through F12. According to cell F11, whenever a machine breaks down, it is out of operation for an average of 17.98 hours. Of this total down time, cell F10 indicates that the machine spends approximately 10 hours waiting for service to begin. Cell F9 indicates that approximately 1.524 machines are out of operation at any point in time.

We used columns H through J of the worksheet to calculate the economic consequences of the current situation. There is one server (or service technician) in this problem who is paid $20 per hour. According to cell F9, an average of approximately 1.524 machines are broken in any given hour. Because the company loses $100 each hour a machine is inoperable, cell J9 indicates the company is presently losing about

Figure 14.13
Results of an M/M/1 model with a finite population of 10 machines for Miller Manufacturing's machine repair problem.

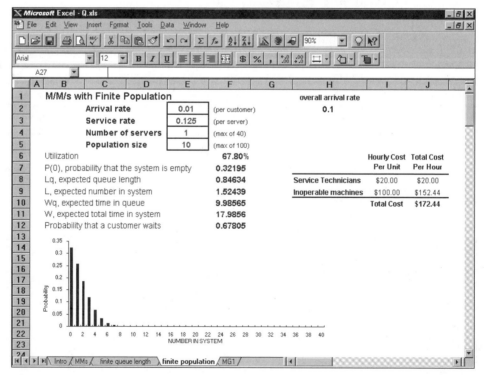

Software Note

The Q.xls file comes "protected" so that you will not inadvertently write over or delete important formulas in this template. Sometimes you may want to turn off this protection on a sheet so you can do your own calculations off to the side or format your results (as shown in Figure 14.13). To do this,

1. Click Tools.
2. Click Protection.
3. Select Unprotect Sheet.

If you unprotect a sheet, you should take special care not to alter any of the formulas on the sheet.

$152.44 per hour due to machine down-time. Thus, with a single service technician the company is incurring costs at the rate of $172.44 per hour.

14.8.3 Adding Servers

Figure 14.14 shows the expected operation of this system if Miller Manufacturing adds another service technician.

Cell F10 indicates that when a machine breaks down, repairs start, on average, in only 0.82 hours (or approximately 49 minutes), in comparison to the 10-hour waiting time with only one technician. Similarly, cell F9 indicates that with two technicians,

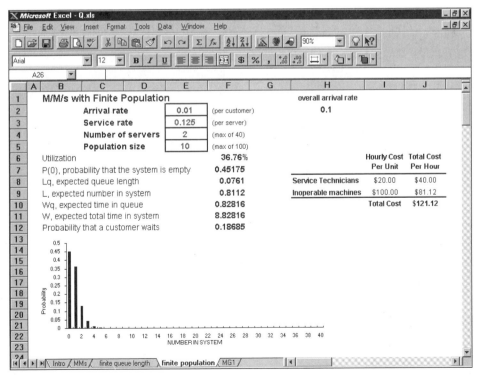

Figure 14.14
Results of an M/M/2 model with a finite population of 10 machines for Miller Manufacturing's machine repair problem.

an average of only 0.81 machines are out of operation at any point in time. Thus, by adding another repair technician, Miller Manufacturing can keep approximately one more machine in operation at all times. Thus, while the additional service technician increases the total hourly cost by $40, the decrease in the average number of machines in the system saves the company $71.32 per hour (i.e., 152.44 − 81.12 = 71.32). The net effect is a cost savings of $51.32 as the total hourly cost in cell J10 drops to $121.12.

Figure 14.15 shows the results of adding a third service technician for this problem. Notice that this has the effect of increasing labor costs by $20 per hour over the solution shown in Figure 14.14 while reducing the losses due to idle machines by only $6.36. So as we go from two to three service technicians the total hourly cost increases from $121.12 to $134.76 per hour. Thus, the optimal solution is for Miller Manufacturing to employ two service technicians because this results in the smallest total hourly cost.

14.9   THE M/G/1 MODEL

All the models presented so far assume that service times follow an exponential distribution. As noted earlier in Figure 14.4, random service times from an exponential distribution can assume *any* positive value. However, in some situations this assumption is unrealistic. For example, consider the time required to change the oil in a car at an auto service center. This service probably requires *at least* 10 minutes and might require up to 30, 45, or even 60 minutes, depending on the service being performed. The M/G/1 queuing model enables us to analyze queuing problems in which service times cannot be modeled accurately using an exponential distribution. The formulas describing the operating characteristics of an M/G/1 queue are summarized in Figure 14.16.

Figure 14.15
Results of an M/M/3 model with a finite population of 10 machines for Miller Manufacturing's machine repair problem.

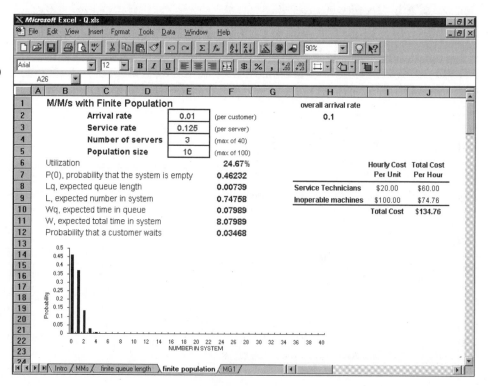

$$P_0 = 1 - \lambda/\mu$$

$$L_q = \frac{\lambda^2\sigma^2 + (\lambda/\mu)^2}{2(1 - \lambda/\mu)}$$

$$L = L_q + \lambda/\mu$$

$$W_q = L_q/\lambda$$

$$W = W_q + 1/\mu$$

$$P_w = \lambda/\mu$$

Figure 14.16
Formulas describing the operating characteristics of an M/G/1 queue.

The M/G/1 queuing model is quite remarkable because it can be used to compute the operating characteristics for *any* one-server queuing system where arrivals follow a Poisson distribution and the mean μ and standard deviation σ of the service times are known. That is, the formulas in Figure 14.16 do not require that service times follow one specific probability distribution. The following example illustrates the use of the M/G/1 queuing model.

Zippy-Lube is a drive-through automotive oil change business that operates 10 hours a day, 6 days a week. The profit margin on an oil change at Zippy-Lube is $15. Cars arrive randomly at the Zippy-Lube oil change center following a Poisson distribution at an average rate of 3.5 cars per hour. After reviewing the historical data on operations at this business, the owner of Zippy-Lube, Olie Boe, has determined that the average service time per car is 15 minutes (or 0.25 hours) with a standard deviation of 2 minutes (or 0.0333 hours). Olie has the opportunity to purchase a new automated oil dispensing device that costs $5,000. The manufacturer's representative claims this device will reduce the average service time by 3 minutes per car. (Currently, Olie's employees manually open and pour individual cans of oil.) Olie would like to analyze the impact the new automated device would have on his business and determine the payback period for this device.

14.9.1   The Current Situation

We can model Olie's current service facility as an M/G/1 queue. The operating characteristics of this facility are shown in Figure 14.17.

Cell E3 contains the average arrival rate of 3.5 cars per hour. The average service time per car (also in hours) is indicated in cell E4, and the standard deviation of the service time (in hours) is indicated in cell E5. Cell F11 shows that an average of about

Figure 14.17
Results of an
M/G/1 model for
the original
Zippy-Lube
problem.

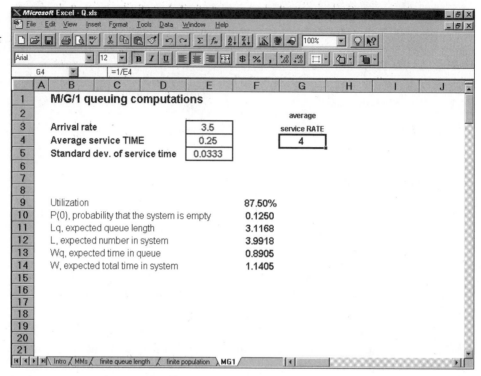

3.12 cars wait for service at any given point in time. Cell F14 indicates that, on average, 1.14 hours (or about 68 minutes) elapse between the time a car arrives and leaves the system.

14.9.2   Adding the Automated Dispensing Device

If Olie purchases the automated oil dispensing device, the average service time per car should drop to 12 minutes (or 0.20 hours). Figure 14.18 shows the impact this would have if the arrival rate remained constant at 3.5 cars per hour.

The value in cell F14 indicates that going to the automated oil dispensing device reduces the amount of time a car spends in the system from 1.14 hours to 0.4398 hours (or about 26 minutes). Cell F11 indicates that the expected queue in front of the service bay consists of only 0.8393 cars, on average. Thus, the addition of a new oil dispensing device would significantly improve customer service.

The shorter queue at Zippy-Lube resulting from the acquisition of the automated dispensing device would likely result in an increase in the arrival rate, because customers who previously balked when confronted with a lengthy queue might now consider stopping for service. Thus, Olie might be interested in determining just how much the arrival rate could increase before the average queue length returned to its original level of about 3.12 shown in Figure 14.17. We can use the Goal Seek tool to answer this question. To do this,

1. Click Tools.
2. Click Goal Seek.
3. Fill in the Goal Seek dialog box as shown in Figure 14.19.
4. Click OK.

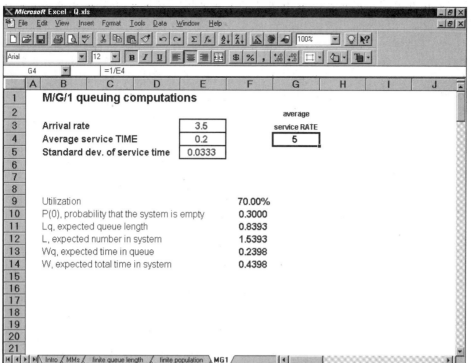

Figure 14.18
Results of an
M/G/1 model for
the Zippy-Lube
problem after
purchasing the
automatic oil
dispensing
machine and
assuming an
increase in
arrivals.

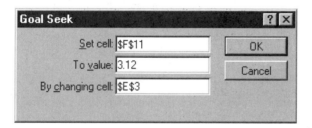

Figure 14.19
Goal Seek
settings to
determine the
arrival rate that
produces an
average queue
length of 3.12
cars.

The results of this Goal Seek analysis are shown in Figure 14.20. Here we see that if the arrival rate increases to 4.37 cars per hour, the average length of the queue will return to approximately 3.12. Thus, by purchasing the automatic oil dispensing machine it is reasonable to expect that the average number of cars arriving for service at Zippy-Lube might increase from 3.5 per hour to approximately 4.371.

Column I in Figure 14.20 summarizes the financial impact of purchasing the new oil dispensing machine. Because the arrival rate may be expected to increase by approximately 0.871 cars per hour, weekly profits should increase by approximately $783.63 per week. If this increase in profits occurs, the pay-back period for the new machine will be approximately 6.38 weeks.

14.10 THE M/D/1 MODEL

The M/G/1 model can be used when service times are random with known mean and standard deviation. However, service times might not be random in some queuing

Figure 14.20
Results of an
M/G/1 model for
the Zippy-Lube
problem after
purchasing the
automatic oil
dispensing
machine and
assuming arrival
rate will
increase.

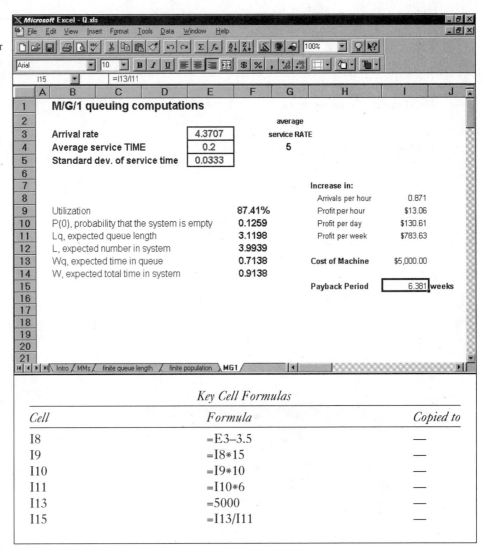

Cell	Formula	Copied to
I8	=E3–3.5	—
I9	=I8*15	—
I10	=I9*10	—
I11	=I10*6	—
I13	=5000	—
I15	=I13/I11	—

systems. For example, in a manufacturing environment it is not unusual to have a queue of material or subassemblies waiting to be serviced by a certain machine. The machine time required to perform the service might be very predictable—such as exactly 10 seconds of machine time per piece. Similarly, an automatic car wash might spend exactly the same amount of time on each car it services. The M/D/1 model can be used in these types of situations where the service times are deterministic (not random).

The results for an M/D/1 model can be obtained using the M/G/1 model by setting the standard deviation of the service time to 0 ($\sigma = 0$). Setting $\sigma = 0$ indicates that no variability exists in the service times and, therefore, the service time for each unit is equal to the average service time μ.

14.11   SIMULATING QUEUES

Queuing theory is one of the oldest and most well-researched areas of management science. Discussions of other types of queuing models can be found in advanced texts on management science and in texts devoted solely to queuing theory. However, keep in mind that the technique of simulation can be used to analyze virtually any queuing problem you might encounter. Indeed, not all queuing models have closed-form equations to describe their operating characteristics. So simulation is often the only means available for analyzing complex queuing systems where customers balk (don't join a queue upon arrival), renege (leave a queue before being served), or jockey (switch from one queue to another).

14.12 THE STEADY-STATE ASSUMPTION

The formulas used in this chapter describe the *steady-state* operations of the various queuing systems presented. At the beginning of each day, most queuing systems start in an "empty and idle" condition and go through a transient period as business activity gradually builds up to reach the normal, or **steady-state**, level of operation. The queuing models presented describe only the behavior of the system in its steady-state level of operation. A queuing system can have different levels of steady-state operations at different times throughout the day. For example, a restaurant might have one steady-state level of operation for breakfast, and different steady-state levels at lunch and dinner. So before using the models in this chapter, it is important to identify the arrival rate and service rate for the specific steady-state level of operation you want to study. If an analysis of the transient phase is needed or if you want to model the operation of the system across different steady-state levels, you should use simulation.

THE WORLD OF MANAGEMENT SCIENCE
"Wait Watchers" Try to
Take Stress Out of Standing in Line

© Kathleen Doheny, a Los Angeles journalist. Reprinted with permission from the *Los Angeles Times*, 7/15/91, V110 pB3 14 col in.

Standing in Line—at the bank, the market, the movies—is the time-waster everyone loves to hate. Stand in just one 15-minute line a day, every day, and kiss goodbye four days of idle time by year's end.

While we've been waiting and grumbling, researchers have been analyzing lines with an eye to making them, if not shorter, at least less stressful.

The field of line analysis—more scientifically known as queuing theory—began in the early 1900s when a Danish telephone engineer devised a mathematical approach to help design phone switches. Researchers found that the principles developed through that system, which helped process calls more efficiently, could be applied to help move people through lines more efficiently.

The concept has spread from the communications and computer industries to other fields, helping modern researchers predict such things as how long customers might wait for a restaurant lunch or how many customers might visit a bank ATM at noon on Saturday. Now, some researchers have gone beyond a mere mathematical analysis of lines, focusing as well on our psychological reactions.

In one recent study, Richard Larson, a professor of electrical engineering at the Massachusetts Institute of Technology, wanted to determine which of two approaches would be more tolerable to Bank of Boston customers. As Larson's researchers filmed the customers, one group watched an electronic news board while waiting in line; the other group was advised via an electric clock how long the wait would be before each one entered the line. About 300 customers, nearly a third of those filmed, were interviewed after they finished their transactions. The findings, published in the *Sloan Management Review,* an MIT publication circulated to corporate managers, showed that:

- Customers in both lines overestimated their waits by nearly a minute; those who watched the news board overestimated the most. On average, customers thought they waited 5.1 minutes to see a teller but actually waited 4.2 minutes.
- Watching the news board did not change customers' perceptions of their waiting time. But it did make the time spent more palatable, customers reported. (After the bank removed the news board, many customers asked that it be reinstalled.)
- The news board also seemed to make customers less fidgety. Without it, they touched their faces and played with their hair. With the news board in view, they stood still with their arms at their sides.
- Customers who were advised of the length of the line via an electronic clock at the entry did not find the experience less stressful than those not told the expected waiting time, much to Larson's surprise. Nor were they more satisfied than the other group with the service. The electronic clock's display of waiting time may backfire, Larson speculates, by making respondents even more aware of time wasted standing in line.
- Customers in the lines with the clock tended to play "beat the clock." They felt they had "won" if they spent less time in line than predicted. The clock also seemed to make more customers balk at joining the line if the predicted delay was lengthy.
- In both lines, customers altered their definition of a "reasonable" wait depending on their time of arrival. They were willing to wait longer during lunch time than during other times of day.

Larson's recent findings bear out a formula published in 1984 by David Maister, a former Harvard Business School faculty member and now a business consultant. When it comes to lines, Maister said, satisfaction is tied to both perception and expectation.

"Nowhere in that [equation] does reality appear," Maister said with a laugh during a telephone interview. Giving a personal example of how perception influences reaction, he said he would wait "40 minutes for a performance by a world-class musician but less than 30 seconds for a hamburger."

Larson, a professional "wait watcher" for 20 years, puts it a bit differently: "When it comes to customer satisfaction, perception is reality."

If those concepts are true, taming customer unrest does not necessarily mean a business must beef up its staff to eliminate lines, Larson and Maister contend. It's much more a matter of "perception management," they say. "People in the service industries who think they have a line problem may be able virtually to

erase customer dissatisfaction and customer complaints not by changing the statistic of the wait but by changing the environment of it," Larson said.

He points to a number of companies already actively wooing waiters. Some
companies use a "queue delay guarantee," giving customers free dessert or
money if the wait exceeds a preset time period.

Larson predicts customers can expect lines that segment them by personality type. Impatient souls may have the option of paying more to join an automated express line; "people watchers" could opt to wait for less expensive,
friendlier human service.

SUMMARY

Waiting lines, or queues, are a common occurrence in many types of businesses. The
study of the operating characteristics of waiting lines is known as queuing theory.
Numerous mathematical models are available to represent and study the behavior of
different types of queues. These models have different assumptions about the nature
of the arrival process to the queuing system, the allowable size and nature of the
queuing discipline, and the service process within the system. For many models,
closed-form equations have been developed to describe various operating characteristics of the system. When closed-form solutions are not possible, the technique of
simulation must be used to analyze the behavior of the system.

QUESTIONS AND PROBLEMS

1. Consider the three queuing configurations shown in Figure 14.2. For each con-
    figuration, describe a situation (besides the examples mentioned in the chapter)
    in which you have encountered or observed the same type of queuing system.

2. Of the queuing configurations shown in Figure 14.2, which would you prefer to
    wait in? Explain your response.

3. This chapter implies that customers find waiting in line to be an unpleasant expe-
    rience. In addition to reducing the length of the wait itself, what other steps could
    a business take to reduce the frustration customers experience while waiting?
    Give specific examples.

4. Describe a situation in which a business might want customers to wait some
    amount of time before receiving service.

5. Tri-Cities Bank has a single drive-in teller window. On Friday mornings, cus-
    tomers arrive at the drive-in window randomly, following a Poisson distribution at
    an average rate of 30 per hour.

    a. How many customers arrive per minute, on average?
    b. How many customers would you expect to arrive in a 10-minute interval?
    c. Use equation 14.1 to determine the probability of exactly 0, 1, 2, and 3 arrivals
        in a 10-minute interval. (You can verify your answers using the POISSON( )
        function in Excel.)
    d. What is the probability of more than three arrivals occurring in a 10-minute
        interval?

6. Refer to question 5. Suppose that service at the drive-in window is provided at a rate of 40 customers per hour and follows an exponential distribution.

   a. What is the expected service time per customer?
   b. Use equation 14.2 to determine the probability that a customer's service time is one minute or less. (Verify your answer using the EXPONDIST( ) function in Excel.)
   c. Compute the probabilities that the customer's service time is: between two and five minutes, less than four minutes, and more than three minutes.

7. Refer to questions 5 and 6 and answer the following questions:

   a. What is the probability that the drive-in window is empty?
   b. What is the probability that a customer must wait for service?
   c. On average, how many cars wait for service?
   d. On average, what is the total length of time a customer spends in the system?
   e. On average, what is the total length of time a customer spends in the queue?
   f. What service rate would be required to reduce the average total time in the system to two minutes? (Hint: You can use Solver or simple what-if analysis to answer this question.)

8. The manager of the Radford Credit Union (RCU) wants to determine how many part-time tellers to employ to cover the peak demand time in its lobby from 11:00 A.M. to 2:00 P.M. RCU currently has three full-time tellers that handle the demand during the rest of the day, but during this peak demand time customers have been complaining that the wait time for service is too long. The manager at RCU has determined that customers arrive according to a Poisson distribution with an average of 60 arrivals per hour during the peak period. Each teller services customers at a rate of 24 per hour, with service times following an exponential distribution.

   a. On average, how long must customers wait in line before service begins?
   b. Once service begins for a customer, how long does it take to complete the transaction, on average?
   c. If one part-time teller is hired to work during the peak time period, what effect would this have on the average amount of time a customer spends waiting in the queue?
   d. If one part-time teller is hired to work during the peak time period, what effect would this have on the average amount of time it takes to serve a customer?

9. The Westland Title Insurance Company leases one copying machine for $45 per day that is used by all individuals at their office. An average of five persons per hour arrive to use this machine, with each person using it for an average of eight minutes. Assume the interarrival times and copying times are exponentially distributed.

   a. What is the probability that a person arriving to use the machine will find it idle?
   b. On average, how long will a person have to wait before getting to use the machine?
   c. On average, how many people will be using or waiting to use the copy machine?
   d. Suppose that the people who use the copy machine are paid an average of $9 per hour. On average, how much does the company spend in wages during

each eight-hour day paying the people who are using or waiting to use the copy machine?

e. If the company can lease another copying machine for $45 per day, should they do it?

10. The Orange Blossom Marathon takes place in Orlando, Florida, each December. The organizers of this race are trying to solve a problem that occurs at the finish line each year. Thousands of runners take part in this race. The fastest runners finish the 26-mile course in just over 2 hours, but the majority of the runners finish about 1 1/2 hours later. After runners enter the finish area, they go through one of four finish chutes where their times and places are recorded. (Each chute has its own queue.) During the time in which the majority of the runners finish the race, the chutes become backlogged and significant delays occur. The race organizers want to determine how many chutes should be added to eliminate this problem. At the time in question, runners arrive at the finish area at a rate of 50 per minute according to a Poisson distribution, and they randomly select one of the four chutes. The time required to record the necessary information for each finishing runner at any chute is an exponentially distributed random variable with a mean of four seconds.

a. On average, how many runners arrive at each chute per minute?
b. Under the current arrangement with four chutes, what is the expected length of the queue at each chute?
c. Under the current arrangement, what is the average length of time a runner waits before being processed?
d. How many chutes should be added if the race organizers want to reduce the queue time at each chute to an average of five seconds?

11. State University allows students and faculty to access its mainframe computer by modem. The university has 15 modem connections that can be used. When all of the modem connections are in use, the phone system can keep up to 10 callers on hold waiting for a modem connection to become available. If all 15 modem connections are in use and 10 calls are already holding, a new caller receives a busy signal. Calls to the modem pool follow a Poisson distribution and occur at an average rate of 60 per hour. The length of each session with the mainframe is an exponential random variable with a mean of 15 minutes—therefore, each modem services an average of four callers per hour.

a. On average, how many callers are on hold waiting for a modem connection?
b. On average, how long is a caller kept on hold before receiving a modem connection?
c. What is the probability that a caller receives a busy signal?
d. How many modem connections would the university need to add to its modem pool in order for there to be no more than a 1% chance of a caller receiving a busy signal?

12. On Friday nights, patients arrive at the emergency room at Mercy Hospital following a Poisson distribution at an average rate of seven per hour. Assume that an emergency-room physician can treat an average of three patients per hour, and that the treatment times follow an exponential distribution. The board of directors for Mercy Hospital wants patients arriving at the emergency room to wait no more than five minutes before seeing a doctor. How many emergency-room doctors should be scheduled on Friday nights to achieve this objective?

13. During tax season the IRS hires seasonal workers to help answer the questions of taxpayers who call a special 800 telephone number for tax information. Suppose that calls to this line occur at a rate of 60 per hour and follow a Poisson distribution. The IRS workers manning the phone lines can answer an average of five calls per hour with the actual service times following an exponential distribution. Assume that 10 IRS workers are available and, when they are all busy, the phone system can keep five additional callers on hold.

   a. What is the probability that a caller receives a busy signal?
   b. What is the probability that a caller is put on hold before receiving service?
   c. On average, how long must a caller wait before speaking with an IRS agent?
   d. How many additional workers would be required if the IRS wants no more than a 5% chance of a caller receiving a busy signal?

14. Several hundred personal computers (PCs) are in use at the corporate headquarters for National Insurance Corporation. The pattern of breakdowns for these PCs follows a Poisson distribution with an average rate of 4.5 breakdowns per five-day work week. The company has a repair technician on staff to repair the PCs. The average time required to repair a PC varies somewhat, but takes an average of one day with a standard deviation of 0.5 days.

   a. What is the average service time in terms of a five-day work week?
   b. What is the standard deviation of the service times in terms of a five-day work week?
   c. On average, how many PCs are either being repaired or waiting to be repaired?
   d. On average, how much time transpires from the time a PC breaks down to the time it is repaired?

15. Refer to question 14. Suppose that National Insurance estimates it loses $40 a day in productivity and efficiency for each PC that is out of service. How much should the company be willing to pay to increase service capacity to the point where an average of seven PCs a week could be repaired?

16. A manufacturer of engine belts uses multipurpose manufacturing equipment to produce a variety of products. A technician is employed to perform the setup operations needed to change the machines over from one product to the next. The amount of time required to set up the machines is a random variable that follows an exponential distribution with a mean of 20 minutes. The number of machines requiring a new setup is a Poisson random variable with an average of two machines per hour requiring setup. The technician is responsible for setups on five machines.

   a. What percentage of time is the technician idle, or not involved in setting up a machine?
   b. What should the technician do during this idle time?
   c. On average, how long is a machine out of operation while waiting for the next setup to be completed?
   d. If the company hires another, equally capable technician to perform setups on these machines, how long on average would a machine be out of operation while waiting for the next setup to be completed?

17. DeColores Paint Company owns 10 trucks that it uses to deliver paint and decorating supplies to builders. On average, each truck returns to the company's sin-

gle loading dock at a rate of three times per eight-hour day (or at a rate of 3/8 = 0.375 times per hour). The times between arrivals at the dock follow an exponential distribution. The loading dock can service an average of four trucks per hour with actual service times following an exponential distribution.

a. What is the probability that a truck must wait for service to begin?
b. On average, how many trucks wait for service to begin at any point in time?
c. On average, how long must a truck wait before service begins?
d. If the company builds and staffs another loading dock, how would your answers to parts a, b, and c change?

18. Suppose that arrivals to a queuing system with one server follow a Poisson distribution with an average of $\lambda = 5$ per time period, and that service times follow an exponential distribution with an average service rate of $\mu = 6$ per time period.

a. Compute the operating characteristics for this system using the M/M/s model with $s = 1$.
b. Compute the operating characteristics for this system using the M/G/1 model. (Note that the average service time for the exponential random variable is $1/\mu$ and the standard deviation of the service time is also $1/\mu$.)
c. Compare the results obtained from the M/M/1 and M/G/1 models. (They should be the same.) Explain why they are the same.

19. Calls arrive at a rate of 150 per hour to the 800 number for the Land's Beginning mail-order catalog company. The company currently employs 20 operators who are paid $10 per hour in wages and benefits and can each handle an average of six calls per hour. Assume that interarrival times and service times follow the exponential distribution. A maximum of 20 calls can be placed on hold when all the operators are busy. The company estimates that it costs $25 in lost sales whenever a customer calls and receives a busy signal.

a. On average, how many customers are waiting on hold at any point in time?
b. What is the probability that a customer will receive a busy signal?
c. If the number of operators plus the number of calls placed on hold cannot exceed 40, how many operators should the company employ?
d. If the company implements your answer to part c, on average, how many customers will be waiting on hold at any point in time and what is the probability that a customer will receive a busy signal?

REFERENCES

Gilliam, R. "An Application of Queuing Theory to Airport Passenger Security Screening." *Interfaces*, vol. 9, 1979.

Gross, D. and C. Harris. *Fundamentals of Queueing Theory*. New York: Wiley, 1985.

Hall, R. *Queuing Methods for Service and Manufacturing*. Englewood Cliffs, NJ: Prentice Hall, 1991.

Kolesar, P. "A Quick and Dirty Response to the Quick and Dirty Crowd: Particularly to Jack Byrd's 'The Value of Queuing Theory'." *Interfaces*, vol. 9, 1979.

Quinn, P., et al. "Allocating Telecommunications Resources at LL Bean, Inc." *Interfaces*, vol. 21, 1991.

Mann, L. "Queue Culture: The Waiting Line as a Social System." *American Journal of Sociology*, vol. 75, 1969.

CHAPTER 15

Project Management

At some point, almost every manager assumes responsibility for the completion of some type of project. The project might be relatively simple—such as planning a company picnic or producing an employee newsletter—or it might be more complex—such as planning the launch of a space shuttle, designing and implementing a large computer information system, or constructing a multistory office building. Successfully completing a project of any size requires a thorough analysis of the tasks involved, accurate estimates of the time and resources required, and a good understanding of the physical and logical interdependencies. Keeping track of all these details for even a relatively small project can be overwhelming.

This chapter presents two techniques that were developed to help managers plan, organize, and control projects: the **Critical Path Method** (CPM) and the **Program Evaluation and Review Technique** (PERT). Both techniques were developed concurrently but independently during the 1950s. CPM was developed by representatives of DuPont and Sperry-Rand to assist in the management of industrial projects where the time required to perform each activity in the project could be estimated with a high degree of accuracy. The focus of CPM is to determine when a project should be completed and to schedule when each activity in the project must begin in order to keep the project on schedule. PERT was developed jointly by representatives of the U.S. Navy, Lockheed, and the consulting firm of Booz, Allen and Hamilton working on the Polaris missile. Because many of the tasks required in the development of the Polaris had never been done before, the time required to complete the tasks was uncertain. Thus, PERT was designed for projects where the time required to perform each activity is essentially a random variable. PERT focuses on estimating the probability of completing a project by a given deadline.

Over the years, the two techniques have blended together, so that most practitioners today refer to them collectively as PERT/CPM or CPM/PERT. The fact that these techniques have stood the test of time and are still widely used is a tribute to their usefulness and simplicity. Indeed, the basic ideas behind PERT/CPM provide the underpinnings for a number of project management software tools that you can find at your local software store or advertised in any computer magazine. Although we'll explore the fundamental concepts of CPM and PERT using a spreadsheet, keep in mind that specialized project management software tools are more effective and efficient than spreadsheets for managing a project of any significant size.

15.1 AN EXAMPLE

One of the key ideas in both CPM and PERT is that any project can be broken down into component activities that require different amounts of time and that must be accomplished in a specific order. The major difference between CPM and PERT involves how the time element of the activities is determined. However, both CPM and PERT require a detailed network of the project that clearly indicates each of the main activities in the project and their precedence relationships. The following example illustrates how to create such a project network.

> Tom Lightner is the owner of Lightner Construction, a general contracting company that specializes in the construction of single-family residences and small office buildings. Tom frequently has numerous construction projects going on at the same time and needs a formal procedure for planning, monitoring, and controlling each project. He is aware of various project scheduling techniques but has never used them. He wants to see how he might apply such techniques to one of the home-building projects he will be undertaking in the near future. Tom has identified each of the major activities required for this project and has estimated how much time each activity will require. Figure 15.1 summarizes this information along with the precedence relationships among the activities.

15.2 CREATING THE PROJECT NETWORK

The activities in a project can be represented as a network in one of two ways. As noted in Chapter 5, a network is a set of nodes that are connected in various ways by directed arcs. Thus, if we let the nodes in a network represent the activities in a project, we are employing the **Activity-On-Node** (AON) network design. Figure 15.2 shows this type of network for our example problem.

The nodes in the network shown in Figure 15.2 correspond to each project activity in Figure 15.1. The arcs in this network indicate the precedence relationships between the activities (or nodes). For example, Figure 15.2 shows that we cannot start laying the foundation (activity B) until the excavation (activity A) is complete. Similarly, the arcs leading into node H indicate that the sheet rock cannot be installed until the activities represented by nodes C, E, F, and G are *all* complete.

In this type of network, activity A is called the **immediate predecessor** of activity B, and activities C and D are called the **immediate successors** of activity B. Throughout this chapter, we use the shortened terms **predecessor** and **successor** to mean immediate predecessor and immediate successor.

The second way to represent a project as a network is the **Activity-On-Arc** (AOA) design, in which the arcs represent the project's activities. Figure 15.3 shows an AOA network for our example problem.

Figure 15.1
Activities for the
Lightner
Construction
home-building
project.

Activity	Description	Time Required (in days)	Immediate Predecessor Activity
A	excavate	3	—
B	lay foundation	4	A
C	rough plumbing	3	B
D	frame	10	B
E	finish exterior	8	D
F	install HVAC	4	D
G	rough electric	6	D
H	sheet rock	8	C, E, F, G
I	install cabinets	5	H
J	paint	5	H
K	final plumbing	4	I
L	final electric	2	J
M	install flooring	4	K, L

Figure 15.2
Activity-On-
Node (AON)
representation of
the home-
building project.

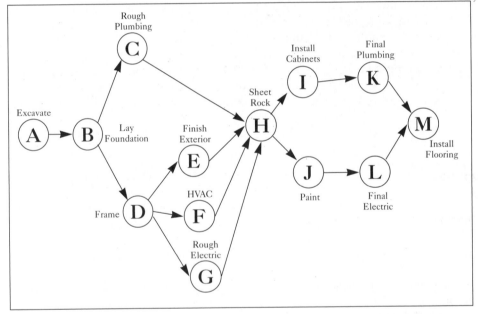

The nodes in an AOA network represent the start and finish points (or milestones) for each activity. For example, in Figure 15.3 activity A starts at node 1 and ends at node 2. Activity B starts at node 2 and ends at node 3, and so on. Unfortunately, an AOA representation often produces a more complicated network when multiple activities start and end at common nodes. For example, because activity H (which begins at node 8) cannot begin until activities C, E, F, and G are complete, we might be inclined to draw the arcs for activities E, F, and G as starting at node 4 and finishing at node 8 (eliminating nodes 5, 6, and 7). However, an AOA network does not allow multiple arcs with common start and finish nodes. To get around this problem, we must include the "phantom" activities indicated by the dashed lines connecting nodes 5, 6, and 7 to node 8. AOA networks are mentioned here so that you will be aware of their existence (and shortcomings). In this chapter we'll use only the AON network representation, which many believe to be superior.

15.2.1 A Note on Start and Finish Points

The techniques discussed in this chapter require that all projects have one unique start activity and one unique finish activity. This requirement is met by our example project shown in Figure 15.2 where activity A is the unique start point and activity M is the unique finish point. However, some projects involve multiple start and/or finish activities, as illustrated in Figure 15.4.

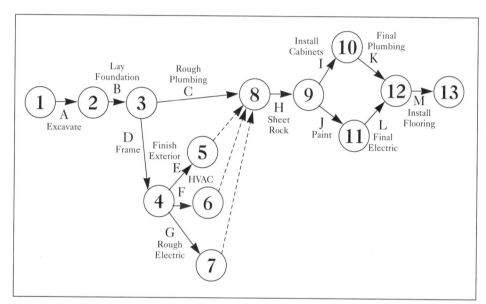

Figure 15.3 Activity-On-Arc (AOA) representation of the home-building project.

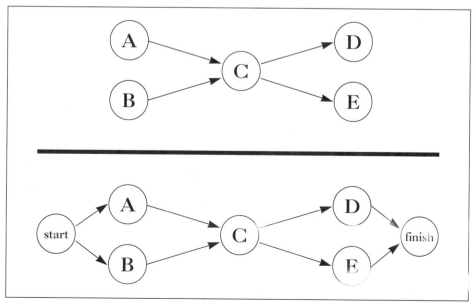

Figure 15.4 Using artificial start and finish activities to produce a network with unique start and finish points.

The first network shown in Figure 15.4 represents a project with five activities: A, B, C, D, and E. However, this project does not have a unique start or finish activity. In such cases, it is necessary to create artificial start and/or finish activities, as shown by the second network in Figure 15.4. Here, we created an artificial start activity that precedes activities A and B. Similarly, we inserted an artificial finish activity that follows the completion of activities D and E. These activities are artificial because they require no time to complete and merely serve to give a project a unique start and finish point. Thus, by using artificial start and finish activities, we can ensure that the network for any project has a unique start and finish point.

15.3   CPM: AN OVERVIEW

After creating a network representation of a project, the next step in the CPM technique is to determine the earliest time that each activity in the network can start and finish. We determine these times by making what is called a **forward pass** through the network. Ultimately, this analysis determines the earliest time that the project itself can be completed. Next, we make a **backward pass** through the network to determine the latest time that each activity can start and finish without delaying the completion of the project.

One of the primary goals in CPM is to determine the critical path through the network. Figure 15.2 shows several paths that could be followed from the initial activity (node A) to the final activity (node M). For example, one path is given by the following set of activities: A→B→C→H→I→K→M. Another path through the network is given by: A→B→D→F→H→J→L→M. Figure 15.2 shows a total of eight paths through the network, each representing a set of activities that must be completed before the project is complete. Therefore, the earliest time that the project can be completed is the time required to complete the set of activities along the *longest* path through the network. The **critical path** is the longest path through a project network.

Any delays in the start or finish times of the activities on the critical path (also known as **critical activities**) delay the completion of the project. A project manager should always identify the critical activities in a project to focus attention on these activities and to avoid delays on these activities when possible.

In conducting the forward pass through the network, we will use the activity times to determine the earliest *possible* start time and the earliest *possible* finish time for each activity. The following notations represent these quantities:

$$t_i = \text{amount of time required to perform activity } i$$

$$EST_i = \text{earliest possible start time for activity } i$$

$$EFT_i = \text{earliest possible finish time for activity } i$$

During the backward pass, we'll determine the latest time that each activity can be started and finished without delaying the project. These quantities are represented as:

$$LST_i = \text{latest possible start time for activity } i$$

$$LFT_i = \text{latest possible finish time for activity } i$$

We'll record all the information about each project activity on the corresponding network node in the format shown in Figure 15.5.

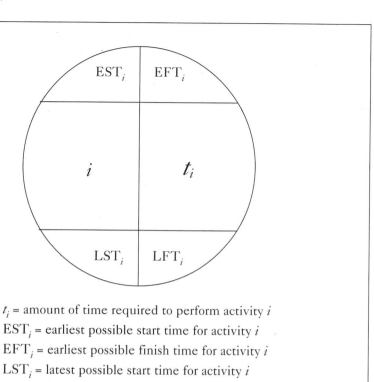

Figure 15.5
Information recorded on the node for each project activity.

t_i = amount of time required to perform activity i

EST_i = earliest possible start time for activity i

EFT_i = earliest possible finish time for activity i

LST_i = latest possible start time for activity i

LFT_i = latest possible finish time for activity i

15.4 THE FORWARD PASS

The first step in the CPM technique (after constructing the project network) is to determine the earliest time at which each activity in the network can start and finish. The term **time zero** identifies the time period at which the first project activity begins—just as the time on a stopwatch starts from zero. Thus, in our example problem, the earliest time at which activity A (excavation) can begin is time zero, or $EST_A = 0$.

In general, the earliest time at which an activity can finish is the earliest time at which it can start plus the expected time required to perform the activity. That is, for any activity i:

$$EFT_i = EST_i + t_i$$

For activity A, $EFT_A = EST_A + t_A = 0 + 3 = 3$. The project network in Figure 15.6 shows the earliest start and finish times for activity A.

Now let's consider activity B. Because activity A must be completed before activity B can begin, the earliest start time for activity B equals the earliest finish time for activity A. That is, $EST_B = EFT_A = 3$. Activity B is expected to take four units of time; therefore, its earliest finish time is $EFT_B = EST_B + t_B = 3 + 4 = 7$.

Now let's consider activity C. Because activity B must be completed before activity C can begin, the earliest start time for activity C equals the earliest finish time for activity B. That is, $EST_C = EFT_B = 7$. Activity C is expected to take three units of time; therefore, its earliest finish time is $EFT_C = EST_C + t_C = 7 + 3 = 10$.

Figure 15.6
Results of
forward pass
calculation of
earliest start and
finish times.

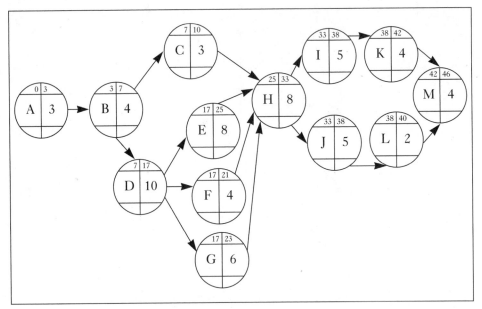

As you can see from these examples, calculating the earliest start and finish times for activities with a single predecessor activity is a simple process. We could apply this same logic to determine the earliest start and finish times for activities D, E, F, and G shown in Figure 15.6. You should verify the calculations for these activities on your own to make sure you understand the process. Figure 15.7 provides details of all the forward pass calculations for this example.

Notice that the calculation of the earliest start time for activity H differs from the previous activities because it has *multiple* predecessors rather than a single predecessor. Activity H cannot begin until activities C, E, F, and G are *all* completed. Thus, if we consider the earliest finish times of activities C, E, F, and G, the latest of these times determines the earliest time at which activity H can start:

$$EST_H = MAX(EFT_C, EFT_E, EFT_F, EFT_G) = MAX(10, 25, 21, 23) = 25$$

The earliest start time of an activity is equal to the latest (or maximum) early finish time of the activities directly preceding it. This is true regardless of the number of predecessors an activity has.

The earliest start and finish times for the remaining activities are calculated using this same logic. Notice that the earliest start times for nodes I, J, K, and L are the earliest finish times of their respective predecessor activities. Because activity M has multiple predecessor activities, its earliest start time is the maximum of the earliest finish times of activities K and L.

Key Points: The Forward Pass

- The earliest start time for the initial activity in a project is time zero.
- The earliest start time of an activity is equal to the latest (or maximum) early finish time of the activities directly preceding it.
- The earliest finish time of an activity is equal to its earliest start time plus the time required to perform the activity.

Figure 15.7
Summary of
forward pass
calculations.

Earliest Start Times   *Earliest Finish Times*

$EST_A = 0$ $EFT_A = EST_A + t_A = 0 + 3 = 3$

$EST_B = EFT_A = 3$ $EFT_B = EST_B + t_B = 3 + 4 = 7$

$EST_C = EFT_B = 7$ $EFT_C = EST_C + t_C = 7 + 3 = 10$

$EST_D = EFT_B = 7$ $EFT_D = EST_D + t_D = 7 + 10 = 17$

$EST_E = EFT_D = 17$ $EFT_E = EST_E + t_E = 17 + 8 = 25$

$EST_F = EFT_D = 17$ $EFT_F = EST_F + t_F = 17 + 4 = 21$

$EST_G = EFT_D = 17$ $EFT_G = EST_G + t_G = 17 + 6 = 23$

$EST_H = MAX(EFT_C, EFT_E, EFT_F, EFT_G)$ $EFT_H = EST_H + t_H = 25 + 8 = 33$
$\quad = MAX(10, 25, 21, 23) = 25$

$EST_I = EFT_H = 33$ $EFT_I = EST_I + t_I = 33 + 5 = 38$

$EST_J = EFT_H = 33$ $EFT_J = EST_J + t_J = 33 + 5 = 38$

$EST_K = EFT_I = 38$ $EFT_K = EST_K + t_K = 38 + 4 = 42$

$EST_L = EFT_J = 38$ $EFT_L = EST_L + t_L = 38 + 2 = 40$

$EST_M = MAX(EFT_K, EFT_L)$ $EFT_M = EST_M + t_M = 42 + 4 = 46$
$\quad = MAX(42, 40) = 42$

At the end of our forward pass, we have determined the earliest possible start and finish times of each activity in the network. Note that the last activity in the project, activity M, can be completed no earlier than 46 time units (in this case, days) from the beginning of the project. Thus, the earliest the project can be completed is 46 days.

15.5   THE BACKWARD PASS

After completing the forward pass, the next step in the CPM technique is to make a **backward pass** to determine the *latest* times at which the project activities can start and finish without delaying the project. This process identifies those activities that *must* start and finish at their earliest possible times in order to complete the project in the minimum possible time identified by the forward pass. These activities constitute the critical path through the network.

The logic behind the backward pass is similar to that of the forward pass. Here, however, we start at the final activity in the network and work backwards through the network to determine the latest time at which each activity could be finished without delaying the project. Consider activity M. If the project can be completed within 46 days, the latest finish time for activity M is 46, or $LFT_M = 46$.

In general, the latest time at which an activity can start without delaying a project is the latest time by which it must be finished minus the time required to perform the activity. That is, for any activity i:

$$LST_i = LFT_i - t_i$$

For activity M, $LST_M = LFT_M - t_M = 46 - 4 = 42$. Figure 15.8 shows the latest start and finish times for activity M.

Figure 15.8
Results of
backward pass
calculation of
latest start and
finish times.

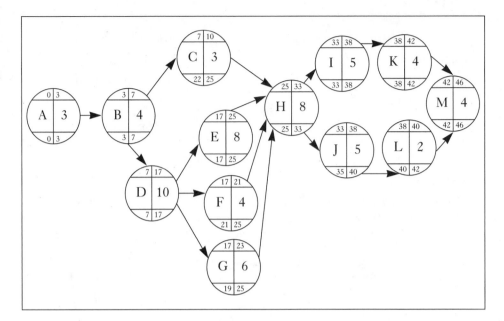

Now let's consider activity L. Because activity L must be completed before activity M can begin, and activity M must begin no later than time period 42, activity L must be finished no later than time period 42. That is, $LFT_L = LST_M = 42$. Activity L is scheduled to take two units of time; therefore, the latest time at which this activity could start without delaying the project is $LST_L = LFT_L - t_L = 42 - 2 = 40$.

As another example, consider activity J. Because activity J must be completed before activity L can begin, and activity L must begin no later than time period 40, activity J must be finished no later than time period 40. That is, $LFT_J = LST_L = 40$. Activity J is scheduled to take five units of time; therefore, the latest time at which this activity could start without delaying the project is $LST_J = LFT_J - t_J = 40 - 5 = 35$.

Calculating the latest start and finish times for activities with a single successor activity is a simple process. We could apply this same logic to determine the earliest start and finish times for activities I and K, as shown in Figure 15.8. Again, you should verify the calculations for these activities on your own to make sure you understand the process. Figure 15.9 provides the details of the backward pass calculations for this example.

Notice that the calculation of the latest finish time for activity H differs from the previous activities because it has *multiple* successors rather than a single successor. Activity H must be finished in time for activities I and J to begin by their latest start times. Thus, if we consider the latest start times for activities I and J, the earliest of these times determines the latest time by which activity H must be finished:

$$LFT_H = MIN(LST_I, LST_J) = MIN(33, 35) = 33$$

The latest finish time of an activity is equal to the earliest (or minimum) late start time of the activities directly following (or succeeding) it. This is true regardless of the number of successors an activity has.

The latest start and finish times for the remaining activities are calculated using this same logic. Notice that the latest finish times for nodes C, E, F, and G are the latest start times of their successor activities. Because activity D has multiple successor activities, its latest finish time is the minimum of the latest start times of activities E,

Figure 15.9
Summary of
backward pass
calculations.

Latest Finish Times	*Latest Start Times*
$LFT_M = EFT_M = 46$	$LST_M = LFT_M - t_M = 46 - 4 = 42$
$LFT_L = LST_M = 42$	$LST_L = LFT_L - t_L = 42 - 2 = 40$
$LFT_K = LST_M = 42$	$LST_K = LFT_K - t_K = 42 - 4 = 38$
$LFT_J = LST_L = 40$	$LST_J = LFT_J - t_J = 40 - 5 = 35$
$LFT_I = LST_K = 38$	$LST_I = LFT_I - t_I = 38 - 5 = 33$
$LFT_H = MIN(LST_I, LST_J)$ $= MIN(33, 35) = 33$	$LST_H = LFT_H - t_H = 33 - 8 = 25$
$LFT_G = LST_H = 25$	$LST_G = LFT_G - t_G = 25 - 6 = 19$
$LFT_F = LST_H = 25$	$LST_F = LFT_F - t_F = 25 - 4 = 21$
$LFT_E = LST_H = 25$	$LST_E = LFT_E - t_E = 25 - 8 = 17$
$LFT_D = MIN(LST_E, LST_F, LST_G)$ $= MIN(17, 21, 19) = 17$	$LST_D = LFT_D - t_D = 17 - 10 = 7$
$LFT_C = LST_H = 25$	$LST_C = LFT_C - t_C = 25 - 3 = 22$
$LFT_B = MIN(LST_C, LST_D)$ $= MIN(22, 7) = 7$	$LST_B = LFT_B - t_B = 7 - 4 = 3$
$LFT_A = LST_B = 3$	$LST_A = LFT_A - t_A = 3 - 3 = 0$

F, and G. Similarly, because activity B has multiple successor activities, its latest finish time is the minimum of the latest start times of activities C and D. Finally, the latest finish time for activity A is the latest start time for activity B ($LFT_A = LST_B = 3$), and the latest start time for activity A is then determined by $LST_A = LFT_A - t_A = 0$.

Key Points: The Backward Pass

- The latest finish time for the final activity in a project is equal to its earliest finish time as determined by the forward pass.
- The latest finish time for any other activity is equal to the earliest (or minimum) late start time of the activities directly following (or succeeding) it.
- The latest start time of an activity is equal to its latest finish time minus the time required to perform the activity.

15.6 DETERMINING THE CRITICAL PATH

As mentioned earlier, one of the key objectives of CPM is to determine the critical path through a project network. The critical path consists of the set of activities that, if delayed in any way, would cause a delay in the completion of the entire project. The activities on the critical path can be identified easily from the results of the forward pass and backward pass. Specifically, the activities whose latest start times equal their earliest start times make up the critical path (or, equivalently, whose latest finish times equal their earliest finish times). As shown by the heavier arcs in Figure 15.10, the critical path of activities in our example problem is:

$$A \rightarrow B \rightarrow D \rightarrow E \rightarrow H \rightarrow I \rightarrow K \rightarrow M$$

If any of the activities in this path do not start by their earliest start time, the overall time required to complete the project will increase (unless management intervenes in some way). (Note that it is possible for an activity network to have more than one critical path, although this is not illustrated in our example.)

The noncritical activities in a project are distinguished by the presence of slack. **Slack** is the amount of time by which the start of an activity can be delayed without delaying the project. Critical activities have zero slack and noncritical activities have slack values that are strictly positive. The amount of slack for any activity i is defined as:

$$\text{Slack for activity } i = \text{LST}_i - \text{EST}_i$$

or, equivalently, as:

$$\text{Slack for activity } i = \text{LFT}_i - \text{EFT}_i$$

In our example, activities C, F, G, J, and L are noncritical. Thus, we compute the slack for activity C as:

$$\text{Slack for activity C} = \text{LST}_C - \text{EST}_C = 22 - 7 = 15$$

This indicates that activity C could be delayed up to 15 days beyond its earliest start time without delaying the project. The slack for activities F, G, J, and L are:

$$\text{Slack for activity F} = \text{LST}_F - \text{EST}_F = 21 - 17 = 4$$
$$\text{Slack for activity G} = \text{LST}_G - \text{EST}_G = 19 - 17 = 2$$
$$\text{Slack for activity J} = \text{LST}_J - \text{EST}_J = 35 - 33 = 2$$
$$\text{Slack for activity L} = \text{LST}_L - \text{EST}_L = 40 - 38 = 2$$

Figure 15.10
The critical path and slack conditions.

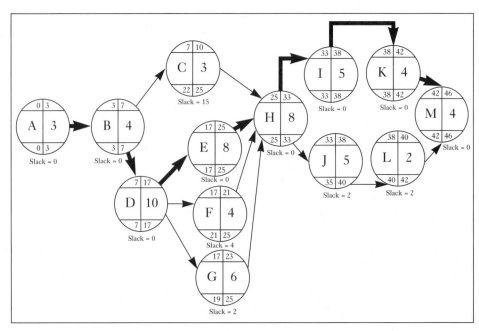

15.6.1   A Note on Slack

In Figure 15.10, note that activities J and L both appear to have two units of slack. Now suppose that the start of activity J is delayed for two time periods and does not start until time period 35. Because it takes five units of time to perform activity J, this activity should be complete at time period 40. Thus, activity L cannot start any sooner than time period 40. So does activity L still have two units of slack? The answer is *no*.

If the start of activity J is delayed by two time units, the start of activity L is also delayed by two time units. Delaying the start of activity J by two time units depletes the slack available not only for activity J but also for activity L. So the amount of slack available at activity L depends on the amount of slack used at activity J.

You must be careful in interpreting how much slack is available for a given activity. To be precise, slack represents the amount of time by which the start of an activity can be delayed without delaying the entire project, *assuming that all predecessor activities start at their earliest start times*. If any activity on a noncritical path starts late, the slack available along the rest of the noncritical path is reduced. For this reason, it is safer to focus on the latest start times of each activity (rather than on slack) because if all activities start by their latest start times, the project should not be delayed.

Key Points: Determining the Critical Path

- Critical activities have zero slack and cannot be delayed without delaying the completion of the project.
- Noncritical activities have some positive amount of slack that represents the amount of time by which the start times of these activities can be delayed without delaying the completion of the entire project, assuming that all predecessor activities start at their earliest start times.

15.7   PROJECT MANAGEMENT USING SPREADSHEETS

We can use a spreadsheet in a variety of ways to manage a project. As shown in Figure 15.11 (and in the file FIG15-11.xls on your data disk), we can use a spreadsheet to perform all of the calculations required to determine the earliest and latest start and finish times for the project activities in our example problem, though this is a somewhat cumbersome process.

To create the spreadsheet in Figure 15.11, we first entered all the labels and the activity times. The earliest finish times in column E are calculated as the earliest start time for each activity plus the time required to perform the activity. The latest start times in column F are calculated as the latest finish time of each activity minus the time required to perform the activity. Unfortunately, no one formula can calculate the earliest start times shown in column D. Each cell in column D required an individual formula to implement the logic of the forward pass described earlier (and summarized in Figure 15.7). Similarly, each of the latest finish times in column G required a unique formula to implement the logic described earlier for the backward pass (summarized in Figure 15.9). The slack values in column H are calculated as the difference between the latest and earliest start times for each activity.

Figure 15.11
Spreadsheet
calculations of
start and finish
times, slack, and
critical activities.

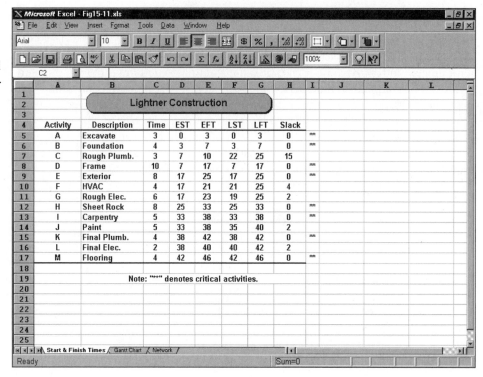

Although the spreadsheet approach is feasible for small projects, it would be tedious and impractical to build custom formulas to calculate the earliest start times and latest finish times for each activity in a large project. Section 15.8 describes another, more efficient, approach for calculating earliest and latest start and finish times for larger projects.

A **Gantt chart** is a popular technique for portraying the schedule of a project's activities over time. Figure 15.12 shows the earliest start and finish times for each activity in our example problem displayed in a Gantt chart. This type of chart is useful in helping a project manager see when activities can begin and end, and in keeping track of which activities are underway at any point in time.

Creating Gantt Charts in Excel

The Gantt chart in Figure 15.12 is a stacked horizontal bar chart that plots the EST and the time required to perform each activity. However, the bars for the EST for each activity are formatted so that they do not appear on the graph—giving the illusion that only the activity times are being graphed. To create a Gantt chart like the one shown in Figure 15.12:

1. Select the range B5 through D17 (shown in Figure 15.11).
2. Click the Insert menu.
3. Click Chart.
4. Click As New Sheet.

continued

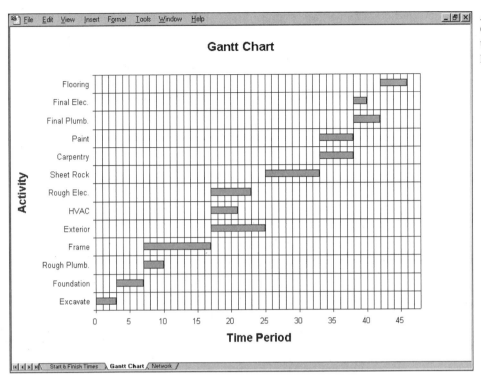

Figure 15.12
Gantt chart for the example problem.

Excel's ChartWizard then prompts you to make a number of selections concerning the type of chart you want and how it should be formatted. Select the options to display a stacked horizontal bar chart. When finished with the ChartWizard, you need to reverse the order in which the bars are displayed on the graph. To do this:

1. Click the Format menu.
2. Click Bar Group.
3. Click Series Order.
4. Click Move Down (to reverse the order of the bars).

Finally, double-click any of the bars representing the EST of any activity, select the Patterns option, and indicate that you want no border or area patterns. The basic Gantt chart is now complete. You can continue to customize the chart by clicking any element and specifying options in the resulting dialog boxes.

A weakness of both the Gantt chart and the table of start and finish times shown earlier in Figure 15.11 is that they do not show the precedence relationships between the activities in a project. For example, the Gantt chart shows that the painting and carpentry activities should both end at time period 38, and that the final electrical and final plumbing activities should begin at that point. But what happens if the painting activity is delayed? Would this prevent both the final electrical *and* final plumbing activities from starting on time? To answer this question, we need to know if painting is a predecessor for both the final plumbing and final electrical activities. The Gantt chart does not provide this information. Thus, although the Gantt chart is a valuable monitoring tool, it does not tell the whole story about the precedence relationships among project activities.

As shown in Figure 15.13, we can display the network structure of a project in a spreadsheet. Here, we used the relationships in Figures 15.7 and 15.9 to calculate the earliest and latest start and finish times for each activity. Then we used Excel's drawing tool to draw arrows indicating the precedence relationships between activities. Again, this approach is feasible for small projects, but larger projects require specialized project management software tools.

15.8   DETERMINING EARLIEST AND LATEST START TIMES USING LP

As mentioned earlier, the process of creating spreadsheet formulas to calculate the earliest and latest start and finish times for project activities can be overwhelming for all but the smallest of projects. Fortunately, a simple LP approach exists for determining earliest and latest start times for projects of any size. If we know these start times, we can determine the earliest and latest finish times as:

$$EFT_i = EST_i + t_i$$
$$LFT_i = LST_i + t_i$$

Figure 15.13 Project network implemented in a spreadsheet.

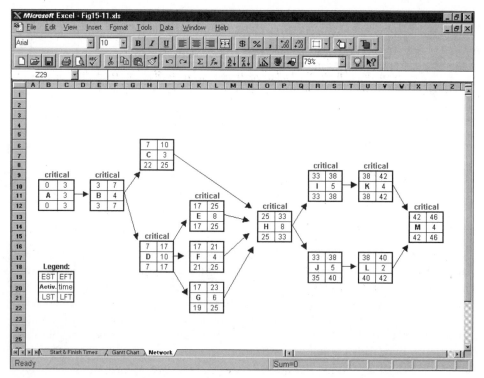

15.8.1　An LP Model for Earliest Start Times

The logic behind the LP approach parallels that of the forward and backward passes described earlier. To explain this approach, we'll let T_i represent the time at which activity i begins, and let t_i represent the amount of time required to perform activity i. The LP model that determines the earliest start time for each activity in our example problem is:

$$
\begin{aligned}
\text{MIN:} \quad & T_A + T_B + \dots + T_M \\
\text{Subject to:} \quad & T_B \geq T_A + t_A \\
& T_C \geq T_B + t_B \\
& T_D \geq T_B + t_B \\
& T_E \geq T_D + t_D \\
& T_F \geq T_D + t_D \\
& T_G \geq T_D + t_D \\
& T_H \geq T_C + t_C \\
& T_H \geq T_E + t_E \\
& T_H \geq T_F + t_F \\
& T_H \geq T_G + t_G \\
& T_I \geq T_H + t_H \\
& T_J \geq T_H + t_H \\
& T_K \geq T_I + t_I \\
& T_L \geq T_J + t_J \\
& T_M \geq T_K + t_K \\
& T_M \geq T_L + t_L \\
& T_i \geq 0, \text{ for all } i
\end{aligned}
$$

To understand the formulation of this model, consider the first constraint: $T_B \geq T_A + t_A$. This constraint indicates that the time at which activity B begins (T_B) must be greater than or equal to the time at which activity A begins (T_A), plus the time required to perform activity A (t_A). This follows logically from the project network shown in Figure 15.13 and our earlier discussion of the forward pass. Similarly, the second constraint indicates that the time at which activity C begins (T_C) must be greater than or equal to the time at which activity B begins (T_B), plus the time required to perform activity B (t_B).

If you compare this LP model with the project network in Figure 15.13, you will notice that each constraint in this model corresponds to one of the arcs representing the precedence relationships in the project network. Each arc in the network goes *from* one node *to* another node. In general, if an arc goes *from* activity i to activity j, the constraint takes the form:

$$
T_j \geq T_i + t_i
$$

This constraint indicates that the time at which activity j begins must be greater than or equal to the time at which activity i begins plus the time required to perform activity i. Because the objective function in this model seeks to minimize the sum of the start times of each activity, the solution to this model will provide the *earliest* possible start time for each activity in the project.

15.8.2   *Implementing the Model in a Spreadsheet*

Each constraint in our LP model takes the form:

$$T_j \geq T_i + t_i$$

or, equivalently:

$$T_j - T_i \geq t_i$$

where i represents the *from* node and j represents a *to* node of a particular arc in the network. The second form of the constraint indicates that the time between the start of activity j and activity i must be greater than or equal to the time required to perform activity i. We'll use the second form of the constraints to implement our model in the spreadsheet.

The type of spreadsheet layout needed to implement this model is shown in Figure 15.14 (and in the file FIG15-14.xls on your data disk). To implement the constraints for this model, we need a list of the *from* and *to* nodes of all the arcs in the project network, and a list of the activities in the network and the time required to complete them (the t_i).

Figure 15.14
Spreadsheet model for the LP formulation of earliest start times.

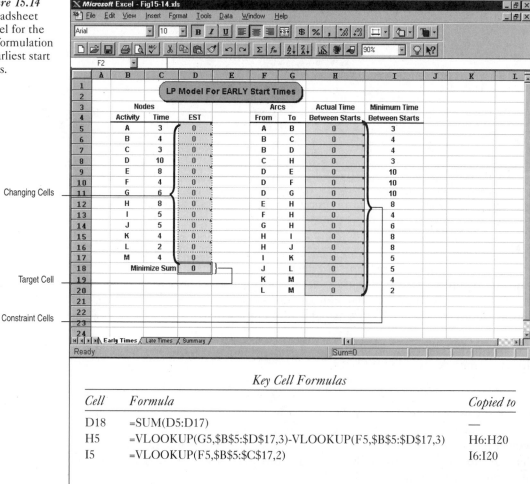

Key Cell Formulas

Cell	Formula	Copied to
D18	=SUM(D5:D17)	—
H5	=VLOOKUP(G5,$B$5:$D$17,3)-VLOOKUP(F5,$B$5:$D$17,3)	H6:H20
I5	=VLOOKUP(F5,$B$5:$C$17,2)	I6:I20

In Figure 15.14, cells D5 through D17 represent the T_i variables in our algebraic model (that is, D5 indicates the time at which activity A starts, D6 indicates the time at which activity B starts, and so on). The objective function is implemented in cell D18 as:

Formula for cell D18:   =SUM(D5:D17)

The LHS of the constraints are implemented in column H. Specifically, the LHS of the first constraint $(T_B - T_A)$ is implemented in cell H5 then copied to cells H6 through H20 as:

Formula for cell H5:   =VLOOKUP(G5,$B$5:$D$17,3)-
(Copy to H6 through H20.)   VLOOKUP(F5,$B$5:$D$17,3)

The first VLOOKUP function in this formula corresponds to the value of T_B. The first VLOOKUP function takes the contents of cell G5 (the letter B) and looks for its match in the first column of the range $B$5:$D$17 (the match is in cell B6), then returns the value in the third column of the range—or the value in cell D6. Cell D6 corresponds to T_B. The second VLOOKUP function works in a similar way to return the appropriate value for T_A. The difference between the values of these two VLOOKUP functions represents the amount of time between the start of activities A and B.

The RHS values for each LHS formula in column H are implemented in column I as:

Formula for cell I5:   =VLOOKUP(F5,$B$5:$C$17,2)
(Copy to I6 through I20.)

The formula in cell I5 returns the value t_A—or the amount of time required to perform activity A. Thus, after entering the data for the problem, we can use three simple formulas to implement the LP model regardless of the number of nodes and arcs in the project network.

15.8.3   Solving the Model

Figure 15.15 shows the Solver parameters and options used to solve this problem. The optimal solution is shown in Figure 15.16. Notice that the earliest start times shown in Figure 15.16 correspond to those calculated earlier in Figure 15.13. In particular, the earliest start time for activity M is 42. Because it takes four units of time to perform this activity, its earliest finish time corresponds to time period 46.

15.8.4   An LP Model for Latest Start Times

We can use the LP model for determining the earliest start times to also determine the latest start times if we make two simple modifications. First, we must change the objective from a minimization to a maximization. Second, we must include one additional constraint to ensure that the latest start time of the final project activity equals the earliest start time for this activity, identified from the solution to the previous model. Thus, the LP model for determining the latest start time for each activity in our example problem is:

Figure 15.15
Solver
parameters and
options for the
earliest start
times.

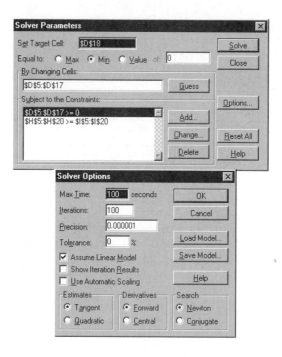

Figure 15.16
Optimal solution
for the earliest
start times.

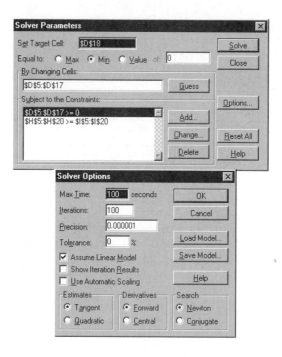

$$\text{MAX:} \qquad T_A + T_B + \dots + T_M$$

Subject to:

$T_B \geq T_A + t_A$	$T_H \geq T_G + t_G$
$T_C \geq T_B + t_B$	$T_I \geq T_H + t_H$
$T_D \geq T_B + t_B$	$T_J \geq T_H + t_H$
$T_E \geq T_D + t_D$	$T_K \geq T_I + t_I$
$T_F \geq T_D + t_D$	$T_L \geq T_J + t_J$
$T_G \geq T_D + t_D$	$T_M \geq T_K + t_K$
$T_H \geq T_C + t_C$	$T_M \geq T_L + t_L$
$T_H \geq T_E + t_E$	$T_M = 42$
$T_H \geq T_F + t_F$	$T_i \geq 0$, for all i

Because the objective function in this model seeks to maximize the sum of the activity start times, the solution will provide the *latest* possible start time for each activity, subject to the additional constraint that activity M starts no later than time period 42 ($T_M = 42$). Thus, the solution to this problem should reveal the latest time at which each activity can begin without delaying the earliest possible completion of the entire project.

15.8.5   Implementing and Solving the Model in a Spreadsheet

We can implement the model to determine the latest start times in exactly the same way as described for the earliest start time model. Figure 15.17 illustrates the spreadsheet implementation of the latest start time model for our example problem.

Figure 15.18 shows the Solver parameters and options required to solve this problem. Notice that the maximization option (Max) is selected and an extra constraint is included to force the latest start time for activity M (represented by cell D17) to equal 42. The optimal solution to this problem is shown in Figure 15.19. The latest start times shown here correspond to those calculated earlier in Figure 15.13.

15.8.6   Summarizing the Results

The results of our two LP models are summarized in the report shown in Figure 15.20. This summary sheet reads the earliest and latest start times from the sheets shown in Figures 15.16 and 15.19. These values are used to calculate the earliest and latest finish times for each activity. The slack time for each activity is calculated in the usual way, and critical activities are highlighted.

The LP approach to determining earliest and latest start and finish times is quite simple and can be applied to small, medium, or large projects. However, keep in mind that if any of the estimated activity times change, the LP model must be updated and re-solved to identify the impact of the change on the start and finish times throughout the project network.

Figure 15.17
Spreadsheet
model for the
LP formulation
of the latest start
times.

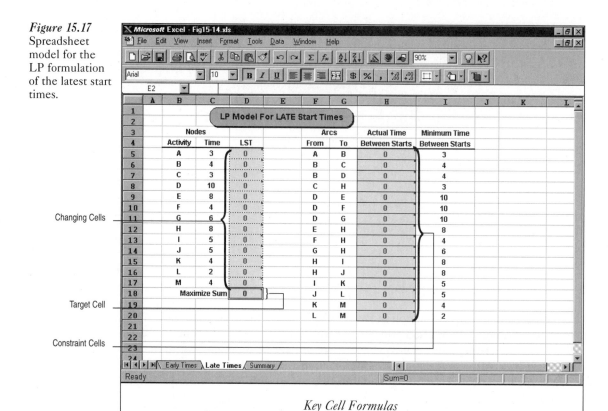

Changing Cells

Target Cell

Constraint Cells

Key Cell Formulas

Cell	Formula	Copied to
D18	=SUM(D5:D17)	—
H5	=VLOOKUP(G5,$B$5:$D$17,3)-VLOOKUP(F5,$B$5:$D$17,3)	H6:H20
I5	=VLOOKUP(F5,$B$5:$C$17,2)	I6:I20

Figure 15.18
Solver
parameters and
options for the
latest start times.

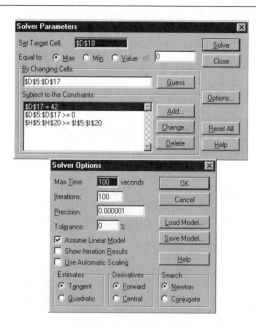

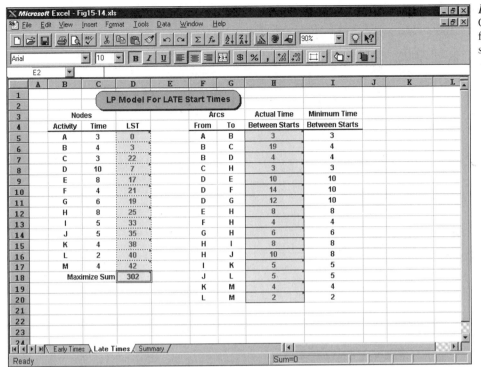

Figure 15.19
Optimal solution for the latest start times.

15.9 PROJECT CRASHING

With the CPM technique, we can use the times required to perform each activity to determine the least amount of time required to complete the entire project. However, the time required to complete an activity can often be shortened, or crashed. For example, suppose that the amount of time it takes to paint a house is *normally* five days. But, by hiring more painters or asking the existing painters to work overtime, it might be possible to paint the same house in two days. Thus, activities can have normal times and crash times.

The **normal time** of an activity represents the ordinary amount of time required to complete the activity with the usual amount of resources and effort. The **crash time** of an activity represents the least amount of time in which an activity can be accomplished if extra effort and resources are applied to the activity. The extra effort and resources required to crash certain activities usually increase the cost of performing these activities.

In managing projects, we often need to evaluate the trade-offs between the cost of crashing certain activities and the benefit of accomplishing these activities in less than normal time. For example, in our problem we determined that it takes 46 working days to complete the construction of the house. But what if the buyer wants the house built in 35 days? We need some way to determine if this can be done and, if so, how much additional cost will be involved. Similarly, it is not unusual for some critical activities in a project to take more than their normal time. After all, projects are not immune to Murphy's Law, which states that if something can go wrong, it will go wrong. When a critical activity is delayed, the completion of the project will be delayed unless management chooses to crash some of the remaining critical activities.

Figure 15.20
Summary of
earliest and
latest start and
finish times.

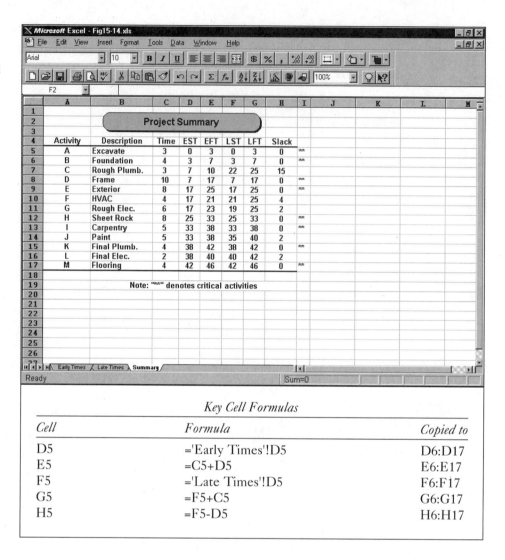

Key Cell Formulas

Cell	Formula	Copied to
D5	='Early Times'!D5	D6:D17
E5	=C5+D5	E6:E17
F5	='Late Times'!D5	F6:F17
G5	=F5+C5	G6:G17
H5	=F5-D5	H6:H17

Cashing In On a Project Crash

In early 1973, TRW (a large government defense contractor) was in trouble. TRW held a contract to develop software for several DEC PDP-10 computers to analyze the power needs of the Northwest region and control the amount of electricity generated by hydroelectric dams on the Columbia River. But the PDP-10 software was infested with bugs and the project soon fell behind schedule. If TRW couldn't get the bugs fixed quickly, it would have to pay substantial contract penalties—so it was time to crash the project. An urgent request from TRW's headquarters to DEC for bug-hunting experts led to a surprising suggestion—a high school senior named Bill Gates at Seattle's exclusive Lakeside prep school. Bill and his friend, Paul Allen, had debugged DEC software for Seattle's Computer Center Corporation in exchange for free time to "play" with the computers. But TRW offered to compensate Gates and Allen with real money—$165 per week. Gates and Allen took the job. Two years later Bill Gates and Paul Allen teamed up again on a slightly more profitable software venture—the founding of the Microsoft Corporation.

Source: James Wallace and Jim Erickson, *HARDDRIVE*, Harper Business, 1992.

15.9.1 An LP Approach to Crashing

We can use LP to help determine the least costly way of crashing a project to meet certain deadlines. To do this, we first must determine the normal time, normal cost, crash time, and crash cost for each project activity. Suppose that Tom asked his subcontractors to estimate crash times and costs for activities involved in our example problem. This information is summarized in Figure 15.21 (and in the file FIG15-21.xls on your data disk), along with the normal times and normal costs that Tom originally estimated for each activity.

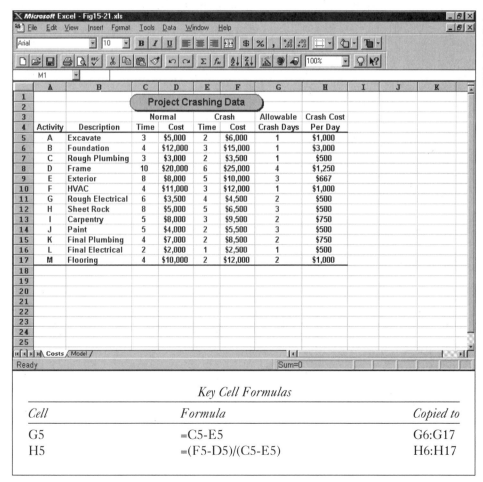

Figure 15.21
Summary of normal and crash times and costs for the home-building project.

		Normal		Crash		Allowable	Crash Cost
Activity	Description	Time	Cost	Time	Cost	Crash Days	Per Day
A	Excavate	3	$5,000	2	$6,000	1	$1,000
B	Foundation	4	$12,000	3	$15,000	1	$3,000
C	Rough Plumbing	3	$3,000	2	$3,500	1	$500
D	Frame	10	$20,000	6	$25,000	4	$1,250
E	Exterior	8	$8,000	5	$10,000	3	$667
F	HVAC	4	$11,000	3	$12,000	1	$1,000
G	Rough Electrical	6	$3,500	4	$4,500	2	$500
H	Sheet Rock	8	$5,000	5	$6,500	3	$500
I	Carpentry	5	$8,000	3	$9,500	2	$750
J	Paint	5	$4,000	2	$5,500	3	$500
K	Final Plumbing	4	$7,000	2	$8,500	2	$750
L	Final Electrical	2	$2,000	1	$2,500	1	$500
M	Flooring	4	$10,000	2	$12,000	2	$1,000

Key Cell Formulas

Cell	Formula	Copied to
G5	=C5-E5	G6:G17
H5	=(F5-D5)/(C5-E5)	H6:H17

As shown in Figure 15.21, in his original plan Tom estimated that the framing activity (activity D) would take 10 days and cost $20,000. However, the subcontractor indicated that if this activity were crashed by the maximum amount, it could be completed in only 6 days but at a cost of $25,000. For planning purposes, Tom might assume that the time required to complete the framing activity can be reduced from its normal time of 10 days by no more than 4 days (10 − 6 = 4). This value is indicated in Figure 15.21 in the Allowable Crash Days column. Tom might also assume that each day this activity is crashed will increase the cost of the activity by approximately $1,250 (($25,000 − $20,000)/4 = $1,250). This value is shown for the framing activity in the Crash Cost Per Day column. The allowable number of crash days and crash costs per day for the remaining activities are determined in a similar way and are shown in Figure 15.21.

15.9.2   Determining the Earliest Crash Completion Time

Tom might want to know the earliest possible date that the project could be completed and by what amount each activity would need to be crashed in order to achieve this date. An LP formulation of this problem is represented as:

$$\text{MIN:} \quad T_M + t_M - C_M$$

$$\text{Subject to:} \quad T_B - T_A \geq t_A - C_A$$

$$T_C - T_B \geq t_B - C_B$$

$$T_D - T_B \geq t_B - C_B$$

$$T_E - T_D \geq t_D - C_D$$

$$T_F - T_D \geq t_D - C_D$$

$$T_G - T_D \geq t_D - C_D$$

$$T_H - T_C \geq t_C - C_C$$

$$T_H - T_E \geq t_E - C_E$$

$$T_H - T_F \geq t_F - C_F$$

$$T_H - T_G \geq t_G - C_G$$

$$T_I - T_H \geq t_H - C_H$$

$$T_J - T_H \geq t_H - C_H$$

$$T_K - T_I \geq t_I - C_I$$

$$T_L - T_J \geq t_J - C_J$$

$$T_M - T_K \geq t_K - C_K$$

$$T_M - T_L \geq t_L - C_L$$

$$C_i \leq \text{allowable crash days for activity } i$$

$$T_i, C_i \geq 0, \text{ for all } i$$

where

$$T_i = \text{the time at which activity } i \text{ begins}$$

$$t_i = \text{the normal activity time of activity } i$$

$$C_i = \text{amount of time by which activity } i \text{ is crashed}$$

This LP model is similar to the models discussed in the previous section except that this model allows for the project activities to be crashed. For example, the first time constraint indicates that the difference between the start times of activities A and B must be greater than or equal to the normal time for activity A minus the amount be which activity A is crashed. The rest of the time constraints can be interpreted in a similar way. Also note that this model places appropriate upper limits on the amount of time by which each activity can be crashed. Finally, the objective function in this problem attempts to minimize the final completion time of the project (which is equal to the start time for activity M, plus its normal activity time, minus the amount by which this activity is crashed). Thus, the solution to this model should indicate the earliest possible time at which the project can be completed if activities are crashed.

15.9.3 Implementing the Model

One approach to implementing this model in a spreadsheet is shown on the Model sheet in Figure 15.22. In this spreadsheet, the values in column D represent the start time of each activity (the T_i) and the values in column E correspond to the amount by which each activity is crashed (the C_i).

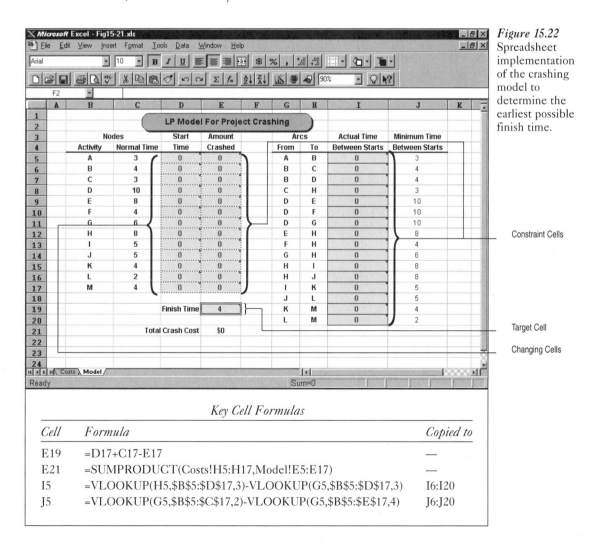

Figure 15.22
Spreadsheet implementation of the crashing model to determine the earliest possible finish time.

Key Cell Formulas

Cell	Formula	Copied to
E19	=D17+C17-E17	—
E21	=SUMPRODUCT(Costs!H5:H17,Model!E5:E17)	—
I5	=VLOOKUP(H5,$B$5:$D$17,3)-VLOOKUP(G5,$B$5:$D$17,3)	I6:I20
J5	=VLOOKUP(G5,$B$5:$C$17,2)-VLOOKUP(G5,$B$5:$E$17,4)	J6:J20

The LHS formulas for the time constraints are implemented in column I in the same manner as described in the previous section. Specifically, cell I5 contains the following formula, which is copied to cells I6 through I20:

Formula for cell I5:   =VLOOKUP(H5,$B$5:$D$17,3)-
(Copy to I6 though I20.)   VLOOKUP(G5,$B$5:$D$17,3)

This formula first finds the cell in column D that corresponds to the start time for activity B and then subtracts the cell in column D that represents the start time for activity A. The value returned by this formula represents the actual amount of time between the start of activity A and the start of activity B.

The RHS values of the time constraints are implemented in column J as:

Formula for cell J5:   =VLOOKUP(G5,$B$5:$C$17,2)-
(Copy to J6 though J20.)   VLOOKUP(G5,$B$5:$E$17,4)

This formula first finds the cell in column C corresponding to the normal time for activity A, then subtracts the cell in column E corresponding to the time by which activity A will be crashed.

The objective function for this problem is implemented in cell E19 with the following formula:

Formula for cell E19:   =D17+C17-E17

This value represents the time at which the project will be completed. Finally, for informational purposes (and future reference), in cell E21, we implement the following formula to calculate the total cost associated with crashing the project:

Formula for cell E21:   =SUMPRODUCT(Costs!H5:H17,Model!E5:E17)

This formula calculates the sum of products between the crash cost per day for each activity (calculated in cells H5 through H17 on the Costs sheet shown in Figure 15.21) and the amount by which each activity is crashed (represented by cells E5 through E17 on the Model sheet shown in Figure 15.22).

15.9.4   Solving the Model

Figure 15.23 shows the Solver parameters and options used to solve this model. In defining the constraints for this problem, the values of cells E5 through E17 (the C_j) are required to be less than or equal to their maximum allowable values calculated earlier on the Costs sheet.

The optimal solution for this problem, shown in Figure 15.24, indicates that by crashing various activities, the project could be completed within 28 days rather than 46. However, the Total Crash Cost figure indicates this would raise the cost of the project by $19,000. (Note that in general, the total crash cost obtained when solving this type of model is not necessarily the minimum crash cost because the model minimizes completion time, not crash costs. Because alternate optimal solutions can occur, another crash schedule might also allow the project to be completed within 28 days but at a lower total crash cost. Thus, to verify that the minimum total crash cost is $19,000, we need to add a constraint to hold the finish time at 28 days and attempt to minimize the total crash cost. In this case, the solution shown in Figure 15.24 is optimal and the minimum total crash cost is, in fact, $19,000.)

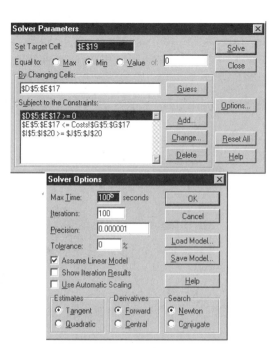

Figure 15.23
Solver
parameters and
options for the
earliest possible
finish times.

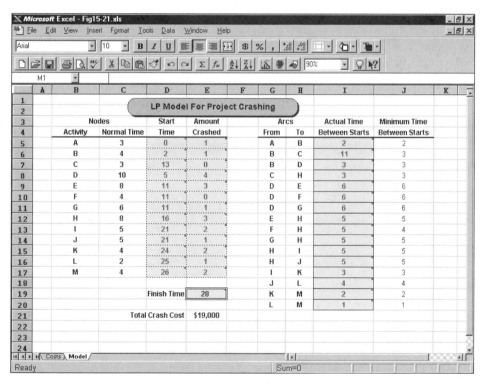

Figure 15.24
Optimal solution
for the earliest
possible finish
times.

15.9.5 Determining a Least Costly Crash Schedule

Another use of a crashing model is to determine the least costly way to complete a
project at some time earlier than would be possible using normal activity times. For

example, if the home buyer insists on the house being built within 35 days, we might want to determine the least costly way of crashing the schedule to meet this deadline.

We can solve this type of problem easily using the existing model. In this case, we would simply add a constraint to hold the project completion time at 35 days and attempt to minimize the total crash cost. The Solver parameters and options required to accomplish this are shown in Figure 15.25, and the optimal solution is shown in Figure 15.26.

The solution shown in Figure 15.26 indicates that it would cost an additional $8,500 to crash the project so that it could be completed within 35 days. The values in the Amount Crashed column indicate the amounts by which each activity must be crashed in order to implement this schedule.

15.9.6   Crashing as an MOLP

As we have seen, two objectives can be pursued in our crashing model. On the one hand, we might want to minimize the finish time of the project. On the other hand, we might want to minimize the cost of crashing the project. These two objectives are in conflict with one another because reducing the completion time of the project increases the crash costs. Thus, we could use the techniques for MOLPs described in Chapter 7 if we want to study the cost/time trade-offs more formally in this type of problem.

Another way to study the cost/time trade-offs is to re-solve the problem several times to determine the minimum crash cost for each possible completion time. A graph showing the minimum crash cost for each possible completion time is useful in evaluating the trade-offs involved in crashing. Figure 15.27 shows such a graph for our example problem.

Figure 15.25
Solver parameters and options for the least costly crash schedule to complete the project by time period 35.

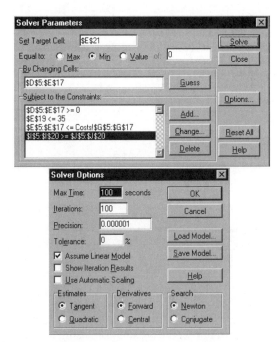

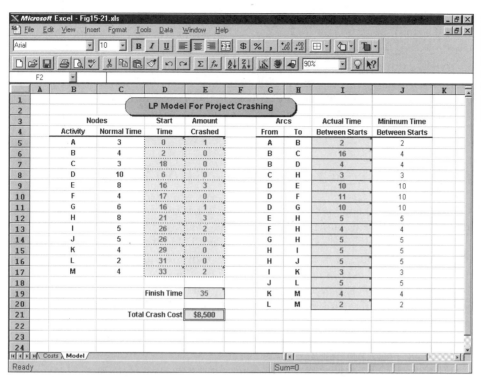

Figure 15.26
Optimal solution for the least costly crash schedule to complete the project by time period 35.

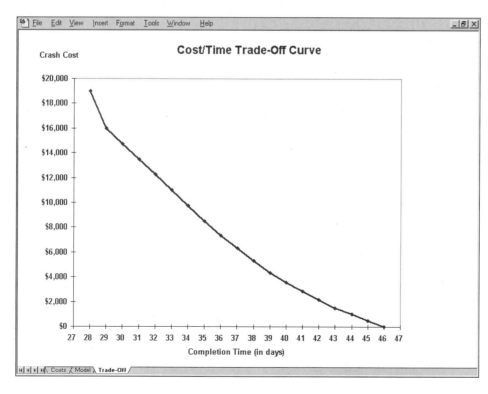

Figure 15.27
Graph of the relationship between crash time and completion time.

According to this graph, no crash costs will be incurred if the project is completed in its normal time of 46 days, but crash costs of $19,000 will be incurred if we complete the project in the least amount of time (28 days). Although it is relatively inexpensive to crash the project by a few days, the graph shows that it becomes increasingly expensive to crash the project by additional amounts. Note that a rather substantial increase in cost is incurred to complete the project in 28 days rather than 29. So this type of graph gives us a clear picture of the cost/time trade-offs involved in crashing a project.

15.10 CERTAINTY VS. UNCERTAINTY

Throughout our discussion of CPM, we assumed that the times required to complete project activities were known with certainty or could, at least, be estimated with a high degree of accuracy. This assumption does not hold for all projects. For example, consider the schedule of activities required to design and build the first space shuttle. Because no one had ever built a space shuttle before, no historical data were available for estimating how long it would take to perform many of the creative tasks required by this project. Even in projects where the same or similar tasks have been performed before, the amount of time required to perform them might be different. PERT was developed as an attempt to deal with uncertainty in activity times.

In recent years, a number of problems have surfaced regarding the PERT technique, causing many to question the wisdom of using this technique at all. The following discussion of PERT focuses on illuminating these weaknesses. We will then briefly consider how to overcome some of these problems using the technique of simulation.

15.11 PERT: AN OVERVIEW

PERT differs from CPM in that it assumes the times required to perform the project activities are *not* known with certainty. PERT assumes that the activity times are random variables that have some mean, or expected, value and some variance. However, rather than specifying a mean and variance for each activity, we must give three time estimates for each activity in the project. Specifically, for each activity PERT requires estimates of:

a_i = estimate of the duration of activity i assuming the most favorable conditions

b_i = estimate of the duration of activity i assuming the least favorable conditions

m_i = estimate of the most likely duration of activity i

We can think of a_i, b_i, and m_i as representing, respectively, the best case, worst case, and most likely times required to perform activity i. PERT uses these values to calculate the expected duration of each activity as:

$$t_i = \frac{a_i + 4m_i + b_i}{6}$$

and estimates the variance of each activity's duration as:

$$v_i = \frac{(b_i - a_i)^2}{36}$$

The preceding formulas are based on the assumption that the times required to perform each activity are random variables that follow the beta probability distribution. An in-depth understanding of the beta distribution is not necessary for our purposes. The beta distribution can be used to describe a wide variety of random variables, and is a reasonable choice for describing the behavior of most activity times when their true distributions are unknown.

After calculating the expected times for each activity, the next step in PERT is to identify the critical path for the project. In most project networks, a variety of paths can be followed to get from the start activity to the finish activity. Each path represents a sequence of activities that must be performed in order to complete the project. Because PERT assumes that the times required to perform the activities along a path are random variables, the time required to complete a given path is also a random variable with some mean and variance.

The expected (or mean) time required to complete any path in the network is simply the sum of the expected times (the t_i) of the activities on the path. If we assume that the individual activity times in a project are independent of one another (as does PERT), we may also calculate the variance of the completion time for any path as the sum of the variances (the v_i) of the activities on the path. Because all the paths through a project network must be completed in order for the project to be completed, PERT deems the path with the largest expected completion time to be the most critical—the critical path.

The expected completion time and variance for the critical path are used in PERT to estimate the probability of completing the project by various dates and to assist in negotiating and setting deadlines for the project's completion. Many projects impose financial penalties for each day, week, or month a project is late; therefore, it is often important to identify a deadline for a project that management is confident will not be exceeded. Thus, in addition to identifying a critical path for management to scrutinize, PERT also claims to offer assistance in estimating and setting deadlines for a project.

15.11.1   The Problems with PERT

The PERT technique presents a number of problems that should cause us to approach it with caution. First, as indicated above, PERT assumes that the time required to perform project activities are random variables that are independent of one another. Although this assumption makes it easy to complete the calculations in PERT, it is probably not a realistic assumption. For example, if one activity along the critical path (or any other path) runs a bit over its expected time, a diligent project manager will make sure that one or more of the subsequent activities run a bit under their expected times to catch up on the schedule. To the extent that these over- and under-runs offset one another, the expected completion time of the project should not be affected seriously. However, the variance of the completion times of the paths through the network will be reduced as a result.

The more serious problem in PERT involves the identification of the critical path. As described earlier, PERT identifies the critical path as the path with the longest expected completion time. Thus, an unsuspecting project manager might focus on the activities on the critical path, believing that they are the activities most likely to delay the completion of the project. In reality, activities not on the critical path can pose a greater risk of delaying the project. Consider the activity network shown in Figure 15.28.

Figure 15.28
Example of a
PERT network.

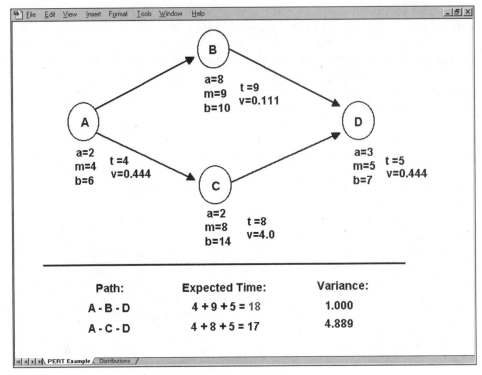

The network in Figure 15.28 represents a simple project consisting of only four activities. The three time estimates (a, b, and m) required by PERT are given for each activity. The expected time and variance (t and v) are calculated for each activity. Only two paths run through this network: A to B to D, and A to C to D. The expected times and variances for each path are calculated as shown in Figure 15.28. The path consisting of A-B-D has an expected time of 18 and variance of 1.0. The path consisting of A-C-D has an expected time of 17 and variance of 4.889. Thus, PERT would identify A-B-D as the critical path and use its expected value and variance to make estimates about when the project will be completed.

Earlier, we indicated that the time to complete any path in a PERT network is a random variable. We can view the time to complete path A-B-D and the time to complete path A-C-D as two separate random variables whose probability distributions are similar to those shown in Figure 15.29. Notice that the distribution of the critical A-B-D path is centered at its expected value of 18 and has a relatively small variance. The distribution of the noncritical A-C-D path is centered at its expected value of 17 and has a much larger variance.

If we focus only on the distribution of the critical path shown in Figure 15.29, it appears that almost no chance exists that completing this path will take more than 21 time periods. Thus, if we apply the PERT technique to this project, we would conclude that the project can almost certainly be completed within 21 time units. However, the distribution of times for path A-C-D indicates a fairly significant probability that this noncritical path will take more than 21 days. So which path is really the critical path—the one with the longest expected completion time or the one with the smallest probability of completion by the desired deadline? And which activity in this project is really more critical—B or C? The fact that PERT causes us to ask such

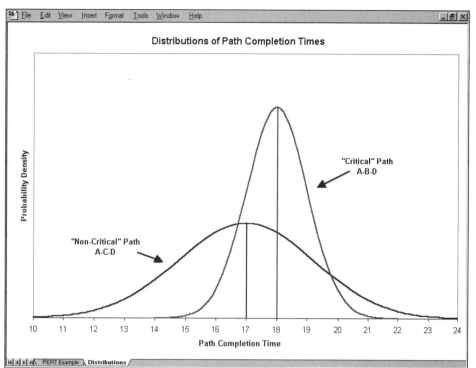

Figure 15.29
Graph of the distributions of completion times for each path through the PERT network.

questions, and fails to answer them, should raise serious concerns about the wisdom of using this technique.

15.11.2   Implications

The preceding discussion makes it clear that activities not on PERT's critical path might, in fact, be more critical to the completion of a project than the activities PERT identifies as critical. Indeed, *every* activity in a project has some probability of being critical. For some activities, this probability might be near 0; for others, it might be closer to 1. A project manager would want to focus on the activities with the highest probability of being critical—regardless of whether or not they fall on the critical path. Unfortunately, PERT does little to help us identify the project activities that are truly the most critical.

15.12   SIMULATING PROJECT NETWORKS

Although the PERT technique has serious drawbacks, it does highlight an important point—activity times in a project are likely to be somewhat random. Although CPM ignores this point entirely, by calculating the earliest and latest start times for each activity it at least shows which activities are likely to be critical if the actual activity times deviate from their expected values.

    The best way to evaluate the impact of variability in activity times on the critical path and the completion time of a project involves the technique of simulation described in Chapters 12 and 13. To simulate a project, we need to generate random times from appropriate probability distributions for each project activity. For the given set of random activity times, we can determine the critical path and the time required to complete the project. If we repeat this process many times, we can determine the frequency with which the project activities fall on the critical path. We could also analyze the resulting distribution project completion times to estimate more accurately the probability of completing the project within various time periods.

15.12.1   An Example

The following example, which is a modification of our earlier home-building example, illustrates the mechanics of simulating the duration of a project.

> Tom has asked the subcontractors for each activity in the home-building process to supply a best-case, most-likely-case, and worst-case estimate of the amount of time required to complete each activity. Figure 15.30 shows these time estimates.
>
> Tom wants to use these time estimates to conduct a simulation study of the project. In particular, he wants to determine how critical each activity is—that is, the probability of each activity falling on the critical path. He also wants to determine the number of days it will take to complete the entire project.

15.12.2   Generating Random Activity Times

To simulate the duration of this project, we first must identify probability distributions that describe the behavior of the random activity times. Because the three time estimates for each activity correspond to the best-case, most-likely-case, and worst-case scenarios for each activity, we might assume that the random behavior of the activity times can be approximated by a triangular probability distribution such as the

Figure 15.30
Summary of time estimates for activities in the home-building project.

	Time Estimates		
Activity	*a* Best Case	*m* Most Likely Case	*b* Worst Case
A	2	3	5
B	3	4	6
C	2	3	7
D	8	10	14
E	6	8	10
F	3	4	5
G	4	6	8
H	7	8	10
I	4	5	7
J	3	5	9
K	3	4	6
L	1	2	4
M	3	4	6

one shown in Figure 15.31 for activity A. Notice that the shape of the triangular distribution varies depending on the parameters *a*, *m*, and *b*, which correspond (respectively) to the best-case, most-likely-case, and worst-case time estimates for a given activity.

15.12.3   Implementing the Model

A spreadsheet model for this problem is shown in Figure 15.32 (and in the file FIG15-32.xls on your data disk).

   The three times for each project activity are entered in columns B, C, and D. The formula to generate the random values representing the time required for activities in column A are implemented in column E as follows:

> Formula for cell E6:   =RNGTriang(B6,C6,D6)
> (Copy to E7 through E18.)

   (Note: In order to use the RNGTriang( ) function, the RNG.xla add-in must be installed as described in Chapter 12.) Using the randomly generated activity times, we can create formulas to calculate the earliest and latest start and finish times and the amount of slack available for each activity. We would accomplish this in the same manner as described earlier with respect to Figure 15.11. The activities on the critical path are indicated by slack values of 0.

15.12.4   Running the Simulation

We can use the Data Table command (as described in Chapter 12) to replicate this model repeatedly. To do so, we must identify the values in the model that we want to

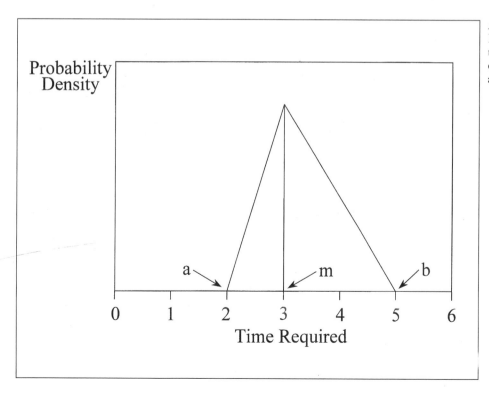

Figure 15.31
Example of a triangular distribution of activity times.

Figure 15.32
Spreadsheet
model for the
home-building
project with
random activity
times.

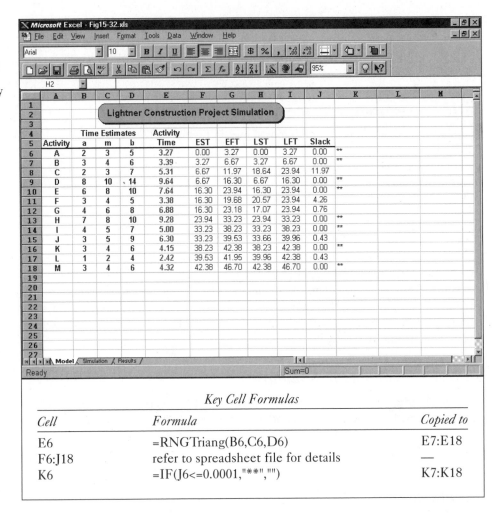

Key Cell Formulas

Cell	Formula	Copied to
E6	=RNGTriang(B6,C6,D6)	E7:E18
F6:J18	refer to spreadsheet file for details	—
K6	=IF(J6<=0.0001,"**","")	K7:K18

track. One objective in our problem is to determine how critical each activity is. Because critical activities are indicated by slack values of 0, we want to track the values in the Slack column for each activity in our model. However, because all paths go through activities A, B, H, and M, we know that these activities will always be critical, so there is no point in tracking their slack values. Thus, the slack value for activity C in the Model sheet in Figure 15.32 is repeated in cell B3 of the Simulation sheet shown in Figure 15.33 using the following formula:

Formula for cell B3:   =VLOOKUP(B2,Model!$A$6:$J$18,10)
(Copy to C3 through J3.)

This formula is copied to cells C3 through J3 to provide the slack values for activities D, E, F, G, I, J, K, and L, respectively.

A second objective in our problem is to estimate the amount of time required to complete the project—or the finish time of activity M. This value is tracked in column K on the Simulation sheet shown in Figure 15.33 through the following formula in cell K3:

Formula for cell K3:   =Model!I18

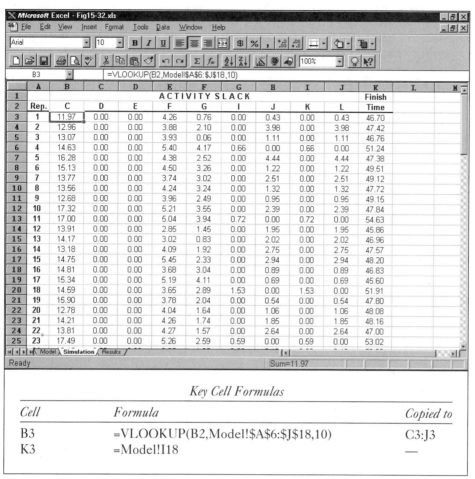

Figure 15.33
Spreadsheet model for the home-building project with random activity times.

			Key Cell Formulas		
Cell		Formula			Copied to
B3		=VLOOKUP(B2,Model!$A$6:$J$18,10)			C3:J3
K3		=Model!I18			—

The remainder of the spreadsheet shown in Figure 15.33 is completed using the Data Table command. Each row in this table represents the amount of slack for the activities and the project completion times that were observed in each replication of our project activity model. The simulation shown in Figure 15.33 consists of 100 such replications.

15.12.5   *Analyzing the Results*

The Results sheet shown in Figure 15.34 provides the results of the simulation. In the top portion of this sheet, we used the AVERAGE( ) function to calculate the average amount of slack observed for each activity during the simulation. We also calculated the percentage of time each activity was critical during the 100 replications performed on the model. For example, this sheet indicates that activity D was on the critical path (or had 0 slack) in 100% of the replications, activity E was critical in 95% of the replications, and so on. Thus, this sheet clearly shows which activities are most likely to be critical and warrant the most attention.

The average and variance of the finish times observed during the simulation are shown in cells F8 and F9, respectively. Assuming that the finish times are normally distributed, there is roughly a 50% chance that the actual project completion time will

Figure 15.34
Results of the
simulation.

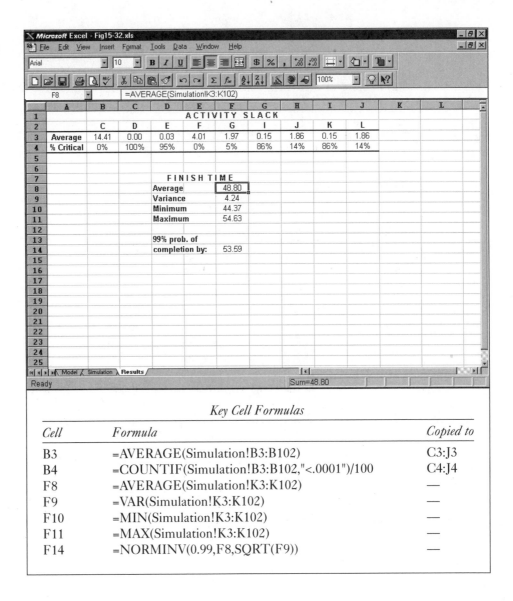

exceed 48.8 time periods. Thus, we might want to determine the amount of time within which it is virtually certain that the project will be completed. That is, we might want to determine the 99th percentile of the distribution of project completion times. This is calculated in cell F14 as:

Formula in cell F14:   =NORMINV(0.99,F8,SQRT(F9))

The result of this formula indicates a 99% chance exists that a normally distributed random variable with a mean of 48.8 and standard deviation of $\sqrt{4.24}$ will assume a value less than or equal to 53.59. Notice that this is consistent with the maximum finish time (shown in cell F11) observed during the simulation. Thus, we could be reasonably confident that the project can be completed within 54 time periods.

THE WORLD OF MANAGEMENT SCIENCE
Food and Drug Administration Uses PERT to Control the Timeliness of Research and Development Projects

The National Center for Drug Analysis develops automated drug testing procedures for the U.S. Food and Drug Administration (FDA). The FDA uses these procedures to conduct production studies of drugs selected on the basis of therapeutic significance and how widely they are used.

To allocate personnel and facilities efficiently to drug testing studies, it is important to have a good estimate of when a new, automated testing procedure will be ready. If a method is not ready at the time samples are collected, either the samples must be analyzed manually or existing schedules must be reworked, causing serious disruptions.

The FDA chose PERT to manage methods of development projects because it treats activity completion times as random variables. This is appropriate for research and development activities, many of which are being done for the first time.

The PERT network for a development project consists of 24 nodes and 31 arcs. The network is updated weekly, giving management access to probabilities of completion times, activities on the critical path and second most critical path, slack times for noncritical activities, a list of completed activities, and so on. This information makes it easy to review and adjust personnel assignments and to control completion times. The PERT plans and reports are also useful to the individual chemists, providing a more comprehensive procedure for planning and organizing their work.

The director of the center successfully implemented the use of PERT by developing appropriate forms and computer programs, thoroughly training staff members on how to use PERT, and then incrementally introducing the procedure in a series of pilot tests. The pilot test results suggested some improvements, which were incorporated as the center proceeded with full implementation.

Source: N. K. Kwak and Lawrence Jones, "An Application of PERT to R&D Scheduling," *Information Processing and Management*, vol. 14, no. 2, 1978, pp. 121–131.

SUMMARY

This chapter presented a variety of techniques for managing projects by representing and analyzing a project in the form of a network. When the activity times in a project can be estimated with a reasonable amount of certainty, CPM can be applied to determine the earliest start and finish times for each activity and the earliest time for completing the entire project. CPM can also be used to determine the latest possible times that activities can start and finish without delaying the completion of the project. The slack in a project helps to distinguish between critical and noncritical activities. Various LP techniques can be used to analyze CPM networks and determine optimal crash schedules for projects that must be completed ahead of schedule.

When activity times cannot be estimated with certainty, they must be modeled as random variables. Although the PERT technique was designed to address these types of problems, it has some serious theoretical and practical shortcomings. However, simulation can be used to provide a more complete and accurate analysis of activity networks containing random activity times.

QUESTIONS AND PROBLEMS

1. In this chapter, we stated that the longest path through an activity network is the critical path. Why isn't the completion time for a project defined by the shortest path through the network? Explain your answer.

2. Throughout this chapter, we assumed that a project manager identifies and organizes the activities in a project, estimates the time required for each activity, then determines how quickly the project can be completed. However, the deadlines for some projects are fixed before any planning begins. For example, consider the planning of a New Year's Eve celebration in the downtown area of a major city. Which, if any, of the techniques described in this chapter might be helpful in planning such an event?

3. In illustrating how to simulate an activity network, we used a triangular distribution based on three time estimates to generate random activity times. What problem might be encountered if we assume that activity times were normally distributed? (Hint: Consider the values that a normally distributed random variable with a mean of 5 and variance of 3 might assume.)

4. Consider the CPM network for the following set of activities:

Activity	Predecessor Activities
A	—
B	A
C	A, B

Is it necessary to draw an arc from the node for activity A to the node for activity C? Why or why not?

5. Consider the following set of activities:

Activity	Days Required	Predecessor Activities
A	3	—
B	2	A
C	5	A
D	8	B, C
E	4	B, C
F	2	D, E

a. Draw the CPM network for this problem.
b. Manually determine the earliest and latest start and finish times for each activity and the amount of slack for each activity.
c. What is the critical path?
d. How long should it take to complete the project?

6. Consider the following set of activities:

Activity	Days Required	Predecessor Activities
A	3	—
B	2	—
C	5	A, B
D	8	A, B
E	4	D

a. Draw the CPM network for this problem. (Remember that a CPM network requires unique start and finish nodes.)
b. Manually determine the earliest and latest start and finish times for each activity and the amount of slack for each activity.
c. What is the critical path?
d. How long should it take to complete the project?

7. Consider the following set of activities:

Activity	Time Required	Predecessor Activities
A	5	—
B	4	A
C	5	B
D	8	B
E	9	C
F	6	C, D
G	8	D
H	3	E, F, G

a. Draw the CPM network for this problem.
b. Identify each path through the network and its expected length.
c. What is the critical path?

8. Aerobatic, Inc. custom-designs and manufactures light aircraft. The activities involved in this process are summarized below (where the time required is expressed in number of weeks).

Activity	Description	Time Required	Predecessor Activities
A	design	4	—
B	order and receive materials	5	A
C	construct frame	8	B
D	prepare engine	6	B
E	prepare avionics	5	B
F	cover frame	4	C
G	install engine	2	E, F
H	paint	2	F
I	install avionics	2	D, G, H
J	test	1	I

a. Draw the activity network for this problem.
b. Use LP to determine the earliest start time for each activity.
c. What is the earliest this project can be finished?

    d. Use LP to determine the latest start time for each activity.

    e. Create a spreadsheet to summarize the earliest and latest start and finish times, the slack for each activity, and the critical activities.

9. Linda Madison owns Creations, a business that provides hair and nail care services in a small college town. Recently, Linda has decided to expand her business to include tanning and massage services for her clients. In order to accommodate these new services and the additional clients they are expected to attract, Linda is relocating her business to a larger facility. However, the new location will require some renovation before she can relocate there. Linda has identified the following activities that must be performed before she can open at her new location.

Activity	Description	Days Required	Predecessor Activities
A	install new plumbing	10	—
B	order and receive furniture	20	—
C	order and receive flooring	15	—
D	construct partitions	5	—
E	paint and wallpaper	5	A, D
F	install furniture	3	E, B
G	install flooring	4	E, C
H	move inventory and records	2	F, G
I	clean old shop	2	H

    a. Draw the activity network for this problem.

    b. Use LP to determine the earliest start time for each activity.

    c. What is the earliest this project can be finished?

    d. Use LP to determine the latest start time for each activity.

    e. Create a spreadsheet to summarize the earliest and latest start and finish times, the slack for each activity, and the critical activities.

10. Refer to question 9. Suppose that Linda's lease on her current facility expires in 20 days. The normal and crash times and costs for each activity in her moving project are summarized below. By what amount should each activity be crashed in order for her to complete the move within 20 days?

	Normal		Crash	
Activity	Time	Cost	Time	Cost
A	10	$11,000	7	$15,000
B	20	5,000	18	6,000
C	15	3,000	12	3,500
D	5	1,500	3	2,000
E	5	750	2	1,200
F	3	600	1	1,200
G	4	1,000	2	1,500
H	2	250	1	450
I	2	200	1	300

11. The activities required to service a car at Zippy-Lube can be viewed as a mini-project as summarized on the next page.

Activity	Description	Predecessor Activity	Min.	Avg.	Max.
			Time Required		
A	drain oil	—	2	3.5	5
B	replace filter	A	1	2	3
C	refill oil	B, E	2	2.5	4
D	check tires	—	2	3	4
E	wash windows	D	2	3	5
F	fill fluids	E	2	3	4
G	final test	C, F	0.5	1	1.5

The variability in the time required to perform each activity is due to the different types, sizes, and condition of the cars to be serviced.

a. Draw the activity network for this problem.
b. Use PERT to identify the expected time and variance for each activity.
c. What is the critical path? What is the expected time and variance of the critical path?

12. Refer to question 11. Create a spreadsheet model to simulate the completion times for servicing cars. Assume that activity times follow a triangular distribution and perform 300 replications on the model.

a. Estimate the probability of each activity falling on the critical path.
b. On average, how long should it take to finish servicing a car?
c. Suppose that the manager of this business wants to guarantee that your car will be ready within 10 minutes or you will receive a coupon worth $5 off your next visit. What proportion of customers would receive the coupon?

13. The activities summarized below must be performed by the promoter of a country music concert in Dallas.

Activity	Description	Predecessor Activity	Min.	Avg.	Max.
			Days Required		
A	find location	—	2	4	7
B	hire opening act	A	3	6	10
C	hire technicians	A	1	2	3
D	set up radio ads	B	2	4	6
E	distribute tickets	B	2	3	5
F	rent sound and lights	B, C	3	4	6
G	set up newspaper ads	B	1	2	4
H	hire security	F	2	3	4
I	conduct rehearsal	F ,H	1	1.5	2
J	final details	I	2	3	4

a. Draw the activity network for this problem.
b. According to PERT, what is the expected length of time required to accomplish these activities?
c. Assume that the durations of the activities are random variables that follow triangular distributions. Create a spreadsheet model of the project and use sim-

ulation to create 300 replications of the project. Rank the activities according to how critical they are.

d. When should the promoter begin working on the concert to have a 99% chance of completing the project by August 15?

14. Consider the following set of activities:

Activity	Days Required	Predecessor Activities	Activity	Days Required	Predecessor Activities
A	3	—	G	6	B
B	4	A	H	5	F ,C, E
C	4	A	I	6	G, H
D	3	A	J	4	F, C, E
E	3	D	K	2	D
F	4	B	L	6	I, J, K

a. Draw the CPM network for this problem.
b. Use LP to identify the earliest start time for each activity.
c. What is the earliest time that the project can be completed?
d. Use LP to identify the latest start time for each activity.
e. Create a spreadsheet to summarize the earliest and latest start and finish times, the slack for each activity, and the critical activities.

15. The following data summarize the per-day cost of crashing the activities in the problem described in question 14.

Activity	Crash Cost per Day	Maximum Crash Days	Activity	Crash Cost per Day	Maximum Crash Days
A	$50	2	G	$65	5
B	60	3	H	55	2
C	57	1	I	28	4
D	45	2	J	33	3
E	25	3	K	40	1
F	30	2	L	37	2

a. Create an LP model to determine the least costly way of crashing the project to complete it within 20 days.
b. By how much should each activity be crashed, and what is the total crashing cost?

CASE 15.1   IMAGINATION TOY CORPORATION

Amy White is the director of marketing for the Imagination Toy Corporation (ITC). She just received a phone call from her boss indicating that the company's board of directors gave final approval for the production and marketing of the Mighty Morphin' Monkeys—a new product line of action play toys for ITC. Amy worked hard in developing the concept for this product line and is thrilled that her ideas will become reality. But this news also means that she must get busy developing the marketing and sales force training materials needed to launch this new product line successfully. Amy's boss wants to know how soon she can have the sales staff trained and equipped to handle the new line.

The development of marketing materials and training of the sales staff for the new product line constitute a project. Amy identifies 10 specific project tasks that need to be accomplished before she can roll out the marketing program for this product line. First, Amy needs to collect information about the details of the decisions made by the board of directors. She can start this task (task A) immediately, and she estimates that it will take five days to determine exactly which items and accessories will be included in the first offering of the product line. After she completes this task, she will request prototypes of all items from the engineering department (task B), which she expects will take 10 working days. While waiting for the prototypes, she can begin laying out the marketing program (task C). She expects this activity to take eight days. Once the prototypes (task B) are available, Amy estimates that it will take seven days to prepare instructions (task D) on the operation and use of the items in the product line and nine days to design its packaging (task E). When the marketing program (task C) is finished, it must be approved (task F) by the president of the company. Amy expects this approval to take three days.

Amy plans to hold a two-day training course (task G) for the sales force once the operating instructions (task D) and the packaging design (task E) are completed. When the operating instructions (task D) are finished and the marketing plan is approved (task F), Amy will develop an information guide (task H) that the sales force can distribute to retailers. Amy expects to take eight days to complete the information guide. Also, as part of the marketing plan, Amy wants to hire a number of actors to portray Mighty Morphin' Monkeys (task I) at various promotional events around the country. Hiring and training these actors is expected to take eight days and can be done only after the marketing plan is approved (task F). Finally, after the marketing plan (task F) has been approved and the packaging for the product has been designed (task E), special point-of-sale display racks must be manufactured (task J). Amy expects this activity to take 12 working days.

1. Develop an AON network for this problem.

2. Use Solver to determine the earliest and latest start and finish times for each activity.

3. Identify the critical path.

4. If Amy starts working immediately, how long will it take her to complete this project?

5. Suppose that the engineering department can create the prototypes in only eight days if the engineers work overtime on this activity. Would this help reduce the length of time required to complete this project?

REFERENCES

Golenko, G. "On the Distribution of Activity Times in PERT." *Journal of the Operational Research Society*, vol. 39, August 1988.

Levy, F., A. Thompson, and S. Weist. "The ABCs of the Critical Path Method." *Harvard Business Review*, vol. 41, September-October 1963.

Meredith, J. and S. Mantel. *Project Management: A Managerial Approach*. New York: Wiley, 1985.

Phillips, C. and E. Davis. *Project Management with CPM, PERT, and Precedence Diagramming*. New York: Van Nostrand Reinhold, 1983.

Ragsdale, C. "The Current State of Network Simulation in Project Management Theory and Practice." *OMEGA*, vol. 17, no. 1, 1989.

Schonberger, R. "Why Projects Are 'Always' Late: A Rationale Based on Manual Simulation of a PERT/CPM Network." *Interfaces*, vol. 11, no. 5, 1981.

CHAPTER 16

Decision Analysis

The previous chapters in this book describe a variety of modeling techniques that can help managers gain insight and understanding about the decision problems they face. But models do not make decisions—people do. Although the insight and understanding gained by modeling problems can be helpful, decision making often remains a difficult task. The two primary causes for this difficulty are uncertainty regarding the future and conflicting values or objectives.

For example, suppose that when you graduate from college you receive job offers from two companies. One company (company A) is in a relatively new industry that offers potential for spectacular growth—or rapid bankruptcy. The salary offered by this company is somewhat lower than you'd like, but would increase rapidly if the company grows. This company is located in the city that is home to your favorite professional sports team and close to your friends and family.

The other job offer is from an established company (company B) that is known for its financial strength and long-term commitment to its employees. It has offered you a starting salary that is 10% more than you asked, but you suspect it would take longer for you to advance in this organization. Also, if you work for this company, you would have to move to a distant part of the country that offers few of the cultural and sporting activities that you enjoy.

Which offer would you accept? Or would you reject both offers and continue looking for employment with other companies? For many, this might be a difficult decision. If you accept the job with company A, you might be promoted twice within a year—or you could be unemployed in six months. With company B, you can be reasonably sure of having a secure job for the foreseeable future. But if you accept the job with company B and then company A grows rapidly, you might regret not accepting the position with company A. Thus, the uncertainty associated with the future of company A makes this decision difficult.

To further complicate the decision, company A offers a more desirable location than company B, but the starting salary with company A is lower. How can you assess the trade-offs between starting salary, location, job security, and potential for advancement in order to make a good decision? There is no easy answer to this question, but this chapter describes a number of techniques that can help you structure and analyze difficult decision problems in a logical manner.

16.1 GOOD DECISIONS VS. GOOD OUTCOMES

The goal of decision analysis is to help individuals make good decisions. But good decisions do not always result in good outcomes. For example, suppose that after carefully considering all the factors involved in the two job offers, you decide to accept the position with company B. After working for this company for nine months, it suddenly announces that, in an effort to cut costs, it is closing the office in which you work and eliminating your job. Did you make a bad decision? Probably not. Unforeseeable circumstances beyond your control caused you to experience a bad outcome, but it would be unfair to say that you made a bad decision. Good decisions sometimes result in bad outcomes.

The techniques for decision analysis presented in this chapter can help you make good decisions, but cannot guarantee that good outcomes will always occur as a result of those decisions. Even when a good decision is made, luck often plays a role in determining whether a good or bad outcome occurs. However, using a structured approach to make decisions should give us enhanced insight and sharper intuition about the decision problems we face. As a result, it is reasonable to expect good outcomes to occur more frequently when using a structured approach to decision making than if we make decisions in a more haphazard manner.

16.2 CHARACTERISTICS OF DECISION PROBLEMS

Although all decision problems are somewhat different, they share certain characteristics. For example, a decision must involve at least two alternatives for addressing or solving a problem. An **alternative** is a course of action intended to solve a problem. The job selection example described earlier involves three alternatives: you could accept the offer from company A, accept the offer from company B, or reject both offers and continue searching for a better one.

Alternatives are evaluated on the basis of the value they add to one or more decision criteria. The **criteria** in a decision problem represent various factors that are important to the decision maker and influenced by the alternatives. For example, the criteria used to evaluate the job offer alternatives might include starting salary, expected salary growth, desirability of job location, opportunity for promotion and career advancement, and so on. The impact of the alternatives on the criteria is of primary importance to the decision maker. Note that not all criteria can be expressed in terms of monetary value, making comparisons of the alternatives more difficult.

Finally, the values assumed by the various decision criteria under each alternative depend on the different states of nature that can occur. The **states of nature** in a decision problem correspond to future events that are not under the decision maker's control. For example, company A could experience spectacular growth, or it might go bankrupt. Each of these contingencies represents a possible state of nature for the problem. Many other states of nature are possible for the company; for example, it could grow slowly, or not grow at all. Thus, an infinite number of possible states of nature could exist in this, and many other, decision problems. However, in decision analysis, we often use a relatively small, discrete set of representative states of nature to summarize the future events that might occur.

16.3   AN EXAMPLE

The following example illustrates some of the issues and difficulties that arise in decision problems.

Hartsfield International Airport in Atlanta, Georgia, is one of the busiest airports in the world. During the past 30 years, the airport has expanded again and again to accommodate the increasing number of flights being routed through Atlanta. Analysts project that this increase will continue well into the next century. However, commercial development around the airport prevents it from building additional runways to handle the future air-traffic demands. As a solution to this problem, plans are being developed to build another airport outside the city limits. Two possible locations for the new airport have been identified, but a final decision on the new location is not expected to be made for another year.

The Magnolia Inns hotel chain intends to build a new facility near the new airport once its site is determined. Barbara Monroe is responsible for real estate acquisition for the company, and she faces a difficult decision about where to buy land. Currently, land values around the two possible sites for the new airport are increasing as investors speculate that property values will increase greatly in the vicinity of the new airport. The spreadsheet in Figure 16.1 (and in the file FIG16-1.xls on your data disk) summarizes the current price of each parcel of land, the estimated present value of the future cash flows that a hotel would generate at each site if the airport is ultimately located at the site, and the present value of the amount for which the company believes it can resell each parcel if the airport is not built at the site.

The company can buy either site, both sites, or neither site. Barbara must decide which sites, if any, the company should purchase.

16.4   THE PAYOFF MATRIX

A common way of analyzing this type of decision problem is to construct a payoff matrix. A **payoff matrix** is a table that summarizes the final outcome (or payoff) for each decision alternative under each possible state of nature. To construct a payoff matrix, we need to identify each decision alternative and each possible state of nature. The following four decision alternatives are available to the decision maker in our example problem:

16.4.1   Decision Alternatives

1. Buy the parcel at location A.
2. Buy the parcel at location B.
3. Buy the parcels at locations A and B.
4. Buy nothing.

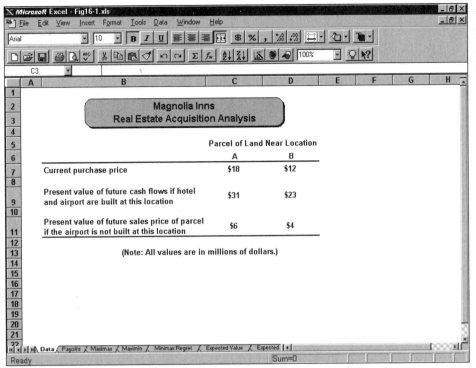

Figure 16.1
Data for the
Magnolia Inns
decision
problem.

Regardless of which parcel or parcels Magnolia Inns decides to purchase, two possible states of nature can occur:

16.4.2   States of Nature

1. The new airport is built at location A.
2. The new airport is built at location B.

Figure 16.2 shows the payoff matrix for this problem. The rows in this spreadsheet represent the possible decision alternatives, and the columns correspond to the states of nature that might occur. Each value in this table indicates the financial payoff (in millions of dollars) expected for each possible decision under each state of nature.

16.4.3   The Payoff Values

The value in cell B5 in Figure 16.2 indicates that if the company buys the parcel of land near location A, and the airport is built in this area, Magnolia Inns can expect to receive a payoff of $13 million. This figure of $13 million is computed from the data shown in Figure 16.1 as:

	Present value of future cash flows if hotel and airport are built at location A	$31,000,000
minus:	Current purchase price of hotel site at location A	−$18,000,000
		$13,000,000

Figure 16.2
Payoff matrix for
the Magnolia
Inns decision
problem.

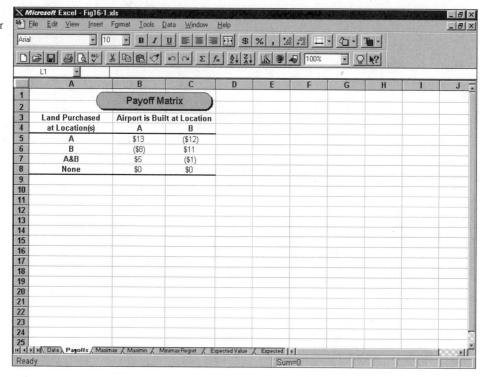

The value in cell C5 in Figure 16.2 indicates that if Magnolia Inns buys the parcel of land at location A (for $18 million), and the airport is built at location B, the company would later resell the parcel at location A for only $6 million, incurring a loss of $12 million.

The calculations of the payoffs for the parcel near location B are done using similar logic. The value in cell C6 in Figure 16.2 indicates that if the company buys the parcel of land near location B, and the airport is built in this area, Magnolia Inns can expect to receive a payoff of $11 million. The value in cell B6 in Figure 16.2 indicates that if Magnolia Inns buys the parcel of land at location B (for $12 million), and the airport is built at location A, the company would later resell the parcel at location B for only $4 million, incurring a loss of $8 million.

Let's now consider the payoffs if the parcels at both locations A and B are purchased. The value in cell B7 in Figure 16.2 indicates that a payoff of $5 million will result if both parcels are purchased and the airport is built at location A. This payoff value is computed as:

	Present value of future cash flows if hotel and airport are built at location A	$31,000,000
plus:	Present value of future sales price for the unused parcel at location B	+ $ 4,000,000
minus:	Current purchase price of hotel site at location A	– $18,000,000
minus:	Current purchase price of hotel site at location B	– $12,000,000
		$ 5,000,000

The value in cell C7 indicates that a loss of $1 million will occur if the parcels at both locations A and B are purchased, and the airport is built at location B.

The final alternative available to Magnolia Inns is to not buy either property at this point in time. This alternative guarantees that the company will neither gain nor lose anything, regardless of where the airport is located. Thus, cells B8 and C8 indicate that this alternative has a payoff of $0 regardless of what state of nature occurs.

16.5   DECISION RULES

Now that the payoffs for each alternative under each state of nature have been determined, if Barbara knew with certainty where the airport was going to be built, it would be a simple matter for her to select the most desirable alternative. For example, if she knew the airport was going to be built at location A, a maximum payoff of $13 million could be obtained by purchasing the parcel of land at that location. Similarly, if she knew the airport was going to be built at location B, Magnolia Inns could achieve the maximum payoff of $11 million by purchasing the parcel at that location. The problem is that Barbara does not know where the airport is going to be built.

Several decision rules can be used to help a decision maker choose the best alternative. No one of these decision rules works best in all situations and, as you will see, each has some weaknesses. However, these rules help to enhance our insight and sharpen our intuition about decision problems so that we can make more informed decisions.

16.6   NONPROBABILISTIC METHODS

The decision rules we'll discuss can be divided into two categories: those that assume that probabilities of occurrence can be assigned to the states of nature in a decision problem (**probabilistic methods**), and those that do not (**nonprobabilistic methods**). We'll discuss the nonprobabilistic methods first.

16.6.1   The Maximax Decision Rule

As shown in Figure 16.2, the largest possible payoff will occur if Magnolia Inns buys the parcel at location A and the airport is built at this location. Thus, if the company optimistically believes that nature will always be "on its side" regardless of what decision it makes, the company should buy the parcel at location A because it leads to the largest possible payoff. This type of reasoning is reflected in the **maximax decision rule,** which determines the maximum payoff for each alternative and then selects the alternative associated with the largest payoff. Figure 16.3 illustrates the results of the maximax decision rule on our example problem.

Although the alternative suggested by the maximax decision rule enables Magnolia Inns to realize the best possible payoff, it does not guarantee that this payoff will occur. The actual payoff depends on where the airport is ultimately located. If we follow the maximax decision rule and the airport is built at location A, the company would receive $13 million; but if the airport is built at location B, the company would lose $12 million.

Figure 16.3
The maximax
decision rule for
the Magnolia
Inns decision
problem.

	Key Cell Formulas	
Cell	Formula	Copied to
D5	=MAX(B5:C5)	D6:D8

In some situations, the maximax decision rule leads to poor decisions. For example, consider the following payoff matrix:

		State of Nature		
Decision	1	2	MAX	
A	30	−10000	30	← maximum
B	29	29	29	

In this problem, alternative A would be selected using the maximax decision rule. However, many decision makers would prefer alternative B because its guaranteed payoff is only slightly less than the maximum possible payoff, and it avoids the potential large loss involved with alternative A if the second state of nature occurs.

16.6.2   The Maximin Decision Rule

A more conservative approach to decision making is given by the **maximin decision rule,** which pessimistically assumes that nature will always be "against us" regardless of what decision we make. This decision rule can be used to hedge against the worst possible outcome of a decision. Figure 16.4 illustrates the effect of the maximin decision rule on our example problem.

To apply the maximin decision rule, we first determine the minimum possible payoff for each alternative and then select the alternative with the largest minimum payoff (or the maximum of the minimum payoffs—hence the term "maximin"). Column D in Figure 16.4 lists the minimum payoff for each alternative. The largest (maximum) value in column D is the payoff of $0 associated with not buying any land. Thus, the maximin decision rule suggests that Magnolia Inns should not buy either parcel because, in the worst case, the other alternatives result in losses whereas this alternative does not.

The maximin decision rule can also lead to poor decision making. For example, consider the following payoff matrix:

	State of Nature			
Decision	1	2	MIN	
A	1000	28	28	
B	29	29	29	← maximum

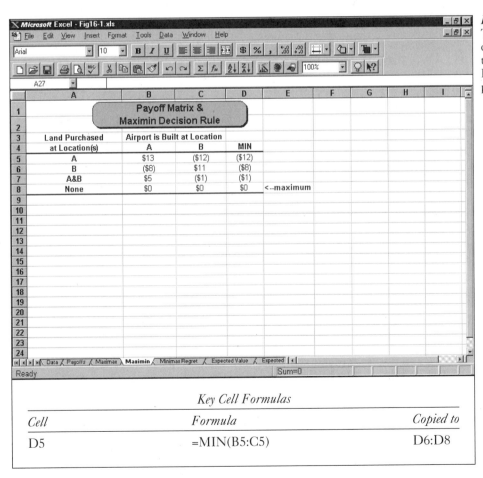

Figure 16.4
The maximin decision rule for the Magnolia Inns decision problem.

Key Cell Formulas		
Cell	*Formula*	*Copied to*
D5	=MIN(B5:C5)	D6:D8

In this problem, alternative B would be selected using the maximin decision rule. However, many decision makers would prefer alternative A because its worst-case payoff is only slightly less than that of alternative B, and it provides the potential for a much larger payoff if the first state of nature occurs.

16.6.3   The Minimax Regret Decision Rule

Another way of approaching decision problems involves the concept of **regret,** or opportunity loss. For example, suppose that Magnolia Inns decides to buy the parcel of land at location A as suggested by the maximax decision rule. If the airport is built at location A, the company will not regret this decision at all because it provides the largest possible payoff under the state of nature that occurred. However, what if the company buys the parcel at location A and the airport is built at location B? In this case, the company would experience a regret, or opportunity loss, of $23 million. If Magnolia Inns had bought the parcel at location B, it would have earned a payoff of $11 million, and the decision to buy the parcel at location A resulted in a loss of $12 million. Thus, there is a difference of $23 million in the payoffs between these two alternatives under this state of nature.

To use the minimax regret decision rule, we must first convert our payoff matrix into a regret matrix that summarizes the possible opportunity losses that could result from each decision alternative under each state of nature. Figure 16.5 shows the regret matrix for our example problem.

The entries in the regret matrix are generated from the payoff matrix as:

Formula for cell B5:   =MAX(Payoffs!B$5:B$8)–Payoffs!B5
(Copy to B5 through C8.)

Each entry in the regret matrix shows the difference between the maximum payoff that can occur under a given state of nature and the payoff that would be realized from each alternative under the same state of nature. For example, if Magnolia Inns buys the parcel of land at location A and the airport is built at this location, cell B5 indicates that the company experiences 0 regret. However, if the company buys the parcel at location B and the airport is built at location A, the company experiences an opportunity loss (or regret) of $21 million ($13 - (-8) = 21$).

Column D in Figure 16.5 summarizes the maximum regret that could be experienced with each decision alternative. The minimax regret decision corresponds to the alternative with the smallest (or minimum) maximum regret. As indicated in Figure 16.5, the minimax regret decision in our example problem is to buy the parcels at both sites. The maximum regret that could be experienced by implementing this decision is $12 million, whereas all other decisions could cause a larger regret.

The minimax regret decision rule can lead to peculiar decision making. For example, consider the following payoff matrix:

	State of Nature	
Decision	1	2
A	9	2
B	4	6

The regret matrix and minimax regret decision for this problem are represented by:

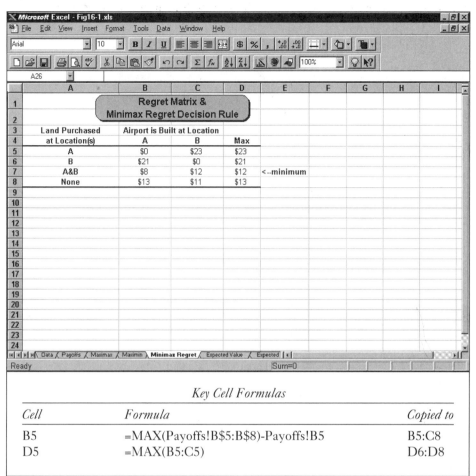

Figure 16.5
The minimax regret decision rule for the Magnolia Inns decision problem.

Key Cell Formulas

Cell	Formula	Copied to
B5	=MAX(Payoffs!B$5:B$8)-Payoffs!B5	B5:C8
D5	=MAX(B5:C5)	D6:D8

	State of Nature			
Decision	*1*	*2*	*MAX*	
A	0	4	4	← minimum
B	5	0	5	

Thus, if the alternatives are given by A and B, the minimax regret decision rule would select alternative A. Now, suppose that we add a new alternative to this decision problem to obtain the following payoff matrix:

	State of Nature	
Decision	*1*	*2*
A	9	2
B	4	6
C	3	9

Notice that the payoffs for alternatives A and B have not changed—we simply added a new alternative (C). The regret matrix and minimax regret decision for the revised problem are represented by:

	State of Nature			
Decision	1	2	MAX	
A	0	7	7	
B	5	3	5	← minimum
C	6	0	6	

The minimax regret decision is now given by alternative B. Some decision makers are troubled that the addition of a new alternative, which is not selected as the final decision, can change the relative preferences of the original alternatives. For example, suppose that a person prefers apples to oranges, but would prefer oranges if given the options of apples, oranges, and bananas. This person's reasoning is somewhat inconsistent or incoherent. But such reversals in preferences are a natural consequence of the minimax regret decision rule.

16.7   PROBABILISTIC METHODS

Probabilistic decision rules can be used if the states of nature in a decision problem can be assigned probabilities that represent their likelihood of occurrence. For decision problems that occur more than once, it is often possible to estimate these probabilities from historical data. However, many decision problems (such as the Magnolia Inns problem) represent one-time decisions where historical data for estimating probabilities are unlikely to exist. In these cases, probabilities are often assigned subjectively based on interviews with one or more domain experts. Highly structured interviewing techniques exist to solicit probability estimates that are reasonably accurate and free of the unconscious biases that may impact an expert's opinions. These interviewing techniques are described in several of the references at the end of this chapter. Here, we will focus on the techniques that can be used once appropriate probability estimates have been obtained either from historical data or expert interviews.

16.7.1   Expected Monetary Value

The **expected monetary value decision rule** selects the decision alternative with the largest expected monetary value (EMV). The EMV of alternative i in a decision problem is defined as:

$$EMV_i = \sum_j r_{ij}p_j$$

where

$$r_{ij} = \text{the payoff for alternative } i \text{ under the } j\text{th state of nature}$$

$$p_j = \text{the probability of the } j\text{th state of nature}$$

Figure 16.6 illustrates the EMV decision rule for our example problem. In this case, Magnolia Inns estimates a 40% chance that the airport will be built at location A and a 60% chance that it will be built at location B.

The probabilities for each state of nature are entered in cells B10 and C10, respectively. Using these probabilities, the EMV for each decision alternative is calculated in column D as:

Formula for cell D5:   =SUMPRODUCT(B5:C5,$B$10:$C$10)
(Copy to D6 through D8.)

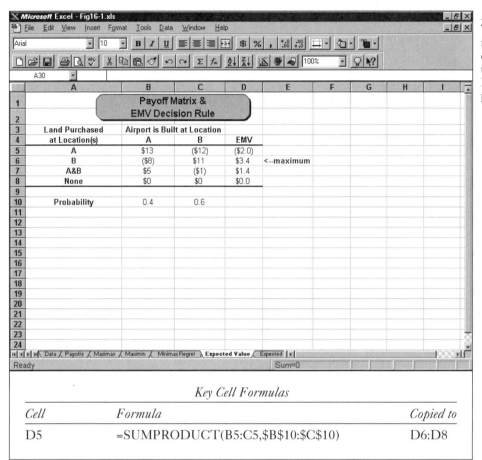

Figure 16.6
The expected monetary value decision rule for the Magnolia Inns decision problem.

Cell	Formula	Copied to
D5	=SUMPRODUCT(B5:C5,$B$10:$C$10)	D6:D8

The largest EMV is associated with the decision to purchase the parcel of land at location B. Thus, this is the decision suggested according to the EMV decision rule.

Let's consider the meaning of the figures in the EMV column in Figure 16.6. For example, the decision to purchase the parcel at location B has an EMV of $3.4 million. What does this figure represent? The payoff table indicates that Magnolia Inns will receive a payoff of $11 million if it buys this land and the airport is built there, or it will lose $8 million if it buys this land and the airport is built at the other location. So there does not appear to be any way for the company to receive a payoff of $3.4 million if it buys the land at location B. However, imagine that Magnolia Inns faces this same decision not just once, but over and over again (perhaps on a weekly basis). If the company always decides to purchase the land at location B, we would expect it to receive a payoff of $11 million 60% of the time, and incur a loss of $8 million 40% of the time. Over the long run, then, the decision to purchase land at location B results in an average payoff of $3.4 million.

The EMV for a given decision alternative indicates the average payoff we would receive if we encounter the identical decision problem repeatedly and always select this alternative. Selecting the alternative with the highest EMV makes sense in situations where the identical decision problem will be faced repeatedly and we can "play the averages." However, this decision rule can be very risky in decision problems encountered only once (such as our example problem). For example, consider the following problem:

Decision	State of Nature 1	State of Nature 2	EMV	
A	15,000	–5,000	5,000	← maximum
B	5,000	4,000	4,500	
Probability	0.5	0.5		

If we face a decision with these payoffs and probabilities repeatedly and always select decision A, the payoff over the long run would average to $5,000. Because this is larger than decision B's average long-run payoff of $4,500, it would be best to always select decision A. But what if we face this decision problem only once? If we select decision A, we are equally likely to receive $15,000 or lose $5,000. If we select decision B, we are equally likely to receive payoffs of $5,000 or $4,000. In this case, decision A is more risky. Yet this type of risk is ignored completely by the EMV decision rule. Later, we'll discuss a technique—known as the utility theory—that allows us to account for this type of risk in our decision making.

16.7.2   Expected Regret

We can also use the probability of the states of nature to compute the **expected regret,** or **expected opportunity loss** (EOL), for each alternative in a decision problem. Figure 16.7 illustrates this process for our example problem.

The calculations in Figure 16.7 are identical to those used in computing the EMVs, only here we substitute regret values (or opportunity losses) for the payoffs. As shown in Figure 16.7, the decision to purchase the parcel at location B results in the smallest EOL. It is not a coincidence that this same decision also resulted in the largest EMV in Figure 16.6. The decision with the smallest EOL will also have the largest EMV. Thus, the EMV and EOL decision rules always result in the selection of the same decision alternative.

Key Point

The expected monetary value (EMV) and expected opportunity loss (EOL) decision rules always result in the selection of the same decision alternative.

16.8   THE EXPECTED VALUE OF PERFECT INFORMATION

One of the primary difficulties in decision making is that we usually do not know which state of nature will occur. As we've seen, estimates of the probability of each state of nature can be used to calculate the EMV of various decision alternatives. However, probabilities do not tell us which state of nature will occur—they only indicate the likelihood of the various states of nature.

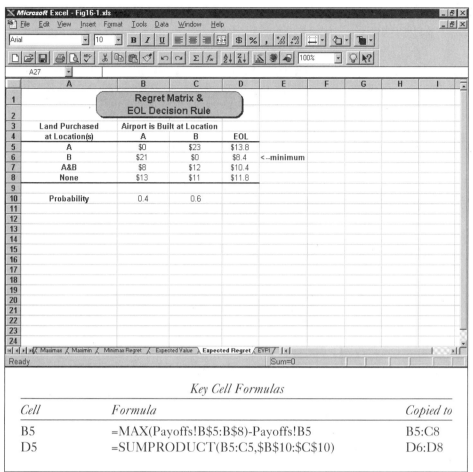

Figure 16.7
The expected
regret decision
rule for the
Magnolia Inns
decision
problem.

Cell	Formula	Copied to
B5	=MAX(Payoffs!B$5:B$8)-Payoffs!B5	B5:C8
D5	=SUMPRODUCT(B5:C5,$B$10:$C$10)	D6:D8

Key Cell Formulas

Suppose that we could hire a consultant who could tell us in advance and with 100% accuracy which state of nature will occur. If our example problem were a repeatable decision problem, 40% of the time the consultant would indicate that the airport will be built at location A, and the company would buy the parcel of land at location A and receive a payoff of $13 million. Similarly, 60% of the time the consultant would indicate that the airport will be built at location B, and the company would buy the parcel at location B and receive a payoff of $11 million. Thus, with advance perfect information about where the airport is going to be built, the average payoff would be:

Expected value *with* perfect information = $0.40 \times \$13 + 0.60 \times \$11 = \$11.8$ (in millions)

So how much should Magnolia Inns be willing to pay this consultant for such information? From Figure 16.6 we know that *without* the services of this consultant, the best decision identified results in an EMV of $3.4 million. Therefore, the information provided by the consultant would enable the company to make decisions that increase the EMV by $8.4 million ($11.8 – $3.4 = $8.4). Thus, the company should be willing to pay the consultant up to $8.4 million for providing perfect information.

The **expected value of perfect information** (EVPI) is the expected value obtained with perfect information minus the expected value obtained without perfect information (which is given by the maximum EMV); that is:

$$\text{Expected value } of \atop \text{perfect information} = \text{Expected value } with \atop \text{perfect information} - \text{maximum EMV}$$

Figure 16.8 summarizes the EVPI calculation for our example problem. Cell D6 in Figure 16.8 shows the calculation of the maximum EMV of $3.4 million, which was described earlier in our discussion of the EMV decision rule. The payoffs of the decisions made under each state of nature with perfect information are calculated in cells B12 and C12 as:

Formula for cell B12:   =MAX(B5:B8)
(Copy to C12.)

The expected value *with* perfect information is calculated in cell D12 as:

Formula for cell D12   =SUMPRODUCT(B12:C12,$B$10:$C$10)

Finally, the expected value *of* perfect information is computed in cell D14 as:

Formula for cell D14:   =D12-MAX(D5:D8)

Figure 16.8
The expected value of perfect information for the Magnolia Inns decision problem.

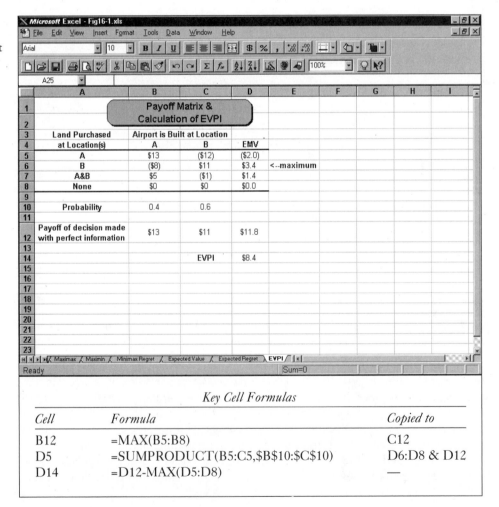

Key Cell Formulas		
Cell	*Formula*	*Copied to*
B12	=MAX(B5:B8)	C12
D5	=SUMPRODUCT(B5:C5,$B$10:$C$10)	D6:D8 & D12
D14	=D12-MAX(D5:D8)	—

Notice that the $8.4 million EVPI figure in cell D14 is identical to the minimum EOL shown earlier in Figure 16.7. This is *not* just a coincidence. The minimum EOL in a decision problem will always equal the EVPI.

Key Point

The expected value of perfect information (EVPI) is equivalent to the minimum expected opportunity loss (EOL).

16.9 DECISION TREES

Although some decision problems can be represented and analyzed effectively using payoff tables, we can also represent decision problems in a graphical form known as a **decision tree**. Figure 16.9 shows the decision problem for Magnolia Inns represented in this format.

As shown in Figure 16.9, a decision tree is composed of a collection of nodes (represented by circles and squares) interconnected by branches (represented by lines). A square node is called a **decision node** because it represents a decision. Branches emanating from a decision node represent the different alternatives for a particular decision. In Figure 16.9, a single decision node (node 0) represents the decision Magnolia Inns faces about where to buy land. The four branches coming out of this decision node represent the four alternatives under consideration. The cash flow associated

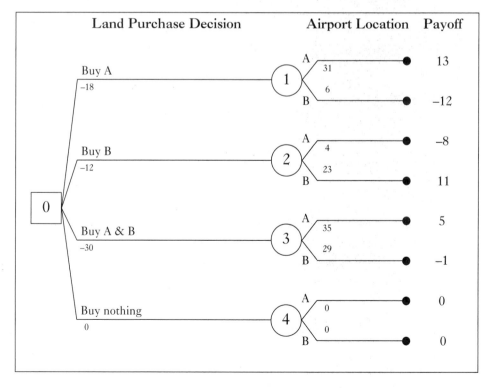

Land Purchase Decision	Airport Location	Payoff

Figure 16.9
The decision tree representation of the Magnolia Inns problem.

with each alternative is also listed. For example, the value –18 below the alternative labeled "Buy A" indicates that if the company purchases the parcel at location A, it must pay $18 million.

The circular nodes in a decision tree are called **event nodes** because they represent uncertain events. The branches emanating from event nodes (called **event branches**) correspond to the possible states of nature or the possible outcomes of an uncertain event. Figure 16.9 shows that each decision alternative emanating from node 0 is followed by an uncertain event represented by the event nodes 1, 2, 3, and 4. The branches from each event node represent possible locations of the new airport. In each case, the airport can be built at location A or B. The value next to each branch from the event nodes indicates the cash flow that will occur for that decision/event combination. For example, at node 1 the value 31 next to the first event branch indicates that if the company buys the parcel at location A and the airport is built at this location, a cash flow of $31 million will occur.

The various branches in a decision tree end at the small black dots called **leaves.** Because each leaf corresponds to one way in which the decision problem can terminate, leaves are also referred to as **terminal nodes.** Each leaf in Figure 16.9 corresponds to an entry in the payoff table in Figure 16.2. The payoff occurring at each leaf is computed by summing the cash flows along the set of branches leading to each leaf. For example, following the uppermost branches through the tree, a payoff of $13 million results if the decision to buy the parcel at location A is followed by the new airport being built at this location (–18 + 31 = 13). You should verify the cash-flow values on each branch and at each leaf before continuing.

16.9.1   Rolling Back a Decision Tree

After computing the payoffs at each leaf, we can apply any of the decision rules described earlier. For example, we could identify the maximum possible payoff for each decision and apply the maximax decision rule. However, decision trees are used most often to implement the EMV decision rule—that is, to identify the decision with the largest EMV.

We can apply a process known as **rolling back** to a decision tree to determine the decision with the largest EMV. Figure 16.10 illustrates this process for our example problem.

Because the EMV decision rule is a probabilistic method, Figure 16.10 indicates the probabilities associated with each event branch emanating from each event node (that is, a 0.4 probability exists of the new airport being built at location A, and a 0.6 probability exists of it being built at location B). To roll back this decision tree, we start with the payoffs and work our way from right to left, back through the decision tree, computing the expected values for each node. For example, the event represented by node 1 has a 0.4 probability of resulting in a payoff of $13 million, and a 0.6 probability of resulting in a loss of $12 million. Thus, the EMV at node 1 is calculated as:

$$\text{EMV at node 1} = 0.4 \times 13 + 0.6 \times -12 = -2.0$$

The expected value calculations for the remaining event nodes in Figure 16.10 are summarized as:

$$\text{EMV at node 2} = 0.4 \times -8 + 0.6 \times 11 = 3.4$$
$$\text{EMV at node 3} = 0.4 \times 5 + 0.6 \times -1 = 1.4$$
$$\text{EMV at node 4} = 0.4 \times 0 + 0.6 \times 0 = 0.0$$

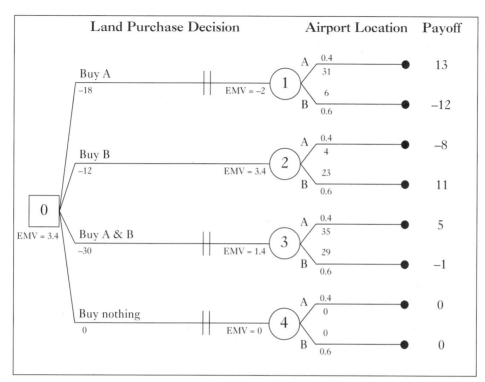

Figure 16.10
Rolling back the
decision tree for
the Magnolia
Inns decision
problem.

The EMV for a decision node is computed in a different way. For example, at node 0 we face a decision among four alternatives that lead to events with expected values of –2, 3.4, 1.4, and 0, respectively. At a decision node we always select the alternative that leads to the best EMV. Thus, the EMV at node 0 is 3.4, which corresponds to the EMV resulting from the decision to buy land at location B. The optimal alternative at a decision node is sometimes indicated by "pruning" the suboptimal branches. The pruned branches in Figure 16.10 are indicated by the double vertical lines (‖) shown on the suboptimal alternatives emanating from node 0.

The relationship between the decision tree in Figure 16.10 and the payoff table in Figure 16.2 should now be clear. However, you might wonder if it is necessary to include event node 4 in the tree shown in Figure 16.10. If Magnolia Inns decides not to buy either property, the payoff it receives does not depend on where the airport is ultimately built—regardless of where the airport is built, the company will receive a payoff of 0.

Figure 16.11 shows an alternate, and perhaps more efficient, way of representing this problem as a decision tree where it is clear that the decision not to purchase either parcel leads to a definite payoff of 0.

16.10   USING TREEPLAN

A spreadsheet add-in called **TreePlan** can help us create and analyze decision trees in Excel. We will use TreePlan to implement the decision tree shown in Figure 16.11 in Excel.

Figure 16.11
Alternate
decision tree
representation of
the Magnolia
Inns decision
problem.

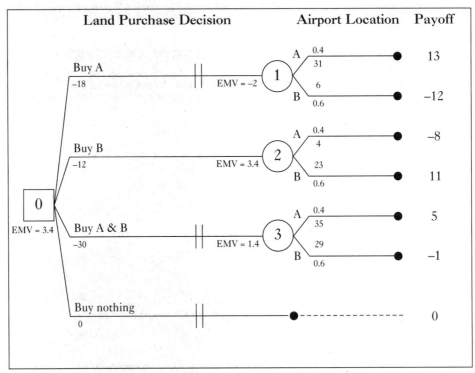

To attach the TreePlan add-in, choose the Open command from the File menu and open the file named TREEPLAN.xla provided on your data disk. To create a decision tree using TreePlan, open a new workbook, then invoke TreePlan by choosing the TreePlan command from the Tools menu (or by pressing [Ctrl][t]). In response, TreePlan displays the dialog box shown in Figure 16.12.

If you click the New Tree button, TreePlan creates a tree diagram with one initial decision node and two decision branches. As shown in Figure 16.13, this initial tree diagram is inserted in the spreadsheet near the cell that is active when TreePlan is invoked. Also note that TreePlan uses the triangular symbols shown in cells F3 and F8 to denote the leaves (or terminal nodes) in a decision problem.

TreePlan automatically labels the branches in the tree as Decision 1 and Decision 2. Later, we'll change these labels to describe more accurately the decisions in our example problem. First, we'll add two more decision branches to the initial tree shown in Figure 16.13.

16.10.1   Adding Branches

To add a new decision branch to our tree:

1. Click the decision node (cell B5).
2. Press [Ctrl][t] to invoke TreePlan.

The dialog box shown in Figure 16.14 appears. Because we selected a decision node before invoking TreePlan, this dialog box displays the options for working on a selected decision node. Different dialog boxes appear if we select an event node or terminal node and then invoke TreePlan. It is important to understand that TreePlan

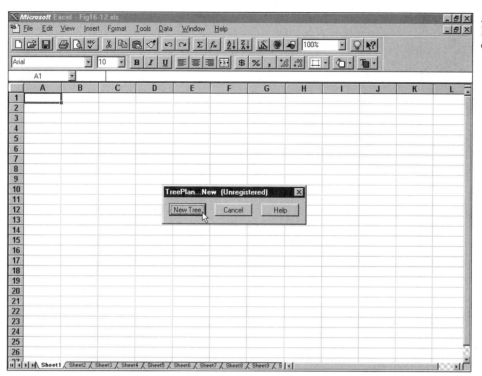

Figure 16.12
Initial TreePlan
dialog box.

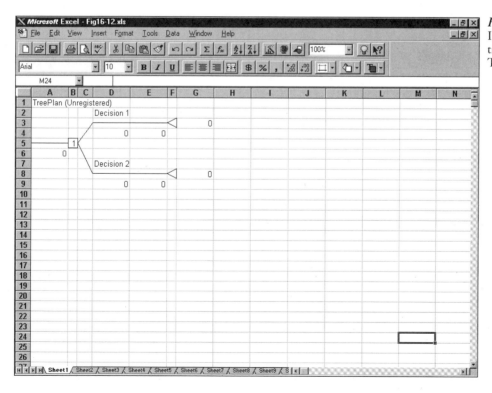

Figure 16.13
Initial decision
tree created by
TreePlan.

is context-sensitive—that is, the dialog box that appears when you invoke TreePlan depends on what cell is selected when TreePlan is invoked.

To add a branch to the currently selected decision node, click the Add branch option, then click OK. A third branch is added to the tree, as shown in Figure 16.15.

To add the fourth decision branch to the tree, we can follow the same procedure:

1. Click the decision node (cell B8).
2. Press [Ctrl][t] to invoke TreePlan.
3. Click Add branch.
4. Click OK.

The four decision branches for this problem appear as shown in Figure 16.16. Notice that we changed the label on each branch to reflect the decision alternatives for Magnolia Inns.

16.10.2   Adding Event Nodes

Each of the first three decision branches in Figure 16.11 leads to an event node with two event branches. Thus, we need to add similar event nodes to the decision tree shown in Figure 16.16. To add an event node:

1. Select the terminal node for the branch labeled Buy A (cell F3).
2. Press [Ctrl][t] to invoke TreePlan.

Because we selected a terminal node before invoking TreePlan, the TreePlan Terminal dialog box appears as shown in Figure 16.17.

Figure 16.14
TreePlan
Decision dialog
box.

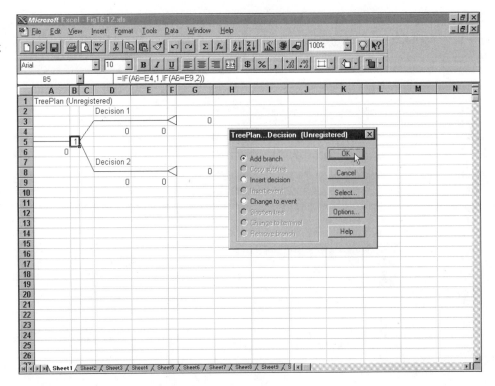

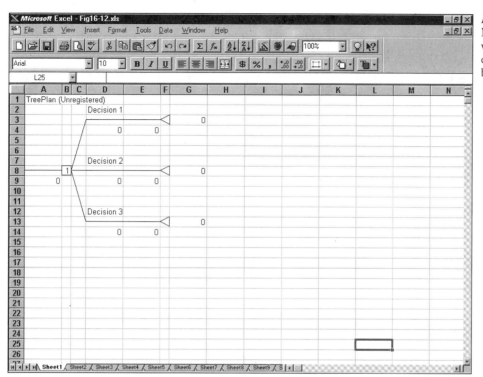

Figure 16.15
Modified tree
with three
decision
branches.

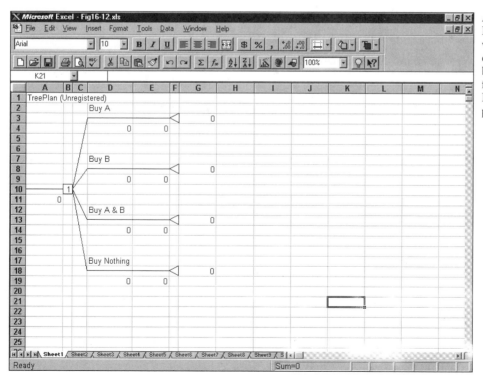

Figure 16.16
Modified tree
with four
decision
branches labeled
for the Magnolia
Inns decision
problem.

This dialog box displays the options for working on a terminal node. In this case, we want to change the selected terminal node into an event node with two branches, as shown in Figure 16.17. The resulting spreadsheet is shown in Figure 16.18.

Figure 16.17
TreePlan
Terminal dialog
box.

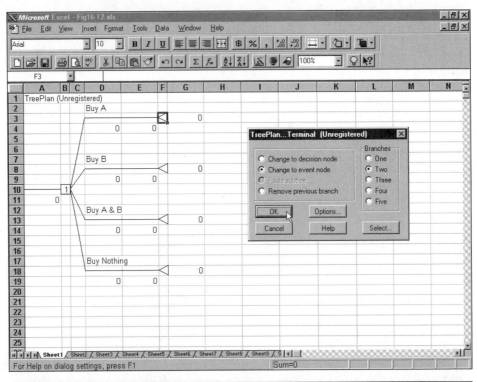

Figure 16.18
Modified tree
with an event
node.

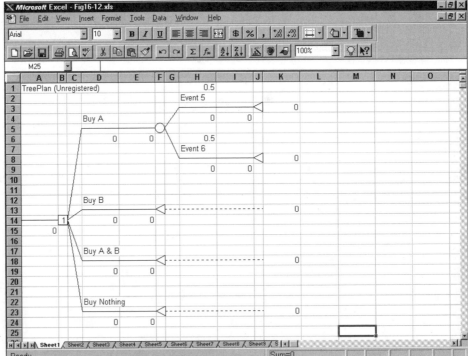

In Figure 16.18, an event node with two event branches now follows the decision to purchase the parcel at location A. TreePlan automatically labels these branches as Event 5 and Event 6, but we can change the labels to whatever we want. The cells immediately above each event branch label (cells H1 and H6) are reserved to represent the probability of each event. By default, TreePlan assumes that the events have equal probability (0.5), but we can change these values to whatever is appropriate for our particular problem.

In Figure 16.19, we changed the labels and probabilities of the event branches to correspond to the events occurring in the Magnolia Inns problem. The procedure used to create the event node for the Buy A decision could be repeated to create event nodes for the decisions corresponding to Buy B and Buy A & B. However, because all of the event nodes are identical in this problem, we can simply copy the existing event node.

You might be tempted to copy and paste the existing event node using the standard Excel commands—but if you use the standard Excel commands, TreePlan cannot update the tree settings properly. As indicated in Figure 16.19, TreePlan provides a built-in option that allows you to copy a section, or **subtree,** of a decision tree to another part of the tree. It is important to copy subtrees using this command so that TreePlan can update the appropriate formulas in the spreadsheet. To create a copy of the event node:

1. Select the event node you want to copy (cell F5).
2. Press [Ctrl][t] to invoke TreePlan.
3. Click Copy subtree.
4. Click OK.

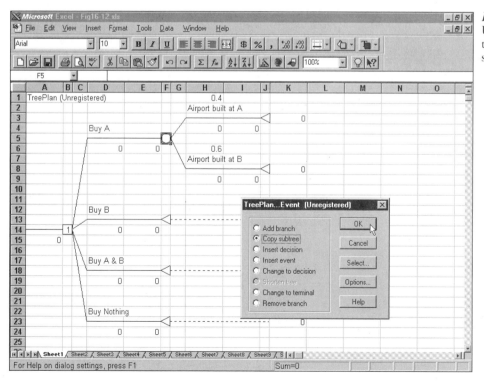

Figure 16.19
Using TreePlan to copy a subtree.

This creates a copy of the selected event node on the clipboard. As shown in Figure 16.20, to paste a copy of this subtree into the decision tree:

1.   Select the target cell location (cell F13).
2.   Press [Ctrl][t] to invoke TreePlan.
3.   Click Paste subtree.
4.   Click OK.

We can repeat this copy-and-paste procedure to create the third event node needed for the decision to buy the parcels at both locations A and B. Figure 16.21 shows the resulting spreadsheet.

16.10.3   Adding the Cash Flows

To complete the decision tree, we need to add the cash flows that are associated with each decision and event. TreePlan reserves the first cell below each branch to represent the partial cash flow associated with that branch. For example, in Figure 16.22 (and in the file FIG16-22.xls on your data disk) cell D6 represents the partial cash flow that occurs if Magnolia Inns buys the parcel at location A, and cell H4 represents the partial cash flow that occurs if the company buys the parcel at location A and the airport is built at that location. The remaining partial cash flows for each decision are entered in the appropriate cells in Figure 16.22 in a similar manner.

16.10.4   Determining the Payoffs and EMVs

Next to each terminal node, TreePlan automatically created a formula that sums the payoffs along the branches leading to that node. For example, cell K3 in Figure 16.22

Figure 16.20
Using TreePlan to paste the copied subtree.

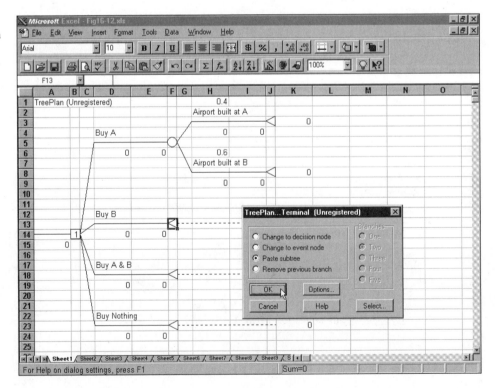

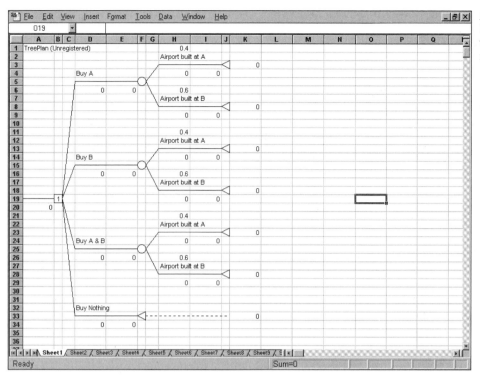

Figure 16.21
Decision tree with three event nodes.

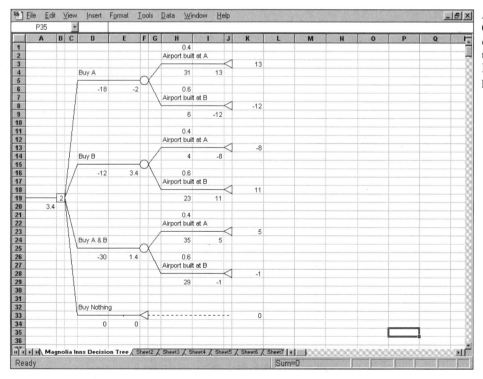

Figure 16.22
Completed decision tree for the Magnolia Inns decision problem.

contains the formula =SUM(H4,D6). Thus, when we enter or change the partial cash flows for the branches in the decision tree, the payoffs are updated automatically.

Immediately below and to the left of each node, TreePlan created formulas that compute the EMV at each node in the same way as described earlier in our discussion of rolling back a decision tree. Thus, cell A20 in Figure 16.22 indicates that the largest EMV at the decision node is $3.4 million. The value 2 in the decision node (cell B19) indicates that this maximum EMV is obtained by selecting the second decision alternative (that is, by purchasing the parcel at location B).

16.10.5   Other Features

The preceding discussion of TreePlan was intended to give you an overview of how TreePlan operates, its capabilities, and some of its options. Most of the other TreePlan options are self-explanatory, and you can obtain descriptions of them by clicking the Help button available in all the TreePlan dialog boxes. The Select and Options buttons available in all the TreePlan dialog boxes presented earlier lead, respectively, to the two dialog boxes shown in Figure 16.23.

At times we might want to select all the instances of a certain type of element in a decision tree. For example, we might want to select all the partial cash flows and display them in a currency format, or we might want to hide all the EMV values. The TreePlan Select dialog box shown in Figure 16.23 is designed to simplify this process. By selecting an option in this dialog box, all the elements of the type chosen will be selected automatically in the spreadsheet, enabling us to format them all at the same time.

The TreePlan Options dialog box serves two purposes. By default, TreePlan assumes that we want to analyze the decision tree using expected values. However, another technique (described later) uses exponential utility functions in place of expected values. Thus, this dialog box provides options for selecting whether TreePlan should use expected values or exponential utility functions. Also by default, TreePlan assumes that the EMVs it calculates represent profit values and that we want to identify the decision with the largest EMV. However, in some decision trees the expected values could represent costs that we want to minimize. Thus, this dialog box provides options for maximizing profits or minimizing costs.

Figure 16.23
TreePlan Select
and TreePlan
Options dialog
boxes.

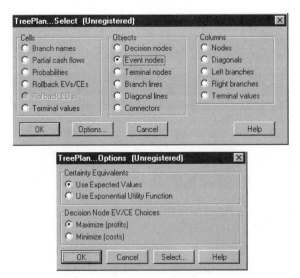

16.11   MULTISTAGE DECISION PROBLEMS

To this point, our discussion of decision analysis has considered only **single-stage** decision problems—that is, problems in which a single decision must be made. However, most decisions that we face lead to other decisions. As a simple example, consider the decision of whether or not to go out to dinner. If you decide to go out to dinner, you must then decide how much to spend, where to go, and how to get there. Thus, before you actually decide to go out to dinner, you'll probably consider the other issues and decisions that must be made if you choose that alternative. These types of problems are called **multistage** decision problems. The following example illustrates how a multistage decision problem can be modeled and analyzed using a decision tree.

The Occupational Safety and Health Administration (OSHA) has recently announced it will award an $85,000 research grant to the person or company submitting the best proposal for using wireless communications technology to enhance safety in the coal-mining industry. Steve Hinton, the owner of COM-TECH, a small communications research firm located just outside of Raleigh, North Carolina, is considering whether or not to apply for this grant. Steve estimates he would spend approximately $5,000 preparing his grant proposal and that he has about a 50-50 chance of actually receiving the grant. If he is awarded the grant, he would then need to decide whether to use microwave, cellular, or infrared communications technology. He has some experience in all three areas but would need to acquire some new equipment depending on which technology is used. The cost of the equipment needed for each technology is summarized as:

Technology	Equipment Cost
Microwave	$4,000
Cellular	$5,000
Infrared	$4,000

In addition to the equipment costs, Steve knows he will spend money in research and development (R&D) to carry out the research proposal, but he doesn't know exactly what the R&D costs will be. For simplicity, Steve estimates the following best-case and worst-case R&D costs associated with using each technology, and he assigns probabilities (shown on the next page) to each outcome based on his degree of expertise in each area.

	Possible R&D Costs			
	Best Case		Worst Case	
	Cost	Prob.	Cost	Prob.
Microwave	$30,000	0.4	$60,000	0.6
Cellular	$40,000	0.8	$70,000	0.2
Infrared	$40,000	0.9	$80,000	0.1

Steve needs to synthesize all the factors in this problem to decide whether or not to submit a grant proposal to OSHA.

16.11.1   A MultiStage Decision Tree

The immediate decision in this example problem is whether or not to submit a grant proposal. To make this decision, Steve must also consider the technology selection decision that he will face if he receives the grant. So this is a multistage decision problem. Figure 16.24 (and the file FIG16.24.xls on your data disk) shows the decision tree representation of this problem where, for clarity, we have temporarily hidden the rollback EMVs at each event and decision node in the tree.

This decision tree clearly shows that the first decision Steve faces is whether or not to submit a proposal, and that submitting the proposal will cost $5,000. If a proposal is submitted, we then encounter an event node showing a 0.5 probability of

Figure 16.24
Multistage decision tree for COM-TECH's grant proposal problem.

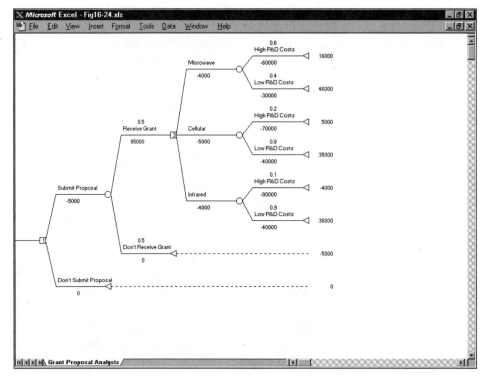

receiving the grant (and a payoff of $85,000), and a 0.5 probability of not receiving the grant (leading to a net loss of $5,000). If the grant is received, we then encounter a decision about which technology to pursue. Each of the three technology options has an event node representing the best-case (lowest) and worst-case (highest) R&D costs that might be incurred. The final (terminal) payoffs associated with each set of decisions and outcomes are listed next to each terminal node. For example, if Steve submits a proposal, receives the grant, employs cellular technology, and encounters low R&D costs, he will receive a net payoff of $35,000.

In Figure 16.24, note that the probabilities on the branches at any event node must always sum to 1 because these branches represent all the events that could occur. The R&D costs that would actually occur using a given technology could assume an infinite number of values. Some might argue that these costs could be modeled more accurately by some continuous random variable. However, our aim is to estimate the expected value of this random variable. Most decision makers probably would find it easier to assign subjective probabilities to a small, discrete set of representative outcomes for a variable such as R&D costs rather than try to identify an appropriate probability distribution for this variable.

Figure 16.25 (and the file FIG16-25.xls on your data disk) shows the completed decision tree for our example problem, including the EMV at each node. According to this decision tree, Steve should submit a proposal because the expected value of this decision is $13,500 and the expected value of not submitting a proposal is $0. The decision tree also indicates that if Steve receives the grant, he should pursue the infrared communications technology because the expected value of this decision ($32,000) is larger than the expected values for the other technologies.

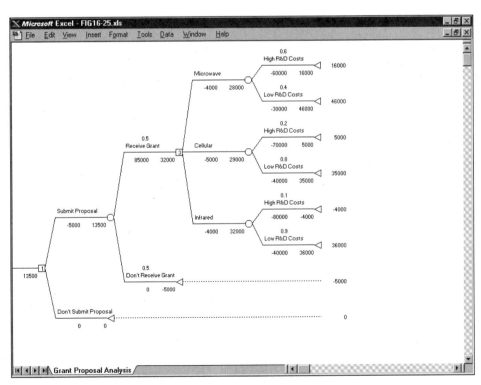

Figure 16.25
Multistage decision tree with EMVs for COM-TECH's grant proposal problem.

16.12   ANALYZING RISK IN A DECISION TREE

Before implementing the decision to submit a grant proposal as suggested by the previous analysis, Steve would be wise to consider how sensitive the recommended decision is to changes in values in the decision tree. For example, Steve estimated that a 50-50 chance exists that he will receive the grant if he submits a proposal. But what if that probability assessment is wrong? What if only a 30%, 20%, or 10% chance exists of receiving the grant? Should he still submit the proposal?

Using a decision tree implemented in a spreadsheet, it is fairly easy to determine how much any of the values in the decision tree can change before the indicated decision would change. For example, Figure 16.26 shows how we can use Solver to determine how small the probability of receiving the grant would need to be before it would no longer be wise to submit the grant proposal (according to the EMV decision rule).

In this spreadsheet we are using cell H14 (the probability of receiving the grant) as both our target cell and our changing cell. In cell H32 we entered the following formula to compute the probability of not receiving the grant:

Formula for cell H32:   =1-H14

Minimizing the value in cell H14 while constraining the value of B32 to equal 1 determines the probability of receiving the grant where the EMV of submitting the grant is zero. This gives the decision maker some idea of how sensitive the decision is to changes in the value of cell H14.

If the EMV of submitting the grant is zero, most decision makers would probably not want to submit the grant proposal. Indeed, even with an EMV of $13,500 (as

Figure 16.26
Using Solver to determine the sensitivity of a decision to changes in probabilities.

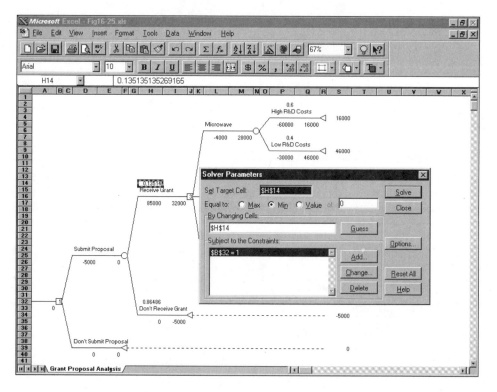

shown in Figure 16.25) some decision makers would still not want to submit the grant proposal because there is still a risk that the proposal would be turned down and a $5,000 loss incurred. As mentioned earlier, the EMV decision rule is most appropriately applied when we face a decision that will be made repeatedly and the results of bad outcomes can be balanced or averaged out with good outcomes. When using decision trees to analyze one-time decision problems, it is particularly helpful to develop a risk profile to make the sure the decision maker understands all the possible outcomes that might occur. A *risk profile* is simply a graph or tree that shows the chances associated with possible outcomes. Figure 6.27 shows the risk profile associated with not submitting the proposal and that of the optimal EMV decision-making strategy (submitting the proposal and using infrared technology) identified from Figure 16.25.

From Figure 16.27 it is clear that if the proposal is not submitted, the payoff will be $0. If the proposal is submitted, there is a 0.50 chance of not receiving the grant and incurring a loss of $5,000. If the proposal is submitted, there is a 0.05 chance (0.5 × 0.1=0.05) of receiving the grant but incurring high R&D costs and suffering a $4,000 loss. Finally, if the proposal is submitted, there is a 0.45 chance (0.5 × 0.9=0.45) of receiving the grant, enjoying small R&D costs and making a $36,000 profit.

A risk profile is an effective tool for breaking an EMV into its component parts and communicating information about the actual outcomes that can occur as the result of various decisions. By looking at Figure 16.27, a decision maker could reasonably decide that the risks (or chances) of losing money if a proposal is submitted are not worth the potential benefit to be gained if the proposal is accepted and low R&D costs occur. These risks would not be apparent if the decision maker was provided only with information about the EMV of each decision.

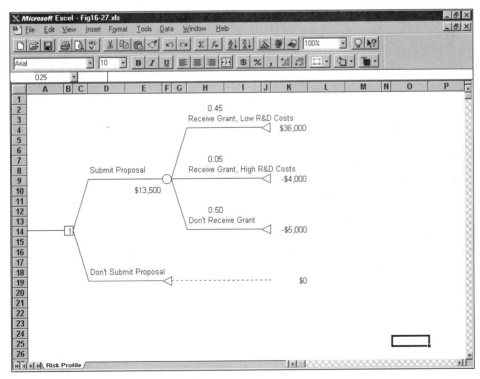

Figure 16.27
A risk profile for the alternatives of submitting or not submitting the proposal.

16.13   USING SAMPLE INFORMATION IN DECISION MAKING

In many decision problems, we have the opportunity to obtain additional information about the decision before we actually make the decision. For example, in the Magnolia Inns decision problem, the company could have hired a consultant to study the economic, environmental, and political issues surrounding the site selection process and predict which site will be selected for the new airport by the planning council. This information might help Magnolia Inns make a better (or more informed) decision. The potential for using this type of additional sample information in decision making raises a number of interesting issues that are illustrated using the following example.

> Colonial Motors (CM) is trying to determine what size of manufacturing plant to build for a new car it is developing. Only two plant sizes are under consideration: large and small. The cost of constructing a large plant is $25 million and the cost of constructing a small plant is $15 million. CM believes a 70% chance exists that the demand for this new car will be high and a 30% chance that it will be low. The following table summarizes the payoffs (in millions of dollars) the company expects to receive for each factory size and demand combination (not counting the cost of the factory).
>
> | | Demand | |
> | Factory Size | High | Low |
> | --- | --- | --- |
> | Large | $175 | $95 |
> | Small | $125 | $105 |

A decision tree for this problem is shown in Figure 16.28 (and in the file FIG16-28.xls on your data disk). The decision tree indicates that the optimal decision is to build the large plant and that this alternative has an EMV of $126 million.

Now suppose that before making the plant size decision, CM conducts a survey to assess consumer attitudes about the new car. For simplicity, we'll assume that the results of this survey indicate either a favorable or unfavorable attitude about the new car. A revised decision tree for this problem is shown in Figure 16.29 (and in the file FIG16-29.xls on your data disk).

The decision tree in Figure 16.29 begins with a decision node with a single branch representing the decision to conduct the market survey. For now, assume that this survey can be done at no cost. An event node follows, corresponding to the outcome of the market survey, which can indicate either favorable or unfavorable attitudes about the new car. We assume that CM believes that the probability of a favorable response is 0.67 and the probability of an unfavorable response is 0.33.

16.13.1   Conditional Probabilities

Once the survey results are known, the decision nodes in the tree indicate that a decision must be made about whether to build a large plant or a small plant. Following each decision branch, event nodes occur with branches representing the market demands for the car that could occur. Four event nodes represent the market demand

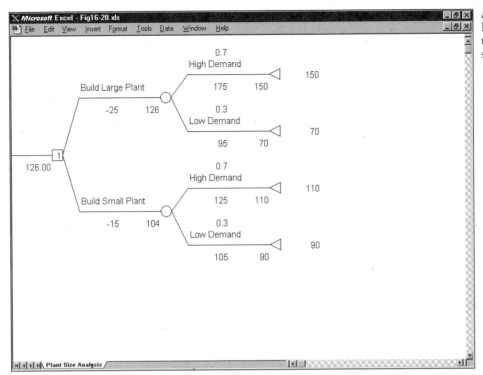

Figure 16.28
Decision tree for the CM plant size problem.

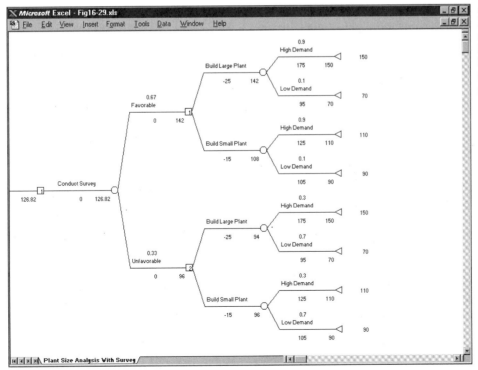

Figure 16.29
Decision tree if consumer survey is conducted before CM makes a plant size decision.

that might occur for this car. However, the probabilities we assign to the branches of these nodes are likely to differ depending on the results of the market survey.

Earlier we indicated that CM believed a 0.70 probability exists that demand for the new car will be high, expressed mathematically as:

$$P(\text{high demand}) = 0.7$$

In this formula $P(A) = X$ is read, "the probability of A is X." If the market survey indicates that consumers have a favorable impression of the new car, this will raise expectations that demand will be high for the car. Thus, given a favorable survey response, we might increase the probability assessment for a high market demand to 0.90. This is expressed mathematically as the following *conditional* probability:

$$P(\text{high demand} \mid \text{favorable response}) = 0.90$$

In this formula $P(A \mid B) = X$ is read, "the probability of A given B is X."

As noted earlier, the probabilities on the branches at any event node must always sum to 1. If the favorable survey response increases the probability assessment of a high demand occurring, it must decrease the probability assessment of a low demand given this survey result. Thus, the probability of a low demand given a favorable response on the survey is:

$$
\begin{aligned}
P(\text{low demand} \mid \text{favorable response}) &= 1 - P(\text{high demand} \mid \text{favorable response}) \\
&= 1 - 0.90 = 0.10
\end{aligned}
$$

These conditional probabilities are shown in Figure 16.29 on the first four event branches representing high and low demands given a favorable survey response.

If the market survey indicates consumers have an unfavorable response to the new car, this will lower expectations for high market demand. Thus, given an unfavorable survey response, we might reduce the probability assessment of a high market demand to 0.30:

$$P(\text{high demand} \mid \text{unfavorable response}) = 0.30$$

We must also revise the probability assessment for a low market demand given an unfavorable market response as:

$$
\begin{aligned}
P(\text{low demand} \mid \text{unfavorable response}) &= 1 - P(\text{high demand} \mid \text{unfavorable response}) \\
&= 1 - 0.3 = 0.70
\end{aligned}
$$

These conditional probabilities are shown on the last four demand branches in Figure 16.29. Later, we'll discuss a more objective method for determining these types of conditional probabilities.

16.13.2   The Expected Value of Sample Information

The additional information made available by the market survey allows us to make more precise estimates of the probabilities associated with the uncertain market demand. This, in turn, allows us to make more precise decisions. For example, Figure 16.29 indicates that if the survey results are favorable, CM should build a large plant; and if the survey results are unfavorable, it should build a small plant. The expected value of this decision-making strategy is $126.82 million, assuming that the survey can be done at no cost—which is unlikely. So, how much should CM be willing to pay to perform this survey? The answer to this question is provided by the expected value of sample information (EVSI), which is defined as:

$$\text{EVSI} = \begin{pmatrix} \text{Expected value of the best} \\ \text{decision with sample infor-} \\ \text{mation (obtained at no cost)} \end{pmatrix} - \begin{pmatrix} \text{Expected value of the best} \\ \text{decision without sample} \\ \text{information} \end{pmatrix}$$

The EVSI represents the *maximum* amount we should be willing to pay to obtain sample information. From Figure 16.29, we know that the expected value of the best decision *with* sample information for our example problem is $126.82 million. From Figure 16.28, we know that the expected value of the best decision *without* sample information is $126 million. So for our example problem, the EVSI is determined as:

$$\text{EVSI} = \$126.82 \text{ million} - \$126 \text{ million} = \$0.82 \text{ million}$$

Thus, CM should be willing to spend up to $820,000 to perform the market survey.

16.14   COMPUTING CONDITIONAL PROBABILITIES

In our example problem, we assumed that the values of the conditional probabilities were assigned subjectively by the decision makers at CM. However, a company often has data available from which it can compute these probabilities. We'll illustrate this process for the CM example. To simplify our notation, we'll use the following abbreviations:

H = high demand

L = low demand

F = favorable response

U = unfavorable response

To complete the decision tree in Figure 16.29, we determined values for the following six probabilities:

- $P(F)$
- $P(U)$
- $P(H\,|\,F)$
- $P(L\,|\,F)$
- $P(H\,|\,U)$
- $P(L\,|\,U)$

Assuming that CM has been in the auto business for some time, it undoubtedly has performed other market surveys prior to introducing other new models. Some of these models probably achieved high consumer demand, whereas others achieved only low demand. Thus, CM can use historical data to construct the joint probability table shown at the top of Figure 16.30 (and in the file FIG16-30.xls on your data disk).

The value in cell B4 indicates that of all the new car models CM developed and performed market surveys on, 60% received a favorable survey response and subsequently enjoyed high demand. This is expressed mathematically as:

$$P(F \cap H) = 0.60$$

In this formula $P(A \cap B) = X$ is read, "the probability of A *and* B is X." Similarly, in the joint probability table we see that:

$$P(F \cap L) = 0.067$$

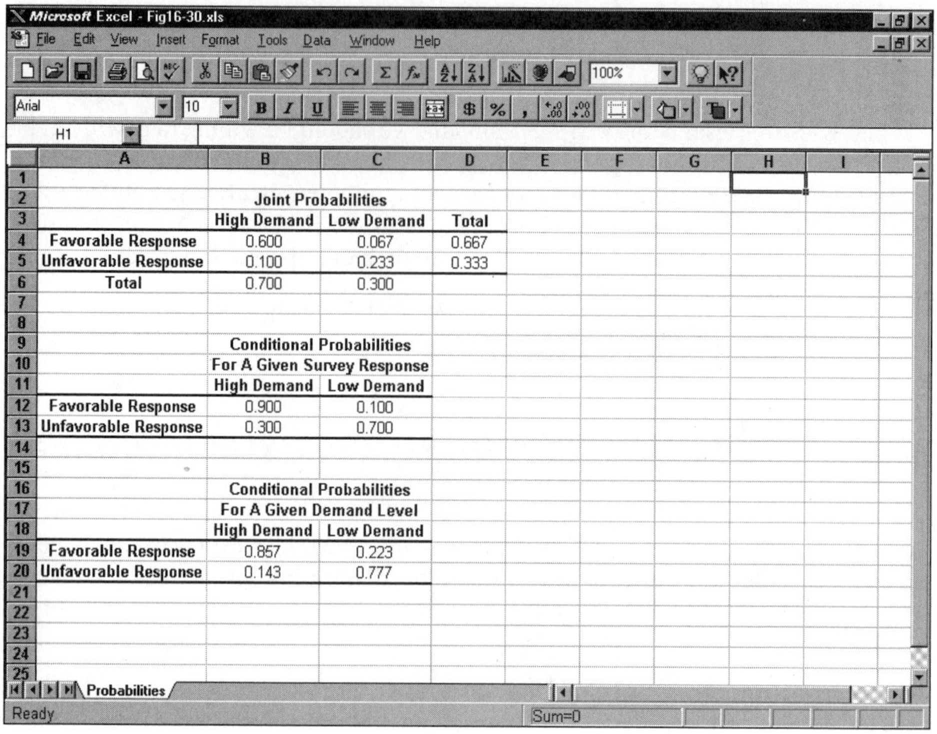

Figure 16.30
The calculation
of conditional
probabilities for
the CM decision
problem.

	A	B	C	D	E	F	G	H	I
1									
2		**Joint Probabilities**							
3		**High Demand**	**Low Demand**	**Total**					
4	**Favorable Response**	0.600	0.067	0.667					
5	**Unfavorable Response**	0.100	0.233	0.333					
6	**Total**	0.700	0.300						
7									
8									
9		**Conditional Probabilities**							
10		**For A Given Survey Response**							
11		**High Demand**	**Low Demand**						
12	**Favorable Response**	0.900	0.100						
13	**Unfavorable Response**	0.300	0.700						
14									
15									
16		**Conditional Probabilities**							
17		**For A Given Demand Level**							
18		**High Demand**	**Low Demand**						
19	**Favorable Response**	0.857	0.223						
20	**Unfavorable Response**	0.143	0.777						
21									
22									
23									
24									
25									

$$P(U \cap H) = 0.10$$

$$P(U \cap L) = 0.233$$

The column totals in cells B6 and C6 represent, respectively, the estimated probabilities of high and low demands as:

$$P(H) = 0.70$$

$$P(L) = 0.30$$

The row totals in cells D4 and D5 represent, respectively, the estimated probabilities of a favorable and unfavorable response. These values correspond to the first two of the six probability values listed earlier; that is:

$$P(F) = 0.667$$

$$P(U) = 0.333$$

With these values, we are now ready to compute the necessary conditional probabilities. One general definition of a conditional probability is:

$$P(A \mid B) = \frac{P(A \cap B)}{P(B)}$$

We can use this definition, along with the values in the joint probability table, to compute the conditional probabilities required for Figure 16.29 as:

$$P(H \mid F) = \frac{P(H \cap F)}{P(F)} = \frac{0.60}{0.667} = 0.90$$

$$P(L \mid F) = \frac{P(L \cap F)}{P(F)} = \frac{0.067}{0.667} = 0.10$$

$$P(H \mid U) = \frac{P(H \cap U)}{PU} = \frac{0.10}{0.333} = 0.30$$

$$P(L \mid U) = \frac{P(L \cap U)}{PU} = \frac{0.233}{0.333} = 0.70$$

We can calculate these conditional probabilities of the demand levels for a given survey response in the spreadsheet. This is done in the second table in Figure 16.30 using the following formula:

Formula for cell B12:   =B4/$D4
(Copy to B12 through C13.)

Although not required for Figure 16.29, we can also compute the conditional probabilities of the survey responses for a given level of demand as:

$$P(F \mid H) = \frac{P(H \cap F)}{P(H)} = \frac{0.60}{0.70} = 0.857$$

$$P(U \mid H) = \frac{P(H \cap U)}{P(H)} = \frac{0.10}{0.70} = 0.143$$

$$P(F \mid L) = \frac{P(L \cap F)}{P(L)} = \frac{0.067}{0.30} = 0.223$$

$$P(U \mid L) = \frac{P(L \cap U)}{P(L)} = \frac{0.233}{0.30} = 0.777$$

The third table in Figure 16.30 calculates conditional probabilities of the survey responses for a given level of demand using the following formula:

Formula for cell B19:   =B4/B$6
(Copy to B19 through C20.)

16.14.1 Bayes's Theorem

Bayes's Theorem provides another definition of conditional probability that is sometimes useful. This definition is:

$$P(A \mid B) = \frac{P(B \mid A)P(A)}{P(B \mid A)P(A) + P(B \mid \overline{A})P(\overline{A})}$$

In this formula, A and B represent any two events, and $\overline{A}$ is the complement of A. To see how this formula might be used, suppose that we want to determine $P(H \mid F)$ but we do not have access to the joint probability table in Figure 16.30. According to Bayes's Theorem, we know that:

$$P(H \mid F) = \frac{P(F \mid H)P(H)}{P(F \mid H)P(H) + P(F \mid L)P(L)}$$

If we know the values for the various quantities on the RHS of this equation, we can compute $P(H \mid F)$ as in the following example:

$$P(H \mid F) = \frac{P(F \mid H)P(H)}{P(F \mid H)P(H) + P(F \mid L)P(L)} = \frac{(0.857)(0.70)}{(0.857)(0.70) + (0.223)(0.30)} = 0.90$$

This result is consistent with the value of $P(H \mid F)$ shown in cell B12 in Figure 16.30.

16.15   UTILITY THEORY

Although the EMV decision rule is widely used, sometimes the decision alternative with the highest EMV is not the most desirable or most preferred alternative by the decision maker. For example, suppose that we could buy either of the two companies listed in the following payoff table for exactly the same price:

| | State of Nature | | |
Company	1	2	EMV
A	150,000	–30,000	60,000	← maximum
B	70,000	40,000	55,000
Probability	0.5	0.5	

The payoff values listed in this table represent the annual profits expected from this business. Thus, in any year, a 50% chance exists that company A will generate a profit of $150,000 and a 50% chance that it will generate a loss of $30,000. On the other hand, in each year, a 50% chance exists that company B will generate a profit of $70,000 and a 50% chance that it will generate a profit of $40,000.

According to the EMV decision rule, we should buy company A because it has the highest EMV. However, company A represents a far more risky investment than company B. Although company A would generate the highest EMV over the long run, we might not have the financial resources to withstand the potential losses of $30,000 per year that could occur in the short run with this alternative. With company B, we can be sure of making at least $40,000 each year. Although company B's EMV over the long run might not be as great as that of company A, for many decision makers, this is more than offset by the increased peace of mind associated with company B's relatively stable profit level. However, other decision makers might be willing to accept the greater risk associated with company A in hopes of achieving the higher potential payoffs this alternative provides.

As this example illustrates, the EMVs of different decision alternatives do not necessarily reflect the relative attractiveness of the alternatives to a particular decision maker. Utility theory provides a way to incorporate the decision maker's attitudes and preferences toward risk and return in the decision analysis process so that the most desirable decision alternative is identified.

16.15.1   Utility Functions

Utility theory assumes that every decision maker uses a **utility function** that translates each of the possible payoffs in a decision problem into a nonmonetary measure known as a utility. The **utility** of a payoff represents the total worth, value, or desirability of the outcome of a decision alternative to the decision maker. For convenience, we'll begin by representing utilities on a scale from 0 to 1, where 0 represents the least value and 1 represents the most.

Different decision makers have different attitudes and preferences toward risk and return. Those who are "risk neutral" tend to make decisions using the maximum EMV decision rule. However, some decision makers are risk avoiders (or "risk averse") and others look for risk (or are "risk seekers"). The utility functions typically associated with these three types of decision makers are shown in Figure 16.31.

Figure 16.31 illustrates how the same monetary payoff might produce different levels of utility for three different decision makers. A "risk averse" decision maker assigns the largest relative utility to any payoff but has a diminishing marginal utility for increased payoffs (that is, every additional dollar in payoff results in smaller increases in utility). The "risk seeking" decision maker assigns the smallest utility to any payoff but has an increasing marginal utility for increased payoffs (that is, every additional dollar in payoff results in larger increases in utility). The "risk neutral" decision maker (who follows the EMV decision rule) falls in between these two extremes and has a constant marginal utility for increased payoffs (that is, every additional dollar in payoff results in the same amount of increase in utility). The utility curves in Figure 16.31 are not the only ones that can occur. In general, utility curves can assume virtually any form depending on the preferences of the decision maker.

16.15.2   Constructing Utility Functions

Assuming that decision makers use utility functions (perhaps at a subconscious level) to make decisions, how can we determine what a given decision maker's utility function

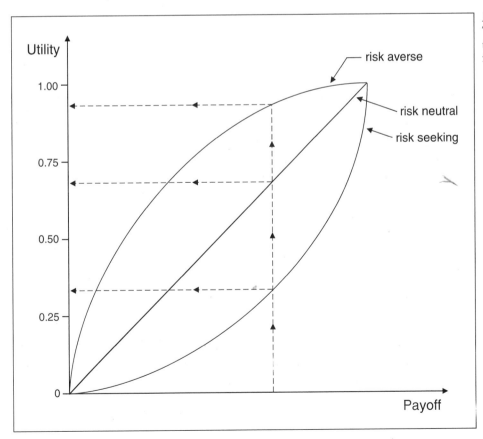

Figure 16.31
Three common types of utility functions.

looks like? One approach involves assigning a utility value of 0 to the worst outcome in a decision problem and a utility value of 1 to the best outcome. All other payoffs are assigned utility values between 0 and 1. (Although it is convenient to use endpoint values of 0 and 1, we can use any values provided that the utility value assigned to the worst payoff is less than the utility value assigned to the best payoff.)

We'll let $U(x)$ represent the utility associated with a payoff of x. Thus, for the decision about whether to buy company A or B, described earlier, we have:

$$U(-30,000) = 0$$
$$U(150,000) = 1$$

Now suppose that we want to find the utility associated with the payoff of $70,000 in our example. To do this, we must identify the probability p at which the decision maker is indifferent between the following two alternatives:

Alternative 1. Receive $70,000 with certainty.

Alternative 2. Receive $150,000 with probability p and lose $30,000 with probability $(1 - p)$.

If $p = 0$, most decision makers would choose alternative 1 because they would prefer to receive a payoff of $70,000 rather than lose $30,000. On the other hand, if $p = 1$, most decision makers would choose alternative 2 because they would prefer to receive a payoff of $150,000 rather than $70,000. So as p increases from 0 to 1, it reaches a point—p^*—at which the decision maker is indifferent between the two alternatives. That is, if $p < p^*$, the decision maker prefers alternative 1, and if $p > p^*$, the decision maker prefers alternative 2. The point of indifference, p^*, varies from one decision maker to another, depending on his or her attitude toward risk and according to his or her ability to sustain a loss of $30,000.

In our example, suppose that the decision maker is indifferent between alternative 1 and 2 when $p = 0.8$ (so that $p^* = 0.8$). The utility of the $70,000 payoff for this decision maker is computed as:

$$U(70,000) = U(150,000)p^* + U(-30,000)(1 - p^*) = 1p^* + 0(1 - p^*) = p^* = 0.8$$

Notice that when $p = 0.8$, the expected value of alternative 2 is:

$$\$150,000 \times 0.8 - \$30,000 \times 0.2 = \$114,000$$

Because the decision maker is indifferent between a risky decision (alternative 2) that has an EMV of $114,000 and a nonrisky decision (alternative 1) that has a certain payoff of $70,000, this decision maker is "risk averse." That is, the decision maker is willing to accept only $70,000 to avoid the risk associated with a decision that has an EMV of $114,000.

The term **certainty equivalent** refers to the amount of money that is equivalent in a decision maker's mind to a situation that involves uncertainty. For example, $70,000 is the decision maker's certainty equivalent for the uncertain situation represented by alternative 2 when $p = 0.8$. A closely related term, **risk premium,** refers to the EMV that a decision maker is willing to give up (or pay) in order to avoid a risky decision. In our example, the risk premium is $114,000 - $70,000 = $44,000; that is:

$$\text{Risk premium} \quad = \quad (\text{EMV of an uncertain situation}) \quad - \quad \begin{pmatrix} \text{certainty equivalent of the} \\ \text{same uncertain situation} \end{pmatrix}$$

To find the utility associated with the $40,000 payoff in our example, we must identify the probability p at which the decision maker is indifferent between the following two alternatives:

Alternative 1. Receive $40,000 with certainty.

Alternative 2. Receive $150,000 with probability p and lose $30,000 with probability $(1-p)$.

Because we reduced the payoff amount listed in alternative 1 from its earlier value of $70,000, we expect that the value of p at which the decision maker is indifferent would also be reduced. In this case, suppose that the decision maker is indifferent between the two alternatives when $p = 0.65$ (so that $p^* = 0.65$). The utility associated with a payoff of $40,000 is:

$$U(40,000) = U(150,000)p^* + U(-30,000)(1-p^*) = 1p^* + 0(1-p^*) = p^* = 0.65$$

Again the utility associated with the amount given in alternative 1 is equivalent to the decision maker's indifference point p^*. This is not a coincidence.

Key Point

When utilities are expressed on a scale from 0 to 1, the probability p^* at which the decision maker is indifferent between alternatives 1 and 2 always corresponds to the decision maker's utility for the amount listed in alternative 1.

Notice that when $p = 0.65$, the expected value of alternative 2 is:

$$\$150,000 \times 0.65 - \$30,000 \times 0.35 = \$87,000$$

Again this is "risk averse" behavior because the decision maker is willing to accept only $40,000 (or pay a risk premium of $47,000) to avoid the risk associated with a decision that has an EMV of $87,000.

For our example, the utilities associated with payoffs of -$30,000, $40,000, $70,000, and $150,000 are 0.0, 0.65, 0.80, and 1.0, respectively. If we plot these values on a graph and connect the points with straight lines, we can estimate the shape of the decision maker's utility function for this decision problem, as shown in Figure 16.32. Note that the shape of this utility function is consistent with the general shape of the utility function for a "risk averse" decision maker given in Figure 16.31.

16.15.3 Using Utilities to Make Decisions

After determining the utility value of each possible monetary payoff, we can apply the standard tools of decision analysis to determine the alternative that provides the highest expected utility. We do so using utility values in place of monetary values in payoff tables or decision trees. For our current example, we substitute the appropriate utilities in the payoff table and compute the expected utility for each decision alternative as:

Figure 16.32
An estimated
utility function
for the example
problem.

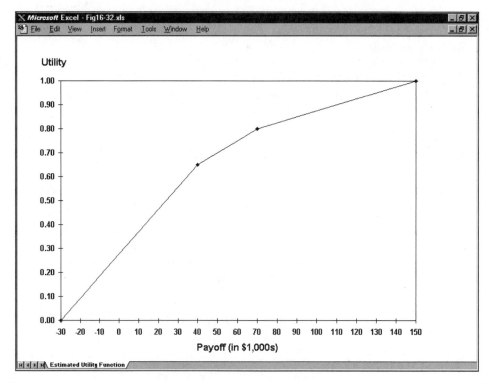

Company	State of Nature		Expected Utility	
	1	2		
A	1.00	0.00	0.500	
B	0.80	0.65	0.725	← maximum
Probability	0.5	0.5		

In this case, the decision to purchase company B provides the greatest expected level of utility to this decision maker—even though our earlier analysis indicated that its EMV of $55,000 is less than company A's EMV of $60,000. Thus, by using utilities decision makers can identify the alternative that is most attractive given their personal attitudes about risk and return.

16.15.4   The Exponential Utility Function

In a complicated decision problem with numerous possible payoff values, it might be difficult and time consuming for a decision maker to determine the different values for p^* that are required to determine the utility for each payoff. However, if the decision maker is "risk averse," the **exponential utility function** can be used as an approximation of the decision maker's actual utility function. The general form of the exponential utility function is:

$$U(x) = 1 - e^{-x/R}$$

In this formula, e is the base of the natural logarithm ($e = 2.718281 \ldots$) and R is a parameter that controls the shape of the utility function according to a decision maker's risk tolerance. Figure 16.33 shows examples of the graph of this function for several values of R. Note that as R increases, the shape of the utility curve becomes flatter (or less "risk averse"). Also note that as x becomes large, $U(x)$ approaches 1, when $x = 0$, then $U(x) = 0$; and if x is less than 0, then $U(x) < 0$.

To use the exponential utility function, we must determine a reasonable value for the risk tolerance parameter R. One method for doing so involves determining the maximum value of Y for which the decision maker is willing to participate in a game of chance with the following possible outcomes:

Win $Y with probability 0.5

Lose $Y/2 with probability 0.5

The maximum value of Y for which the decision maker would accept the above gamble should give us a reasonable estimate of R. Note that a decision maker willing to accept this gamble only at very small values of Y is "risk averse," whereas a decision maker willing to play for larger values of Y is less "risk averse." This corresponds with the relationship between the utility curves and values of R shown in Figure 16.33.

16.15.5 *Incorporating Utilities in TreePlan*

The TreePlan add-in provides a simple way to use the exponential utility function to model "risk averse" decision preferences in a decision tree. We will illustrate this using the decision tree developed earlier for Magnolia Inns, where Barbara needs to decide which parcel of land to purchase. The decision tree developed for this problem is shown in Figure 16.34 (and in the file FIG16-34.xls on your data disk).

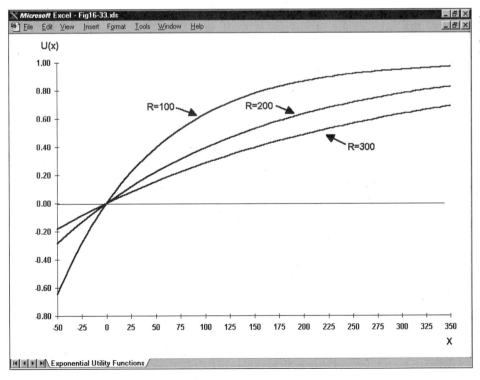

Figure 16.33
Examples of the exponential utility function.

Figure 16.34
Decision tree for
the Magnolia
Inns land
purchase
problem.

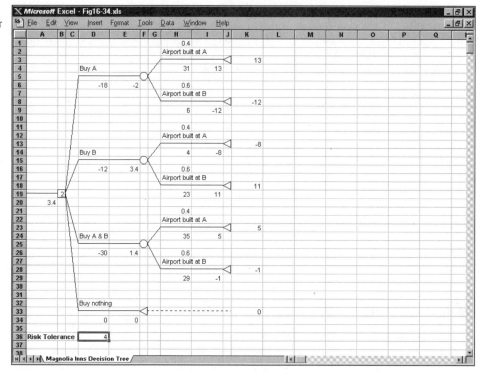

To use the exponential utility function, we first construct a decision tree in the usual way. We then determine the risk tolerance value of *R* for the decision maker using the technique described earlier. Because Barbara is making this decision on behalf of Magnolia Inns, it is important that she provide an estimated value of *R* based on the acceptable risk levels of the corporation—not her own personal risk tolerance level.

In this case, let's assume that $4 million is the maximum value of Y for which Barbara believes Magnolia Inns is willing to gamble winning $Y with probability 0.5 and losing $Y/2 with probability 0.5. Therefore, *R* = Y = 4. (Note that the value of *R* should be expressed in the same units as the payoffs in the decision tree.)

TreePlan requires that we enter the value of *R* in a cell named "RT" (short for Risk Tolerance). (This cell must be outside of the rectangular region containing the decision tree.) Cell D36 in Figure 16.34 serves this purpose. To assign the name "RT" to this cell:

1. Click cell D36.
2. Click the Insert menu.
3. Click Name.
4. Click Define.
5. Type RT.
6. Click OK.

We can now instruct TreePlan to use an exponential utility function to determine the optimal decision. To do this:

1. Click cell D3.
2. Press [Ctrl][t] to invoke TreePlan.
3. Click the Options button.

4. Click Use Exponential Utility Function.
5. Click OK.

TreePlan automatically converts the decision tree so that the rollback operation is performed using expected utilities rather than EMVs. The resulting tree is shown in Figure 16.35. The certainty equivalent at each node appears in the cell directly below and to the left of each node (previously the location of the EMVs). The expected utility at each node appears immediately below the certainty equivalents. According to this tree, the decision to buy the parcels at locations A and B provides the highest expected utility for Magnolia Inns.

16.16 MULTICRITERIA DECISION MAKING

A decision maker often uses more than one criterion or objective to evaluate the alternatives in a decision problem. Sometimes these criteria conflict with one another. For example, consider again the criteria of risk and return. Most decision makers desire high levels of return and low levels of risk. But high returns are usually accompanied by high risks, and low levels of return are associated with low risk levels. In making investment decisions, a decision maker must assess the trade-offs between risk and return to identify the decision that achieves the most satisfying balance of these two criteria. As we have seen, utility theory represents one approach to assessing the trade-offs between the criteria of risk and return.

Many other types of decision problems involve multiple conflicting criteria. For example, in choosing between two or more different job offers, you must evaluate the alternatives on the basis of starting salary, opportunity for advancement, job security,

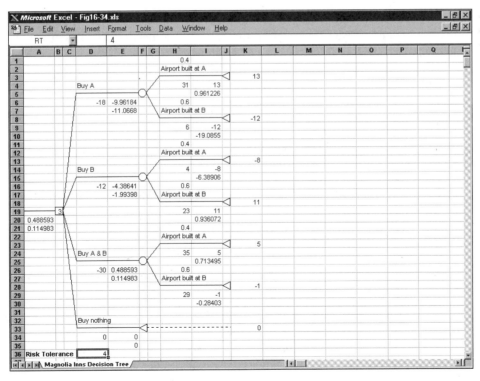

Figure 16.35
Analysis of the Magnolia Inns decision tree using an exponential utility function.

location, and so on. If you purchase a video camcorder, you must evaluate a number of different models based on the manufacturer's reputation, price, warranty, size, weight, zoom capability, lighting requirements, and a host of other features. If you must decide whom to hire to fill a vacancy in your organization, you will likely have to evaluate a number of candidates on the basis of education, experience, references, and personality. This section presents two techniques that can be used in decision problems that involve multiple criteria.

16.17   THE MULTICRITERIA SCORING MODEL

The **multicriteria scoring model** is a simple procedure in which we score (or rate) each alternative in a decision problem based on each criterion. The score for alternative j on criterion i is denoted by s_{ij}. Weights (denoted by w_i) are assigned to each criterion indicating its relative importance to the decision maker. For each alternative, we then compute a weighted average score as:

$$\text{Weighted average score for alternative } j = \sum_i w_i s_{ij}$$

We then select the alternative with the largest weighted average score.

The beginning of this chapter described a situation that many students face when they graduate from college—choosing between two job offers. The spreadsheet in Figure 16.36 (and in the file FIG16-36.xls on your data disk) illustrates how we might use a multicriteria scoring model to help in this problem.

In choosing between two (or more) job offers, we would evaluate criteria for each alternative such as the starting salary, potential for career development, job security, location of the job, and perhaps other factors as well. The idea in a scoring model is to assign a value from 0 to 1 to each decision alternative that reflects its relative worth on each criterion. These values can be thought of as subjective assessments of the utility that each alternative provides on the various criteria.

In Figure 16.36, the starting salary offered by company B provides the greatest value, but the salary offered by company A is not much worse. (Note that these scores do not necessarily mean that the starting salary offered by company B was the highest. These scores reflect the value of the salaries to the decision maker, taking into account such factors as the cost of living in the different locations.) The remaining scores in the table indicate that company A provides the greatest potential for career advancement and is in the most attractive location, but provides considerably less job security than that offered by company B.

Next, the decision maker must specify weights that indicate the relative importance of each criterion. Again, this is done subjectively. Hypothetical weights for each criterion in this example are shown in column F in Figure 16.36. Note that these weights must sum to 1. Weighted average scores for each alternative are calculated in cells C9 and D9 as:

Formula for cell C9:   =SUMPRODUCT(C5:C8,$F$5:$F$8)
(Copy to D9.)

In this case, the weighted average scores for company A and B are 0.84 and 0.77, respectively. Thus, this model indicates that the decision maker should accept the job with company A because it has the largest weighted average score.

Figure 16.36
A multicriteria
scoring model.

Key Cell Formulas		
Cell	*Formula*	*Copied to*
C9	=SUMPRODUCT(C5:C8,$F$5:$F$8)	D9
F9	=SUM(F5:F8)	—

16.18 THE ANALYTIC HIERARCHY PROCESS

Sometimes a decision maker finds it difficult to subjectively determine the criterion scores and weights needed in the multicriteria scoring model. In this case, the **analytic hierarchy process** (AHP) can be helpful. **AHP** provides a more structured approach for determining the scores and weights for the multicriteria scoring model described earlier.

To illustrate AHP, suppose that a company wants to purchase a new payroll and personnel records information system and is considering three systems, identified as X, Y, and Z. The systems differ with respect to three key criteria: price, user support, and ease of use.

16.18.1 Pairwise Comparisons

The first step in AHP is to create a pairwise comparison matrix for each alternative on each criterion. We'll illustrate the details of this process for the price criterion. The values shown in Figure 16.37 are used in AHP to describe the decision maker's preferences between two alternatives on a given criterion.

Figure 16.37
Scale for
pairwise
comparisons in
AHP.

Value	Preference
1	Equally Preferred
2	Equally to Moderately Preferred
3	Moderately Preferred
4	Moderately to Strongly Preferred
5	Strongly Preferred
6	Strongly to Very Strongly Preferred
7	Very Strongly Preferred
8	Very Strongly to Extremely Preferred
9	Extremely Preferred

To create a pairwise comparison matrix for the price criterion, we must perform pairwise comparisons of the prices of systems X, Y, and Z using the values shown in Figure 16.37. Let P_{ij} denote the extent to which we prefer alternative i to alternative j on a given criterion. For example, suppose that when comparing system X to Y, the decision maker strongly prefers the price of X. In this case, $P_{XY} = 5$. Similarly, suppose that when comparing system X to Z, the decision maker very strongly prefers the price of X, and when comparing Y to Z, the decision maker moderately prefers the price of Y. In this case, $P_{XZ} = 7$ and $P_{YZ} = 3$. We used the values of these pairwise comparisons to create the pairwise comparison matrix shown in Figure 16.38.

The values of P_{XY}, P_{XZ}, and P_{YZ} are shown in cells D4, E4, and E5 in Figure 16.38. We entered the value 1 along the main diagonal in Figure 16.38 to indicate that if an alternative is compared against itself, the decision maker should equally prefer either alternative (because they are the same).

The entries in cells C5, C6, and D6 correspond to P_{YX}, P_{ZX}, and P_{ZY}, respectively. To determine these values we could obtain the decision maker's preferences between Y and X, Z and X, and Z and Y. However, if we already know the decision maker's preference between X and Y (P_{XY}), we can conclude that the decision maker's preference between Y and X (P_{YX}) is the reciprocal of the preference between X and Y; that is, $P_{YX} = 1/P_{XY}$. So, in general, we have:

$$P_{ji} = \frac{1}{P_{ij}}$$

Thus, the values in cells C5, C6, and D6 are computed as:

Formula for cell C5: =1/D4

Formula for cell C6: =1/E4

Formula for cell D6: =1/E5

16.18.2   Normalizing the Comparisons

The next step in AHP is to normalize the matrix of pairwise comparisons. To do this, we first calculate the sum of each column in the pairwise comparison matrix. We then divide each entry in the matrix by its column sum. Figure 16.39 shows the resulting normalized matrix.

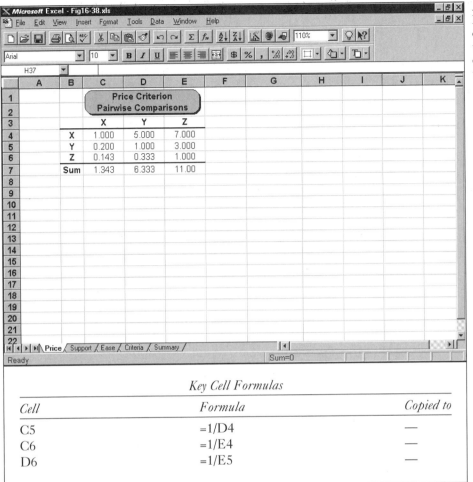

Figure 16.38
Pairwise comparisons of the price criterion for the three systems.

		Key Cell Formulas	
Cell		*Formula*	*Copied to*
C5		=1/D4	—
C6		=1/E4	—
D6		=1/E5	—

We'll use the average of each row in the normalized matrix as the score for each alternative on the criterion under consideration. For example, cells F11, F12, and F13 indicate that the average scores on the price criterion for X, Y, and Z are 0.724, 0.193, and 0.083, respectively. These scores indicate the relative desirability of the three alternatives to the decision maker with respect to price. The score for X indicates that this is by far the most attractive alternative with respect to price, and alternative Y is somewhat more attractive than Z. Note that these scores reflect the preferences expressed by the decision maker in the pairwise comparison matrix.

16.18.3   Consistency

In applying AHP, the decision maker should be consistent in the preference ratings given in the pairwise comparison matrix. For example, if the decision maker strongly prefers the price of X to that of Y, and strongly prefers the price of Y to that of Z, it would be inconsistent for the decision maker to indicate indifference (or equal preference) regarding the price of X and Z. Thus, before using the scores derived from the normalized comparison matrix, the preferences indicated in the original pairwise comparison matrix should be checked for consistency.

Figure 16.39
Price scores
obtained from
the normalized
comparison
matrix.

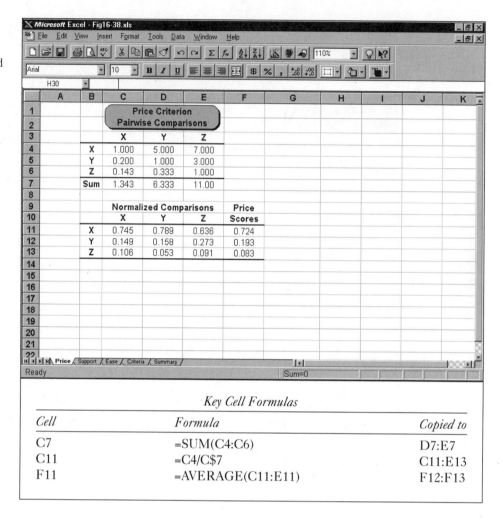

A consistency measure for each alternative is obtained as:

$$\text{Consistency measure for X} = \frac{0.724 \times 1 + 0.193 \times 5 + 0.083 \times 7}{0.724} = 3.141$$

$$\text{Consistency measure for Y} = \frac{0.724 \times 0.2 + 0.193 \times 1 + 0.083 \times 3}{0.193} = 3.043$$

$$\text{Consistency measure for Z} = \frac{0.724 \times 0.143 + 0.193 \times 0.333 + 0.083 \times 1}{0.083} = 3.014$$

The numerator in each of these calculations multiplies the scores obtained from the normalized matrix by the preferences given in one of the rows of the original pairwise comparison matrix. The products are summed and then divided by the score for the alternative in question. These consistency measures are shown in Figure 16.40 in cells G11 through G13.

If the decision maker is perfectly consistent in stating preferences, each consistency measure will equal the number of alternatives in the problem (which, in this case,

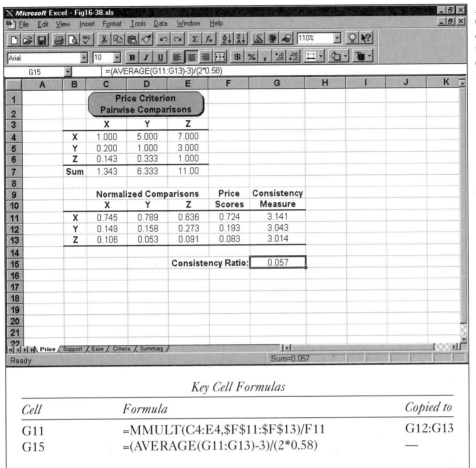

Figure 16.40
Checking the
consistency of
the pairwise
comparisons.

Key Cell Formulas

Cell	Formula	Copied to
G11	=MMULT(C4:E4,$F$11:$F$13)/F11	G12:G13
G15	=(AVERAGE(G11:G13)-3)/(2*0.58)	—

is three). So there appears to be some amount of inconsistency in the preferences given in the pairwise comparison matrix. This is not unusual. It is difficult for a decision maker to be perfectly consistent in stating preferences between a large number of pairwise comparisons. Provided that the amount of inconsistency is not excessive, the scores obtained from the normalized matrix will be reasonably accurate. To determine whether or not the inconsistency is excessive, we compute the following quantities:

$$\text{Consistency Index (CI)} = \frac{\lambda - n}{n - 1}$$

$$\text{Consistency Ratio (CR)} = \frac{\text{CI}}{\text{RI}}$$

where:

λ = the average consistency measure for all alternatives

n = the number of alternatives

RI = the appropriate random index from Figure 16.41

Figure 16.41
Values of RI for
use in AHP.

n	RI
2	0.00
3	0.58
4	0.90
5	1.12
6	1.24
7	1.32
8	1.41

If the pairwise comparison matrix is perfectly consistent, then $\lambda = n$ and the consistency ratio is 0. The values of RI in Figure 16.41 give the average value of CI if all the entries in the pairwise comparison matrix were chosen at random, given that all the diagonal entries equal 1 and $P_{ij} = 1/P_{ji}$. If CR ≤ 0.10, the degree of consistency in the pairwise comparison matrix is satisfactory. However, if CR > 0.10, serious inconsistencies might exist and AHP might not yield meaningful results. The value for CR shown in cell G15 in Figure 16.40 indicates that the pairwise comparison matrix for the price criterion is reasonably consistent. Therefore, we can assume that the scores for the price criterion obtained from the normalized matrix are reasonably accurate.

16.18.4   Obtaining Scores for the Remaining Criteria

We can repeat the process for obtaining the price criterion scores to obtain scores for the user support and ease-of-use criteria. Hypothetical results for these criteria are shown in Figures 16.42 and 16.43, respectively.

We can create these two spreadsheets easily by copying the spreadsheet for the price criterion (shown in Figure 16.40) and having the decision maker fill in the pairwise comparison matrices with preferences related to the user support and ease-of-use criteria. Notice that the preferences given in Figures 16.42 and 16.43 appear to be consistent.

16.18.5   Obtaining Criterion Weights

The scores shown in Figures 16.40, 16.42, and 16.43 indicate how the alternatives compare with respect to the price, user support, and ease-of-use criteria. Before we can use these values in a scoring model, we must also determine weights that indicate the relative importance of the three criteria to the decision maker. The pairwise comparison process used earlier to generate scores for the alternative on each criteria can also be used to generate criterion weights.

The pairwise comparison matrix in Figure 16.44 shows the decision maker's preferences for the three criteria. The values in cells C5 and C6 indicate that the decision maker finds user support and ease of use to be more important (or more preferred) than price, and cell D6 indicates that ease of use is somewhat more important than user support. These relative preferences are reflected in the criterion weights shown in cells F11 through F13.

User Support Criterion Pairwise Comparisons

	X	Y	Z
X	1.000	0.333	2.000
Y	3.000	1.000	5.000
Z	0.500	0.200	1.000
Sum	4.500	1.533	8.000

	Normalized Comparisons X	Y	Z	Support Score	Consistency Measure
X	0.222	0.217	0.250	0.230	3.003
Y	0.667	0.652	0.625	0.648	3.007
Z	0.111	0.130	0.125	0.122	3.001

Consistency Ratio: 0.003

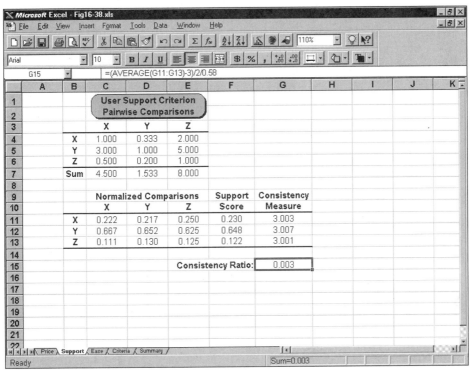

Figure 16.42 Spreadsheet used to calculate scores for the user support criterion.

Ease-of-Use Criterion Pairwise Comparisons

	X	Y	Z
X	1.000	0.500	0.333
Y	2.000	1.000	0.500
Z	3.000	2.000	1.000
Sum	6.000	3.500	1.833

	Normalized Comparisons X	Y	Z	Ease Score	Consistency Measure
X	0.167	0.143	0.182	0.164	3.004
Y	0.333	0.286	0.273	0.297	3.008
Z	0.500	0.571	0.545	0.539	3.015

Consistency Ratio: 0.008

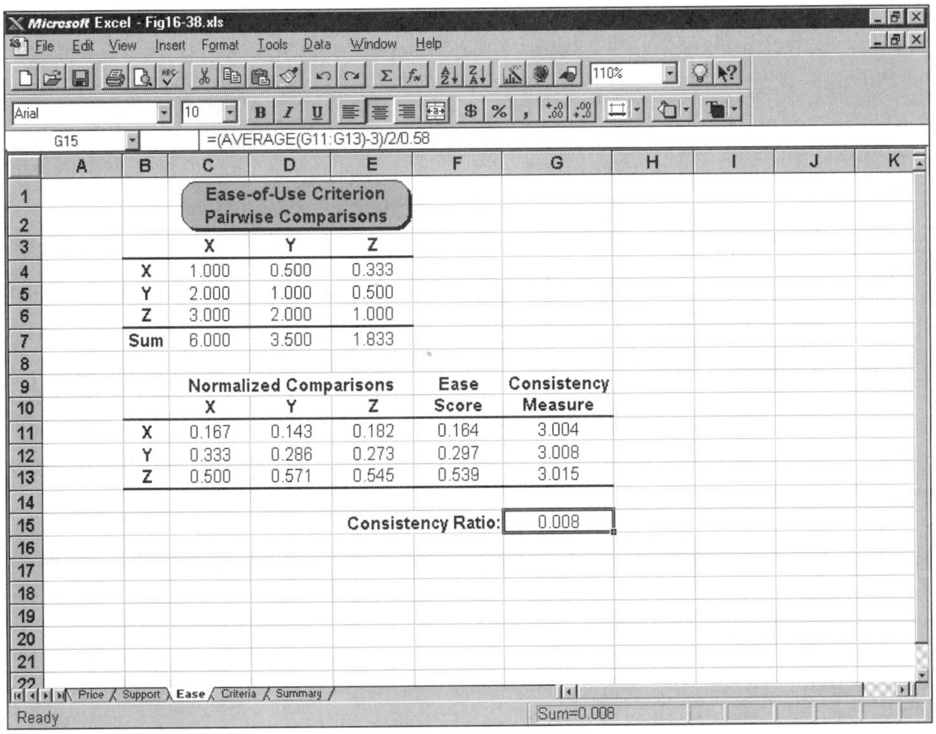

Figure 16.43 Spreadsheet used to calculate scores for the ease-of-use criterion.

Figure 16.44
Spreadsheet
used to
determine the
criterion
weights.

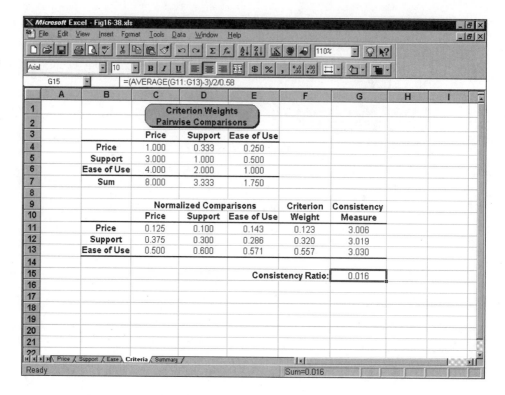

16.18.6   *Implementing the Scoring Model*

We now have all the elements required to analyze this decision problem using a scoring model. Thus, the last step in AHP is to calculate the weighted average scores for each decision alternative. The weighted average scores are shown in cells C8 through E8 in Figure 16.45. According to these scores, alternative Y should be selected.

SUMMARY

This chapter presented a number of techniques for analyzing a variety of decision problems. First it discussed how a payoff table can be used to summarize the alternatives in a single-stage decision problem. Then a number of nonprobabilistic and probabilistic decision rules were presented. No one decision rule works best in all situations, but together, the rules help to highlight different aspects of a problem and can help develop and sharpen a decision maker's insight and intuition about a problem so that better decisions can be made. When probabilities of occurrence can be estimated for the alternatives in a problem, the EMV decision rule is the most commonly used technique.

Decision trees are particularly helpful in expressing multistage decision problems in which a series of decisions must be considered. Each terminal node in a decision tree is associated with the net payoff that results from each possible sequence of decisions. A rollback technique determines the alternative that results in the highest EMV. Because different decision makers derive different levels of value from the same monetary payoff, the chapter also discussed how utility theory can be applied to decision problems to account for these differences.

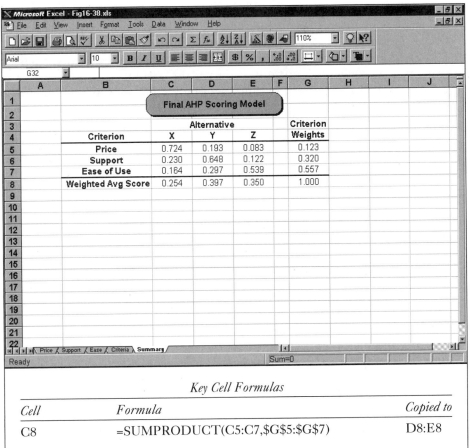

Figure 16.45
Final scoring model for selecting the information system.

Key Cell Formulas		
Cell	*Formula*	*Copied to*
C8	=SUMPRODUCT(C5:C7,$G$5:$G$7)	D8:E8

Finally, the chapter discussed two procedures for dealing with decision problems that involve multiple conflicting decision criteria. The multicriteria scoring model requires the decision maker to assign a score for each alternative on each criterion. Weights are then assigned to represent the relative importance of the criteria, and a weighted average score is computed for each alternative. The alternative with the highest score is the recommended alternative. AHP provides a structured approach to determining the scores and weights used in a multicriteria scoring model if the decision maker has difficulty specifying these values.

THE WORLD OF MANAGEMENT SCIENCE
Decision Theory Helps
Hallmark Trim Discards

Many items distributed by Hallmark Cards, Incorporated can be sold only during a single season. Leftovers, or discards, must then be disposed of outside normal dealer channels. For example, table items such as napkins can be used in the company's cafeteria, donated to charity, or sold without the brand name to volume discounters. Other items have no salvage value at all.

A product manager deciding the size of a production run or quantity to purchase from a supplier faces two risks. First is the consequence of choosing a quantity that is larger than the eventual demand for the product. Products that have been paid for must be discarded, and the salvage value (if any) might not make up for the cost. The second risk is that the quantity might be less than demand, in which case revenues are lost.

A substantial increase in the dollar volume of discards prompted Hallmark management to initiate a training program for product managers and inventory controllers. They were taught to use product cost and selling price together with a probability distribution of demand to make order quantity decisions. The format for conducting the analysis was a payoff matrix in which rows represented order quantities and columns represented demand levels. Each cell in the payoff matrix contained a computed contribution to profit.

Salvage values and shortage costs were not included in the values of the payoff matrix cells. Instead, sensitivity analysis provided ranges of values within which the order quantity was still optimal.

Although some probability distributions could be estimated from sales data for previous years, it was sometimes necessary to use subjective probabilities. This was especially true for special promotions that had no relevant product history. For this reason, product managers were trained in specifying subjective probabilities. Although direct assessment of a cumulative distribution function would have tied into the order quantity decision more efficiently, it turned out that the managers became more adept at estimating a discrete probability function.

Enough managers adopted the payoff matrix technique, with positive results, that the training program has been continued and expanded within the company.

Source: F. Hutton Barron, "Payoff Matrices Pay Off at Hallmark," *Interfaces*, vol. 15, no. 4, August 1985, pages 20–25.

QUESTIONS AND PROBLEMS

1. This chapter presented the problem of having to decide between two job offers. The decision maker could accept the job with company A, accept the job with company B, or reject both offers and hope for a better one. What other alternatives can you think of for this problem?

2. Give an example of a national business, political, or military leader who made a good decision that resulted in a bad outcome, or a bad decision that resulted in a good outcome.

3. Consider the following payoff matrix:

| | State of Nature | | |
Decision	1	2	3
A	50	75	35
B	40	50	60
C	40	35	30

Should a decision maker ever select decision alternative C? Explain your answer.

4. Brenda Kelley runs a specialty ski clothing shop outside of Boone, North Carolina. She must place her order for ski parkas well in advance of ski season because the manufacturer produces them in the summer months. Brenda needs to determine whether to place a large, medium, or small order for parkas. The number sold will depend largely on whether the area receives a heavy, normal, or light amount of snow during the ski season. The following table summarizes the payoffs Brenda expects to receive under each scenario.

	Amount of Snow		
Size of Order	Heavy	Normal	Light
Large	10	7	3
Medium	8	8	6
Small	4	4	4

Payoffs (in $1000s)

Brenda estimates the probability of heavy, normal, and light snowfalls as 0.25, 0.6, and 0.15, respectively.

a. What decision should be made according to the maximax decision rule?
b. What decision should be made according to the maximin decision rule?
c. What decision should be made according to the minimax regret decision rule?
d. What decision should be made according to the EMV decision rule?
e. What decision should be made according to the EOL decision rule?

5. One of Philip Mahn's investments is going to mature, and he wants to determine how to invest the proceeds of $30,000. Philip is considering two new investments: a stock mutual fund and a one-year certificate of deposit (CD). The CD is guaranteed to pay an 8% return. Philip estimates the return on the stock mutual fund as 16%, 9%, or –2%, depending on whether market conditions are good, average, or poor, respectively. Philip estimates the probability of a good, average, and poor market to be 0.1, 0.85, and 0.05, respectively.

a. Construct a payoff matrix for this problem.
b. What decision should be made according to the maximax decision rule?
c. What decision should be made according to the maximin decision rule?
d. What decision should be made according to the minimax regret decision rule?
e. What decision should be made according to the EMV decision rule?
f. What decision should be made according to the EOL decision rule?
g. How much should Philip be willing to pay to obtain a market forecast that is 100% accurate?

6. The Fish House (TFH) in Norfolk, Virginia, sells fresh fish and seafood. TFH receives daily shipments of farm-raised trout from a nearby supplier. Each trout costs $2.45 and is sold for $3.95. To maintain its reputation for freshness, at the end of the day TFH sells any leftover trout to a local pet food manufacturer for $1.25 each. The owner of TFH wants to determine how many trout to order each day. Historically, the daily demand for trout is:

Demand:	10	11	12	13	14	15	16	17	18	19	20
Probability:	0.02	0.06	0.09	0.11	0.13	0.15	0.18	0.11	0.07	0.05	0.03

a. Construct a payoff matrix for this problem.
b. What decision should be made according to the maximax decision rule?
c. What decision should be made according to the maximin decision rule?
d. What decision should be made according to the minimax regret decision rule?
e. What decision should be made according to the EMV decision rule?
f. What decision should be made according to the EOL decision rule?
g. How much should the owner of TFH be willing to pay to obtain a demand forecast that is 100% accurate?
h. Which decision rule would you recommend TFH use in this case? Why?

7. Refer to question 6. Suppose that TFH receives a quantity discount that reduces the price to $2.25 per trout if it purchases 15 or more. How many trout would you recommend TFH order each day in this case?

8. Bob Farrell, owner of Farrell Motors, is trying to decide whether or not to buy an insurance policy to cover hail damage on his inventory of more than 200 cars and trucks. Thunderstorms occur frequently and they sometimes produce golfball-sized hail that can severely damage automobiles. Bob estimates the potential damage from hail in the next year as:

Hail Damage (in $1,000s):	0	15	30	45	60	75	90	105
Probability:	0.25	0.08	0.10	0.12	0.15	0.12	0.10	0.08

Bob is considering the following three alternatives for dealing with this risk:

- Bob can buy an insurance policy for $47,000 that would cover 100% of any losses that occur.
- Bob can buy an insurance policy for $25,000 that would cover all losses in excess of $35,000.
- Bob can choose to self-insure, in which case he will not have to pay any insurance premium but will pay for any losses that occur.

a. Construct a payoff matrix for this problem.
b. What decision should be made according to the maximax decision rule?
c. What decision should be made according to the maximin decision rule?
d. What decision should be made according to the minimax regret decision rule?
e. What decision should be made according to the EMV decision rule?
f. What decision should be made according to the EOL decision rule?

9. Morley Properties is planning to build a condominium development on St. Simons Island, Georgia. The company is trying to decide between building a small, medium, or large development. The payoffs received for each size of development will depend on the market demand for condominiums in the area, which could be low, medium, or high. The payoff matrix for this decision problem is:

	Market Demand		
Size of Development	Low	Medium	High
Small	400	400	400
Medium	200	500	500
Large	-400	300	800

Payoffs in $1,000s

The owner of the company estimates a 21.75% chance that market demand will be low, a 35.5% chance that it will be medium, and a 42.75% chance that it will be high.

a. What decision should be made according to the maximax decision rule?
b. What decision should be made according to the maximin decision rule?
c. What decision should be made according to the minimax regret decision rule?
d. What decision should be made according to the EMV decision rule?
e. What decision should be made according to the EOL decision rule?

10. Refer to question 9. Morley Properties can hire a consultant to predict the most likely level of demand for this project. This consultant has done many similar studies and has provided Morley Properties with the following joint probability table summarizing the accuracy of the results:

| | Actual Demand | | |
Forecasted Demand	Low	Medium	High
Low	0.1600	0.0300	0.0100
Medium	0.0350	0.2800	0.0350
High	0.0225	0.0450	0.3825

The sum of the entries on the main diagonal of this table indicates that the consultant's forecast is correct about 82.25% of the time, overall.

a. Construct the conditional probability table showing the probabilities of the various actual demands given each of the forecasted demands.
b. What is the EMV of the optimal decision without the consultant's assistance?
c. Construct a decision tree Morley Properties would use to analyze the decision problem if the consultant is hired at a cost of $0.
d. What is the EMV of the optimal decision with the consultant's free assistance?
e. What is the maximum price Morley Properties should be willing to pay the consultant?

11. MicroProducts, Incorporated (MPI) manufactures printed circuit boards for a major PC manufacturer. Before a board is sent to the customer, three key components must be tested. These components can be tested in any order. If any of the components fail, the entire board must be scrapped. The costs of testing the three components are given below, along with the probability of each component failing the test:

Component	Cost of Test	Probability of Failure
X	$1.75	0.125
Y	$2.00	0.075
Z	$2.40	0.140

a. Create a decision tree for this problem that could be used to determine the order in which the components should be tested to minimize the expected cost of performing the tests.
b. In which order should the components be tested?
c. What is the expected cost of performing the tests in this sequence?

12. Refer to question 11. A manufacturing engineer for MPI collected the following
    data on the failure rates of components X, Y, and Z in a random sample of 1,000
    circuit boards:

X	Y	Z	Number of Boards
p	p	p	710
p	f	p	45
p	p	f	110
p	f	f	10
f	p	p	95
f	f	p	10
f	p	f	10
f	f	f	10
		Total:	1000

(p=pass, f=fail)

For example, the first row in this table indicates that components X, Y, and Z all
passed their inspections in 710 out of the 1,000 boards checked. The second row
indicates that 45 boards passed inspection on components X and Z, but failed on
component Y. The remaining rows can be interpreted similarly.

a. Using these data, compute conditional probabilities for the decision tree you
    developed in question 11. (Note that $P(A \mid B) = P(A \cap B)/P(B)$ and $P(A \mid B \cap C)$
    $= P(A \cap B \cap C)/P(B \cap C)$.)
b. According to the revised probabilities, in which order should the components
    be tested?
c. What is the expected cost of performing the tests in this sequence?

13. The Banisco Corporation is negotiating a contract to borrow $300,000 to be repaid
    in a lump sum at the end of nine years. Interest payments will be made on the
    loan at the end of each year. The company is considering the following three
    financing arrangements:

• The company can borrow the money using a fixed rate loan (FRL) that
  requires interest payments of 9% per year.
• The company can borrow the money using an adjustable rate loan (ARL) that
  requires interest payments of 6% at the end of each of the first five years. At
  the beginning of the sixth year, the interest rate on the loan could change to
  7%, 9%, or 11% with probabilities of 0.1, 0.25, and 0.65, respectively.
• The company can borrow the money using an ARL that requires interest payments of 4% at the end of each of the first three years. At the beginning of the
  fourth year, the interest rate on the loan could change to 6%, 8%, or 10% with
  probabilities of 0.05, 0.30, and 0.65, respectively. At the beginning of the sev-
  enth year, the interest rate could decrease by 1 percentage point with a probability of 0.1, increase by 1 percentage point with a probability of 0.2, or
  increase by 3 percentage points with a probability of 0.7.

a. Create a decision tree for this problem, computing the total interest paid
    under each possible scenario.
b. Which decision should the company make if it wants to minimize its expect-
    ed total interest payments?

14. Refer to question 13. The present value (PV) of a future cash-flow value (FV) is defined as:

$$PV = \frac{FV}{(1 + r)^n}$$

where n is the number of years into the future in which the cash flow occurs and r is the discount rate. Suppose that the discount rate for Banisco is 10% ($r = 0.1$).

   a. Create a decision tree for this problem, computing the PV of the total interest paid under each possible scenario.
   b. Which decision should the company make if it wants to minimize the expected PV of its total interest payments?

15. Medical studies have shown that 10 out of 100 adults have heart disease. When a person with heart disease is given an EKG test, a 0.9 probability exists that the test will indicate the presence of heart disease. When a person without heart disease is given an EKG test, a 0.95 probability exists that the test will indicate the person does not have heart disease. Suppose that a person arrives at an emergency room complaining of chest pains. An EKG is given and indicates that the person has heart disease. What is the probability that the person actually has heart disease?

16. From industry statistics, a credit card company knows that 0.8 of its potential card holders are good credit risks and 0.2 are bad credit risks. The company uses discriminant analysis to screen credit card applicants and determine which ones should receive credit cards. The company awards credit cards to 70% of those who apply. The company has found that of those awarded credit cards, 95% turn out to be good credit risks. What is the probability that an applicant who is a bad credit risk will be denied a credit card?

17. Suppose that you are given the following two alternatives:

   Alternative 1:   Receive $200 with certainty.
   Alternative 2:   Receive $1,000 with probability p or lose $250 with probability $1 - p$.

   a. At what value of p would you be indifferent between these two alternatives?
   b. Given your response to part a, would you be classified as risk averse, risk neutral, or risk seeking?
   c. Suppose that alternative 2 changed so that you would receive $1,000 with probability p or lose $0 with probability $(1 - p)$. At what value of p would you now be indifferent between these alternatives?
   d. Given your response to part c, would you be classified as risk averse, risk neutral, or risk seeking?

18. Refer to question 9. Suppose that the utility function for the owner of Morley Properties can be approximated by the exponential utility function:

$$U(x) = 1 - e^{-x/R}$$

where the risk tolerance value $R = 100$ (in $1,000s).

   a. Convert the payoff matrix to utility values.
   b. What decision provides the owner of the company with the largest expected utility?

19. Refer to question 10. Suppose that the consultant's fee is $5,000 and the utility function for the owner of Morley Properties can be approximated by the exponential utility function:

$$U(x) = 1 - e^{-x/R}$$

where the risk tolerance value $R = 100$ (in $1,000s).

a. What expected level of utility is realized if Morley Properties hires the consultant?
b. What expected level of utility is realized if Morley Properties does not hire the consultant?
c. Based on this analysis, should Morley Properties hire the consultant?

20. The president of Pegasus Corporation is trying to decide which of three candidates (denoted as candidates A, B, and C) to hire as the firm's new vice president of Marketing. The primary criteria the president is considering are each candidate's leadership ability, interpersonal skills, and administrative ability. After carefully considering their qualifications, the president used AHP to create the following pairwise comparison matrices for the three candidates on the various criteria:

Leadership Ability

	A	B	C
A	1	3	4
B	1/3	1	2
C	1/4	1/2	1

Interpersonal Skills

	A	B	C
A	1	1/2	3
B	2	1	8
C	1/3	1/8	1

Administrative Ability

	A	B	C
A	1	1/5	1/8
B	5	1	1/3
C	8	3	1

Next, the president of Pegasus considered the relative importance of the three criteria. This resulted in the following pairwise comparison matrix:

Criteria

	Leadership Ability	Interpersonal Skills	Administrative Ability
Leadership Ability	1	1/3	1/4
Interpersonal Skills	3	1	1/2
Administrative Ability	4	2	1

a. Use AHP to compute scores for each candidate on each of the three criteria, and to compute weights for each of the criteria.

   b. Was the president consistent in making pairwise comparisons?

   c. Compute the weighted average score for each candidate. Which candidate should be selected according to your results?

21. Kathy Jones is planning to buy a new minivan but, after narrowing her choices down to three models (X, Y, and Z) within her price range, she is having difficulty deciding which one to buy. Kathy has compared each model against the others on the basis of four criteria: price, safety, economy, and comfort. Her comparisons are summarized as:

Price	X	Y	Z
X	1	1/4	3
Y	4	1	7
Z	1/3	1/7	1

Safety	X	Y	Z
X	1	1/2	3
Y	2	1	8
Z	1/3	1/8	1

Economy	X	Y	Z
X	1	1/3	1/6
Y	3	1	1/3
Z	6	3	1

Comfort	X	Y	Z
X	1	1/4	1/8
Y	4	1	1/3
Z	8	3	1

Kathy wants to incorporate all of these criteria into her final decision, but not all of the criteria are equally important. The following matrix summarizes Kathy's comparisons of the importance of the criteria:

Criteria	Price	Safety	Economy	Comfort
Price	1	1/7	1/2	1/5
Safety	7	1	4	2
Economy	2	1/4	1	1/2
Comfort	5	1/2	2	1

   a. Use AHP to compute scores for each minivan on each of the four criteria, and to compute weights for each of the criteria.

   b.   Was Kathy consistent in making pairwise comparisons?

   c.   Compute the weighted average score for each minivan. Based on this analysis, which minivan should Kathy buy?

22. Identify a consumer electronics product that you want to purchase (for example, a TV, VCR, camcorder, personal computer, and so on). Identify at least three models of this product that you would consider purchasing. Identify at least three criteria on which these models differ (for example, price, quality, warranty, options). Use AHP to determine scores for each model on each of the criteria and to determine weights for the criteria. Which model should you choose according to the AHP results?

CASE 16.1   THE SPREADSHEET WARS

Contributed by Jack Yurkiewicz, Lubin School of Business, Pace University, New York.

Sam Ellis is worried. As president and CEO of Forward Software, Sam introduced a new spreadsheet product, Cinco, to the market last year. Forward Software has been developing and marketing high-quality software packages for more than five years, but these products are mostly computer software language interpreters, similar to Pascal, FORTRAN, and C. These products received excellent critical reviews, and because of Forward's aggressive pricing and marketing, the company quickly captured a major share of that software market. Buoyed by its wide acceptance, last year Forward decided to enter the applications arena for the IBM and compatible audience, leading off with Cinco and following up with a word processing application, Fast.

The spreadsheet market is dominated by Focus Software, whose product—Focus A-B-C—has an 80% market share. Focus A-B-C was released in 1981, shortly after the IBM personal computer (PC) was introduced, and the two products had an immediate symbiotic effect. The spreadsheet was a major advance over what was available at the time, but required the extra 16-bit processing power that the IBM PC offered. IBM, on the other hand, needed an application that would make its PC a "must buy." Sales of Focus A-B-C and the IBM PC took off as a result of their near-simultaneous release.

At the time of its release, Focus A-B-C was a superb product, but it did have flaws. For example, because the software was copy-protected, it could be installed on a hard disk, but the original floppy disk had to be inserted each time before the software could run. Many users found this step an annoyance. Another problem with A-B-C was printing graphs. In order to print a graph, users had to exit the software and load a new program, called Printgraf, which would then print the graph. Finally, the product had a list price of $495, and the best discounted price available was approximately $300.

However, Focus A-B-C had a unique menu system that was intuitive and easy to use. Pressing the slash key (/) displayed the menu system at the top of the spreadsheet. The menu allowed the user to make choices and provided a one-line explanation of each menu option. Compared to the cryptic commands or keystrokes users had to enter in other products, the Focus A-B-C menu system was a model of simplicity and clarity. Millions of users became accustomed to the menu system and hailed its use.

Another advantage of Focus A-B-C was its ability to let users write their own macros. Literally a program, a macro allowed a user to automate spreadsheet tasks and then run them with a keystroke or two.

In 1985, a small company named Discount Software introduced its own spreadsheet to the market. Called VIP Scheduler, the product looked and worked exactly the same as Focus A-B-C. Pressing the slash key displayed the identical menu as found in Focus A-B-C, and the product could read any macros developed with Focus A-B-C. VIP Scheduler was designed to look and work exactly as Focus A-B-C so that users would not have to learn a new system and could start productive work immediately. VIP Scheduler also offered two advantages over Focus A-B-C: its list price was $99, and the software was not copy-protected. Sales for VIP Scheduler were strong, but many consumers, perhaps feeling safer with the Focus name, did not buy the product, even though critical reviews were positive. VIP Scheduler did find a receptive market in academia.

When Forward released its first spreadsheet product, Cinco, it was hailed by critics as a better all-around product than Focus A-B-C. It had better graphics, allowed users to print graphs from within Cinco, and was 100% compatible with Focus A-B-C. Cinco had its own menu system, which was as flexible as the Focus A-B-C system, but the menus and options were arranged more intuitively. For users who did not want to invest the time to learn a new menu system, Cinco could emulate the Focus A-B-C menu system. Both menus were activated by pressing the slash key, and users could specify easily which menu system they wanted. All macros written for Focus A-B-C ran perfectly on Cinco, provided that the Focus A-B-C menu system was being used. Because of favorable reviews and aggressive marketing by Forward, Cinco quickly gained market share.

In a move that surprised the industry, Focus recently sued Discount Software, publisher of VIP Scheduler, for copyright infringement. Focus claimed that its menu system was an original work, and that VIP Scheduler, by incorporating that menu system in its product, had violated copyright laws. Focus claimed that the look and feel of its menu system could not be used in another product without permission. Sam is certain that Focus initiated this lawsuit because Cinco has made such dramatic progress in gaining a share of the spreadsheet market. Sam also is sure that Focus's target is not really VIP Scheduler, because it has such a small market share, but Cinco.

After discussions with Forward's attorneys, Sam thinks that if he makes a quiet overture to Focus to settle out of court, Focus would be amenable to such a proposal. This would stave off potential negative publicity if Focus wins its suit against Discount Software and then follows up with a lawsuit against Forward. Based on projections of Cinco's sales, Forward's attorneys think that Focus could ask for $5, $8, or as much as $15 million in damages. Sam believes that the probability of Focus agreeing to $5 million is 50%, $8 million is 30%, and $15 million is 20%.

Sam knows that settling now means an immediate loss of income, in the amount of one of the three estimates given, plus an admission of defeat and guilt for Forward. On the other hand, Sam could wait for the outcome of the Focus versus Discount Software unit. Forward's attorneys believe that Focus has a 40% chance of winning its lawsuit against Discount Software. With a win, Focus would have its legal precedent to sue Forward. It is by no means certain that Focus would institute a lawsuit against Forward because Forward is a much larger company than Discount Software and could afford a vigorous legal defense. Also the case against Forward is not as clear cut because Cinco has its own menu system as the primary mode of operation and offers the Focus A-B-C menu system for those who want to use it. VIP Scheduler provides only the Focus A-B-C menu system. However, Forward's attorneys believe there is an 80% chance that Focus would initiate a lawsuit against Forward if Focus wins its suit against Discount Software.

Sam believes that even if Focus sues Forward, he could still try to settle the case out of court at that time or decide to go to trial. An attempt to settle out of court at that time would be more expensive for Forward because Focus would feel secure that it would win its case against Forward, having already won its lawsuit against Discount Software. Thus Forward's attorneys think that Focus would settle for no less than $7 million, possibly asking for $10 million or even $12 million. The respective probabilities that Focus would settle for these amounts ($7, $10, and $12 million) are estimated to be 30%, 40%, and 30%. Also, Forward would have to pay its attorneys roughly $1 million to go through the settling process.

However, if Focus sues Forward and Forward decides to go to trial instead of initiating settlement proceedings, Forward could lose the case. Forward's attorneys estimate there is an 80% chance that Forward would lose the trial, resulting in a judgment of either $10 million, $12 million, or $18 million against Forward, with probabilities of 10%, 20%, and 70%, respectively. The attorneys also estimate that their fees for a trial could run as high as $1.5 million.

Use decision analysis to determine what Sam's optimal strategy should be. Create the decision tree for this problem, including all costs and probabilities, and find the optimal decision strategy and expected cost for that strategy. Consider Sam to be "risk neutral" in this analysis.

REFERENCES

Clemen, R. *Making Hard Decisions: An Introduction to Decision Analysis.* Boston: PWS-KENT Publishing Company, 1991.

Corner and Kirkwood. "Decision Analysis Applications in the Operations Research Literature 1970-1989." *Operations Research*, vol. 39, no. 2, 1991.

Coyle, R. *Decision Analysis.* London: Nelson, 1972.

Heian, B. and J. Gale. "Mortgage Selection Using a Decision-Tree Approach: An Extension." *Interfaces*, vol. 18, July-August 1988.

Keeney, R. and H. Raiffa. *Decision With Multiple Objectives.* New York: Wiley, 1976.

Keeney, R. *Value-Focused Thinking.* Cambridge, MA: Harvard University Press, 1992.

Merkhofer, M.W. "Quantifying Judgmental Uncertainty: Methodology, Experiences & Insights." *IEEE Transactions on Systems, Man, and Cybernetics*, vol. 17, pp. 741-752, 1987.

Wenstop, F., and A. Carlsen. "Ranking Hydroelectric Power Projects with Multicriteria Decision Analysis." *Interfaces*, vol. 18, no. 4, 1988.

Zahedi, F. "The Analytic Hierarchy Process—A Survey of the Method and Its Applications." *Interfaces*, vol. 16, no. 4, 1986.

Index